INTERNATIONAL TRADE

INTER- NATIONAL TRADE

GOODS, PEOPLE, AND IDEAS

Wendell C. Gordon

DEPARTMENT OF ECONOMICS

THE UNIVERSITY OF TEXAS

NEW YORK ⚑ ALFRED A. KNOPF ⚑ 1958

L.C. catalog card number: 58-5047
© *Wendell C. Gordon, 1958*

THIS IS A BORZOI BOOK
PUBLISHED BY ALFRED A. KNOPF, INC.

FIRST EDITION

To Gertrude Mills Gordon

Preface

THIS BOOK tries to accomplish three different yet related purposes.

It tries to integrate current thinking in the field of international economic relations into a coherent whole. This is difficult since not all of the thinking has, by any means, been pointed in the same direction. The chief works incorporated in the material of this book which have not generally been included in survey works on international economics up to this time are, on the one hand, the work of J. E. Meade and, on the other, those parts of the institutional theory of Thorstein Veblen and C. E. Ayres which are especially pertinent to the theory of growth.

Second, the book tries to suggest a co-ordinated pattern of policies which would make possible the existence of a viable world economy that would make it somewhat less likely that the human race will blow itself apart in the next few years.

Third, this book tries to present the materials in a readable form. I hope that the presentation can be understood both by the well-informed lay reader and also by the junior or senior social-science student in college. All of the technical economic terms have been defined in the book. A few may present some difficulty so far as the casual reader is concerned. But the general argument of the book is not dependent on the manipulation of the more abstruse, technical concepts.

There are numerous acknowledgments that I must make to those who have helped me in the preparation of this book. Mrs. Bonnie Whittier toiled on a draft which was once distributed to my junior class in lieu of a text. S. L. McDonald and E. E. Hale have read various sections of the manuscript. Charles McCord, Arthur Massey, and Jeff Clark have worked with the statistical data. A grant from the University of Texas Research Institute was of assistance in facilitating work on parts of the study. Ray Ginger's criticism of the analytical material has been a real service.

WENDELL GORDON

University of Texas

Contents

PART III: BALANCE OF PAYMENTS AND NATIONAL INCOME THEORY

PART IV: THE MOVEMENT OF GOODS AND SERVICES (OR, THE YANKEE TRADER OUTDOES HIMSELF)

Contents

PART V: MONEY, SHORT-TERM FUNDS, AND THE BUSINESS CYCLE PROBLEM

PART VII: GROWTH

PART VIII: TOWARD AN INTEGRATED PROGRAM

Tables

Charts

INTERNATIONAL TRADE

Introduction

❦ ❦ ❦

*The study of international economic relations is a study of the most
important factors influencing the manner in which people and nations live together on this planet.*

*Human motivation involves as central goals (a) higher material levels
of living, (b) freedom, and (c) security.*

*Conflicts among the goals can only be resolved satisfactorily by the will
of the majority, expressed through the democratic process.*

❦ ❦ ❦

I N STUDYING international economic relations we are dealing
with a topic which influences mightily, for good or ill, the destiny
of the human race. Nations have fought wars for outlets to markets or for sources of raw materials. Confusion in international
finance can affect the national income of countries, however much those
countries would like to stay aloof from the troubles of others. Restrictions on the free movement of goods, people, and ideas from country
to country should be a matter of concern to all of us. They affect our
whole way of life whether we approve them or not.

And yet there is much confusion as to the manner in which international economic forces operate. The National Opinion Research Center
conducted a poll in 1946. One question ran as follows:[1]

> Do you think we should try to make the people in Japan
> pay us in some way or other for our cost of this war, or don't
> you think we should try to get repaid?

The answers to this question ran: 79 per cent, try; 14 per cent, do not
try; 7 per cent, undecided.

Another question in the same survey was:

> If the only way Japan could pay us for our cost of the war
> would be in goods, would you be willing for our country to
> accept any goods which would be sold cheaper than similar
> goods we make in this country?

[1] John Lee Coulter, *Public Opinion in the United States on Foreign Trade*
(American Tariff League, Publication No. 117 [New York, 1946]), pp. 15, 18.

And the answers to this question ran: 21 per cent, willing to accept; 68 per cent, not willing; 11 per cent, undecided.

These replies are inconsistent. The answers to the second question bar payment by the only channel through which it is at all feasible to make payment. But the answers to the first question support the view that we wanted to get something of value by way of payment from the Japanese.

This illustration suggests that the study of international economics should proceed with care and effort at thoughtful understanding. What purposes do we desire that international economic relations should serve? Will certain policies and procedures serve these goals? Much of this book is devoted to analysis of various policies and procedures. But before we can proceed with their discussion, it is necessary to make an effort to clarify the nature of the goals which are to be served.

THE VALUE THEORY

General Motivation (Non-homogeneous Values) [2]

In this book the dogmatic assumption is made that the human race, in some sense, is trying to bring about, or should be trying to bring about, that combination of (a) higher material level of living, (b) greater individual freedom of action and expression, and (c) increased security, which the race considers most desirable.

(a) The meaning of higher material level of living—having more of the material good things of life—is ostensibly clear. But difficulties exist both in absolute measurement and in the weighing of various degrees of inequality in income distribution against the highest possible gross income. The more desirable income distribution may not correlate with the highest possible gross income.

(b) Individual freedom of action involves the freedom of human beings to move from place to place, to work where they choose, to work in the profession they choose, and to have and express such ideas as they choose—with the proviso that some people's mouths should be washed out with soap occasionally.

Freedom of action is not license. It includes freedom to do "the decent thing." Perhaps the nature of the decent thing will change as the years pass. But in any given epoch the person who follows this precept will get more genuine private satisfaction from living than the person who does not. Respect for the "rights" of one's fellows is an aspect of doing

[2] The argument over value has been central in the work of many of the leading economists. The comments presented here hardly make a major contribution to the subject; but it may be useful to the reader of this book to know in advance the author's bias.

the decent thing. The freedom of expression and action enjoyed by businessmen in the free competitive market (if we had it) would be only
one aspect of the general freedom of all people to practice the religion
they prefer, go on a fishing trip if they wish, engage in a political
argument, marry whomever they wish (if they can get the other party
to agree), and so on. The freedom of businessmen, as an aspect of freedom, is desirable and should be allowed to express itself, unless and until
it limits other freedoms or does not make a reasonable contribution to
raising the level of living—as may be the case when depressions get out
of hand or when monopolies curtail production in order to make more
profits.

(c) Security is a concept which involves both national security against
war and individual security against old age, illness, and loss of income.
But the people in our country who are most concerned about war (and
Communism) are a quite different group of people from those most
concerned about social security.

There are difficulties involved in the effort to add together the elements
which serve these goals. They are quite different in kind. Human freedom
cannot be measured in dollars and added to a certain number of dollars
of money income and a certain number of units of security for purposes
of measuring the merit of one situation by comparison with another. The
values involved are not homogeneous.

There is even difficulty in objectively adding the elements making up
level of living alone. How should the significance of inequality in the
distribution of income be allowed for? How can one tell which is more
desirable, a high total income and great inequality in its distribution or
a somewhat lower total income more evenly distributed?

And the difficulty is compounded when an effort is made to add level
of living to freedom of action, and the two to security. Even more so here,
the addition cannot be accomplished by any presently known additive
techniques. If a double negative may be permitted, this does not mean
that the problem cannot be handled. But the solution will not be provided
by engineers and physical scientists with their techniques for adding and
dividing physical quantities.

At any rate, the optimum combination of level of living, freedom of
action, and security, however difficult to evaluate, will be called in this
book the "better," "fuller," or "good" life, or the maximum social well-
being.

Role of the Democratic Process

Anyone willing to accept the general welfare goals of higher level of
living, greater freedom of action, and security should also be willing to
agree that conflicts can only be resolved by the people themselves, adding

and appraising the various factors *subjectively* as best they can and expressing their decisions through the democratic process.[3] In any event this book is written on the assumption that whatever combination of these several goals is subjectively decided upon by the people acting through the democratic process represents at any one time the most authoritative opinion as to how things should be done. Individuals are privileged to disagree in their minds and to express their disagreement in words; but as long as they live in society their overt actions should conform to society's rules—pending the acceptance by the people of the divergent ideas of the dissidents.

Presumably society is justified in preventing one individual from using his freedom of action in such a way as to lessen the well-being of someone else. And society must be the judge of the relative value of the freedom of action lost in one case and the well-being gained (or retained) in the other. This problem could be dealt with in large measure if in our society we emphasized ordinary decency in respect for the rights of others. In the United States today the greatest disservice which parents do to their children is the failure to teach them to be considerate of their fellow men—as a first principle.

Ministers of the gospel frequently point out that we should look beyond our stomachs to our eternal souls. That may be rather much to expect of the two-thirds of the population of the world that is in an endemic state of starvation.[4] Or it may represent the only real solace and comfort in a life for which, otherwise, not much can be said. One should not be scornful of the real service which religion renders to the poor, even though many of them are as "entitled" as their richer brethren to other pleasures in life.

Real satisfaction in life is surely gained from a wide range of activity, and from interest in, and understanding of, the many and varied things going on around us. Stagnation and dissatisfaction follow from doing nothing or from repeating the same old activities in the same old way. This is true of the worker in the mass production industry who has no hobbies and no other interests, but even more true of the social dilettante with nothing better to do than follow the night club circuit till four in the morning.

The shortening of the working day has been a tremendous boon to the worker in giving him the leisure time to express himself in other ways—whether it be spent in the beer parlor or in building a boat. We have to

[3] Of course there is argument as to the most satisfactory channels through which the democratic process may express itself: majority vote, Hare preferential voting, etc. But surely there would not be a *major* problem in this area if all were really agreed that decision making should be done through the democratic process—however much minor disagreement there might be about the details.

[4] American Geographical Society (Medical Geographical Department), *Study in Human Starvation* (New York, 1953).

judge that the general result is gain even though some facets of the result appear questionable. As for the social dilettante, if he (or she) is neither a fighting nor a nauseated drunk, one might well say: "Let him stew in his own juice or drown in his own whiskey. He may even be amusing while he is stewing." And what would we do without the goings-on described in the tabloids to give us a healthy contempt for our fellow men and an appreciation of how good we are ourselves? Something in the American culture does lead many of us to use our spare time and increasing freedom of action in ways that do not reflect much credit on us and, what is more important, tend to restrict the other fellow's freedom of action. The teen-age (male or female) recipient of an unearned convertible may show rather slight regard for the freedom of action (or even the life) of others.

Much of the current plea for allowing free private enterprise and competition (of sorts) to run wild is really a plea for a policy which would increase the freedom of some at the expense of the freedom of the great many. In governing ourselves, in making democracy work, we do not have the problem of choosing once and for all between freewheeling enterprise and paternalistic government, but the continuing problem of weighing each decision our society makes in the light of the total impact, in the light of the desirable balance between let-it-alone-to-take-care-of-itself and group or government planning. And we determine, or should determine, relative desirability, if there seems to be a conflict between level of living and freedom of action, by a subjective evaluation expressed through the democratic process. If we are not capable of satisfactory decision making in this way, we shall have only ourselves to thank for the dictatorship which may descend on the world and make itself permanent and effective with the powerful new tools at its disposal (propaganda techniques, radio and television, Gestapo-type methods, and the ability to manipulate great masses of people).

Earlier comments about the not particularly edifying use that some people have made of their leisure time and opportunities do not, must not, refute the fundamental proposition that our goals are to raise the level of living and to increase the freedom of action and security of people. Society must use coercion to restrain anyone who would use his freedom to reduce that of others. But we cannot take the position that higher levels of living and greater freedom of action and security are undesirable goals without at the same time taking the position that the human race is not worth fooling with at all. If these are not the worthwhile goals for the race, the sooner it makes a mistake and blows itself up with an A-bomb, or an H-bomb, or a C-bomb, the better. But since we are the race involved, that position is ruled out for us.

Any human individual, who chooses to take the contrary position that he has certain rights to wealth or to engage in independent, arbitrary action that may be harmful to the rest of the race, forfeits his claim on the protection of society.

The position, that there are some supermen who are entitled to establish themselves in a position of hegemony and express themselves while lording it over the rest of a servile mankind, is hardly one that the self-designated supermen can expect the great mass of the race to respect.

Which brings us back to raising the level of living and increasing freedom of action and security as desirable goals.

Multiple Motivation Theory

The foregoing may be described as a multiple motivation or multiple goal theory in which social development is assumed to be guided fundamentally by the democratic process—rather than by the self-regulating market. It should be noted, however, that emphasis on the fact of multiple motivation is called for—not because there has been an artificial classification of the value goals of society into several rather than one—but because the values are non-homogeneous. Elements of the one set of values cannot be objectively added to elements of the other.

This theory does not give precise answers. It does not state in any absolute sense what the optimum population is, nor does it offer any precise measure for the general well-being. Each generation can reappraise these matters and change the prevailing attitude accordingly. The only unchanging element is the idea that the decision should be democratically made.

PART I

Background

Chapter 1

WHY AND HOW

> ⊭ ⊭ ⊭

In international trade, as in domestic trade, buyers and sellers are motivated chiefly but not exclusively by the desire for profit.

In determining international trade policies, national governments and the world as a whole should be motivated chiefly by the desire to achieve a better life for their citizens.

But the fact is that pressure groups often exert more influence than the general population in determining the policies of any government.

If governments were to follow the proper objectives, they would in general promote international specialization, which would inevitably break down national isolation.

But international specialization will conflict in many instances with the desire of individuals for profit.

> ⊭ ⊭ ⊭

THE BASIC assumption of this book is that the maximization of a combination of (1) level of living, (2) individual freedom of action, and (3) security, is desirable.

It is all very well to insist upon the desirability of these goals. But for an intelligent understanding of the process by which they may be achieved, there must be an awareness of the actual motivations of the different institutions which make significant decisions affecting international economic relations.

MOTIVES AT VARIOUS LEVELS OF DECISION MAKING

In connection with study of the international trade problem, the complex world of decision making may be simplified into three levels: (1) the individual (or corporate) traders, (2) nations, and (3) the world.

The Individual (or Corporate) Trader

The individual (or corporate) trader is mainly interested in maximizing monetary profit in his home-country currency. An American engaged in international trade finds the trading worthwhile if he derives from it a substantial profit in dollars. He is not especially interested in ending up in physical possession of the goods in which he is trading. Nor does it benefit him to secure a profit in the non-transferable currency of another country, unless perhaps he can arrange to go to that country as a tourist—hardly the customary situation.

It is not quite true that the only influence motivating international traders is monetary profit, any more than it is true that the only influence motivating people in general is monetary profit. Goods may be shipped for sentimental reasons. People in the United States may make a gift, via the Red Cross, to aid in relief after a Chilean earthquake. Or trade in certain commodities may conceivably continue by force of habit long after alternatives have become more profitable. Or the tourist may bring home with him the "import of a service," which includes the cost of the trip to view the scenery, without having any precise conception of the money value of the thing he is buying. Nevertheless, it will be assumed through much of this book that the individual trader is primarily interested in maximizing monetary profit in his home-currency.

National Motivation

National currency can be created or destroyed arbitrarily by a national government, but not by indivduals. Federal Reserve notes and demand deposits can be created or canceled by the Federal Reserve Banks. Of course, there are rules governing the process; and the creation of money may be related to the incurring and paying off of public debt and to the import and export of gold. But the government (the nation) can directly influence the quantity of money within the nation, while the private citizen cannot legally counterfeit money. He has to obtain it from others by "good works." Consequently the nation cannot be interested in maximizing monetary profit in the sense that the individual is.

If a nation is behaving with intelligent selfishness (a rather uncommon procedure for nations), if it is intelligently representing an intelligent citizenry, it will be concerned with helping them to attain the fuller life (higher level of living, more freedom of action, and greater security). It will endeavor to co-ordinate international trade with domestic production in order to obtain the largest possible amount of consumer goods, proper allowance being made for freedom of action and security. Of course, if this better life is to be prolonged and extended, attention must be given to the problem of maintaining and expanding the supply of capital equipment. But the capital equipment serves as "means" and not as "end."

The ultimate desirability of having more goods for consumption within a country need not imply the desirability of an import surplus of the largest possible size. Perhaps the largest possible import balance would go hand in hand with a rather small volume of total trade, which would mean that little benefit was being gained, in actuality, from the trading operations. A far larger volume of total trade, in a setting where exports roughly equaled imports, might result in more goods being available for consumption within the country. This might be possible because the volume of trade was a factor in expanding internal production. At all events the proposition that an export trade balance (more exports than imports) is desirable is the most doubtful contention of all.

A government is not certain to be the effective agent of an intelligent citizenry. In fact, a government's day-to-day behavior may be described more accurately as a response to the combination of pressures exerted upon it than as a response to considerations of intelligent selfishness. The people operating through the ballot are only one of these pressures. Many special-interest pressure groups operate on the government and on legislators with varying degrees of subtlety and insistence. When one trade association representative after another has told a legislator that this or that industry is in desperate need of tariff protection, it is little wonder that the legislator forgets the consumers' need for more goods at lower prices. Although it is contrary to intelligent national motivation, the government is not unlikely to end up as the cat's paw of individual traders whose intelligent self-interest is served by ceaseless efforts to increase their own monetary profit.

There is, thus, considerable complication in the answer to the question as to national motive in terms of what *ought* to be and in terms of what *is*. Whereas a government ought to give effect to the decisions of the people as expressed through the democratic process, and whereas an effectively operating democratic process would surely demand emphasis on the maximization of social well-being, actually a government is much influenced by the wishes of sometimes disinterested, more often self-seeking, pressure groups.

The "World"

The world as a whole has, or should have, no especial interest in the monetary profits of one individual as compared with those of another; neither should the world care which nation has relatively more of what goods there are, or which is preparing most efficiently for war, or which is the most servile creature of its pressure groups. The world should be interested in a better life for the citizenry of the whole world, the meaning of "the better life" being determined by the people themselves, speaking through an effectively operating world-wide democratic process. Such would be the desirable state of affairs.

But an international government, like a national government, will probably respond to the pressures which create it, select its officials, and operate on it from day to day. This is observably true of the present United

Nations, the delegates to which are strictly the creatures of their respective national governments.

APPLICATION TO INTERNATIONAL TRADE

The foregoing has been a brief discussion of *why* the interested parties to the international trading process behave as they do. The conditions that control *how* the desirable goals may be accomplished involve certain considerations of a different sort.

Specialization

In the international sphere the general proposition might be that if there is more specialization and more trading, more total production and a higher level of living will result. If there is less restriction on travel and migration, the people themselves will have more freedom of action. Moreover, the stability which the world would gain from such activities would contribute to security. On the other hand, the measures people take in an effort to increase their monetary profits tend to decrease the amount of specialization and to inhibit the free movement of goods.

One type of specialization is based on differences in geographical endowment (*geographical specialization*). In the absence of international trade there would be virtually no tin produced in Malaya, Indonesia, and Bolivia, since the domestic market (the size of the market) for tin in those countries is extremely limited. Only because there is an extensive market for tin in the United States, England, and France is the extensive production of tin possible and desirable. Much the same argument applies to other natural resources. The areas where they can be effectively produced or grown are rather limited. If Canada were to try growing coffee, it could be done, possibly, in hothouses; but the time and effort spent in doing it would net relatively little coffee by comparison with the quantity that Brazil can produce with the same amount of effort. Time spent on nickel production is more remunerative in Canada—more remunerative in the sense that there is probably more coffee plus nickel in the world available for consumer use than would have been the case in the absence of such specialization, and incidentally more of the combination of the two in Canada and in Brazil.

The argument for specialization has a much greater range of validity than is indicated by the preceding examples. The advantages are not limited to situations where the production of the particular commodity is virtually impossible in a second country. Maximum total productivity for different kinds of goods requires complicated production patterns involving various combinations of raw materials, labor, and capital equipment. And more production results if individual countries specialize in the development of a limited number of production patterns—rather than dissipating their energies in an effort to develop all. Production is greater and more efficient if there are certain broad areas of specialization in different countries (if there is *division of labor*) whether or not those areas are determined by a relatively favorable endowment of raw materials or climate, although one or the other of those considerations is likely to indicate the direction of specialization. Some well-known areas of specialization are Swiss watches, Panama (Ecuadorean) hats, Scotch whiskey, English worsteds, and French perfumes. Each country in the world could insist on producing its own supply of each of these things. In fact, many countries have as good a potential for producing some of them as the country which happens to be the specialist. But if each insisted on producing all things, the combined supply available to the people of the world would be smaller.

There would be no sense in all countries the size of El Salvador having steel industries of efficient size. But this is not to say that Cuba should grow nothing but sugar, Brazil nothing but coffee; and it certainly does not follow that all steel and all automobiles should be produced in the United States. Some competition from other countries may have a stimulating effect on efficiency, even in naturally well-endowed countries.

Interaction vs. Isolation

The world is going to grow as a unit. Technical progress will evolve as the knowledge of scientists in one country interacts with the knowledge of scientists elsewhere. Levels of living in the world at large will rise as this interacting process continues. And certainly freedom of action and expression is furthered by such interchange. There will also be more genuine security in a world which is working effectively as a unit than in one which is a complex of "biting and scrapping" sovereign nations. In such a process of growth, the country that will progress furthest and fastest is the country that participates most effectively in this interacting process and not the country that retires behind a Chinese wall.[1]

CONCLUSION

This chapter has attempted to identify the purposes of the international trading process. In the next chapter an effort will be made to identify some of the statistical tools that may be used in analyzing trading problems. Also a rough picture will be presented, in figures, of the chief international trade relations.

[1] That a country grows by participating in active interchange and not by restrictions is an ancient and respectable proposition. See the comments of Lewes Roberts, *The Treasure of Traffike* (London, 1641), as reproduced in J. R. McCulloch (ed.), *Early English Tracts on Commerce*, pp. 49–113. Roberts attributed Spanish stagnation to restrictions, and Florentine and English development to active interchange.

Chapter 2

THE MEASUREMENT OF
INTERNATIONAL TRADE

Since the real value of goods cannot be measured directly, statistics of international trade are based on (a) money value, (b) physical quantity, or (c) quantum.

The total and the per capita values of international trade have increased historically, but they have increased less rapidly than income.

Since 1913, the shares of the various countries in world trade have remained surprisingly stable.

Trade does not depend on the existence of some industrial and some non-industrial countries, but the patterns of world trade do change as different countries develop.

The relative importance of international trade to a country depends chiefly on the size of the country.

Even a very large country, such as the United States, would be adversely affected if it prevented all trade across its national boundaries.

C HAPTER 1 made an attempt to identify the purpose of the international trading process. This chapter gives a general statistical description of various international trade relations. Thus the two chapters provide background to the theoretical material of Part II and to the problems that will be discussed thereafter.

UNITS OF MEASUREMENT

Much of the difficulty in the study of international trade, and of economics as a whole for that matter, stems from the problems involved in measuring the relevant data. The possible units of measurement are, essentially, the following: (1) real value, (2) money value, (3) physical quantity, and (4) the quantum (quantity) index. Combinations of these units of measurement will be used in later chapters to develop concepts such as the "terms of trade."

Real Value

In measuring international trade, it would be desirable to measure the *real value* of the goods involved. But as yet no satisfactory technique has been found for doing this. The classical economists, led by David Ricardo, attempted to appraise value in terms of the labor time required to produce the goods in question. But this procedure has involved at least two difficulties. There has been no general agreement that labor time is a satisfactory measure of value. And as a practical matter the concept cannot be handled statistically. How could one compute the labor time required to produce any article? How much labor time should be imputed to the machinery which is used, for example? More complicated concepts of real value present even greater difficulties. In short, although it would be desirable to have the measurements in terms of real value, this is not possible in the present "state of the statistical arts"; and one is reduced to measuring trade by other units of measurement: money value, physical quantity, and index numbers of quantum.

Money Value

A country's trade may be measured in the national currency: United States dollars, British pounds sterling, French francs, etc. This can be done with considerable precision in spite of the difficulty involved in making some decisions, such as whether to use a c.i.f., f.o.b., or f.a.s. basis for assigning value.[1]

Table 1 shows the annual dollar value of United States exports, averaged by decades until 1910, by five-year periods from 1911 to 1950, and by single years thereafter. The dollar value of United States exports multiplied to become 330 times as great in 1955 as in 1791–1800—clearly a phenomenal rate of increase.

Table 2 shows the money value of the exports and imports of various countries for 1955—or in some cases for other years. The figures are first given in the national currency of the country concerned and are then translated into United States dollars—at the foreign exchange rates which the United Nations experts consider most appropriate. We can compare the exports and imports of any country by measuring both in terms of the national currency of that country. But the value of the trade of one coun-

---

[1] *C.i.f.* (cost-insurance-freight) means that the value assigned to the goods is considered to include not only their actual price or cost in the country from which they are coming, but also the insurance and freight costs involved in the international shipment. *F.o.b.* (free on board) does not include insurance and freight, but merely the purchase price and the cost of getting the goods on the means of transportation. *F.a.s.* (free alongside) valuation is the original price of the goods plus the cost of getting the goods on the wharf alongside the ship.

try cannot be compared with that of another until both values are translated into some common denominator—in this case United States dollars. The dollar figures indicate that the United States is the most important trading nation.

The usefulness of money figures is subject to certain limitations. To illustrate: the exports of the United States from 1891 to 1900 averaged

TABLE 1

MONEY VALUE OF UNITED STATES EXPORTS AND
IMPORTS, 1791 TO DATE

(ANNUAL AVERAGES OR ANNUAL TOTALS)
($1,000,000)

	TOTAL EXPORTS [1]	GENERAL IMPORTS
1791–1800	47	59
1801–1810	75	93
1811–1820	59	81
1821–1830	69	73
1831–1840	104	120
1841–1850	123	121
1851–1860	249	284
1861–1870	254	332
1871–1880	589	535
1881–1890	765	692
1891–1900	1,025	763
1901–1910	1,616	1,158
1911–1915 [2]	2,371	1,712
1915–1920 [2]	6,521	3,358
1921–1925	4,397	3,450
1926–1930	4,777	4,033
1931–1935	2,025	1,713
1936–1940	3,220	2,482
1941–1945	10,051	3,514
1946–1950	11,829	6,659
1951	15,032	10,967
1952	15,201	10,717
1953	15,774	10,873
1954	15,077	10,208
1955	15,538	11,384
1956	18,987	12,590

[1] Including re-exports; [2] There is a slight overlap here.
Source: *Statistical Abstract, 1955*, p. 900; and table 2.

$1,025 million per year; in 1951 they were $15,032 million. Is one justified in saying that the real value of exports was approximately fifteen times as large in 1951 as in the 1890's? The fact that the index number of the price level in the United States was 48.8 in 1895 and 180.4 in 1951 suggests that the real value of exports in 1951 was about four times the 1895 real value, not fifteen times, a rather considerable difference. Such a comparison indicates the amount of error that may result if comparisons of the changes in money value through time are used to measure changes in real value.

However, a comparison of money values at a given time is rather meaningful as a *guide* to differences in "real" value. For example, it can be stated that the "real" value of United States exports in 1955 was twenty-three times the Mexican, on the basis of the fact that the money value of United States exports was $15,538 million, of Mexican exports, $669 million.

TABLE 2

MONEY VALUE OF EXPORTS AND IMPORTS BY COUNTRIES, 1955

| | MILLIONS IN NATIONAL CURRENCY | | MILLIONS IN U.S. DOLLARS | |
	EXPORTS	IMPORTS	EXPORTS (F.O.B.)	IMPORTS (C.I.F.)
NORTH AMERICAN GROUP:				
United States (dollar)	15,538	11,384	15,538	11,384
Canada (dollar)	4,517	4,712	4,763	5,165
LATIN AMERICAN GROUP:				
Argentina (peso)			1,000	1,100
Brazil (cruzeiro)	54,520	60,230	1,423	1,307
Cuba (peso)	594	496	594	535
Mexico (peso)	8,357	9,899	669	792
Venezuela (bolivar) [2]	5,661	2,998	1,690	1,002
(Latin America—total)			7,930	7,140
OTHER:				
China (yuan) [3]			170	387
France (franc)	1,679,000	1,641,000	4,800	4,688
Germany, Federal Republic (Deutsche mark)	25,676	24,358	6,119	5,798
India (rupee)	6,055	6,483	1,271	1,361
Italy (lira)	1,161,000	1,691,000	1,857	2,706
U.S.S.R. (ruble) [3]			880	2,055
United Kingdom (£)	3,024	3,886	8,467	10,881
WORLD TOTAL [1]			83,870	87,820

[1] World total does not include Albania, Bulgaria, Mainland China, Czechoslovakia, Eastern Germany, Poland, Rumania, and the U.S.S.R.; [2] 1954; [3] 1948.

Source: *International Financial Statistics,* May, 1956, pp. 28–31 and *passim.*

This is a useful and meaningful comparison which can legitimately be drawn from the money value figures, even though the comparison may not be *precisely* accurate. For example, to illustrate a conditioning difficulty, the conversion of the value of Mexican trade from a peso base to a dollar base involves the use of a prevailing peso-dollar foreign exchange rate that may only approximately reflect the difference in price levels in the two countries. Are errors from this source likely to be as misleading as errors resulting from changes in price levels over a period of time? In general: No, not by far.

In appraisal of money value statistics, it may be said that they have a real usefulness for comparison at a given moment but a very limited usefulness for comparisons through time, unless corrected by the use of index numbers which accurately reflect the change in price levels. To get slightly ahead of the story, this is what the quantum indexes attempt to do.

Physical Quantity

Another basis of measurement that may be used is *physical quantity* (weight or volume in the literal sense—or number of bags). Data of this sort can be compiled with relative ease and are compiled in many countries for specific commodities. Thus, Cuba exported 10,681,000,000 pounds of centrifugal raw sugar in 1951. But the usefulness of these figures as a guide to the value of total trade suffers from the fact that the real values of goods are surely not in proportion to either weight or physical quantity; for example, a comparison of weight would hardly be a reasonable basis for comparing the value of diamonds and of coal. South Africa's exports have been largely gold and diamonds, whereas England's chief export has been coal. Thus, for the comparison of values at a given time, physical volume or weight would provide little clue to the relative value of British and South African exports. Consequently, physical quantity figures are useful for comparisons through time of the amount of trade in a particular commodity, but they are not generally added up to describe the total amount of trade—although they may be. Port authorities like to use a figure describing the physical quantities of the goods they handle. For example, the port of Houston handled 3,527,257 short tons of cargo in November, 1954.

Quantum

There has been an effort to compile an index number series (variously called *quantum, quantity,* or *volume*) that would correct money value figures for changes in the price level. The resulting index would be a more accurate indication of changes in real value than are the crude money value figures. The League of Nations developed such an index number which has been called "quantum" in League and United Nations statistics; has been called, for some strange reason, "quantity" in United States statistics; and has been called, for equally obscure reasons, "volume" in British statistics.

This figure, perforce, is not an absolute figure like $10,000,000 or £2,000,000. It is an index number which offers a clue to change and relative rate of change, not to absolute values. To compute the index number showing the change in the quantum (quantity) of United States exports, as in Table 3:

TABLE 3

OTHER MEASUREMENTS OF TRADE (UNITED STATES)

(1923–1925 EQUALS 100)

YEAR	I INDEX NUMBER OF TOTAL MONEY VALUE OF EXPORTS	II INDEX NUMBER OF UNIT VALUE OF EXPORTS	III INDEX NUMBER OF QUANTUM (QUAN- TITY) OF EXPORTS (I/II × 100)
1913	55	65	85
(1923–1925)	100	100	100
1929	115	87	132
1930	85	78	109
1931	53	60	88
1932	35	51	69
1933	37	54	69
1934	47	63	75
1935	50	65	77
1936	54	66	82
1937	74	70	106
1938	68	65	105
1939	70	64	109
1940	88	68	129
1941	112	73	153
1942	179	89	201
1943	287	98	293
1944	317	112	283
1945	215	112	192
1946	213	106	201
1947	319	126	253
1948	280	134	209
1949	267	125	214
1950	227	121	188
1951	333	138	241
1952	337	138	244
1953	350	137	255
1954	335	135	248
1955	344	137	251

Source: *Statistical Abstract, 1955*, p. 905. Some of the data is derived from other issues of the *Statistical Abstract*.

Take	Index number showing *total* money value of exports;
Divide by	Index number showing *unit* money value of exports (i.e., showing changes in price level);
Multiply by	100.

What does this mean? Let us suppose that we have an index series of total money exports; this series is based on 1920 when the total value of all exports of Country X was $10 million. Thus $10 million gives the index number 100. Further suppose that in 1950 the total value, at 1950 prices, of all exports of Country X is $20 million. Thus we have an index number for 1950 of 200. Now let us take an entirely different series of index numbers—one showing changes in the average prices of the goods exported—also based on the average price of exports in 1920 as the index number 100. Now suppose that, from 1920 to 1950, the average price of exports doubled, so that the index number for 1950 is 200. Look back at the formula given above. If we take the index number showing total money value of exports in 1950—that is, 200—and divide it by the index number showing the unit value of exports in 1950—that is, 200—we get a result of 1, which, multiplied by 100, is 100. This tells us that the total value of exports from Country X was exactly the same in 1950 as in 1920, *if both are valued at 1920 prices.*

A quantum index number series of this sort is far more accurate as a description of the change in the real value of trade through time than are the uncorrected money value figures of Table 1.

The statement that the amount of United States exports increased three-fold between 1913 and 1951—derived from the quantum index—is more meaningful than the statement that United States exports increased six-fold—derived from the change in the total money value.

LONG-RUN CHANGE IN THE IMPORTANCE OF TRADE

In spite of all the studies that have been made of international trade—and probably there have been more statistics compiled in this area than in any other field of economics—there is imperfect knowledge of some of the major trends. For example, what is the relationship between the change in the amount of international trade and the change in world income or world production? German economists, such as Werner Sombart, as early as the last decade of the nineteenth century, went so far as to develop a so-called "law of the falling export quota." It alleged that "the volume of foreign trade, though increasing in absolute terms, tends to constitute a declining proportion of the total social product." [2]

If we want to test this hypothesis statistically, the nearest thing to really relevant data for the world as a whole is the comparison of world industrial production and the quantum of international trade (Chart 1). It gives support to the proposition that world industrial production is rising at a faster rate than the quantum of world trade. Additional relevant data may be obtained from the trade and income statistics of certain countries. Table 4 states United States imports as a percentage of total United States national income. This data indicates a decline in the ratio of imports

[2] See the discussion in Carl Iversen, *Aspects of the Theory of International Capital Movements* (Copenhagen: Levin and Munksgaard, 1936), p. 183. A similar proposition has been stated more recently by Norman S. Buchanan, *Rebuilding the World Economy* (New York: Twentieth Century Fund, 1947), p. 43.

to income, thereby providing further evidence that the importance of international trade, at least for the United States, is declining.

Another means of appraising the importance of international trade is to make an estimate of the change in the real per capita value of such trade. Table 5 represents such an estimate carrying the real per capita value of United States imports back to 1790. The captions in the table indicate how the figures were derived. The wholesale price index is, perhaps, not the best index for correcting money value changes in the effort to obtain real value changes; but it is the most satisfactory available index covering such a long period of time. The figures indicate—and in this they are no doubt accurate—a long-run rise in the real value of imports.

In summary, it may be alleged that over the last century and a half the real value of international trade has risen in terms of both per capita and total figures. But the real value of world trade has not increased as rapidly as world real income—and this is true whether the figures are given as totals or on a per capita basis. In this sense, international trade has become less important.

Why? Is it a result of the "rash" of trade restrictions in recent years? Probably—in part. Is it a result of a change in the number of politically sovereign nations in the world? Probably not—since the number has been increasing rather than decreasing. And, other things equal, with the same number of ton-miles of traffic over the same routes, the larger the number of countries, the more international trade there would be. Postan may well have a better explanation for the pattern of changes—assuming that the nineteenth century actually represented a peak in the trade-to-income ratio:[3]

> For all we know, the record of international trade in the nineteenth century may well turn out to have been a mere aberration in the economic development of the world. It has been argued that in the course of that century factors of production—land, labour, capital—were distributed more unequally over the face of the globe than in any other period of world history. As a result, interregional trade may have been greater in relation to total income than it would have been had the movable resources and especially capital been more evenly spread. By the same argument the international flow of resources has been slowly reducing the relative importance of trade. . . .

[3] M. Postan and E. E. Rich (eds.), *Trade and Industry in the Middle Ages* (The Cambridge Economic History of Europe, Vol. II; Cambridge: University Press, 1952), p. 132. By permission of the Cambridge University Press.

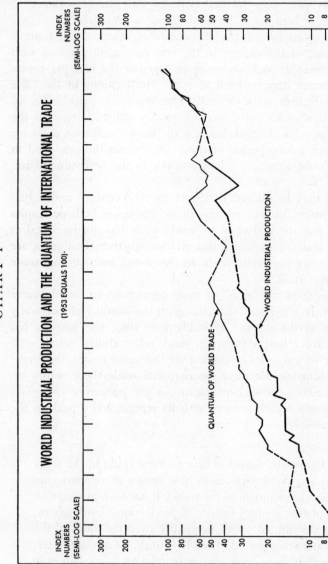

CHART 1

WORLD INDUSTRIAL PRODUCTION AND THE QUANTUM OF INTERNATIONAL TRADE

(1953 EQUALS 100)

INDEX NUMBERS (SEMI-LOG SCALE)

WORLD INDUSTRIAL PRODUCTION

QUANTUM OF WORLD TRADE

Sources: *Statistical Yearbook*; League of Nations, *Review of World Trade*; Warren and Pearson, *Prices*, p. 48; Woytinsky and Woytinsky, *World Commerce and Governments, Trends and Outlook*, p. 38.

TABLE 4

RATIO OF IMPORTS TO NATIONAL INCOME THROUGH TIME FOR THE UNITED STATES (IMPORT COEFFICIENTS)

	I MONEY VALUE OF UNITED STATES IMPORTS ($1,000,000)	II NATIONAL INCOME [1] ($1,000,000)	III IMPORT COEFFICIENT (PERCENTAGE) I/II
1799	79	677	11.7
1809	59	915	6.4
1819	87	876	9.9
1829	67	975	6.9
1839	156	1,631	9.6
1849	141	2,420	5.8
1859	331	4,311	7.7
1869	418	6,827	6.1
1879	446	7,227	6.2
1889	745	10,701	7.0
1899	697	15,364	4.5
1900	850	16,158	5.3
1905	1,118	21,428	5.2
1910	1,557	28,166	5.5
1915	1,674	32,533	5.1
1920	5,278	68,434	7.7
1925	4,227	70,051	6.0
1930	3,061	72,398	4.2
1935	2,047	57,057	3.6
1938	1,960	67,581	2.9
1940	2,625	81,634	3.2
1945	4,159	181,248	2.3
1950	8,852	239,956	3.7
1951	10,967	277,041	4.0
1952	10,717	289,537	3.7
1953	10,873	303,648	3.6
1954	10,208	299,673	3.4
1955	11,368	322,300	3.5
1956	12,590	342,400	3.7

[1] National income figures from 1799 to 1930 are from the National Industrial Conference Board, from 1935 to date from the Department of Commerce.

Sources: National Industrial Conference Board, *Conference Board Studies in Enterprise and Social Progress* (New York: N.I.C.B., 1939), p. 79; *Statistical Abstract,* various issues; *Survey of Current Business,* various issues.

TABLE 5
REAL PER CAPITA VALUE OF UNITED STATES IMPORTS THROUGH TIME

	I PER CAPITA VALUE OF IMPORTS (U.S. DOLLARS)	II WHOLESALE PRICE INDEX (1926 = 100)	III REAL PER CAPITA VALUE OF IMPORTS (CONSTANT DOLLARS AT 1926 PUR- CHASING POWER) (I/II)
1790	5.90	67 [1]	8.80
1795	15.20	97 [1]	15.70
1800	17.20	95 [1]	17.90
1805	19.33	104.2	18.60
1810	11.80	107.7	11.00
1815	13.40	121.5	11.00
1820	7.70	76.6	10.10
1825	8.00	71.8	11.10
1830	4.88	65.6	7.40
1835	9.10	74.6	12.20
1840	5.70	71.1	8.00
1845	5.60	62.6	8.90
1850	7.50	62.3	12.00
1855	9.40	68.9	13.60
1860	11.20	60.9	18.40
1865	6.70	132.0	5.10
1870	10.90	86.7	12.60
1875	11.80	77.7	15.20
1880	13.30	65.1	20.40
1885	10.20	56.6	18.00
1890	12.50	56.2	22.20
1895	10.50	48.8	21.50
1900	11.20	56.1	20.00
1905	13.30	60.1	22.10
1910	16.84	70.4	23.90
1915	16.46 [3]	69.5	23.70
1920	47.16	154.4	30.50
1925	35.80	103.5	34.60
1930	24.90	86.4	28.80
1935	15.75	80.0	19.70
1940	18.89	78.6	24.00
1945	28.66	105.8	27.10
1950	56.58	161.5	35.00
1955	67.38	171.0 [2]	39.40

[1] Warren and Pearson figures with base changed. [2] Bureau of Labor Statistics figures with the base changed. [3] After 1915 the per capita figures are obtained directly from the *Statistical Abstract*.

Sources: *Historical Statistics*, p. 26 (population), pp. 233–4 (wholesale price index); *Statistical Abstract*, various issues.

CHANGE IN NATIONAL SHARES OF WORLD TRADE

Another comparison of considerable importance relates to the change in the shares of various countries in world trade. In terms of power politics this is an extremely important comparison.

TABLE 6

CHANGE IN SHARES OF WORLD TRADE, 1913–55

(EXPORTS AS PERCENTAGES OF WORLD TOTAL EXPORTS)

	1913	1929	1937	1948	1952	1955 [2]
I. Sterling Area			25.0	26.3	24.1	24.4
United Kingdom	13.9	10.7	11.0 [2]	12.1 [2]	9.9 [2]	10.1
II. Western Europe			31.1	21.6	29.5	29.1
Germany, West	13.1	9.7	6.3 [2]	1.1 [2]	5.5 [2]	7.3
France	7.2	5.9	4.1 [2]	3.8 [2]	5.4 [2]	5.7
III. Eastern Europe and China			6.0	6.6 [3]		
U.S.S.R.	4.2	1.4	1.4	1.5 [3]		
IV. Middle East			1.7	3.0	2.0	
V. United States	13.3	15.6	13.2	23.3	20.6	18.5
VI. Canada	2.3	3.7	4.4	5.6	6.0	5.7
VII. Latin America	8.4	8.9	9.0	12.2	9.8	9.5
VIII. Far East, n.e.s.[1]			7.7	2.1	4.1	
Japan	1.7	2.9	5.1 [2]	0.5 [2]	1.8 [2]	2.5
IX. Rest of the World			1.9	2.4	2.0	

[1] n.e.s.: not elsewhere specified; [2] percentages of a world total which does not include the Eastern European countries and Mainland China; [3] based on International Monetary Fund data.

Sources: *Monthly Bulletin of Statistics*, August, 1953, p. ix; *Statistical Yearbook, 1953*, pp. 368–75; *Statistical Yearbook* (League of Nations), 1937/38, pp. 224–5; *International Statistical Yearbook* (League of Nations), 1927, pp. 128–9; *International Financial Statistics*, May, 1956, pp. 28–31.

The percentage figures given in Table 6 indicate that United States exports have risen substantially as a percentage share of world exports, although there is reason to believe that the United States share is now in process of falling slightly. The share of Eastern Europe and the U.S.S.R. in the total is not large. Perhaps it is the trade restrictions at the Iron Curtain which are keeping those figures small. The United Kingdom's share of world exports has declined somewhat since 1913. The German share of world exports has jumped up and down violently, sharply declining each time Germany has lost a war. But neither during the notorious German trade drive of the middle 1930's nor at present do German exports approach the percentage of that faraway year 1913. Perhaps successive German trade drives have alarmed their competitors more because of the accompanying noise than because of the real success of the drives. The French share of world trade has declined perceptibly in forty years. The Japanese, like the Germans, felt the adverse effects of losing World

War II; but the Japanese share of world trade has since recovered somewhat, as has the German. Whether the share of the underdeveloped countries—and in particular of Latin America—has risen to any marked extent is not established by the data. The Latin American decline between 1948 and 1955 would seem to be a more important development than the relatively minor gain in the forty years since 1913.

But perhaps the most significant conclusion to be drawn from Table 6 is that the changes in shares have actually been very slight. Even the most pronounced change—the rise of the United States—may well be more ephemeral than we now tend to believe.

TYPES OF COMMODITIES

Industrialization and Trade

Still another comparison, and one which is also related to the degree of industrial development of a country, is based upon the types of commodities that move in international trade. One runs into such statements as: the trading pattern involves the exchange of temperate zone products for tropical products, or the exchange of the products of industrialized countries for raw materials. And it is true that patterns can be worked out showing these relationships in many cases. There is a pattern for Britain, for example, involving import of raw materials and export of manufactured goods.

It is useful to identify these patterns. But the conclusion should not be drawn that a pattern of this type is necessary for trade to exist. Some misunderstanding of the international trade process arises from the idea that simple trading patterns of this sort adequately explain why trade occurs.

A person in England in the early part of the nineteenth century, working on the assumption that it takes a pattern such as this to motivate trade, would have found it difficult to believe that much of England's trade would develop with other industrialized countries such as the United States and Germany. Nevertheless, as manufacturing developed in Germany, France, and the United States, the quantity of trade between those countries and England increased tremendously; and the proportion of total world trade which is among the industrialized countries has certainly increased over the last hundred-and-fifty years. Thus although we tend to speak of trade as involving the exchange of raw materials for manufactured goods, that is not necessarily true at all. As manufacturing developed in the United States, American citizens with expanded incomes were able to buy more of England's specialized manufactures.

The crude statement that a country will lose its export markets because of the development of manufacturing in other countries is not an accurate description of what has happened in the evolution of international trade, nor does it offer a reliable indication of what is likely to happen.

Changing Patterns of Trade

A changing pattern of exports and imports is the order of the day for a developing, dynamic, expanding economy. Table 7 shows the changing relative importance of various American industries in the foreign trade picture. There has been a steady long-range decline in the importance of

TABLE 7

CHANGING COMPOSITION OF UNITED STATES TRADE, 1820–1955

(EXPORTS, OR IMPORTS, OF CLASS IN QUESTION AS A PERCENTAGE OF TOTAL EXPORTS OR IMPORTS)

EXPORTS

	Crude Materials	Crude Foodstuffs	Manu-factured Foodstuffs	Semi-Manu-factures	Finished Manu-factures
1820	60.62%	4.79%	19.51%	9.42%	5.66%
1871–1880	38.59	19.70	21.99	4.61	15.10
1901–1910	30.98	10.55	20.14	12.77	25.57
1926–1930	24.40	6.40	9.72	14.14	45.35
1931–1935	30.23	3.85	8.83	14.51	42.57
1946–1950	13.96	8.33	9.95	11.10	56.66
1954	12.69	4.95	5.08	12.12	65.16
1955	12.36	6.04	5.48	14.96	61.17

IMPORTS

	Crude Materials	Crude Foodstuffs	Manu-factured Foodstuffs	Semi-Manu-factures	Finished Manu-factures
1820	4.66	11.15	19.85	7.48	56.86
1871–1880	17.24	15.98	20.72	13.05	33.01
1901–1910	34.07	11.80	12.04	17.32	24.77
1926–1930	36.80	12.56	9.88	18.89	21.88
1931–1935	28.91	15.61	13.73	18.72	23.03
1946–1950	30.26	18.79	10.72	22.34	17.89
1954	23.57	21.50	10.90	22.58	21.45
1955	25.14	17.62	9.84	24.48	22.91

Source: *Statistical Abstract, 1955*, p. 903.

crude materials exports. This does not necessarily mean that the production of crude materials—copper, lead, and zinc, and uranium ore—is less profitable to the people engaged in those activities than was the case one hundred and thirty years ago. Nor, even, does it mean that there has been an absolute decline in business activity in the area of raw commodity production or export. It simply means that a smaller proportion of total exports involves the export of those commodities. There has been little over-all change in the relative importance of exports of crude foodstuffs, and of semi-manufactured goods. The relative importance of manufactured foodstuffs has declined considerably. Meanwhile, manufactured goods exports have increased in about the same proportion as crude materials exports have contracted.

The expansion in crude materials imports is probably a natural result of the development of manufacturing. Manufacturing and other activities in this country simply require some materials which can be obtained more cheaply abroad; thus a rise in the percentage of total imports represented by crude materials seems to be a natural corollary of industrialization. The contraction in the proportion of imports which are finished manufactures would also seem to be a natural result of the expansion of manufacturing relative to other activity in this country, but is probably also due in part to the extensive tariffs on manufactured goods.

The circumstances connected with some of the major shifts can be identified. The expansion in crude foodstuff exports between 1860 and 1880 was due to a tremendous expansion in agricultural production, especially of wheat in the Northwest. As a result, low-cost American wheat moved onto the world market. But in later years, with the expansion of Argentine and Australian production, and also the expansion of domestic demand in the United States, foodstuff exports dropped in relative importance. One of the shorter run patterns (1927–1935, years of transition from prosperity to depression) is also revealing. During those years manufacturing exports suffered, relatively speaking, and crude materials gained. Indicative of the likely futility of trade restrictions, the tariffs on imports (obtained in the Hawley-Smoot Act of 1930), although cutting down the absolute money value of manufactured goods imports, did not reduce the proportion of imports of manufactured goods. In fact, there was a slight increase in the proportion of manufactured goods imports in those years (whether one considers finished manufactures alone or takes into account manufactured foodstuffs and semi-manufactures as well as finished manufactures).

Some Specific Commodities

A very limited number of raw commodities account for a high proportion of all world trade. The thirteen listed in Table 8, for example, alone account for one fourth of all world trade, and petroleum alone represents almost one twentieth of all international trade. Cotton, coffee, and wheat also represent large figures. However, one should note that the categories used tend to minimize the importance of manufactured goods because they are less homogeneous than the raw commodities; a tractor and an automobile are different commodities in the trade figures.[4]

[4] Tremendous classification difficulties exist, especially in connection with manufactured goods. The United Nations has tried to deal with this problem by developing the Standard International Trade Classification. But the difficulties are still great. See R. G. D. Allen and J. Edward Ely, *International Trade Statistics* (New York: John Wiley, 1953).

The relative importance of all manufactured goods in international trade by comparison with all raw commodities is another matter. Table 7 gives the comparative figures for the United States. Manufactures are a large proportion of exports but only 23 per cent of imports.

TABLE 8

CHIEF WORLD TRADE COMMODITIES

COMMODITY	% OF TOTAL WORLD EXPORTS REPRESENTED BY COMMODITY (1953)	CHIEF EXPORTING COUNTRIES	% OF WORLD EXPORTS COMING FROM COUNTRY INDICATED (1952)	% OF COUNTRY'S EXPORTS REPRESENTED BY COMMODITY IN QUESTION (1952)
Petroleum	4.52%	Venezuela	44%	95%
		Saudi Arabia	18	87
		Kuwait	17	100
Cotton	2.81	United States	42	6
		Egypt	17	87
		Pakistan	13	49
Coffee	2.70	Brazil	52	74
Wheat	2.44	United States	52	6
		Canada	41	17
Pulp and Paper	2.36	Canada	51	20
Wool	1.90	Australia	58	48
		New Zealand	16	34
		Union of South Africa	14	20
Rubber	1.52	Malaya	40	48
		Indonesia	38	44
Timber, Lumber	1.48	x		
Coal	1.25	United States	57	3
		Germany	26	6
		United Kingdom	17	2
Sugar	1.19	Cuba	67	85
		Philippines	10	26
Copper	1.05	Chile	37	63
		Northern Rhodesia	26	87
		Canada	11	2
Rice	.85	Burma	31	74
		United States	25	1
Tobacco	.76	United States	48	2
		Turkey	11	17

Source: *International Financial Statistics*, February, 1955, pp. 22–5, 32.

In any event it is a fact that relatively few raw commodities account for a significantly large proportion of world trade, and when any one of these commodities is singled out, an extremely large proportion of the trade comes from one or two countries. Moreover, the export of that commodity is likely to represent a very large proportion of the total exports of the country in question. The term applied to this state of affairs is *monoculture*. The combination of world dependence on a few sources for supplies of certain commodities with the dependence of the supplying nation on one or two commodities for much of its exports creates a delicate situation. Developments on the world market in the price of one commodity are thrown back with compounded effect (for good or ill, prosperity or depression) on the economies of one or two countries. Some implications of this situation will be discussed in Chapter 13.

IMPORTANCE OF TRADE TO DIFFERENT COUNTRIES

Probably the most satisfactory technique for measuring the significance of trade to any country is to relate imports to national income (or exports to national income, a comparison which would give substantially the same results). If one is interested in determining the importance of trade to a country, the total money value of the trade of one country should not be compared directly with the total money value of the trade of other countries. It should be obvious that international trade is not necessarily more important to the United States than to Cuba simply because the money value of the United States trade is larger. Such a comparison merely shows the relative importance of the United States on the world scene. In an important sense international trade is not more essential to the United States than to Cuba. In fact the United States could probably discontinue trade with less attendant economic disruption than would be the case in Cuba.

Relation to Stage of Development

It has sometimes been argued that there is a connection between the degree of industrialization in a country and that country's dependence on international trade. But actually there seems to be no such correlation between stage of development and dependence on trade. Table 9 indicates that there are industrially developed countries with great dependence on foreign trade (Belgium, Denmark, and the Netherlands); and there are industrialized countries with virtually no dependence on foreign trade (the United States). There are underdeveloped countries (China and India) with little dependence and underdeveloped countries (Cuba) with great dependence. If a country's dependence on foreign trade is not essentially related to its stage of industrial development, to what is it related?

Relation to Size

On the basis of the figures in Table 9, it would seem that the correlation is actually with the size of the country. Of course, "size" is a bit ambiguous. It is probably, in some sense, a combination of resources,

TABLE 9

IMPORTS AS A PERCENTAGE OF NATIONAL INCOME FOR
DIFFERENT COUNTRIES, 1954

	%
I. SMALL COUNTRIES	
Developed	
Belgium	38
Denmark	34
Netherlands	52
Norway	39
Switzerland	26
Sweden	24
Underdeveloped	
Cuba	29
Ireland	40
Philippines	12
Dominican Republic	18
Ecuador	15
Greece	21
Portugal	22
II. MIDDLE-SIZED COUNTRIES	
Developed	
Japan	14
Italy	15
France	13
United Kingdom	21
Germany	17
Underdeveloped	
Canada	22
Mexico	14
Brazil	13
III. LARGE COUNTRIES	
Developed	
U.S.S.R.	1.4 (1938)
U.S.	3
Underdeveloped	
China	4.5 (1936)
India	7.3 (1948)

Sources: Compiled from *Monthly Bulletin of Statistics*, October, 1955, pp. 92–100, 142–4; *International Financial Statistics, passim; Statistical Yearbook, 1952.* (The data on China, the U.S.S.R., and India are from the latter source.)

area, population, and national income. The classification used in the accompanying table represents a rather crude attempt to take into account all of these factors. On the whole, the small countries listed are small in area, resources, population, and national income; but some of the so-called middle-sized countries have quite a large area although a rather sparse population (for example, Australia and Canada), or a high national income and small area (United Kingdom). The large countries— the United States, the Soviet Union, China, and India—are large in varying respects, although not necessarily characterized by high per capita income. In some cases the correlation will be disturbed by using different criteria of size, but on the whole it makes surprisingly little difference. And the general conclusion is that there is an inverse correlation between size and dependence on trade: the larger the country, the less the dependence on trade.

Perhaps the reason for this will be a little clearer if one considers the hemispheres, rather than individual countries, as the basic trading units. Take the Western Hemisphere or the Eastern Hemisphere and compare the value of the imports of the region (a figure which does not include trade between the countries within the region) with the national income of the region. The resulting figure may well be something like one per cent for the Western Hemisphere. If the world as a whole is taken, the figure is zero, all of the world's international trade being contained within the world.

One moderately important qualification should be made to this line of argument. Certain rather small countries, in which the working population is engaged primarily in subsistence agriculture and in which there has been no significant development of mining, seem to have relatively little dependence on international trade (a low ratio of trade to income). It might be argued that they are "little worlds unto themselves" and thus, in a sense, fit the pattern. How prevalent this situation may be remains a question, because these are just the countries without adequate national income figures.

Dependence on international trade is a function of size, and it is natural that this should be so. The observation that a country or a certain type of country is more or less dependent on foreign trade is chiefly an indication of whether it is big or little, not an indication of whether it is developed or undeveloped, raw material producing or industrialized.

This observation has certain implications for policy making. It means literally that the United States could get along without international trade without too much sacrifice. It would not make much difference to the level of living in the United States if international trade were eliminated. One may argue that to obtain coffee (for the nerves) or to obtain tin or uranium (for the stockpile of strategic materials) is extremely crucial, far more important than the size of the trade figures indicates. And mercury, antimony, tungsten, tin, and manganese are examples of minerals that the United States does not have in adequate quantities according to present estimates. What would be the consequences if those things were kept out? There would be some re-adjustment in manufacturing techniques, and a somewhat lower level of living, but there is no reason to think that these changes would be very significant. The country would still be here, the level of living would be only slightly lower, and people would soon become accustomed to some other beverage than coffee.

The Case Against Autarchy

Consequently, if it were true that practicing autarchy could keep a country out of war, it might be worth the sacrifice for the United States. But could it? The United States, for better or worse, is in the world. And there are at least two different sets of circumstances that would make autarchy for the United States extremely undesirable, even downright unstatesmanlike.

International trade could not be eliminated for most of the small countries without a tremendous shake-up in the organization of their economies and, probably, a very drastic decline in the level of living. In a country like Belgium, which is a highly industrialized, manufacturing country, the economy would have to be completely reorganized if international trade were eliminated. Probably there would have to be wholesale emigration and the country would be forced to return to a predominantly agricultural organization. For Belgium, and for Cuba, the elimination of international trade would be a death-sentence on the present way of life. Clearly, it would be unwise for the United States to eliminate its trade, because of the terrific impact which that step would have on the little countries now highly dependent on the United States market. And the large country could hardly avoid becoming embroiled in the political consequences of the desperate conditions that resulted in the small countries.

But another aspect of this question may be even more significant. Surely the practice of self-sufficiency, and the eliminating or restricting of contact with others, is harmful to the country that is doing it. A country must remain in contact with the other countries of the world, especially in contact with their technical progress, if its own economy is not to stagnate. China probably was ripe for exploitation by the countries of western Europe in the middle of the nineteenth century because she had fallen behind the technical progress and productivity of the rest of the world. And this was in large part a result of a policy of isolation. China was at a disadvantage because of technical backwardness and not because of lack of population or lack of raw materials or lack of intelligence. There have surely been periods in China's development when that country was technically more advanced than western Europe—but not in the later nineteenth century.

Applying this line of argument to the United States, it would seem that the best way for this country to *lose* its dominant political position and unmatched level of living is to rely on artificial protective barriers, instead of a dynamic policy of development, to maintain leadership. The United States can do itself a far greater service by being an active participant in world affairs and by being at the forefront in economic development and adjustment. It is, of course, the dynamic and flexible nature of the United States economy—the fact that by comparison with other countries it has been singularly uninhibited by institutional drag on development—which in large measure accounts for the remarkable development of the United States.

Old and inefficient industries must be replaced by newer, more efficient ones. And it surely is true that the exchange of goods is an extremely important element in the exchange of technical knowledge. The United States synthetic rubber industry, which had purposely delayed its development in the 1930's and then found it necessary to develop all at once in the early years of World War II, provides an illustration of the handicaps under which a laggard industry may find itself.[5] There should be not only exchange of goods, but also exchange of ideas and people. How far would the United States have advanced in her atomic energy program without the help of European scientists like Einstein and Fermi? The United States has a reputation for lagging behind in pure theory and moving ahead in practical application and mass production. If we should shut ourselves off from the basic research of the world, denying to other countries our knowledge in the atomic field and consequently being excluded from their knowledge in other fields, it might not be very long before we would be outdistanced in crucially important areas, in spite of our ability to mass-produce. All this is essentially a plea for working out problems by mutual contact in a setting that includes consideration of "the other fellow's side."

The balance is in favor of contact, the interchange of ideas, and goods, and people. And the person or nation making most intelligent use of *all the world's knowledge,* and of as much of the world's goods as it can get, will be the one with the highest level of living.

BALANCE OF TRADE

Much of the policy making designed to influence international trade has been associated with the effort to achieve a so-called *favorable balance of trade.* It would be better to call this phenomenon an *export* balance of trade, since it has yet to be established that there is anything particularly "favorable" about it. But the term is frequently misused in newspaper editorials and political speeches and lobbying efforts, for the idea still prevails in some quarters that there is something good about it.

The term is generally used to apply to a situation in which the money value of goods exported exceeds the money value of goods imported. And in the case of an unfavorable balance of trade, the money value of

[5] George W. Stocking and Myron W. Watkins, *Cartels in Action* (New York: Twentieth Century Fund, 1947), pp. 56–117.

goods imported would exceed the money value of goods exported. But for analytical purposes it would be more meaningful if the term export (favorable) balance of trade were applied whenever the money value of exports of all goods *and services* (i.e., things of value, including shipping services, insurance, etc.) exceeded the money value of the imports of all goods and services.

One reason why data is frequently given in terms of the goods balance alone is because such data is easier to obtain. In fact, for the period before World War II it is the only accurate data available for most countries. And it is still true that for many countries accurate data on services is not available. As a consequence Table 10 deals with the balance of goods or commodity trade for the United States and not with the goods-and-services balance. But Table 36 (in Chapter 25) gives sketchy data on the goods and services balance for the United States during the period from 1850 to World War I and detailed data for the period since 1919. Chart 19, in the same chapter, gives data on the goods balance for Great Britain.

On the whole Tables 10 and 36 give a similar picture of balance of trade developments, with one notable exception. According to the "goods only" statement, the United States shifted over from having a typical import balance to an export balance in the period 1873 to 1875. According to the "goods and services" statement, that development did not occur until the 1890's. Probably this difference in timing is due largely to the fact that one set of figures includes "import of shipping services" from foreigners, since from 1875 to 1895 much of United States trade was being carried in foreign bottoms.

NETWORK OF WORLD TRADE

Although it is impossible for any one country to have continuing inequality in the value of its exports and imports in trade relations with the rest of the world, this does not apply to either the long run or the short run of the relationship between any one country and any other country. United States shipments to England, year after year, could exceed English shipments to the United States—and yet no giving, lending, or gold movements might be involved. In fact, this is an extremely important basic possibility. England could have an export balance with Brazil, and Brazil an export balance with the United States, that would continue indefinitely.

Chart 2 hints at the extremely complicated nature of the trade network of the world. Within this complex pattern—even though in a given year one country's exports to another do not equal its imports from that coun-

TABLE 10

BALANCE OF TRADE (GOODS OR MERCHANDISE ONLY) FOR
THE UNITED STATES

($1,000,000)

(EXPORT BALANCE: NO SIGN; IMPORT BALANCE: —)

1790— 3	1835— 22	1880 168	1925 683
1791—10	1836— 52	1881 260	1926 378
1792—11	1837— 19	1882 26	1927 681
1793— 5	1838 9	1883 101	1928 1,037
1794— 2	1839— 44	1884 73	1929 842
1795—22	1840 25	1885 165	1930 782
1796—23	1841— 11	1886 44	1931 334
1797—24	1842 4	1887 24	1932 288
1798— 7	1843 40	1888— 28	1933 225
1799— .4	1844 3	1889— 3	1934 478
1800—20	1845— 7	1890 69	1935 235
1801—18	1846— 8	1891 40	1936 33
1802— 4	1847 34	1892 203	1937 265
1803— 9	1848— 10	1893— 19	1938 1,134
1804— 7	1849— 1	1894 237	1939 859
1805—25	1850— 29	1895 76	1940 1,396
1806—28	1851— 22	1896 103	1941 1,802
1807—30	1852— 40	1897 286	1942 5,323
1808—35	1853— 60	1898 615	1943 9,583
1809— 7	1854— 61	1899 530	1944 10,330
1810—19	1855— 39	1900 545	1945 5,646
1811 8	1856— 29	1901 665	1946 4,796
1812—39	1857— 55	1902 478	1947 8,673
1813 6	1858 9	1903 394	1948 5,529
1814— 6	1859— 38	1904 470	1949 5,429
1815—60	1860— 20	1905 401	1950 1,423
1816—65	1861— 70	1906 517	1951 4,065
1817—12	1862 1	1907 446	1952 4,483
1818—28	1863— 39	1908 666	1953 4,900
1819—17	1864—158	1909 351	1954 4,869
1820— 5	1865— 73	1910 188	1955 4,163
1821— .03	1866— 86	1911 522	1956 6,397
1822—19	1867—101	1912 551	
1823— 4	1868— 75	1913 653	
1824— 3	1869—131	1914 471	
1825 1	1870— 43	1915 1,094	
1826— 5	1871— 77	1916 3,091	
1827 3	1872—182	1917 3,281	
1828—17	1873—120	1918 3,118	
1829 .3	1874 19	1919 4,016	
1830 9	1875— 20	1920 2,950	
1831—24	1876 80	1921 1,976	
1832—14	1877 151	1922 719	
1833—14	1878 258	1923 375	
1834— 6	1879 265	1924 981	

Source: *Statistical Abstract, 1955*, p. 901.

CHART 2

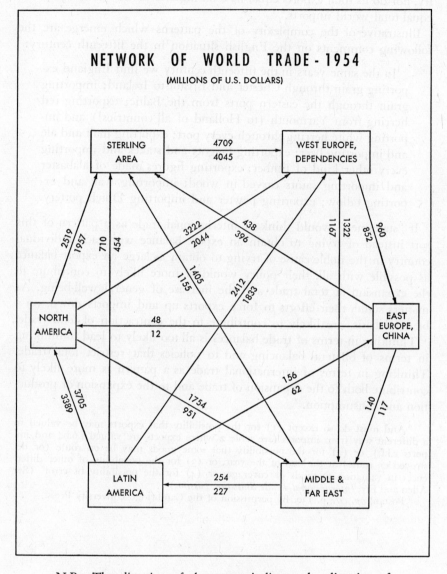

NETWORK OF WORLD TRADE - 1954

(MILLIONS OF U.S. DOLLARS)

N.B.: The direction of the arrow indicates the direction of movement of the larger of the two figures.

Source: *Monthly Bulletin of Statistics,* August, 1955, pp. viii–xix.

try, nor do its total exports equal its total imports—total world exports do equal total world imports.[6]

Illustrative of the complexity of the patterns which emerge are the following comments on the English situation in the fifteenth century:[7]

> In the same years in the fifteenth century we find England exporting grain through Chester and Bristol to Ireland; importing grain through the eastern ports from the Baltic; exporting red herring from Yarmouth (to Holland of all countries!) and importing white herring through every port; exporting malt and ale and importing beer; exporting faggots and stakes and importing every other kind of timber; exporting figures made of alabaster and importing saints carved in wood; importing wax and exporting tallow; exporting pewter and importing Dutch pottery.

If "statesmen" would think of international trade as a pattern of this sort instead of trying to obtain an export balance with each individual country in the noble cause of trying to obtain as large an export balance as possible with all, their policy would be more likely to contribute to the expansion of total trade and the increase of general well-being. As matters stand, their efforts to force exports up and imports down, on a bilateral basis, are likely to contribute to the contraction of total trade.

Thinking in terms of trade balances is all too likely to lead to thinking in terms of bilateral balancing and to policies that restrict total trade. Thinking in terms of international trade as a pattern is more likely to contribute both to the expansion of trade and to the expansion of production and consumption.

[6] And must do so except (1) for the possibility that exports may be valued in a different way from imports (see table 2 where exports are valued f.o.b., and imports c.i.f.), or (2) for the possibility that some goods may be en route (or destroyed en route) at the end of the year, or (3) for the possibility of other differences in valuation methods or coverage, or (4) for the possibility of error. (See Allen and Ely, *International Trade Statistics, passim.*)

[7] Postan, *op. cit.,* p. 130. By permission of the Cambridge University Press.

PART II

The Traditional Theory

Chapter 3

MERCANTILISM

🙚 🙚 🙚

*Until about the fifteenth century, nations conducted their foreign trade
so as to obtain as much goods as possible.*

*During the mercantilist period from 1500 to 1750, nations planned their
foreign trade in an effort to have an export balance and accumulate
gold.*

*They desired gold perhaps because they thought it was wealth, perhaps
as a temporary store of wealth, perhaps as a stimulus to trade.*

*Mercantilists believed in holding down wages in order to make it pos-
sible to sell exports at lower prices.*

*English development during the mercantilist period owes much to the
fact that demand for English goods was stimulated by low English prices, which were the result of England's being less well supplied with gold than were other countries.*

🙚 🙚 🙚

PART II is in some respects historical, representing an effort to
trace the evolution of the main theoretical concepts which have
influenced man's attitude toward international economic problems. This chapter attempts to trace the earlier evolution
through the mercantilist period and down to the time of Adam Smith
and the American Revolution.

HISTORICAL BACKGROUND (PRE-MERCANTILISM)

Nowhere in the literature of the ancient world does one find a "fear
of goods" psychology expressed. Governments as well as individuals
tried to get as much goods and give as little in exchange as they could.
Organized effort to keep goods out of a nation and to export as much
as possible was hardly characteristic of those earlier times.

That the Romans operated in this frame of reference is indicated by
the importance to Rome of the grain shipments from Egypt. The Roman
was not interested in working to provide goods for export to the regions

he had conquered. His interest was the rationally selfish one of getting as much goods as possible from others so as to have more time for the spectacles at the Colosseum. Exploitation and pleasure were the keynotes; modern movies on ancient Rome are clear on this point. Such a method of behavior might be considered a rather low form of the intelligent selfishness alluded to in Chapter 1.

Then during the Middle Ages the attitude toward trade was conditioned by the moral attitude of the Catholic Church. In the realm of buying and selling the dominant concept was the *just price,* which had as a corollary disapproval of cheating one's neighbor. It might be argued that getting more "value" of imports in exchange for less "value" of exports (the Roman procedure) would involve cheating the other countries in a manner opposed to the just price concept. Consequently one might not expect to find a plea for an import balance of trade in medieval writing. Nevertheless, a very sophisticated understanding of the trading process is found in some of the writing of the period. Ricardus de Media Villa (Richard of Middletown), who died about 1306, for example, wrote the following: [1]

> Let us envisage two countries, A and B, unequally endowed by nature. A produces corn in abundance, but little wine, while country B has an abundance of wine and a deficiency of corn. We know that the market price or the just price of a commodity varies according to its plentifulness or scarcity. The same commodity when plentiful is less appreciated than when it is scarce. In this manner a sextarium of corn in country A will be cheaper than in country B, while conversely a dolium of wine in country A will be dearer than in Country B. Now, it is natural for the business of trade and commerce to equalize supply. The merchant, then, buys corn cheap in country A and sells it at the higher market price that is ruling in country B, or he buys wine cheap in country B and sells it at the higher market price that is ruling in country A, so that in reality the consumer is not in the least overcharged, for he pays for each commodity the normal price, the just price, which is ruling in his respective country. The exchanges are equal, yet the merchant earns his profit, and he does so rightfully, for, *far from having injured either country, he brought benefit to both.* His profit is therefore neither usury nor turpe lucrum. The same rule of equality of exchanges which we find in international trade applies also to the business transactions of individuals in their own country. The commodity which

[1] See Max Beer, *Early British Economics* (London: George Allen and Unwin, 1938), pp. 42–3. Beer quotes from Ricardus de Media Villa, *Quodlibeta* II, questio 23, articulus I; and *Sententiae* III, distinctio 33, articulus 3, questio 4). Quoted with the kind permission of the publisher.

the consumer receives is of more immediate utility to him than the money he gives for it, while to the merchant the money he receives for his commodity is of greater immediate utility than the commodity which he surrenders, so that both draw equal benefits from the exchange. (Italics added)

A modern economist might quibble with some of the details of the argument of Ricardus, but the general idea of gain to both countries as a result of the trading process is a significant part of the statement —even though the merchants in the two countries, seemingly, carry off the gain and even though the just price is rather arbitrarily alleged to be the price prevailing in the country of sale.

The foregoing comments would seem to indicate that in ancient times people were selfish and rational; and in the Middle Ages they were moral and reasonably rational But a great change came over economic thinking during the centuries of the Commercial Revolution in Tudor England, Bourbon France, and Hapsburg Spain and Germany. Men were no less selfish than in ancient times, and possibly no less intelligent, at least in terms of "native" intelligence. But they seem to have become less moral and their selfishness was less intelligently directed. Changes in the institutional organization of western European society led to an international trade policy called mercantilism which involved a change over to a "fear of goods" psychology which still prevails, coloring our attitude on such subjects as the balance of trade. These are important, new attitudes that were completely lacking before the Commercial Revolution.

SMITH'S STATEMENT

The conception prevailing in his time of what mercantilism had been was briefly stated by Adam Smith in 1776:[2]

> The two principles being established, however, that wealth consisted in gold and silver, and that those metals could be brought into a country which had no mines only by the balance of trade, or by exporting to a greater value than it imported; it necessarily became the great object of political economy to diminish as much as possible the importation of foreign goods for home consumption, and to increase as much as possible the exportation of the produce of domestic industry. Its two great engines for enriching the country, therefore, were restraints upon importation, and encouragements to exportation.

[2] Adam Smith, . . . *The Wealth of Nations* (Modern Library ed.; New York: Random House, 1937), p. 418.

SOPHISTICATED STATEMENT

Smith's attack on mercantilism was aimed chiefly at the identification of gold with wealth of which he accused the writers of that school. Recent writers have pointed out at some length that the mercantilists were not quite as simple as Smith charged and that their doctrines do not depend upon a crude identification of gold and wealth.[3] These writers in exploring the actual content of the writings of the mercantilist period have found many statements which show flashes of very considerable insight into economic processes. It is even possible, with the use of some imagination, to find the Keynesian system anticipated in mercantilist writing.

Leading mercantilist writers included Thomas Mun (*England's Treasure by Forraign Trade, or the Ballance of our Forraign Trade is the Rule of our Treasure,* c. 1630), Edward Misselden (*The Circle of Commerce, or the Ballance of Trade,* 1623), Gerard Malynes (*A Treatise of the Canker of England's Common Wealth,* 1601), and Antonio Serra (*Breve Trattato delle Cause che Possono Far Abbondare li Regni d'oro e d'Argento dove non Sono Miniere,* 1613). Leading practitioners of mercantilism were Oliver Cromwell, Lord Protector of England from 1653 to 1658, and author of the Navigation Act of 1651; Jean Baptiste Colbert, controller general of the finances of Louis XIV from 1662 to 1683; and Philip II, king of Spain from 1556 till 1598.

Probably all of the mercantilist writers were agreed as to the desirability of a favorable or export balance of trade. It was, in fact, during this period that the expression "favorable" came into vogue to describe an export trade balance. They were also in agreement as to the desirability of the gold inflow which would result. And they were further agreed that a substantial amount of national government regulation was desirable in order to effect the favorable balance of trade.[4] Such regulatory measures included, on the one hand, customs duties (and in some cases absolute prohibitions) to impede imports and, on the other hand, subsidies and bounties to encourage exports. Privileged markets for exports were also sought when commercial treaties were negotiated. The desire to obtain access to markets on favorable terms represented one of the chief reasons for obtaining colonies; the desire to obtain precious metals was another.

[3] For example, see: Jacob Viner, *Studies in the Theory of International Trade* (New York: Harper, 1937), chapters 1 and 2, pp. 1–118.

[4] The mercantilists also favored a considerable amount of government regulation of internal production, trade, and commerce. This was the age of the developing nation state, and it was thought that all possible effort should be devoted to the strengthening and aggrandizing of the nation and its king. See: Eli Heckscher, *Mercantilism* (London: George Allen and Unwin, 1935).

Motives for Desiring Gold

The mercantilists were in agreement as to the desirability of a gold inflow but were not in agreement as to why it was desirable. Among the reasons alleged for desiring gold were these:

(1) *Gold is wealth.* It is difficult to find a categorical statement to this effect in mercantilist writing. It is necessary to go to the critic of mercantilism, Adam Smith, to find the statement clearly made. Nevertheless, it may have been and probably was a widely held popular belief which colored to the point of dominating mercantilist writing. But it remains rather hard for a thoughtful person to convince himself that the obtaining of gold with the view of holding it in perpetuity (this being the necessary meaning of the expression gold *is* wealth), with no intention of using it in any way, could represent a real gain to a community. The more intelligent mercantilist writers seem to have sensed this and to have shied away from the categorical statement that "gold is wealth." Hence they searched about for other reasons that would justify the desire to bring in gold.

(2) *Gold is a temporary store of wealth.* It is very convenient for a sovereign to have a reserve of gold in the event of war, particularly in the event of a war which is to be fought with foreign mercenaries. It may be noted that if this was the mercantilist argument for having an export trade balance, then it was not true that they considered a favorable balance of trade to be permanently desirable. It was merely desirable in the short run; when they needed to pay the mercenaries in the next war, they expected that the gold would flow out in payment for the import of their service—the service of the mercenary Hessians fighting England's battles beyond the sea. But this argument cannot serve as the basis for alleging that a favorable balance of trade is good or desirable as a final goal. In this setting the import of the gold becomes merely a temporary expedient.

(3) *Gold is a stimulus to trade.* Another argument for a favorable balance of trade that is found in the mercantilist writings runs to the effect that a gold inflow will in some sense stimulate trade (meaning by "trade," it would seem, the amount of internal business activity).

The anonymous author of *Considerations on the East-India Trade* (1701) wrote:[5]

> The *East-India* Trade is the most likely way not only to increase the business in the former Manufactures, it is also the way to introduce new Manufactures, new Imployments, into *England,* by

[5] The text of the pamphlet is reproduced in J. R. McCulloch (ed.), *A Select Collection of Early English Tracts on Commerce. . . .* (London: Political Economy Club, 1856), p. 594. The publication was reissued by the Cambridge University Press in 1954.

creating a greater plenty of Money for this purpose; the greater the plenty shall be of Money, the same will be less likely to be hoarded, less likely to lye still; wanton Purses will be always open to build, beautifie, and improve the Kingdom; Shipping and Navigation will every day increase, new Trades will be discover'd.

In general terms, the idea of additional money being a stimulus to increased production foreshadows Keynes' argument that increased investment of funds will lead to an increase in national income. Or, more specifically, it foreshadows the argument which has been elaborated by certain Keynesians that a boost in exports (with consequent increase in payments received) will have the same effect as an increase in domestic investment in expanding national income. It is interesting that such an idea was present in mercantilist literature even though the argument was not developed in a logically detailed or conclusive fashion. Of recent years it has become quite the fashion in some quarters to imply that mercantilist awareness that an export balance can stimulate internal trade is evidence of how advanced and enlightened they were. There has been a sort of rebirth of respect for mercantilist doctrine. But this surely can be overdone, too, for the mercantilists who made such comments did not analyze in any satisfactory way the process by which the result could be brought about.

Views on Labor

On the other hand, mercantilist views of the place of labor in the economy open to question whether the mercantilists had any conception of the fuller life for ordinary citizens as the worth-while goal of the economic process. They believed that in order to have an increasing supply of goods available for export it was necessary to have a larger and larger labor force; [6] and in order to compete effectively for sales in foreign markets it was necessary to have low export prices; therefore, in order to afford low export prices it was desirable to pay as low wages as possible. This is not a particularly pretty picture, at least in terms of the end result of low wages.

Present-day advocates of trade barriers to stimulate exports and discourage imports can well do a little soul-searching to ascertain whether the measures they advocate will actually sacrifice the internal level of living and the level of real wages in exchange for a "pot of gold" or in exchange for larger monetary profits for a limited segment of the population—specifically, the producer-exporter-fearer-of-foreign-competition.

[6] For reference see: Edgar S. Furniss, *The Position of the Laborer in a System of Nationalism* (Boston: Houghton Mifflin, 1920). He particularly cites Josiah Tucker, Henry Fielding, William Petty, Thomas Mun, and Arthur Young.

Adam Smith for his part was not at a loss to explain the motives of the mercantilists. He said:[7]

> It cannot be very difficult to determine who have been the contrivers of this whole mercantile system; not the consumers, we may believe, whose interest has been entirely neglected; but the producers, whose interest has been so carefully attended to; and among this latter class our merchants and manufacturers have been by far the principal architects.

ROLE OF GOLD AND PRICES UNDERLYING DEVELOPMENT

Thoughts of the above sort may suggest certain questions. Why did western European history follow the path it did during the three hundred years from 1500 to 1800? Why did England, while practicing mercantilism, change from a not particularly advanced country to the site of the Industrial Revolution? Why did other countries, such as Spain, which also practiced mercantilism, lag?

Stated in broad terms, the basic explanation for this surprising English development must lie in a fortunate juxtaposition of technical knowledge, institutional arrangements, and resources.[8] If the sudden acquisition of gold or money can explain development, the Industrial Revolution should have started in Spain, not England.

Spain, as a result of the great discoveries following 1492, acquired great quantities of silver and gold from the New World.[9] The increased supply of money resulted in substantial price rises not only in Spain but also in France and the Low Countries, to which nations quantities of the gold soon spread. But the gold spread with a perceptible lag to England,[10] so that there was a considerable interval during which prices had risen farther and faster on the continent, and particularly in Spain, than in England. The continent was relatively high priced, England relatively low priced; hence England was the more attractive place in

---

[7] Smith, *op. cit.,* p. 626.

[8] Technical knowledge (which western Europe had begged, borrowed, or stolen), such as printing, Arabic numerals, gunpowder, the horse collar, etc.; favorable institutional arrangements such as the more friendly attitude toward the taking of interest which was ushered in by the Protestant Reformation; resources such as coking coal and the humid climate of Manchester. (There is additional discussion of the factors affecting development in Part VII.)

[9] See Earl J. Hamilton, *American Treasure and the Price Revolution in Spain, 1501-1650* (Cambridge: Harvard University Press, 1934.)

[10] Max Beer, *op. cit.,* pp. 95-121; and Richard Cantillon, *Essai sur la Nature du Commerce en Général* (Paris: Institut National d'Etudes Démographiques, 1952). (Text of the 1755 edition.) The most amazing document of all, however, considering its date, was the work of a Spaniard, Martín González de Cellorigo.

which to buy. Some of the impetus which English industry received during the sixteenth and seventeenth centuries was clearly a result of the fact that England *did not have gold*. That the obtaining of gold and silver does not automatically cause industrialization is amply attested by the history of Spain during those years. The varying development of Spain and England rather demonstrated the advantage of being a low-priced country with the appropriate raw materials, an institutional organization that permitted development, and access to the accumulated technical knowledge of the age.

If the English mercantilists had really understood what was going on, they should have been deeply thankful that England did not start this period in 1500 as the possessor of large stocks of gold. But unmindful of their blessings, they spent their energies trying to achieve a favorable balance of trade which would, they hoped, bring in the much-desired gold that Spain had and England lacked.

EVALUATION

Mercantilism should not be left on this negative note. Mercantilism was a stage in history and as such cannot be arbitrarily judged as "good" or "bad." It was a period when the "strait-jacket" rules of the guild system were being thrown off—and along with the inhibitory rules, the guild standards of quality workmanship as well. But the new, important merchant and manufacturer classes, at the same time that they were throwing off the shackles of the guild regulations, were turning to the national sovereign with demands for "aid to the detriment of others" as well as for "aid in throwing off the shackles." The national sovereign in his turn was trying to centralize in his own hands the great powers that had formerly been divided among the feudal barons. It was in this setting that the regulation of trade and production by nation states occurred in the sixteenth and seventeenth centuries. And it is interesting to note that, in contrast to the situation in our time, national government regulation of business was desired by the businessmen. The governments and the rising business groups established a kind of partnership to the detriment of the old, dominant barons and also to the detriment of the mass of the population.

Mercantilism, and the Commercial Revolution of which it was an aspect, may more adequately be called a phase of human history than an economic theory. Nevertheless, even though one may wish to avoid describing mercantilist policies as "good" or "bad" in any absolute sense divorced from the setting, one may well be less kind to one's contemporaries who call for a reversion to mercantilist policies "because they were good."

From a somewhat different point of view, however, and bearing in mind the similarity of certain twentieth-century opinions with those of the mercantilists, one might say with the Frenchman, "le plus ce change, le plus c'est la même chose."

In fact, the statement that the classical, competitive, free private enterprise economics of Smith and Ricardo is dominant today is only a half-truth. In those cases where the national interest in more goods at lower prices conflicts with the interest of free private enterprise in money profits we are all still "little mercantilists" at heart, ready to call on the government for aid, instead of stalwart, independent practitioners of competition.

Chapter 4

CLASSICAL THEORY

⩗ ⩗ ⩗

Adam Smith emphasized that goods rather than gold are the true wealth of a nation.

He advocated free trade as a means of encouraging geographical specialization and division of labor, in order to increase the supply of goods.

Ricardo argued that even if one country had an absolute advantage over another in the production of all commodities, both countries would benefit from specialization and trade: the more efficient of the two should concentrate on those commodities in the production of which it had the greatest comparative advantage, and the less efficient in those areas where it had the least comparative disadvantage.

⩗ ⩗ ⩗

DAVID HUME, in his *Political Discourses* (1752), and Adam Smith, in the *Wealth of Nations* (1776), offered powerful arguments in refutation of the mercantilist position on the balance of trade, gold, and wealth.[1] They laid the groundwork for classical, orthodox, laissez-faire, competitive theory.

ADAM SMITH

Adam Smith took the position that goods, rather than gold stocks, are wealth:[2] "The revenue of the person to whom it is paid, does not so properly consist in the piece of gold, as in what he can get for it, or in what he can exchange it for." This is literally the reason for the title he gave to his book: *An Inquiry into the Nature and Causes of the*

---

[1] Hume's chief contribution, the specie-flow explanation of the operation of the adjustment process under the gold standard, is discussed in Chapter 18. Suffice it to say here that this explanation goes far toward indicating the futility of government planning in the effort to have a permanent net gold inflow.

[2] Adam Smith, . . . *The Wealth of Nations* (Modern Library ed.; New York: Random House, 1937), p. 275.

Wealth of Nations. Smith saw no merit in acquiring increasing amounts of gold for the sake of the gold; rather he considered that what was desirable was the obtaining of more goods. "According therefore, as this produce, or what is purchased with it, bears a greater or smaller proportion to the number of those who are to consume it, the nation will be better or worse supplied with all the necessaries and conveniences for which it has occasion."[3] The idea was not new; but it could stand restating in 1776.

Basic Theories

Smith believed that in the world as a whole there would be more goods to consume if the *division of labor* was practiced. "The division of labour . . . occasions, in every art, a proportionable increase of the productive powers of labour."[4] Smith's classic example concerned the advantages of division of labor in the manufacture of pins.

In connection with the closely related question of *geographical specialization,* Smith said:[5] "If a foreign country can supply us with a commodity cheaper than we ourselves can make it, better buy it of them with some part of the produce of our own industry, employed in a way in which we have some advantage." Smith takes as an example the production of grapes in Scotland:[6]

> By means of glasses, hotbeds, and hotwalls, very good grapes can be raised in Scotland, and very good wine too can be made of them at about thirty times the expence for which at least equally good can be brought from foreign countries. Would it be a reasonable law to prohibit the importation of all foreign wines, merely to encourage the making of claret and burgundy in Scotland? But if there would be a manifest absurdity in turning towards any employment, thirty times more of the capital and industry of the country, than would be necessary to purchase from foreign countries an equal quantity of the commodities wanted, there must be an absurdity, though not altogether so glaring, yet exactly of the same kind, in turning towards any such employment a thirtieth, or even a three hundredth part more of either. . . . As long as the one country has those advantages, and the other wants them, it will always be more advantageous for the latter, rather to buy of the former than to make.

[3] *Ibid.,* p. lvii.

[4] *Ibid.,* p. 5. Appreciation of the gain from the division of labor goes back to Plato.

[5] *Ibid.,* p. 424. This idea, also, was not entirely original with Smith. See the anonymously authored *Considerations on the East-India Trade* (London, 1701), pp. 42–43, as quoted in J. R. McCulloch (ed.), *Early English Tracts on Commerce,* p. 590.

[6] Smith, *op. cit.,* pp. 425–6.

It was through *free trade* that the benefits of geographical specialization and the division of labor were to be divided among the nations.

According to Smith the only valid situations justifying trade restrictions were (1) the encouragement of an industry necessary for national defense, Smith's example being ocean shipping; and (2) a tax on imports to counterbalance an already imposed tax burdening internal commerce (the compensatory duty), so that there would not be a greater tax burden on domestically produced goods than on foreign-produced goods.[7]

Assuming for the moment everything that Smith assumed, how do his ideas bear on the desirability of an export balance of trade? One might expect him to say that an *import balance* would be desirable because it would involve acquiring more goods; and goods are wealth. But this Smith did not say, because of an additional feature of the argument. He was probably a bit more realistic about the nature of the trade process than were the mercantilists and consequently understood that exports must equal imports.[8]

Evaluation

In evaluating the contribution of Adam Smith to the theory of international trade, it may be said that several of his ideas were borrowed from others and many of them are now so commonly held that it is rather difficult to appreciate the genuine importance of their introduction into general economic thinking, which was the great contribution of Smith. The idea that goods rather than mere gold constitute basic wealth, that division of labor and geographical specialization increase total productivity, that as a corollary substantial freedom of trade is necessary, and that "plotting" to obtain a permanent export trade balance is a self-defeating process because exports must equal imports, are ideas of tremendous basic significance.

DAVID RICARDO

Ricardo is, at least in some quarters, credited with being a more important member of the classical school than Adam Smith, probably in large part because his logic is supposed to have been better. Taking Adam

[7] Smith, *op. cit.,* pp. 420–39. Smith was explicit in denying the validity of the infant industry argument for tariffs. And if he be granted his assumptions of full employment, free competition, and "mobility of the factors," there is considerable merit in his argument. Smith also thought that tariffs might be a matter of discretion in situations calling for retaliation against a foreign country and that high prevailing tariffs should be removed only gradually. (The infant industry argument is discussed at greater length in Chapter 9.)

[8] See Chapter 6, p. 77.

Smith's ideas as a basis, he refined them into the precise logical form in which they were expressed as classical economics for the next hundred years. In the field of international trade, Ricardo's contribution was the doctrine of comparative cost.

The Comparative-Cost Argument

In developing the comparative-cost argument, Ricardo selected as an example trade between Portugal and England in cloth and wine. This was an earthy example in 1817. The Portuguese-English trade was important in those days; it had been so, in fact, at least since the Methuen Treaty of 1703. And the trade was characterized by the exchange of port wine from Oporto for English woolens. So, at least in some respects, Ricardo's example might be called realistic—although in other respects it was as unrealistic as could possibly be imagined. (For example, it assumed that Portugal had an absolute advantage over England in the production of all things.)

The following arithmetic example was used as the basis for developing the comparative-cost argument:

	Number of man years of labor required to produce one unit of:	
	CLOTH	WINE
In Portugal	90	80
In England	100	120

In the words of Ricardo:[9]

England may be so circumstanced that to produce the cloth may require the labour of 100 men for one year; and if she attempted to make the wine, it might require the labour of 120 men for the same time. England would therefore find it her interest to import wine, and to purchase it by the exportation of cloth.

To produce the wine in Portugal might require only the labour of 80 men for one year, and to produce the cloth in the same country might require the labour of 90 men for the same time. It would therefore be advantageous for her to export wine in exchange for cloth. The exchange might even take place notwithstanding that the commodity imported by Portugal could be produced there with less labour than in England. Though she could make the cloth with the labour of 90 men, she would import it from a country where it required the labour of 100 men to produce it, *because it would be advantageous to her rather to em-*

[9] David Ricardo, *The Principles of Political Economy and Taxation* (Everyman's Library ed.; London: J. M. Dent, 1911), p. 82. The work was originally published in 1817.

*ploy her capital in the production of wine, for which she would
obtain more cloth from England than she could produce by di-
verting a portion of her capital from the cultivation of wines
to the manufacture of cloth.* (Italics added)

Ricardo does not actually identify the forces which determine the precise quantity of cloth that will be exchanged for one unit of wine. He
merely assumes that there is a range within which there is advantage
to both parties in trade.

Assuming for the moment, however, that one unit of cloth exchanges
for one unit of wine, the argument might run somewhat as follows:
The Portuguese would be producing wine at an expenditure of 80 units
of labor per barrel. If they devoted their efforts to cloth production, it
would take 90 units of effort to produce a bolt of cloth. In the absence of
international trade, a bolt of cloth would cost more to produce in Portugal
than would a barrel of wine; hence it would cost more than a barrel of
wine to obtain a bolt of cloth. Therefore the Portuguese would relish
the idea of being able to obtain a bolt of cloth from England for only
one barrel of wine.

But would the Englishman be willing to provide a bolt of cloth for
only one barrel of wine? It costs Englishmen 100 units of effort to produce a bolt of cloth and substantially more, 120 units of effort, to produce
a barrel of wine. In the absence of international trade, it would take
more than one bolt of cloth to buy a barrel of wine in England. Therefore the Englishman also will relish the idea of being able to obtain, via
international trade, a barrel of wine for only one bolt of cloth.

Both countries will gain from trade if cloth is exchanged for wine
at a "one-to-one" ratio. And this is true in spite of the fact that the
Portuguese can produce both cloth and wine more cheaply, in terms of
real effort, than can the English. Even if one country has an absolute
advantage over another in the production of all commodities, both countries will benefit from specialization and trade if the more efficient of
the two concentrates on those commodities in the production of which it
has the greatest relative or *comparative advantage.*

It is no refutation of this theory that the data cannot be substantiated
in an actual study—that is, that figures for cost of production in terms
of labor time cannot, in practice, be computed. But this consideration
certainly renders the theory less useful for application to real-life problems.
Refutation of the theory would take the form of proving one of two
things: either that the assumptions on which it is based are contrary to
fact, or that the logic is bad.

The logic of the theory of comparative cost is impeccable. It remains
to evaluate the assumptions on which the theory rests.

Mobility of Productive Factors

Land, labor, and capital are immobile internationally, though labor and capital (if not land) are mobile internally. Ricardo refers, for example, to "the difficulty with which capital moves from one country to another, to seek a more profitable employment," and to the facility with which it moves within a country.[10]

Ricardo took the position, then, that labor and capital can move freely within any country. This meant that if the wages paid in Lancashire were higher than the wages paid in Essex, then laborers would move from Essex to Lancashire. If the interest rate were higher in London than in Lancashire, then the capital supply would move to London. Capital and labor would move, and move freely, internally; as a consequence, wages and interest rates would be uniform throughout England. The assumption of the free movement of labor and capital was at the very heart of the classical theory of the working of the internal economy.

Ricardo was aware that the productive factors did not work that way in all situations—that there was not always completely free movement. Nevertheless, for the purposes of his analysis of an internal economy, he assumed that movement was free. He compensated for this unreality in his theory of international trade, where he assumed the contrary— that labor and capital could not move. English labor could not go to Portugal, nor could English capital, even though they would be more productive there.[11]

This assumption of the international immobility of capital and labor is necessary to the logic of the comparative cost argument because, if English capital and labor could move from England to Portugal, they would continue to do so as long as Portuguese production costs were lower. And in the situation described in Ricardo's numerical example— Portugal having a permanent advantage over England in the production of all things—England would eventually be depopulated. This result could be prevented only by assuming that productive factors could not cross national boundaries. Thus the assumption was necessary to the theory, whether or not it represented an accurate description of conditions in the real world.

If he had chosen to see, Ricardo had before him at the very time he wrote, in refutation of his position, the example of Englishmen emigrating to the thirteen colonies in North America. However, this consideration does not necessarily discredit Ricardo's assumption. He could not deal theoretically with all possible circumstances. Accordingly, he chose to deal with the two extreme situations—complete mobility of labor and

[10] Ricardo, *op. cit.,* p. 83.
[11] And the climate would be more agreeable.

capital on the one hand and complete immobility on the other. For analytical convenience he dealt with one in his internal theory and with the other in his international theory. But he was probably aware that it would be necessary to blend and compromise the two views as part of a reasonably accurate description of either an internal or an international situation. Alfred Marshall later did the same thing in developing his price theory; he described the competitive situation and the monopoly situation, knowing full well that an accurate description of most situations would lie somewhere between. If the theoretical description of two extremes proves useful, even though the reader must fit actual cases in somewhere between, Ricardo is entitled to some credit for having analyzed the two extreme situations of complete mobility and complete immobility of labor and capital in presenting his theories on the internal and international economies.[12]

Labor Theory of Value

A second basic element in Ricardo's premises was the *labor theory of value*. Those classical economists Ricardo and Karl Marx dealt with the theory of value in much the same way. Looking behind money prices, which are—or have been up to now—unsatisfactory as a measure of real value, Ricardo (and Marx) speculated as to the nature of true, basic, and fundamental value. They decided that the way to measure or compare value was in terms of the amount of labor time going into the production of the goods whose values were being compared. Ricardo wrote: "I affirm only that their relative values will be governed by the relative quantities of labour bestowed on their production."[13]

Ricardo did not affirm that the labor theory of value determined either (1) absolute value in any measurable sense or (2) the immediate money price, but merely that it determined *in the long run* the relationship among the money prices of different goods. Thus, to use Ricardo's example the long-run exchange ratio between cloth and wine, in the absence of international trade, would be determined by comparison of the amount of labor required to produce each. In England, a unit of wine would be slightly more valuable than a unit of cloth, as determined by the ratio of 120 to 100.

It should be noted, however, that for goods moving in international trade the exchange ratio is not determined by the relationship between labor costs. It cannot be, since that relationship is different in the two

[12] But Ricardo might have done better to describe his theory of comparative advantage merely as the counterpart of his competitive theory, rather than setting it up as a theory of international trade. The logic of Ricardo's argument is applicable to any situation involving immobility, whether in international trade or not. And to the extent that there is mobility of capital and labor in international trade, it is not applicable to such trade.

[13] Ricardo, *op. cit.*, pp. 29–30.

countries. The exchange ratio is, however, set *within the limits* which are determined by the relationship between the labor time costs of production in the two countries. The Englishman will not be willing to give more than 1.2 bolts of cloth for a barrel of wine; and the Portuguese will not be willing to give more than nine-eighths of a barrel of wine for a bolt of cloth.

A work on international economics is hardly the place for a detailed critique of the controversial labor theory of value. However, certain aspects of the theory are pertinent to the international trade problem.

(a) It has not been possible, up to now, to keep reliable accounting records in terms of labor time. There are various reasons for this. It is difficult not only to make allowance for the varying degrees of skill involved in different types of work, but also to evaluate the labor time that went into the capital equipment being used.

(b) Substantially the same problem remains if a real cost theory of value, adding capital and land to labor time, is substituted for the labor theory. Actual computation of the real value of a combination of these diverse elements (if money prices are not a satisfactory measure of real value) is difficult to manage.[14]

(c) Nevertheless, whether labor cost or real cost may be measured or not, and whether or not they are objectively determined, they may still represent the important basic influences that underlie and control the direction and amount of trade.

Two Country–Two Commodity Assumption

Another of Ricardo's premises was the so-called *two country–two commodity assumption*. Ricardo, in his example, literally assumed that Portugal and England were the only countries in the world, and that cloth and wine were their only products. This assumption immensely simplified the example. Whether this simplification destroys the validity of the theory has been much discussed. Probably it does not. Nevertheless, in dealing with the tremendously complicated problems of the real world, with its many countries and many commodities, it would be difficult to test for a situation containing a clear example of comparative advantage, even if the labor theory of value had not, by its very nature, virtually precluded such testing.

Constant Cost

The fourth of the Ricardian assumptions was the assumption of *constant cost*. In Ricardo's example, it was assumed that it would take 100

---

[14] One may believe that certain real cost values underlie the productive process and still be skeptical of a value theory that, while alleging objectivity, is incapable of being used in making accurate measurements. The actual trouble may well be that "real" value originates in the minds of men rather than in concrete objects.

man-years of labor to produce a unit of cloth in England, however much or however little cloth might be produced altogether.

Assuming the possibility of rising and falling costs (and U-shaped cost curves), the volume of production of many lines of goods in different countries would tend to adjust so that the marginal cost of production would be the same in different countries. In this modified situation the difference in the cost of producing the early units would control the volume of production in the different countries, but there would be no ultimate difference in marginal cost among them, once the production and trading patterns were established.

Adjustment of this sort, if it went on to any considerable extent, would reduce the number of instances in which it would be possible to identify an actual comparative-cost situation. Marginal costs would be equal, and the *direction of trade* in a particular commodity would be a corollary of the different *volumes* of production (and consumption) in the different countries. This would reduce the importance of the comparative-cost type of situation, although it is still conceivable that such a relationship could exist if the volume of production was not sufficiently great to equalize marginal costs.[15]

Evaluation

Even if the constant-cost assumption is disallowed, Ricardo's theory is not basically discredited. But evidence of the underlying cost differences will be indicated by the differing production volumes and not by marginal cost differences.

From the preceding discussion of the assumptions underlying the theory of comparative cost, it is evident that their validity cannot be clearly established. Nonetheless, the theory of comparative cost itself may be fundamentally true. For there must be, in some sense, real values and real costs, although it may turn out that they must be determined in a subjective rather than an objective manner.

Immobilities, or difficulties of movement and adjustment, should be taken into account in international trade theory. This the comparative-cost argument attempts to do.

But in the area of the practical, the theory, as a guide to policy making, is little improvement over Adam Smith's less sophisticated argument based on absolute rather than comparative differences in cost. All either theory tells the policy maker is that, in general, goods should be produced in the most economical places, and that substantial freedom of trade is desirable.

[15] For the short run there is perhaps a certain amount of truth in a constant-cost assumption. A recent careful study in the steel industry indicates that costs are likely to be fairly constant over the range in which the firms are actually operating. But since Ricardo was primarily concerned with long-run adjustment, this evidence can hardly be considered to support his theory.

Ricardo's comparative-cost doctrine continued to provide the basis for the accepted description of the forces regulating international trade until as late as the 1930's. For example, Frank W. Taussig, possibly the leading American economist of the 1920's, in his *International Trade* worked from the comparative-cost approach.[16] And that approach still represents a major topic in international economics texts, even though much of the descriptive and analytical material which fills the balance of the books cannot be handled in such terms.

Ricardo's ideas provide a motivation for trade, but they do not indicate on what terms the trade will occur. Will Portugal or England gain most from the trade? How much cloth will it actually take to buy a little wine? In Ricardo's example will they exchange at a one-to-one ratio or some other? John Stuart Mill, writing in the middle of the nineteenth century, attempted to answer these questions.

[16] Frank W. Taussig, *International Trade* (New York: Macmillan, 1928).

Chapter 5

TERMS OF TRADE

❦ ❦ ❦

According to Mill, the division of the gain from trade favored the nation whose demand was less intense.

The unit (or net barter) terms of trade concept involves a comparison of import and export prices.

Despite much controversy, it is not established that the unit terms of trade tend to move favorably for developed countries by comparison with underdeveloped countries. On the other hand, it is possible for the terms of trade of all countries to improve at once.

❦ ❦ ❦

RICARDO'S argument had not determined the exact ratio at which cloth would be exchanged for wine. Ricardo's figures established merely the outside limits within which the exchange ratios of cloth to wine could fluctuate and still be profitable to both parties. But where is the price (or the exchange ratio) going to be established between these extremes after international trade begins? And how have these "terms of trade" evolved through the years?

MILL'S THEORY OF RECIPROCAL DEMAND

In an effort to answer the first question, John Stuart Mill wrote in 1829:[1]

> It may be considered, therefore, as established, that when two countries trade together in two commodities, the exchangeable value of these commodities relatively to each other will adjust itself to the inclinations and circumstances of the consumers on both sides, in such manner that the quantities required by each country of the article which it imports from its neighbor, shall be exactly sufficient to pay for one another.

[1] John Stuart Mill, *Essays on Some Unsettled Questions of Political Economy* (London: Parker, 1844), p. 12. The work was originally written in 1829 but not published till 1844. It was reprinted by the London School of Economics and Political Science in 1948.

In this early formulation, the only factors mentioned as influencing the result were factors on the demand side—"the inclinations and circumstances of the consumers." No mention was made of the role of supply. The conditioning factor, that exports must equal imports in value, was hardly new with Mill.

Later, in his *Principles,* Mill gave a place in the proposition to supply (capital) factors; but he did not emphasize them.[2]

The argument behind the theory of reciprocal demand may be stated somewhat as follows: England at the time had cloth to offer, and a certain amount of desire for wine. Portugal, on the contrary, had wine to offer and a certain amount of desire for cloth. Let us assume that Englishmen "just cannot get along" without wine (a likely assumption), whereas the Portuguese do not care whether they are clothed or not. In that case, Portugal is going to profit most from the trade in terms of the ratio of exchange in the average transaction. That is to say, the country with the less intense demand is going to profit most. And this is true because the country which is desperately in need of the other country's products is going to be willing to give relatively more of what it has to offer (in terms of labor time) in exchange for a unit of what the other country has to sell. The country with the more intense demand is going to gain less from the trade. Under this hypothesis, Portugal gains more from the trade—not because she is the country with the lower costs, but because she is the country with the less intense demand. If Portugal were desperate for cloth and Englishmen did not care whether or not they drank port wine, the exchange ratio would move in a direction favorable to England. England would have to give less cloth for a unit of wine; consequently England would enjoy more favorable terms of trade even though she had the higher real costs of production in connection with both commodities. In the doctrine of John Stuart Mill, the "inclinations and circumstances of the consumers" thus became the chief factors in determining who would gain most from a given volume of trade. And the possibility that supply conditions could influence the result was added as an afterthought.

THE TERMS OF TRADE

Such was the classical identification of the forces controlling the division of the gain from trade. Geographical specialization, full employment, and optimum use of resources would assure the existence of such gain. The problems with which Mill was concerned, handled in a somewhat different way as the "terms of trade," have in recent

[2] John Stuart Mill, *Principles of Political Economy* (New impression of the 6th ed.; London: Longmans, Green, 1904), p. 365.

years become increasingly important and (strangely enough) statistically manageable.

Various statistical methods have been used in trying to evaluate the terms of trade. Probably the four most important are (1) the net (barter) terms of trade which might better be called the unit terms of trade, (2) the gross (barter) terms of trade, (3) the double factoral terms of trade, and (4) the income terms of trade (or the index of the capacity to import).[3]

Unit Terms of Trade

When the expression *terms of trade* is used, it generally refers to the unit terms of trade. This index is computed by relating the index numbers of import prices and export prices (unit values of imports and exports). Using the figures in Table 11, the unit terms are obtained by dividing the export price index (unit value of exports) by the import price index (unit value of imports). Rising figures indicate improving terms of trade (i.e., a country is getting more value of import in exchange for each unit of whatever it exports), and falling figures indicate worsening terms of trade.

The methods for computing the terms of trade were standardized to a considerable extent by Frank W. Taussig in the late 1920's.[4]

Charts 3 and 4 show the unit (and gross) terms of trade for the United States from 1879 to date and for Great Britain for the longer period from 1798 to date.

Terms of Trade and Stage of Industrial Development

These figures may be analyzed in various ways. But one of the most significant issues was raised by John Stuart Mill. He alleged that "the richest countries, coeteris paribus, gain the least by a given amount of foreign commerce: since, having a greater demand for commodities generally, they are likely to have a greater demand for foreign-commodities, and thus modify the terms of interchange to their own disadvantage."[5]

An opposing position was taken by the Economic Commission for Latin America in a 1949 study entitled *Relative Prices of Exports and Imports of Under-developed Countries.* That study, the heart of which is the comparison of United Kingdom export and import prices from

[3] See Allen and Ely, *International Trade Statistics,* pp. 207–11. The unit terms of trade are discussed in the following text; the other three concepts are discussed in the supplementary note at the end of the chapter.

[4] Taussig, *International Trade,* pp. 411–19. The method shown in the above illustration does not represent exactly Taussig's mechanics, but the resulting concept is substantially the same as his, except that in Taussig's formulation falling, rather than rising, figures indicated improving terms.

[5] Mill, *Principles . . . ,* p. 365. Mill's proposition is theoretically suspect on the ground that he has confused total purchasing power and intensity of demand.

CHART 3

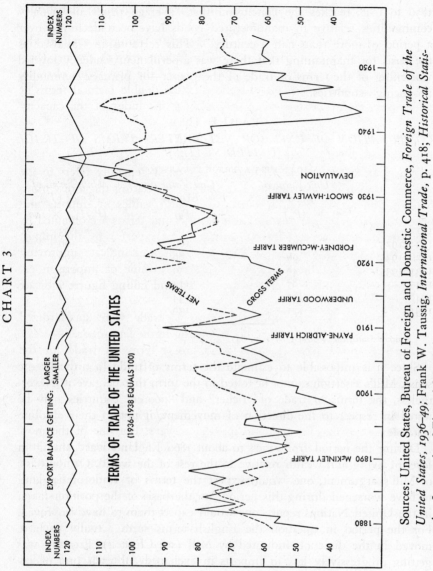

TERMS OF TRADE OF THE UNITED STATES
(1936-1938 EQUALS 100)

Sources: United States, Bureau of Foreign and Domestic Commerce, *Foreign Trade of the United States, 1936-49;* Frank W. Taussig, *International Trade,* p. 418; *Historical Statistics; International Financial Statistics.*

1876 to 1948, reaches the conclusion that "average prices of primary commodities relative to manufactured goods have been declining over a period of more than half a century."[6] This relationship was used as the basis for maintaining that there was a permanent tendency toward worsening of the terms of trade of the poorer—or primary commodity producing—countries.

TABLE 11

COMPUTATION OF UNIT (OR NET BARTER) TERMS OF TRADE (UNITED STATES)

(1923–1925 AVERAGE EQUALS 100)

	Unit Value of Imports (P_m)	Unit Value of Exports (P_x)	Unit Terms of Trade (T_u) $(P_x/P_m) \times 100$
1913	70	65	93
1923–1925	100	100	100
1926–1930	90	86	96
1931–1935	48	59	123
1945	87	112	129
1948	132	134	102
1951	171	138	81

Source: *Statistical Abstract, 1952,* p. 847.

Since it is impossible to estimate the terms of trade in any absolute sense, Mill's assertion cannot be tested in the form that he gave it. Nevertheless, the terms of trade of "richer" and "poorer" countries may be tested in respect to the direction of movement, if not to their absolute state.

During the period from 1798 to about 1860 England was gaining in level of living and wealth relative to the rest of the world. On the basis of Mill's argument, one would expect the terms of trade of England to have worsened during this period; on the basis of the position taken in the United Nations report, one would expect them to have improved. For the period in question the English terms seem actually to have moved in the direction indicated by Mill (see Chart 4). England was getting progressively less in imports in exchange for each unit of exports during the period when, as a consequence of the Industrial Revolution, she was taking world leadership in economic development.[7]

[6] United Nations, Economic Commission for Latin America, *Relative Prices of Exports and Imports of Under-developed Countries* (Lake Success, 1949), pp. 22–23; and United Nations, Economic Commission for Latin America, *The Economic Development of Latin America and Its Principal Problems* (Lake Success, 1950). Raúl Prebisch is largely responsible for the studies.

[7] One may guess that Mill was wrong as to the reason. It was not so much the greatness of English demand as the tremendously expanded English supply and the declining production costs in England which contributed to the result.

CHART 4

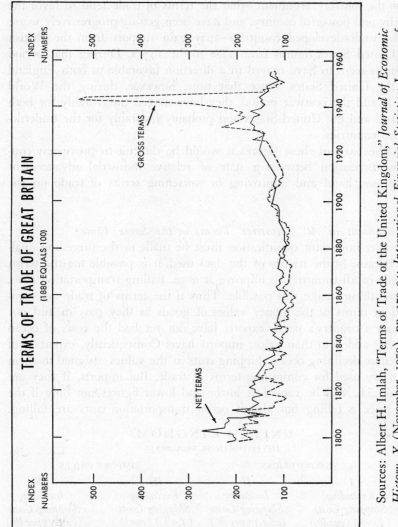

TERMS OF TRADE OF GREAT BRITAIN
(1880 EQUALS 100)

Sources: Albert H. Imlah, "Terms of Trade of the United Kingdom," *Journal of Economic History*, X (November, 1950), pp. 170–94; *International Financial Statistics*; League of Nations, *Review of World Trade*; Great Britain, General Statistical Office, *Annual Abstract of Statistics*; *Yearbook of International Trade Statistics*; *Monthly Bulletin of Statistics*.

But the contrary argument—that the terms of trade tend to favor the wealthy and powerful country, and have been getting progressively worse for the underdeveloped countries—may gain support from the British and United States figures from 1880 to the 1930's. During that period the terms seem to have moved in a direction favorable to both England and the United States. Since that time, however, during the World War II and the postwar period, they have moved unfavorably for both England and the United States and probably favorably for the underdeveloped countries.

On the basis of these figures it would be difficult to prove any consistent correlation between a state of relative industrial advancement on the one hand and improving or worsening terms of trade on the other.

Improvement in All Countries' Terms at the Same Time

Another important qualification must be made to the preceding analysis. Because of the nature of the data used, it is possible for the terms of trade of all countries to improve at once. Falling transportation costs, for one thing, make this possible. Thus if the terms of trade are computed in terms of the money values of goods as they pass in and out through a country's ports, exports have not yet had the costs of ocean shipping added to their price; imports have. Consequently, exports will not reflect declining ocean shipping costs in the values assigned to them which are used for computing terms of trade. But imports, if they are valued c.i.f., will be valued at lower and lower figures not only if the f.o.b. price is falling but also if ocean transportation costs are falling.

UNITED KINGDOM
(HYPOTHETICAL FIGURES)

	EXPORT PRICES		IMPORT PRICES	
	I Excluding Shipping Costs (f.o.b.) (per lb.)	*II* Including Shipping Costs (c.i.f.) (per lb.)	*III* Excluding Shipping Costs (f.o.b.) (per lb.)	*IV* Including Shipping Costs (c.i.f.) (per lb.)
1910	£1.00 (100)	£1.20 (100)	£1.00 (100)	£1.20 (100)
1920	1.00 (100)	1.10 (92)	1.00 (100)	1.10 (92)

(The figures in parentheses are the money prices converted to index numbers, using 1910 as the base year: 1910 equals 100.)

In the above table, f.o.b. export prices for the United Kingdom remain unchanged between 1910 and 1920, although c.i.f. prices are falling. On the import side c.i.f. prices are falling, although f.o.b. import prices remain unchanged. If f.o.b. prices for both exports and imports were used in computing the terms of trade, the terms would remain unchanged at 100 (100/100 × 100) in 1920 by comparison with 1910. But if f.o.b. export prices and c.i.f. import prices were used, the terms of trade of Britain would appear to have improved from 100 to 109 (100/92 × 100). Assuming Latin American terms of trade to be the reverse of the British, as was done by the Economic Commission for Latin America, evidence such as this would indicate that the Latin American terms had worsened. But if the British c.i.f. export price and the British f.o.b. import price were used as evidence of the trend in the Latin American terms, then one would conclude that the Latin American terms had improved from 100 to 109. The latter procedure gives a fairer comparison with British terms when they are computed from f.o.b. export prices and c.i.f. import prices.

In the terms of trade computation, falling shipping costs are more likely to be reflected in the import data than in the export data; this could produce a situation in which the terms of trade of two countries trading exclusively with each other would improve at the same time if the same method were used in both calculations.

These considerations suggest a possible flaw in the argument of the Economic Commission for Latin America—apart from the fact that figures covering a longer period do not seem to confirm the conclusions drawn from the 1876–1938 data. Because of the inadequacy of the statistics from the Latin American countries, the Commission has assumed that improvement in the terms of trade of Britain and the United States meant that the terms of trade of Latin America were worsening. But this conclusion does not follow, at least insofar as the British–Latin American relationship is concerned. The Latin American terms may have been improving at the same time that the British terms were improving.

Most countries assign f.o.b. prices to exports and c.i.f. prices to imports in computing terms of trade.[8] Britain does this, for example. And in such cases the preceding comments are valid. The United States and Canada, however, use f.o.b. values for both exports and imports. For them, the preceding comments would not be valid.

Hidden Qualitative Changes

Another, and perhaps more important, weakness in the long-run data on change in terms of trade results from the improvement in quality of manufactured goods, as well as from the change in their identity. British worsteds, for example, are better cloth now than they were two hundred years ago. Also, there is a tremendously increased variety of new manufactured goods available for buying. Index numbers do not

[8] C. P. Kindleberger, "Industrial Europe's Terms of Trade on Current Account," *Economic Journal*, LXV (March, 1955), p. 19.

accurately reflect changes of this sort—and it should be noted that the quality and variety of the manufactured goods exported by countries like England have probably changed more than the quality and variety of the raw commodities exported by countries like Chile.

If these two considerations (improved quality and greater variety) were properly taken into account, Britain's terms of trade probably would be shown to have moved in a direction less favorable to Britain than currently used figures indicate.

CONCLUSION

These reservations are not intended to refute the usefulness of the terms-of-trade concept. However, the concepts used in analyzing international trade must be employed with caution, with a reasonable awareness of what they mean, and with respect for the difficulties involved in making the figures accurate. It is only very recently that statistical data of this sort has become available for analyzing trade problems. There are now prospects of greatly enlarging our understanding of the trading process. But by the same token, both the data-gathering methods and the meaning of the data must be studied closely.

SUPPLEMENTARY NOTE: ADDITIONAL TERMS OF TRADE CONCEPTS

Gross Terms of Trade

The concept of the gross terms of trade involves an effort to compare the *change* in the relationship between the real value of aggregate imports and the real value of aggregate exports. It thus combines the information derived from total exports and imports with that obtained from the unit terms of trade.

In Table 3 the figures for the money value of exports have been converted into a series of index numbers in the first column. The second column contains index number figures indicating the change in the price level of exports. Division of the price level figures into the appropriate money value figures (I/II) gives a series of index numbers representing the *change* in the "real" value of exports; a similar calculation could be made for imports. This method may be used to secure a series of index numbers for the change in "real" value (quantum or quantity or volume) of exports or imports.

The table on page 71 contains a series of such quantum figures for the United States. The gross (barter) terms of trade are then computed by dividing the index of the quantum of imports by the index of the quantum of exports.

The gross terms of trade, thus computed, show whether the "real" value of imports is rising or falling relative to the "real" value of exports. A rising figure indicates that the value of imports is increasing relative to exports. But the figures do not provide assurance at any given time that the terms of trade are either favorable or unfavorable to a given country—merely that they have been getting more or less favorable with the passage of time. For example, one does not know

	Quantum of Imports (Q_m)	Quantum of Exports (Q_x)	Gross Terms of Trade (T_g) $(Q_m/Q_x) \times 100$
1913	66	84	79
1923–1925	100	100	100
1926–1930	116	122	95
1931–1935	92	76	121
1945	122	192	64
1948	141	208	68
1951	165	241	68

whether in 1923–25 (the base years) the "real value" of imports actually equaled the "real value" of exports. The two 100's in the table are merely due to the fact that the value of both imports and exports for 1923–25 has been arbitrarily equated to 100. If different base years were used, the computed figures would be different. But, regardless of the base year, the direction of movement of the figures should be the same for any given period of years.

Double Factoral Terms of Trade

Another factor to be taken into account is the increased productivity of labor (and perhaps of capital) in the various countries. Raúl Prebisch has argued:[9]

> During the period covered by that research—the forty years preceding the Second World War—manufacturing production costs declined regularly and persistently. The movement of prices did not follow this pattern at all. *The increase in productivity was not reflected in prices but in income. Wages and salaries rose as real costs fell.*

[9] United Nations, Economic Commission for Latin America, *The Economic Development of Latin America and its Principal Problems,* pp. 15, 16; H. W. Singer, "The Distribution of Gains between Investing and Borrowing Countries," *American Economic Review, Papers . . . ,* XL (May, 1950), pp. 473–86.

> . . . . *since prices do not keep pace with productivity, indus-*
> *trialization is the only means by which the Latin-American*
> *countries may fully obtain the advantages of technical progress.*

The double factoral terms of trade represent an effort to take these additional complexities into account. They are derived from the net barter (unit) terms of trade multiplied by the relative change in productivity in the export sector of a given country and then divided by productivity in foreign industries engaged in producing its imports.

Double factoral terms of trade $= ($Unit terms of trade $\times \dfrac{Z_x}{Z_m})$

where:

Z_x is the productivity in the export sector of a given country, and Z_m is the productivity in foreign industries engaged in producing its imports.[10]

There follows a computation of the movement of the double factoral terms of trade of industrial Europe relative to the tropical, underdeveloped countries of Latin America, Africa, Asia, and the Middle East (designated by Kindleberger as "all other" countries), which is based upon Kindleberger's rough estimates of productivity.[11]

	I Productivity of Industrial Europe (Z_x)	II Productivity of "All Other" (Z_m)	III Productivity of IE rela- tive to AO $(I/II)100$	IV Net Terms of Trade of IE relative to AO	V Double Fac- toral Terms of Trade of IE relative to AO $(III \times IV)/100$
1872	55	80	69	123	85
1900	75	90	83	122	101
1913	100	100	100	100	100
1928	135	110	123	119	147
1938	170	120	142	176	250
1952	170	125	136	155	210

[10] Charles P. Kindleberger, *The Terms of Trade: A European Case Study* (New York: The Technology Press of Massachusetts Institute of Technology and John Wiley, 1956), p. 6; Jacob Viner, *Studies in the Theory of International Trade*, p. 561. I have inverted the productivity part of the index relative to the position suggested by Kindleberger and Viner. It seems reasonable that increased productivity is gain for the one whose productivity is increasing. Kindleberger discusses the problem of estimating productivity (pp. 223–227) and the computation of the double factoral terms of trade for industrial Europe (p. 240). He does not place much confidence in the estimates of productivity nor in the accuracy of the double factoral terms of trade which he computes. But he seems to feel that the computation is worthwhile because it indicates how the computation might be made with more accurate data.

[11] Kindleberger, *Terms of Trade*, pp. 227 and 234; the figures do not entirely correspond with those of Kindleberger on p. 240.

From this computation it appears that the position of industrial Europe is improving relative to that of the underdeveloped countries as the result of a combination of increasing productivity (Column III) and increasingly advantageous prices (Column IV).

Whether the benefits of increased productivity should be passed along is not established by the double factoral terms of trade concept per se. Perhaps the person whose productivity increases should be the beneficiary of that increase. Whether he should be or not, Prebisch seems to feel that he is, and that the only way for the underdeveloped countries to deal with the problem is by industrializing themselves.

Capacity to Import

One other concept closely related to the terms of trade is the "capacity to import" concept, sometimes called the income terms of trade.[12] The index of the capacity to import is the product of the unit terms of trade and the quantum index of exports divided by 100. It is computed for the United States for various years in the following table:

	Quantum of Exports (Q_x)	Unit Terms of Trade (T_u)	Income Terms of Trade $(T_{inc.})$ $(Q_x \times T_u)/100$
1913	84	93	78
1923–1925	100	100	100
1926–1930	122	96	117
1931–1935	76	123	93
1945	192	129	248
1948	208	102	212
1951	241	81	195

The usefulness of this concept lies in the fact that it places emphasis where intelligent selfishness indicates it ought to be. Exports and the terms of trade in combination determine how much capacity to import (foreign exchange, etc.) a country will possess in implementing its selfish desire for more goods (imports).

This concept is better called "capacity to import" than "income terms of trade," if the expression *terms of trade* is applied only to situations involving the division of the gain from trade. In contrast with the gross and unit terms, which will tend to fluctuate around 100 if the base year is intelligently selected (and if the possibility of secular decline in transport cost is temporarily forgotten), the capacity to import can be expected to rise as a long-run trend. Moreover, it may rise for all countries at the same time. Chart 5 gives the data for the United States for a long enough period of time to indicate a secular trend up-

[12] Allen, *op. cit.,* pp. 208–9; G. S. Dorrance, "The Income Terms of Trade," *Review of Economic Studies,* XVI (1948–49), pp. 50–6.

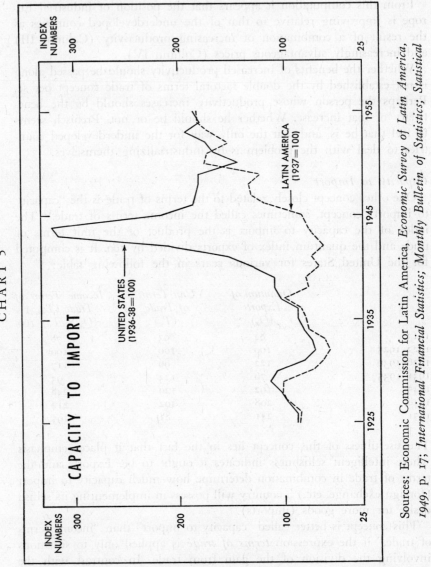

CHART 5

CAPACITY TO IMPORT

INDEX NUMBERS

300

200

100

25

UNITED STATES
(1936-38=100)

LATIN AMERICA
(1937=100)

1925   1935   1945   1955

INDEX NUMBERS

300

200

100

25

Sources: Economic Commission for Latin America, *Economic Survey of Latin America,
1949*, p. 17; *International Financial Statistics; Monthly Bulletin of Statistics; Statistical
Abstract*.

ward. But there is nothing about this development which need alarm the confirmed American "pusher of exports." It is precisely the increase in United States exports which is responsible, in large measure, for the increase in capacity to import.

During World War II the real value of Latin American exports remained below 1937 levels; and the Latin American terms of trade did not improve; all of which meant that during the war years the Latin American countries were "suffering" in terms of capacity to import. (Only the capacity-to-import figures are shown in Chart 5.) But the foreign exchange reserves built up during those years by the Latin American countries (one of the outstanding wartime developments) were not the result of "wartime profiteering" due to relatively high prices. The terms of trade indicate that Latin American export prices were relatively low by comparison with the prices the Latin American countries had to pay for imports. Rather, those countries built up foreign exchange reserves because they were doing very little importing in quantitative terms. The Latin American countries went on their buying spree after the wartime export controls were lifted by the United States and other countries during the postwar years when they (the Latin American countries) had everything in their favor: the foreign exchange reserves of the war years, a rising quantum index of exports, improving terms of trade, and a rising capacity to import. Nevertheless, in the years following the war, the rise in imports was of such magnitude that the Latin American countries got into payment difficulties in spite of all these favorable factors—in spite of the rising capacity to import.

The usefulness of the concept (quantum index of exports times unit terms of trade) as a guide to actual capacity to import is limited by the fact that the quantum index of exports and the terms of trade take into account, at best, only what is happening to goods and the prices of goods—and only during the particular year in question. In actual fact the export of services (such as tourist expenditures in Latin America) and foreign lending may provide the region with considerable capacity to import; also, a nation may finance imports with the foreign exchange reserves acquired in earlier years. An even more serious difficulty, however, is indicated by what happened to the United States capacity to import during World War II. The chart indicates a phenomenal rise; and yet much of that rise was due to lend-lease shipments, which did not give the United States a claim on foreign exchange such as would really increase her capacity to import.[13]

---

[13] To deal with these difficulties, the Economic Commission for Latin America has reformulated its procedures for computing capacity to import. See *Economic Survey of Latin America*, 1954, pp. 8–9, as well as United Nations, Department of Economic and Social Affairs, *Analyses and Projections of Economic Development, I. An Introduction to the Technique of Programming* (New York, 1955), p. 25. The formula now used by ECLA takes into account exports of goods and services, effect of the terms of trade, and net inflow of foreign capital.

Chapter 6

"MODERN" THEORY

⚑ ⚑ ⚑

According to Ohlin, money costs and monetarily expressed demand interact in the foreign-exchange market in a "mutually interdependent" process to determine that goods are produced and exported from the lowest money-cost source.

The identity of the goods moving in international trade, their quantity, and the direction in which they will move depend on the supply elasticities, demand elasticities, and national-income forces in both countries.

There is, according to neo-classical price theory as applied to international trade, a tendency for the prices of given commodities to be the same all over the world.

However the tendency to price equalization is so retarded by the existence of transfer costs as to permit very substantial price discrepancies between different countries.

The "constructive free trade" position is based on the premise that neither pure free trade nor the operation of market forces as now known will assure maximum well-being throughout the world.

⚑ ⚑ ⚑

PRICE theory and general equilibrium analysis, for which Alfred Marshall, Cournot, Walras, and Pareto are largely responsible, involve the use of demand and supply analysis to determine the forces that will interact to set price and volume of production for each individual commodity and for all commodities together. This theory has been applied to international trade in the analysis of Bertil Ohlin and others.

In various economic writings of the last twenty-five years the application of price theory to international trade has frequently been called the "modern" theory. In Ohlin's own formulation it is generally called the mutual interdependence theory. The argument in the early part of this chapter is chiefly based on Ohlin.[1]

[1] Bertil Ohlin, *Interregional and International Trade* (Cambridge: Harvard University Press, 1933). There is amazing anticipation of Ohlin in Augustin Cournot,

MONEY PRICES, SUPPLY, AND DEMAND

Ohlin continued to base his theory on many of the assumptions of Ricardo. He assumed competition (with qualifications), free private enterprise, and laissez faire (with reservations). But internal mobility and international immobility of resources—far from being an assumption—became a problem in his analysis, as will be seen. And instead of using a labor theory of value or a real-cost theory of value, he presented a money-cost theory of value and based his argument upon money prices, demand, and supply. He said that any one country would export those commodities which it produced at lower money costs and would import the goods that other countries produced at lower money costs.[2]

The supporting analysis involves appraisal of the underlying factors affecting (1) money costs (supply), (2) market demand, and (3) foreign exchange rates. But these factors, Ohlin stresses, are mutually interdependent. Domestic money costs cannot be determined except as part of the process which, at the same time, is conditioning demand and foreign exchange rates.

Several elements must be taken into account before money costs can be known. There must be a theory for analyzing the forces that influence internal money costs and demand; and there must be a technique (the foreign-exchange rate) for comparing money costs and demands in different countries. To make matters more difficult, the foreign exchange rate, in its turn, is not predetermined, but rather is set as part of the process determining costs and demand.

Supply Costs

In the determination of supply conditions, according to Ohlin, the problems are the same as those that enter into the construction of an ordinary supply curve in orthodox domestic price theory. Remuneration is paid to the various factors of production: labor gets a wage, capital gets interest, land receives rent, and the entrepreneur receives profits. Each is bargaining for his share in the competitive market and getting as much as he can. Entering into the businessman's decision as to the relative quantities of the different factors which he will use are the total costs which result at different levels of output as the factors of

---

Recherches sur les Principes Mathématiques de la Théorie des Richesses (Paris: Marcel Rivière, 1938), pp. 134–45, 173–98. The work was originally published in 1838.

[2] However belated, the "modern" theory of international trade represented an important development. And the use of money costs and money prices as the fundamental variables in the analysis gives an element of reality to international trade analysis which was not present during the years of adherence to a labor cost or a real cost theory of value.

production are combined in various possible proportions. Then, too, costs are dependent on the size of plant, and on the production techniques and methods which are used.

In the international field there is an important qualification which complicates the role of supply costs. The quantities of the various factors of production available for use (and consequently the marginal prices which will be paid for them) are influenced by whether the goods are internationally traded or not. It is not possible, by means of a simple analysis of cost conditions in different countries, to determine relative costs with any assurance *before international trade begins.* The fact of trade itself must be taken into account as a factor conditioning the relative availability of the different factors. Also, unlike the spokesmen for classical theory, Ohlin assumed that capital and labor could move internationally, if only at certain costs. This, too, would affect the prices of the various factors in the different countries.

Demand

As for the elements on the demand side, that complicated subject will be slighted with the comment that the domestic and foreign demand patterns which exist after trade has begun (and which are not determined until trade has begun) are the effective demand patterns.

Foreign Exchange Rates

The handling of the rate of exchange represents the third factor in the theory. The price differences—determined by costs in dollars and costs in francs, and demand in dollars and demand in francs—are only potential price differences, not actual price differences, until the exchange rate is set. What is a franc going to be worth: twenty United States cents, or one cent, or one third of a cent, or what? Ohlin answered the question by saying that the rate of exchange "depends on the conditions of supply and demand, transport and prices in such wise that imports and exports and other elements that enter into the balance of payments (including, above all, capital transactions) create an equality between the supply of and demand for exchange in this situation." [3]

In the foreign exchange markets, if such markets actually were free, people would be haggling and bargaining to see who could get most and give least. It would be possible to draw a curve representing the demand for dollars and the supply of francs, for example, much like any other supply-and-demand curve. The exchange rate would equilibrate

[3] Bertil Ohlin, *Comercio Exterior y Politica Comercial* (Madrid: Aguilar, 1948), p. 89. It may be noted that in this formulation of the doctrine Ohlin is allowing for foreign investments as a possibility making it unnecessary that imports exactly equal exports; but essentially this is still the position of Adam Smith and of John Stuart Mill—that the adjustment will take place in such wise that exports equal imports.

the demand for and the supply of foreign exchange. This argument involves little more than the application of demand-and-supply analysis to national currencies. But, according to the "modern" theory, the demand for and supply of the currencies are conditioned by the production costs and demand schedules; and these in turn are not determined until the exchange rate is set. After the exchange rate, demand, and supply have been set by their *interaction* on each other, it is possible—and only then is it possible—to state that the cost of production of something in the United States is higher or lower than the cost of production of something in France, and consequently to state where production will occur and in which direction various goods will move.

A slight qualification should be added. Actually, according to price theory, production tends to expand in the low-cost location and contract in the high-cost location until prices (except for a margin permitted by transfer costs) are equal in both places. If the process actually reaches this point, the cost advantages in the different countries will be overtly visible in the statistics on differences in volume rather than in the statistics on price. But since the tendency to cost and price equality is only a tendency, meaningful differences in costs and prices will frequently be observable. Ohlin was most realistic in arguing that a tendency toward equilibrium and price uniformity does not insure that such equilibrium and uniformity are the prevailing situation.

Ohlin, Ricardo, and Adam Smith

What effect does this theory have, if any, on Ricardo's comparative-cost doctrine? It should be noted that Ohlin's theory ignores the comparative-cost situation; therefore, neither the truth nor the falsity of the comparative-cost doctrine is established. According to Ohlin, one country will have lower money costs in some things, another country will have lower money costs in other things. There is thus an absolute difference (not a comparative difference) in money costs. There may or may not be a difference in comparative real costs underlying this difference in money costs; no one is in a position to say. Ohlin is dealing with money-price data that can be assembled, rather than with real-value data which cannot. And when money-value figures are used, an *absolute* difference in money price or cost will motivate trade.

The ideas underlying Ohlin's theory were very similar to those of Adam Smith. According to Ohlin, as well as Smith, the relative abundance or scarcity of the different factors of production in different countries is the fundamental force in determining the place of specialization. However, Ohlin did not assume an almost complete immobility of labor and capital, as Smith had done; instead he substituted transfer costs in his theory and analyzed the ways in which the transfer costs influence the process. Presumably industries will be located relative to markets so that total costs, including transfer costs, are kept as low as possible relative to receipts.[4]

Ohlin thus made a sophisticated statement of demand-price and supply-price analysis and applied it to the theory of international trade.

PRICE ELASTICITY

Ordinary Meaning

In ordinary price theory the concept of price elasticity refers to the relationship between the rate of change in quantity (demanded or supplied) and the rate of change in price. If quantity demanded or supplied is quite sensitive to price changes, we speak of elastic supply or elastic demand. If quantity is insensitive to price changes, we speak of an inelastic demand or an inelastic supply. On the demand side the borderline between elastic and inelastic demand is called unit elasticity. It describes a situation in which buyers are willing to spend the same total amount of money on the purchase of the type of goods in question regardless of price. On the supply side, unit elasticity merely means that a certain percentage change in price will call for the same percentage change in output.

Algebraically the relation may be represented by the equation:

$$Elasticity = \frac{\% \text{ change in Quantity}}{\% \text{ change in Price}}$$

The more refined concept correlates an extremely small percentage change in quantity with a correspondingly small change in price. Thus if the quantity supplied will rise .000002 per cent when the price rises .000001 per cent, then the elasticity of supply is 2.

$$\frac{.000002}{.000001} = 2$$

In applying the concept of price elasticity, it is valuable to conceive of a situation as it appears to those involved. Thus a producer, in deciding how much of his product to supply, will consider the possible prices to be paid to him in his own currency. The buyer will likewise demand goods on the basis of the prices he must pay in his own currency.

Meaning as Applied to International Trade

These concepts may be reasonably definite and meaningful when applied to a single commodity in the domestic market. It is tempting

[4] For Ohlin transfer costs included not only transportation costs but trade barriers as well.

to apply them straightway to international trade. And much useful analysis may occur as a result. But the fundamental nature of the *price elasticity* concept changes significantly when it is applied to international trade in the customary manner.

Applied to international trade, the concept no longer refers to what happens to an individual commodity when price changes; it refers to what happens to all the exports or all the imports of a country when price *levels* change (or when currencies are devalued).

Elastic demand for a country's exports means that, if their price level falls, the total amount which foreigners will spend on them will increase. But there are subtle variations to this proposition that keep it from being as simple as the similar proposition applied to the internal demand for a particular commodity. For example, is the money value involved to be measured in the currency of the selling or of the buying country? This difference is important in cases where currency devaluation has been the device which effected the price-level change. For example, let us assume that the United States devalues the dollar so that the number of francs which would yesterday buy $100,000,000 of United States goods will today buy $200,000,000 worth. In this situation the French will have to double the dollar value of their purchases to effect a situation of unit elasticity in terms of francs. This adjustment must occur to keep the franc expenditure as large as it was before the devaluation. Consequently, dollar expenditure would have to be more than doubled to justify saying that there is elastic demand in terms of francs.

But if elastic demand merely means that, consequent on a currency devaluation of the sort mentioned, the French are willing to buy at least $100,000,001 of United States goods, the situation is quite different. They can manage that with an expenditure of only slightly more than half as many francs as they previously spent on United States goods.[5]

Factors Determining Trading Pattern

In the case of the price elasticity of internal demand for one commodity, the analysis may legitimately assume that national income does not change. It can also assume that the forces influencing the demand situation are independent of the forces influencing the supply conditions. There is merit, under certain circumstances, in making the above assumptions and then considering how changes in demand and supply conditions will affect the quantity of a particular commodity which is sold.

But when the elasticity concept is applied to international trade, the circumstances are materially altered. No longer is one commodity being

[5] In connection with the discussion of currency devaluation in Chapter 19, there is additional discussion of the problem of making practical use of the concept of elasticities.

analyzed alone. The price-level changes affecting the quantity of all exports of a country are being analyzed all at once. It is no longer valid to assume that changes affecting these large blocks of commodities will have no effect on national income. It is no longer valid to assume that the factors affecting the demand conditions are independent of the factors influencing the supply conditions. After all, *total* demand and *total* supply are not determined independently; they are large or small together.

In dealing with the international trade elasticities, therefore, it is not particularly meaningful to isolate one elasticity and evaluate the effect of that one elasticity on exports (let us say) alone.

A complex of factors needs to be taken into account in determining what goods and in what quantities will move in international trade. These elements include:

(1) the elasticity of demand (in country B) for exports (from country A);
(2) the elasticity of demand (in country A) for imports (from country B);
(3) the elasticity of supply in A;
(4) the elasticity of supply in B;
(5) and various effects on national income in both countries which react back to influence the demand and supply conditions a second time.

THE TENDENCY OF PRICES TO EQUALIZE

Neo-Classical Theory

Ordinary price theory, when applied to international trade, has several things to say about comparative prices and price levels. For one thing, there is a tendency for the money price of a particular type of goods to be equal in different countries. For another, there is a tendency for price levels to come together or equalize. And the tendency toward equality of commodity prices is facilitated by a tendency toward equality of the prices paid for the factors of production.

To the extent that the factors of production (labor and capital but not, as a rule, land) are mobile internationally, they will migrate until the price paid for them—proper allowance being made for foreign exchange rates and for transfer costs—is the same in all countries. The resulting equality of factor prices in different countries will tend to equalize the prices of products. However, to the extent that a factor cannot move internationally (land generally being cited as an example of this), the price paid for it in different countries will not completely equalize. But even then, since the products can move from the countries where they are produced at low cost to the countries where production costs are higher, prices of the final product in the different countries tend to become equal. Moreover, this combination of developments tends to equalize the prices paid for all the factors, including the immobile factors such as land.[6]

If a certain type of land is relatively high priced in one country, so that the commodity produced on it is also high priced, there will be a tendency in that country to buy that commodity abroad. Consequently, the demand for the domestically produced commodity will fall and the price which that type of domestic land can command will fall. It will fall toward the level which that type of land commands in the country where production is "lower cost." Thus there is a tendency toward equalization of the price paid in various countries for even the immobile factor of production land. As a result, everything tends toward equality in this most equal of all possible worlds.

There is a large element of belaboring the obvious, some element of important truth, and some positive misrepresentation in these assertions of neo-classical price theory when they are applied to international trade.

Of course, neo-classical price theoreticians have recognized that trade barriers, tariffs, quotas, transportation costs, non-comparability of the factors used in different countries, and the like, mitigate against complete equalization of factor costs and prices. But these possibilities are generally listed parenthetically *as exceptions* to the general rule that prices tend to equality.

Evidence of Inequality

Inequality seems to have been more prevalent and more of a problem than the foregoing would indicate. Wages, both real wages and money

[6] Ohlin, *Interregional and International Trade, passim;* Paul A. Samuelson, "International Trade and the Equalisation of Factor Prices," *Economic Journal,* LVIII (June, 1948), 163–84; Paul A. Samuelson, "International Factor Price Equalisation Once Again," *Economic Journal,* LIX (June, 1949), 181–97; Carl Iversen, *Aspects of the Theory of International Capital Movements* (Copenhagen: Levin and Munksgoard, 1936), *passim.* Ohlin, Samuelson, and Iversen have expressed awareness of the difficulties and frictions which beset the operation of the process they describe. But they still assume that it is worth while to build a theory on the "tendency to equalization." Professor Samuelson, apparently concerned about some of the complications of his 1948 article, stated at the beginning of his 1949 article: "My recent paper attempting to show that free commodity trade will, under certain specified conditions, inevitably lead to complete factor price equalisation appears to be in need of further amplification." But worse, in this field of study, is the inclination, once the theory is centered on the "tendency to equalization," to assume that facts follow the theory and to make certain deductive judgments, as Ohlin does, for example (p. 344): "The foreign borrowing of Denmark was to some extent used to reorganise agriculture and transform it to a butter and bacon industry—which must have reduced the supply prices of these goods in Great Britain."

wages, have consistently been higher in the developed countries that have taken the leadership in the Industrial Revolution than in the under-developed tropical and subsistence-agriculture countries. English labor has enjoyed such an advantage from the eighteenth century on. As early as 1701, the anonymous author of *Considerations on the East India Trade* went so far as to allege that ". . . a King of India is not so well lodg'd, and fed, and cloath'd, as a Day-labourer of England." [7] This statement is, no doubt, exaggerated, but it is indicative of a re-lationship that informed people knew to exist. Englishmen, even then, were better off than Indians—if not than Indian kings. The United States, now the dominant industrial country, for many years has enjoyed higher real and money wages [8] than the rest of the world.

Money prices in general—allowance being made for the prevailing foreign-exchange rate—are probably also higher in developed than in underdeveloped countries. [9] Money prices are perhaps generally higher in the United States than in the rest of the world and already were higher long before World War II. Enough travelers have noticed this phenomenon to make it credible, even though professional statisticians find it difficult to give precise expression to the relationship. It is also probable that higher prices prevailed in England during the eighteenth and nineteenth centuries than in the less developed parts of the world.

Reasons for Inequality

Why are persistent discrepancies possible between the wage rates in different countries and between individual commodity prices and price levels in different countries? The answer would seem to be that a different social and institutional milieu makes possible a different pat-tern of economic values. If it were simply that raw material resources, techniques, and capital plant were quantitatively present in different proportions, and if there were no other differences, one would expect the "tendency toward equalization" postulated in classical theory. But something more is required to explain the difference; and that additional element would seem to be slow-dying cultural and institutional differ-ences. The transfer costs (transport costs, tariffs, trade barriers), which merely permit the differences and do not cause them, will not explain

---

[7] McCulloch, *A Select Collection . . .* , p. 594.

[8] The use of the money-wage comparison in this context means merely that, if the prevailing foreign-exchange rate is allowed for, there is such a money-wage dif-ference.

[9] If anyone really feels inclined to question the truth of this, I shall hedge and say that the theory which follows is relevant for price differences without regard to which way the difference is. Various international agencies are engaged in statistical work designed to compare directly the cost of living in different coun-tries. But the work has not gone very far as yet. However, see: United Nations, Statistical Office, *Retail Price Comparisons for International Salary Determination* (Statistical Papers, series M, no. 14 [New York, 1952]).

why wages tend to be higher in the developed than in the underdeveloped countries.

A specific factor which might help to explain why the general level of prices is higher in developed than in underdeveloped countries is market differentiation. This type of discrimination is impossible in competitive markets but is common in monopolistic situations. If monopolies were spread evenly over the globe, market discrimination would account for specific, isolated price differences, though it could not explain why the entire price level is higher in one area than in another. But the fact is that powerful monopolies in manufacturing are characteristic of the institutional structure of some countries and not of others; this difference in the pattern of social organization makes it possible to identify a type of economy which may well be characterized by higher prices.

Another explanatory factor is the dumping of goods—that is, selling a commodity at a lower price in foreign markets than at home. Cartels, enjoying a monopoly in the domestic market (partly because of artificial barriers against imports which have been erected largely as a result of pressures from corporations and trade associations), keep prices high there. But in the foreign market they have to compete more extensively. Consequently the prices are lower abroad. As a possible but not necessary result of this combination of circumstances, the price levels could be higher in the developed than in the underdeveloped countries, even though the terms of trade were unfavorable to the developed country.

Other examples of institutional differences could be cited. The difference in institutional structure makes United States investors fearful that their money is not safe in Latin America. The attitudes toward investment in real estate are quite different in the two areas, and so are the organization of the credit system, the attitude toward women's wearing shorts, the attitude toward eating meat on Friday, the attitude toward having household servants or letting the wife do the housework. Such examples could be multiplied many times over. When combined they mean that the pattern of demand for goods and services is going to be quite different in the areas under consideration. The price that will be paid for caviar is going to bear a different relation to the price that will be paid for wheat in the two countries, and this is quite aside from the question of what it would cost to produce caviar, wheat, potatoes, rice, or West Highland white terriers in different areas. Within the range of price differences permitted by transfer costs, individual prices vary as they do between countries. And there is nothing in this scheme of things which will tend to make the average of all prices the same in the various countries. The general price levels in the different countries may therefore vary within the limits set by the transfer costs. The fact that the consumption habits of people differ appreciably in different areas is enough to establish that the prices will probably not be completely comparable—as long as there are transfer costs. And by the same token, as those habits and customs change in different directions, in the natural course of events, the prices will not necessarily vary together.

These comments in no wise disprove the part played by trade barriers and transfer costs in perpetuating price differences among "world trade" commodities. But the trade barriers, transportation costs, and immobility elements involved are of such an order of magnitude as to permit price-level differences of great size. Another theory is required to explain why and where the price-level differences will settle (if they do settle) within the range of difference which transfer costs permit.

THE CASE FOR "CONSTRUCTIVE FREE TRADE"

Given free competition, an effectively working price system, a tendency for prices to equalize, and so on, the international trade theories of Smith, Ricardo, and Ohlin all led to the conclusion that free trade (in a setting permitting geographical specialization) was conducive to the optimum pattern of goods production and distribution. But in the world as we know it, this argument can be accepted only with certain qualifications and modifications.

James E. Meade has recently reformulated the free-trade argument to take account of certain qualifications which seem to be indicated:[10]

> We will call the position which is reached with all the interventions which are required to lead to a maximum of world real income (but without any interventions which may be undertaken solely to affect the distribution of world real income between the various countries or solely in order to put the balance of payments into equilibrium) the "modified free-trade position."

The chief difficulty in arriving at such a desirable situation rises from the fact that most planning is done by private citizens thinking in terms of money profits, whereas the interest of society is in general well-being as distinct from money profits. A distinction between social costs and money costs is involved. Production should occur, for example, at the lowest social cost, not necessarily at the lowest money cost. Complete free trade à la Smith, Ricardo, and Ohlin, in the setting of a completely unregulated market, could bring about the lowest money costs without necessarily achieving the lowest social costs.

[10] J. E. Meade, *A Geometry of International Trade* (London: George Allen and Unwin, 1952), pp. 44–97; J. E. Meade, *Balance of Payments* (London: Oxford, 1951), p. 326; J. E. Meade, *Trade and Welfare* (London: Oxford, 1955), *passim*.

The international trading policy which modifies the pure free-trade position to the extent necessary to achieve maximum world well-being might be called the "constructive free trade" position.[11] It is necessary to deviate somewhat from the pure free-trade position (and from the conditions prevailing in the world's markets as we have known them) in order to achieve maximum well-being for various reasons: (1) because of the nature of the process of structural change, (2) because of the implications of monopoly power, (3) because of external economies and diseconomies, (4) because of equity considerations in income distribution, and (5) in certain cases, because of the implications of a "second best" situation. (6) Government tax and spending policies, depending on their nature, may or may not play a constructive role.

Structural Change

Important developments in the growth process occur spasmodically. They do not occur in the small marginal quantities that the private enterpriser can intelligently handle in his search to maximize his monetary profits. The development of atomic power or the growth of a Tennessee Valley may contribute tremendously to the social welfare and help establish a new setting in which the private enterpriser will find his small-scale activities more remunerative than before. Yet the basic decision to develop atomic power or TVA in all probability was utterly beyond the power of any individual enterpriser. To put the matter a little differently, in a setting where there are significant economies of large-scale production, getting a desirable new product into production may present great difficulties.

Meade has pointed out that major international movements of labor and capital, which may make a significant long-run contribution to social betterment, may not be profitable in the beginning. Consequently, such a movement of labor or capital may never come about if it must depend upon the stimulation of private profit expectations.[12] Major and desirable changes may not occur if the process of change is left strictly to private and marginal considerations.

Monopoly Power

A very considerable element of monopoly power does exist in our society. As long as that is the case, competition and free trade cannot operate freely to bring the results that might be possible under more nearly ideal conditions. Of course, this is not specifically an argument against free trade in the classical sense. But it does mean that we

---

[11] It is probably best not to use Meade's term, the "modified free trade position," because it is desirable to give the concept somewhat broader coverage than Meade imputes to his concept.

[12] Meade, *Trade and Welfare*, p. 427.

might very possibly obtain results more desirable than we are now obtaining by some interference with the market process as we now know it.

External Economies and Diseconomies

There are economies and diseconomies external to the private firm on both the production side and the consumption side.

On the production side what is meant "is a divergence between the social and the private net product of a factor."[13] There may be a difference between what the "factor produces for the benefit of society and what it produces for the enjoyment of its employer." An example, of the type Meade calls "atmosphere creation," would be a forestation project engaged in by a private company in the expectation of making money from timber sales, which had the by-product effect of increasing rainfall to the benefit of farmers down the valley. On the other hand, soot from a factory smokestack may cause considerable expense to miscellaneous private citizens who have to get their suits cleaned more often in consequence. Yet the suit-cleaning cost will not appear on the factory's books as a cost. Smog in Los Angeles presents a similar problem.

There must be some sort of social interference with the free-market process if any sort of allowance, however imperfect, is going to be made for external economies and diseconomies.

Income Distribution

How unequally should income be distributed? One degree of inequality will get more goods produced. Another degree seems more equitable. Yet another degree actually results from the operation of competitive market forces. What is to be done? The answer is not easy. The problem has a domestic facet and an international facet.

Perhaps all that can fruitfully be said on this point here is that the people acting through the democratic process primarily should decide what shall be done. But the objective which they choose may well call for some intervention by society in the free-market process, perhaps by progressive taxes and a spending program calculated to favor poorer people.

Internationally, the problem of income distribution is chiefly the problem of implementing economic growth in the underdeveloped areas. However, even if all countries were equally developed but income distribution patterns remained quite different as between the countries, total world welfare might be increased by some interference with the free-trade pattern.

[13] *Ibid.*, p. 13.

The "Second-Best" Argument

A measure which would be undesirable in an ideal world may be necessary to improve matters in an imperfect world. A sanitary embargo at an international frontier to stop the spread of disease may be desirable even though it would be better to have the embargo line drawn around the area where the disease actually is concentrated.

Government Fiscal Policy

Government fiscal policies may be conducive to an improvement in welfare—or they may not be. It depends on what the policies are. If they are not, it behooves the people to speak up and see that they are changed. In this book (and especially in Chapters 15 and 36), the discussion of fiscal policy is chiefly in terms of what it should be rather than in terms of how wrong it has been in the past.

Conclusion

Free trade (and free competition) do not necessarily yield the best results in terms of level of living. Therefore free trade may not give the best results in terms of the most desirable combination of level of living, freedom of action, and security.

These observations are important, but are not necessarily a defense of trade barriers as we now know them. In the present setting their chief contributions seem to be in raising prices to consumers and in increasing the money profits of domestic producers rather than in improving the level of living.

The present complex of trade restrictions and non-comparable prices makes it absolutely impossible to evaluate a situation and say that certain regulations would be desirable. We need a properly functioning system, free of pressure-group-motivated restrictions, with data set up to give as good comparability as possible; then, we would be in a position to consider the desirability of certain restrictions.

In Chapters 15, 23, and 36 an effort will be made to indicate a pattern of policies which, with as little regimentation and interference as possible, would provide for the deviations from the pure free-competition free-trade position which seem called for by this discussion.

PART III

Balance of Payments
and
National Income Theory

Chapter 7

BALANCE OF PAYMENTS
STATEMENTS

⚑ ⚑ ⚑

*The balance of payments statement is simply a statement of the inter-
national commercial and financial transactions of a nation with the
outside world during the course of a year.*

*This statement must balance for much the same reason that the debits
and credits in ordinary double-entry bookkeeping balance.*

*On the one hand the statement carries information as to the value of
goods and services shipments.*

*On the other hand it carries information as to how the financial re-
sources to pay for those goods and services were acquired.*

*In a given year the money value of goods and services exports may
not equal the money value of goods and services imports because
of the possibility of (1) international lending at (a) long term or
(b) short term, (2) unilateral transfers, (3) gold movements, or
(4) errors and omissions.*

⚑ ⚑ ⚑

FOR the most part the theoretical material of Part II assumed the
necessity for equality between exports and imports—at least basically and in the long run. But when we attempt to be somewhat
more realistic about the manner in which the trading process
works, especially in the short run, it becomes obvious that financing is required and that lending, and even giving, can make possible at least temporary inequality between exports and imports. As a preliminary to the
effort in Parts IV, V, and VI to be more realistic about the relationship
between trade and financing, this chapter is devoted to analysis of the
accounting-type statements which are used to describe the relationship
among exports, imports, financing, lending, and gold movements for one
country in a given year.

Such accounting statements take various forms and are prepared by
several different agencies: (1a) balance of payments statements for individual countries prepared by the governments of those countries, (1b)

similar statements for the individual countries prepared by the International Monetary Fund, and (2) statements relating international trade to national income.

THE UNITED STATES BALANCE OF PAYMENTS STATEMENT

Most governments prepare such statements annually to describe their trade with the rest of the world. The Department of Commerce (and within the Department, the Bureau of Foreign Commerce) has been preparing such a statement for the United States annually since the early twenties.

The major parts of the present statement are (1) the export and import of goods and services, (2) unilateral transfers, (3) international lending at long term and short term, and (4) the movement of gold. *The goods and services relationships are the basic categories.* Unilateral transfers, lending, and gold movements are the available devices for financing a discrepancy between such exports and imports.

When a country buys goods or services from abroad, in a basic sense it must pay in foreign currencies. These foreign currencies may be obtained in several ways:

    1. As payment for the export of goods or services;
    2. As gifts from foreigners;
    3. As loans from foreigners;
    4. As payment for gold exports.

When a country sells goods or services to foreigners, it obtains foreign currencies. These foreign currencies may be used in various ways:

    1. As payment for the import of goods or services;
    2. As gifts to foreigners;
    3. As loans to foreigners;
    4. As payment for gold imports.

International sales, like domestic sales, involve payment arrangements. A businessman has indeed been guilty of a grievous oversight (unless he is being intentionally charitable) if he ships merchandise to a foreign country without making an arrangement for being paid. An export balance of trade cannot exist in a vacuum.

On page 93 is an abbreviated presentation of the United States balance of payments for 1955 set up to indicate the balancing nature of the statement. The statement in full in the form currently used by the United States Department of Commerce is presented as Table 12 later in the chapter.

From the accounting point of view the crux of the matter, insofar as understanding the statement is concerned, lies in the use which is

	In Millions of Dollars	
	Pluses	*Minuses*
1. Exports of goods and services, total	22,049	
13. Imports of goods and services, total		− 17,923
24. Unilateral transfers, net [to foreign countries (−)]: total		− 4,596
30. United States capital, net [outflow of funds (−)]: total		− 1,455
41. Foreign capital, net [outflow of funds (−)]: total	1,433	
46. Gold sales [purchases (−)]	41	
48. Errors and omissions [receipts by foreign areas (−)], net	451	
	23,974	−23,974

made of the "plus" and "minus" signs. (Customarily the absence of a sign implies a plus.) A *plus* entry involves a transaction that increases the amount of foreign funds available to the United States or to United States citizens. A *minus* entry involves a transaction which increases the amount of dollars available to foreigners. The expressions *credits* and *debits* are frequently used with the same meaning as plus and minus: credit (plus) and debit (minus).

Exports of Goods and Services

The first major group of entries in the balance of payments statement of the United States is exports of goods and services, totaling $22 billion in 1955:

	In Millions of Dollars	
1. Exports of goods and services, total		22,049
2. Military transfers under grants, net, total	2,134	
3. Other goods and services, total	19,915	
4. Merchandise, adjusted, excluding military	14,264	
5. Transportation	1,336	
6. Travel	645	
Miscellaneous services:		
7. Private	825	
8. Government, excluding military	131	
9. Military transactions	202	
Income on investments:		
10. Direct investments	1,978	
11. Other private	260	
12. Government	274	

These are plus entries; and it might be said that the figures represent not so much exports themselves as the amount of money that United States exporters were paid by foreigners for the exports. In the statements of the last three or four years it has become the practice to set up the basic merchandise export entry (item 4) to exclude considerable exports of military equipment which are included in item 2. The more conventional figure for total United States merchandise exports in 1955 is $15,538 million (see Table 2). In consequence of the modified procedure of recent years, there is no figure in the United States balance of payments statement which corresponds with the conventional total merchandise exports.

The transportation figure of $1,336 million involves the carrying of goods for foreigners by United States ships and the consequent payment for that service by foreigners. This is what is meant by the *export of a service,* the service of shipping facilities being provided by the United States to the foreigner. The travel entry total of $645 million involves the traveling that foreigners are doing in the United States, as a by-product of which they make their currency available to Americans in exchange for the services which they receive in this country: hotel rooms, curios, etc. Although this is counted, once again, as the export of a service, the service is not actually exported at all—it is merely sold in the United States to persons who pay this country with foreign funds.

The next entries are miscellaneous services, private and governmental. If insurance, for example, is the service involved, one might ask who is selling insurance to whom—the answer in this case being that the United States insurance company is paid premiums by the foreigner for the insurance protection which the United States company is extending. A wide range of other services rendered by private citizens and by the United States government makes up the total figures of $825 and $131 million. Military transactions (item 9) include only transactions of this type in connection with which the foreign country is making an actual payment to the United States. This entry thus is separate and distinct from the grants or gifts of item 2.

The next items are income on investments. This is *not* a figure that summarizes the making of new investments or the repayment of old ones, nor does it state the amount of investment outstanding. It is merely a figure covering such interest and profit on investments as happened to be remitted internationally during the year in question. In this case it is the income which United States citizens and the United States government are receiving from investments abroad. The United States oil companies operating in Venezuela may be bringing home profits, and the Export-Import Bank may be receiving interest on its loans to Latin America. The existence of an outstanding foreign investment, during the year in question, is taken to represent the providing of a service by the creditor to the debtor country, and the interest is payment for the service. One anomalous feature of the income-on-investments entry should be noted. The entry includes only such profits and interest as are transferred internationally. Profits earned abroad but plowed back into plant expansion abroad would not appear in the balance of payments statement as at present formulated.

Imports of Goods and Services

Analysis of the items in the section on imports of goods and services involves just the opposite line of argument:

		In Millions of Dollars
13.	Imports of goods and services, total	−17,923
14.	Merchandise, adjusted, excluding military	−11,516
15.	Transportation	−1,202
16.	Travel	−1,155
	Miscellaneous services:	
17.	Private	−489
18.	Government, excluding military	−245
19.	Military expenditures	−2,804
	Income on investments:	
20.	Private	−418
21.	Government	−94

Americans are making dollars available to foreigners in exchange for imports, transportation service provided by foreign ships, the travel of United States citizens abroad, the payment of premiums on insurance protection obtained from Lloyd's of London, and so on. Income on investments is the interest paid by United States borrowers on investments which foreigners have in this country.

In speaking of a country's balance of trade and whether it involves an export (favorable) balance or an import (unfavorable) balance, there is the possibility of confusion. The reference may be to the merchandise balance only, or to the balance on goods *and services*. For the United States in 1955 the merchandise balance cannot be computed directly from the balance of payments statement because of the way military goods are handled; but from other data it appears that the United States had a merchandise export balance of $4,048 million, whereas the export balance on goods and services totaled $4,126 million—a figure which is available as item 22 in the statement:

		In Millions of Dollars
	Balance on goods and services:	
22.	Total	4,126
23.	Excluding military transfers	1,992

When a figure for the balance of trade is given in the newspapers, it will generally include the merchandise balance alone. But this is true simply because figures for the merchandise balance are more readily available—and for many countries are the only data available—not because they are necessarily the more significant figures. It is desirable in any particular discussion about the balance of trade to keep clearly in mind which concept is involved and which concept will be more useful in connection with the question under consideration. In many cases, perhaps most cases, it will be the goods and services balance rather than the balance on goods alone that will be the more significant to work with. This is especially true if one is studying the relationship between the export and the import of "things of value" and attempting to relate (a) the exchange of things of value to (b) the means of financing. In fact, the last half of the balance of payments statement is devoted to *explaining how the discrepancy between the exports and the imports of goods and services (things of value) is financed.*

Unilateral Transfers

The first major entry in the group explaining the financing of the discrepancy is unilateral transfers:

In Millions of Dollars

Unilateral transfers, net [to foreign countries (−)]:

24.	Total	−4,596
25.	Excluding military supplies and services	−2,462
26.	Private remittances	−456
	Government:	
27.	Military supplies and services	−2,134
28.	Other grants	−1,865
29.	Pensions and other transfers	−141

Unilateral transfers are gifts: The entries include such things as private Red Cross aid, immigrant remittances back to the "old country," and the large bloc of Marshall Plan (Mutual Security or Foreign Operations) aid which the United States government is extending to certain countries. It may be deduced from these figures that the United States government provided somewhat more military supplies and services than other grants (economic and development aid) to foreign countries in 1955. As is customary in these statements, the providing of money by Americans to foreigners (such as Mutual Security aid) is represented by a minus sign. If foreigners were providing more aid to the United States than the United States is providing abroad, there would be plus signs in this section, since the figures are all "net." But in the present instance, these funds provide the dollars with which to pay for United States exports. In fact, the figure of $4,596 million of net unilateral transfers to foreign countries is more than enough to finance the export surplus of $4,126 million. To that extent unilateral transfers overfinanced United States exports in 1955. (It should be emphasized that the actual shipments of goods which were financed by this $4,596 million of aid are incorporated in the $22,049 million figure for total goods and services exports.)

Since gifts do not require financing in the ordinary sense of the word, if the books are to balance there must be a more-or-less artificial entry to explain the financing. Thus one might say that the unilateral transfers entry does not represent the gift-of-goods shipment itself but is rather an offsetting entry, arbitrarily made to explain the financing. It is also desirable to have the total amount of such aid available in a separate entry rather than lost in the total figure for goods and services shipments.

Next there is the problem of explaining the financing of the discrepancy between exports and imports which is not accounted for by gifts or unilateral transfers (or, for 1955, the problem of explaining away the over-financing of exports which seems to have existed after unilateral transfers are allowed for). Capital movements provide part of the explanation.

United States Capital and Movement of Funds

The next entry is United States capital (net), which includes both private and governmental funds.

In Millions of Dollars

30. United States capital, net (outflow of funds [−]).			−1,455
31. Private, net, total		−1,153	
32. Direct investments, net	−679		
33. New issues	−124		
34. Redemptions	203		
35. Other long-term, net	−359		
36. Short-term, net	−194		
37. Government, net, total		−302	
38. Long-term capital, outflow	−375		
39. Repayments	416		
40. Short-term, net	−343		

These figures contain both the outgo and the return of foreign investments made by the United States and its residents. Are Americans lending more or being repaid more? If a minus sign precedes the figure, more United States capital is being loaned, or is "flowing out," and is available to finance exports, than is being repaid. A plus sign, on the other hand, would indicate an excess of repayment. In 1955, the export of capital funds, or the movement of funds from the United States, apparently exceeded the repatriation of such funds by $1,455 million, revealing that the export trade balance of the United States was overfinanced by even more than seemed to be indicated by unilateral transfers alone.

It may be well to digress at this point to discuss the significance of the expression, "the movement of funds." We tend to speak very glibly of the movement of funds as though they actually moved. As a matter of fact, they seldom do.

To take several examples: A case of direct private investment might involve the shipment by the Standard Oil Company from itself in the United States to itself in Venezuela of a drilling rig worth $100,000. The $100,000 would be included in the merchandise exports figure. The offset would be entered with a minus sign in the private direct investments figure even though there was actually no financial transaction, no "movement of funds" of any sort connected with the transfer.

Another example of a long-term private investment might be a bond issue. What the United States investor has to lend is dollars. But dollars, as such, are of no use to the foreigner in the foreign country. The chances are that the foreign borrower wants to end up either with goods obtained from the United States in exchange for his dollars or with his own currency. The dollars are not likely to move in a literal sense (although they may). If the borrower uses the dollars, as he probably will, to buy goods in this country, the goods appear under merchandise exports. And even though no money moves, the loan appears as a minus entry under new issues (No. 33).

Another way to look at this complicated problem is as follows: If a long-term loan were made and entered as such and if the borrower did not use the money but left it on deposit in a bank in the United States, such funds would appear with a minus sign under long-term lending from the United States; but at the same time they would probably reappear under short-term lending by foreigners (foreign capital) to the United States with a plus sign. The short-term loan to the United States bank, where the funds are on deposit, would at least temporarily cancel out the long-term loan. This is the development frequently referred to in the literature as an "equalising short-term capital movement." No over-all net movement of capital occurs until the short-term balances are used.

To be more specific about short-term funds, they appear in two places under United States capital (No. 36 and No. 40) and also under foreign capital (No. 44 and No. 45). Again a minus sign has to represent (as it did in the case of the long-term lending) a net movement of short-term funds *from* the United States—that is, the providing of United States dollars to foreigners.

Under United States capital (net) the minus figures for private ($194 million) and government ($343 million) short-term capital probably indicate chiefly an increase in the balances held in foreign banks by either United States banks or the United States government. Such sums could be obtained in the first instance as the proceeds from the sale of United States exports in those countries. (A plus sign would have indicated that such foreign balances were being reduced.)

Almost all goods and services movements—the $22,049 million of exports and the $17,923 million of imports—are likely to involve the use of short-term funds. Consequently, if a figure for *gross* transactions in short-term funds were given instead of the net figures, it would probably be as large as or larger than exports and imports of goods and services taken together. It may be in part for this reason that the figures pertaining to short-term funds are presented as net rather than as gross figures.

Foreign Capital

In 1955 there was a net movement to the United States of $1,433 million in foreign capital (item 41).

		In Millions of Dollars
41.	Foreign capital, net (outflow of funds [−]), total	1,433
42.	Direct and long-term portfolio investments other than U.S. government securities	344
43.	Transactions in U.S. government securities	529
44.	Short-term liabilities to foreign banks and official institutions	700
45.	Other short-term liabilities	− 140

Thus the net movement of United States capital abroad exceeded the net movement of foreign capital to this country by only $22 million. In other words, there was virtually no net lending by the United States to foreigners—and there has been little or none during the last five or six years.

Part of the motivation for the foreign lending to the United States seems clear enough in spite of the so-called "dollar shortage." Foreigners may want to have a little "nest egg" in this country "just in case." The figure for foreign short-term capital, which is a plus $700 million reduced by a minus $140 million, indicates that foreigners are placing their short-term funds at our disposal to the extent of $560 million. In 1955 this meant primarily that they were increasing their deposits in American banks. A substantial proportion of these funds was probably drawn directly or indirectly from unexpended monies derived from Marshall Plan aid, United States government lending, or private United States lending. This is, in large part, the answer to the enigma of the overfinancing of United States exports which appeared when only unilateral transfers and United States capital were taken into account.

Movement of Gold

The only remaining possibility (aside from errors and omissions) in explaining the financing of the goods and services balance is gold movements.

		In Millions of Dollars
46.	Gold sales (purchases [−])	41
47.	Foreign capital and gold, total	1,474
48.	Errors and omissions (receipts by foreign areas [−]), net.	451

If gold had been handled as goods and had not been singled out for special treatment because of its monetary role, the pluses and minuses *would necessarily balance* (again "except for errors and omissions") after the gifts and loans had been taken into account. Since gold shipments are actually goods shipments (things of intrinsic value which must be paid for) isolated in a special part of the statement, it is natural that they should carry the same sign as other goods shipments. Gold exports from the United States, which make foreign currencies available to Americans, carry a plus sign; and gold imports carry a minus sign. In recent years, gold imports have generally exceeded gold exports. However, in 1955 there was a small net outflow of $41 million of gold valued at $35 an ounce.

Errors and Omissions

Since the statement has tried to take everything into account, and theoretically has done so, but still does not balance, it follows that there must be an error or errors totaling $451 million in the statement. Some of the possibilities for error result from the fact that some significant information is not available, given the present methods for gathering data. Difficulties also arise from: [1]

(1) changes of domicile from foreign to domestic by persons with deposits in United States banks;

(2) foreign purchase of real estate and other assets not included in the current reporting mechanisms;

(3) foreign purchase of securities and holdings of cash balances by agents who are not included among those reporting currently; and

(4) deposits held by non-reporting persons in the United States for foreign accounts.

The balance of payments statement is a summation of all the transactions which occur during the year, and all the goods movements have to be financed in one way or another. If they are not financed by goods (including gold) moving the other way, or by loans (either long-term or short-term), they must involve gifts. Consequently, if there are entries for gifts and for loans (and for gold shipments) offsetting the discrepancy between goods and services imports and exports, then the statement must balance, except for errors and omissions.

Limitations of the Balance of Payments Statement

The discussion up to this point is of little use in dealing with some fundamental problems of cause and effect. The statement, as it stands, cannot tell us whether the export balance of trade came first, and the

[1] United States, Treasury Department, *Census of Foreign-Owned Assets in the United States* (Washington: Government Printing Office, 1945), p. 49.

financing adjusted to it; or whether the financing occurred first, and the discrepancy between goods imports and exports was a result of the financing. That is to say, it is possible that an international loan will occur because the lender is attracted by higher interest rates abroad, the goods movement occurring as a result of this; or, on the contrary, the goods movement may be decided on first because of price differences between the countries involved, with the financing arranged later. What actually is cause and what is effect? It is easy, and substantially correct, to say that the goods balance must correlate with financing. But where is the meaningful decision made? And how does the adjustment process work itself out, to equate financing to goods movement or goods movement to financing? Parts V and VI of this book, dealing with money and short-term funds and with long-term capital movements, involve analysis of the problems connected with this sort of speculation.

Table 12 represents only one way that the balance of payments of the

TABLE 12

BALANCE OF PAYMENTS OF THE UNITED STATES, 1955

(MILLIONS OF DOLLARS)

1.	Exports of goods and services, total		22,049
2.	Military transfers under grants, net, total	2,134	
3.	Other goods and services, total	19,915	
4.	Merchandise, adjusted, excluding military	14,264	
5.	Transportation	1,336	
6.	Travel	645	
	Miscellaneous services:		
7.	Private	825	
8.	Government, excluding military	131	
9.	Military transactions	202	
	Income on investments:		
10.	Direct investments	1,978	
11.	Other private	260	
12.	Government	274	
13.	Imports of goods and services, total		−17,923
14.	Merchandise, adjusted, excluding military	−11,516	
15.	Transportation	−1,202	
16.	Travel	−1,155	
	Miscellaneous services:		
17.	Private	−489	
18.	Government, excluding military	−245	
19.	Military expenditures	−2,804	
	Income on investments:		
20.	Private	−418	
21.	Government	−94	
	Balance on goods and services:		
22.	Total		4,126
23.	Excluding military transfers	1,992	
	Unilateral transfers, net (to foreign countries [−]):		
24.	Total		−4,596

TABLE 12 (*continued*)

25.	Excluding military supplies and services	−2,462	
26.	Private remittances		−456
	Government:		
27.	Military supplies and services		−2,134
28.	Other grants		−1,865
29.	Pensions and other transfers		−141
30.	United States capital, net (outflow of funds [−])		−1,455
31.	Private, net, total		−1,153
32.	Direct investments, net	−679	
33.	New issues	−124	
34.	Redemptions	203	
35.	Other long-term, net	−359	
36.	Short-term, net	−194	
37.	Government, net, total		−302
38.	Long-term capital, outflow	−375	
39.	Repayments	416	
40.	Short-term, net	−343	
41.	Foreign capital, net (outflow of funds [−]), total		1,433
42.	Direct and long-term portfolio investments other than U.S. government securities	344	
43.	Transactions in U.S. government securities	529	
44.	Short-term liabilities to foreign banks and official institutions	700	
45.	Other short-term liabilities	−140	
46.	Gold sales (purchases [−])		41
47.	Foreign capital and gold, total		1,474
48.	Errors and omissions (receipts by foreign areas [−]), net		451

Source: *Survey of Current Business*, June, 1956, p. 24.

United States might be organized. As was mentioned above, the International Monetary Fund prepares statements slightly different in form for many countries. Also, many individual governments prepare balance of payments statements in a variety of forms on their own initiative.

INTERNATIONAL TRADE BOOKKEEPING IN RELATION TO NATIONAL INCOME

In addition to the problem of preparing a balance of payments statement to summarize many aspects of international economic relations, there is the problem of integrating the international figures with the ordinary internal national income and product accounts. It is necessary to work out such an integration, if the interaction between international trade and national income is to be shown.

The basic elements in the gross national product of the United States for 1955 were (in millions of dollars):

Personal consumption expenditures	$253,971
Gross private domestic investment	60,557
Net foreign investment	−470
Government purchases of goods and services	76,802
Gross national product	$390,860

Net Foreign Investment

The net foreign investment figure is computed as follows from the data in the balance of payments statement:

	In Millions of Dollars
24. Unilateral transfers, net, total	−4,596
22. Balance on goods and services, total	4,126
	−470

It thus represents the balance on goods and services with allowance made for unilateral transfers. Presumably, what is left after this balance is struck is capital movement one way or the other. Gold movements and errors and omissions are thus included in this rather artificial net-foreign-investment figure. Computed in this way, there was a net foreign investment into the United States of $470 million in 1955.

Rest of the World Account

The so-called net-foreign-investment item is broken down in the "rest of the world account," which is published annually as one of the auxiliary accounts in the national income data prepared by the Department of Commerce (see Table 13).

Items 2 through 16 in the rest of the world account analyze the payments made in connection with financing United States exports and imports to determine whether payments go as remuneration directly to labor, capital, and enterprise (items 2 through 6) or whether they involve purchases or sales by business, government, or individuals (items 7 through 16). The United States, as a result of the transactions summarized in items 2 through 16, receives $470 million more than it pays—if $4,596 million of unilateral transfers is disregarded.

This $470 million of capital movement to the United States (item 17) may take the form, as was indicated above, of genuine lending operations (at long term or short term), gold movements, or errors and omissions.

TABLE 13

REST OF THE WORLD ACCOUNT (UNITED STATES), 1955

(MILLIONS OF DOLLARS)

1.	Net current payments to the United States		−470
2.	Net payments of factor income		2,021
3.	Wages and salaries	21	
4.	Interest	380	
5.	Dividends	505	
6.	Branch profits	1,115	
7.	Net purchases from the United States		−2,491
8.	Net purchases from United States business	3,829	
9.	Purchases from United States business	16,955	
10.	Sales to United States business	13,126	
11.	Net purchases from United States Government		−3,919
12.	Purchases from United States Government	311	
13.	Sales to United States Government	4,230	
14.	Net purchases from United States persons		−2,401
15.	Purchases from United States persons	28	
16.	Sales to United States persons	2,429	
17.	Net capital movement to the United States		470
18.	Long-term		−45
19.	Short-term		23
20.	Change in gold stock		41
21.	Errors and omissions		451
22.	Adjustment for United States territories and possessions		...

Source: *Survey of Current Business,* July, 1956, p. 15.

Limitations of Available Figures

The statisticians have undoubtedly rendered a real service in compiling this data. However, the economist, primarily interested in the impact of international trade on a country's level of living, might well wish (1) that the international trade data was presented on a gross rather than a net basis at the point where it enters the general stream of the national income accounting, (2) that the balance on goods and services was emphasized rather than this rather odd definition of net foreign investment, and (3) that the national income accounts emphasized personal consumption expenditures rather than gross national product or national income.

(1) Gross international trade figures are accounted for elsewhere in the national income statistics so that inclusion only of net foreign investment

in the gross national product figures does not mean that there is a sum of goods and services entering trade which is not reflected in the national income statistics. But the arrangement used does imply that it is through the *net* figure that international trade has its impact on national income and product.

It should be obvious that the effect of international trade on national income may be quite different in the two cases that follow:

Case I	Exports	$1,100,000,000
	Imports	1,000,000,000
	Export Surplus	$ 100,000,000
Case II	Exports	$ 200,000,000
	Imports	100,000,000
	Export Surplus	$ 100,000,000

Even though the size of the export surplus is the same in both cases, the net figures would not accurately reflect the importance of international trade relative to purely domestic activities. This is even more obviously true in two cases where changes of the following sort may occur:

		1948	1949
Case III	Exports	$500,000,000	$1,100,000,000
	Imports	500,000,000	1,000,000,000
	Export Surplus	None	$ 100,000,000
Case IV	Exports	$100,000,000	$ 200,000,000
	Imports	100,000,000	100,000,000
	Export Surplus	None	$ 100,000,000

And if the *reductio ad absurdum* is needed there is the following case:

Case V	Exports	$200,000,000	$ 200,000,000
	Imports	200,000,000	100,000,000
	Export Surplus	None	$ 100,000,000

When only net figures are given, all of the above cases look the same: during the course of the year an export surplus of $100 million was acquired, where previously there had been none. The question, of course, is whether the stimulating effect on national income is the same in cases III, IV, and V. If it is the same, the net figures for "balance only" do represent a satisfactory vehicle for stating the impact of international trade on national income. But if the stimulating effect of the three situations may be different, the net basis does not give a satisfactory picture of the impact of trade.

(2) But even if net figures were the significant ones for analyzing the impact of trade on national income, the rest of the world account would

not give the proper net figures for purposes of national income analysis. According to the balance of payments statements, the export balances (goods and services) of the United States were the following (and these are the figures that indicate the difference between what American exporters are being paid and what American importers are paying—the significant data for national income purposes, if any net data is relevant):

1948	$6,310,000,000
1949	6,983,000,000
1952	4,973,000,000

According to the rest of the world account, the net foreign investment figures (net current payments to the United States) were:

1948	$1,901,000,000
1949	528,000,000
1952	−235,000,000

The discrepancy (aside from some statistical corrections of minor size) is due to the fact that the net current payments (net foreign investment) figure is computed after allowance is made for the offsetting unilateral transfers entry. The resultant figure thus does not include Marshall Plan aid. If the stimulating effect of international economic activity on national income is to be studied, gifts and unilateral transfers should be included in the international trade data as items which result in increased income to Americans.

Consequently, and strangely, the balance on goods and services figure in the balance of payments statement is more useful for national income studies (if a net figure is usable at all), and the total figures in the balance of payments statement are more useful for other purposes, than is the net foreign investment figure or any other figure in the national income and product accounts. (The implications of this statement will be elaborated in the following chapter.)

(3) Which entry in the national income accounts corresponds most closely to high level of living?

For the closed economy, which has no international trade, it would be justifiable to say that an increase in national income, *or* in gross national product, *or* in net national product, *or* in personal consumption expenditures shows an increase in the level of living, provided the figure is adjusted for changes in the price level and for increases or decreases in population.

But this does not continue to be the case when international trade enters the picture. Gross national product is not a satisfactory concept for maximization by international trade devices because it is increased by exports and decreased by imports. National income also is increased by exports and decreased by imports. So is net national product. But exports decrease real income (goods are lost) and imports increase real income (goods are gained). Consequently, if the analyst is concerned with the role of international trade in maximizing real per capita income, he is not justified in using gross national product, or national income, or net national product (as those concepts are currently defined in national income accounting) as the factor which should be maximized.

Personal Consumption Expenditures

Perhaps the closest we can come to identifying a single factor, the maximization of which would correspond with increase in income, is to consider personal consumption expenditures. In national income accounting personal consumption expenditures are increased by imports; for 1955, these expenditures ran as follows:

	Millions of Dollars
Purchases of direct services:	
Compensation of employees:	
Wages and salaries paid	8,746
Supplements paid:	
Employer contributions for social insurance	114
Other labor income	103
Interest paid	3,729
Net purchases from business	238,878
Net purchases from abroad	2,401
Personal consumption expenditures	253,971

There is much merit in the oversimplification that personal consumption expenditures should be singled out of national income accounting as the item to be maximized. But even here, certain reservations should be noted. We really want to maximize personal consumption expenditures (a) stated in real and not monetary terms (b) on a per capita basis (c) with suitable income distribution. Also there is the problem of discounting the future. Because more investment now may increase real per capita income in the future, current investment cannot be left out of account. But investment in this setting assumes a secondary rather than a primary role.

CONCLUSION

Though criticism has been offered of some of the specific techniques used in the preparation of the balance of payments statements, the mere fact that they are prepared has increased tremendously during recent years our understanding of the relations involved in the international trading process.

Chapter 8

NATIONAL-INCOME THEORY—
A GENERAL STATEMENT

❧ ❧ ❧

It has become the practice in recent years to consider an increase in exports as desirable—at least in fighting a depression—on the grounds that it will increase domestic income in much the same manner as an increase in domestic investment.

The practical value of such efforts to increase exports is limited for several reasons: (1) Foreign retaliation is likely to render futile an artificial effort to increase exports. (2) If anything really useful could be done along these lines, the government could achieve the same effect by paying the producer (or exporter) for the goods and then destroying them. (3) The parallel drawn between goods destruction and an export surplus suggests the desirability of the alternative course of getting goods into the hands of those people within the country who need them.

A more constructive application of national-income theory to the field of international trade can be made through the maintenance of imports by the country where the depression starts.

Maintenance of imports by the country where the depression starts may inhibit somewhat the tendency of the depression to spread via reduced imports, reduced income to foreign exporters, etc.

Arguments relating the balance of trade to national income tend to have only a short-run (or a business-cycle-run) validity at best because of the necessity that exports, in the long run, must equal imports.

❧ ❧ ❧

THE IMPORTANCE OF KEYNESIAN THEORY

IN the theory of Smith, Ricardo, Mill, Marshall, Pareto, Meade, and Ohlin, there has been, for the most part, an assumption of full employment. But if, at a given moment, not all people have jobs, or if resources are not most fully and effectively employed—in short, if there are business cycles or longer-run periods of stagnation—the problem assumes a different aspect. Economic theory has needed to consider the measures which will help to effect fuller, more productive use of resources at times of underemployment—that is, most of the time.

John Maynard Keynes noted that a major amount of unemployment obviously has persisted over long periods of time.[1] Working from that fact, he attempted to develop a theory that would explain how to solve the unemployment problem and increase national income in the process.

What follows is an effort to evaluate the application of Keynesian or national-income theory to international trade. The theory has come to have such extensive ramifications that hardly any problem in the international-trade field can be analyzed without reference to the tools of national-income theory.

In its internal aspects the argument runs to the effect that, if there is a given amount of new investment, a multiplier will operate to increase national income a certain number of times more than the amount of the new investment. If the multiplier were three, new investment of $1,000,000,000 would increase national income by $3,000,000,000.

It was thought that some such result would flow from the new investment, as it was used by the investor to hire labor, to buy raw materials, and to expand plant and other facilities, thereby giving additional jobs and wages to labor and additional revenue to the enterprises from which raw materials were purchased. The recipients of the additional revenue, in their turn, would spend most of their new income and save a fraction. The proportion they spent would then be new income for others. The recipients of the new income, once again, would spend a fraction and save a fraction. And so the process would go on.

There is probably little point in considering, at this stage in the argument, whether or not the multiplier (or the propensity to save) is an exact and stable constant. It very well may not be. Nevertheless the process, roughly as described, surely is of tremendous importance. And in domestic terms, investment, or the failure of investment, is a major force controlling the size of national income.

APPLICATION TO INTERNATIONAL TRADE

Theoretical Argument

Keynes himself did not go through the analysis involved in the application of the theory to international trade. That has been done by others on the general assumption that an increase in exports (or an "improvement" in the trade balance) is comparable to an increase in domestic investment.[2]

---

[1] John Maynard Keynes, *The General Theory of Employment, Interest, and Money* (New York: Harcourt, Brace, 1936). Keynes centered attention on human unemployment rather than on less than optimum use of other resources.

[2] Fritz Machlup, *International Trade and the National Income Multiplier* (Philadelphia: Blakiston, 1943); J. E. Meade, *The Balance of Payments;* Hans Neisser

Table 14 may help to clarify the process involved. In the example, a sudden increase in exports of 100 (perhaps $100,000,000) is assumed. Perhaps the spurt is caused by the fact that the country in question has some remarkable or important new export—such as uranium or television

TABLE 14
APPLICATION OF NATIONAL-INCOME THEORY TO INTERNATIONAL TRADE

I PERIOD	II AUTONO-MOUS IN-CREASE IN EXPORTS	III RESULT-ANT IN-CREASE IN NATIONAL INCOME	IV RESULT-ANT SAV-ING [1]	V RESULTANT SPENDING ON GOODS: *Internal* [2]	VI *Imports* [3]	VII *Total of v & vi*
1	100	100	20	70	10	80
2		70	14	49	7	56
3		49	9.8	34.3	4.9	39.2
4		34.3	6.9	24	3.4	27.4
5		24	4.8	16.8	2.4	19.2
6		16.8	3.4	11.8	1.7	13.5
7		11.8	2.3	8.2	1.2	9.4
8		8.2	1.6	5.8	.8	6.6
etc.		etc.	etc.	etc.	etc.	etc.
Cumulative Total	100	333.3 [4]	66.7	233.3	33.3	266.6

N.B.: Apparent export surplus resulting from the operation: 66.67 (100 − 33.33), the autonomous increase in exports minus the resultant spending on imports.

[1] Assuming marginal propensity to save of $1/5$.

[2] Assuming marginal propensity to consume domestic goods of $7/10$.

[3] Assuming marginal propensity to spend on imports of $1/10$.

[4] The multiplier is apparently 3.33. The multiplier could be computed from the formula: $M = \dfrac{1}{1 - MPC}$, where MPC is the marginal propensity to consume domestically produced goods. Thus $M = \dfrac{1}{1 - .7} = 3\frac{1}{3}$.

sets. In any event, as a result of such an autonomous increase in exports the receipts of exporters are expanded by 100 ($100,000,000) over what they would otherwise have been.

It is worth pausing at this point to note that, for this development to represent a potential gain of any sort to the nation concerned, these increased exports must be surplus goods or goods produced by otherwise idle labor and raw materials—that is, they must come from a setting

and Franco Modigliani, *National Incomes and International Trade* (Urbana: University of Illinois Press, 1953); J. J. Polak, *An International Economic System* (London: George Allen and Unwin, 1954).

where resources are underemployed. Otherwise the exporters' income might just as well have been increased the 100 by domestic sale of the good in question with the additional selfish advantage (from the viewpoint of the nation) that the goods would be consumed by domestic users. Under somewhat different circumstances—full-employment conditions—the increase in exports might indeed represent 100 of additional gross receipts to the exporters; but it would also involve a reduction in the total goods available to the whole population. The balance of the population can hardly be expected to sympathize with the motives of the exporter in such a case, even though the exporters' receipts would be increased by the increase in exports.

But to return to the earlier assumption that the export spurt has been made possible by putting otherwise unemployed resources to work: in Table 14 the income of exporters is assumed to have increased by 100. At this point the additional assumption is made that, out of an increase in income, $7/10$ will be spent on domestic goods, $1/10$ on imports (marginal propensity to import), and $2/10$ will be saved (marginal propensity to save).

Given the assumed propensities, the exporters who receive the additional 100 of income (which at the point when they receive it also increases national income by 100, national income being the sum of all individual incomes) can be expected on the average to save 20, spend 70 on domestic goods, and spend 10 on foreign goods. The 70 which is spent on domestic goods increases the revenues of the recipients, and consequently national income, by 70. The recipients, motivated on the average by the same propensities, dispose of their 70 of additional income, 14 $(2/10)$ on saving, 49 $(7/10)$ on domestic goods, 7 $(1/10)$ on imports. The 49 is then increased income to a new group of recipients, as well as increased national income. The process continues progressively as the money is spent, becomes other people's income, and then is either spent again or saved by them. But each time the turnover occurs the sums involved become smaller and by about the tenth go around the sums involved are so small as to be of no particular significance. Thus a given quantity of autonomous exports or of new investment will have most of its effect on national income, spending, and saving fairly quickly—even though it may be Judgment Day before all of the effects of the operation are worked out. And all the money and purchasing power now being spent and saved is the result of some long-past autonomous increase in investment or export or some such thing, turning over for the nth time and being partly saved and partly spent. In the illustration, the *full* effect (increasing national income by 333.33) of the original spurt in exports of 100 would not have worked itself out within the lifetimes of the people responsible for the autonomous increase in exports. Nevertheless, national income would have been increased by most of that amount, 314, after only eight turnovers.

Other end results of the original spurt in exports of 100 are an increase in savings of 66.7; an increase in internal spending of 233.3, an increase in imports of 33.3, and an increase in total spending of 266.6. These totals can be computed directly by multiplying the initial increase in imports by the multiplier (as computed in Table 14) to get the change in national income from which the other changes can be calculated.

Limitations of Export Stimulation

This would seem to be a convincing demonstration that export increase is a fine way to increase national income, and by substantially more than the value of the exports in most cases. But there are "several jokers in the deck," some of which are discussed below.

Most countries are affected by a major depression at about the same time. If any country is justified in trying to stimulate its exports relative to its imports, then every country is so justified. But not all countries can do this at the same time. Somebody has to have an increasing import balance to correspond with the other country's rising export balance, even in the short run. In terms of what a country can do in "this world of sin and woe," it may be noted that it is quite possible for a government to take positive measures that will prevent imports. A country can establish a quota or tariff or even an embargo that will cut down imports or eliminate them altogether. That is half of the operation of increasing exports relative to imports; but as for the other half of the operation—the stimulation of exports—that is something else again. It is not possible for a country performing that maneuver to be at all certain of the outcome. The United States may subsidize the export of cotton, but no one can be compelled to buy the cotton. Another country, thinking in the same terms and desiring to fight its own depression by curtailing imports relative to exports, may raise its tariff on cotton or establish a quota limiting import, and the measure that will probably prevail will be the one designed to keep goods out. The application of the export stimulation argument assumes the ability of each country to take measures to encourage exports and discourage imports. But, since the only measures that are effective are the ones to keep goods out, the countries end up with more or less the same trade balance that they started with. There will merely be less total trade and consequently less mutual benefit from geographical specialization. And that was literally the result of the activities of the 1930's, when most governments were trying to build up export surpluses. This form of activity has frequently been called "exporting your depression to your neighbor"—or trying to! In this setting very few countries obtained the sort of multiplier stimulation from increased exports which they had hoped to obtain. Depressions have not been exported—they were aggravated—by such measures. Artificial stimulation of exports frequently has a close resemblance to kicking a brick wall with a bare toe.

If what a country wants is new investment to stimulate its internal economy, would it not achieve the same result by government purchase of the goods, with money specially created for the purpose through the banking system? The government might then ship the goods out and sink them in the middle of the ocean. At least the ocean would take the goods. Why try to force them on the unwilling, especially since there are other ways to obtain the stimulating effect of new investment? Advocates of tariffs, who are bitterly opposed to destroying potatoes, should ponder these relations. Is there something about the psychology of our race and time that makes us require the fiction of a legitimate business deal to camouflage waste? We should not plow under every third row of cotton; but neither should we subsidize the sale of cotton to unwilling foreign nations.

It reflects sadly on our ability to solve problems if it is necessary for us to destroy goods at a time when there is widespread want. But the motives of advocates of government commodity purchases and crop destruction in the early 1930's were the same as those of the advocates of a favorable balance of trade, and *the sin was the same.* "Get the goods out of our economic system. They are 'running down' prices and profits." But need either of these procedures be followed? There must be some process for distributing surplus goods in depression times to the people who really need them. And there must be some way of running an economic system so that the premium is on producing more goods and working out effective means of distribution—rather than on a fear of goods.

Perhaps a valid case could be made for export stimulation in a situation where one country was afflicted by a depression and all other countries were prosperous—with the further assumption that internal institutional barriers to solving the distribution problem were genuinely insurmountable. The one country afflicted by depression could proceed to engage in export stimulation. The process then might work out, roughly, as described in the theory, in the sense that other countries would not throw up insurmountable barriers to receiving the goods. But it is not certain that they would be willing recipients even then. At all events, if there is any stimulation to be gained by new investment, it can be gained far more easily and directly by government spending or private investment internally than by artificial export stimulation.

But there is a difference between a natural increase in exports (and probably in imports too, at the same time, since the two go together), which is likely to be a corollary of rising national income, and artificial efforts to increase exports relative to imports. Efforts of the latter kind, far from giving the simple results of Table 14, are likely to decrease imports, exports, national income, and world income all at one fell swoop. Thus, in spite of the validity of the argument (that an increase in exports will increase national income) in a certain setting, it is probable that Keynesian doctrine is inapplicable to most international situations. Indeed, possibly the two leading Keynesians—Keynes himself, before he died, and Alvin Hansen—have both deplored the misapplication of the theory to international trade to justify effort to stimulate exports relative to imports. Keynes apparently went through quite a change in his own views on the subject between 1931 and 1946. In 1931 he was in favor of British devaluation to increase exports relative to imports in order to fight Britain's depression. But in the period immediately following World War II, he quite definitely maintained that his theory had been used to cover a multitude of sins and malpractices in the foreign-trade field.

Propensities and Income Elasticities

The analytical tools used in the application of national-income theory to international trade include (a) the average propensity to import, (b) the marginal propensity to import, and (c) the income elasticity of demand for imports.

(a) *The average propensity to import* (sometimes called the import coefficient) is obtained by dividing the money value of imports in a given year by the national income or the gross national product (or perhaps the industrial output) for that year. It would be necessary to check any particular statistical compilation to determine whether national income or gross national product or some similar concept had been used. But for present purposes it does not especially matter as long as there is consistency. Examples of the average propensity to import are shown in Tables 4 and 9, and Chart 6. This figure is obviously not a constant through time for the United States; and, as Table 9 indicates, it is certainly not the same figure for different countries at the same time.

(b) The meaning of the *marginal propensity to import* varies, depending on whether an instantaneous multiplier of the type Keynes himself used is involved or whether period analysis of the type developed in Table 14 is used.

Presumably the marginal propensity to import, in either case, would be the ratio between a change in imports and a change in national income. But in the case of Keynes' instantaneous multiplier, the complete effect of the autonomous increase in exports is assumed to work itself out at once. If the process actually developed in this way, it would give a color

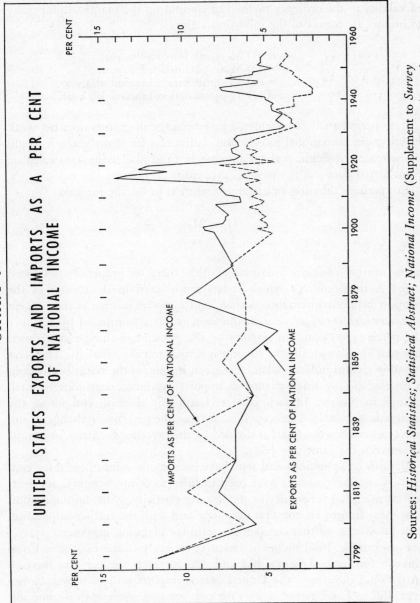

CHART 6

UNITED STATES EXPORTS AND IMPORTS AS A PER CENT
OF NATIONAL INCOME

IMPORTS AS PER CENT OF NATIONAL INCOME

EXPORTS AS PER CENT OF NATIONAL INCOME

PER CENT

15

10

5

1799   1819   1839   1859   1879   1900   1920   1940   1960

Sources: *Historical Statistics; Statistical Abstract; National Income* (Supplement to *Survey of Current Business*); National Industrial Conference Board, *Studies in Enterprise and Social Progress*, p. 79.

of validity to the ordinary method of computing the marginal propensity to import, by means of the following ratio:

$$\frac{M_1 - M_0}{Y_1 - Y_0}$$

where (1) M_1 equals imports this year,
(2) M_0 equals imports last year,
(3) Y_1 equals national income this year,
and (4) Y_0 equals national income last year.

If, as period analysis indicates, a given change in exports does not work its effect out on national income and on imports for many years, it would be extremely difficult, perhaps impossible (and also useless) to calculate from actual data a true marginal propensity to import.

But perhaps the most practical procedure is to use the formula

$$\frac{M_1 - M_0}{Y_1 - Y_0}$$

as the nearest feasible approximation of the marginal propensity to import.

(c) A third concept which is frequently used in discussions of the relation between international trade and national income is the concept of *income elasticity of demand for imports*. It is computed by dividing the percentage change in imports by the percentage change in national income. Mathematically the concept is similar to price elasticity. The computation should indicate what, at a given instant, is the result of dividing a microscopically small change in imports by the correspondingly small change in income. In fact, what is frequently done in computing the figures is shown in Table 15. In that table the percentage change in imports as between two years is divided by the percentage change in income as between the same two years.

Various computations and tests have been made using these three concepts. Certain economists have been inclined to compute figures for average or marginal propensity or for income elasticity, with the implication that those figures are constant over time and with the further implication that knowledge of that constant is useful for planning purposes.

For example, Raúl Prebisch, executive-secretary of the Economic Commission for Latin America, has said that for each one per cent increase in national income in the United States, imports will increase 0.66 per cent. But in Latin America for each one per cent increase in income imports tend to increase by 1.8 per cent.[3] C. P. Kindleberger has stated that for Brazil the average propensity to import is low but the marginal propensity is probably high.[4] Kindleberger also says that for the United

[3] Raúl Prebisch, "Exposición . . . ," *Trimestre Económico*, XX (April, 1953), p. 353.
[4] C. P. Kindleberger, *International Economics* (Homewood, Ill.: Irwin, 1953), pp. 156–7.

TABLE 15
(CRUDE) MARGINAL PROPENSITY TO IMPORT AND (CRUDE) INCOME
ELASTICITY OF DEMAND FOR IMPORTS
FOR THE UNITED STATES

	I (CRUDE) MARGINAL PROPENSITY TO IMPORT ($\triangle$M/$\triangle$NI) [3] %	II (CRUDE) INCOME ELASTICITY OF DEMAND FOR IMPORTS (%$\triangle$M/%$\triangle$NI) [4]		I %	II
1900 [1]	19.3	4.2	1930 [2]	11.1	2.2
1901	(Perverse) [5]	(Perverse)	1931	6.1	1.5
1902	6.3	1.3	1932	4.5	1.3
1903	10.7	2.1	1933	(Perverse)	(Perverse)
1904	(Perverse)	(Perverse)	1934	2.3	0.6
1905	9.5	1.9	1935	4.8	1.4
1906	6.3	1.1	1936	4.8	1.3
1907	16.7	3.2	1937	7.6	2.0
1908	25.4	4.3	1938	18.6	4.4
1909	3.9	0.8	1939	6.9	2.4
1910	11.4	2.3	1940	3.5	1.1
1911	(Perverse)	(Perverse)	1941	3.1	0.8
1912	9.6	1.7	1942	(Perverse)	(Perverse)
1913	7.9	1.4	1943	1.9	1.0
1914	(Perverse)	(Perverse)	1944	4.4	2.2
1915	(Perverse)	(Perverse)	1945	(Perverse)	(Perverse)
1916	11.6	2.3	1946	(Perverse)	(Perverse)
1917	7.3	1.2	1947	4.6	1.7
1918	0.7	0.1	1948	5.6	1.9
1919	14.6	2.7	1949	9.2	2.8
1920	25.0	4.1	1950	9.4	3.1
1921	23.6	3.1	1951	5.7	1.5
1922	125.8	30.2	1952	(Perverse)	(Perverse)
1923	0.8	0.1	1953	1.1	0.3
1924	(Perverse)	(Perverse)	1954	17.0	4.7
1925	20.2	3.8	1955 [2]	5.1	1.5
1926	5.9	1.0			
1927	(Perverse)	(Perverse)			
1928	(Perverse)	(Perverse)			
1929 [1]	8.6	1.6			

[1] Data through 1929 is based on NICB income estimates. [2] Data from 1929 on is based on Department of Commerce income estimates. [3] Change in imports by comparison with preceding year divided by change in income by comparison with preceding year. Thus, imports in 1900 were $153,000,000 larger than in 1899 and national income was $794,000,000 larger. $153,000,000/$794,000,000 equals 19.3%. [4] Imports were 22.0% higher in 1900 than in 1899 and national income was 5.2% higher. 22.0/5.2 equals 4.2. [5] "Perverse" means that change in the import figures was in the opposite direction from change in the national-income figures.

Source: Same as Chart 6.

Kingdom the average propensity to import is high and marginal propensity is low. He states, further, that the average propensity of the United States to import is 3 per cent and the marginal propensity is 4 per cent.

But one of these figures taken in isolation can have little meaning. And it certainly has little predictive value at a given time. As Table 15 indicates, there is tremendous variation in these figures over time in the case of the United States. And the following compilation for the United Kingdom indicates a similar state of affairs so far as that country is concerned.[5]

	1946	*1947*	*1948*	*1949*	*1950*	*1951*	*1952*
Average propensity to import (imports divided by national income)	.15	.19	.20	.21	.23	.31	.23
Marginal propensity to import $\dfrac{(M_1 - M_0)}{(Y_1 - Y_0)}$	1.23	.84	.29	.28	.56	1.12	(see below)[6]

Planners need to beware of thinking that particular changes in investment or trade will have any certain result as indicated by these constants. However, comparisons between these figures may be useful if the variations are great enough, particularly in connection with the effort to master business fluctuations. But the rough estimates of long-run average or marginal propensity or elasticity contribute little to that end; it is considerably more important to have some conception of how the figures vary over time.

The propensity to import seems rather consistently to be higher in prosperity than in depression. The Randall Commission singled out the following data for the United States:[7]

United States Imports as a Percentage of United States Gross National Product

Prosperity	1920	5.6%
Depression	1921	3.5
Prosperity	1927–29	4.2
Depression	1930–33	2.8
Prosperity	1937	3.3
Depression	1938	2.3

Imports fluctuate more violently than does domestic production.[8] Don Humphrey finds a partial explanation for such fluctuations in the propo-

[5] Derived from data in *International Financial Statistics,* March, 1954, pp. 166–9.

[6] And in 1952, by comparison with 1951, national income rose by £977,000,000 and imports fell by £425,000,000. The latter inconsistent development seems to call for a specific observation rather than a figure.

[7] United States, Commission on Foreign Economic Policy, *Staff Papers,* p. 313.

[8] Don D. Humphrey, *American Imports* (New York: Twentieth Century Fund, 1955), p. 49.

sition that competitive imports are more unstable than non-competitive imports. Apparently American manufacturers can and do take effective action to keep out competition during depressions. They would seem to be less energetic or less successful in this respect during prosperous periods. On the other hand, non-competitive imports are less subject to the restrictive measures of the depression years.[9]

Is the Multiplier a Constant?

The possibility remains that estimates of the size of the constants have usefulness in analyzing growth as distinct from business fluctuations.

Let us return for a moment to the assumption that the multiplier is a constant, that it does not change in size as the economic process goes on and on through time. That can be true only if the average (or marginal) propensity to import and the average (or marginal) propensity to save are both constants. And there is little reason to believe this to be so.

In fact, although the propensity to save conceivably could be a constant (but is not), the foreign trade multiplier *cannot* be a constant under any circumstances. The necessity that exports must pay for imports and imports for exports is a more fundamental force; therefore in many cases the relations between trade and income which are suggested by the constant-multiplier assumption simply cannot prevail.[10]

But refutation of the idea that the multiplier is a constant is no denial of the major importance of national income theory, nor does it discredit the idea that a change in exports or investment may change national income. It does mean that the multiplier process cannot be used with any accuracy for purposes of prediction, and it also means that the economic system is not heading with uncontrollable force in any particular direction as the result of the operation of these constants.

A theory of long-run economic development simply cannot be built on a money-oriented constant multiplier—although the data derived from national-income theory may be used in studying long-run problems.

The Rate of Turnover and Identification of the Injection Point

To turn from the standard model used in national-income theory: Much of the trouble involved in business fluctuations is probably not so much the result of decline in net *new* investment (although that is a notoriously violent fluctuator) as it is the result of decline in the rate at which the sums in circulation as the result of *earlier* investments are turning over. This is the turnover problem.

[9] Some ramifications of this line of argument are developed in the chapter: "Subsidies, Dumping, Cartels, and Raw Commodity Control Schemes."

[10] The logic of this difficulty may be avoided by saying that national-income theory, as applied to international trade (with constant-multiplier assumptions) is short-run and not long-run theory. That is to say, it is valid until the foreign exchange reserves run out. This line of thought raises serious questions as to the validity of applying the theory to growth problems.

Another factor that is perhaps more important: New funds may enter the spending-saving-producing complex at many different points—not just in connection with new investment or increased exports. In a given situation new funds in the hands of consumers may have a more stimulating effect—being entirely spent in the first go-around of the money—than new funds put into the complex at some other point. The giving of new funds to exporters may well be one of the least effective and desirable methods to inject new funds into the complex.

The question is not *whether* new funds shall be used to fight depressions. The question is *who* shall get the benefit of this subsidy in the first instance: manufacturers, bankrupt railroads, exporters, wage earners, consumers, or some other group. Anyone who feels skeptical about the "trickle-down" theory, on the ground that he does not like to be "dripped on," may find greater merit in suggestions for placing the initial increase in purchasing power in the hands of wage earners and consumers.[11]

What Should Be Maximized?

The ordinary presentation of the Keynesian theory implies that the thing to be maximized is national income. There may be some justification for this implication in the case of the closed economy, the country with no international trade. At least the justification might run: "Yes, we are fundamentally interested in the highest per capita real income or level of living. But increasing national money income does increase national real income during periods of unemployment and of underemployed resources." The argument would go on to assert that new investment funds serve to put otherwise idle people to work. As a consequence of the additional money invested, there will be additional production and more goods to be purchased. It follows that, in such a setting, the increase in money investment is not particularly inflationary, for there is a high degree of correlation between change in national money income, change in national real income, and change in level of living.[12]

But this high positive correlation between changes in money income and in real income simply does not exist when the theory is stated in terms of an economy that engages in international trade (an open economy) rather than in terms of a closed economy that does not. The increase in money income that goes with an export increase is a corollary of loss of goods. Consequently there is gain in real income in the coun-

[11] The trickle-down theory, now much in vogue among businessmen and favored by Secretary of the Treasury George Humphrey, seems to embody the specific claim that if wealthy people have their taxes cut, the benefits of their resultant increase in spending will eventually reach everybody.

[12] But if new investment funds were pumped into a full-employment situation in which goods production could not be increased, the new funds would have a volatile, inflationary impact.

try with the export surplus *only if the resultant increase in real domestic consumption* is *larger than the increase in goods exports.*[13]

The figures in Table 14, which are in money terms, give little indication whether real national income has risen by 333.33 or whether there has been a marked price inflation as a consequence of the increase in the money supply and the loss of goods.

If maximizing domestic goods consumption is a better working approach than maximizing national money income, it would follow that maximizing column VII in Table 14 is more desirable than trying to maximize column III. Maximizing domestic purchases of domestically produced goods plus domestic purchases of goods from abroad (imports) makes far better sense than trying to maximize exports or national income.[14]

The export-balance-of-trade fetish is an amazing, irrational phenomenon. Intelligent selfishness calls for maximizing the consumption of domestically produced goods plus imports. Realization of the fuller life for as many people as possible in the nation calls for tempering that maximization with other considerations. Making the world a viable place in which each individual nation may enjoy such benefits calls for these maximizations on a world-wide scale.

Argument for Import Maintenance

What is the basic relationship between national income and imports and exports? Probably if national income rises in a country there will be a tendency for that country to increase its imports. If national income falls there will be a tendency for the country where the fall occurs to decrease its imports. More purchasing power (or less purchasing power) will be used (or not used) in various ways; and the impact will be divided between domestic and foreign purchases. It is hard to conceive, though theoretically possible, that all of the impact of a change in income might fall on domestic purchases or all on imports. But we are probably justified in assuming that in virtually all real situations the impact will be divided. How much or how little a given change in income will affect imports, we cannot say *a priori*. But we can say with reasonable certainty that there will be an influence.

It stands to reason that, if there is a connection between depressions in different countries, they are going to start somewhere and spread. They may spread rather rapidly and reach an acute stage everywhere at almost the same time, but there still must be a chain of causation. And the depression is more likely to start in a large, important country than

[13] Allowance also being made for import changes.

[14] An article by Warren L. Smith, "Effects of Exchange Rate Adjustments on the Standard of Living," *American Economic Review,* XLIV (December, 1954), 808–25, states somewhat this same proposition. A variation of this argument has already been presented in Chapter 7.

anywhere else, if it is to affect the whole world. It has been argued, in recent years, that the major country where a depression is most likely to begin is the United States; and the opinion is widely held in many other countries that the American economy is very unstable, being characterized by great swings up and down, great rises in productivity followed by sharp drops. When the drops occur, the rest of the world suffers as a result.

Can it be that the real key in explaining the process by which depressions spread is the decline in imports of the country where a depression starts? This argument has been refined into a precise theory as to the nature of the "cause-and-effect process" by a United Nations study group.[15] The argument developed by the group ran to the effect that a depression may start in a large country, such as the United States, and be characterized by large-scale unemployment, a decline in demand, and a decline in national income. Applying the multiplier in reverse to this situation, imports will be decreased by a certain amount as a result of the decrease in national income. Then, by application of the Keynesian analysis in reverse, the beginning of a depression will involve a decline in imports into the country where it began.

According to this line of argument, it is as a result of the decline in imports that the depression spreads. Less importation into the United States means less export from France and other countries, and consequently less production in France, less employment in France, lower national income in France. Ultimately, as a result of the decline in national income, France has less demand for imports of United States goods, with a consequent decline in exports from the United States. The result of this is to make the depression still worse in the United States. Thus a depression, becoming world-wide, generates a vicious spiral downward: declining income, declining trade, and declining employment.

On the basis of this argument, it would seem that if the United States (or the country where the depression starts, whatever country it may be) could maintain its imports so that its depression would not spread, depressions could be confined to the country where they originate. There might be several possible methods for effecting such a quarantine. The country where the depression begins might take prompt measures (increase internal investment or internal spending) to lessen unemployment and maintain the national income. If national income could be so maintained, *by the national government operating at the national level,* the decline in imports would not occur to start the world-wide downward spiral. This seems to be the reason why other countries are concerned

[15] United Nations, Department of Economic Affairs, *National and International Measures for Full Employment* (Lake Success, 1949). The members of the committee were J. M. Clark, Arthur Smithies, Nicholas Kaldor, Pierre Uri, and E. Ronald Walker, the latter being the chairman of the group.

about the maintenance of full employment in the United States. But foreigners are not particularly optimistic that the United States can achieve this goal. The feeling is widespread even in non-Russian and non-Communist circles—although it is certainly purveyed in Communist circles, too—that the United States, economically organized as it is, is not capable of maintaining full employment.

And perhaps it is true, given the institutional structures of this country, that employment will continue to fluctuate. In that case, what is to be done? Or what should be the stand-by arrangement in case the United States does prove incapable of maintaining full employment? In the United Nations report, referred to above, it is suggested that the problem could be dealt with by establishing an obligation on the part of nations to maintain imports whether they maintain domestic full employment or not. Thus the United States might assume an obligation to maintain imports at a certain level, after a depression had begun internally. Such an effort to isolate a depression in the United States would, of course, call for artificial measures.

Proposals for Import Maintenance

Is the United States prepared to make the gesture of appropriating enough money during a period of depression to keep imports at or near pre-depression levels? It would be financially feasible; it would probably cost no more than Marshall Plan aid is costing now.

Perhaps a workable formula would be for the government to take measures insuring the purchase of sufficient foreign goods to keep total imports in any one year from falling more than 5 per cent below the preceding year's total. (The most United States imports have ever varied between one year and the next is $2,700 million.) It might even be desirable, in addition to the measures affecting total trade, to maintain the importation of particular commodities, and total imports from particular countries, by preventing their decline by more than 5 per cent in any single year.[16]

Another question is whether it would be politically possible to get such a program through Congress. It is the kind of program which intelligent selfishness indicates may well be in the national interest. Who can say for sure whether or not it would be possible to pass such a proposal until it is tried?

Another possibility, if the governments of importing countries are not prepared to maintain imports, would be to set up an international agency charged with the responsibility for maintaining the value of trade

---

[16] Planning measures designed to slow down the rate of change are discussed in a slightly different setting in Chapter 13. Suffice it to say here that the difficulties posed by structural change in the cost of production relationships as between various supplying countries would be eased by the slow rate of change under the 5 per cent formula.

(within 5 per cent of the figure of the preceding year). Such an agency might commit itself to buy and stockpile the exports of each country in such amounts that the total exports of a country in any given year would be at least 95 per cent of the total for the preceding year.[17]

A third possibility would be for the government of the exporting country to make purchases from its own exporters who are losing markets. This latter proposal would have the advantage of being politically feasible. In fact, governments are doing this sort of thing all the time.[18] On the negative side, this procedure does not contribute substantially toward getting the goods into the possession of people who really want them.

All things considered, either maintenance of imports by the importing country or trade maintenance and stockpiling by an international agency would seem to be a more desirable procedure.

There are problems in attempting to deal artificially with the maintenance of imports, but it is worth noting that, in essence, these measures are no more difficult and involved, and no more objectionable, than measures such as crop destruction, which the United States has found it possible to implement in the past. Artificially maintaining imports should be no more objectionable than artificially maintaining exports, and far more useful.

Some of the policy tools which are available to a national government are actually available to the United Nations, and all are potentially available. Perhaps the most useful single addition to the "kit of tools" available to the United Nations would be the power to create credit—via some such international agency as the International Monetary Fund. This would solve the problem of financing if the United Nations were to assume the obligation of maintaining export purchases from different countries. But powers of taxation, borrowing, or commercial policy might serve equally well.[19]

United Nations proposals looking toward the maintenance of imports in countries where depressions start are much more statesmanlike than many measures which have been taken in the past to combat depressions (such as the competitive devaluations to stimulate exports of the 1930's). They indicate that no country should fight its depression by

---

[17] The financial implications of such a scheme can hardly be appraised before the discussion of money and short-term funds in Part V.

[18] But the program would need to be financed by "tax and spend" rather than by deficit financing—in order to avoid giving a boost also to imports, a boost which would make the trade balance situation yet more unbalanced. If the purchase program were financed by borrowing (deficit financing), the process would put more money into circulation; the price level would almost certainly rise; and imports would be encouraged at the same time that exports were falling off—a process which would have the effect of unbalancing the trade balance yet further. (The implications of situations of this sort are discussed more fully in Part V.)

[19] The issue of giving an international agency the power to create credit is discussed further in Chapters 22 and 23.

measures which have the effect of making things worse in other countries. While this is all to the good, it does not necessarily prove that depressions spread via the mechanism described in the United Nations report. Perhaps, for example, they spread by the power of suggestion. When businessmen in one country hear of the beginning of a depression in another country, their activities may be affected by that knowledge alone, and their consequent actions may lead to depression in their country without the intermediation of declining imports.

Statistical testing of the theory that depressions spread in the manner described in the United Nations report has not as yet established the truth or falsity of the theory. But there is some evidence that the implied sequence of events has not always occurred in connection with the international spread of depressions.[20]

In any event, whether or not the United Nations theory is adequate as a complete description of the forces influencing the international movement of depressions, it is certainly not vicious in its impact, as the Keynesian argument may be when used to justify the stimulation of exports relative to imports. And if there is any substantial element of truth in the United Nations argument, it may serve as a guide to policies which might well be followed. The maintenance of imports is desirable whenever declining national income tends to decrease imports and presents a threat of world-wide depression. Even if such measures do not neutralize all the forces transmitting depressions internationally, that is no argument against maintenance of imports to neutralize one of the processes by which depressions may spread.

There may be still stronger arguments for import stimulation rather than export stimulation. The implementation of domestic investment in a country may require certain imports of raw materials or machinery. For this reason an increase in imports may be essential to increased domestic investment, increased material income, and a generally desirable situation.[21]

In the face of the threat of foreign retaliation, and bearing in mind the statesmanship involved in import maintenance, as well as the possibility of a favorable import effect on investment, it becomes all the harder to understand the general opinion that "an increase in exports relative to imports is by law of nature a good thing."

EVALUATION

The data on the relationship among exports and imports and national income presented in the supplementary note to this chapter sug-

---

[20] See the supplementary note to this chapter.

[21] A. O. Hirschman, "Disinflation, Discrimination, and the Dollar Shortage," *American Economic Review*, XXXV (December, 1948), p. 887. Hirschman has hinted at this effect in an article in which he is primarily concerned with inflation and the dollar shortage.

gests that there is a closer connection between imports and national-income changes than there is between exports and national income. If true, this gives some support to the proposition that the more statesman-like way to use the tools of national-income theory involves working from the assumption that maintenance of imports is a better approach to depression fighting than artificial stimulation of exports.

But one may surmise, although the data of this chapter are not set up to show it, that the important meaningful relationship is that total exports, total imports, national income, and world income rise and fall together.[22]

SUPPLEMENTARY NOTE: FOREIGN REPERCUSSIONS AND THE TIMING PROBLEM

Foreign Repercussions

Table 14 does not allow for what have come to be called "foreign repercussions." The changes in imports and exports described in the table must affect income and consequently imports and exports in other countries. There would then be secondary effects on the exports and imports of the country where the process started.[23] But for a multi-country world the mathematics is almost unmanageable—even with the constant-multiplier assumption. And with the dropping of the constant-multiplier assumption, it would seem that the resulting complex situation can be handled about as well in words as in figures.

The Timing Problem

But it is probably also true that the timing of changes—the timing of changes in developed countries relative to the timing of changes in the underdeveloped countries, and the timing of income turns relative to the timing of trade turns—is a more important subject for study than are the numerical figures for the actual multiplier magnitudes. Some of the implications of the problem of timing are discussed below. The observations cover all of the testable sequences of events covered in the United Nations Statistical Office's *Yearbook of International Trade Statistics, 1952*, and *Statistical Yearbook, 1952*, except for the war years, which are excluded. Otherwise the period covered is roughly 1939 to 1952.

To begin with, the situation at the bottom of a depression was analyzed to determine whether a rise in national income followed a rise in exports. The first test involved the identification of twenty situations where ex-

---

[22] Table 1 and Charts 1 and 7, however, will support the generalization.

[23] Meade takes this problem into account for a two-country world in a series of ingenious simultaneous equations. Meade, *Balance . . .* , pp. 125–48.

ports were low. Data for exports and for national income were then centered on the low years as illustrated in the following Cuban example:

		Exports	National Income
Cuba	1948	709.9	1,702
(million pesos)	1949	578.3	1,578
	1950	642.0	1,683
	1951	766.1	1,860

The low year for exports and the low year for national income were then identified, with the following results:

(1) an upturn in national income followed an upturn in exports in   2 cases;
(2) an upturn in national income occurred in the same year as an upturn in exports in   6 cases;
(3) an upturn in national income occurred prior to the upturn in exports in   3 cases;
(4) and there was no trough at all in national income to correspond with the trough in exports in   9 cases.

In the two cases where the national income and exports turned upward in the same year, it remains a question which development came first. In the cases where national income rose (or fell) steadily through the whole period under observation, the data do not disprove the possibility that the export timing affected the rate of change in national income. But it is still rather amazing that, out of this group of examples, there should emerge three cases where the upturning national income preceded the rise in exports and only two cases where the upturn in exports preceded the upturn in national income.

The next test involved taking the eleven cases where a trough in national income could be identified and observing whether there was a related upturn in imports. The results were as follows:

(1) an upturn in imports followed an upturn in national income in   4 cases;
(2) an upturn in imports occurred in the same year as an upturn in national income in   6 cases;
(3) an upturn in imports occurred prior to the upturn in national income in   1 case;
(4) and there was no trough in imports to correspond with the trough in national income in   0 cases.

The next test involved taking eighteen cases where export peaks could be identified. The question was then asked whether national-income peaks preceded or followed. The results were as follows:

(1) a downturn in national income followed a downturn
in exports in   2 cases;
(2) a downturn in national income occurred in the same
year as a downturn in exports in   7 cases;
(3) a downturn in national income preceded a downturn
in exports in   1 case;
(4) and there was no peak in national income to corre-
spond with the peak in exports in   8 cases.

The fourth test involved taking the ten cases where a national-income peak could be identified and testing to see whether a peak in imports preceded or followed. The results were as follows:

(1) a downturn in imports followed a downturn in na-
tional income in   2 cases;
(2) a downturn in imports occurred in the same year as a
downturn in national income in   8 cases;
(3) a downturn in imports preceded a downturn in na-
tional income in   0 cases;
(4) and there was no peak in imports to correspond with
the peak in national income in   0 cases.

The fifth test involved identifying eleven cases of troughs in national income and observing the evolution of the balance of trade with respect to them. The results were as follows:

(1) an upturn in the balance of trade (increase in exports
relative to imports) preceded the upturn in national
income in   0 cases;
(2) an upturn in the balance of trade occurred in the same
year as the upturn in national income in   3 cases;
(3) an upturn in the balance of trade followed the upturn
in national income in   3 cases;
(4) the balance of trade turned downward the same year
(or the year following) a downturn in national in-
come in   3 cases;
(5) and there was no trough in the balance of trade to
correspond with the trough in national income in 2 cases.

The sixth case involved identifying seven cases of peaks in national income and observing the evolution of the balance of trade with respect to them. The results were as follows:

(1) a downturn in national income preceded a downturn
in the balance of trade (decrease in exports relative
to imports) in   2 cases;

(2) a downturn in national income occurred in the same
　　year as a downturn in the balance of trade in　　　2 cases;
(3) a downturn in national income followed a downturn in
　　the balance of trade in　　　2 cases;
(4) the national income turned downward in the same
　　year that the balance of trade turned upward in　　　1 case;
(5) there was no peak in the balance of trade to corre-
　　spond with the peak in national income in　　　0 cases.

On the whole none of the relationships studied seem to be very certain in their connection.

PART IV

The Movement of Goods
and Services
(or, the Yankee Trader
Outdoes Himself)

Chapter 9

ARGUMENTS ON RESTRICTIONS: I. VARIOUS ARGUMENTS AND ESPECIALLY THE INFANT-INDUSTRY ARGUMENT

❧ ❧ ❧

Since governments can control the domestic money supply, arguments for tariffs based on the desirability of having more money at home are largely without merit.

The Ricardian doctrine of comparative cost—combined with the long-run necessity for exports to equal imports—indicates the fundamental fallacy of the cheap-foreign-labor argument for tariffs.

Any argument for keeping out imports which is based on military preparedness is basically suspect, for wars are fought, after all, with tremendous quantities of matériel.

The protection of weak domestic industries, and the consequent inhibition of change and adaptation, is hardly a proper procedure for a dynamic, growing economy—which wants to keep its economic leadership.

Industries injured by import increases, and especially the labor forces of industries injured by import increases, are entitled to constructive assistance by the government in making the transition to new lines of activity.

Young or infant industries may well require some form of assistance against the competition of older and financially stronger enterprises in other countries. But this assistance might better take the form of production subsidies rather than tariffs.

Comparison of significant periods when nations have made extensive use of trade restrictions with periods of substantial economic growth and development within those countries reveals little connection between protectionism and economic growth.

❧ ❧ ❧

PART IV deals with measures, policies, and theories directly affecting the international movement of things of value: goods and services. The nature of the financing of trade, which indirectly has an important effect in determining whether there is trade, is left for Part V. In Part IV itself, Chapters 9 and 10 evaluate various arguments for trade restrictions. Chapters 11 through 14 are largely descriptive of the measures, practices, and policies of governments and of private enterprises. Chapters 15, 23, and 36 attempt to establish a co-ordinated pattern of policies which would make for a viable international economy serving the general welfare.

In the main, the arguments discussed in this chapter advocate "doing something for" a particular industry. The person advancing the argument may not be primarily interested in an export trade balance. He is likely to be more specifically interested in some special privilege for himself: some help in promoting his exports or some deterrent against imports that might compete with his product. But such people are also rather likely to advocate a favorable balance of trade—if the topic comes up. And when many individuals advocate measures encouraging some particular export or discouraging some particular import, the result is that the government takes a combination of measures which tend to encourage exports relative to imports. But since, as a rough truth, exports must equal imports, the real, ultimate effect of all these pressures is a decline in total trade.

KEEP THE MONEY AT HOME

The plea to "keep the money at home" in some quarters would be called a "high-toned argument calculated to appeal to low-toned people." It is a variation of an argument much used in the anti-chain-store crusade of the early 1930's: "Buy from your local merchants and keep the money at home." There is a classic statement of this doctrine which is attributed, probably mistakenly, to Abraham Lincoln: "I do not know much about the tariff, but I know this much—when we buy manufactured goods abroad, we get the goods and the foreigner gets the money. When we buy the manufactured goods at home, we get both the goods and the money." There is some truth in this statement, but it is chiefly concentrated in the first part of the first sentence.

To analyze this proposition at all it is necessary to know what is meant by money. Is the reference to gold or paper? If gold, the question becomes: Is the stockpiling of gold desirable? The United States has plenty of gold piled up at Fort Knox, Kentucky; and this circumstance may provide empirical evidence that there is no necessary merit in having a lot of gold for its own sake. But common sense, also, should indicate that the accumulation of gold is no end in itself.[1] Lewes Roberts in 1641 observed that a country grows by engaging actively in production and commerce and not by hoarding gold. He pointed out that Spain had gold but England lacked the yellow "blessing" in the sixteenth and early seventeenth centuries. Yet, as he pointed out, England was progressing while Spain was stagnating.[2]

On the other hand, if what is meant by money is paper money, there is even less of a problem. If a country is suffering from a lack of paper money, it can print some; or, more properly put, it can expand the supply of money and credit through its credit control powers. Therefore, it need not go to great trouble to arrange for an export balance of trade —perhaps risking failure in the effort to get such a balance. So much for the "keep the money at home" argument, which has little or no merit.

CHEAP FOREIGN LABOR

Since United States wages are higher than the wages in Canada, Argentina, Germany, and Japan,[3] a "wage gap" undoubtedly exists. This difference is a combination of a substantial difference in money wages and a somewhat less marked but still substantial difference in real wages or real level of living.

Based upon this difference, the cheap-foreign-labor argument, as applied to wool, runs somewhat as follows: It costs forty cents a head to shear sheep in the United States and only twelve cents a head in Australia.[4] This, it is argued, represents unfair competition.

The standard example of this sort of thing was found in Japan in the 1930's. Japanese labor was so cheap that a tariff was considered necessary to protect the United States textile industry against Japanese competition. A comparison of textile wages in the two countries would undoubtedly reveal that both the pay scale and the level of living of the United States workers were substantially higher than those of the Japanese.

[1] The mercantilist arguments connected with the desirability of hoarding gold were discussed in Chapters 3 and 4.

[2] Lewes Roberts, *The Treasure of Traffike or a Discourse of Forraigne Trade* (London, 1641), as reproduced in J. R. McCulloch (ed.), *Early English Tracts on Commerce*, pp. 49–113.

[3] American Tariff League, *What About the Wage Gap?* (Publication No. 134 [New York, 1954]), p. 1.

[4] United States Congress, Senate, Committee on Agriculture and Forestry, *Foreign Trade in Agricultural Products* (1953), part 3, pp. 470–1. The argument is that of Mr. Ray Willoughby.

A more recent application of the cheap-foreign-labor argument involves the Westinghouse Electric Corporation.[5] It seemed, according to company spokesmen, that Westinghouse could underbid its foreign competitors in selling assembly-line products, but not in selling custom-built generators and transformers. The latter process involves a very high proportion of labor cost in the total cost. Since skilled foreign labor costs less, it developed that the foreign concerns could provide the generators and transformers more cheaply and did offer to sell some to the United States government at a price 30 per cent under a Westinghouse bid. In the interest of economy in government it might have seemed desirable to accept the bid of the Swiss firm, Brown, Boveri and Company. But Westinghouse proceeded to organize in East Pittsburgh a demonstration of some 8,000 workers to protest the granting of the contract to the Swiss. In view of the fact that Westinghouse in the preceding eighteen months had lost $7,000,000 in government orders to foreign companies, it might appear that the protest was justified. But it was also true that Westinghouse International had done a $110,000,000 export business the preceding year. How well advised, then, were the company's efforts to throttle trade, even from the company's own point of view?

Since a high level of living in the United States is obviously desirable, the argument that the tariff is necessary to protect it has sounded plausible. But the cheap-foreign-labor argument may be criticized on two counts: as generally stated it involves an incomplete theory of cost, and it confuses cause and effect in relation to the high level of living in the United States.

Labor cost is not the only cost; and in producing goods in the United States the use of more efficient machinery and of artificial power permits considerable saving in labor. The United States thus can produce many lines of goods at total costs lower than the corresponding foreign goods and still pay higher wages while doing so, because of the more important role of capital equipment and technical knowledge. Surely what is important is total average cost, and not the average wage, in appraising the menace of foreign competition.

With regard to wage and cost differentials, the Public Advisory Board for Mutual Security has said:[6] "The exceptional productivity of American industry means, in fact, that wage costs per unit of output in manufacturing are generally lower in the United States than abroad. It is only in certain limited fields that American manufacturers are faced

---

[5] *Fortune,* July, 1953, pp. 46 and 67–8. A different example drawn from the electric equipment field is cited in Chapter 12.

[6] United States, Public Advisory Board for Mutual Security, *A Trade and Tariff Policy in the National Interest* (1953), p. 17.

with serious competition." Howard S. Piquet has identified the type of industry where this may be the case.[7]

> American producers, *as a whole,* have little to fear from import competition. Most of such competition comes from smaller and less efficient foreign industries. Generally speaking, the lines of production in the United States having most to fear from import competition are those that employ a large proportion of hand labor, *which must be paid high wages because of alternative opportunities in more fortunately situated domestic industries,* or that have not kept pace with technological or other changes.

Accordingly, the sheepmen are in trouble because they are trying to hire herders away from other more productive employment within the United States, not because of the menace of unfair foreign competition.

But discussion of the wool problem should not be left on this negative note. Is the wool industry really a dying industry? If so, let it die; at the same time, however, set up a program calculated to help those now in the sheep business to shift to other lines of activity. But perhaps the industry, in spite of the weeping and wailing of the representatives from the mountain states, is not dying. Perhaps wool is a by-product of mutton and the sheep people are "making plenty" from their mutton (and from their wool, too, for that matter). They are merely engaged in an effort—which is the right of every free private enterpriser—to get the government to set up a situation which will enable them to make a little more.

For the sake of argument, let us say that the wool industry is neither dying nor well—it is just plain sick. And probably this is the real belief of the wool industry lobbyists. Is a tariff what this situation calls for? The makers of woolen textiles are at a disadvantage these days as a result of the competition of orlon, dacron, and what not. A high tariff and a high domestic price for wool means high wool costs for the woolen textile mills and the loss of another round by the wool industry in the fight with synthetics. One might well say to the sheepmen arguing for a tariff on wool: "Let's not cut our own throats, boys." Clearly, this is a case where, if any government aid is called for, the aid should take the form of subsidies, not tariffs. Keep the prices low to keep the wool industry competitive, instead of keeping them high to insure a slow and agonizing death.

The cheap-foreign-labor argument should not be dismissed without

[7] Howard S. Piquet, *Aid, Trade and the Tariff* (New York: Crowell, 1953), p. 60. Copyright 1953 by the Thomas Y. Crowell Company. Reprinted by permission.

discussing its fundamental implications. The assumption is that any one who opposes tariffs because of opposition to this argument favors a low wage scale for American workers. Sinclair Weeks, President Eisenhower's Secretary of Commerce, has said:[8] "I am willing for American industry to face the competition of any industry anywhere with respect to all save the labor factor. I am not, however, willing to have American industry compete at the expense of the standard of living of American labor." The solicitude which people with business backgrounds show for labor in some circumstances is most gratifying, even though labor's general interest in more goods at lower prices is forgotten in the confusion of arguments.

In connection with the cheap-foreign-labor argument there is a basic confusion of cause and effect. Are wages in the United States higher than those in Japan because of the tariff protection, or for some other reason? Did the tariff barriers make possible the high level of living and the higher United States wages? If there is any truth in the proposition that tariffs had such an effect, it is to be found in the infant-industry argument and not in the cheap-foreign-labor argument. Is it not true that the general wage scale in the United States is higher because of the greater productivity and lower costs in many lines of American industry? It then becomes pertinent to inquire why United States industry is more productive than the Japanese. It did not get that way by putting a large part of the productive energy into lines of activity where the United States was less efficient than foreign countries. If one industry in a prosperous country is chronically sick, this is an argument for getting out of that industry. If all industry is sick in a sick country, the cheap-foreign-labor argument will not be relevant, because labor in that country will be universally cheap.

To cite an example, the chemical industry in the United States apparently takes the position that it is a sick industry in a well country (unless it thinks the country is sick). To quote Calvin A. Campbell, vice president of the Dow Chemical Company,[9] "We know that in isolated instances we excel in technology or other advantages to a degree sufficient to offset the wage differential. But—we also know that in other instances (and this is true in regard to chemical production) we have no such superiority." Apparently the chemical industry (along with agriculture, oil, iron, and textiles) is sick. Where does American industrial supremacy in the world come from, if in this day and age no American industry can compete with its foreign counterparts? Maybe some of these people should read the London *Economist:*[10]

[8] *Foreign Commerce Weekly,* November 23, 1953, p. 14.
[9] American Tariff League, *Let's Not Import Depression* (New York, 1953), p. 11.
[10] December 19, 1953, p. 874. Reprinted with the kind permission of the London *Economist.*

The House of Commons last week debated the Order increasing import duties on fruit and vegetables in an atmosphere of sweet reasonableness and inter-party amity. The irrepressible voice of Sir Waldron Smithers spoke up for free trade and cheap food; otherwise, differences of emphasis and approach hardly flawed the surface of a virtual unanimity. In part, this reflects the generally accepted view that Britain must, even at a fairly heavy price, be more self sufficient in food production than comparative international costs would dictate. This is reasonable enough. What is disheartening is the list of unspoken assumptions that serve as justification for any and every piece of international barrier-building.

The debate showed, for example, the assumption that "the" industry—horticultural or other—is a homogeneous concern each of whose components is equally efficient, equally vulnerable to price fluctuations, and equally sacrosanct; the notion that a fringe of marginal producers might be "driven out of business" (i.e., induced to turn to some other job) without simultaneous ruin for producers in general is apparently too abstruse and academic to be ever entertained, let alone given weight.

The really important factors determining United States productive superiority have been mentioned before; but it may be well to repeat them here. The important variables are technical knowledge, institutional organization, and appropriateness of the available raw materials. The United States has been fortunate in having natural resources especially appropriate for the technical processes which have become important during the last hundred-and-fifty years. In addition, institutional barriers to technical development probably have been less strong than elsewhere, and initiative has consequently had more of a chance in the United States.

Consider the growth of the steel industry in this country in the latter part of the nineteenth century. The development occurred because the United States had the coal and the iron ore (relatively accessible and relatively high grade), such technical knowledge as there was, and an institutional organization which was less inhibitory than the institutional organization in many other areas. The use of the tariff against steel imports from Britain in the early part of the nineteenth century may have been a factor encouraging development of the industry in the United States by offering protection against the dumping tactics of British industry (infant-industry argument), but certainly it was no factor in helping the steel industry in the United States to withstand the competition of the Japanese steel industry (cheap-foreign-labor argument).

The cheap-foreign-labor argument is generally aimed at less developed countries that are beginning to develop and not at the more developed countries, which are likely to be paying higher wages (as was probably the case with Britain in the early part of the nineteenth century). This is a "kick the fellow who is down" type of argument. But it is surely because of the fact that an economy is dynamic and expanding that its real-wage scale is high relative to those of other countries. The higher real wage in the United States is a result of greater productivity, rather than a result of cheap-foreign-labor motivated tariffs.

With regard to the international differences between wages on the one hand and productivity on the other, the Randall Commission has this to say: [11]

> . . . the wage relatives country by country bear a close resemblance to the productivity relatives. This means that the average American worker turns out three times as much per year as the average European worker and is also paid, on the average about three times as much per year. This similarity between relative wages and productivities is probably more of an effect than a cause of productivity differences. However, the close correlation suggests that relative wages can be taken as a first indicator of relative productivities.

But there are those who, in the face of the general superiority of American industry, may still choose to worry about the consequences of freer foreign competition: "Even though our level of living is higher, we will lose foreign markets because our costs turn out higher." A person arguing in these terms forgets that the value of a country's exports must equal the value of its imports, unless someone is willing to finance a discrepancy.

Ricardo's doctrine of comparative cost may also give comfort to a person worrying in these terms. All that is necessary is to take at face value the statement of the lobbyists that cheap foreign labor is undercutting United States producers right and left. This amounts to assuming a comparative-cost type of situation. And the doctrine of comparative cost tells us that trade may go on even though one country has an advantage in the production of all things. The result is that, in spite of the fact that Portugal can produce all things more cheaply than England, as much money value of goods goes from England to Portugal as goes from Portugal to England. By the same principle, as much money value of goods goes out of the United States as comes in, unless somebody is willing to finance a discrepancy.

It is true, of course, especially in an economy that has had the

[11] United States, Commission on Foreign Economic Policy, *Staff Papers*, p. 430, quoting from a study *Research in Industry*, published by the Stanford Research Institute, Stanford, California, November 1953.

"benefit" of numerous tariffs, that certain industries could be undersold by foreign competitors if the tariffs were removed (even though other domestic industries would be benefited by a more than compensating amount). Undoubtedly there are certain United States industries that would suffer if the United States eliminated certain tariffs. But since the dominance of the United States in the world today is due to the fact that this country can produce more things more cheaply than any other country, surely we need not worry about the possibility that other countries, paying cheap wages, can undersell the United States on most things, or even on many things. The United States may have an adjustment problem; it does not have a problem in terms of "general" marketing disadvantage. Both low total costs in this country and the comparative-cost argument indicate the correctness of this statement.

It goes without saying that the workers of China or Japan do not like their low real wages. They would rather consume the goods themselves than ship them to the United States. The cure for the problem posed by the cheap-foreign-labor argument (the real problem being the suffering in those areas and not the suffering in the United States) is higher wages and a higher level of living in the underdeveloped areas. And the people in those areas will surely co-operate in any such program.

EQUALIZATION OF COST OF PRODUCTION

Closely related to the cheap-foreign-labor argument, but erected on even less closely packed sand, is the equalization-of-cost-of-production argument. In its own innocent way it is probably the most spurious of the arguments for protection, for this is the argument that ostensibly is based on fairness. The proposition runs to the effect that, if a United States company has a cost of $10 in producing a certain item, and if the French industry has a cost of $6 in producing the same item, then a tariff of $4 would equalize the cost of production. It would bring the French cost of production up to the United States cost of production, and would place each on an equal footing in facing the American consumer. What could be fairer than that; all producers should start on an equal basis in offering their goods for sale, should they not? There is no question about the pervasiveness of this idea, for it has been written into the United States tariff law. And the Tariff Commission in the early 1920's was instructed to make studies of the costs of production of United States industries for comparison with the costs in foreign industries with a view to changing the tariff rates to correspond with the difference. The argument has thus been something more than an academic doctrine.

The equalization-of-cost-of-production clause, as embodied in the Smoot-Hawley Act of 1930, reads: [12]

> If the commission finds it shown by the investigation that the duties expressly fixed by statute do not equalize the differences in the costs of production of the domestic article and the like or similar foreign article when produced in the principal competing country, the commission shall specify in its report such increases or decreases in rates of duty expressly fixed by statute (including any necessary change in classification) as it finds shown by the investigation to be necessary to equalize such differences. In no case shall the total increase or decrease of such rates of duty exceed 50 per centum of the rates expressly fixed by statute.

If the President found the Tariff Commission's factual data to be accurate, he was required to place the recommended rate changes in effect. But the 50 per cent limitation on duty change provided at least a slight restraint on the all-pervasiveness of the equalization-of-cost concept. The argument could not be used to make the American consumer pay in excess of 50 per cent "more."

Of course the Tariff Commission ran into trouble. Foreign nations and corporations were no more interested in facilitating the work of the United States Tariff Commission than their United States counterparts would have been if the shoe had been on the other foot. And accurate studies of foreign production costs proved extremely difficult.[13] But even if the Tariff Commission could have made such studies, the results would have been very inconclusive. What production costs should be used? Different companies have different costs. Some are more efficient than others. And even within a given company, production costs depend on the volume of production. Should the tariff take into account the lowest-cost foreign firm and the highest-cost domestic firm? Should it relate the lowest-cost domestic firm to the highest-cost (or even the lowest-cost) foreign firm? Should it attempt to strike some kind of an average? At any rate, how to do this has never been satisfactorily worked out. And if you add to these considerations the fact

[12] United States Code (1952 edition), Title 19, par. 1336 (a). The Fordney-McCumber Act of 1922 contained a similar clause.

[13] Such studies are still being attempted. Certain unfortunate by-product effects of one such study were cited recently by the *New York Times* (October 3, 1954, p. 9). "The Soviet Union is profiting directly from the vagaries of the United States foreign trade policy in its impact on Italy. . . . The situation is considerably eased for the Soviet by the United States practice of sending in teams of investigators to report on Italian costs and conditions of production as the basis for tariff or other action to protect American producers. These teams are sent in quite openly and are remarked upon by all those concerned with whatever industry may be involved."

that all such costs are changing continually, it appears unlikely that the government can ever work out a satisfactory formula for keeping its records up to date.

It remains, however, to point out the fundamental objection to the equalization-of-cost-of-production argument, which would remain even though the administrative difficulties were resolved. Could there be any occasion for goods moving in international trade if this doctrine were effectively applied? It would seem that there would be literally no point in a ship leaving port. What the doctrine would do, if applied, would be to eliminate the gain from geographical specialization and from international trade. Such a tariff would remove the reason for buying goods abroad, since they could not be cheaper than domestic goods. International trade would be rendered pointless.[14]

PERIL POINT AND ESCAPE CLAUSE

In point of fact there is at present little effort to apply the equalization-of-cost-of-production formula as such. Rather, businessmen are attempting to induce the executive branch to apply the peril-point and escape-clause provisions (and farmers are attempting to obtain application of the provisions of the agricultural laws which permit quota limitations when imports seem to represent a threat to the parity price support program of the Department of Agriculture).[15]

A fairly standard escape clause has been included in reciprocal trade agreements since 1947. The clause was originally placed there by executive action; but in 1951 Congress provided by law that the escape clause must be included in all agreements. Under the peril-point provision, tariff reductions cannot go beyond the point of "causing or threatening serious injury to the domestic industry producing like or directly competitive articles" at the time new agreements are concluded. While this provision has been in and out of the law, it has remained in the law since 1951. The basic criteria of the escape-clause and peril-point provisions are roughly the same; they merely apply to different stages in the process.

The June, 1951, revision of the tariff law provided that the following escape clause must be included in all reciprocal trade agreements:

No . . . concession . . . shall be permitted . . . to continue in
effect . . . when the product on which the concession has been

---

[14] N. I. Stone, *One Man's Crusade for an Honest Tariff* (Appleton, Wis.: Lawrence College Press, 1952). This tract is the saga of Herbert E. Miles, "father" of the Tariff Commission, who believed that the equalization-of-cost-of-production approach was better than some other evils.

[15] The peril-point idea and the escape clause are also discussed in Chapter 11.

granted is, as a result, . . . of the . . . concession, being imported into the United States in such increased quantities, either
actual or relative, as to cause or threaten serious injury to the
domestic industry producing like or directly competitive products.

This clause seems to give a domestic business group a vested interest
in its position, both absolute and relative, regardless of how inefficient
and high cost it may be, regardless of changes in demand patterns, and
regardless of changes in relative cost conditions as between countries.

However, as is well-known, in such cases much depends on the manner of administration. It is a bit difficult to measure the influence
which the peril point has had in connection with the negotiation of
new agreements. But the escape clause, between 1948 and 1953, was
"called to witness" by domestic producers in fifty-one cases. The Tariff
Commission sided with the complainants in seven cases. Eight cases
(the law providing that one additional case in which there was a tied
vote also be submitted) were submitted to the President for implementation. The President granted the desired relief in only three cases—namely,
women's fur felt hats and hat bodies, hatters' fur, and dried figs.[16]

Congress seems to have intended that the escape-clause and peril-point
provisions should be invoked if domestic industry were "pinched" even
a little. The Tariff Commission has been reluctant to invoke the escape
clause and the President has been somewhat more reluctant to implement the "invocation," but he has nevertheless done so several times.
However, given the state of the world during the last few years, why
should United States industry be "hurting" at all? Relative to foreign
industries, United States industry is never going to be better off than it
has been for the last ten years.

The concept of injury to domestic industry, as a basis for determining
whether or not trade barriers should be lowered or whether reductions
should be continued, is a nebulous thing. For example, in connection
with women's fur felt hats (an industry that has obtained relief under
the escape clause), the Randall Commission has reported: [17]

> The basic problem of the industry was the fact that many
> women have given up wearing hats, and that women's hat
> styles have changed to fabrics other than felt.

Relief for the domestic watchmaking industry was recommended by
the Tariff Commission, not granted by the President at first, but finally

[16] Irving B. Kravis, "The Trade Agreements Escape Clause," *American Economic
Review*, XL (June, 1954), pp. 319–38. Watches and bicycles should now be added
to the list of industries which have received relief.
[17] United States, Commission on Foreign Economic Policy, *Staff Papers*, p. 284.

granted in 1954 after tremendous pressure had been exerted. With regard to the watchmakers, the Randall Commission said: [18]

It has been widely contended that the American watch industry has been too slow to adopt the aggressive merchandising methods of its Swiss competitors—methods which have changed sales of watches in the last 15 years from a luxury trade to a mass-merchandising industry—and too slow in matching such Swiss innovations as second-sweep hands, shock-proof movements, and the like.

Don Humphrey has written in condemnation of these procedures: [19]

One reason why tariff concessions have been rather ineffective may be the uncertainty that attends the escape clause principle. . . . the escape clause places the interest of a single industry, narrowly defined, above the national interest. This is the most important issue in American commercial policy today.

Humphrey points out that the increase in imports into the United States has been very moderate in recent years in spite of very substantial tariff reductions. Foreigners are simply afraid to try to develop a market from which they know they will be cut off by operation of the escape clause if they have any success in developing it.

This, then, is a most nebulous formula which "depends on administration" for implementation within a range of latitude that virtually runs from "no implementation" to "application to everything."

SENESCENT INDUSTRIES

Closely related to the type of thinking which has gone into many of the complaints filed by industry under the peril-point and escape-clause provisions is a phenomenon that might well be called the senescent-industry argument for tariffs.

An old, long-established United States industry finds that it is afflicted by declining sales—and declining profits. Imports may be increasing —but not by enough to account for the decline in sales. Or imports may be declining but "enjoying" a rising proportion of the falling market. Fur felt hats and hat bodies and toweling (of flax, hemp, or ramie) seem to have been examples of this sort of thing. Instead of considering this situation as one calling for some intelligent adjustments, the domestic industry is likely to call for higher tariffs.[20] In some cases the industry

---

[18] *Ibid.*, p. 285.
[19] Don D. Humphrey, *American Imports*, p. 386.
[20] United States, Tariff Commission, *Toweling, of Flax, Hemp, or Ramie.*

which is senescent on the American scene may be profitable in other countries. Humphrey has pointed out that technological progress in the United States has given this country a great comparative advantage in new lines of activity at the same time that it has brought a loss of comparative advantage in certain lines of activity where the United States formerly had an advantage.[21]

This is a natural result of the working of the law of comparative cost and of the necessity that exports equal imports. But the American industries adversely affected—which are chiefly those making relatively large use of low-paid labor (low-paid as the American wage scale goes) —naturally object. The government, instead of catering to their difficulties by tariff increases which solve no fundamental problems, should consider thoughtfully what can be done about the situation.

MILITARY NECESSITY (TRADE RESTRICTIONS FOR DEFENSE)

Military necessity is a potent argument which anybody may use as a justification for doing almost anything he has in mind. Everything is necessary for defense, especially cheese.[22] The defense argument is advanced customarily as a reason for tariff protection. But, to test its validity, try sitting down and making a list of the tariff measures which the United States should take if it were looking forward to the possibility of a war sometime during the next ten or twenty years. Should the copper tariff be low in order to encourage imports and safeguard domestic reserves; or should it be high to make domestic copper production more profitable? Ask the same question about crude oil, lead, zinc, or what you will. Probably in such a list, if it be at all comprehensive, you will find far more situations calling for the encouragement of imports than for their discouragement. But when private interests use the military-necessity argument it is almost invariably to justify curtailment of the importation of competing goods. It would be interesting to see the day when a private-industry spokesman goes down to Washington and uses the national-defense argument to justify import expansion.

Military danger may be considered from two points of view; one can anticipate either a long-drawn-out series of minor clashes or a general war.[23]

---

[21] Humphrey, *American Imports*, pp. 461, 463.

[22] *New York Times*, March 4, 1955, p. 13.

[23] See the testimony by Col. Richard L. Leghorn before the United States Congress, Joint Committee on the Economic Report, *Foreign Economic Policy*, Hearings, 84th Cong., 1st Sess. (Washington: G. P. O., 1955), pp. 308–19.

If the military defense problem is appraised in the form that it is likely to take for the United States during the next few (or not so few) years while the "cold war" lasts, one may well envisage *a long series of squabbles and minor clashes* with the Russians scattered over the surface of the globe, but with no general war ever breaking out. If one thinks in those terms, surely the military-necessity argument boils down to the taking of measures which will make the maximum supply of goods available to the United States. In this setting tariffs protecting uneconomical industries do not look like very intelligent measures.

Apropos of the national-defense argument for tariffs, it may not be amiss to cite the case of wool, since wool growers never tire of claiming that their industry should be protected in the interest of national defense. To cite the *Staff Papers* of the Randall Commission: [24]

> Are recent levels of sheep numbers and wool production too low from the standard of the national interest? Under pressure from the wool growers, the Congress was so persuaded in 1949 . . .
>
> The main arguments put forward are that wool is an "essential," "critical," and "strategic" material, that requirements for it rise sharply in wartime, and that in the event of war the supply of imported wool, most of which comes by sea over long distances, could be cut off.
>
> This plausible argument is not supported by our war experience. Early in World War II the British stockpiled a large amount of Australian wool in the United States; most of this was shipped out of the country between VE-Day and July 1947. The Defense Supplies Corporation purchased part of this stockpile in 1941, and later acquired small quantities of other imported wools by purchase or exchange; these were mostly disposed of in 1944 and 1945. Very large military requirements were met without serious difficulty, in considerable measure from current imports and almost wholly from *foreign sources;* and only moderate and perhaps unnecessary restrictions were imposed on civilian uses of wool. In fact, a large part of the domestic clips accumulated in the hands of the CCC during 1943-47, when it purchased domestic wool at OPA ceiling prices, well above the prices of comparable imported wool. It was on the postwar sale of these stocks, mostly for export that most of the [previously mentioned] $92 million loss was incurred . . .
>
> Experience during and after World War II, however, indi-

[24] United States, Commission of Foreign Economic Policy, *Staff Papers,* pp. 184–87.

cated that stockpiling of wool is feasible, indeed, that it can easily be overdone. Deterioration in storage, even for several years, is inconsequential under proper management. The cost of stockpiling, though by no means negligible, is not prohibitive . . .

In short, little or no justification for price supports on domestic wool or equivalent measures, can properly be sought in the defense arguments . . .

The interests of the woolen manufacturing industry [within the United States], and of the Defense Department, lie in having the maximum freedom to choose among the various types and grades of domestic and imported wools, undisturbed by changes in Government policy and changing holdings of Government stocks . . .

[In this connection it is not inappropriate to add:] The quality of American wools is generally inferior to that of imported wools.

It would be better for us to buy wool from the cheapest source instead of protecting an uneconomical local sheep raising industry (*if* the local industry *is* uneconomical).

The sugar industry provides further proof that tariff and quota protection do not necessarily assure supplies in wartime, even if the domestic industry has argued that it needs such protection as a military necessity. In spite of all the protection of the 1930's, not only was domestic production of sugar inadequate to meet wartime needs, but domestic production *fell off* during the war years. The industry did not deliver the goods in spite of the favoritism of which it had been the beneficiary. The falling off of sugar production during World War II was due in large part to the fact that underpaid labor in the beet fields preferred to go into better paying jobs in manufacturing; this is an explanation for what happened but not a justification for the trade barriers of the 1930's. Cuba, the chief sufferer from the prewar trade barriers, had to be called on during World War II to engage in a large-scale program of expanding sugar production. Nonetheless, in the Sugar Act of 1948, Cuba was given the same low basic quota in the United States market which she had been given in the 1930's (roughly 28 per cent). But since Cuba had been our staunch ally during the war, we made a concession: during the years of high demand we agreed that Cuba should have a much larger share than 28 per cent of the larger demand. We thus assured that the Cuban economy would be operating on a "boom and bust" basis, but did no particular disservice to the United States industry, which has not shown itself very effective in expanding production in response to a rise in demand, anyway.

Similarly, the use of the military-defense argument by the watch-makers might be a little more convincing if the domestic industry had been a little more adaptable and efficient. As was mentioned in connection with the cheap-foreign-labor argument, the Randall Commission has found the domestic industry "too slow in matching such Swiss innovations as second-sweep hands, shock-proof movements, and the like." [25]

But to turn to the really dynamite-laden issue, the use of the military necessity argument to justify tariffs on metallic minerals, petroleum, and related raw materials: At a recent conference in Denver, lead and zinc industry spokesmen resolved as follows: [26]

> The National Emergency Committee on Lead and Zinc in conference at Denver, Colorado, on February 10 and 11, 1953, has concluded that, in the interest of National defense and security, constructive legislation as stated below is needed without delay for the preservation of the Mining Industry engaged in the production of Lead and Zinc.
>
> 1. Whenever the respective market prices of these metals are below the prices required to perpetuate the domestic mining industry, a sliding scale stabilization import tax on lead and zinc must be provided . . .

This measure would prevent American consumers from buying the cheaper foreign lead and zinc which they would prefer to buy under such conditions.

But here is an American industry in trouble as a result of rising costs and falling prices. Some adjustment, and some aid, are probably called for. But not in this form. Moreover, the industry is not entitled to make the decision as to whether special assistance *in the interest of national defense* is called for in its case. That decision should be made by experts in national defense. And in fact a clause calling for legislation that "should be made effective *for not less than* the life of the Defense Act," shows that the proponents of the legislation have something more than national defense in mind.

Of course, an industry such as zinc and lead mining, if it has information on likely future production and prices which it thinks may affect national defense, is performing a patriotic service by making

[25] For some evidence on both sides of the question of the essentialness of a domestic watch industry for national defense see: *New York Times,* March 4, 1955, p. 13; February 15, 1955, p. 4; July 28, 1954, p. 1; *Austin American,* March 22, 1955, p. 15; and United States Congress, Senate, Committee on Armed Services, *Essentiality of the American Watch and Clock Industry,* Report of Preparedness Subcommittee No. 6 (Washington: Government Printing Office, 1954).

[26] *Mining Engineering* (AIME), March, 1953, p. 269. Reprinted with the kind permission of the publisher.

such data available to those responsible for planning national defense.[27] The only grounds for by-passing the responsible planners, as industrial spokesmen do when they go to Congress and argue for a tariff, would be that they have knowledge to the effect that said planners are incompetent. But then the data they submit to Congress should pertain to the incompetence of the Defense Department and not to their claim for special privilege in the name of defense, a claim which neither they nor members of Congress are competent to appraise.

The quoted resolution also leaves completely ambiguous the level of domestic mining activity which it is desirable to protect. In fact, it turns out that the industry spokesmen are not protecting a level of activity at all, but a price. And the scheme is intended (it develops as it is elaborated) to effect a domestic price for lead and zinc which will rise and fall proportionately "with the BLS index of primary market prices for all commodities other than farm and food." Neither lead nor zinc (nor any other commodity) is entitled to such protection of a relative position in the industry. What if changes in technology decrease the usefulness of lead and zinc? What if large new discoveries either in the United States or abroad tend to make the industry more profitable at lower prices? The implications of this line of argument are discussed in Chapter 13 in connection with the parity price formula.

Not much can be said for an industry's claim for aid on the basis of military necessity. But the industry may have a genuine problem which can be mitigated by direct subsidy (if it is a short-run problem, or if it is genuinely desirable to maintain a certain level of activity in the industry in the interest of national defense), or by change-over aid if the industry really is due for a decline in importance.

Nevertheless, the Domestic Minerals Program Extension Act of 1953 included the following provision:

> Sec. 2. It is hereby recognized that the continued dependence on overseas sources of supply for strategic or critical minerals and metals during periods of threatening world conflict or of political instability within those nations controlling the sources of supply of such materials gravely endangers the present and future economy and security of the United States. It is therefore declared to be the policy of the Congress that each department and agency of the Federal Government charged with responsibilities concerning the discovery, development, production, and acquisition of strategic or critical minerals and metals shall undertake to decrease further and to eliminate where possible

---

[27] The Defense Department either is or had better become competent in these matters. Defense Department personnel have been so bombarded by private enterprise in this context that Defense Department officials sometimes talk like the industry spokesmen.

the dependency of the United States on overseas sources of supply of each such material.

All of this is without regard to whether the measures favoring domestic industry would actually increase the available supply of strategic and critical minerals. Surely the basic approach should call for measures to increase the supply of vital materials available for use within the United States. It should even call for increasing domestic reserves; but self-sufficiency should at most be an additional consideration—not the fundamental norm.

The United States is largely or wholly dependent on foreign sources for many militarily important minerals and materials: antimony, asbestos, chromium, cobalt, corundum, graphite, industrial diamonds, manganese, mica, nickel, platinum, quartz crystals, radium, tantalum, thorium, and tin. It is markedly dependent on foreign sources for bauxite, bismuth, cadmium, lead, mercury, silver, tungsten, vanadium, and zinc. Ergo, we have tariffs: mica (13.7%), manganese (10.9%), mercury (39.5%), graphite (7.7%), tungsten (41.3%), bauxite (13.4%).[28] Before long there will no doubt be a tariff on uranium ore: Or is there one now?

In connection with the current effort to get the tariffs on minerals raised, the Randall Commission has reported:[29]

> An argument that has been advanced for the retention or increase of our trade restrictions on minerals and metals is that existing domestic facilities and resources might be urgently needed in the event of a national emergency because there is a possibility that we might be cut off from foreign sources; hence it is desirable to keep such facilities in operating condition. The security aspect deserves serious consideration; however, the United States is more deficient in minerals than in other resources—except for mineral fuels. Under these circumstances, it is not clear how the interests of national security would be best served if we were to deplete further or exhaust completely our limited reserves of strategic minerals in order to meet peacetime demands.

Certain domestic minerals are in at least temporary difficulties, it is true. But Table 16 indicates a glowing future for the mineral industries, if those industries show even a modicum of adaptability. On the other hand, if foreign mineral sources are tremendously large relative to the domestic, the domestic mining industry may be in trouble and may

[28] United States, Commission on Foreign Economic Policy, *Staff Papers*, p. 231. These tariff rates may not jibe with some of those mentioned in Chapter 11, if they were computed at a different time.

[29] *Ibid.*, pp. 235–6.

have a legitimate claim on Congress for some form of assistance (perhaps aid in change-over to other lines of business)—but the claim cannot be based on the military-necessity argument under the present assumption of a long series of minor wars. What is needed is to get the desirable quantities of the minerals as cheaply and expeditiously as possible from abroad. Therefore, given the assumption of a series of minor wars, military necessity is not a particularly convincing argument for the extensive use of tariffs.

TABLE 16

HOW UNITED STATES CONSUMPTION OF MINERALS MIGHT RISE BY 1975

(ASSUMING NO RELATIVE CHANGE IN PRICES)

	1975 ESTIMATED PER CENT INCREASE OVER 1950
MINERALS, total (except gold)	90
Iron and Ferro-alloys	75
Iron	54
Chromium	100
Cobalt	344
Manganese	50
Molybdenum	170
Nickel	100
Tungsten	150
Non-ferrous Metals, total (except ferro-alloy and gold)	85
Copper	43
Lead	53
Zinc	39
Antimony	81
Bauxite	291
Magnesium	1845
Mercury	25
Platinum	30
Tin	18
Titanium and Cadmium	324
Mineral Fuels, total	97
Coal	54
Petroleum	109
Natural Gas	142

Source: United States, Commission on Foreign Economic Policy, *Staff Papers,* p. 229.

Military necessity *may* be an argument for giving some special favor or encouragement to a particular industry. But military and defense experts should make such decisions; and economists should evaluate the particular assistance device used in terms of whether it is likely to accomplish the result intended; and the decisions should not be made in the maelstrom of special privilege exerting pressure on Capitol Hill.

If qualified people say that military necessity does provide a proper basis for aiding a particular industry, certain conclusions follow. The Randall Commission has said in its report: [30]

> The Commission recommends that tariffs or other import restrictions on raw materials shall be determined on economic grounds. Upon a finding by the Executive that it is necessary on solely military grounds to assure a strictly domestic source of supply, the Commission recommends that the purpose should be accomplished by other means, the cost of which should be borne by the defense budget.

In transmitting the report to Congress, President Eisenhower added his endorsement to these views: [31]

> The Commission also recommended that domestic sources for raw materials required for military purposes should be assured by direct means and not by tariffs and import quotas. I believe that normally this is sound.

But the preceding discussion of the military-necessity argument has been largely predicated upon the likely assumption that there will be a long-drawn-out series of minor clashes. What if there should be a *general war* with Russia involving the use of the atomic bomb? In that case it probably is not going to make much difference whether we have protected the local shoe industry in the interest of "shoes for defense" or not. The general war will surely destroy our institutional organization and way of life. And whether or not we have tariffs now will be irrelevant in determining the form of the society that will emerge from an atomic war—assuming any society emerges.

On this point Liddell Hart has written: [32]

> The H-bomb makes nonsense of the pursuit of "victory" in a "total war." Both terms now become totally absurd. Anyone who now dreams or talks of "winning the war," if war should come, is worse than absurd—a menace to his country and to all humanity.

And Albert Einstein wrote in a letter prepared before his death, which was released by Bertrand Russell and signed by several other famous scientists: [33]

[30] United States, Commission on Foreign Economic Policy, *Report*, p. 44.

[31] *New York Times*, March 31, 1954, p. 18.

[32] B. H. Liddell Hart, "Why the H-Bomb Wipes Off the 'New Look,'" *World, America's Magazine of World Events*, I (June, 1954), p. 13.

[33] *New York Times*, July 10, 1955, p. 25. Reprinted by permission of the *New York Times*.

We have to learn to think in a new way. We have to learn
to ask ourselves, not what steps can be taken to give military
victory to whatever group we prefer, for there no longer are
such steps; the question we have to ask ourselves is: what
steps can be taken to prevent a military contest of which the
issue must be disastrous to all parties? . . .

IMPROVE TERMS OF TRADE

The preceding arguments for tariffs have been pushed by "practical,
realistic" people. But as one might expect, the academicians also have
succeeded in finding an intellectually satisfying argument for tariffs.
The argument runs to the effect that tariffs improve the unit terms of
trade. The argument may well be logically correct (academicians should
at least be capable of logical correctness) without thereby giving a valid
excuse for imposing tariffs.

The argument is dependent on the proposition that a new tariff on
any article will affect its price, quantity of production, and quantity of
consumption in a manner which primarily depends on the elasticities
of demand and supply.

Let us assume that the United States is levying the new tariff. Actually, in the event that United States demand is anything short of
completely inelastic, the price paid the foreigner (which is the United
States price minus the tariff) will be lower than it was before imposition
of the tariff, if increasing costs are assumed as characteristic of the
foreign industry. This is what is meant by improvement in the unit
terms of trade.[34]

At first glance, this may seem to be a desirable thing—improvement
in the terms of trade. But in the background are decreased total trade,
decreased benefit from geographical specialization, and smaller imports
into the United States. It is conceivable (and a much called-on con-

---

[34] There are some jokers in this deck: (1) the possibility that the foreign industry is a decreasing cost industry—the decreasing cost possibility is discussed
below—and (2) the possibility that the result of the operation may ultimately
be a lowering of United States export prices. This latter result could occur if
domestic demand for the product on which the tariff is levied is inelastic. More
total money might therefore be spent on that product; less money would be
available for spending on other domestic products; the prices of other domestic
products would tend to fall; and the unit terms of trade might move against
the country imposing the tariff. (This statement might need to be qualified—depending on what the government does with the tax revenue. See Meade, *Trade
and Welfare*, p. 158.)

Other factors need to be taken into account if the restriction is a quota rather
than a tariff. In Chapter 12 it will be alleged that if quotas are used rather than
tariffs, the direction of movement of the terms of trade depends on whether
the quota right is assigned to the foreign exporter or to the domestic importer.

ception)—but unlikely—that the country establishing the tariff would, in spite of the general world loss, come out with gain; but even then, if there is foreign retaliation, the whole operation will only lead to mutual throat cutting, and the tangible result will be less total trade and less total production. And, to be realistic about it, this is the likely result.

The decline in total trade and the consequent decline in supply of goods will probably more than counterbalance the gain from the improvement in the terms of trade, even in the country that starts the process. Moreover, the process is almost certain to be harmful to the world as a whole. Thus it does not follow that there will be more goods available to consumers even in the country levying the tariff, as a result of the improvement in the unit terms of trade. In fact, there are likely to be fewer goods even there. And, to repeat, if the foreign industry happens to be operating under decreasing cost, or if domestic demand happens to be inelastic for the imported goods, the terms of trade may not even be improved.

Kindleberger's statistical studies have established no clear connection between tariffs and improving terms of trade. They do not establish the contrary result, either. But it would seem that, if there is much practical importance to the proposition that tariffs will improve the terms of trade, the result could be observed in the statistics.[35]

On top of all this, if a country takes measures to decrease its imports, those measures ultimately can be expected to decrease exports by about the same amount. This results from the overriding necessity that exports equal imports. All of which emphasizes again the importance of the basic proposition that it is far more important to look to the volume of trade than to the terms or to the balance. All in all, the country planning to levy a tariff to improve its terms of trade is taking a shot in the dark with a rusty shotgun.

Consequently, the argument relating to improvement in the terms of trade, although much used and refined in academic circles, is not so often encountered in the area of practical politics, where the contestants seem to be prepared to sacrifice terms of trade and willing to sacrifice total gain from trade in the interest of a favorable balance of trade or in order to answer the call of those constituents of importance—the "special interests with leverage."

DECREASING-COST INDUSTRIES

A second sophisticated argument for tariffs runs somewhat as follows. If decreasing-cost industries exist in each of two countries and divide the

[35] Charles P. Kindleberger, *Terms of Trade*, p. 72.

market in each, one government might, by imposing a tariff, enable its local industry to obtain the whole local market, reduce costs, sell the product at a lower price, and make the consumers of that country better off in terms of more goods at lower prices, if at the same time the foreign market could be retained.[36]

The argument proves too much. It *is* desirable, in the case of the decreasing-cost industry, that production be concentrated so that it can occur at the lowest possible costs. But the chances are that cut-throat competition will accomplish this result without the assistance of a tariff.

The difficulty with decreasing-cost industries is not the problem of effecting concentration as a preliminary to getting the benefits of greater volume and lower prices. The real difficulty involves regulation of such industries in the public interest—after they have established themselves as monopolies. They are then in a position to gouge the public (whether they got to be monopolies with the assistance of tariffs or with the help of price wars and mergers).

INFANT-INDUSTRY ARGUMENT

By contrast with the preceding arguments, the infant-industry argument is a valid one—but not for tariffs in general. The argument runs to the effect that a new industry, during its formative period, may well need tariff protection.

Thus in the very nature of the doctrine it is not an argument for the protection of every industry, but must be applied in a very few particular situations at a time. One must be wary of the argument which starts off "just protect me"; by the time you have added up all the pleas—"just protect me and the other hazelnut producers"—you may be protecting everybody.

The infant-industry argument would be valid in a setting where the industry is a genuine infant—being not only in the formative stage but also offering promise of eventually becoming a legitimate low-cost industry, even though it may not be so at first.

Underemployment of resources is a third prerequisite for the argument to be valid. It was his assumption of full employment of resources (land, labor, and capital) that led Adam Smith to reject the infant-industry argument. His reasoning ran somewhat as follows: If it were true that a country was using all of its resources in the most efficient possible way, then there was certainly no point in misusing those resources

---

[36] The difficulty is that the other country will raise a tariff, too. Before the sequence of tariffs, each industry sold half of its product in each country; but after the tariff has been imposed, the net effect is that each has lost its foreign market, and each monopolizes its domestic market, while the volume of production costs and prices have not changed.

in an effort to create a new and, by assumption, less productive industry.[37] But if a country has idle resources or is not using its resources in the most effective way, Smith's objection loses its validity. Surely this is the actual situation in most countries most of the time and in the underdeveloped countries all of the time.

Some sort of threat from outside may well be the feature which establishes the immediate need for protection (for example, dumping by the financially stronger industry). The argument in the early days (about 1820) of the United States steel industry was that the old, established, financially strong British steel industry was prepared to dump steel in the United States market in order to embarrass the new American companies which had limited financial resources. It is true that this strategy has been followed over and over again and was, in fact, practiced by the British steel industry at that time.

Duperial is a jointly-owned subsidiary in Argentina of duPont and the British Imperial Chemical Industries. In 1936 the Argentine firm of Bunge and Born was considering going into the manufacture of heavy chemicals, especially sulfuric acid. The Duperial reaction to this is indicated by the following statement of the company manager: [38]

> From the beginning we have felt that our policy toward Bunge and Born should be fixed, having regard more to future than to immediate profits. If we do not accept Mr. Hirsch's [of Bunge and Born] demands, we shall have to face a period of unsatisfactory earnings on our acid, refined sulphur and CS_2 investments, but in the meantime we shall be making the chemical business most unattractive to Bunge and Born and this, in time, can only have the effect of removing all enthusiasm for their making further investments in the field.

Any new industry starting anywhere is faced with the problem of raising enough funds to sustain it through the first few months or years. At this stage, the old established companies may destroy the new company with comparative ease. It is in such circumstances, when the infant is going to be afflicted with what might be called unfair business practices, price cutting, or other similar measures by the old established companies, designed to force it into early bankruptcy, that some governmental protection or aid to the new industry may be especially appropriate.

But have infant-industry tariffs, in the form in which they have generally been enacted, been especially effective instruments in serving the purpose? If what is called for is an antidumping tariff, such a duty needs to be quite flexible. It clearly calls for administrative discretion in impos-

[37] Smith, *Wealth of Nations,* p. 425.
[38] United States Congress, Senate, Committee on Military Affairs, *Economic and Political Aspects of International Cartels* (1944), p. 48.

ing or removing it overnight. In the nature of things, the tariff that is to be useful in this situation is not a permanent tariff with permanently set rates. And yet, to a marked extent, in response to pleas based on the infant-industry argument, legislatures have passed laws providing for permanent tariffs and have made no provision for their ultimate repeal. The infant if left to itself will never admit that it has grown up; on the contrary it will keep pressuring the government for higher rates and will frequently obtain them. In this setting, the least objectionable tariff would be one of the antidumping sort, strictly temporary in nature, but, as will be argued later, there are better ways to aid the infant than tariffs of any sort.

Moreover, it has been the exceptional new industry that has gotten infant-industry protection as the result of an intelligent preliminary study of its likely prospects. By and large, legislatures promptly grant infant-industry protection if they are pressured to do so, rather than giving it as the result of any rational study of that industry in relation to other industries "in prospect."

The basic questions, which should be studied initially, are whether an industry has a reasonable chance of becoming comparatively efficient in a certain locality, and also whether it is among the most promising of those under study. But how does one know? The underdeveloped countries are undoubtedly in a difficult position when they attempt to raise their productivity and their level of living. Some of the infant-industry protection which they have extended has probably been quite misguided. Take the case of the Mexican tire industry. That new industry in recent years has been extended tariff protection on the basis of the infant-industry argument. At present some of the big tire manufacturing companies in the United States are affiliated with Mexican business groups in the joint ownership and operation of plants (Goodrich-Euzkadi, Goodyear-Oxo, etc.). Other United States firms have no such affiliation; so that some are now manufacturing within the Mexican tariff wall and some are not. The real effect of the tariff is to protect one American group from the competition of another. Because of the tariff wall, it is difficult for the American tire-manufacturing companies that do not have plants in Mexico to compete in the Mexican market and bring down the price. And within Mexico, apparently, the mixed Mexican–United States groups that are enjoying the benefit of the infant-industry protection have used their advantage to exploit the market by charging high prices and limiting the supply. In addition, the enterprises involved are hardly entitled to protection on the basis of the infant-industry argument at all. With the great financial resources and technical knowledge of the United States companies behind them, they are extremely precocious infants. Thus, in this case the result of infant-industry protection in Mexico seems to be high prices and small supply. The Mexican government is being "used." If the facts are as described, the infant-industry argument hardly justifies these tariffs.

The Mexican textile industry has also been the beneficiary of protective tariffs. And yet "textile prices have shown a marked tendency to rise more rapidly than general prices." [39]

All of which raises a significant question. Why should assistance be given, even to industries that merit assistance, by devices that seem to lead to restriction of production and to higher prices during the period of transition?

Governments would seem to have two problems in applying the infant-industry argument. They need to identify the industries with the most promising futures and give aid only to them. And they need to have some assurance that the businessmen granted the protection are thinking in terms of long-run expansion of output, and in terms of lowered prices both immediately and in the long run.

It may be that the desired result could better be gotten from direct subsidies or qualitative credit control than from tariffs. There can be little doubt of the merit of qualitative credit control which is discussed further in Chapters 15, 23, and 36; but a few comments about the production subsidy may be in order at this point. It is probably easier to cancel a subsidy than to repeal a tariff. Also a subsidy is much more clearcut in what it involves—a temporary "sacrifice" by the rest of the population in the expectation of long-run gain in the form of more goods at lower prices. But the subsidy has a far more important advantage over the tariff. A subsidy approach, in connection with which imports would be permitted and the world price would prevail, would enable consumers to be protected against price gouging and restricted supply while the development program was going on. [40]

The relative desirability of various control measures should be appraised not so much in terms of whether each of them would have the desired effect under conditions of static equilibrium. In this complex changing world each measure should be judged in terms of whether its initial impact is desirable or undesirable.

On the basis of this criterion, subsidies to domestic production clearly must be preferred to tariffs as devices for encouraging new production,

[39] Combined Mexican Working Party, *Economic Development of Mexico* (Baltimore: Johns Hopkins Press, 1953), p. 68.

[40] But such an arrangement calls for another measure to insure that the subsidies will be removed in time. This development simply cannot be trusted to the later passage of a law removing the subsidy. The producers will raise an outcry and defeat the law by logrolling tactics, just as the tariff beneficiaries have done in the past. The provision for removing the subsidy has to be in the original law. The producers will accept it then in their desire to get the subsidy. A workable formula in many cases might be to eliminate 20 per cent of the original amount of the subsidy each year from the third to the eighth year of the company's operation.

although possibly qualitative credit control should be preferred to production subsidies.[41]

In conclusion, it should be emphasized that the infant-industry argument does justify artificial aid to new industries in many cases. But from the standpoint of the country granting the aid more discriminating use would be advisable. To yield the desired result of increased national income, it needs to be applied selectively and not "across the board" and "without time limit." Also the aid given should be of a type calculated to keep prices to consumers low while the transition is in process. Tariffs have not been a particularly satisfactory tool in serving these ends, as the following attempt to place the use of protective tariffs in historical perspective may indicate.

HISTORICAL COMPARISON

The following is a more or less general comparison involving the United Kingdom, Spain and Portugal, the Latin American countries, and the United States, in the period between 1500 and the present day. When one compares Spain and Great Britain in about 1500, it would appear that the accumulation of technical knowledge and the level of living in Spain were at least as high, if not higher than in England. Movement of technical knowledge in early modern times was northward out of Spain into France, the Netherlands, and thence to England. The indebtedness of medieval western Europe to the Arabs, who were not finally expelled from Spain until 1492, is well known. This provides evidence that there are no inherent physical qualities in the Anglo-Saxon that assure him of continued technical superiority over other races.

Following 1500 for a period of 250 or 300 years, until about the time of the French Revolution, both Spain and England practiced mercantilism—mercantilism involving the use of a whole combination of government controls to regulate the internal economy, to effect an export trade balance, and to bring in gold. Friedrich List gave much of the credit for English industrial development to those measures.[42]

It would be difficult to prove whether England or Spain was more energetic in such activities. Yet, by 1800, England had moved substantially ahead of Spain in terms of technical knowledge, productivity, and level of living. Since both countries were practicing mercantilism, the use of trading restrictions would not seem to offer an adequate explanation of the discrepancy.[43]

[41] See Chapters 15, 23, and 36.

[42] Friedrich List, *National System of Political Economy* (London: Longmans, Green, 1928). The work was originally published in German in 1841.

[43] Although an appropriate combination of such technical knowledge as there was, weak institutional barriers to innovation, and raw materials appropriate to that stage of industrial development may explain the English development, and also the developments later to be described in this section.

Then during the period from the Napoleonic wars to World War I, England was the chief, perhaps the only, example of a country making really extensive use of free-trade practices. Spain, the Latin American countries, and the United States were all making increasing, if unsystematic, use of trade barriers. England, in comparison with either Spain or Latin America, during this period increased her relative advantage in technical knowledge, productivity, and level of living. This was, of course, the golden age (the Victorian era) of English hegemony on the world scene. In spite of extensive protectionism, the economies of Latin America and Spain stagnated during the same period. Thus the tariffs of the nineteenth century seem to have been of little use to those areas. But at the same time that tariffs were proving so useless to Latin America and Spain, the United States was making extensive use of unsystematic but high tariffs and was gaining on England, industrially speaking. By citing the United States and forgetting Latin America, one can fortify the argument for protective tariffs. But the United States and Latin America were doing the same thing in the nineteenth century, just as Britain and Spain were doing the same thing from 1500 to 1800. In Latin America it was doing no good but in the United States a very substantial industrial development was occurring. One might surmise that the real explanation for the long-run trend must be found elsewhere than in the tariff policies.

Then again, take the period since World War I and particularly since 1930. Latin America has changed its policy to some extent. It is now making an effort at over-all planning of a sort that was not characteristic of its nineteenth-century activities. But it is a planning that involves the extensive, rather than selective, use of tariffs to encourage industrial development. By contrast the United States, at least since 1933, has reduced its use of tariffs very substantially as part of the reciprocal trade agreements program. Yet during this period a greater increase in productivity has occurred in the United States than in Latin America. This relative increase has occurred whether the figures are compared absolutely, as a percentage of earlier production, or on a per capita basis.

The comment may be worth repeating that the wholesale use of protection is no substitute for the intelligent planning of economic development, case by case. And development is part of the process of expansion, not part of the process of restriction. If a government wants to encourage industry it can do so much more effectively by deciding just what industries have a better future and giving them direct and effective assistance. Sweeping use of tariffs—a negative sort of stimulus at best—does not seem to provide an effective push.[44]

[44] Nor does that other negative approach, the non-taxing of profits, seem to provide the answer. In this country it has almost become an assumption that taxes on profits should be low to encourage risk-taking. The idea that the wealthy save a larger proportion of their income than the poor lends support to this

It is also worth noting that England since World War I has returned to the extensive use of trade restrictions, yet her relative position in the world has slipped considerably—probably not cause and effect, but interesting. Thus the developments of the last twenty years are hardly a strong argument for protective tariffs, any more than were the developments of the preceding four hundred.

CONCLUSION

Tariffs are to be condemned. But the condemnation cannot properly be based on the grounds that free trade and perfect competition will necessarily yield better results in terms of level of living. It will be recalled that the discussion of Chapter 6 indicated the existence of several types of situation which may call for some interference with the operation of free market forces. These included (1) the nature of the process of structural change, (2) the implications of monopoly power, (3) external economies and diseconomies, and (4) equity considerations in income distribution.

Specifically on the point of equity considerations in income distribution, Meade has argued that although the terms of trade may be improved by the use of trade barriers,[45] "there is no *a priori* reason to believe that the poor countries will possess exceptionally strong, and the rich countries exceptionally weak, bargaining power."

But tariffs and such regulatory devices as have customarily been used to influence international trade are to be condemned as a control device in most situations because they raise prices and limit supplies to domestic consumers. It is foolish to use a control device that brings these results, *since better measures are available.*

The evaluation of the arguments pro and con with regard to tariffs and trade restrictions indicates that measures to encourage selected industries have a useful place. But the wholesale use of trade restrictions cannot be trusted to stimulate development.

If we want to encourage selected industries, that can be done far more effectively by subsidies or qualitative credit control than by tariffs. If

way of thinking. All of this makes it hard to understand what has happened in Mexico in recent years. There a disproportionate amount of the rise in national income has gone to the enterpriser group. According to the theory, they should consequently have increased saving and investment very substantially by their own independent action. And yet, to quote from the United Nations, Economic Commission for Latin America, *Economic Survey of Latin America,* 1951–1952, p. 88: "It was seen that the coefficient of saving of the group obtaining the greatest advantage from the shift in income distribution did not improve. Instead, the savings coefficient tended to decrease over most of the period under review." People are "sure hard to predict," unless the innate contrariness of their nature is allowed for—something which it is hard for a constant multiplier to do.

[45] Meade, *Trade and Welfare,* p. 566.

the former measures are used, the consumer is benefited as well as the new producer who needs protection. Prices tend to be low. Demand for a larger quantity of goods at the low prices encourages the new industry. This effect is far more desirable than the market contraction which results from the high prices prevailing behind an infant-industry tariff wall. After all, if it is possible to encourage infant industry and expand consumption at the same time, why not do it? The use of the subsidy in preference to the tariff prevents the industries enjoying infant-industry protection from engaging in high price–low output tactics.

Another aspect of the problem—the fear of foreign competition—has elicited much concern in the United States, but the *Staff Papers* presented to the Randall Commission offer reassurance: [46]

> The conclusion seems warranted that the area of "potential injury" to domestic producers would be quite limited even if all tariffs were to be suspended.

Personally, I should be inclined to say that the area of potential injury depends very much on the producers themselves. If they have it set in their minds that they will be injured and there is nothing they can do about it, then they will behave in a manner that actually results in the injury they anticipate. But the elimination of tariffs and the consequent trade expansion will open up a tremendous new market potential for those with enough of the good-old-American spirit of enterprise to take advantage of the situation.

Even so, where there is injury and a difficult problem of transition, the role of the government should be to provide intelligent aid in making the transition, not to provide aid in preventing development and dynamic change.

Possession of a high level of living is dependent on positive action (productivity increase), not on negative action (abstaining from enjoying the fruits of the foreigner's productivity). It was observed three hundred years ago by Lewes Roberts, who was looking at Holland, Venice, Florence, and Genoa as examples, that a country in its stage of greatest power and affluence and greatest development of manufacturing is likely to be a financial and commercial mart of importance—consequent on the maintenance of low barriers to trade.[47] England in the nineteenth century followed the same policy at the height of its power. The China of the Boxer uprising was an example of the contrary trade policy—and the results were not happy for China.

[46] United States, Commission on Foreign Economic Policy, *Staff Papers*, p. 310.
[47] Lewes Roberts, *The Treasure of Traffike, passim.*

Chapter 10

ARGUMENTS ON RESTRICTIONS:
II. MARX, HOBSON, AND THE
RELATIVE STRENGTH OF
PRESSURE GROUPS

⊭ ⊭ ⊭

Marxists such as Lenin have argued that declining profits at home force capitalists into a desperate search for foreign markets.

Empirical data at present gives little support to the proposition of the declining rate of profit; nor is there revealed a rise in the importance of exports relative to national income in the capitalist countries.

The actual reason why countries try to have an export balance of trade (as distinguished from the theoretical arguments advanced) is probably to be found in the relative strength of pressure groups.

Producers are better organized than consumers. On the international scene this means that they are better organized to promote measures to aid them in their marketing than consumers are to promote their interest in more imports—and in more goods at lower prices generally.

⊭ ⊭ ⊭

IF THERE is no good reason for a country's using trade restrictions and trying continually to increase exports relative to imports, why is it that countries continue to make the effort? [1]

---

[1] Several reasons, which have been advanced in various times and places, for favoring exports have been discussed in previous chapters. During the period 1500 to 1800 the mercantilists favored an export balance in order to obtain a gold inflow. That argument was discussed in Chapter 3. The application of Keynesian theory to international trade was based originally on the idea that increasing exports would raise national income. That position was discussed in Chapter 8. Miscellaneous additional arguments for protection were discussed in Chapter 9.

MARXIAN THEORY OF ECONOMIC IMPERIALISM

An argument that has not yet been discussed is the Marxian one. It runs to the effect that producers are constrained to push exports because of the need to find a profitable market for their expanding production. This expanding production is the product resulting from the accumulation of surplus value (capital)—surplus value which the capitalists have "gotten" but which the workers have "produced." As a result of the accumulation of surplus value in the form of capital goods, the consequent expanding production, and the disproportion in purchasing power between laborers and capitalists, the profit rate falls in the capitalistic country. Foreign markets and foreign investments then look to be relatively more profitable than formerly. And as the domestic profit rate falls further as a result of the relative paucity of effective purchasing power at home, the capitalists compete for the foreign markets with more and more desperation.[2]

Marx said in the *Communist Manifesto:* "The need of a constantly expanding market for its products chases the bourgeoisie over the whole surface of the globe." And further on he said:[3]

> Modern bourgeois society with its relations of production, of exchange and of property, a society that has conjured up such gigantic means of production and of exchange, is like the sorcerer who is no longer able to control the powers of the nether world whom he has called up by his spells. For many a decade past the history of industry and commerce is but the history of the revolt of modern productive forces against modern conditions of production, against the property relations that are the conditions for the existence of the bourgeoisie and of its rule. It is enough to mention the commercial crises that by their periodical return put the existence of the entire bourgeois society on trial, each time more threateningly. In these crises a great part not only of the existing products, but also of the previously created productive forces, are periodically destroyed. In these crises there breaks out an epidemic that, in all earlier epochs would have seemed an absurdity—the epidemic of over-production. Society suddenly finds

[2] Karl Marx and Friedrich Engels, *The Communist Manifesto* (New York: International Publishers, 1948). The work was originally published in 1848. V. I. Lenin, *Imperialism, the Highest Stage of Capitalism,* revised translation (New York: International Publishers, 1933). This pamphlet was written in Zurich in the spring of 1916. E. M. Winslow, *Pattern of Imperialism* (New York: Columbia University Press, 1948). Paul M. Sweezy, *Theory of Capitalist Development* (New York: Oxford, 1942). Karl Marx, *Capital: A Critique of Political Economy,* trans. Ernest Untermann (4th German ed.; 3 vols.; Chicago: Kerr, 1906–1909).

[3] Marx and Engels, *Communist Manifesto,* pp. 12, 14–15.

itself put back into a state of momentary barbarism; it appears as if a famine, a universal war of devastation had cut off the supply of every means of subsistence; industry and commerce seem to be destroyed. And why? Because there is too much civilisation, too much means of subsistence, too much industry, too much commerce. The productive forces at the disposal of society no longer tend to further the development of the conditions of bourgeois property; on the contrary, they have become too powerful for these conditions, by which they are fettered, and no sooner do they overcome these fetters than they bring disorder into the whole of bourgeois society, endanger the existence of bourgeois property. The conditions of bourgeois society are too narrow to comprise the wealth created by them. And how does the bourgeoisie get over these crises? On the one hand by enforced destruction of a mass of productive forces; on the other, by the conquest of new markets, and by the more thorough exploitation of the old ones. That is to say, by paving the way for more extensive and more destructive crises, and by diminishing the means whereby crises are prevented.

The idea that the profit rate in the industrially developed countries is falling relative to the profit rate in the underdeveloped countries has a plausible ring as an explanation for vigorous competition for export markets among different companies and among different countries. Lenin thought this process would lead to collusion among the national groups in different lines of activity as they co-operated among themselves but competed bitterly against foreign national groups doing the same thing. This, to Lenin, was the "highest stage of capitalism." And he vigorously attacked Karl Kautsky as a "deviationist" when Kautsky argued that there might be another step: international cartels and co-operation among the exporting groups of different countries.[4] One may be inclined to guess that the German "deviationist" was a better prophet, and perhaps a better Marxist, than the Russian.

The Marxist theory, then, implies certain things for the evolution of the profit rate. The argument that the capitalist countries are becoming desperate in their search for markets also carries an implication that for those countries there is an increase in exports relative to national income.[5] Furthermore, the power-politics allegations and economic-

---

[4] Lenin, *Imperialism*, pp. 68–9.

[5] Lenin argued in his *Imperialism* (p. 57) that in the latter part of the nineteenth century the export of goods was replaced by the export of capital as the chief manifestation of these forces. The argument in Chapter 24 will indicate that an export of capital must have as a corollary an export of goods. Therefore Lenin's differentiation between the export of goods and the export of capital seems to be a distinction without a difference. But even if the argument is

imperialism implications of the Marxian analysis would indicate that the developed countries are in a position to force their goods on under-developed countries if they desired to do so. It should be possible to test various of these propositions statistically to determine whether the facts are behaving as the theory indicates they should.

Is the profit rate falling in industrially developed countries? As important as this proposition is, one would think that a tremendous amount of careful study would have been made of the subject and that the answer would be definitely known. On the contrary, there has been remarkably little statistical work done on the subject, and such as has been done is inconclusive.

The ratio of net profits to total capital accounts for national banks in the United States showed no secular trend downward for the period 1869 to date. The yield on British consols, which was 2.86 per cent in 1753, was 4.08 per cent in 1953.[6] The data in Table 17 on net income after taxes of various United States corporations for the period 1925 to 1954, also, hardly shows a downward trend—although the period covered is not long enough to be conclusive.

On the other hand, Steindl and Valavanis-Vail have assembled some information indicating that there has been a downward secular trend.[7] Valavanis-Vail's study indicates a fall in the profit rate from 11 per cent in the decade 1869–1878 to 5 per cent in the decade 1939–1948. It also indicates a significant fall in the marginal productivity of capital.

The comments of Alfred Marshall on this point are also suitably vague as to trend. He said that the rate of interest on new investments:[8]

> . . . was reported to be 10 per cent. during a great part of the middle ages; but it fell to 3 per cent. in the earlier half of the eighteenth century. The subsequent vast industrial and political demand for capital raised it again, and it was relatively high during the great war [the Napoleonic Wars].

stated in terms of the export of capital instead of in terms of the export of goods, the statement would merely be changed to read that there was desperate effort on the part of the developed countries to export capital to regions where it could earn more interest. The statistical evidence would indicate that this has not happened, either. There has been no substantial increase in the importance of capital export during the last sixty-five years—certainly no increase that would remotely correspond with what the Marxist thesis calls for. If anything, capital export has declined in importance relative to the variables which can be measured, such as the national income of the developed countries.

[6] George F. Warren and Frank A. Pearson, *Gold and Prices* (New York: John Wiley, 1935), p. 403; *International Financial Statistics.*

[7] Stefan Valavanis-Vail, "An Econometric Model of Growth—U.S.A., 1869–1953," *American Economic Review, Papers and Proceedings,* XLV (May, 1955), p. 217; J. Steindl, *Maturity and Stagnation in American Capitalism,* Oxford University Institute of Statistics, Monograph No. 4 (Oxford: Blackwell, 1952), pp. 169–75, especially table on p. 173.

[8] Alfred Marshall, *Principles of Economics* (6th ed.; London: Macmillan, 1910), p. 681.

TABLE 17

NET INCOME AFTER TAXES OF VARIOUS UNITED STATES CORPORATIONS

	% RETURN ON NET ASSETS FOR A SAMPLE OF LEADING CORPORATIONS (1,860 IN 1928; 3,442 IN 1954)	% RETURN ON NET ASSETS FOR A SAMPLE OF MANUFACTURING CORPORATIONS (1,205 IN 1925; 1,778 IN 1954)
1925		10.7
1926		10.8
1927		9.0
1928	10.0	11.5
1929	10.6	12.8
1930	5.7	6.4
1931	2.4	2.3
1932	0.2	−0.5 (deficit)
1933	2.1	2.5
1934	3.6	4.3
1935	5.1	6.7
1936	7.4	10.4
1937	7.2	10.8
1938	3.8	4.8
1939	6.2	8.5
1940	7.4	10.3
1941	9.2	12.4
1942	8.7	10.1
1943	8.6	9.9
1944	8.2	9.8
1945	7.6	9.1
1946	9.5	12.1
1947	12.2	17.0
1948	14.0	18.9
1949	11.0	13.8
1950	13.3	17.1
1951	11.4	14.4
1952	10.3	12.3
1953	10.6	12.7
1954	10.3	12.4
1955	11.9	14.9
1956	11.3	13.9

Source: First National City Bank of New York tabulation of published shareholders' reports contained in the Bank's *Monthly Letter: Business and Economic Conditions.*

The Russians are caught in a dilemma. There is nothing they like better than to denounce the capitalists for making fantastic profits at home and abroad—for present purposes abroad. L. Fitooni wrote: [9]

A large part of the national income of underdeveloped countries is gained by monopolies of the United States, England,

[9] L. Fitooni, "Ob Ekonomicheskoi Pomoshchi Slaborazvitim Stranam," *Voprosi Ekonomiki,* November, 1953, p. 80; see also: V. Solodovnikov, "Vivoz Kapitala . . . ," *Voprosi Ekonomiki,* January, 1953, pp. 76–90.

France, and the other imperialist dominions, extracting the maximum profits by means of enslavement and the systematic looting of the people of the remaining nations.

And yet the Marxist theory in establishing the inevitability of the demise of capitalism does it by attempting to establish that the fall of the domestic profit rate, the turning to foreign markets, and the ultimate fall of all profits leads to a situation from which the system cannot extricate itself. The quotation from Marx may be recalled: "The need of a constantly expanding market for its products chases the bourgeoisie over the whole surface of the globe." Like a lot of other people, the Russians want to have their cake and eat it too—intellectually speaking. They want to damn capitalism both for taking things of value away from the exploited countries and for foisting things of value upon them.

Also, according to Marxist theory, United States exports should be rising at a rapid rate and probably rising as a proportion of national income (and the same thing should hold true, of course, for the other industrialized countries). It may be argued that the rise in the absolute value of United States exports gives some slight support to the Marxist thesis. But when the comparison is made which relates trade to national income, no support at all is gained. United States exports as a percentage of United States national income have been falling as a long-run trend. The same thing is true of the British. In fact there is the related evidence of Chart 1 that for the world as a whole trade is falling relative to production.

This might simply mean a rise in trade barriers in the underdeveloped areas as they effectively keep out United States goods. But if this be so, where is the vaunted power of capitalist imperialism? Moreover, if the capitalists have been thwarted in their search for foreign markets, one would expect, from the Marxian analysis, an even more pronounced fall in the domestic profit rate. And the evidence of that is certainly lacking.

HOBSON'S UNDERCONSUMPTION ARGUMENT

A "bourgeois" economist, J. A. Hobson, anticipated Lenin by arguing in 1902 that economic imperialism was part of the desperate search for markets in which the capitalist countries were engaged because of the unsalable surpluses.[10] The unsalable surpluses existed, he maintained, because of forces explained by the underconsumption theory. Marxists, for the most part, have avoided a simple underconsumption theory in favor of the logically more elegant argument that culminates in the declining rate of profit.

[10] J. A. Hobson, *Imperialism, A Study* (3rd ed.; London: Allen and Unwin, 1938). The first edition was published in 1902.

The application of the underconsumption argument to explain export promotion probably would be nearer to the truth if the argument were only restated to run that there *could be* a failure of effective demand (due to the manner of operation of the expansion and contraction of credit by the banking system) rather than that there must be such a failure. A detailed discussion of Hobson's underconsumption theory is not called for here; but a quotation will indicate the flavor of the argument: [11]

> The volume of production has been constantly rising owing to the development of modern machinery. There are two main channels to carry off these products—one channel carrying off the product destined to be consumed by the workers, and the other channel carrying off the remainder to the rich. The workers' channel is in rockbound banks that cannot enlarge, owing to the competitive wage system preventing wages rising *pro rata* with increased efficiency. Wages are based upon cost of living, and not upon efficiency of labour. The miner in the poor mine gets the same wages per day as the miner in the adjoining rich mine. The owner of the rich mine gets the advantage—not his labourer. The channel which conveys the goods destined to supply the rich is itself divided into two streams. One stream carries off what the rich 'spend' on themselves for the necessities and luxuries of life. The other is simply an 'overflow' stream carrying off their 'savings.' The channel for spending, i.e. the amount wasted by the rich in luxuries, may broaden somewhat, but owing to the small number of those rich enough to indulge in whims it can never be greatly enlarged, and at any rate it bears such a small proportion to the other channel that in no event can much hope of avoiding a flood of capital be hoped for from this division. The rich will never be so ingenious as to spend enough to prevent overproduction.
>
> Thus we reach the conclusion that Imperialism is the endeavour of the great controllers of industry to broaden the channel for the flow of their surplus wealth by seeking foreign markets and foreign investments to take off the goods and capital they cannot sell or use at home. . . .
>
> It is not industrial progress that demands the opening up of new markets and areas of investments, but mal-distribution of consuming power which prevents the absorption of commodities and capital within the country.

Obviously there are unsalable surpluses which sporadically—if not chronically—glut the market and lead to distress selling by producers.

[11] *Ibid.*, pp. 83–5. Reprinted with the kind permission of George Allen & Unwin, the publisher.

Whether a theoretical proof can be built to demonstrate that such surpluses are inevitable is a different matter. And Hobson does not allege they are inevitable—if income could be re-distributed.

THE RELATIVE STRENGTH OF PRESSURE GROUPS

The Communists are correct about some things, if for the wrong reasons. They are correct in stating that the United States and most capitalist countries set great store by the desirability of having a favorable or an export balance of trade. And such countries are continually enacting measures calculated to encourage exports relative to imports. In spite of Adam Smith they have continued to do so. Probably no capitalistic country, except possibly England during the latter part of the nineteenth century, has made any real effort to practice free trade. Most countries most of the time have had measures on the statute books which, if taken in toto, have been intended to stimulate exports relative to imports, or have been intended directly to discourage imports. Why have they done so, if the arguments for an export balance are, in general, not valid?

The reason is rather obvious and has frequently been stated by non-theoreticians, although the important theoretical implications of the proposition seem to be generally overlooked. Enough motivation to explain the adoption of these measures can be found in the "practical politics," as it were, of the situation. The nature of these "practical" considerations results from the institutional organization of our society. To be specific, it is the result of the fact that producer groups are more effectively organized than consumer groups. In an economy such as ours, there is a rather limited number of producers in most lines of activity, whether the line be the automobile industry, petroleum, or steel, or any other field of manufacturing activity, or barbers, or grocers, or what have you. The number of producers is sufficiently limited so that it is feasible for them to organize effectively; a substantial degree of organization is not only possible, but seems to occur in the natural development of the production side of most industries.[12] And so there result the great, effective trade associations: the National Association of Manufacturers, the American Petroleum Institute, and legions more. On the other hand, it is not feasible for all the buyers of automobiles to organize to tell Ford or General Motors what they will pay for cars, nor for the buyers of gasoline to organize to tell the oil companies what they will pay, nor for those who are shorn to tell the barbers what they will pay for the shearing. Prices are

[12] Adam Smith wrote in the Wealth of Nations (p. 128 of the Modern Library edition): "People of the same trade seldom meet together, even for merriment and diversion, but the conversation ends in a conspiracy against the public, or in some contrivance to raise prices."

typically set by producers or sellers (administered prices)—though set temporarily and subject to change. Buyers must "take it or leave it"; they cannot possibly organize to tell the producers of cars and aspirin tablets what prices they will pay for those articles. The difficulty is an organizational difficulty.

This is true in spite of the fact that the population as a whole has just as much interest, in its role of consumer, in getting more goods at lower prices as it has, in its role of producer, in charging higher prices and getting higher wages and profits. It is pointless to say that there is a conspiracy by a little group of producers to exploit consumers. In a sense, we are all producers and all consumers, but we are all more effectively organized to promote our own interests as producers than our own interests as consumers. Here we are analyzing a disservice which we are doing to ourselves, whether we be painters dragging out the painting process or bricklayers limiting the number of men in our organization or manufacturers trying to curtail imports. People are more effectively organized as producers to make the most of their role as producers than as consumers to get more for their money as consumers. And as is well-known, this aim is achieved in large part through co-operation in trade associations and discussions at businessmen's luncheons. Intercorporate *contracts* in restraint of trade need not be involved in such arrangements.

In applying this argument to the international field, it is possible to identify a little more specifically the people and organizations involved. Even though it is difficult to appraise the relative strength of the pressures with any exactness, some very significant "rough evaluations" can be made. It is possible to count registered lobbyists and to know in a general way whether they are representing producer or consumer interests. On the basis of such a count (see Table 18), there were in the United States in the spring of 1953 about 586 lobbying groups obviously representing producer interests as opposed to sixty-two which, by some stretch of the imagination, could be said to represent consumer interests. The powerful labor unions probably represent producer interest more effectively than consumer interest, although it may well be true that they come to the defense of the consumer more frequently than do the manufacturers.

The grouping of labor unions with trade associations may call for some explanation or justification. It is true that labor's national leadership is on record as favoring increased trade.[13] But unions are primarily interested in wage increases and in fringe benefits obtainable from employers. In pursuit of higher wages, they want the corporations for which

[13] According to *Fortune,* May, 1953, p. 74, both George Meany of the A.F. of L. and James Carey of the C.I.O. have signed the Bell report (United States, Public Advisory Board for Mutual Security, *A Trade and Tariff Policy in the National Interest* [Washington: Government Printing Office, 1953]) with its recommendations for liberalizing tariffs.

TABLE 18

CLASSIFICATION OF PRESSURE GROUPS

I. Producer Interest:

Trade associations, manufacturers, farmers, wholesal-
ers, and retailers   298
Labor unions   61
Professional associations   71
Sellers of services (railroads, brokers, airlines, etc.   156

Producer Interest Total   586

II. Consumer Interest:

A. Consumer interest specifically

In general   11
Importers   22
Ocean shippers   12

Subtotal   45

B. Organizations with a genuine interest in the general
welfare (in a sense which would include lobbying for
consumer interest)   17

Consumer Interest Total   62

III. Other (War and Peace, Indian Tribes, Humane Society,
etc.)   126

Total coverage   774

Note: Obviously a major classification difficulty is involved. But the author is convinced of the general accuracy of the result, even though many of the particular
classifications could well be questioned.

Source: Compiled from list of registered lobbyists: United States Congress, *Congressional Record*, June 15, 1953, pp. 6783–6816.

they work to sell more goods and to increase their profits. Consequently,
although the union leadership may make broad statements in favor of
lower tariffs, individual unions are likely to lobby for tariffs to protect
their particular product from foreign competition. Thus John L. Lewis
and the coal miners have been vehement in opposition to the importation
of residual fuel oil. Workers in the watchmaking industry have backed
the watch manufacturers in their recent demands for protection against
the Swiss. The Textile Workers Union (C.I.O.) has favored quota limitation of textile imports. To illustrate how acute one's comprehension
can be when the other fellow is involved and how dull when self-interest
enters the picture, the maritime unions, although they favor increased
trade, also favor "cargo preference" laws which would require certain
shipments to be made only in American ships. In addition, several American Federation of Labor unions belong to the National Labor-Manage-
ment Council on Foreign Trade Policy (or the Nation-Wide Committee
of Industry, Agriculture and Labor on Import-Export Policy), a group
fighting tariff reductions.

As to the interest of such powerful lobbies as the National Association
of Manufacturers, the United States Chamber of Commerce, the American Farm Bureau Federation, the Independent Petroleum Association

of America, the Iron and Steel Institute, and the hundreds of other trade associations, there can be no doubt. Their prime concern as producers is with making greater profit. And each in his individual case can see that curtailment of the imports that compete with his products and encouragement of the export of his products will help him. Such groups have legitimate problems which ought to be given consideration in government decision-making. This argument is not intended as a denial of that. But the interests and problems of the consumer should be given equal weight. All too frequently this is not the case.

The luckless congressman is going to be influenced in his decisions by what he hears. After the oil lobby has "gone over" a congressman or a legislator from thirteen different points of view and pointed out that the industry is having to lay off men in West Texas fields because of oil imports from Venezuela, that the production of oil in Texas is being cut because of such imports, and that oil revenues that go to finance the schools are suffering as a result of oil imports, it is not strange that a congressman may weaken—in just this one case—and favor an import excise on oil, even though the United States petroleum industry is the strongest in the world, and it would be hard to justify an oil tariff if one were thinking primarily of the interests of automobile drivers.

Thus far the congressman has weakened only in respect to oil (while consoling himself with the thought that the chemical industry, at least, is a strong pillar in the American industrial structure, even if the oil industry is not) but then other things begin to happen. He is presently informed that removal of tariffs on chemical products would cripple "Monsanto and other chemical producers" and that "adequate tariffs must be maintained on chemicals because the American chemical industry, on which national security, peacetime economy and full employment depend, would be seriously damaged by an influx of foreign chemical products." [14] After the steel industry, electrical equipment industry, automobile industry, and textile industry people have also gone to work on him, the poor congressman might well believe that he has been living in a fool's paradise all these years deluding himself with the idea that the United States is an industrial giant, when everyone knows that the only American industry that can stand foreign competition is the real-estate business.

Evidence from a slightly different source gives further indication of the omnipresence of producer lobbies and the relative absence of consumer lobbies. The American Tariff League appraised the hearings on President Eisenhower's bill to implement the Randall Commission report as follows: [15]

[14] *New York Times,* November 15, 1953, p. 36.

[15] ATL *Topics,* January, 1955, p. 1. The hearings were before the House Committee on Ways and Means in January, 1955. The bill in question was H. R. 1.

Witnesses testifying in opposition to H.R. 1 far outnumbered the proponents of the trade extension bill and represented a comprehensive cross-section of the U.S. domestic economy, including some of the largest, as well as the smallest industries, and agricultural producers.

On top of everything else, the legislator has to vote for tariffs for industries whose pressures he might otherwise be able to resist in order to get support from other legislators for the tariffs in which some of his constituents are vitally interested. This is the practice known as logrolling.

Such results follow from the type of economic organization we have. Someone has suggested that we kill all the lobbyists or build a high fence around Congress, or that there should be a gentlemen's understanding that congressmen would not take free meals or go to barbecues or accept free vacations in Colorado. Maybe each legislative hall should have a big bulletin board on which each legislator registers, when he gets back, the names of those who paid for his lunch. Ignorant as the lawyer-legislator may remain in the face of such precautions, his ignorant but honest vote may be more intelligently cast, in the sense of taking better account of consumers' interest, than it is likely to be after he has heard an energetic statement of the case only from the producer's side. He would have fewer facts but a clearer head. This may seem like a strange recommendation, but it is entirely reasonable.[16] When one has heard arguments presented in an unbalanced way, five arguments on one side to one argument on the other, though both sides ought to be considered of the same importance, the resulting evaluation is going to be equally lopsided. The lawyer-legislator is not to be blamed for the result (or is he?); but the result will nevertheless leave much to be desired. Tariff rates are going to be high. And the barriers to the international flow of goods are going to increase.

The effort countries make to achieve an export balance is a result of the relative strength of the pressures that are operating on the government. It is rather interesting that Adam Smith, who was most outspoken in his belief that the free forces of the competitive market could be trusted to regulate the economy, wrote as follows: "It cannot be very difficult to determine who have been the contrivers of this whole mercantile system; not the consumers, we may believe, whose interest has been entirely neglected; but the producers, whose interest has been so carefully attended to; and among this latter class our merchants and manufacturers have been by far the principal architects."[17] Smith thus described the impact of the relative strength of pressure groups upon

---

[16] Although, of course, properly put, this should not be a plea for ignorance but for balanced knowledge.

[17] Smith, *Wealth of Nations,* p. 626.

decision making in the society with which he was familiar. The situation does not seem to have changed markedly between 1776 and the present.

If this is all true, it seems to follow that an economy organized roughly like that of the United States will *try* to have an export trade balance, whether it can implement the attempt or not. And it would continue to try even if none of the arguments for tariffs led to results which would promote the general welfare.

It is also possible to interpret the measures now being taken to promote industrial development in the underdeveloped areas in terms of the relative strength of pressure groups. Industrialization is being encouraged by tariffs and other restrictions on imports and by stimulation of exports because these devices will raise the money profit of the new power group. The new entrepreneur-capitalist in the underdeveloped countries has the timeless and perennial interest in money profits. Accordingly, the governments in those countries encourage industrialization by the measures that tend to increase money profits. More desirable means of encouragement that would at the same time lower prices to consumers are not used because the pressure group with an interest in them happens to be "just the people as a whole."

ACCESS TO RAW MATERIALS

All of this has an important bearing on the argument which was current in the 1930's, regarding access to raw materials. During those years Italians and Germans conceived of themselves as "have-not" peoples who lacked raw materials. Their prime targets were the United States and England, countries which seemed to have unlimited access to raw materials. They argued that the invasions of Ethiopia and the Ukraine were justified as efforts to compensate for this lack of raw materials.

What truth, if any, is there in the proposition that a country has more difficulty in obtaining raw materials if it does not own colonies? Coffee, copper, cotton, wheat, tin, and rubber are among the typical materials involved when one talks about access to raw materials. Did Germans have to pay more for those things; was Germany's access to those things more limited or more difficult than that of the United States citizen buying them? Let us take one example which is rather near home: cotton. One might ask whether the United States, during the late 1930's, was actually making cotton relatively more or relatively less available to Germans than to United States citizens. The United States government paid an export subsidy on cotton much of the time, a subsidy which tended to increase the availability to Germany of United States cotton since the price to Germans was made lower than the price to United States citizens. From this it would not appear that Germany had any valid complaint about access to cotton.

It should be recalled that the United States showed no liking for Germany at that time and ostensibly was taking anti-German measures. In view of these facts, the measures that were actually taken seem rather odd. Germany was put on the "black list," which amounted to applying the highest tariff rates of the Smoot-Hawley Act to imports from Germany. This was done at a time when tariffs were being lowered on imports from most countries as a part of the reciprocal trade agreements program. But the anti-German measures consisted in keeping out goods coming from Germany and at the same time making more United States goods available to Germany. Keep out German lenses and help the Germans produce guncotton. That was our so-called anti-German policy.

Evidence indicates that export prices are generally lower than domestic prices more often than not (see Chapter 13). Strangely enough, countries fall all over themselves to make their products available to foreigners more cheaply than they are available at home. And this is especially true during hard times—the times about which there is chief concern. In such a setting there is little support for the access-to-raw-materials argument.

But let us return to the problem of access to raw materials from underdeveloped countries. The question arises regarding raw materials which can be provided by a country such as Brazil (coffee) or Chile (copper): To what extent was there any justification for Germany's trying to get political control in those or other areas in order to gain access to such raw materials? True, Brazil was engaged in a price-raising scheme in connection with coffee. And the international copper cartel was doing the same thing with copper. These measures, which were common enough in connection with other raw commodities, would lend some credence to the German charge that Germany was being exploited. But by and large the raw commodity control schemes were not aimed at Germans per se. They were aimed at consumers per se, and it would probably be difficult to prove that Germans suffered more than other people from their operation.

From the foregoing comments it should not be concluded that the arrangements for export of a particular material could never involve discrimination against foreigners. Many countries practice discrimination to encourage processing at home. There may be an export duty on the raw material that will have a heavier impact than the export duties on the finished product, while export of the finished product is still being encouraged, even subsidized. Such measures do not reduce the ultimate availability of the finished product to foreign consumers. But it is true that, to the extent that such discriminatory export tariffs cause the processing to occur in less efficient places, prices will be higher to consumers than they otherwise would be—but higher to consumers generally, and not just to Germans.

What Germany really was worried about, and perhaps very intelligently, was national power considerations. The Germans were than and always have been impressed by the argument that national power depends upon having productive facilities in one's own country. On the basis of this argument it is desirable to be the country where the processing occurs, and national productive capacity is a thing to be desired. So, to the extent that raw-material-producing countries levy export taxes to encourage processing in their country instead of abroad, there may be something to the access-to-raw-materials argument. Put in this way, however, the nature of the argument is greatly changed.

When the argument is set in these terms, the "chief offenders" are poor backward countries or nations which are primarily raw material producing and which are trying to develop manufacturing—and not the so-called "have nations," the United States and England. What Germany was aiming at, if the argument is placed in this setting, was prevention of the development of processing in underdeveloped countries, hardly the noblest of enterprises.

The access-to-raw-materials argument is sometimes put in still another form, the allegation being that political control is necessary if the availability of materials is to be assured in wartime. But even here there is doubt as to the real merit of the argument. Neutrals are notoriously willing to sell to both parties, though at as large a profit as possible. Thus political control of a country is not necessary in order to obtain exports from a neutral. But an open shipping lane *is* necessary. And if the shipping lane is closed after the war begins, or if the colony is occupied by the enemy, all the prior political control in the world is of no use, as the British and Americans found out in the case of Malayan tin and rubber during World War II.[18]

All of this is not meant to suggest that there is never discrimination against buyers by exporters. But it would appear that in the past such discrimination has been of minor importance in connection with exports—albeit of considerable importance in its effect on imports.

[18] Another German argument, that she was short of foreign exchange in the 1920's because of the reparations burden, would have been more relevant if there had been any reparations burden. But since German foreign borrowing exceeded her payment of reparations, such was not the case. Even if she had been paying reparations, it might well be said that any inability to buy raw materials which she was suffering was a small price for having started and lost World War I. See Chapter 25.

CONCLUSION

In a society organized as ours is producer pressure groups on the whole are stronger and better organized than consumer pressure groups. As a result, in spite of the fact that people in general are just as interested in more goods at lower prices as in higher wages and profits, the balance of pressures, at least in countries organized on a basis of free private enterprise, is actually better calculated to further producer interests than consumer interests. Therefore countries try to encourage exports relative to imports even though the effort is (1) largely futile, since in a general sense exports must pay for imports, and (2) not particularly farsighted, if society is really interested in a higher level of living (intelligent selfishness), or in greater freedom of action and choice for all people.

The foregoing represents an attempt to explain why nations organized on a free private enterprise basis actually have trade barriers. Chapter 9 contained refutation—or attempted refutation—of several of the standard pro-tariff arguments. This is not to say that perfect competition and free trade would necessarily get the best results in terms of the social goals on which this book is premised. To repeat a concluding comment of Chapter 9, there are circumstances that may call for planned deviation away from the conditions that freely operating market forces and free trade would create. An artificially created situation deviating somewhat from the competitive free trade position may contribute more to the desirable goals—this was called in Chapter 6 "the constructive free-trade position."

Nevertheless, it seems to be true that virtually none of the trade restrictions now practiced were planned in this setting. Rather they are the chaotic result of miscellaneous pressures.

Chapter 11

TARIFFS

❦ ❦ ❦

Ad valorem tariffs give more effective protection during periods of rising prices than do specific tariffs.

In spite of world dominance in manufacturing, the United States has consistently granted fuller tariff protection to manufacturing than to mining and agriculture.

Britain made extensive use of tariffs and other trade barriers until the Napoleonic era; she practiced virtual free trade from the mid-nineteenth century until World War I; she has returned to the extensive practice of protection since that time.

Britain is the only country to make a significant experiment with free trade in modern times.

United States tariffs rose erratically but steadily from 1789 to 1930. Since the passage of the Reciprocal Trade Agreements Act in 1934, the United States has been engaged in a major program of tariff reduction.

Most tariff negotiations that have occurred since 1948 have occurred within the organizational framework of the General Agreement on Tariffs and Trade.

Foreign countries have not taken as much advantage of lowered United States tariffs as they might have because of the fear that, if they should increase substantially their shipments to the United States, the United States would again raise barriers against them.

❦ ❦ ❦

TARIFFS, which are the prime concern of the present chapter, are duties or taxes imposed by a government on goods as they are imported or exported. A more limited, legalistic definition, however, might include only the collections made by so-called "customs bureaus," thus leaving out import excises which are collected by some other government agency.

CLASSIFICATION BY "PURPOSE AND EFFECT"

Quite different purposes and effects may underlie the various tariff provisions now in force. Tariffs may be classified in terms of whether they are (1) for revenue, or (2) for protection, and (3) by their effect in the redistribution of income.

Tariffs for revenue have much the same virtues and vices—chiefly vices—as do internal sales or excise taxes. They tend to be regressive taxes, falling primarily on the people in the lower income brackets. But, of course, this is not necessarily and always the case. A tariff may be levied on a luxury item such as French perfume or European-made sport cars. Nevertheless, without going into the detailed argument, the conclusion may be alleged that sales taxes, excises, and duties on goods moving through the channels of trade are not very satisfactory ways for governments to raise money, if money raising is the object.

United States tariffs, which provided nine tenths of the revenue of the Federal government in the early days of this country's history, have dropped very considerably in relative importance until they now provide only about 1 per cent of the revenue. The tariff, then, is no longer a significant source of revenue for the United States government, although it continues to serve this purpose for many underdeveloped countries, providing a fourth to two thirds of the revenue for the governments of such countries as Chile, Egypt, Guatemala, Mexico, Brazil, Peru, and India.

But the protective tariff, which is designed to protect the domestic market for certain home industries, is intended to influence the quantity of trade and not to raise money.

Revenue raising and protection are, in a sense, contradictory. To the extent that the tariff is effectively protective, it will not raise revenue. However, in most cases tariffs operate in an area somewhere between these extremes. And even though tariff rates are high enough to discourage much importation, some foreign enterprises have costs low enough to justify sending some goods in, despite the high rates—and consequently some revenue is raised.

A third important economic effect of a tariff is the income redistribution which results within the country that levies the duty. As a consequence of tariffs, some people have to pay more for certain goods they buy, other people make more money profits, and others are benefited or hurt by the revised government taxing-spending policy which is a by-product of the tariff. One of the amazing things about tariffs is the myth that the protection seekers have built up to give the impression that the tariff is merely a deterrent to "foreign scoundrels," who for some unworthy reason can undersell good, 100-per-cent Americans; and that it is, therefore, a patriotic act to keep the foreign goods out. But it would be as accurate to say that protection seeking is an unpatriotic act designed to make less goods available, at higher prices, to good, 100-per-cent Americans.

CLASSIFICATION BY BASE ON WHICH TARIFF IS COMPUTED

But classification by purpose and effect is only one of the ways in which tariffs may be classified. Another classification can be made in terms of the base on which the tariff is computed.

Specific, Ad Valorem, and Compound

In classifying tariffs in this manner, there are two chief possibilities, and one other possibility which is a mixture of the two: (a) specific, (b) ad valorem, and (c) compound. The *specific* tariff takes the form of a flat rate per unit of the commodity being taxed, perhaps 5 cents per pound, or 10 cents per cubic foot, or a dollar per bag. For example, the United States tariff on phosphorous imports has been 4 cents a pound. In the case of the *ad valorem* duty, the tariff is computed as a percentage of the money value. For example, the United States tariff on smokeless powder was lowered from 60 per cent to 30 per cent of the money value by the Torquay General Agreement of 1951. A *compound* tariff combines elements of the specific and the ad valorem. Examples are the United States tariff on woolen cloth of 25 cents per pound plus 25 per cent ad valorem and the tariff on tungsten of 50 cents per pound plus 50 per cent ad valorem.

The specific tariff has the advantage of being definite. After the government has set up its classification and labeled everything, the customs officials need merely check the physical quantity; the amount of the tariff is then set. The necessary work can be done at the warehouse where the goods enter the country. It is easy (easier than the ad valorem) to administer, and especially advantageous, although not foolproof, in countries where the customs agents are of dubious integrity and graft prevails. It was probably thinking along these lines that led most governments in the underdeveloped areas, during their early history, to make general use of specific rates.

Valuation Problems

By contrast, the ad valorem tariff poses serious administrative problems. How can customs officials ascertain value?[1] A large part of the

---

[1] For a study of these problems see: Ralph Elberton Smith, *Customs Valuation in the United States.* (Chicago: University of Chicago Press, 1948); and the

difficulty has been a result of the complicated criteria used in ad valorem valuation. The tariff law, until 1956, provided:[2]

> . . . 5 different methods of determining value. First, imports must be valued on the basis both of *foreign value* (that is, the price in the domestic markets of the exporting country) and *export value* (that is, the price for export to the United States). [Export value is the prevailing price in the foreign market in connection with exports to the United States, and not the price at which the transaction actually occurred.] The higher of these becomes the statutory basis for the calculation of duties. If neither export nor foreign value can be ascertained, then *United States value* is used. This indirect method of approximating foreign value starts with the selling price of an imported product in the United States and arrives at a foreign value by deducting the duty, transportation, and certain charges and amounts not to exceed 8 percent for profits, 6 percent for commissions, etc. If this figure also is not ascertainable, then *cost of production* is the basis for valuation. This too is specifically defined by statute and includes minimum requirements for profits, general expenses, etc. For a few commodities, the most important of which are coal-tar products, the rate of duty is assessed on the basis of *American selling price* of competitive goods produced in the United States. (Italics added.)

The Randall Commission in 1954 strongly recommended the use of "actual invoice price [not foreign value, not export value, and not any of the other three methods of valuation in actual use] of imported goods for valuation purposes in transactions between a buyer and a seller who are independent of each other."[3]

Then the so-called Customs Simplification Act of 1956 was passed. It stipulated:

> Except as otherwise specifically provided for in this Act, the value of imported merchandise for the purposes of this Act shall be—
> (1) the export value, or
> (2) if the export value cannot be determined satisfactorily, then the United States value, or

---

United States, Public Advisory Board for Mutual Security, *A Trade and Tariff Policy in the National Interest* (Washington, 1953), Chap. VII.

[2] United States, Public Advisory Board . . . , *A Trade and Tariff Policy . . . ,* p. 48.

[3] United States, Commission on Foreign Economic Policy (Randall Commission), *Report*, p. 51.

(3) if neither the export value nor the United States value can be determined satisfactorily, then the constructed value;[4] except that, in the case of an imported article subject to a rate of duty based on the American selling price of a domestic article, such value shall be—

(4) the American selling price of such domestic article.

Thus the only major change is the substitution in the new law of export value for the "whichever is higher, foreign value or export value" of the old law. But Congress could not bring itself to make even this modest simplification without equivocating. A non-revisable list is to be compiled of those articles whose valuation would be decreased by

TABLE 19

AVERAGE RATE OF DUTY (1954) ON IMPORTED DUTIABLE MERCHANDISE BY TARIFF SCHEDULES

	%
I. Chemicals, oils, and paints	14.15
II. Earths, earthenware, and glassware	24.50
III. Metals and manufactures	11.96
IV. Wood and manufactures	6.00
V. Sugar, molasses, and manufactures	9.80
VI. Tobacco and manufactures	20.23
VII. Agricultural products and provisions	9.18
VIII. Spirits, wines, and other beverages	23.39
IX. Cotton manufactures	21.15
X. Flax, hemp, jute, and manufactures	7.13
XI. Wool and manufactures	21.27
XII. Silk manufactures	30.09
XIII. Rayon and other synthetic textiles, manufactures	22.12
XIV. Pulp, paper, and books	9.67
XV. Sundries	20.03
Free list, but taxable	3.79
Ratio of duties calculated to total free and dutiable imports	5.17
Ratio of duties calculated to total dutiable imports only	11.58

Source: *Statistical Abstract, 1955*, pp. 924–6.

more than five per cent under the new rules. The listed articles will then be valued for tariff-paying purposes under the old rules. Consequently all of the valuation procedures remain to complicate the law.

Whether export value or invoice value is better may be debatable. But there seems little question that the other methods of valuation should be thrown out completely and without equivocation or procrastination. The consequent reduction in the amount of Bureau of Customs paper work would be tremendous. Congressmen and businessmen are

[4] Constructed value corresponds roughly with cost of production under the old system.

fond of complaining about the administrative arm of government in matters of this sort, but it is the way the lawyers in Congress have written the laws that frequently necessitates the inordinate amount of paper work.

Height of Tariffs

As to the height of the tariffs which result from the combination of specific, ad valorem, and compound duties, Tables 19 and 20 give some clues. In Table 19 the entry "ratio of duties calculated to total free and dutiable imports" indicates that in 1954 tariff receipts amounted to 5.17 per cent of the total value of all imports. The entry "ratio of duties calculated to total dutiable imports only" indicates that tariff receipts were 11.58 per cent of the combined value of all dutiable imports. The entry for "chemicals, oils, and paints," indicates that the tariffs levied on those items represented 14.15 per cent of their combined value, etc.

A brief comparison of the extent of tariff protection granted by the United States to (1) manufacturing, (2) agricultural commodities, and (3) metals and minerals may not be amiss.[5]

(a) MANUFACTURING: The Public Advisory Board for Mutual Security makes this observation: "No other sector of the American economy has been so consistently and markedly successful in getting tariff barriers set up against imports as has manufacturing." And yet the strength of the American economy is supposed to lie in manufacturing. We make goods so efficiently by mass production and by extensive use of capital equipment "that American manufactured goods dominate the export markets of the world."[6] Among the industries so strong that they hold leading positions in world export markets, yet still claim and receive tariff protection, are electric products (refrigerators, ranges, vacuum cleaners, radios, and television), the automobile industry, machine-making and machine tools, etc.[7]

To add to the troubles of importers: "One feature of the tariff on manufacturing is the great differentiation in duties made on the basis of minor differences in size, value, or ornamentation. Different rates are applied to plate glass depending on the thickness and area. Different rates are applied to watches according to the size of the movement and the number of jewels contained in the movement and the adjustments."[8]

[5] There is much interesting detail on individual tariff rates as they apply to particular commodities in Howard S. Piquet, *Aid, Trade and the Tariff* (New York: Crowell, 1953).

[6] United States, Public Advisory Board . . . , *A Trade and Tariff Policy* . . . , p. 17.

[7] Chapter 13 discusses, in connection with cartels, a possible reason why such tariffs are desirable to the companies concerned.

[8] United States, Public Advisory Board . . . , *A Trade and Tariff Policy* . . . , p. 21.

TABLE 20
SOME SELECTED (WITH MALICE) UNITED STATES TARIFF RATES, 1954

	R.T.A.R.[1]	BASIC RATE [2]
1. Abdominal supporters	27½%	75%
2. Arsenic acid	3¢ lb.	3¢ lb.
3. Address books	25%	25%
4. Agate balls, marbles	35%	70%
5. Ethyl alcohol for beverages		
If from Cuba	$1.75 pf. gal.[3]	
Otherwise	$2.25 pf. gal.[3]	$5.00 pf. gal.[3]
6. Airplanes	15%	30%
7. Alfalfa hay	$1.25 ton	$5.00 ton
8. Sturgeon caviar, boiled, packed in airtight containers	30%	30%
9. Catsup	17½%	35%
10. Passenger automobiles	10%	10%
11. Avocados		
If from Cuba	Free	
Otherwise	7½¢ lb.	15¢ lb.
12. Golf balls	15%	30%
13. Bathtubs	2½¢ lb. plus 7½%	5¢ lb. plus 30%
14. Birds' eggs	Free	Free
15. Books, American authorship	10%	25%
16. Books, foreign, bona fide	5%	15%
17. Books, printed in foreign language	Free	Free
18. Scotch whiskey, containers not over one gallon (in cases)	$1.50 pf. gal.[3]	$5.00 pf. gal.[3]
19. Still wine, from grapes, over 14%, not over 24% alcohol, containers not over one gallon	$1.00 gal.[4]	$1.25 gal.[4]
20. Steel rails	½₀¢ lb.	⅒¢ lb.
21. Uranium metal	25%	25%
22. Uranium ore	Free	Free
23. Teeth, artificial, vitrified	50¢ doz. (but not under 45% nor over 70%)	70%
24. Thumbtacks	⁹⁄₁₀¢ lb.	⁹⁄₁₀¢ lb.
25. Dice of ivory, bone or other material	25%	50%

[1] Reciprocal Trade Agreements rates applied to most countries; [2] Smoot-Hawley rates currently applied to goods coming from certain countries; [3] proof gallon; [4] $1.00 a gallon rate applied to Cuba only; $1.25 to all others.

Source: *Custom House Guide, 1955*, pp. 617–894.

Especially frequent use is also made of the complications of compound duties in connection with tariffs on manufacturing industries. Table 20 only begins to suggest the infinite range of the complications which have been devised by the ingenious mind of man.

(b) Agricultural Commodities present a somewhat different situation from manufactured goods. There are some major imports such as coffee on the free list. But the tariff and other restrictive measures on sugar are among the most complex in the whole field of import restrictions. The sugar tariff is one-half cent per pound if the sugar comes from Cuba, five-eights of a cent if it comes from other foreign countries (except the Philippines). In addition, there is an import excise tax of one-half a cent. The proceeds of this latter burden on imports are used to subsidize domestic beet and cane producers. Then, on top of this, there are quotas on sugar imports, which are changed every year by the Secretary of Agriculture on the basis of a complicated formula which is provided by law and involves estimating future demand. Other restrictions discriminate even more positively against the import of refined sugar. Other notorious agricultural (and livestock) tariffs include those on dairy products, wool, groundfish fillets (cod), and tuna.

But for the most part, quotas are more important in restricting agricultural imports than are tariffs. Quotas are discussed at length in Chapter 12.

(c) Metals and Minerals, like agricultural commodities, present a mixed picture. There is a tariff of two cents a pound on copper ore and concentrates; but it is temporarily suspended in deference to World War II and the "cold war." The tariff on lead ore and concentrates, ad valorem equivalent, is 5.7 per cent; on zinc it is 8.2 per cent. But there is strong pressure from the lead and zinc producers for increases in the tariffs on those products. Those industries are arguing for increases on the grounds that the costs of producing lower grade ores are rising. The Public Advisory Board for Mutual Security, however, seems to feel that: "Incentive is not provided by a tariff as such, but by an expanding market at profitable prices." The report adds that: "The use of tariffs to encourage exploitation of low-grade ores now is particularly objectionable." [9] Why not use up the foreigner's ore?

In practice, the tariffs on ores are generally lower than the tariffs on smelted, or refined, or manufactured products. This is intended to encourage processing in the United States. Such procedure is standard all over the world. Countries commonly have higher import tariffs on manufactured goods than on raw materials. And they tend to have higher export duties on raw materials than on manufactured goods—to encourage processing domestically. But if the exporting country has higher tariffs on ore exports and lower tariffs on the export of refined products; and the importing country has higher tariffs on manufactured-goods imports and lower tariffs on raw-commodity imports, the two sets of tariffs more or less cancel out so far as influencing the loca-

[9] *Ibid.*, pp. 34–5.

tion of the processing is concerned. But they have, when added together, a great effect in cutting down the total amount of trade.

(d) MISCELLANEOUS TARIFFS: Comment on some miscellaneous tariffs follows: [10]

The tariff on opium runs to 28 per cent. This does not make sense. Opium coming in for medical purposes should come in duty free; opium coming in for other purposes—should not come.

The duty on mica runs between 12 and 25 per cent, even though mica is a critically important strategic material which is in short supply in the United States.

The poor are penalized by a formula under which tariffs on low priced "earthenware and chinaware, table and artware" runs to 67 per cent in comparison with tariffs on higher priced ware of this sort which run to 32 per cent.

Manganese pays a tariff of 11 per cent. Manganese is a strategic mineral which is indispensable in the manufacture of steel. It is not produced in sufficient quantity in the United States, nor is there any likelihood that it will be.

Molybdenum mining in the United States is on an export basis. The United States has the largest reserves in the world. Therefore there is a 44 per cent tariff on its import. Does the tariff tend to keep the domestic price high?

There is a tariff of 1.2 per cent on hardwood lumber. It must cost about as much to collect this tariff as it brings in.

Why the American tobacco industry, which is also on an export basis, needs a 27 per cent tariff on cigarette leaf tobacco is a mystery.

There is a butter tariff of 7 cents a pound, which rises to 14 cents a pound if the imports exceed 50,000,000 pounds a year. Granted the Wisconsin dairy industry is in bad shape, is tariff protection the proper answer?

Similarly, potatoes are favored with tariff protection of roughly 28.5 per cent. Tomatoes are favored with rates varying from 22 to 44 per cent. Whether the staggering of the rates on tomatoes on a seasonal basis (to give more protection when the American crop is being harvested) works as intended—or merely adds to the confusion—is open to question. And last but not least, whiskey pays 28 per cent.

(e) INTERNATIONAL COMPARISON: But the United States is not the only country with high tariffs; other countries have them; and in many cases the rates are higher, more extensive, and more inhibitory of trade. From Panama to Suez and from London to the Cape, governments and their

[10] Some of the data is derived from table 20, some from Piquet, *op. cit., passim.* The percentages in the discussion that follows are either ad valorem or ad valorem equivalent (computed by dividing the amount of tariff receipts by the value of imports) in some recent year.

businessmen coadjutors seem to feel the higher the tariffs the better, the more tariffs the better, the more complicated the administration of the tariff law the better. Some one of the measures might keep a nickel's worth of goods out—and what could be finer? According to *Foreign Commerce Weekly* of May 3, 1954, the duties under the new Costa Rican tariff law average 34 per cent, whatever that means. Anyway, the tariff on epsom salts was in the process of being lowered from 98 per cent to 32 per cent.

Precise statistical comparison of the height of the tariff walls in different countries is rather difficult to achieve. It is impossible to strike a simple average of tariff rates and compare the averages because of the difference in importance of different types of goods. It is impossible to measure the importance (for use in weighting the averages) of different types of goods by the quantities being traded because the success of a protective tariff is a result of its efficacy in keeping important goods from moving internationally. But, still and all, some rough generalizations can be made. Many countries have extremely high tariffs, and some are obviously more restrictive of trade than others. The United States tariff wall is a long way from being the highest in the world—but it is still high. Others are higher. A notorious one is Venezuela's.

Tariffs and Inflation

To return to the distinction between specific and ad valorem duties: If a country is interested in protection and if prices are rising—a common situation, it may be added—the ad valorem tariff gives more effective protection than the specific. The protectiveness of the specific rates becomes less and less as the price rises. To illustrate, the United States tariff on Cuban raw sugar was .75¢ per pound in 1942, when the price averaged 2.988¢ per pound. In 1947 the price averaged 5.45¢ per pound but the tariff was the same. This tariff was, obviously, less of a deterrent to importation in 1947 than it was in 1942; it represented a smaller percentage of the value. But an ad valorem tariff of perhaps 25%, approximately what the specific rate amounted to in 1942, would have been the equivalent of a specific rate of about 1.26¢ per pound in 1947. Quite a difference! Because of such considerations, underdeveloped countries have tended, of recent years, to make increased use of ad valorem and compound tariffs and less use of specific tariffs. They have done so in spite of the administrative difficulties involved in assessing an ad valorem tariff.

CLASSIFICATION BY MANNER OF ENACTMENT

Another way to classify tariffs is on the basis of the manner of enactment. The basic possibilities are that they be determined (1) by legislative action, (2) by executive action, or (3) by treaty or other international agreement. But most tariff making involves complicated combinations of these possibilities. Different countries enact tariffs in different ways. A tariff may be enacted outright by the legislature's passing a law stating that the import duty on sugar will be three quarters of a cent per pound, or on Scotch whiskey, 50 per cent. Such provisions may appear in detail in the law; and it will be *in detail*. Through much of the history of the United States, that is the way tariffs have been enacted. Congress passed a law and provided specifically what the rates should be. But tariffs imposed in that way are rather inflexible. If what a country wants to get out of its tariff is protection on the one hand and bargaining leverage on the other, it is desirable to have some process by which the rates can be changed in a hurry. To deal with this problem, the legislature may pass a law that provides basically for certain rates but permits the executive branch of the government to change the rates within certain limits. The law also may provide that the executive can negotiate rate changes with foreign governments in exchange for rate changes by them. Governments can then bargain with each other for tariff reductions, at least within certain limits. "I'll lower my rate on your product if you will lower your rate on my product." It is literally never the other way round. What is involved is one country's effort to increase its exports by trying to get concessions from other countries but willing to make only a limited amount of concession on imports in exchange. That this procedure is typical of the bargaining process is plain enough indication that governments tend to think in terms of the encouragement of exports and discouragement of imports. Strange, is it not, that we should work from the presumption that we are doing the foreigner a favor by taking his goods? And yet this is the procedure that the United States government has been following since 1934 in the setting of United States tariff rates under the Reciprocal Trade Agreements program.

MISCELLANEOUS DEFINITIONS

Most-Favored-Nation Clause

In connection with the classification of tariffs it may be well to define an oft-used term: *the most-favored-nation clause*. The clause, which has occupied an important place in international treaties relating to tariffs, may be either "conditional" or "unconditional."

If a treaty had been signed between the United States and France containing a conditional most-favored-nation clause, and if the United States later were to sign a trade treaty with the United Kingdom providing for a reduction of the United States tariff on, say, worsteds, then that lower duty would be generalized by the United States to worsteds coming from France only if France made to the United States a concession of the same order of magnitude as that which the United Kingdom had made in negotiating the treaty between the United States and England. The United States used the conditional interpretation of the most-favored-nation clause until 1923, but since that time has used the unconditional interpretation, as do most other countries.

In the case of the unconditional most-favored-nation clause, if the United States had signed a treaty with France containing such a clause and then had signed a treaty with England providing for reduction of the tariff on worsteds, the lower rate would also be applied to worsteds coming from France without the necessity that France make any further concession. Trade treaty negotiations are very complicated at best; many things are talked about at once, and it is sometimes difficult to know just what concession is made for what. The unconditional most-favored-nation clause, in such a setting, appears as a tremendously desirable simplifying element by comparison with the conditional interpretation of the clause.

A sample unconditional most-favored-nation clause, Article XIV, paragraph 1, of the Treaty of Friendship, Commerce and Navigation between the United States and Japan, signed April 2, 1953, and entered into force October 30, 1953, reads as follows:

> Each Party shall accord most-favored-nation treatment to products of the other Party, from whatever place and by whatever type of carrier arriving, and to products destined for exportation to the territories of such other Party, by whatever route and by whatever type of carrier, with respect to customs duties and charges of any kind imposed on or in connection with importation or exportation or imposed on the international transfer of payments for imports or exports, and with respect to the method of levying such duties and charges, and with respect to all rules and formalities in connection with importation and exportation.

The United States ostensibly uses the unconditional interpretation now. Actually that does not seem to be precisely what it does, although, when it writes a trade treaty, it generally incorporates an unconditional most-favored-nation clause in the document. The application is, in reality, somewhat more liberal than this. Concessions are generalized to all the nations of the world, whether there has been a treaty containing an unconditional most-favored-nation clause signed with them or not, except for countries which are on a positive blacklist. Thus the approach is positive rather than negative, and a few countries may receive the "benefit" of United States tariff concessions without having signed with the United States trade treaties containing the clause.

At the moment the Soviet Union and various of her so-called satellite countries grace the blacklist. This is another example of a strange manner of thinking: the idea that you are doing something prejudicial to your opponent by keeping his goods out of your country. The Soviet goods now pay the highest rates of the Smoot-Hawley tariff, just as did German goods during the late 1930's. However, in one respect current policy is more rational than it was in the thirties. Then the United States actually subsidized the export of many things, such as cotton, to Germany; now exports to Russia are closely controlled. We are effectively limiting the trade both ways now, whereas we just limited it one way before.

Compensatory Duty

Another much used term is *compensatory duty*. A compensatory duty is a tariff that a country levies to match some other tax which it has imposed.[11] If a government already had an internal processing tax on the milling of wheat flour, and thus placed domestic flour at a slight disadvantage relative to foreign flour, it might well place a tariff on wheat flour coming in from abroad to match the internal tax. A tariff of this sort is not protective; it merely avoids placing the domestic producers at a disadvantage. The compensatory duty was the only sort of tariff levied by England during the latter part of the nineteenth century, when she was virtually on a free-trade basis.

Import Excise

Another type of duty is the import excise tax, which is essentially a tariff under another name. The tax is paid on imported goods, but ostensibly it is an internal excise tax, and is likely to be collected by a bureau of internal revenue (or the equivalent) rather than by the customs (or the bureau that customarily collects tariffs). However, it amounts to the same thing as a tariff so far as the actual burden is concerned. Some of the more notorious United States tariffs are actually import excises rather than tariffs—for example, the import excise on crude oil. By and large, foreign countries quickly inform themselves of such situations and in subsequent international tariff negotiations import excise taxes are discussed right along with the tariffs. All that is gained is a complication.

Countervailing (Anti-Dumping) Duty

Another type of tariff is the countervailing duty. This is sometimes called an "anti-dumping" tariff.[12] It is a duty levied in the importing

[11] The term might also be applied to a tariff, intended to encourage domestic processing, which is levied on the import of a manufactured product (e.g., linen cloth) to compensate domestic manufacturers of linen cloth for the hardship they might be under as a result of the fact that there was already a tariff on the raw material (flax).

[12] Dumping is the sale to the importing country of a product at a price lower than that at which it is sold for domestic consumption in the exporting country;

country to counteract either a government bounty paid by the exporting country—a bounty such as that which the United States has frequently paid to support cotton exports—or dumping by private foreign corporations. It is the type of tariff that properly should be used, on the basis of the infant-industry argument—if that argument justified a tariff at all.

The justifiability of countervailing tariffs as practiced by the United States is also conditioned by the manner in which they have been used. According to the Public Advisory Board, domestic manufacturers have a tendency to file "complaints of dumping" against competing imports. But only a very small percentage of such complaints are justified. Nevertheless they hamstring and delay imports: [13]

> American producers can also create difficulties for importers merely by filing a complaint of dumping. When this happens, appraisement of merchandise may be withheld and trade interrupted. Only a very small proportion of dumping complaints are found to be justified, and it has been proposed that domestic producers be required to show prima facie evidence of injury from dumping before appraisement is withheld.

Drawback

Yet another standard term in tariff jargon is the drawback. It is the refund of a tariff paid on imports which is made when the goods are subsequently exported—if they are. Countries are likely to favor doing as much manufacturing and processing of goods as they can within their own borders. For this reason many countries, although they are "against imports," like to import, process, and re-export. So, the government may permit enterprises to import raw materials, pay the tariff, and then, if the goods are subsequently exported (even though in a more highly processed form), give them a refund of part or all of the tariff.

Single-Column and Multiple-Column Tariffs

A single-column tariff structure provides for only one set of rates regardless of the source of the goods or other possible grounds on which there might be discrimination. A multiple-column tariff provides for the possibility of two or more rates being applied to each classification of goods. It may be that some countries will get the benefit of the column of lowest rates. Imports from other countries, against which the country with the multiple-column rate structure desires to discriminate, will pay the higher rates contained in another column of figures.

---

or it might be said to involve sale to the importing country at a price lower than that indicated as appropriate after all proper costs and a reasonable profit margin are taken into account. United States law says that dumping is sale at less than fair value—a concept susceptible of varied interpretations.

[13] United States, Public Advisory Board . . . , *A Trade and Tariff Policy* . . . , p. 51.

The United States gives a tariff preference to goods coming from Cuba, an arrangement which comes close to representing another column in the tariff. It also applies the highest rates of the Smoot-Hawley Act of 1930 to countries on the blacklist, such as Russia and her satellites. But lower rates resulting from the negotiation of reciprocal trade agreements are applied to most countries. It might be argued that this amounts to a three-column tariff so far as the United States is concerned.

TARIFF HISTORY

A brief sketch of the tariff history of Great Britain and the United States should prove useful.

Great Britain

British tariff history has followed a pattern very different from that of the United States. Britain practiced mercantilism and made extensive use of tariffs and other controls to keep out imports for at least three centuries before the Industrial Revolution. Adam Smith's *Wealth of Nations* (1776) was a plea for a change in that policy. And the repeal of the Corn Laws, which did not occur until 1846, finally implemented the change. Such a change was possible in England because the rising manufacturing class had at that time no effective foreign competition against which it needed to be protected. Therefore it was not lobbying for tariff protection for itself. But that same rising class, influenced by Ricardo, felt that it was desirable to reduce the tariff on food and necessities so that the price of food could be kept low, and consequently wages could be kept low, and profits would be higher. In this single isolated case, the influence of pressure groups combined to get tariffs removed; it seems to have been almost the only occasion in history when there has been a powerful combination of producer pressures interested in such removal.

England from that time until World War I practiced something closely approximating free trade. There were tariffs on some things, but they were very low compensatory duties designed to place as much burden on imports as was being placed on domestic producers by internal excises. By 1900, however, Germany and the United States had become important manufacturing countries, and particular British manufacturers and Joseph Chamberlain were beginning to think in terms of the need for tariff protection from foreign competition. Shortly after 1900 the movement to re-establish protective tariffs in Britain was well under way. The McKenna duties of 1915 established 33⅓ per cent ad valorem rates on certain luxury goods, and the Safeguarding of Industries Act of 1921 extended the tariff somewhat further. Thus England during the 1920's had some protective tariffs, but they were not extensive in coverage. It was the Import Duties Act of 1932 that placed Britain back with the rest of the world squarely in the protective tariff camp. That law provided for a 10 per cent duty on all imports, except for an enumerated free list. It also provided for a wide range of higher rates and for the establishment of an Import Duties Advisory Committee to supervise the whole protective-tariff process. The Committee was to engage in extensive consultation with business groups in the course of its work. Particulary, it was to consult (and it did) with the steel industry about steel tariffs. They were forthcoming.

Another characteristic of the revived British tariff system has been "imperial preference," which has meant allowing goods coming in from other parts of the Empire to enter at a lower rate than goods coming from non-Empire countries. The chief manifestation of this policy has been the exemption of "Empire goods" from the basic 10 per cent duty. Other Empire countries have made similar concessions to each other.

United States

Tariff history began for the United States after the Revolutionary War, at a time when there was a strong reaction against British mercantilist policy. It was not strange that the United States, where the Boston Tea Party had been staged, should begin by practicing the theories that Adam Smith had developed, calling for comparative freedom of trade. In fact the United States in its first tariff law, that of 1789, provided for a revenue tariff of 5 per cent on everything; there was no free list. But the sojourn of the United States near the free-trade camp was very brief. The tariffs were raised somewhat in 1790; and Alexander Hamilton, in his *Report on Manufactures* in 1791, presented the classic statement of the infant-industry argument, and also attempted to justify tariffs on the basis of the military-necessity argument.[14] For the United States in those early years the infant-industry argument had a very real validity because certain British industries, such as steel, were dumping in the United States market as a matter of policy to prevent the development of competing industries in this country. However, it was not until 1816 that Congress enacted a tariff law which was clearly protective in nature. And it was the high rates of the Morrill Act of 1861 which established the Republican party as the party of high tariffs. From that date until the early 1930's a series of tariff acts consistently (except for the Wilson-Gorman Act of 1894 and the Underwood Act of 1913) raised the rates; by 1930, in the Smoot-Hawley Act, the United States had a tariff wall that roughly averaged 60 per cent when converted to an ad valorem base.[15]

[14] The *Report* is reprinted in: *The Works of Alexander Hamilton,* ed. Henry Cabot Lodge (New York: Putnam, 1903), Vol. IV.
[15] Tariff collections as a percentage of the value of dutiable imports.

In 1916 the United States set up a Tariff Commission and empowered it to make studies comparing foreign and domestic costs of production. This was part of the effort to make the tariff rates high enough to counteract any advantage that the foreigners might have in terms of production cost. However, this approach proved extremely difficult to implement (see Chapter 9).

The Smoot-Hawley Act, which raised tariffs to the highest levels they have ever reached in the United States, was especially ill-timed. The great depression had begun in the fall of 1929; United States foreign lending had markedly fallen off; and foreigners needed to increase their shipments to the United States if they were to acquire the dollars necessary to pay the interest on earlier loans. But the passage of the Smoot-Hawley Act tended to inhibit that development. The Act was followed very quickly by formal protest from over thirty different countries; and it did much to justify debtor countries in shrugging their shoulders and declining to trouble themselves particularly about paying their debts in the early 1930's.

The Reciprocal Trade Agreements Act of 1934, sponsored by Cordell Hull, represented a major break in the history of rising tariffs which had been evolving since 1789 and a major change in tariff-making procedure in the United States. The new tariff-making procedure involved:[16]

(a) TARIFF MAKING BY INTERNATIONAL AGREEMENT: One provision of the act was that tariff rates should be set by international agreement rather than by domestic legislation. Previously international trade treaties as signed by the United States had contained the most-favored-nation clause, but they had not generally specified what the rates should be. It had been left to Congress to set the actual rates. And the President as a rule had not been authorized to sign treaties with foreign countries providing for tariff changes.

(b) THE RATE REDUCTION FORMULA: After 1934, the executive branch of the government was permitted to vary the rates by 50 per cent from the rates as set by the Smoot-Hawley Act. This provision was subsequently changed to permit a change of 50 per cent from the rates prevailing on January 1, 1945. And this provision was further modified in 1955 to permit a reduction of 15 per cent (5 per cent a year for three years) from the rates prevailing on January 1, 1955. The 1955 law thus permitted a further 15 per cent reduction in such of the rates as had already been lowered 75 per cent since 1934. This provision makes possible a cumulative reduction of rates, since 1934, of 78.75 per cent.

[16] United States, Tariff Commission, *Trade Agreements Manual—A Summary of Selected Data Relating to Trade Agreements That the United States Has Negotiated Since 1934* (Washington, 1955).

However, in the case of items which did not receive a rate reduction under the earlier laws, the total reduction possible is now only the current 15 per cent. And the 15 per cent reduction must be exercised at the rate of 5 per cent per year during the three-year period or it is lost.

Another provision of the 1955 law permits rate reduction in certain cases down to the equivalent of 50 per cent ad valorem, even though such reduction may total more than 15 per cent. This provision will permit, but not compel, a substantial reduction in certain very high rates.

(c) THE PRINCIPAL SUPPLIER RULE: As a third feature of the reciprocal trade agreements program, negotiation regarding the tariff rate on a particular commodity is to be with the principal supplier of that commodity. This is a logical procedure in a world where governments are interested in obtaining the greatest possible reduction in rates from the other country in exchange for the least possible rate reduction on their part. It stands to reason that the United States can get the most concession from the country that is the chief supplier. Thus, it would not serve any particularly useful purpose to talk about crude oil with Cuba. The Cubans will not offer anything in exchange for a reduction by the United States of its crude-oil import excise; but the Venezuelans will.

(d) THE GENERALIZATION OF CONCESSIONS: A fourth characteristic of the reciprocal trade agreements is that the concessions, once made, are generalized to every country except those on a positive blacklist. The blacklist now consists chiefly of Russia and the countries associated with Russia. Thus, although the reciprocal trade agreements contain most-favored-nation clauses, the concessions are likely to be generalized somewhat more widely than would be the case if they were extended only to the countries with which such treaties have been signed.

(e) RESORT TO MULTILATERAL AGREEMENTS: The fifth and last of this incomplete list of characteristics is that negotiations have generally taken place, since World War II, at international conferences. This was not true of the agreements of the 1930's, which were on a strictly bilateral basis. But, since the General Agreement on Tariffs and Trade of 1947, there has been a series of conferences, first at Geneva, then at Annecy, and at Torquay, and back in Geneva, in which as many as thirty-four nations have participated.

So far as the United States is concerned, ratification of these multilateral agreements is handled in the same way as were the earlier bilateral agreements. Reductions are negotiated under the powers granted by Congress to the executive branch in the Reciprocal Trade Agreements Acts. In fact, tariff reductions of very considerable magnitude were negotiated by this procedure during the three or four years following 1947. But since about 1951, very little has been done along the line of further tariff reductions. However, the GATT negotiations of 1956 did result in the application of the "15 per cent in three years" formula by the United States to about $650,000,000 worth of imports, roughly one twentieth of all United States imports.[17]

The GATT agreement itself has been under heavy attack both in the United States and elsewhere (Great Britain, France, Brazil, Mexico, and so on), and certain Senators have been very critical of the executive branch for not submitting GATT itself, or the later tariff reductions negotiated in the GATT framework, to the Senate for ratification. Indications of the rough road which tariff reduction has had in the United States during the last five years are (1) the "peril-point" clause, (2) the escape-clause controversy,[18] and (3) the provision making it mandatory to apply the highest rates of the Smoot-Hawley Act to Russia and her affiliated countries.

It has been remarked that European countries have not increased their sales in the United States very markedly in response to the tariff reductions of recent years and in response to the "15 per cent in three years" formula of 1955. This is hardly strange. There in plain view are the peril-point and escape-clause provisions, waiting to be invoked if European exports to this country actually do increase. Little wonder that the European countries are somewhat skeptical with regard to United States protestations as to the desirability of lowering trade barriers. And European policy has not included encouragement of exports to the United States—as a solution for the "dollar shortage"—as much as it might have.

EFFECT OF TARIFFS ON EXPORTS AND IMPORTS

The reciprocal trade agreements program plus the General Agreement on Tariffs and Trade have effected a major lowering of the United States tariff wall. Tariff collections as a percentage of the value of dutiable imports were 59 per cent in 1932 and only 12 per cent in 1954. But taxes of 12 per cent applicable to some 40 per cent of United States imports still represented a rather considerable tax—without taking into account all the imports that have not come in at all because the tariffs are there, and without taking into account the quotas, licenses, and embargoes which are the subject of Chapter 12.

In conjunction with the discussion in Chapter 9 on the effect of trade restrictions, something should be said here about the relationship between tariffs and developing trade. Chart 7 is intended to show the rise and fall of exports and imports that attended on increases and decreases in the tariffs. The symbol "P" indicates that the tariff law of that year in-

[17] *New York Times,* June 8, 1956, p. 1.
[18] The theoretical implications of this are discussed more fully in Chapter 9.

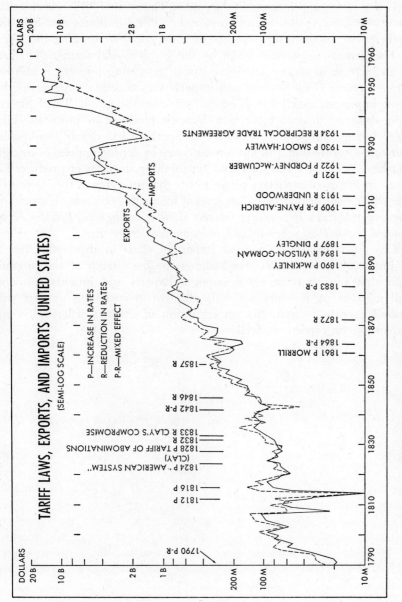

CHART 7

TARIFF LAWS, EXPORTS, AND IMPORTS (UNITED STATES)

(SEMI-LOG SCALE)

P—INCREASE IN RATES
R—REDUCTION IN RATES
P-R—MIXED EFFECT

EXPORTS →

← IMPORTS

1790 P-R

1812 P
1816 P
1824 P · "AMERICAN SYSTEM,"
(CLAY)
1828 P TARIFF OF ABOMINATIONS
1832 P
1833 R CLAY'S COMPROMISE
1842 P-R
1846 R
1857 R
1861 P MORRILL
1864 P-R
1872 R
1883 P-R
1890 P McKINLEY
1894 R WILSON-GORMAN
1897 P DINGLEY
1909 P-R PAYNE-ALDRICH
1913 R UNDERWOOD
1921 P
1922 P FORDNEY-McCUMBER
1930 P SMOOT-HAWLEY
1934 R RECIPROCAL TRADE AGREEMENTS

DOLLARS
20B
10B

2B
1B

200M

100M

10M

1790   1810   1830   1850   1870   1890   1910   1930   1950   1960

DOLLARS
20B
10B

2B
1B

200M

100M

10M

Sources: *Historical Statistics; Statistical Abstract;* Humphrey, *American Imports,* pp. 72–78.

volved a substantial increase in duty rates. The symbol "R" indicates that there was a perceptible reduction in rates. "P/R" indicates that it is difficult to say categorically whether the law raised or lowered the rates.

The general impression given by the graph would seem to be that, if an increase in the rates is successful in restricting imports, *it also restricts exports*. That exports and imports vary together emerges as the most important conclusion to be derived from the graph. Tariff protection, designed to do a favor to a domestic producer by protecting him from foreign competition, will do other, perhaps less clearly identifiable, *but equally American,* producers a disservice by depriving them of foreign markets. Even for those who insist on thinking in terms of producer interest in increased monetary profit, rather than in terms of the interest of the whole population in a higher level of living, this observation should be meaningful. *Even if producer interest alone is considered, Peter is being robbed to pay Paul when trade restriction devices are used.*

Chart 7 is probably the most important chart in the book. And it is important precisely because it shows the basic truth of the proposition that exports must equal imports. Exports and imports rise and fall together. A measure which is effective in curtailing imports will curtail exports as well. But an expansion of imports will involve an expansion of exports as well.

Chapter 12

QUOTAS, LICENSES, AND EMBARGOES (QUANTITATIVE CONTROLS AND DISCRIMINATION)

☙ ☙ ☙

Quotas differ from tariffs chiefly in that they give a certain measure of monopolistic pricing power to the recipient of the quota. At least this is true unless the government taxes the monopoly profit away, controls resale prices, or sells the quotas at auction.

Quotas, licenses, and embargoes are frequently administered in a manner that discriminates against the goods coming from certain countries.

They also may be used to discriminate in favor of necessities, industrial raw materials, or capital equipment.

Some planned distortion away from the free-trade pattern may well be desirable, but it is doubtful that discrimination as between nations is the best means to achieve this.

Discrimination creates ill will between countries; it is also likely to reduce price comparability and to result in less total trade.

☙ ☙ ☙

TARIFFS were the most common type of restriction on trade from the early nineteenth century until the beginning of the 1930's. That is probably the reason why much of the literature analyzing the effect of trade restrictions has been couched in terms of tariffs. It is only since 1930 that such things as quotas, licensing, and embargoes have again assumed major importance; and the theoretical analysis of the implications of restrictions is slowly being reformulated to take them into account.

QUOTAS

Following the passage of the hyper-protectionist Smoot-Hawley tariff in the United States in 1930, other countries looked about for some quick means of retaliation. France is frequently credited with being the leader in rediscovering the possibility of the quota as a handy administrative device especially adapted to quick action in curtailing imports. And in 1931 France established a quota that had as a principal purpose to keep out United States wheat. By 1934 twenty-five or thirty nations were making extensive use of quotas—and still are.

The quota is a quantitative control stating how much of some commodity can enter a country. This sounds rather simple, but working out the criteria to be used in setting quotas has proved to be complicated.

One formula has been to establish *global quotas* stating the total amount of a commodity which could enter the country during a certain time period. Such a quota might provide that 7,000,000 bushels of wheat could enter a country during the next year. An example of such a quota, as applied by Great Britain, involved the provision that a global quota of 1,000,000 standards of timber could be brought into the United Kingdom in 1953.[1]

A major difficulty with the use of global quotas has been that the traders, when they became aware of the size of the quota, would rush their shipments in order to get in under the quota. Hence there would be large shipments during the early part of the quota period and nothing at all imported thereafter, when the quota was exhausted. The result has often been confusion. And in some situations more of the commodity may have come in, as a by-product of the initial rush, than would have been the case without the quota. Another difficulty with global quotas has been that goods might make an ocean transit only to be refused entry because the quota was exhausted.

Some of these difficulties have been obviated by improved administration, licensing, etc.; others have caused a turn to more specific criteria in quota setting. Also governments have turned in this latter direction in order to use quotas as administrative devices to implement domestic planning.

After a country had decided to curtail imports by the use of quotas, it was possible to discriminate among (1) the different commodities, (2) the different exporting nations, and (3) the different exporters and importers (foreign and domestic).

(1) THE DIFFERENT COMMODITIES: A country might make a decision involving the relative priority to be given to different types of goods. In the days before quotas, the price mechanism, presumably, determined whether more or less of this or that type of goods would come in.

But the price mechanism might bring in French perfume and other items not particularly useful. The government that was interested in

---

[1] *Foreign Commerce Weekly,* November 3, 1952, p. 9.

positive planning might decide that food for hungry people or machinery to aid in the development of manufacturing should have a priority. In fact, consumption necessities, and materials and machinery used in connection with development programs, have generally received preference in carefully worked out quota systems. It is no mean advantage of quotas in comparison with tariffs that they are more serviceable tools for such positive planning.

Quotas are also used in a variety of other situations in which the identity of the commodity is the prime consideration. United States quotas on oil and agricultural imports will be discussed below.

(2) THE DIFFERENT EXPORTING NATIONS: Refinements in quota setting have also involved *discrimination on the basis of the national origin of the goods (the identity of the exporting nation)*. The years since 1930 have been replete with examples of discrimination on this basis. The United States has been especially irked by the application of such discriminations because it has been the country most likely to be discriminated against—and for several reasons with which we may sympathize even while condemning this particular sort of retaliation. In the 1930's the United States appeared to certain other countries as a creditor country demanding repayment of debts, at the same time that it led the parade of trade restrictions with the Smoot-Hawley Act in 1930. The reaction of other countries was to set relatively small quotas on goods coming in from the United States. Such retaliation in turn did much to confirm the United States in its traditional policy of advocating equal opportunity in international trade and denouncing the use of discriminations, especially as between nations.[2] It confirmed the rather irrational idea that tariffs are all right but quotas and licenses are not.

But what of the propriety of giving a small quota to goods coming from a country with which a trade treaty containing a most-favored-nation clause has been signed? The United States has frequently found occasion to allege that quotas are in violation of the most-favored-nation clause. In cases where this issue has been thrashed out, it has

[2] Official statements on this point are legion: Anson Burlingame in 1867 trying to secure equality of treatment for the commerce of all nations within the Chinese empire; John Hay in 1899 fighting for the "open door" in China; Francis B. Sayre in 1937 trying to get Argentina to discontinue discrimination against the United States before the United States would begin serious negotiations looking toward a reciprocal trade agreement; or Article I, paragraph 4, of the Havana Charter for an International Trade Organization, which was largely the work of the United States delegation. See: United States, Department of State, (*Papers relating to*) *the Foreign Relations of the United States* . . . 1867. Vol. I (Washington: Government Printing Office), p. 449; *ibid.,* 1899, pp. 128–42; *ibid.,* 1937. Vol. V, p. 224; United States, Department of State, *Havana Charter for an International Trade Organization* (Washington: Government Printing Office, 1948), p. 5.

sometimes been decided that the exporting country would be entitled to the same proportion of trade of the importing (quota-imposing) country that it "enjoyed" during some base year. If Japan imposed a quota on United States wheat, for example, the two countries might agree to take the year 1928 as the base; if in that year the United States provided 30 per cent of Japan's wheat imports, then United States traders would be entitled to fill 30 per cent of whatever quota Japan might set for some later year. Such an arrangement generally came to be regarded as being a reasonable fulfillment of the most-favored-nation clause.[3]

The "percentage of the base-period trade" formula may be preferable to some of the alternatives. But it still leaves much to be desired. Is there anything inherent in the nature of things that would justify the United States' providing 30 per cent of Japan's wheat imports year after year, no more and no less? Trading relations between nations are not static; they are continuously changing—and should change in a dynamic world. More satisfactory criteria need to be developed for assigning quotas if quotas are to be used at all. This is the real "problem of the quota," not whether quotas interfere with the operation of the price mechanism—a point discussed below.

The revised GATT agreement of 1955 says with regard to non-discrimination that: "In applying import restrictions to any product, contracting parties shall aim at a distribution of trade in such product approaching as closely as possible the shares which the various contracting parties might be expected to obtain in the absence of such restrictions . . ." It adds that in cases where this cannot be worked out to the satisfaction of all parties the "previous representative period" formula will constitute reasonable fulfillment of the non-discrimination formula. (With time and experience, rules and procedures may improve.)

(3) THE DIFFERENT EXPORTERS AND IMPORTERS: In addition to the difficulties involved in assigning quotas on the basis of the national origin of the goods, there are difficulties connected with the allocation of the quotas among the *different importing and exporting firms*. Part of the solution to this problem also has been found in the allocation of quotas on the basis of the proportion of the trade enjoyed in some earlier period. But the results are as questionable as they were when the same formula was used for assigning the national-origin quotas, since this system tends to discriminate against newer and more efficient firms in favor of the older and less efficient.

[3] United States, Department of State, *Friendship, Commerce and Navigation, Treaty, and Protocol between the United States of America and Japan* (1953). Treaties and Other International Acts Series 2863 (Washington: Government Printing Office, 1954), p. 13 (Article XIV, Paragraph 3[b]).

A disadvantage that is often cited in connection with quotas is that they prevent the operation of competitive price adjustments, whereas tariffs do not. The argument runs somewhat as follows: A tariff will affect the price of goods to a certain extent, but the most it is likely to affect the price is the amount of the tariff itself—or slightly more, depending on markup practices. If the original price of the goods was $3, a tariff of $3 would hardly raise the price to a figure much higher than $6. The volume of trade would be influenced, to be sure, but competitive forces should operate to keep the profit rate of those engaged in the trade much the same. This would be the case because some traders would get out of that particular line of activity if the profit rate tended to drop below the rate prevailing in other lines of business. But with quotas, the situation is fundamentally different—or at least so runs the argument. For example, during World War II, Colombia and the United States had agreed that Colombia should receive a certain limited number of passenger cars each year. This small quota was divided among a few importers who were in a position to resell the cars at fantastic markups. A type of monopoly profit which has come to be called "quota profit" emerges from such situations. Reasonable price and profit adjustments could not emerge because of the element of monopoly power (restriction on freedom of entry) that the granting of the quota established.

But such quota profits need not be a by-product of the operation of quotas. If the resale markups were carefully controlled by the government, the quota profits could be eliminated; and the situation then would be substantially the same as under any effective system of price control, where ration coupons or some other device serve to protect the consumers. Exorbitant profits appear only in situations where they are condoned; but they have been condoned in many cases, especially in countries with weak, ineffective, or corrupt police forces. When quotas are combined with regulation of resale prices, prices can be kept low to consumers. This is a distinct advantage of the quota over the tariff. But it is frequently overlooked by those who defend the tariff on the grounds that it allows the price mechanism to continue to operate freely—albeit in a higher frame of reference.[4]

Before leaving the subject of quota mechanics, an odd phenomenon, the *tariff quota,* should be briefly mentioned. Tariff quotas provide for the entry of a specified quantity of a product at a reduced rate; imports in excess of the specified quantity are then subjected to a higher rate of duty. This type of arrangement currently applies to certain

[4] Another possible device for eliminating quota profits would be to auction the rights to a quota. The government, rather than the quota recipient, would receive the quota profits in that case. But the prices to consumers would be high—the result in that respect being comparable to the situation under a tariff.

agricultural commodities and to that important and controversial commodity: petroleum.

United States Policy Toward Quotas

The United States customarily has denounced the use of quotas by other countries.[5] Political scientists and skeptics of one sort or another have been known to criticize the United States government on the ground that it has no foreign policy. But in fact the United States does have and has had a consistent foreign policy for many years: It has favored tariffs and denounced the use of quotas and other quantitative controls in international trade. And the State Department has been especially consistent in denouncing such quotas as involve discrimination on a national-origin basis.[6] However, since consistency is not required, the United States is not debarred from making use of quotas itself.[7] And the United States has used far-reaching, important, and effective import quota restrictions in connection with a wide range of agricultural commodities from wheat, to almonds, to textiles. The quota on sugar imports, which has been effective since the early 1930's, has been written into special legislation—the Sugar Act of 1948. The Secretary of Agriculture sets absolute quotas on the amount of sugar that can come in from each of the sugar-supplying countries, and does so each year. Thus the sugar quota is on a national-origin basis.

In the mid-1950's, in fact, quotas loom as the most significant United States barrier to imports. Maybe things do change after all, for it would appear that the United States tariff wall is less of a barrier today than it once was. It still has a tremendous nuisance value in keeping goods out and it is still very high in spots; but it is not, on the average, particularly high. Increasingly, the United States is using quotas to establish the restrictions that matter. If agricultural im-

[5] Acting Secretary of State Castle instructed the United States Ambassador in France (January 23, 1932) as follows: ". . . this Government is definitely opposed to any system of quotas, a fact you might well impress upon the French . . ." United States, Department of State, *Foreign Relations . . . , 1932.* Vol. II, p. 197.

[6] The position taken in connection with the discrimination issue would be equally relevant in connection with the tariff discussion of Chapter 11 or the discussion of foreign-exchange controls in Chapter 20.

[7] The demand for consistency, in a basic sense, is unfair to the democratic process. A type of consistency can be expected from a dictatorship, perpetuating itself in power for many years, which cannot be expected in a democracy as parties come and go in power and as politicians come and go in influence. It is not fair to call upon a country to have a consistent, positive foreign policy unless the critic thinks it is proper for the country to be pursuing some ulterior ends abroad. Somehow those who demand a consistent foreign policy have never seemed to think that "minding one's own business" or co-operating with one's neighbors in the interest of running a viable world would qualify as a foreign policy.

ports threaten the domestic price-support program, they are reduced by quota restrictions. This has been done frequently and drastically in recent years under Section 22 of the Agricultural Adjustment Act, which provides that agricultural imports shall be limited by quota restrictions if they are coming in "under such conditions and in such quantities as to render or tend to render ineffective, or materially interfere with, any program or operation undertaken under . . ." the price-support and production and marketing control programs of the Department of Agriculture.[8] Administratively, Section 22 is handled much like the peril-point and escape-clause provisions. If the Secretary of Agriculture believes a relevant situation is in prospect, an investigation and recommendations are made by the Tariff Commission. If the President concurs, he places the import quota restrictions in operation.

The agricultural program in the United States has the effect of making United States agricultural prices higher than world prices.[9] It is only natural, given this price discrepancy, that foreign agricultural products tend to flow to the United States. And this tendency is independent of whether or not the American farmer is more efficient than his foreign competitor. Of course, it is true that agricultural imports cannot be permitted in unlimited amounts—given the present support program. The trouble is, however, with the basic parity-price approach embodied in the present agricultural program. (A possible alternative program is suggested in Chapter 13.)

In recent years the President has frequently concurred in the temporary application of quotas to agricultural imports. Foreigners have cited these quotas as tangible evidence that the United States is not sincere in its ostensible program of trade-barrier reduction. In 1954 the *New York Times* reported on certain new obstacles placed in the way of almond imports from Italy in consequence of the complaint of some California producers. The almonds were raised in a district around Bari, which is both very poor and subject to increasing Communist influence. While the United States was trying to explain this action to the government of Italy, the Soviet Union gained a psychological victory by stepping in and buying up the almond crop.[10]

Quota restrictions under Section 22 are placed in effect on short notice when a problem arises as a result of the crop situation. Then, when the crop that caused the trouble has been handled, the quotas are likely to be lifted. Thus important quotas imposed on oats, barley, and edible tree nuts (e.g., almonds) were later removed. At any

---

[8] *United States Code,* 1952 Edition, Title 7, par. 624.

[9] According to the argument which will be developed in Chapter 15, this is undesirable.

[10] *New York Times,* October 3, 1954, p. 9.

given time, the quotas in effect will apply to a relatively small proportion of ordinary United States agricultural imports. But they stand as a constant threat to foreigners who might engage in energetic marketing in the United States.

The petroleum industry also has been protected by quota provisions. As was mentioned above, a tariff quota arrangement has been applied by law to petroleum. Currently there is much debate as to whether the Federal government should restrict oil imports by much more restrictive quotas or whether the same result should be obtained by private arrangement among the oil companies concerned.[11] A system of voluntary quotas which was established by the governmental Office of Defense Mobilization under the aegis of Arthur Flemming is now policed by the oil companies. Certain of the independent oil companies operating exclusively within the United States, which do not entirely trust the major oil companies (thirteen importing companies) in these matters, have complained that this savors of violation of the Sherman Antitrust Act. A. E. Herrmann of Amarillo, president of the Texas Independent Producers and Royalty Owners Association, has declared that official designation of the thirteen could result in "rendering them . . . invulnerable to prosecution for engaging in collaborative practices which have the effect of lessening competition. . . ."[12]

The United States textile industry has been complaining about textile imports—especially from Japan—much as the oil industry has been complaining about oil imports. There is this difference: United States companies are producing the foreign oil but not the foreign textiles. One might expect, therefore, that the complaint of the United States textile companies would be correspondingly more vociferous. And it has been energetic. In this case a "solution" somewhat different from that used in the oil case has been worked out. In order to avoid drastic controls by the United States, the Japanese have agreed to quota limitation on various of their textile exports. Needless to say, the United States textile industry is not entirely happy with this arrangement.[13]

European Policy

Most European countries have made extensive use of quotas since the early 1930's. However, quite recently there seems to have been a marked change in the attitude of the European countries themselves toward quota restrictions. The Organisation for European Economic Co-operation (the organization of western European governments that was set up to implement the Marshall Plan) has been encouraging the

[11] *New York Times,* March 12, 1955, p. 8.
[12] *Houston Post,* August 19, 1956, sec. 6, p. 5.
[13] *New York Times,* December 22, 1955, p. 35.

various governments to reduce their quota restrictions. And it has been doing this with considerable success.[14] The OEEC's chief complaint has been that the French have been lagging behind the sixteen other member countries in reducing the incidence of quotas.[15]

LICENSING

Licensing is a procedure by which governments may assign shares of quotas to individuals and firms. Licenses may also be used to determine whether goods are imported or exported in a setting where no quota has been established. It is likely to be the central bank or some special agency (e.g., the Bureau of Foreign Commerce in the Department of Commerce of the United States) that actually issues the licenses. And it is possession of the license which assures the entry of the goods into a country—or their exit.

Licensing may represent something more than merely the implementation of quotas. A government may control its trade by licensing even though it has no quota system. In some instances, decisions are made on the basis of the type of goods, the identity of the nation to which the goods are going, or the identity of the would-be licensee, by administrators operating under rules without regard to quotas. But as a rule the quota provides the criterion and the licensing system merely implements the quotas. The United States now has in operation an extensive export licensing system, the primary purpose of which is to keep certain strategic goods from finding their way to Russia and other strategic goods in short supply from leaving the United States. The *New York Times* recently reported that a shipment of five-hundred Chevrolets had been authorized by the Bureau of Foreign Commerce to Bulgaria and said that this was the first shipment of manufactured goods, of any size, to pass the screening of the Bureau in almost six years.[16] On the other hand, Willys-Overland Export Corporation was put on six-month probation by the Bureau of Foreign Commerce in June of 1955 (the same month that the Chevrolet episode occurred) for sending a hundred jeeps to Lebanon which then found their way to Rumania.

Most countries still have import licensing systems applicable to most of their imports. *Foreign Commerce Weekly* carries periodic summaries

[14] Organisation for European Economic Co-operation, *Liberalisation of Europe's Dollar Trade* (Paris, 1956).

[15] *New York Times,* November 16, 1955, p. 51.

[16] See United States, Bureau of Foreign Commerce, *How to Apply for an Export License and How to Use It,* Business Information Service, World Trade Series, No. 565 (Washington, 1954); *New York Times,* June 17, 1955, p. 3.

of these foreign import licensing arrangements as they apply to goods shipped from the United States.

International trade is further complicated by the frequency with which licensing rules such as these are changed. The foreign trader has a difficult job keeping up to date. The mere fact of the tremendous range of complications involved in all this is an "extra" deterrent to trade. But since deterring trade seems to be the desired goal, the procedure may be said to be serving its purpose.

Licenses are frequently required in connection with both imports and exports. However, on the whole, they would seem to operate in a far more restrictive way on imports than on exports. But the same point could well be made about the quota systems in general—they restrict imports more than exports.

EMBARGOES

An embargo could be termed the extreme form of the quota. Instead of limiting the amount of something that can come in, all entry is prohibited, with the great advantage that the quota allocation problem is avoided.

A well-known embargo has been that applied by the United States to chilled and frozen beef coming from countries where the foot-and-mouth disease is found. Argentina is one such country; more recently Mexico has been another. But the complete list of countries included in the foot-and-mouth embargo is far longer than the list of countries from which chilled and frozen beef can be imported into the United States. This is an example of an embargo that is ostensibly imposed for health reasons, but it has frequently been alleged that the ostensible reason is not the real one. This being a fighting issue in the cattle country, perhaps the less said about it the better.

However, it may not be amiss to cite the position which the United States took in the 1880's and '90's when Germany and France, alleging the presence of trichinae in American hogs, forbade their import:

> In a dispatch of November 20, 1897, Mr. Sherman, Secretary of State, requested Mr. White, the American Minister at Berlin, to make representations on the subject to the German Government, in part, as follows:
>
> ". . . You will bring the foregoing to the attention of the Minister for Foreign Affairs, at the same time insisting that—
>
> "1. American pork as sent to Germany is practically harmless and certainly far less dangerous than inspected German pork, as is shown by the medical records of Germany.

"2. The discovery of trichinae in a few pieces of our pork when reëxamined abroad cannot be accepted as evidence of inefficient inspection. The numerous cases of trichinosis in man which have occurred in Germany from eating pork inspected there shows the impossibility of discovering all trichinous meat by the first inspection.

"3. As American pork is carefully inspected here before shipment, it is unjust to our shippers to require them to pay the expense of a second inspection after it arrives in Germany. This expense, together with the damage from unpacking, exposure, and hastily repacking, is a great obstacle to this important branch of our commerce with the German nation." [17]

Another such embargo, which is imposed by the United States for health reasons, has prohibited the import of avocados from Mexico unless the stone or pit has been removed. Any housewife will know how well avocados keep without the pit.

Yet another example of an embargo was that imposed by Mexico, in the late 1940's, on automobile imports from the United States. The reason for the embargo was that the Mexican government thought that her declining supply of foreign exchange could be better spent for machinery or food necessities than for automobiles and other durable consumer goods. Thus the embargo was avowedly intended to discriminate as among commodities, and intended to do a more thorough job of it than the tariff or the quota would do. There is much to be said for the embargo in such a situation. It is even more forthright and honest as a control device than the quota, but needs to be used with judgment and discretion; if used unwisely, the result may be monopoly profits to domestic producers rather than expanding domestic production. (The reader should beware; anything complimentary said about quotas and embargoes in this context involves the sort of situation Meade has described as a choice among the "second-bests.")

The very adverse results that may follow the use of embargoes are indicated by a bit of verse, circa 1808:

> Our ships all in motion once whitened the ocean,
> They sailed and returned with a cargo;
> Now doomed to decay, they have fallen a prey
> To Jefferson, worms, and embargo. [18]

[17] Ellery C. Stowell and Henry F. Munro, *International Cases,* Vol. I, *Peace,* (Boston: Houghton Mifflin, 1916), pp. 294–5. The selection from *International Cases* by Ellery C. Stowell and Henry F. Munro is used by permission of, and arrangement with the publishers, Houghton Mifflin Company.

[18] Popular verse of early nineteenth century quoted in Harry James Carman and Samuel McKee, Jr., *A History of the United States* (Boston: Heath, 1931), I, 490.

MISCELLANEOUS RESTRICTIONS

The list of devices for restricting trade, and especially imports, is only begun with the enumeration of tariffs, quotas, licenses, and embargoes. Part of the trick in connection with measures of this sort is to think of a new and different "angle." And a tremendous amount of ingenuity is constantly devoted to this end. The aspiring young junior executive who thinks of such an angle—which his corporation can "sell" to the government—may find himself a senior executive before you can say seniority. All that will be attempted in this section, however, is the mention of one or two of the more notorious "angles" that have been worked.

The Buy-American Act

This law was peddled to Congress by the manufacturers of electrical equipment under the aegis of Senator Hiram Johnson in February, 1933, while most of the country was thinking about other things. At that time Senator Johnson had this to say on the floor of Congress: [19]

> . . . it would be unwise and it would be ungenerous of the Government of the United States to permit its taxpayers' money [no indication that what the taxpayers chiefly want is their money's worth] to be awarded by a contract with foreign bidders for machinery, and so forth, manufactured abroad for use in that great undertaking [turbines for Boulder dam].
>
> They [the domestic manufacturers of turbines, etc.] did not object if there was great disproportion between the bids; but if their bid was 1 percent or 2 percent or 3 percent or 5 percent higher than the bids from abroad, they thought that it was an outrageous thing that their money that they put up in taxes with the Government of the United States should be paid out upon a governmental project—paid out in the amount of 6 millions, or thereabouts to any foreign country.

Since all the electrical equipment manufacturers were asking for was a fair 5 per cent advantage, Congress naturally passed a law providing that in United States government purchases, preference be given to domestic firms over foreign bidders; and government procurement officers, in implementing the law, generally established that the differential to be applied in favor of domestic products should be 25 per cent,

[19] United States Congress, Senate, Committee on Banking and Currency (Hearings), *Study of the Export-Import Bank and the World Bank* (Washington: Government Printing Office, 1954), Part I, p. 577.

in addition to the advantages that tariffs and transport costs give him.[20]

In application all of this may become rather confusing, or at least it confounded the London *Economist*.[21]

> "We care nothing for mere rhetoric" the President said in his speech before the American Society of Newspaper Editors last week when he demanded that recent Russian gestures should be "attested by deeds." The English Electric Company probably added a fervent "Amen" as it prepared to bid again for the contract for transformers and generators for the Chief Joseph Dam, a power project being developed by the Army Engineers in the State of Washington. At the first attempt, the company's tender had been nearly $1 million below that of the nearest American firm. This case is important not only because it involves more than $5 million worth of business for a foreign industry but also because it provided the first practical test of the sincerity of the new Administration's professed belief that the United States should, as General Eisenhower put it during the campaign last autumn, "seek out opportunities to increase imports of commodities, goods and services which will improve our economy and help make our allies self-supporting." The Administration came out of the test with drooping colours.
>
> Over the last few years those English firms which have been trying to sell electrical equipment in the United States have had some unnerving experiences but they have, until now, had the help of the federal government in their efforts to get fair treatment, and where the government itself had jurisdiction there has been no cause for complaint. Both the Bureau of Reclamation and the Department of the Army have behaved with great fairness, recognising the existence of the Buy American Act, which requires government purchasers to give preference to domestic producers, but interpreting it with reasonable flexibility. In the case of the Chief Joseph Dam, however, the Secretary of the Army, not being willing to take the decision himself, passed it up to the Secretary of Defense. Mr. Charles Wilson, whose ideas on trade policy seem to differ somewhat from those of his late rival in the motor car industry, Mr. Henry Ford, took the problem to a Cabinet meeting.
>
> In spite of all the efforts of General Bedell Smith, the Under Secretary of State, and Mr. Harold Stassen, the Mutual Security Director, Mr. Wilson's arguments won and the English Elec-

[20] *Ibid.*, pp. 574–97.

[21] *Economist*, April 25, 1953, p. 219. Reprinted with the kind permission of the publisher.

tric Company did not get the contract. It was not given at once, however, to the lowest American bidder, as it should have been if the Buy American Act, which is now being quoted in defence of the decision, really made it impossible to award it to a foreign firm. Instead, all the tenders were rejected and everyone is to have the chance to bid again—with the American firms now knowing the figure which they must approach next time.

All this could be dismissed as but one more example of a familiar commercial patriotism if it were not that the President himself made the decision in favour of Mr. Wilson and against Mr. Stassen and General Bedell Smith. The *Washington Post* has suggested that Mr. Eisenhower was unaware that, under the Buy American Act, he had discretionary powers and that he believed that he had no alternative. If so, it is surprising that he was not told by somebody present at the Cabinet meeting of April 3rd, or by one of his staff, that he was not merely a helpless instrument of Mr. Roosevelt's first Congress.

No less a person than Henry Ford II has commented: "Recently for example, a foreign manufacturer, after paying a 45-percent import duty, underbid two American firms by substantially more than 25-percent on an Army contract. In subsequent bids, the Americans, oddly enough, were able to come down by almost 50-percent. That brought them just within the 25-percent Buy American margin. The Army ultimately split the purchase between the American and foreign firms, saving you and me about half of the potential tax costs plus the import duties paid by the foreign firm—but appeasing at the same time the domestic producers." [22]

In defense of the United States government, it should be said that the 25 per cent preference has recently been cut back. In December of 1954, President Eisenhower reduced the degree of preference which United States firms enjoy to 6–12 per cent. Greater preference was to be continued for domestic bidders prepared to produce the goods in question in areas of "substantial unemployment." [23]

The Food, Drug, and Cosmetic Act
This law also acts in a restrictive manner: [24]

Certain requirements in the Food and Drug Act are so rigorous that foreign producers have difficulty in complying. The

[22] Henry Ford II, *The Free World Can't Trade on a One Way Street* (Detroit: Ford Motor Company, 1953), p. 17.

[23] *New York Times,* November 15, 1955, p. 45.

[24] United States, Commission on Foreign Economic Policy, *Staff Papers* (Washington, 1954), p. 321.

requirement that confectionery contain no alcohol in excess of
0.5 percent, which must be derived solely from flavoring ex-
tracts, creates difficulties for regional food specialities. This requirement prevents the import of liqueur chocolates. . . .

The Act classes a food, drug, or cosmetic as adulterated if
it contains a coal-tar color other than one listed as safe for
such use by the Food and Drug Administration, and the dye
in a particular import must be from a batch that has been certi-
fied in accordance with regulations provided by law. As a result, foreign producers have often been forced to use colors
made in the United States since it is impracticable to send
samples from each batch of coal-tar products for testing in the
United States.

Administrative Red Tape

Worst is the red tape that foreign producers must disentangle. For
example, a real administrative headache exists in connection with the
handling of duty-free imports:[25]

A large number of imports are duty free, and in the majority
of cases Customs officers can readily determine that the merchandise being inspected falls within this category. Examples of
these are: . . . crude rubber, coffee, and cocoa beans. Nevertheless, these imports like dutiable imports, must go through
the formal entry procedure involving the filing of numerous
documents, the withholding of a portion of the goods for inspection, and other steps applicable to dutiable goods. Since
the statistical requirements for data on imports could be handled by other means there is no advantage to having these
goods delayed by this requirement.

Another aspect of the importer's difficulties arises from the possibility that domestic producer-competitors may cause him trouble. The
Public Advisory Board for Mutual Security commented: "Importers
also face the risk of being brought into court by an American producer
or trader who contends that the Customs Service's valuation or classification of the importer's goods is improper."[26] In commenting on this
possibility the Board volunteered the opinion that: "Domestic manufacturers have an interest in the administration of the Tariff Act, but
an importer should not have to defend a Government administrative
action at his own expense."

The Public Advisory Board for Mutual Security in its report, *A Trade*

[25] United States, Commission on Foreign Economic Policy, *Staff Papers,* p. 327.
[26] United States, Public Advisory Board . . . , *A Trade and Tariff Policy* . . . ,
p. 51.

and Tariff Policy in the National Interest, dealt rather harshly with the procedures used in collecting United States customs duties: "Present customs procedures are unfair, time consuming, and uncertain." But the blame does not lie so much with the customs collectors as with the laws. "Customs laws are drawn up in such highly specific form that law-enforcement agencies have relatively little discretion." "The pitfalls of importing are so many and the penalties for law infringement so severe that the bulk of trade through customs is now handled by a group of experts on procedure known as customs brokers, who are licensed by the Treasury Department."

To continue with some selected quotations from Chapter VII of the report of the Public Advisory Board for Mutual Security: "The most serious defect of customs administration is the time required for businessmen to learn their first customs liabilities after the goods have been imported into the United States. These delays frequently stretch out into years. . . . Long after an importer has sold his goods the first customs appraisal or classification may assess duties so high as to wipe out profits altogether." The 640,000 entries of dutiable goods included in the backlog of unliquidated customs entries were about equal to one year's entries of dutiable goods.

But that is not all: [27]

> A bolt of cheesecloth, if it is woven so that some cross strands are missing at intervals to indicate where the cloth is to be cut into squares is "braid."

And the tariff rate on braid is higher than the tariff rate on cheesecloth.

The importer has more troubles. The marking requirements are sometimes difficult to observe. According to the Public Advisory Board: [28] "The special marking provisions for surgical and dental instruments, cutlery, scissors, and similar products state that each article 'shall have the name of the maker or purchaser and beneath the same the name of the country of origin die sunk conspicuously and indelibly.' . . . On some goods, like surgical needles and certain surgical instruments, compliance with these restrictions is physically impossible."

On this point Willard L. Thorp, a former Assistant Secretary of State, said: "With safety razor blades, the process of die-stamping required to meet this requirement breaks the blades, therefore none come in. . . . And sterling silver does not gain in beauty by the process of putting the necessary words on each item in a table setting." [29]

[27] United States, Commission on Foreign Economic Policy, *Staff Papers,* p. 335.
[28] United States, Public Advisory Board . . . , *A Trade and Tariff Policy . . . ,* p. 52.
[29] Willard L. Thorp, "The Tariff and the Consumer," *Consumer Reports* (June, 1953), p. 269. It should be confessed that in 1953 the requirement that surgical

Is it not strange that the domestic producer groups who are among the most vociferous opponents of overdone-governmental-bureaucratic-controls should be responsible for these greatly overdone administrative controls which impede imports? But then red tape is a neat inconspicuous means of supplementing the protection of the tariff itself.[30]

On the railroad train coming up from Mexico City to San Antonio it is customary for the passengers to get together and complain about how inefficient the Mexicans are, how late the train is, and how likely it is to have a wreck.[31] Then the complaints are loudly renewed in connection with the delays going through the Mexican customs at Nuevo Laredo, if the customs officials did not go through the train between Monterrey and Nuevo Laredo. All of this makes it a little hard for the die-hard defender of American efficiency to understand why, upon occasion, the train sits just as long, if not longer, in the station at Laredo after it gets across the river. The following statement from the *Staff Papers* of the Randall Commission may help to explain how this can happen:[32]

> The law specifies that overtime shall be paid customs officials at the rate of one-half day's pay for every two hours which the official must spend on duty outside of statutory working hours of 8 a.m. to 5 p.m. If an official is called back for duty after leaving work, overtime is calculated from the end of the work day to the time the official is freed. The importer responsible for causing the overtime must bear the cost of the overtime pay. Night landings of international aircraft, for example, would regularly involve such overtime pay.

"Night landings" by the passenger train in Laredo are perhaps not so likely to result in such overtime pay if the railroad company prefers to wait until 8 a.m.

BILATERAL TRADE TREATIES

During the 1930's the world, or much of the world, went on a bilateral balancing spree. Governments had given primacy to the idea of controlling their trade by unilateral decision. But when a country planned to control trade in an effort to extract the maximum short-run

---

instruments be die-stamped was removed, probably because of the publicity this particular restriction had recently received.

[30] See also Percy W. Bidwell, *The Invisible Tariff* (New York: Council on Foreign Relations, 1939).

[31] Parenthetically I may say that the only wreck I have actually been in on this train was between Laredo and San Antonio in the U.S.A.

[32] United States, Commission on Foreign Economic Policy, *Staff Papers*, p. 326.

advantages, unilateral pressuring and bilateral arguing were likely developments. Since the international agreements that resulted were bilateral, they tended to force trade into a bilateral pattern.[33] A country would buy only from a country that would buy from it and in approximately equal amount.

In connection with the bilateral treaties there was a tendency to balance the trade closer to the lower trade figure. In other words, if Country A had been shipping $100,000,000 of goods to Country B each year, before a treaty was signed, and had been buying $150,000,000 from B, the trade was likely to be balanced at a figure below $125,-000,000—*cuts being easier to plan than increases*. It would be easier to cut A's purchases to $120,000,000 than to raise B's to $130,000,000, as any realist will appreciate. Such will almost certainly be the result of bilateral arrangements. For the result to be anything other than this, B's citizens would probably have to take goods they did not particularly want or at any rate did not want from that source. If buyers are forced to turn to relatively unattractive sources, they are almost certain to buy less.

It has frequently been observed that the prices set on certain commodities in bilateral trade agreements are higher than the prevailing free market prices. One nation gets a higher price for its exports than it could get in a free market; and in exchange it pays a higher price for its imports. Whether there is any real net gain to any nation as a result of this process is doubtful. The result merely seems to be increased non-comparability of prices in general and greater difficulty in making intelligent decisions. Data becomes harder and harder to handle and intelligently analyze as the world is differentiated more and more into economically distinct units. It is no idle and unsubstantiated observation that the commercial world of the mid-twentieth century is a far less homogeneous one than was the commercial world of the mid-nineteenth.

The trend toward bilateral balancing was a major factor in the decline in total world trade and total world real income in the 1930's. Where there is bilateral balancing, trade is almost certain to be balanced, or roughly balanced, at a total quantity of exports and imports that will be smaller than that prevailing when trade was on a multilateral basis. Fundamentally, this results from the fact that "range of choice" is limited.

In almost all the bilateral treaties of the 1930's there was more to be considered than simply the balancing of goods trade. The resump-

[33] Agreements of this sort should be clearly distinguished from the reciprocal trade agreements sort of international agreement advocated by the United States during this period. The generalization of the concessions made in such agreements—via the most-favored-nation clause—made for a significant difference.

tion of payment on defaulted loans was also frequently at issue. And to the extent that such international payments were taken into account, the goods trade was not exactly balanced. However, even in such cases, there tended to be a reduction of total trade as artificial efforts were made to balance goods movement on the one hand with goods movement plus a certain amount of loan repayment on the other. Chapter 20 contains a somewhat more realistic description of the mechanics of these arrangements—in that chapter the implications of the financing arrangements are taken into account.

EFFECT OF TARIFFS AND OF QUANTITATIVE CONTROLS ON THE GAIN FROM TRADE

Non-Discriminatory Measures

Tariffs, presumably, may improve a country's unit (net barter) terms of trade (the foreign exporter being almost certainly forced to sell to the importer in the tariff-imposing country at a price which is somewhat lower—before the tariff is added—than the price would be in the absence of a tariff). But tariffs also can be presumed to reduce the world gain from trade because of their detrimental effect on the total amount of production (and trade) and the consequent loss of some of the advantage of geographical specialization. The analysis of the effect of tariffs would not be complete, without considering the identity of the payer of the tariff and the use which the government makes of the tariff receipts. It may use them to subsidize its own inefficient domestic producers, as the United States does with the proceeds from the import excise tax on sugar.

It is not entirely clear whether quotas, licensing, and embargoes will move the terms of trade in favor of the country which imposes them. They tend to curtail the producers' market and thus might constrain him to lower prices. But there are some complicating possibilities. If the foreign exporter rather than the domestic importer were the one actually granted the quota, he would obtain the quota profit. His gain from such trade as occurred would be large, implying an adverse rather than a favorable movement in the terms of trade. But this is, seemingly, an exceptional case. Generally quotas are granted to importers; by placing the importer in a better bargaining position vis-à-vis the exporter, they tend to contract imports and to reduce the price paid to foreigners. The quota profit then goes to the importer, or is prevented by resale price controls, or is absorbed by the government via auction sales.

But even if the generalization is justified that quantitative restrictions, like tariffs, will improve the unit terms of trade, the desirability of the result is not established—even in terms of the selfish interest of the country imposing the restrictions. Domestic consumers pay higher prices and get less goods in all. This is true unless the restriction corresponds with the criteria developed in Chapter 6.[34] There is little reason to believe, however, that the trade restrictions of the last twenty-five years have been thought out in those terms. And there is every reason to believe that they have had a general inhibitory effect on economic development and a marked effect in lowering the level of living of the generation which imposed them. That the unhappy state of world political relations is part of the same problem, there can be no doubt. This generation is making a mess of running the world on more than one front.

Discrimination

Almost inevitably the use of quotas, licenses, and bilateral trade treaties (as well as tariffs) involves an element of discrimination. Therefore, it becomes pertinent to inquire into the theoretical impact of discrimination.

Discrimination involves some measure of favoritism in the treatment of (a) some type of goods, (b) some individual, or (c) some country by comparison with some other type of goods, individual, or country. One type of goods may pay a lower tariff than another. One individual may be assigned a large quota and another be granted none. Goods coming from one country may be embargoed and those coming from another country may be admitted.

Granted that in many cases discrimination is motivated by spite and truculence, there still remains the question whether it may serve a constructive and useful purpose. May discrimination contribute to raising the level of living? Or, more specifically, are there situations where there may be more total trade under conditions of discrimination than under conditions of non-discrimination?

In Chapter 6 the position was taken that there are various situations in which it is desirable to deviate from the competitive norm. The encouragement of growth, allowance for external and internal economies and diseconomies, allowance for income distribution—any or all of these circumstances may make interference with free market forces desirable.

But on the whole discrimination seems deserving of condemnation, in spite of the possibility that in certain comparable cases more total

---

[34] In Chapter 6 it was argued that some deviation from the free trade position may become desirable because of the circumstances involved in structural change, because of monopoly power, because of external economies and diseconomies, because of income distribution considerations, because of second-best conditions, or because of government fiscal policy.

trade could result from discrimination than from non-discrimination.[35]

Crude discrimination, especially discrimination as between nations, is such a troublemaker in the political area that it should be avoided if there is any reasonable alternative. One of the worst things we, as members of the human race, do to each other is to seek out reasons for discriminating against one another.

Our particular concern at present is with discrimination as among nations in the international trade area. Society as a whole should evaluate and identify non-justifiable discrimination. Neither nations nor individuals can be trusted to discipline themselves in such matters. And nations in some respects seem to be even more helpless victims of their own prejudices than are individuals.

The previous two paragraphs represent a devious approach to the conclusions that multilateral trade, rather than bilateral balancing, is desirable and that nations should not discriminate on the basis of national origin either as to the source of goods or as to their destination (except on the basis of national defense considerations in troubled times, when national defense considerations will have a priority, anyway). A network of multilateral trade is better than bilateral balancing if the world wants to obtain the maximum amount of goods from geographical specialization. The existence of such a network also contributes greatly to freedom of action.

The general conclusion would still seem to be justified that bilateral balancing and discrimination as to source tend to reduce total trade so that the people of the world as a whole get less benefit in terms of total goods than would result if the resources were used more effectively and distributed more freely.

But there has also been a lot of discrimination on the basis of national origin in this old world (New World, too). And the United States has been one of the chief objects of such discrimination. Imports from the United States have been restricted for various alleged reasons: because the country doing the restricting had an unfavorable trade balance with the United States, because it was plagued with a "dollar shortage," because an export balance had to be developed to pay the

---

[35] Ragnar Frisch has demonstrated that there is likely to be more total trade if a disequilibrium situation is dealt with by cutbacks that discriminate against certain nations rather than by cutting back trade with all countries in the same proportion. The latter procedure would involve some such line of action as using base-year quotas to determine the share of the market each country should have and cutting back accordingly. Base-year quotas and proportional cutbacks will be discussed and condemned in connection with the description of raw commodity control schemes in Chapter 13. It is not surprising that a discriminatory procedure can be found which would reduce trade less than such a proportional cutback approach. See Ragnar Frisch, "On the Need for Forecasting a Multilateral Balance of Payments," *American Economic Review,* XXXVII (September, 1947), pp. 535–51.

debts owed to Uncle Sam. There is an element of justification and an element of spuriousness in all these alleged reasons. None alone is necessary and sufficient motivation for discrimination against the United States. But when you add dislike for and jealousy of the power of Uncle Sam to these other factors, it is not difficult to see why discrimination against the United States is an attractive and popular method for dealing with *any* problem.

European countries generally have been less categorical than the United States in their endorsement of non-discrimination as a matter of sweeping principle. But they have frequently agreed—perhaps as frequently as the United States—that non-discrimination should be the formula used in working out the solution of a current problem in international relations. For example, the code of the European Payments Union provides for non-discrimination (except in connection with customs unions and dumping); [36] and the 1955 revision of the GATT agreement calls, in Article I, for the "elimination of discriminatory treatment in international commerce."

To close this chapter on a more affirmative note: Emphasis on the general expansion of trade and on the most extensive interchange possible will make far more of a contribution to popular welfare than any amount of discrimination in an effort to improve matters.

[36] Frederic Boyer and J. P. Sallé, "The Liberalization of Intra-European Trade in the Framework of OEEC," *International Monetary Fund Staff Papers*, IV, (February, 1955), p. 188.

Chapter 13

SUBSIDIES, DUMPING, CARTELS, AND RAW COMMODITY CONTROL SCHEMES

✶ ✶ ✶

United States governmental subsidies to agricultural exports are a major factor in making agricultural prices in the United States higher than world prices.

Private enterprise frequently finds it profitable to dump commodities abroad, especially when it has unused plant capacity. The dumping then is profitable even though it only covers additional variable cost.

Cartels involve international agreements, generally among private firms, on such matters as pricing, division of the market area, etc.

Raw commodity control schemes also involve an effort to control prices, etc.; but they are generally intergovernmental.

Agricultural and raw commodity prices have shown a tendency to fluctuate more violently than prices in general and prices of manufactured goods in particular.

The tendency since World War II, as evidenced in the International Trade Organization articles of agreement and related documents, has been to frown on cartels but, at least under certain circumstances, to endorse raw commodity control schemes.

✶ ✶ ✶

QUOTAS, licenses, and embargoes involve rules that determine, with the backing of the police power of the government, whether goods may cross an international frontier. Subsidies, dumping, cartels, and raw commodity control arrangements exert a somewhat less direct influence on international trade. Monetary payments, price juggling, production control, and such pressures—rather than police power—supply the leverage in these situations.

SUBSIDIES (GOVERNMENT)

Exports

Subsidies, for purposes of the present discussion, involve the direct payment of money by the government to the exporter or importer. For example, the government might establish a subsidy of one cent per pound on cotton exported and make the payment to the exporter. To the extent that it is more common for the subsidy to be paid in connection with exports than in connection with imports, the use of subsidies tends to increase exports relative to imports and therefore to have the same ostensible (if not effective) influence on the balance of trade as most other trade restrictions.

AGRICULTURE: The payment of such a bounty to the exporter by the government enables the exporter to sell abroad at a price lower than the domestic price. This may make it possible for him to compete profitably in the foreign market, whereas he could not otherwise have done so. And such is the purpose of the subsidy. In recent years the United States government, at least sporadically, has subsidized the export of many things, including wheat, wheat flour, raisins (sultanas), prunes, apples, oranges, pears, and cotton. For example, wheat export subsidies, set by the Department of Agriculture on February 16, 1954, ran 51¢ (West Coast), 61¢ or 63¢ depending on destination (Gulf Coast), and 63¢ (East Coast), per bushel.[1]

The procedure may be slightly more indirect. The government may buy some commodity from a domestic producer at a fairly high support price—or acquire title as the result of a lending operation which has much the same effect. The government may then turn around and sell to foreigners at a lower price. The domestic producer is effectively subsidized by this operation. Butter was sold by the United States government to British buyers under such conditions in 1954. In commenting on this transaction, the *New York Times* said:[2]

> The sale to Britain, which was about 41 cents a pound, will permit the British housewife to buy butter at about two-thirds of the price the American consumer pays. The retail price of butter in this country is now about 67 cents a pound.

Or, to cite another example, in the first half of 1956 the Commodity Credit Corporation (United States government) sold about 1,800,000 bales of cotton for export at prices as much as 10 cents a pound below the domestic price. With cotton at 35 cents a pound and with 500 pounds to a bale, it does not take much imagination to sense that

[1] *New York Times,* February 17, 1954, p. 41.
[2] *New York Times,* July 8, 1954, p. 31.

the world price of cotton is going to be affected by such operations.

The United States needs to reconsider its whole agricultural support system, if for no other reason than the disruption of world marketing arrangements being caused by the United States two-price, export-subsidy (dumping) policy. Yet a more extensive use of two-price, export dumping of agricultural commodities is an important part of the program of the Department of Agriculture under Ezra Taft Benson.[3]

Foreign governments are worried about this trend. It not only disrupts their efforts at intelligent planning, but also creates uncertainty in the free commodity markets of the world.

To quote O. B. Jesness, head of the Department of Agricultural Economics at the University of Minnesota:[4]

> While two-price proposals may be workable to a moderate degree under certain circumstances, it is well for Americans to recognize that they constitute dumping as defined in international trade and consequently are subject to the controls and counteractions with which nations rather generally have equipped themselves.

TAX REBATES: Very frequently the export subsidy takes the form of a tax rebate to the exporter. For example, French exporters can claim reimbursement from the French government for social-security and salary taxes in the proportion that export sales bear to total sales. Certain reimbursements from the production and turnover taxes can also be claimed.[5] Austria, Germany, Italy, and Holland engage in similar practices. Strange, is it not, that countries suffering internal shortages as a result of war and complaining that the terms of trade are moving against them in their trade relations with the raw commodity producing countries, should engage in such practices? The United States, however, does very nearly the same thing. The United States government generally does not collect manufacturer's excise taxes and sales taxes in connection with goods sold for export.

If the domestic price is higher than the foreign price as a result of the subsidy, there is danger that the goods may come bounding back unless there are controls to prevent that, such as a tariff on imports. So a program of tariffs and quotas goes along with the subsidies. Subsidies then result in a situation that may involve both money costs to the government of the country which is paying the subsidy and higher prices in that domestic market than prevail elsewhere. The measure is obviously

[3] *New York Times,* February 29, 1956, p. 1.

[4] United States Congress, Joint Committee on the Economic Report, *Foreign Economic Policy,* Hearings, 84th Congress, 1st Sess. (Washington: Government Printing Office, 1955), p. 349.

[5] *Economist,* September 27, 1952, p. 770; *New York Times,* January 5, 1956, p. 35.

immediately beneficial to the recipient of the subsidy. Whether it results in more business, employment, and a higher national income in the country paying the subsidy is open to question.

Ocean Shipping

One special type of subsidy should also be mentioned: the subsidy to ocean shipping. The subsidizing by a government of its merchant marine is common. The defensibility of such action was one of the few concessions made by Adam Smith in his plea for free trade. It is, he conceded, in the interest of national defense to have a strong merchant marine.[6]

The United States is no exception to the general rule that merchant marines are subsidized. It has been argued that such subsidy is necessary in the case of the United States specifically because (1) shipbuilding costs are lower in foreign yards than in United States yards, and (2) crew wages are lower on foreign ships. This boils down to the cheap-foreign-labor argument which was discussed in Chapter 9. But if the industry is of such importance that it is desirable to protect it whether it is economical or not, then the subsidization policy is not condemned by the refutation of the cheap-foreign-labor argument. If it must be done, production subsidies are one of the better ways to do it.[7]

The United States has experimented with various criteria in paying this subsidy (and a similar subsidy to airlines). The shipping companies may be subsidized for carrying the mail. The United States government has sold ships (e.g., Liberties and Victories) which it has owned to private companies (sometimes foreign companies) at bargain prices. The important subsidy currently in effect, however, is the one to help finance shipbuilding. It is intended to help cover the differential in shipbuilding costs between United States and foreign yards (and to cover certain military or armament features in the construction).

A comment on this may be appropriate. Perhaps shipping subsidies are justified since they permit all countries, instead of just a few, to have a fleet—on the grounds of national defense. But why has the subsidy been allowed to have the effect of providing cheap but extremely luxurious ocean travel for the wealthy? Seventh heaven is found in the facilities and services provided in the first-class accommodations on ocean

---

[6] Smith, *Wealth of Nations,* pp. 429–31.

[7] There is an important distinction to be made among subsidies. The production subsidy (or payment to facilitate production) is a different thing from the trade subsidy (which is a monetary payment to traders as goods move through the channels of trade). The subsidy for which an occasional good word is said in this book is the production subsidy. Most of the subsidies discussed in this section, including some of those supporting ocean shipping, are trade subsidies.

liners. Why? Slightly more efficient use of space could make it possible for far more people to travel across the ocean and still do so in comfort. In addition, ocean liners still practice a sort of class distinction, which the best hotels ashore no longer sanction.

DUMPING

Dumping, for present purposes, involves the selling abroad of goods by a private company at a price lower than the domestic price; and in this section we are concerned with circumstances other than government subsidies which may make this possible. Lest anyone be under any delusions as to how common this procedure has been, it may be desirable to mention the monograph of the Temporary National Economic Committee on *Export Prices and Export Cartels.*[8] A study of the price policies of seventy-six business enterprises indicated that export prices tended to be higher than domestic prices for nine firms, equal to domestic prices for twenty-one firms, and lower than domestic prices for forty-six firms. Although the study was published in 1941, and the situation may not at the present time be characterized by quite as large a proportion of dumping, nevertheless the study has indicated the existence of a significantly large amount of such activity. It would almost seem to be the rule rather than the exception. In a similar vein, Bertil Ohlin pointed out that Danish butter has been cheaper in London than in Copenhagen while British coal has been cheaper in Copenhagen than London.[9]

Marxian theory (see Chapter 10) has an explanation of why this result is likely to occur. But Communist propagandists, smearing capitalism on all counts and without any necessary regard for the data, sometimes argue just the opposite. K. Izmailov, for example, has recently written:[10] "The foreign trade of the capitalistic countries with colonial and dependent countries takes place on the basis of unequal exchange: capitalistic monopolies sell their goods in the backward countries at very high prices and even, beyond that, at specially inflated prices applicable to colonial markets."

Assuming the fact of extensive dumping, in spite of K. Izmailov, by what line of logic has the private businessman decided that dumping on

[8] United States, Temporary National Economic Committee, *Investigation of Concentration of Economic Power*, Monograph No. 6, *Export Prices and Export Cartels* (Washington: Government Printing Office, 1941), p. 31.

[9] This was before World War II. See Ohlin, *Interregional and International Trade*, pp. 246, 258.

[10] K. Izmailov, "Torgovlya Imperialisticheskikh Dyerzhav so Slaborazvitimi Stranami—Orodiye Kolonialnogo Grabyezha," *Voprosi Ekonomiki* (September, 1954), p. 96.

such an extensive scale is desirable? He is not being paid to do this; it is his own idea. Sometimes what is involved is temporary dumping in the effort to bankrupt a new business and potential competitor in a foreign country. In that case it is easy to see the motivation. The old business may be willing to operate at a loss for a short period of time to avoid the future competition. But if dumping is as common as the T.N.E.C. study would seem to indicate, more explanation than this is needed.

Another explanation for dumping, which may explain in large part the prevalence of the practice (*permanent or well-nigh permanent dumping*), depends upon the distinction between fixed costs and variable costs. Thomas Edison, who is perhaps as much entitled to credit for being an enterprising businessman as for being an inventor, claimed credit for observing the possibilities of dumping: [11]

> I was the first manufacturer in the United States to adopt the idea of dumping surplus goods upon the foreign market. Thirty years ago my balance sheet showed me that I was not making much money. My manufacturing plant was not running to its full capacity. I couldn't find a market for my products. Then I suggested that we undertake to run our plant on full capacity and sell the surplus products in foreign markets at less than cost of production. Every one of my associates opposed me. I had my experts figure out how much it would add to the cost of operating the plant if we increased this production 25 per cent. The figures showed that we could increase the production 25 per cent at an increased cost of only about 2 per cent. On this basis I sent a man to Europe who sold lamps there at a price less than the cost of production in Europe. By doing this I was able to employ more labor to run my plant to full capacity, and this labor, of course, received high wages. American consumers were not injured in the slightest, and I was enabled to employ 25 per cent more men and get rid of surplus product by dumping it upon the foreign market.

Of course, for the situation described by Edison to exist, there must have been a previous instance of poor judgment in establishing production capacity larger than conditions called for. Edison's plants must have had facilities for producing far more light globes than could be sold at the monopolistic (or semi-monopolistic) prices prevailing in the United States. When he said that dumping would not harm American consumers in the slightest, he meant that it would not harm them more than they were already harmed by his prices (which probably were higher,

[11] *Wall Street Journal*, December 30, 1911. Reprinted with the kind permission of the *Wall Street Journal*.

while his volume of production probably was lower, as a result of his monopoly power, than they might have been had there been effective competition in the United States).

In such a situation, the producer already had unused plant capacity. He was already saddled with the fixed charges for plant, rent, bond interest, overhead, etc. Consequently, so far as the foreign market was concerned, all he had to take into account as cost was the additional variable costs; and it was literally true that if the cost of producing those additional light globes was going to run only, perhaps, one cent per light globe, and if he could sell the lamps abroad at four cents each (a figure well below his average cost and below the domestic price), there was a three cents profit per light globe to be had; and it was real profit and an addition to total profit, even though the average total cost of producing light globes in the United States might have been, say six cents, and higher than the foreign sale price. This was additional real profit, in spite of the fact that the foreign price was below the United States price and also below average total cost.

Another condition that must also exist to make such dumping successful is that there must be some barrier, tariff or otherwise, to keep the goods from rebounding into the selling country. In technical jargon, the markets need to be "differentiated." Buyers of the dumped goods in the foreign country might otherwise be able to ship them back to the United States and sell them at five cents each. Therefore, it is helpful if the dumper's government will connive with the dumper, "sell the domestic consumers down the river," and impede the re-entry of the dumped goods.

Thus the conditions facilitating this type of dumping are (a) surplus capacity, (b) monopoly power, and (c) differentiated markets. And then, to make the operation profitable, only additional variable cost need be covered.

Such a situation goes a long way toward explaining why the infants that long ago grew up (duPont, United States Steel, and General Electric) still have a real interest in protective tariffs—even if United States consumers do not. It is true that they no longer need tariffs on the basis of the infant-industry argument; nevertheless, they still find them useful to facilitate dumping when they have excess capacity, and they lobby briskly to obtain them. Such companies, especially the duPonts, have been very effective in getting and maintaining tariff protection for themselves.

But, lest anyone believe that dumping died with Edison or ceased with World War II (since which time there has been a much-talked-about scarcity of goods), a postwar example should be cited. The Japanese steel industry seems to be at it again:[12]

[12] *International Financial News Survey,* July 31, 1953, p. 37.

The directors of the Japanese Iron and Steel Exporters' Association are reported to have agreed that below-cost exporting of steel was inevitable in the face of intensified international competition, particularly from Western Europe. Export contracts for the first quarter (April-June) of fiscal 1953-54 amounted to only 190,000 tons, and it is feared that, unless the situation improves, total exports in the current fiscal year will fall short of the target of 1.2 million tons; actual exports last year were 1.47 million tons. The directors reached the conclusion about below-cost steel exports after hearing reports from colleagues who recently returned from a tour of Pakistan. Following this visit, five leading Japanese iron and steel makers decided to accept an order from Pakistan for 9,500 tons of iron and steel goods even though the prices offered were much lower than the Japanese quotations.

There may also be other circumstances which will make dumping profitable. But this example should be sufficient to indicate the possibilities.[13]

With regard to the general possibility of different prices on identical goods in different markets (differentiated markets), this comment should be added. If there are barriers (tariffs, quotas, exchange control, or even just plain transport costs) to goods movement, differentiated markets are possible. And if different demand conditions exist in the different markets (this being extremely likely), it is desirable, so far as the sellers are concerned, to differentiate among them. Their profits will thereby be increased. There need not be any difference in cost conditions as a prerequisite.

CARTELS

The traditional analysis of monopoly pricing indicates that the monopolist, unlike the competitor, can control either quantity of production or price (but not both) and that he will do so in the effort to maximize his profits. Actually, if he has the power, the monopolist will break down or differentiate his market into as small units as possible, and charge a monopoly price in each, which probably will not be the same price in all. The smaller the markets, the better! Of course, he may need tariffs and other assistance from the government to manage this—an aspect of the question not mentioned by the monopolist when

[13] A more theoretical statement to describe these possibilities would be that (1) if the markets are differentiated and (2) if the patterns of demand elasticity are different in the different markets, in the interest of profit maximization it will pay to charge different prices in the different markets.

he is complaining, in another setting, about government interference with free private enterprise.

In such a case, the United States price would not necessarily be higher than the foreign price, but it would be different in whichever direction would make profits greater. Actually, the prices probably run higher (rather than lower) in the United States than in the world at large precisely because the most powerful business enterprises in the world are the great United States corporations. Their power is relatively greater domestically in the United States than it is abroad. Therefore they can get away with higher prices in the United States than in the foreign market.

This may explain the likelihood of price differences in a cartelized world.

The essence of the explanation of cartels is: there comes a time in the development of their industries when businessmen decide that there is more to gain from co-operation than from competition. Perhaps the burden of heavy fixed costs has led to a price-cutting war of the sort which was presaged by the example cited above; and then after a period of fighting and financial losses, the corporations decide that it is better to co-operate. Co-operation on an international scale has the same advantages.[14] Once the co-operation has begun, an almost certain result is less production and higher prices. And international cartels and raw commodity control schemes are the devices by which such results are effected on an international level. But in addition, in the international aspect of the problem, there results not only less production and higher prices, but also less trade.

Practices of Cartels

PRICE AGREEMENTS: Prices set as a result of cartel agreements are likely to be higher than those that prevailed, or would have prevailed, in their absence. A standard example is the case of tungsten carbide:[15]

> Tungsten carbide is a hard-metal composition of great industrial importance in cutting tools, extrusion dies, and wear-

[14] And this is true in spite of Lenin, who did not believe international cartels could become genuinely world-wide. Lenin wrote: "Certain bourgeois writers (with whom Kautsky, who has completely betrayed the Marxist position he held, for example, in 1909, is now associated) expressed the opinion that international cartels are one of the most striking expressions of the internationalisation of capital and therefore offer a possible hope of peace among nations under capitalism. In theory his opinion is absolutely absurd, while in practice it is a sophism and a dishonest defence of the worst opportunism." (p. 68). Lenin went on to allege that the capitalists would go down struggling among themselves—not co-operating.

[15] United States Congress, Senate, Committee on Military Affairs, *Economic and Political Aspects of International Cartels*, p. 12.

resistant surfaces. It was sold in the United States in 1927–28 at $50 per pound. At that time General Electric and Friedrich Krupp Aktiengesellschaft formed an agreement by which their patents were pooled. General Electric was given control of the sale price in the United States and Krupp was obligated to observe this price upon its imports. Thereupon the United States' price rose promptly to a maximum of $453 per pound.

An extreme case, no doubt, but illustrative.

Largely with the endorsement, and frequently with the positive assistance of government agencies, most shipping lines enter into shipping conference agreements to regulate rates.[16] Shipping companies in the North Atlantic service or operating on the west coast of South America will agree on a pattern of rates—which is rather effectively observed and which, seemingly, is not very carefully regulated in the general interest. And, in spite of all the effort and subsidies which have gone into building up a national merchant marine in the national interest (of each of the nations concerned), it is a fair guess that the rate structures chiefly serve the interest of the shipping lines (regardless of nationality), to the detriment of the interest of shippers and consumers (regardless of nationality).

International air fares are controlled in a similar way by the International Air Transport Association. The *New York Times* has printed a very frank statement concerning one rate-setting arrangement of the I.A.T.A. to the effect that it represented a compromise among what Pan American, TWA, and the United States Civil Aeronautics Board wanted.[17]

DIVISION OF THE MARKET: Cartel members have frequently divided the market area among them. The situation with regard to radios in 1934 was an example of this.[18] In that year certain United States government officials observed that Sweden seemed to offer an attractive market for radio sets and that United States-made radios were not sharing in the market. The Department of Commerce made considerable effort to encourage the exploitation of this opportunity by United States companies, only to find that the businessmen did not react by taking advantage of the situation. As it turned out, their curious indifference was explained by the existence since 1925 of an agreement dividing the world radio market among International General Electric, Westinghouse, RCA and Dutch Philips. Sweden was in the area reserved for Philips; so the United States companies, General Electric, RCA, and Westinghouse, were not inter-

[16] Daniel Marx, Jr., *International Shipping Cartels* (Princeton: Princeton University Press, 1952).

[17] *New York Times,* July 1, 1956, sec. 6, p. 19.

[18] United States, Senate, Committee on Military Affairs, *Economic and Political Aspects . . . ,* pp. 20, 45.

ested. And the government had wasted some more of the taxpayers' money trying to render a useful service to businessmen.

RESTRICTION OF CAPACITY TO PRODUCE: Very common have been agreements to curtail production. A famous example of this has been the diamond industry. De Beers and the Diamond Trading Company, among their various activities designed to control the quantity of diamonds getting on the market, have worked to restrict the setting up of new centers of diamond cutting.[19]

RESTRICTIONS ON TECHNICAL IMPROVEMENTS: In part because of a desire not to render obsolete or obsolescent still usable equipment, there have been many cases in which companies have resisted the introduction of new, more efficient processes. Patent law has been extensively used in the process of slowing down the introduction of new techniques.

A notorious example of the misuse of power derived from patent rights was the use by General Electric in the 1930's of its patent power to force its licensees to employ production methods which actually were intended to shorten the life of light globes.[20]

QUOTAS, SUBSIDIES, AND BONUSES: One of the most important of the cartels before the second World War was that in steel. Most of the important steel companies in those days thought of their problem as one of excessive ability to produce, and their planning looked to the curtailment of production below capacity in the effort to keep prices up. The international cartel organization in steel attempted to control domestic production in the late 1920's, but during the 1930's it emphasized a system of export quotas. This left the problem of direct production control within the countries to the national member groups. If exporters from a nation belonging to the cartel exceeded their export quota, the member companies were obligated to pay a fine into the treasury of the international steel cartel. Also, in line with the same type of thinking, if a company did not export its quota of steel, it would be paid a bonus from the cartel treasury. There were stages in the game in the late 1920's and early 1930's when the Germans had to pay fines for exceeding their export quotas, but in the middle 1930's, after the German armament program had gathered momentum, the situation changed. Germany just before World War II was no longer filling her export quotas under the international steel cartel agreement and was consequently entitled to a bonus from the organization. Meanwhile the United States national group was paying fines for over-export.[21] In effect, the big United States steel corporations were paying the Germans for curtailing their exports. The fact that the Germans had come to operate on that basis before World War II would make it funny, if it were

[19] *Ibid.,* p. 45.
[20] Stocking and Watkins, *Cartels in Action,* pp. 304–63.
[21] *Ibid.,* p. 202.

not so tragic, that we could in those days even think that raising the tariff on goods coming from Germany, as we then did, was an effective anti-German measure.

Effects of Cartels

The practices of cartels frequently involve the curtailment of production below, and the raising of price above, what would prevail under competition. To the extent that cartel arrangements make goods scarcer and more expensive, they are objectionable because they reduce the level of living. But to the extent that they give stability to production and marketing patterns and contribute to orderly long-run development, they might have a more favorable effect on production and price, in the long run, than the theory of monopoly price in its static form would indicate. However, the burden of proof should be on the shoulders of those who allege that cartels generally have this beneficent effect. And there is little and unsatisfactory empirical evidence to support the ascription of this virtue to them. Maybe all the cartelists really learned from the depression of the 1930's was that they should have been busy conniving to keep down capacity in 1925—hardly the most constructive of lessons.

But whatever the effect of cartels may be on level of living, they are to be condemned by a consideration of more importance: their effect on human freedom. The great private combines are undemocratic in operation and in essence. The great corporations are not even controlled by a democratic vote of their own stockholders and certainly not by a democratic vote of the people. Indeed, the cartels are one step more removed from such democratic control than the corporations. Their undemocratic nature, combined with the importance of cartel decision-making, means that such organizations have no valid place in a democratic world, whatever their effect on production and price.

A standard sophism which is being espoused in management courses in colleges of business, and also by *Time, Life,* and *Fortune,* runs to the effect that we are now blessed with a new type of business executive who is aware of his social responsibilities. He is not, any more, just a profit seeker. He is something better, a trustee of society running a great enterprise. Now, it does not matter whether this is true or not. It is irrelevant whether the great business executives are intelligent profit seekers in the interest of their firms or intelligent promoters of the nation's well-being. The goal of freedom of action is incompatible with the existence of a self-perpetuating oligarchy of business executives who are not responsible through any effective democratic process (corporate or political) to the shareholders or the voters. Whether or not it is possible for a day laborer to work up to president is irrelevant. It is the oligarchs and not the shareholders and not the voters who select which day laborer shall advance.

National Attitudes Toward Cartels

THE UNITED STATES: National governmental attitudes toward cartels and their practices have varied tremendously. The official attitude of the United States is in large part stated in the Sherman Antitrust Act of 1890 as modified by the Webb-Pomerene Act of 1918. The latter Act was passed in part as the result of an energetic argument presented by the big copper companies to the effect that United States companies participating in international trade were crippled by the Sherman Act's requirement that they compete among themselves. They were hamstrung, according to the argument, because their foreign competitors were colluding among themselves in cartels and the United States companies were consequently at a disadvantage in competing against such powerful groups in the world markets because they had to compete among themselves as well as with the foreigners. Congress rarely fails to pass legislation which is briskly promoted by influential pressure groups and which is calculated to harm foreigners. Accordingly, the Webb-Pomerene Act was passed, and it provided that the various United States companies exporting a particular type of goods could get together in export associations and collude in setting the quantities and prices applicable to exports. But the wording of the act was somewhat ambiguous, and it was not made clear whether collusion by United States companies with foreign companies was permitted as well as collusion among the domestic companies. At one stage, in the mid-1920's, the copper producers obtained a ruling from the attorney general of the United States to the effect that collusion *with* the foreigners was allowable. And between World War I and World War II many United States companies, including the steel companies, used this argument as justification for joining with foreigners in international cartels.

It was 1949 before the question of collusion between the export associations and foreign companies was finally adjudicated by a court—the United States Court for the Southern District of New York. It was decided that the Webb-Pomerene Act did not permit United States corporations or export associations to participate in international cartels. The case was between the United States government and the United States Alkali Export Association. And Judge S. H. Kaufman's language was in part as follows: [22]

> Unquestionably the cartelization of the world, if accomplished by the individual corporate defendants separately and not through an association organized under the Webb Act, would be a flagrant transgression of the antitrust laws.

[22] United States, Federal Trade Commission, *Report of the Federal Trade Commission on International Cartels in the Alkali Industry* (Washington: Government Printing Office, 1950), p. 48.

... To remove cartel agreements, if made by export associations organized under the act, from the comprehensive ban of the Sherman Act, while at the same time condemning similar agreements by others, would be to overlook the fact that it was the evil of restraint on commerce which Congress sought to extirpate, and not the creation of a preferred class which was to be free to continue the evil.

... Viewing the Webb Act in the light of contemporaneous interpretation of the antitrust laws, considering the import of the act when read as a whole, and giving careful attention to the entire legislative history of its passage, the conclusion is irresistible that the Webb-Pomerene Act affords no right to export associations to engage on a worldwide scale in practices so antithetical to the American philosophy of free competition. The international agreements between defendants allocating exclusive markets, assigning quotas in sundry markets, fixing prices on an international scale, and selling through joint agents are not those "agreements in the course of export trade" which the Webb Act places beyond the reach of the Sherman Law.

But the official, legal position is not necessarily the popular or the implemented position. In the 1950's in the United States, cartel practices are no longer as unpopular as they were in the early days of World War II. And a college newspaper, which is generally a stronghold of liberal views, is capable of editorializing to the effect that the "domestic oil industry can be protected by voluntary action on the part of importers." [23]

THE UNITED KINGDOM: In the United Kingdom the situation is somewhat different. Despite Britain's being the home of Adam Smith and of free enterprise, the British attitude of late years toward international cartels has been more sympathetic than the American. Sir Alfred Mond (later Lord Melchett), the head of Imperial Chemical Industries, went so far as to declare in 1928: [24]

There can be no denial that there is, in modern economic tendencies, a growth, both in private industry and in public and economic thought, of the idea of the creation of greater economic units, both industrially and internationally, and I would add imperially. That tendency, which we all witness, and in which some of us have been taking part recently, is one which to my mind, it is little use criticising and little use disliking. It is something which is happening and which is bound to continue; which we

[23] *Daily Texan*, October 11, 1953, p. 4.
[24] Sir Alfred Mond, *Industry and Politics* (London: Macmillan, 1928), pp. 275–76. Reprinted with the permission of Macmillan and Company.

have to accept and which we have to see how to fit into our economic life, in industry, in business and imperially.

Great Britain has not, traditionally, tried to regulate restraint of trade by legislation, although the Statute of Monopolies of 1624 did abrogate the royal prerogative of establishing monopolies.[25] Rather the common law rule prevailed that contracts in restraint of trade were illegal and unenforceable. But time modified the application which Britain made of the common-law precept. Since the beginning of the nineteenth century there has been little or no implementation of the precept if the businessmen who are parties are satisfied with the contract. From 1807 to 1948 there was virtually no effective prosecution of restraint of trade practices charging that the *public* interest was adversely affected.[26]

In the early 1930's, an attitude positively favorable to cartel arrangements developed. This attitude was closely related to a desire to help the domestic steel industry in its bargaining with the continental steel cartel. In setting up a cartel, even though the over-all purpose is to reduce production or exports, each national group wants as large a share of the total quota as it can get. The crux of the internal organizational problem among the cartel members, then, is the allocation of quotas among the companies participating, and there is earnest negotiating as the various parties try to get for themselves as large a share of the quota as possible. A company negotiating for a large share of the quota will be effective in relation to the proportion of the market it controls. A member which cannot even answer for its own domestic market is not going to have much influence. The British companies at the beginning of the 1930's did not even control their own domestic market because of Britain's free-trade policies. The continental companies could ship into Britain, but the British had difficulty retaliating because of the continental tariffs. On this point Sir Alfred Mond said:[27] ". . . in negotiation, the man behind the tariff wall always has something with which to bargain, which the man in the Free Trade country has not. Any one who has any practical experience with continental producers knows that the first thing they say is, 'You cannot export to our country, because we have a tariff. How much of your market are you going to give us?'"

In the early 1930's, then, the most important evidence of the friendly attitude of the British government toward cartels may be found in the assistance given to the British steel companies in this difficult situation

[25] United States, Department of State, *Foreign Legislation Concerning Monopoly and Cartel Practices,* Report of the Department of State to the Subcommittee on Monopoly of the Select Committee on Small Business, United States Senate, July 9, 1952, 82d Congress, 2d Sess. (Washington: Government Printing Office, 1952), p. 87.

[26] *Ibid.*

[27] Stocking, *Cartels or Competition,* p. 265.

by means of a tariff on steel imports. In fact, the Import Duties Act of 1932 provided for a general raising of the British tariff wall and for consultation between the British government (the Import Duties Advisory Committee) and British industry as to the most effective measures to take.

Since World War II, Britain has dealt with the monopoly and restraint of trade problems by various new laws. The Restrictive Trade Practices Act of 1956 provides for the registration of contracts containing provisions involving restrictive trade practices affecting prices, terms and conditions of trading, what is to be sold, to whom it is to be sold, and where it is to be sold. The Restrictive Practices Court then reviews the practices. A practice is presumed to be contrary to the public interest unless the person seeking to uphold the agreement can prove the contrary.[28]

British emphasis seems to be on whether the *results* of the practice are contrary to the public interest—not on whether the *practice* itself is specified as illegal in the law. Consequently, the British law provides that a restriction may be permitted to continue if it is necessary for the protection of the public against injury. Thus a restriction providing that medical prescriptions could only be sold by qualified pharmacists would probably be upheld. Other arguments also may be used to justify the continuance of certain practices.

In connection with resale price maintenance, the British law takes exception to arrangements that involve the collective enforcement of the practice by a group of firms. But contracts between manufacturers and retailers, which carry resale price provisions, are enforceable in the ordinary courts.

Restrictive practices involving exports are dealt with through somewhat different procedures involving the supervision of the Monopolies Commission rather than the Restrictive Practices Court. The Monopolies Commission also has jurisdiction over single-firm monopolies, which are defined in British law as being single firms which control at least one third of the market for a particular commodity.

But at the same time that Britain was taking steps in the direction of controlling monopolies and restrictive practices, she was taking another step in another direction. The Industrial Organization Act of 1947 placed the planning of industrial development on a permanent basis and provided for the exercise of an important planning role by the trade associations.[29] The nationalization of certain industries in the years following World War II and the establishment of comprehensive govern-

[28] Lord Meston, "Restrictive Business Practices," *Cartel*, VI (October, 1956), pp. 127–9.

[29] Raymond Vernon, "Postwar Trends in International Business Organization," *American Economic Review: Papers and Proceedings*, XXXVIII (May, 1948), pp. 94–108.

ment regulation of agriculture in the Agriculture Act of 1947 were also moves in the direction of organized planning.

GERMANY: The German Government, before World War II, was frankly sympathetic to cartels, to the extent of sponsoring them (and even requiring membership by law). Since World War II it has hardly been in a position to have an independent policy. The United States has imposed an antitrust law on Germany; but the long-run effect of that measure is far from certain. Since it has been imposed upon her, is Germany more or less likely to retain the law after the country regains real independence of initiative?

OTHER COUNTRIES: In France, Italy, and Japan, companies participated in international cartels before World War II with much franker assistance from their governments than was the case in the United States. And according to the *New Republic,* Japan by 1953 was well on the road to resuming such practices.[30]

The French-sponsored *Schuman Plan* for a European Coal and Steel Community containing the German, French, Belgian, and Italian industries gives the steel situation in particular a somewhat different turn. Maybe future decisions actually will help to develop the European steel industry in the general interest, instead of in the interest of maximum monetary profit to the companies. But it is much too early to say with any certainty whether the Community is the epitome of cartels or a great forward-looking experiment in international government in the public interest. In any event, the steel companies remain private enterprises, and the Community is merely a general planning and regulating organization.

Through the whole range of countries since the war, there has been a great increase in the socialization of industry at the same time that, under the aegis of the United States at least, lip service is being paid to the idea of increasing competition. Whether these two trends are compatible only time can tell. Perhaps, strangely enough, they may be, even though the proponents of each viewpoint do not seem to believe so. And the result may be a decline in the power of private cartels.

Both more and less centralization of economic activity are called for. And this is precisely the area where the implications of that idea are most important. "Eternal vigilance is the price . . ." of more things than one. Constant, careful consideration by all the people of how a particular industry should be organized at any given time, is the only possible worthwhile approach to the problem of business organization. That problem is not going to be worked out by the sweeping application of a simple principle like free private enterprise or socialism to all industries regardless of their nature.

[30] *New Republic,* August 17, 1953, p. 6.

RAW COMMODITY CONTROL SCHEMES

Price Fluctuation Relationships

Cartels of the sort that have been under discussion have been common in connection with manufacturing and mineral raw materials—that is to say, in industries which are typically dominated by a relatively few firms.

But in agriculture the problem is different. There generally are too many producers in the field of agricultural commodities for self-discipline to be feasible. Several hundred thousand farmers growing wheat cannot agree privately, with any facility, on marketing quotas and prices. A second problem, which possibly is a result of the relatively large number of farmers, also intensifies their difficulties. The prices of agricultural products rise higher in good times and sink lower in bad times than do the prices of commodities in general (or of manufactured goods). Table 21 indicates this relationship. Manufacturers are able to look after themselves and make agreements to stabilize prices, although they sacrifice volume in the process. But the farmer is more nearly at the mercy of a competitive market; and a competitive market may be more effective in reducing prices than in reducing volume of production in agriculture. In fact, supply in agriculture is notoriously unresponsive, in the short run, to price.

In connection with demand for raw commodity exports, the institutional setting should not be disregarded. Demand is inelastic in a rather special and highly variable sense. The quantity of the raw materials which will be demanded by the industrial machines of the great manufacturing centers is set by the stage of the business cycle. It will be large and predetermined (inelastic) during the prosperity phase of the cycle in the developed country. It will be small, predetermined, and consequently inelastic during the depression phase. This would seem to mean a high average propensity to import in prosperous times and a lower propensity to import in depression times.

In Table 21 an attempt was made to identify the years of business cycle upswing and of business cycle downswing between 1901 and 1951. Then the average rise in price for the different export products of underdeveloped countries for the years of upswing and the average fall for the years of downswing were computed. It should be noted how much larger was the annual fluctuation in the unit prices of United States imports of the commodities in question (12.7% and 13%) than the average fluctuation in the wholesale price index within the United States. This is strong supporting evidence for the proposition that raw materials (mineral as well as agricultural) are faced with far more violently fluctuating market prices than is the case with commodities in general

TABLE 21

CYCLICAL MOVEMENT IN IMPORT UNIT VALUES,[2] EXPORT VOLUMES, AND EXPORT PROCEEDS, 1901 TO 1951

	DURING BUSINESS CYCLE UPSWING (PERCENTAGE INCREASE PER YEAR)	DURING BUSINESS CYCLE DOWNSWING (PERCENTAGE DECREASE PER YEAR)
I. Average Change in Import Unit Values (U.S.) of 25 raw materials [1]	12.7	13.0
II. Average Change in		
A. Wholesale price index (U.S.)	5.2	7.6
B. Wholesale price index (U.K.)	5.8	9.2
III. Average Change in Export Volumes (Underdeveloped Countries) for 18 [3] Commodities	17.6	16.8
IV. Average Change in Export Proceeds (Underdeveloped Countries) for 18 Commodities [3]	21.6	22.1

[1] Hemp, cotton, copra, cocoa, linseed, rubber, shellac, coffee, wool, tin, rice, jute, sisal, silk, copper, wheat, petroleum, sugar, hides, tobacco, tea, sodium nitrate, manganese, bananas, nickel. [2] Import unit values are values prevailing on import into the United States. [3] Linseed, wheat, hemp, sodium nitrate, cotton, rubber, copper, tin, cocoa, silk, jute, rice, sugar, coffee, petroleum, tobacco, wool, tea.
Sources: United Nations, Department of Economic Affairs, *Instability in Export Markets of Under-developed Countries* (New York, 1952), pp. 16, 34, 55.

in an industrially developed country. But the United Nations study goes on to indicate that, for the underdeveloped countries, the fluctuation in the volume of the exports studied is more violent than the fluctuation in their price.[31] Demand for raw commodities may be inelastic at a given second, but it seems to be highly variable over the business cycle. And as a consequence of the combination of fluctuations, the element which fluctuates most violently of all is the proceeds or receipts which the underdeveloped countries obtain for their exports.

Note the difficult position in which these developments place the underdeveloped countries. They are truly operating on a feast or famine basis. To cite the case of Cuban sugar, the "dance of the millions" is followed by the fighting of a revolution through the halls of a country's finest hotel.

For evidence that the underdeveloped countries are under special difficulties, emphasis may be placed on the facts that (1) agricultural and raw commodity prices fluctuate more violently than manufactured goods prices (for institutionally determined reasons), (2) the Latin American countries produce a high proportion of agricultural commod-

[31] For definition of the volume concept see Table 3.

ities and raw materials, and (3) their international trade is a relatively high proportion of national income. But that, in any measurable sense, underdeveloped countries suffer more during depressions than do developed countries is not established by this argument. They probably suffer in a different way. But they may well be entitled to some special consideration if the forces that cause them to suffer are beyond their power to control—and if this is not the case in countries like the United States.[32]

The problem created by the pattern of price fluctuation of agricultural and manufactured goods is obscured somewhat by the even more pronounced tendency for the prices of goods moving in international trade (whatever they may be) to fluctuate more violently than the domestic prices of the same goods.[33] This circumstance is relevant to a dilemma posed by data which Imlah and Rostow have presented—data which on its face contradicts some of the preceding arguments. For example, their British data give little comfort to the proposition that the unit terms of trade move in a direction favorable to a developed country following the inception of a depression.[34] A study made by Imlah and analyzed by Rostow indicates that, in twenty-one depressions between 1800 and 1914, following the crisis ending the period of prosperity, the terms of trade improved for Britain in ten cases and worsened in eleven. Such data will hardly support a general conclusion that the terms of trade in the early part of a depression move in a direction unfavorable to underdeveloped countries.

Data for the United States gives somewhat more support to the proposition that the terms of trade, after the inception of a depression, move in favor of the developed country. Data used in this comparison are the unit (net barter) terms of trade of Chart 3 and the depression reference dates estimated by Wesley Mitchell.[35] According to this rough comparison the terms of trade have moved in a direction favorable to the United

[32] It does not even seem to be certain that the impact of depression is worse in agriculture than in manufacturing. But the nature of the problem is different in the two areas. That is certain. In manufacturing the impact falls chiefly on unemployed laborers—not on the employers. The unemployed go hungry. The employers cut total production, maintain prices, and by and large do not go hungry. In agriculture there is little or no unemployment. There are substantial drops in prices and income—but not in production volume. There are difficult and *different* functional problems in both places. But which segment of the economy is hardest hit? The evidence is not all in. But when it is, the conclusion may well be that the analysis of the problem in terms of this simple cleavage—where is the impact worse—is rather fruitless.

[33] Humphrey, *American Imports,* p. 45.

[34] W. W. Rostow, *Process of Economic Growth* (New York: Norton, 1952), p. 215. See also: K. Martin and F. D. Thackeray, "The Terms of Trade of Selected Countries 1870–1938," *Bulletin of the Oxford University Institute of Statistics,* X (November, 1948), 373–92.

[35] Wesley C. Mitchell, *Business Cycles: The Problem and Its Setting* (New York: National Bureau of Economic Research, 1927), p. 387.

States following the beginning of nine depressions and in an unfavorable direction following five—during the period covered. This comparison, taken alone, might be said to indicate the likelihood that the terms of trade move favorably to the United States in the early part of a depression. But they hardly indicate a reliable and regular pattern.

But regardless of what is happening to the terms of trade and regardless of the fact that industrialized countries also have problems during depressions, many underdeveloped countries have serious problems because of (1) the violence in the fluctuations of raw commodity prices (2) combined with a high proportion of production devoted to raw commodities and (3) a high ratio of trade to national income.[36]

All of this points up the fact that the difficulties of agriculture vis-à-vis manufacturing are not primarily geographical problems; they are primarily functional problems in a certain institutional setting. Irrespective of national boundaries, commercialized agriculture has certain problems in relation to industry.

Governments of underdeveloped countries might well emphasize the desirability of solving the agricultural problem as a functional problem common to all commercialized farmers, and as a pattern which requires solution by international action. This approach promises better results than to point up the problem as though it were a terms-of-trade problem in international trade or a problem involving basically a geographical issue—exploitation of one geographical area by another. It is a good general rule, in any case, that problems should be posed as functional problems rather than as problems in relations between countries and governments, especially if they really are fundamentally functional rather than geographical in character.

The truth remains that raw commodity producers and farmers have a difficult time during depressions; and they are less capable of doing something about their problem than are manufacturers in large industrialized countries.

History of Control Schemes

Raw commodity producers have problems; and if anything is to be done for them, it is the governments (or international organizations)

---

[36] China and India may not have a legitimate complaint on this particular point because of their low ratios of trade to income. It stands to reason, however, from a knowledge of the institutional arrangements of China and India, that real suffering in those countries is not consequent on bumper crops and low export prices in years when the world is suffering from depression. Whether or not there is worldwide depression has been a matter of considerable indifference to the mass of the population in China and India. What matters is whether the crops are good or bad. And it is a poor crop which means famine or want and suffering in those countries—not good crops and low prices. The violent price change poses a significant problem only for the countries which are significant traders—or rather, which have a high international-trade to national-income ratio.

that must do it because of the practical impossibility of doing it privately.

Plans to deal with these problems are generally referred to as raw commodity control schemes. Essentially, the raw commodity control schemes and the cartels are intended to do the same thing; but in the one case (cartels) the agreements are privately arrived at, and in the other case (raw commodity control schemes) they are governmentally sanctioned, at least as a general rule.

There were such international agreements in the 1930's in connection with many of the major raw commodities that had a world market.[37] Sugar and coffee were striking examples.

There has been a remarkable parallel in the evolution of different raw commodity control schemes—whether they deal with sugar, coffee, or what have you. The evolution is likely to run somewhat as follows: A group of producers in one of the chief centers of production feels the effects of overproduction and low prices. They decide to try to get the assistance of their local government. Envisage the coffee growers of São Paulo in Brazil appealing to the government of São Paulo in the years before World War I and again in the middle 1920's and again to the government of Brazil following 1930. A scheme may then be set up calling for production quotas, and/or provisions for crop destruction, and/or prohibition of new planting. The hope is that the holding of product off the market by this important group of producers will force the world price up. The quotas are (or were in most of the pre-World War II schemes) generally assigned on the basis of the share of the market which a particular producer enjoyed in some earlier selected, more or less representative year.

In fact the holding of some of the product off the market by such schemes is likely to make the industry more profitable—or, at least, less unprofitable than it otherwise would have been. But the chief gain will go to the producers who are not part of the scheme and who have not restricted their marketings. One important result of the Brazilian control schemes was that Colombia, Guatemala, and other countries gained an expanding share of the market during a period of years in

[37] P. T. Bauer, *The Rubber Industry—A Study in Competition and Monopoly* (London: London School of Economics and Political Science, 1948); Joseph S. Davis, H. M. Gibbs, and E. B. Taylor, *Wheat in the World Economy* (Stanford: Stanford University Press [Food Research Institute], 1945); William Y. Elliott, et al., *International Control in the Non-ferrous Metals* (New York: Macmillan, 1937); H. R. G. Greaves, *Raw Materials and International Control* (London: Methuen & Co., 1936); International Labour Office, *Intergovernmental Commodity Control Agreements* (Montreal: 1943); Klaus E. Knorr, *Tin under Control* (Stanford: Stanford University Press [Food Research Institute], 1945); Klaus E. Knorr, *World Rubber and Its Regulation* (Stanford: Stanford University Press [Food Research Institute], 1945); V. D. Wickizer, *Coffee, Tea, and Cocoa—An Economic and Political Analysis* (Palo Alto: Stanford University Press [Food Research Institute], 1951).

the middle 1930's when very nearly half of the total Brazilian production of coffee was destroyed.

But the lesson that the practitioners of restrictions learn from these developments is not that marketing restrictions are bad. Rather, the lesson they learn is that the scheme did not include a large enough percentage of the producers.

If the scheme is a temporary failure, because of the behavior of the non-members, as was the case with the Brazilian coffee control scheme in the late thirties, it may not be long before further price drops convince some of the producers who were not members of the earlier schemes that they need to co-operate. In the case of coffee, Colombia, Guatemala, and other producing countries by 1940 were ready to participate in a general Inter-American coffee control agreement, which established export quotas for the various producing countries and left it to the national governments to allot those quotas among the domestic producers. The quotas, again, in connection with these schemes of larger coverage, are likely to be allotted on the basis of the share of the market enjoyed in some earlier base year. By World War II much of the raw commodity trade of the world was subject to the restrictions of raw commodity control schemes which included most if not all of the producers, which restricted marketing in an effort to raise price, and which allotted quotas by a base-year type of formula.

Few of these schemes have been revived since the end of World War II. Such arrangements thrive on low raw commodity prices, not on high prices. Even so, and in spite of the continued relatively favorable market for raw commodities, major agreements have been concluded in connection with wheat, sugar, and tin. And the producers certainly have not forgotten the days of two-cent-per-pound sugar and seven-cent coffee. Nor do the producers of most raw commodities seem willing to entrust their future to an unregulated market. It is possible to forecast with some assurance that raw commodity control schemes will be back with us in great numbers as soon as the raw commodity price drops which are going to occur, and which have already occurred in some measure, become only slightly more prevalent.

PROPOSED INTERNATIONAL TRADE ORGANIZATION CHARTER

The articles of agreement of the proposed International Trade Organization handle manufacturing cartels and raw commodity control schemes in different ways.

With regard to the manufacturers, the articles took an approach suggested by the Sherman Antitrust Act and frowned on most of the restrictive practices, although the machinery which was planned for dealing with the objectionable practices offered little promise of being effective in operation—publicity being the ultimate sanction established.

But agreements in the raw commodity field, in marked contrast, were not outlawed by the articles of agreement. In fact, they were explicitly sanctioned as devices for dealing with difficult situations. It was recognized that the facts of violent price fluctuations and innumerable producers made the problems in agriculture quite different from those in manufacturing.

According to the articles of agreement, the administrative group set up to regulate a particular raw commodity should contain an equal number of representatives of producer and consumer interests. That is a major change from the producer-dominated schemes of the 1930's. But in any event, the producers have to co-operate when it is the consumers who are in difficulty; and the consumers have to co-operate when it is the producers who are in difficulty.

The committees that are now in existence, under United Nations aegis, are studying different raw commodities. They are in general conforming with the precepts of the articles of agreement—even though that document has not been ratified. On those committees producer and consumer groups have equal representation. Plans are actively being discussed for dealing with the problems of raw commodity surpluses when those problems arise again. And control programs have actually come into operation again, as was mentioned above, in connection with wheat, sugar, and tin. Thus there is in existence the machinery that the articles envisaged for dealing with the raw commodity problem, even though the I.T.O. itself did not come into existence as planned. In fact the signing of the General Agreement on Tariffs and Trade in 1947 bound member governments to the I.T.O. provisions on raw commodities, at least in principle, whether or not they ratified the I.T.O. articles.

Thus machinery for dealing with restrictive business practices in manufacturing is substantially non-existent, but the basic machinery for handling the raw commodity problem is in existence, or is potentially available as envisaged by the I.T.O. articles of agreement, even though that document has not been ratified. But even in connection with the raw commodities, although the machinery exists, there is no agreement on the basic principles to be applied in regulation.

CRITERIA FOR CONTROL SCHEMES

Raw Commodities

There needs to be international agreement on the basic principles to underlie raw commodity controls; and the functional nature of the problem is such that it can be dealt with satisfactorily only at a level that includes substantially all of the producers and consumers.

There is needed an operating formula for regulating production (or marketing) which does not inhibit long-run change in the relative importance of different commodities—and a formula that will involve the minimum of governmental control and regulation of individuals, the minimum of red tape and administrative complication. Neither a parity-price formula (attempting to make the price of a particular commodity vary in a certain relationship to other prices) nor a parity-of-income formula (attempting to maintain the income of people in a certain line of activity in a certain relationship to other incomes) can accomplish this result.

A workable formula might well provide that prices could not be changed by more than 5 per cent in one year by comparison with the figure of the previous year.[38] Under such a formula, a long-run drop in the price of diamonds relative to other prices would be possible. But the adjustment problem would not hit the industry all at once in a single year. South African diamond miners would not be bankrupted suddenly by the discovery of large, new, low-cost deposits or by the discovery of a process for making synthetic diamonds. But they would be required to adjust to these changed conditions.

It is all very well to say that moderation of the violence of price fluctuations is the desirable basic method for dealing with the raw commodity situation; but many problems remain. One such problem is administrative.

Administration very possibly could be organized somewhat as follows. An international agency, liberally endowed with funds (or associated with an international central bank that could create funds), might handle the maintenance of the prices of goods moving in international trade. It might or might not delegate responsibility, within the limitations of the general formula adopted (perhaps the 5 per cent figure) to national governments to handle the administration of the program within their own borders, although it would probably be desirable to do so.

The fact that any national government could completely transfer the burden of the adjustment mechanism to the international agency, merely by exporting its surplus, would mean that the real importance of the international agency would grow in proportion as nation states shirked their responsibility. The situation is somewhat analogous to the assumption of the state debts by the United States government at the suggestion of Alexander Hamilton in the early history of the United

[38] A real advantage of a formula such as this is that it gets away from the base-year quota approach of the 1930's, which was so adverse to the interests of new, more efficient producers. Harrod makes a strong statement along these lines. R. F. Harrod, *Towards a Dynamic Economics* (London: Macmillan, 1948), pp. 122–8.

States. Much of the subsequent extension of federal power in this country has resulted from the refusal on the part of state and local governments to assume responsibility in facing pressing problems. If lower or more decentralized units will perform a useful role in activities of this sort, much bureaucratic centralization can be avoided. But jobs such as this must be done. And if lower levels of government assume a merely negative attitude the job will be done at a higher—perhaps more autocratic—level.

Also, administration of a program such as this should be handled by methods that place a premium on honesty rather than on dishonesty. To assure this, market prices probably should be completely uncontrolled. Buying and selling should be by private enterprise or by government enterprises that are actually engaged in the production or manufacture of the article in question.[39] If the market price falls below the price being supported, the agency with the responsibility for supporting the price would pay the difference to the seller. Since, prima facie, this arrangement would place a premium on dishonest collusion between buyer and seller to understate the sale price, it would probably be desirable that the subsidy be the difference between the quoted market price on the day of the sale and the support price, rather than the difference between the actual sale price and the support price. The seller would then be under inducement to sell at as high a price as he could, and all that would really matter would be certification of the volume of the sale and the date.

It is submitted that some such formula for lessening the violence of fluctuations (but not tending to prevent slow, long-run adjustments in the relative importance of different industries) is the most desirable basic principle for dealing with the raw commodity problem—and many other problems as well.

This plan, as it stands, avoids the chief difficulties presented by the parity price support program in the United States. More particularly, it avoids the problems posed by trying to maintain prices which are different from those prevailing in the rest of the world. One country should not try artificially to maintain a price structure out of line with that prevailing everywhere else. The corollary complications make for a very undesirable situation. A remedy that will establish a setting in which prices are generally uniform is eminently to be desired.

But individuals are injured and have to find new lines of work as a result of the long-run changes which this program permits. And of course individuals should not be forced to pay the bill. Society should

[39] Except for governmental or international agency stockpiling. But it should be added that administrative agencies operating with some discretion could make the stockpiling program carry a good deal of the adjustment impact in connection with violent changes of a strictly temporary nature, if not in connection with the long-run changes. See: Harrod, *op. cit.,* pp. 122–8.

pay it.[40] In part this problem is dealt with by the payment of the subsidies called for in the plan above. Those subsidies mean that change in the relative importance of any product will occur only gradually. The entrepreneur will have the time to make an intelligent adjustment. But the employees should be given considerable additional help (perhaps in the form of retraining programs) in making their adjustment.[41]

Society can hardly be expected to guarantee a certain size of market, and a certain price, and continuing profits forever to the manufacturers of farm wagons, or to the domestic producers of wool. One may well disagree with a certain United States Senator who seems to think there is no middle ground for the people of his state between the continued production of wool on the present scale and migration.[42] If his state is in as bad shape as he implies, the people should move. But of course it is not.

It simply cannot be true at one and the same time (1) that the United States is the most efficient producer of goods in the world, (2) that exports, overall, must equal imports in value, and (3) that low-cost foreign production of goods is a major threat to the United States economy. Our problems are orderly growth, increasing the level of living, and improving the degree of freedom of action which individuals enjoy. Our problem is not how to maintain the old prices and the old production methods in the old places, willy-nilly.

Cartels

Giant corporations and cartel organizations may restrict production and retard development in the interest of profits. On the other hand, they may have a concept of the desirability of development and expansion that overshadows their interest in short-run profits. Or it may be that the behavior in these matters varies from corporation to corporation, from cartel to cartel, and from time to time—especially depending on the phase of the business cycle.

All of these considerations are important; but there is another consideration which is overriding. On freedom-of-action grounds, it is simply not desirable to place the power to make decisions of the importance involved here in the hands of individuals who are not responsible to the democracy nor even to their own stockholders.

---

[40] It may be noted that the bill will not be as high in connection with a program of gradual changes as it would be in connection with a series of violent fluctuations.

[41] One of the worst features of the Randall Commission report is its refusal to face up to this problem. See United States, Commission of Foreign Economic Policy, *Report* (Washington, 1954), p. 59.

[42] United States Congress, Senate, Committee on Agriculture and Forestry, *Foreign Trade in Agricultural Products*, pt. 3, p. 518.

Chapter 14

STATE TRADING

☙ ☙ ☙

Countries with economic systems similar to that of the United States seem generally to be trying to have export balances of trade.

Countries organized like the U.S.S.R. attempt to get as much goods as they can in exchange for as little as possible. However, the U.S.S.R. may have kept the total volume of her foreign trade lower than it would otherwise have been in an effort to avoid entanglement with the business-cycle fluctuations of the capitalistic system.

United States striving for an export balance and Russian striving for an import balance indicate that, at least in the area of "struggle for markets," there will not be major friction between the two countries.

☙ ☙ ☙

STATE trading, for present purposes, means international trade in goods to which a government has title. For the most part, the discussion in the preceding chapters has been concerned with private trading and government measures affecting private trading, rather than trade for the account of a government.[1]

In discussions of trading problems the topic of state trading is likely to be merged into the subject of trade restrictions; and, by implication, the reader is led to believe that the logic which is used to condemn trade restrictions also condemns state trading—a proposition which does not follow.

THEORY

Assumption as to Motive

In a socialist country—country with much nationalized industry and engaged in considerable state trading—it is probably true that the government will respond to the relative strength of the pressures put

---

[1] Of course, much trade may involve a mixed situation—one party to the transaction being a private citizen and the other a government. And the trade of many nations may be partly state trading, partly private trading—could be, should be, and is.

upon it and interpret value in the light of those pressures. But the pressures will be of a far different sort and exert themselves in a quite different way than is the case in a country organized on the basis of free private enterprise. In the economic field, the socialist government will, almost certainly, have a major interest in increasing the value of goods in the country (whether a high value is placed on military goods will depend on circumstances). And there will not be in existence strong pressure groups interested in monetary profit which will be in a position to divert the government from this goal. A socialist government can be expected to be consistently interested in obtaining as much import as possible in exchange for as little export as possible. An unfavorable balance of trade—if attainable—and favorable terms of trade will be striven for. Indicative of the attitude toward the balance of trade which is to be expected from a socialistic country, is the following statement with regard to Czechoslovakia: [2] "It is no longer a question of exporting in order to accumulate gold, or foreign exchange, or foreign balances, or to assure service on the foreign loans, but in order to pay for the imports which are necessary to the execution of the plan."

It is probably best to qualify this argument slightly in the light of Russian policy. Non-economic, political factors would seem now to exert a major influence on the Russians. There is, for example, the Russian phobia about encirclement and her desire not to become dependent on the West for anything really important if she can help it. Whatever we may believe about our own intentions (and we know that we have no dastardly plans in view), the Soviet Union only need believe that our intentions are hostile for its policy to be affected thereby. There is also the Russian fetish to be completely divorced from the effect of the business cycle fluctuations of the western world. Consequently, there is substance to the belief that Russia, under present circumstances, wants to keep the total size of her trade beyond the "iron curtain" at a low figure. This is partially the basis for the statement made from time to time that Russia is "starving herself into greatness." But she will still be interested in getting as much import as possible in exchange for each unit of export; that is, she will be interested in favorable unit terms of trade. And as a general proposition, unless special circumstances such as those now affecting the Russians can be identified, there is no reason to expect that a government engaged in state trading would have an interest in keeping down the total volume of trade.

Since the interest of the state is in a net gain from the combination of exports and imports, it will plan the two together. Exports will be planned in the light of import needs, and decisions on the import of needed goods will be made in the light of export possibilities. These considerations will be related to the over-all planning which is calculated

[2] Guy Braibant, *La Planification en Tchecoslovaquie* (Paris: Colin, 1948), p. 96.

to make the country end up with as much goods as possible internally. And it is just as reasonable (or unreasonable) to believe that the government will be rational and intelligent in such planning as it has been for price theory to assume an economic man.

Application to Russia and Associated Countries

There is considerable ambiguity and uncertainty with regard to how the planning and organization of production is actually conducted in the Soviet sphere.

It seems probable that what the Communist world is doing can be roughly described as follows.[3] Each country individually plans its economic activity for the subsequent planning period. The production patterns which are established call for fixed proportions of the various factors of production and fixed proportions of various raw materials. This sort of planning in the Soviet scheme of things is now called the "materials-balance system." The plans establish certain goals for each productive plant. And engineers determine the amounts of various materials required to meet these output quotas. This sort of planning is far different from planning that would be geared to minor price variations and marginal decisions. However, although the Soviet bloc does not plan on the basis of these factors, it does not follow that they could not. At least Oscar Lange has argued vigorously that socialist countries should make their decisions in that fashion.

Be that as it may, the Soviet sphere countries now seem to use the "materials-balance system." Ames' chief criticism of the implications of this for international trade seems to be that:[4] "The materials-balance system will not in itself provide an answer to planners deciding which industries to develop for export or import-replacing purposes. It will, in principle, permit a country to determine its imports or exports given a particular productive structure, but it will not indicate the sectors of the economy where investment should be concentrated."

So far as the Russians themselves are concerned, it seems that the government of Russia, working within the framework of its over-all plan for the economy, draws up an annual budget of import needs and an estimate of the goods that can best be spared for export. Spulber writes that the basic principle for planning foreign trade has been that:[5] "the output plan commands the dynamics of imports, and that both condition the dynamics of exports."

[3] Edward Ames, "International Trade without Markets—the Soviet Bloc Case," *American Economic Review*, XLIV (December, 1954), pp. 791–807; Nicolas Spulber, "Economic Thinking and its Application and Methodology in Eastern Europe Outside of Soviet Russia," *American Economic Review, Papers . . .*, XLVI (May, 1956), pp. 367–79.

[4] Ames, *loc. cit.*, p. 800.

[5] Spulber, *loc. cit.*, p. 377.

The foreign trade combines, Soyuzneftexport (oil), Soyuzugelexport (coal), etc., on the export side, and Textilimport (textiles), Soyuzemtimport (steel products), etc., on the import side, take orders from the domestic state organizations, co-operatives, and private persons who have been allotted exports or imports under the plan. The foreign trade combines then sell or buy through the Ministry for Foreign Trade, which in turn works through the trade delegations set up by the Soviet Union in different countries.

There are reports of the co-ordination of industrialization programs as among the countries of the Soviet Sphere and of agreements within the framework of the Council for Mutual Economic Aid (Comecon), which was established in 1949.[6] And even as early as the 1945–46 period, various measures were apparently taken involving the relations between Russia on the one hand and at least Hungary and Rumania on the other.[7] A series of agreements, for example, provided for the joint Russian-Rumanian management of certain industries—in Rumania: oil, steel, glass, lumber, airlines, and Danube River traffic. A joint Russian-Rumanian company is a Sovrom.

Comecon may not have brought about effective co-ordination of economic planning in the Communist sphere, but the Russians have certainly continued to think in terms of the desirability of such co-ordinated planning. And in a conference at Warsaw in May, 1955, a Political Consultative Committee was set up which, according to Walter Ulbricht, was to co-ordinate economic planning in the Communist sphere in a process in which Russia would participate as the "first among equals."[8] The fact that such a conference was held can just as well be taken to indicate that Russia has not gone very far, as yet, with co-ordinated planning as that she has. But where there is this much smoke, there may be some fire.

At all events, it remains a question how effective such long-run planning can be in a setting where short-run price comparability is not utilized for planning purposes and where production and trade planning in the short run is on a materials-balance basis.[9]

There is, however, every reason to believe that the "monopolistic trading organizations of unequal bargaining strength" which characterize the Soviet system have a basic interest in improved terms of trade. They desire, insofar as their bargaining strength permits, to obtain more goods for less.

Russian exploitation of the countries associated with her (if there is

[6] *New York Times,* November 3, 1954, p. 32.

[7] Thomas E. M. McKitterick, *Russian Economic Policy in Eastern Europe* . . . (London: Fabian, 1948).

[8] *New York Times,* June 5, 1955, p. 1.

[9] Spulber says that the Soviet bloc planners do not as yet utilize effective cost comparisons.

such in addition to the affront to personal liberty and freedom of action involved in the existing political domination) might occur in two ways: either by terms of trade relatively favorable to Russia (high-priced Russian goods and low-priced satellite goods) or by gifts (reparations or unilateral transfers) from the satellite to Russia. Somewhat more subtly, however, it also might consist of Russian insistence on a trading pattern that could support relatively faster industrialization of Russia than of her smaller associated countries.

Application to United States-Russian Rivalry

If the theory as to motivation suggested earlier in this chapter is applied to Russia–United States trading relations, some odd conclusions follow.

It is worth remembering that the trade war of the late 1930's, especially as it involved the United States and Germany, was thought to be a threat to the peace (and was a threat to the peace) because various countries were struggling against each other for export markets. But such trade wars are likely causes for international difficulties only when they involve more than one country, organized, as is the United States, to push exports to the detriment of imports.

Russia is not likely to enter into a struggle for the privilege of sharing in foreign markets—although she is probably quite capable of taking advantage of an isolated situation to dump some product on the international market if that operation will embarrass a capitalistic country. She might even compete with us for export sales in an effort to capture the friendship of people in underdeveloped areas. But this will not be the ordinary Russian procedure; on the contrary, Russia will not customarily argue with the United States to see who is to have the privilege of having the largest favorable balance of trade. The United States is welcome to it.

Thus it would seem that, whatever the causes for friction may be between the United States and Russia, rivalry for export markets is not one of them. And there is, here at least, one less cause operating to bring about war—for whatever comfort we may draw from such thoughts.

The Mixed Economy and the Theory

Russia and other 100 per cent socialized countries are not the only nations to engage in considerable quantities of state trading. Even the United States government does considerable importing and exporting for its own account. In recent years, it has imported considerable quantities of raw materials for stockpiling purposes. In addition, in connection with ordinary government purchases, as for example generators to be used in government-built power projects, there is nothing to keep foreigners from submitting bids; and occasionally they may actually be awarded a contract. In Argentina, almost half the trading has been done by a government agency, IAPI. In the United Kingdom, about half the total trade has been for the account of the British government, and during the Labor regime virtually all the food imports into the United Kingdom have been made by the government. To a lesser extent, the same thing is true of France and Italy and many other countries on this side of the "iron curtain." It is literally true that a very substantial part of world trade is for the account of governments and is certain to remain so. This circumstance has a significance that we sometimes disregard in the United States when we think of free private enterprise and socialism as being a clear-cut "white versus black" proposition.

In fact, nothing could be farther from the truth than the idea that we are confronted with an absolute choice between state trading and free private enterprise trading. State trading is not a new evil that has obtruded itself into a happy order of private trading. A mixture of government trading and private trading has always characterized international trade and probably always will. The Bible cites Jacob's effort to buy corn from the pharaoh in Egypt.[10]

Theory needs to be modified to handle the implications of this mixed situation. The categorical statement, made above, about Russian interest in an unfavorable balance of trade and favorable terms of trade need not be repeated with regard to the mixed-economy situation. The manner in which a mixed-economy government conducts its affairs while engaging in state trading is dependent upon the nature and strength of the pressures exerted on it. In the mixed situation, private traders still may be a sufficiently vocal and influential group to lead the government into an effort which, on balance, tends to encourage exports relative to imports. English textile-manufacturing and whiskey-making interests may still have been influential enough to obtain government assistance in their search for markets, even in the days of the Labor government. Argentina is undoubtedly influenced by the infant-industry argument for tariffs in spite of a large amount of state trading.

It is, then, possible that a country which engages in some state trading and some private trading, on balance, either may be encouraging exports relative to imports in an effort to aid private traders to maximize monetary profit, or may be trying to maximize the amount of goods available for consumption in the country.

As for what should be done, as distinguished from what is done, eternal vigilance and continual flexibility in adjusting the relationship between private and public trading are called for. There is a presumption in favor of decentralization and private trading as long as the result is consistent with the maxium general well-being and individual freedom of choice. But it is a presumption which should not prevail if it runs

[10] *Genesis,* 42.

contrary to society's appraisal of the combination of measures which will contribute most effectively to general well-being.

Irresponsible Dictatorship

There are in the world a good many dictators (for example, Trujillo and Batista) who actively own, operate, and profit from private businesses within their countries. Also, various of their cohorts are active in business on their own account. Such situations cannot be analyzed in the frame of reference of this chapter. Such individuals may well have a basic interest in monetary profit (and perhaps in monetary profit in a foreign currency—the currency of the country where they plan to take refuge if overthrown). Their interest is probably far from a desire to increase general well-being—although of course it is not inconceivable that such an individual would be genuinely interested in his country's welfare.

The behavior of such dictators therefore cannot be analyzed as state-trading behavior in the meaning of this chapter, nor can it be analyzed, without considerable qualifications, as mixed-economy behavior. The mixture is truly different in kind.

SOME PRACTICES

Russian Trade with the United States

During the 1920's there was a limited amount of trade between the United States and Russia, but, since the United States government did not then recognize the Russian government, it was not conducted on a very orderly basis. Discussions between the two governments had to be conducted through intermediaries.

In spite of these difficulties, the Russians had set up and chartered under the laws of the state of New York in 1924 the Amtorg Trading Corporation. Amtorg sold goods in the United States and with the dollars thus obtained bought United States goods for shipment to Russia.[11] During the 1930's, after the institution of diplomatic relations between the United States and the Soviet Union, Amtorg's activities expanded considerably. Also during this period another sort of "trading relation" between the United States and Russia attained considerable importance. The Soviet government hired large numbers of American technicians to come to Russia and assist with the technical problems connected with the industrialization program.

During and immediately after World War II, Amtorg was a beehive of activity; and the firm, incidentally, enjoyed a very high credit rating and was frequented by United States businessmen for a consider-

---

[11] Considerable additional detail on the financing arrangements is to be found in Chapter 21.

able time after the political relations between the United States and
Russia had gotten extremely cold. But as the cold war became more
serious and the United States embargoed or placed licensing restrictions
on most shipments to Russia, the activities of Amtorg slowed to a
virtual standstill (unless there is a certain amount of espionage activity
being supervised from behind the doors).

United States exports (including re-exports) to and general imports
from the Soviet Union and China were as follows (in $1,000): [12]

	RUSSIA		CHINA	
	US Exports	US Imports	US Exports	US Imports
1947	149,069	77,102	353,605	116,705
1953	19	10,791	—	614

The Amtorg Trading Corporation now occupies offices consisting of
the entire twelfth floor of the Textile Towers building at 49 West 37th
Street in New York City; and it is apparently ready, willing, and
anxious for the resumption of a considerable amount of trading between
Russia and the United States.

Desirability of East-West Trade

There is a presumption in favor of the desirability of trade between
the free-private-enterprise economies and the state-trading agencies, as
long as such trade is handled judiciously on both sides. In fact there is
evidence that the Russians are interested in expanding East-West trade
in general. Georgi Malenkov has suggested the "expansion of trade and
co-operation with other countries irrespective of differences in social
systems . . . [and] . . . restoring the unification of the world market." [13]
Regardless of the sincerity of the proposal, there can be no harm in a
"cagey" Yankee trader going along with the idea as far as the Russians
can, by attrition, be induced to go. Embargoing trade with Russia is
merely confession of our inability to identify a good bargain and of our
fear that the Russians are better traders than we are. And if the
Russians really are pursuing a dastardly scheme to export surpluses to
aggravate the capitalist crisis,[14] our procedure is clear-cut. We do not
solve this problem, ostrich-like, by sticking our head in the sand. We
deal with the problem by making such adjustments in our economic
system as are necessary so that we can enjoy this embarrassment of riches
or at least such of the riches as we really need (like manganese).

[12] United States, Bureau of Foreign Commerce, *United States Trade with European and Asiatic Countries in the Soviet Bloc . . .* , Business Information Service,
International Trade Statistics Series Washington, April, 1954), p. 1; *Statistical Abstract*, 1953, pp. 916, 917.

[13] *International Conciliation*, April, 1953, p. 220. The Russian attitude on this matter does not seem to have changed with Malenkov's loss of influence.

[14] Austin *American-Statesman*, October 5, 1952, p. A-8.

Winston Churchill's position on the matter of trade between Eastern and Western Europe is worth quoting in detail:[15]

> I do not feel that there is any incongruity between building up the strength of E.D.C. and N.A.T.O. and associating with it under the conditions which have been set forth a powerful German contribution on the one hand, and faithfully striving for a workaday understanding with the Russian people and Government on the other.
>
> There is one agency, at any rate, which everyone can see, through which helpful contacts and associations can be developed. The more trade there is through the Iron Curtain and between Great Britain and Soviet Russia and the satellites the better still will be the chances of our living together in increasing comfort. . . .
>
> Friendly infiltration can do nothing but good. We have no reason to fear it and if Communist Russia does not fear it, that, in itself, is a good sign. I was, therefore, very glad to read the measure of success which attended the recent visits by British businessmen to Moscow. I do not suggest that at the present time there should be any traffic in military equipment . . . .

And a representative of American labor has expressed similar views. Mr. David J. McDonald, president of the United Steel Workers and a member of the Randall Commission, dissented from the Commission's report on the issue of East-West trade and said:[16]

> The countries that now comprise the Soviet bloc used to furnish Western Europe with a large part of its import requirements of food, fuel, and other raw materials. Similarly, they were important customers for the manufactured goods of the West. Under these circumstances, it is unwise for the United States to frown upon trade between Western Europe and the countries in the Soviet bloc while, at the same time, failing to take adequate steps to facilitate increased trade between Western Europe and the United States.

But the chief argument for East-West trade is not on the grounds that it is doing somebody else a favor. We will be doing ourselves the greatest favor of all. Infiltration of the Soviet bloc by all possible means is desirable, and if our economic-social-political system is really the best and the strongest, it will help us rather than hurt us.

We are not, or should not be, planning for the great atomic war with Russia; we should rather be planning to avoid it and make a viable

[15] *British Record*, March 15, 1954.
[16] United States, Commission on Foreign Economic Policy, *Report*, p. 77.

world. But even if we were planning for war, a good rule is to "know your enemy." Trade can contribute to this end by being judicious, not by being non-existent.

GATT

The revised General Agreement on Tariffs and Trade of 1955 provides that state trading enterprises shall practice non-discrimination. More specifically, it is required that such enterprises make their "purchases or sales solely in accordance with commercial considerations, including price, quality, availability, marketability, transportation, and other conditions of purchase or sale. . . ." The Soviet Union does not belong to GATT, but it is rather likely to behave in this fashion, anyway.

CONCLUSION

To crystal gaze a bit, let me hazard a guess as to how the cleavage between the United States and Russia may well turn out. There is a real similarity between the present ideological conflict and that between Catholics and Protestants at the time of the Reformation. There was the bitter and bloody Thirty Years' War (1618–1648) to prove that it was a real conflict. But the war destroyed neither Catholics nor Protestants, and as the years went by it developed that both groups could live in the same world. Catholics and Protestants to this day make snide remarks about each other, but they do not fight wars against each other. Perhaps our current difficulties with the Russians may turn into a sort of bitter stalemate which with the passage of time can lead to a situation in which the parties, although not liking each other, will have found out that they can get along; and the businessmen will have discovered once again that there is profit in trade. Whether this is wishful thinking or not, it is the only feasible assumption on which to operate when the alternative is atomic war.

The chief differences between the present situation and the Thirty Years War are these: if war breaks out this time, it will not last thirty years; and instead of ending in a draw that will preserve, with modifications, both the Protestant and Catholic churches, such a war will destroy both Communism and capitalism and thus destroy world society as it now exists.

The great issues of our time do not consist of a life-and-death struggle between good and bad, right and wrong, Communism and capitalism, centralization and individual rights. The great issue is: Can the human race control its environment and itself in its own interest? At present it is enjoying greater success in controlling its environment than in controlling itself.

Chapter 15

POLICY—AFFECTING THE MOVEMENT
OF GOODS

*Price comparability is a useful working tool both for businessmen and
for government planners.*

*If there is any alternative, trade control measures that reduce price
comparability are undesirable on that ground alone.*

*In general, the trade control measures discussed in Part IV are un-
desirable. They are tariffs, quotas, licenses, embargoes, discrimination, export subsidies, dumping, and cartels.*

*In the raw commodity control area, intervention to reduce the violence
of price fluctuations is probably desirable.*

*Otherwise, controls in this area should probably be limited to the
production subsidy and the consumption subsidy.*

*It would be highly desirable to establish an international organization,
such as the International Trade Organization or the Organization for
Trade Co-operation, with certain control powers in this area.*

T HIS chapter is devoted to some preliminary "drawing together
of threads" and some tentative policy judgments. Together with
Chapters 23 and 36, it is intended to build a picture of a combination of economic policies that would contribute to a viable,
growing world economy.

MEANING OF SELFISH GAIN

There has recently been a lot of criticism of the do-gooders and many
demands for an essentially selfish policy on the part of the United States,
much of this by people who have not bothered to analyze the meaning
of intelligent selfishness or the direction in which a policy of intelligent
selfishness would lead a country. It would be well to attempt to identify

the ingredients of intelligent selfishness before we try to be do-gooders or even to serve our own interests.

Turning back to the distinction made in Chapter 1, one classification of those with a stake in the international trading process is: (1) individual traders, (2) nations, and (3) the world. If we assume that each of these entities is thoroughly selfish and motivated by a desire to maximize its own well-being, we get the following results:

The individual trader will concentrate on an effort to maximize his own monetary profit in his own currency, that being the thing he can influence most readily by his own individual actions. Moreover, to the individual, money means command over goods, power, freedom of action, security, and what have you—except possibly affection and genuine human understanding.

The well-being of a nation is a combination of goods consumed (qualified for income distribution), plus freedom of action and security. The nation is well advised to influence its international trade pattern in the manner that will make the greatest ultimate contribution to the supply of goods in the country, unless there is positive evidence of harm on the freedom of action or security side. Pending proof to the contrary, large imports relative to exports increase the supply of goods in the country. And assistance by the government to a few local people who are complaining because foreign competition is hurting their monetary profit may, and probably will, reduce the total supply of goods and services available to the population as a whole.

The third party is the world. And there cannot be any satisfactory order in the world until the world community is in a position to make the world interest in a generally higher world well-being take precedence over national interest—in the rare cases where such a conflict might arise. Most of the fear in the United States of such a conflict of interest is uncalled for. We would probably be better off instead of worse off, in terms of level of living, in a world where the people of the other areas were better off as well. And the world would certainly be a healthier one in which to live—for us, too. Much of the alarm about conflict of interest between the nation and the world is raised by people with a monetary-profit ax to grind. The real conflict generally is between the individual consumer and his fellow citizens, not between the nation and the world at all.

It is easy to muddy the waters. It is also easy to say that a higher level of living is a desirable goal, and that geographical specialization and trade contribute to this goal. At this point the water is clear. Then somebody points out that tariffs may improve the terms of trade, and export stimulation may raise national (money) income. The water is now muddy. One can struggle to get the dirt out of the water by the expenditure of much time and effort; after that is done, the general proposition remains true that a higher level of living is furthered by increased geographical specialization and trade. But the proposition is now sufficiently soiled to permit many businessmen to argue that the special circumstances of his particular situation justify a barrier against foreign competition.

Theory does seem to indicate that a qualified free-trade position—a trading pattern shifted by planning somewhat away from that which would exist if there were genuine competition and laissez-faire—would accomplish better results than a completely free trade-competitive-laissez-faire position. It was argued in Chapter 6 that some interference with market forces may be necessary (1) because of the nature of the process of structural change, (2) because of the implications of monopoly power, (3) because of external economies and diseconomies, (4) because of equity considerations in income distribution, and (5) in certain cases, because of the implications of a "second-best" situation. But there is some reason to believe that few, if any, of the trade regulations now in existence tend to implement the constructive free trade position. Rather, the existing trade regulations as a rule have a restrictive and contracting effect. And the process by which they come into existence—as a result of the pressures of special interests—is not a process which is capable of producing any better result.

The fact that the United States was a large free-trade area undoubtedly facilitated development in the nineteenth century by comparison with what the development would have been if the country had been thirteen or forty-eight separate nations. But to say that the existence of this large tariff-free area facilitated development is not the same thing as saying that the United States developed without some planning aids. It is well known that government played an important role in guiding canal and railroad building across the United States. Examples of this relationship could be multiplied. And it is almost certainly true that American development occurred faster as a result of governmental participation in the process than it would have otherwise. The American case history makes some government participation in the development process (largely via the production subsidy) look desirable. But it makes an extensive free-trade area look very desirable as well.

Altering trade channels by coercive measures—unless a clear gain in well-being can be shown—is undesirable also on freedom-of-action grounds. Trade barriers limit the freedom of consumers to buy where and when they choose. Consumers are entitled to buy the goods they choose where they choose. What right have producers to impede this process? Getting as much as possible from life, tasting and savoring the good things of this world, is facilitated by having access to them.

Considerable judgment, therefore, is needed in the selection of the planning measures that are desirable. The problem has two chief aspects:

(1) selection, from among a broad field of possibilities, of the measures that will directly implement well-being most effectively; and (2) selection, also from among a large number of possibilities, of the measures that will make the economic system work.

To consider the second point first: The measures connected chiefly with the workability of the economic system are for the most part the financial measures which will be discussed and fitted into the picture in Part V. In this chapter, our concern is with the selection of measures that will directly implement well-being most effectively.

TOOLS

Price Comparability

A word should be said first for the desirability of price comparability as an aid in planning.

Price comparability is a situation in which the price of a particular commodity will be the same—except for differences corresponding to legitimate costs of transportation—everywhere in the world.

Price comparability is important for effective planning by both business and government. The private promoter and the government planner have all too few genuinely useful tools to aid them in decision making. A choice between development of this project or that may be much facilitated by reference to a meaningful pattern of raw commodity prices, which have come about in production situations that were influenced by as wide as possible a range of factors. The present fractionated world, which presents a picture of significant price differences for individual commodities as between country and country and as between region and region, can do little but confuse the planner. He cannot count on the meaningfulness of any one of these prices. If a promoter is considering developing a cotton textile mill in an underdeveloped country, but there are ten different prices for raw cotton of a certain staple length in ten different supplying countries, which one should he use for planning purposes? Planning for the future is uncertain enough at best; nothing is gained by the creation of additional, unnecessary uncertainties.

It may be noted that the position taken here with regard to the desirability of price comparability has little in common with the concept that the price of a single commodity in a certain market tends to be uniform at a given time. Rather the present proposition is that there should be effort to effect such uniformity—not that such uniformity automatically tends to come about.

Comparison of prices is the most satisfactory technique we are likely to develop for comparing real value. Consequently, every effort should be exerted to make price comparison as meaningful as possible. Planners, whether they be government officials or corporation executives, need to plan as intelligently as they can. But the world is infinitely complex; the number of factors to be taken into account is legion. Planning is difficult at best. But if prices were at least as comparable as possible, the problem would be to that extent less difficult.

Then man makes the problem worse. Tariffs distort price relations. Quotas, licenses, and embargoes distort price relations—or help monopolists to differentiate between markets and consequently to distort price relations. Multiple exchange rates distort price relations. Tax-free sale of cigarettes on ocean liners distorts price relations. Tax-free sales in United States government commissaries in Panama have, for years, been a disturbing factor in the Panamanian market.

It is difficult to see how government planners—working, say, toward a goal of industrialization—can possibly imagine that their problem is made easier when they destroy the usefulness of the price comparability tool by their own actions in using such a hodgepodge of confusing policy tools. Private businessmen do the same thing to themselves in their efforts to differentiate markets.

If the government wants to do something for its soldiers, it should pay them more instead of setting up tax-free commissaries. If it wants to discriminate in favor of one businessman, it should do it by measures that do not tend to destroy price comparability.

Insofar as they can, businessmen and government officials should use policy measures that are conducive to increased price comparability. They will improve the accuracy of their planning if they do.

If some obviously desirable goal can only be reached in a setting where prices are not comparable, price comparability will have to be dispensed with. But if it is possible to reach all of the desirable goals with other policy tools—then such tools as cause non-comparability of prices should be dispensed with. Effort is made in this chapter and in Chapters 23 and 36 to develop a workable pattern of policies. For the most part this has been done without resort to policies that distort price comparability.

Direct Commercial Controls

In the interest of intelligent planning, it is desirable to make the system of controls as simple as possible. A system of tariffs (involving different or discriminatory rates against different commodities) can be set up to have exactly the same effect as a system of multiple exchange rates. Yet many countries use both control devices—to the infinite confusion of the foreign trader. One of the worst things about the recent United States program for reducing trade barriers has been that it has not eliminated one single control device.[1] We reduce a tariff rate to a low

---

[1] This is barely exaggerated.

figure—half of one per cent—but leave it on the books for what the complication is worth. A wholesale house-cleaning of thousands of direct control devices that have only a nuisance value is long overdue. And recent misnamed customs simplification legislation has done almost nothing along this line.

A lot of rhetoric at the Democratic and Republican conventions has latterly been devoted to the desirability of doing something for the much-put-upon small businessman. Complicated import restrictions are much more of a hindrance to the small businessman than to the large corporation. For a small shipment of tile from Monterrey, Mexico, it is hardly worth his time to find out what the regulations are. The removal of quantitative barriers to trade and of tariffs would be a major service to the small businessman who has any desire to engage in international trade.

It is considerations of these several sorts which lead to the rejection of all of the commercial-policy tools (see Table 50) such as tariffs, quotas, etc., which have been discussed in Part IV. If it should prove impossible to work out a reasonable pattern of co-ordinated policy without the use of the commercial-policy tools, it would be necessary to come back to them. Such is not the case, however. Consequently the use of tariffs and of trade subsidies on exports and imports; the use of quotas, licenses, and other quantitative controls over trade; and the practice of discrimination—all are rejected.

In addition to the above recommended changes, the rejection of discrimination merits special emphasis because it is the tactic which is most likely to call forth unanticipated sorts of violent retaliation.

Impact of Tariff Reduction on United States

Commercial-policy barriers to trade are not removed painlessly overnight. Consequently some consideration of the implications for the United States of a removal of tariffs may be helpful.

Although intelligent selfishness should permit the tariff problem to be handled at the national level, the present institutional arrangements in most countries create a situation which can best be dealt with by international action. The prevailing pattern of pressure-group activities makes it very difficult for a government, such as that of the United States, to practice intelligent selfishness in the interests of its own people. In this setting an international agency conceivably could serve a most beneficial purpose by assisting a national government to do what is actually in its own interest.[2]

[2] The place where restrictions may be appropriate is not the United States but the underdeveloped countries. And in the underdeveloped countries the restrictions called for are production subsidies which will keep prices down (at the same time that infant industries are encouraged) rather than tariffs to keep them up. If the

Intelligent selfishness calls for something approaching free trade on the part of the United States, but this does not mean that free trade can be or should be put into effect overnight—although that might not be as bad an idea as is sometimes alleged. The change-over might have a considerable, stimulating effect, at least temporarily, on business ingenuity. But it is probably desirable that the change-over should be orderly and gradual.

The standard method for effecting a change, which has been suggested in other contexts in this book, should apply. In the case of tariffs, that would mean a certain percentage reduction in all tariffs each year, perhaps 10 per cent of the amount of the tariff in the base year (a procedure which would eliminate all tariffs in ten years). In addition, in the interest of simplicity, it might be well to eliminate the tariff on any particular type of goods the year after it falls below 5 per cent ad valorem.

With regard to the impact of the change-over on individuals, something should be repeated which has been said before. First, the amount of change-over that will be called for is not likely to be as great as alarmists sometimes allege. No less a person than Henry Ford II says this is the case.[3] Few if any industries will be wiped out. Most will be affected little if at all, if management shows true American ingenuity and if community planning or re-planning is well done by an intelligent citizenry at the municipal level.[4]

But this does not justify disregarding the problem of the workers who may be displaced, although it may justify disregarding the problem of the displaced entrepreneur, who, in the American tradition, is assumed to have the ingenuity to look after himself. But free technical and training school re-education should be provided at government expense (free board and room, too) to displaced workers who are older than 25 or 30. The criteria would have to be worked out. Also employers should be required, by law if necessary, to discharge the younger people first. It is better for them to get out of a declining industry as

United States were really practicing free trade, it would be in a stronger position to inveigh against tariffs and import quotas in the underdeveloped countries.

[3] Henry Ford II, *Expanded Trade and World Peace* (Dearborn, Michigan: Ford Motor Company, 1953), p. 9.

[4] Durable-goods industries and new industries in general will probably be least affected. Exposed branches of agriculture and some of the older nondurable-goods industries (such as pottery, chinaware, and handblown glass) may well be adversely affected. (Humphrey, *American Imports,* p. 412). Humphrey says (p. 477): "Those who favor freer trade have given too little attention to the problem of adjustment. It is no use to sugar-coat the import pill. Absolute or relative injury to some is an essential and inevitable result of the shift from a protected market to a free market." The United States Department of Commerce (Business and Defense Services Administration) has begun the publication of a magazine called *Area Development Bulletin* which should help with the analysis of these adjustment problems.

quickly as possible, anyway, if the industry is really declining. It should not be necessary at all to discharge many of the older workers. No specific industry is going to die in an afternoon. In fact a few marginal, high-cost firms are all that would probably be affected initially. If planning is well done, an industry can provide good jobs to fewer workers during its declining years. To repeat, we must provide retraining assistance for workers, industry-wide planning of the period of decline, and community-wide planning for the better things to come.

During the ten-year period of tariff cutting (and even if the tariff cutting proposal is not adopted), the disposition of tariff revenue should be changed. All tariff revenues should be turned over to the United Nations or its appropriate affiliated agency. This is desirable, not out of altruism toward the United Nations, but, again, on the basis of intelligent selfishness in the short run. If one group of businessmen is to be allowed to enhance its monetary profits by having tariff protection (and since exports tend to equal imports) and exports are consequently reduced to the detriment of the monetary profit of the exporters, we are not really injured by turning the dollars received from our import tariffs over to foreigners, via the United Nations, with the hope that they will be used to finance purchases from United States exporters. And they will be. There would be a certain amount of poetic justice involved in such disposition of tariff revenues, in any case. All misguided governments that insist on continuing the use of tariffs should comply with this requirement, to aid their own exporters who are otherwise penalized by the restriction on imports.

Prices, Multilateral Trade, and the Possibility of Substitution

Still another argument indicates the desirability of avoiding tariffs, quotas, licenses, discrimination, and other direct commercial controls over trade. In the event of disequilibrium in the balance of trade (and difficulty in the operation of the financial adjustment mechanisms that will be discussed in Part V), adjustment will occur far more easily if there is a minimum of trade restrictions. If traders have broad freedom of choice in determining what they will buy and to whom they will sell, very moderate price adjustments can solve problems that are almost incapable of solution otherwise (except by bilateral balancing and trade contraction) in a world saturated with direct controls.[5]

In this setting multilateral trade as distinct from bilateral balancing plays an important role.

[5] In terms of the economist's professional jargon, if demand is elastic price adjustments are effective. If demand is quite inelastic, price adjustments may not be very good at effecting adjustment and direct controls may be the only alternative. But the point is precisely that demand will be more elastic if buyers have more freedom of choice. And they have more freedom of choice if there are fewer trade barriers.

Bilateral balancing involves effort by each country to make the money value of its exports to each other country equal the money value of its imports from each other country. This is the state of affairs to which conditions tend when the planners in each country, seeking to make exports as large as they can relative to imports, decide to pressure other countries one at a time in the effort to attain the desired goal. The only differences between exports and imports will be those allowed if the planners decide to permit some debt settlement or some new foreign lending. (Some of the ramifications of these policies are discussed in Chapters 12 and 20.)

Chart 2 suggests that trade does not naturally balance on a country-by-country basis. Some countries want large amounts of the product of countries that do not naturally want large amounts of their goods in return. Everybody may be better off if the United States has an export balance (machinery and wheat) with the United Kingdom, if the United Kingdom has an export balance with the rest of the Empire, and if the rest of the Empire has an export balance (tin and rubber) with the United States.

In a world characterized by multilateral trade, a high degree of substitutability exists as between the products of different countries. And this substitutability facilitates adjustment. Conceivably, it would be impossible to get any satisfactory adjustment without it—even if demand elasticities were fairly high and direct trade control were being used right and left.[6]

Price adjustment, as a policy tool, is desirable if it works smoothly and if a little price adjustment will accomplish a good deal of adjustment in the trading pattern. Balance-of-trade problems are not acute between the regions of a country in the same manner as internationally chiefly because of the many different ways in which price adjustments can occur within a country uncluttered by trade barriers.[7]

Price adjustments pose a serious problem in their effects on the relationship between prices of manufactured goods and prices of raw commodities. In Chapter 13, it was suggested that it might be desirable to use government subsidies to a limited extent to lessen the swiftness of price drops of agricultural commodities. But that is about the only area where government interference with the price mechanism is desirable (in normal times).

---

[6] Meade, *Balance of Payments*, p. 377.

[7] Meade goes a good deal further than this and discusses wage-rate changes on the assumption that they underlie price changes. He makes most of the case for price changes hinge on the possibility that wages may fluctuate up or down. (*Balance of Payments*, Chap. XI). He probably overstresses the closeness of the connection between prices and wages. It is rather doubtful that wage reductions should be extensively used as a device for implementing adjustment. Other segments of the economy can better bear the adjustment sacrifice.

Fiscal and Monetary Policy

The tools discussed up to this point do not lend themselves to use in a positive way by planners in their effort to increase welfare. It will be recalled that problems arise in connection with structural change, monopolies, external economies and diseconomies, and income distribution. It is now the time to attempt, in a constructive way, to identify the tools that may be genuinely serviceable. And the most serviceable policies, by and large, are the fiscal and monetary measures that can be used directly to influence production and distribution. They offer far more promise for making the control pattern as simple and manageable as possible and for accomplishing the desired results of increased production and better income distribution.

In this area, the chief measures available are (1) public works (if it is decided that the government itself should implement a particular project), (2) the production or consumption subsidy (if it is decided that the activity should be in private hands but also that, for one reason or another, its fate should not be left purely to market forces), and (3) quantitative and qualitative credit control (the latter probably being the most useful control of all).

Public works and direct government operation of a business are rather clear-cut operations. The government of the United States decides to build a dam and does it.

The production subsidy calls for a little more comment, especially in terms of its relation to the trade subsidy.[8] The production subsidy is a direct payment by the government to facilitate production. The trade subsidy is a direct payment by the government to traders, perhaps international traders, to facilitate the trading process. Except for the subsidy recommended in Chapter 13, which was intended to slow down the violence of price fluctuations, trade subsidies appear undesirable. If the goals of the economic process are higher level of living, more desirable income distribution, etc., the trade subsidy is an oblique and uncertain method for serving these ends. The same should be said for tariffs and the other direct commercial controls. The warping of the commercial pattern merely tends to destroy price comparability and makes it increasingly difficult to equate social cost to the price paid for goods.

At the other end of the economic process from production is consumption. Especially in times of emergency, it may be most desirable to make direct gifts to consumers. Contributions to the Red Cross in the United States for earthquake relief in Chile are a most commendable action. In general, if interference with the economic process could be limited to one end of the spectrum or the other—could be limited to pro-

[8] See Meade, *Trade and Welfare, passim.*

duction or consumption subsidies to the exclusion of trade subsidies and barriers—it would be easier to analyze and plan the process.

But the foregoing is not necessarily an argument for the direct, wholesale use of the production subsidy. Most of the aid required by businesses, even by new productive enterprises, can probably be obtained from more carefully planned quantitative and qualitative credit controls in the money and banking area.

It may be noted that the fiscal and monetary measures suggested do not, by and large, involve interference with the international trading process, at least not directly. The indirect effects of financial measures on international trade will be discussed in Part V and especially in Chapter 23.

Distribution

Some special comment should be directed at the problem of income distribution. Internally, the government can influence income distribution via the progressiveness of the tax structure and the pattern of government spending (and deficit financing). Internationally, the same sort of thing could be accomplished by a simplified world-wide income tax combined with extensive use of grants-in-aid from the world tax authority (with relatively more of the funds going to the areas which it has been decided on distributional grounds should get more). Much the same result can be accomplished by qualitative credit controls which make more purchasing power available in the countries which it has been decided should be favored on distributional grounds.[9]

Volume vs. Balance

To a disproportionate extent, the discussion of international trade has been concerned with the state of the trade balance and the effort to have an export balance.[10] Actually a better working approach for those in a position to influence international trade would be that any measure which will permit or encourage the volume of either imports or exports to increase is a good thing. It does not matter which. Increase in the volume of one will carry with it an increase in the volume of the other. This is about the only high positive statistical correlation in the field of international trade which is worth anything (see Chart 7).

[9] But detailed discussion of this possibility must wait upon the discussion of finance in Part V.

[10] In truth, there is an underlying tendency for the balance to look after itself—since "cagey" businessmen tend to insist on satisfactory payments arrangements when they make a sale.

AGENCIES

I.T.O., GATT, and O.T.C.

If the preceding ideas are worth implementing, what do they call for in terms of organization?

At the international level, organizations called the International Trade Organization (I.T.O.) and the Organization for Trade Cooperation (O.T.C.) have been proposed to deal with such problems. And an arrangement called the General Agreement on Tariffs and Trade (GATT) is in existence. At the national level the Eisenhower administration is ostensibly working on a program to lower trade barriers.

The I.T.O. was an organization proposed in the immediate post-World War II years and energetically pushed by the State Department, which published its original proposal in December of 1945. A series of international conferences was held in London (1946), Geneva (1947), and Havana (1949); and articles of agreement were drafted for ratification by the legislatures of the participating countries. The articles provided machinery for negotiating tariff reductions, eliminating quantitative restrictions on trade, and regulating cartels, raw commodity control schemes, and state trading. The nations would remain sovereign in determining how much they were prepared to reduce their tariffs. Decisions would be made by negotiation.

Since the organization had been promoted by the United States and United States membership was necessary if the organization was to become an effective, going concern, other governments waited for the ratification of the agreement by the United States government before bothering to submit it to their own legislatures. At least at one time, it was a foregone conclusion that it would be ratified by enough governments to go into effect if it was ratified by the United States. But the United States did not ratify. Why? It seems that strong trade associations which had originally favored the idea changed their mind. After the articles of agreement were finally drafted, when business leaders read them through, they could find clauses that might conceivably be detrimental to their particular firms. One person objected to this clause, another to that. And as a result of this reverse logrolling procedure, they prevented the ratification of the charter. It was almost certainly a significant shift of organized business sentiment in the United States—from favoring the articles as a matter of principle to opposition because of dislike for specific provisions—that led to the rejection by the United States of this chick which had sprung from an egg that it laid. In a minor key, this development compares with the rejection by the United States Senate of the League of Nations following World War I.

The failure to implement the I.T.O. left the General Agreement on

Tariffs and Trade, which is a nebulous sort of thing, as the most important existing organization for regulating commodity trade. At the Geneva conference of 1947, it was appreciated by the delegates (remarkable foresight as it turned out) that it would take time for the I.T.O. to go into operation, and it was thought desirable to implement some of its features sooner. GATT was the result.

GATT is a loose organization which holds multilateral conferences to discuss tariff reductions. The United States government has participated in the work of GATT by executive action under the powers granted by the Reciprocal Trade Agreements Act. Conferences in which twenty to thirty governments have participated have been held since 1947 at Annecy, Torquay, and again at Geneva. And a very respectable reduction of tariffs was effected by 1951. Few reductions have occurred since. Without disparaging the work which GATT has done, it may be said that it is not a general-purpose, permanent organization equipped with any real power to regulate all the features of international trade which should be regulated at the international level.

At a GATT meeting in Geneva in the fall of 1954 in which thirty-four nations participated, a new organization—the Organization for Trade Cooperation—was proposed. This is, substantially, the I.T.O. under another name. Tariff reduction by negotiation—with the individual nations determining whether or not changes in rates will occur—is still the heart of the plan. There is still a general condemnation of quantitative restrictions (not tariffs) on trade. It is provided that trade restrictions, when used, should be non-discriminatory. The generalization of concessions via the unconditional most-favored-nation clause principle is endorsed. In spite of United States insistence on the principle of condemnation of quantitative restrictions, the government of this country requested and succeeded in obtaining a waiver which would permit it to continue to practice quota limitation on agricultural imports coming into this country.[11] Other qualifications of the general principles continue to permit, under controlled conditions, restrictions on imports justified by balance-of-payments considerations. Still others provided considerable latitude for underdeveloped countries to modify tariff rates and impose other restrictions in the interest of economic development.[12]

The negotiations that resulted in the proposal for the Organization for Trade Cooperation also revised the General Agreement on Tariffs and Trade and provided for a "tariff truce" to continue for three years following June, 1955. The United States delegates at the conference, under the powers granted the executive branch by the Reciprocal Trade Agreements Act, committed this government to the revised GATT. The Or-

[11] *New York Times,* April 15, 1955, p. 14.
[12] *International Financial News Survey,* March 25, 1955, p. 294.

ganization for Trade Cooperation itself is provided for in a protocol to the revised GATT which will not be binding without Senate ratification.[13] For a while in the spring of 1956, it appeared that the Eisenhower administration would energetically push ratification of O.T.C. through Congress. The American Tariff League expressed violent opposition; and no action was taken by the Senate.

Agency Powers

A chief function of an international trade regulation organization should be the control of discrimination. American nationalists should not be worried as to the implications of such control actions. If nations come to realize intelligent selfishness calls for getting as much goods and services as possible moving in the channels of trade, they will be much less prone to practice discriminations—which chiefly tend to discourage imports from the lowest cost country.

But it is important that an international trade regulatory authority should be able to prevent unjustified discrimination among nations, even though it may not prove necessary to make extensive use of the authority except possibly in connection with private cartels. As may be recalled from Chapter 13, the private cartels, in their effort to maximize monetary profit (rather than national *real* income) engage in all sorts of discriminatory practices as between different markets. They charge different prices in different markets, and so on. Collusion among private companies that results in discrimination among buyers in different countries must be under the jurisdiction of the international agency if there is to be any prospect of satisfactory regulations in this difficult field. National governments should be interested in avoiding basic policies that restrict production to raise price. Therefore, the international organization might not need to regulate that aspect of the problem, although it should be able to do so if necessary.

Another function of such an organization would be to counsel underdeveloped countries with regard to the implementation of such protection as may be justified on the basis of the infant-industry argument. But since such aid to new industries should chiefly take the form of production subsidies and qualitative credit controls (rather than tariffs, quotas, etc.), the real problem is to help the underdeveloped countries to select the industries which should be given special treatment and to assist with the financing problem. In that event, much of the work in this area would fall within the purview of an expanded International Bank for Reconstruction and Development. It would be a problem of developmental policy rather than a problem of trade in goods.

Nations probably ought to make the decision for themselves as to how much of their trade should be in private hands and how much

[13] *New York Times*, March 22, 1955, p. 1.

should be in the form of state trading. The private trader (without benefit of trade restrictions) and the state-trading government (interested in raising real per capita income) can then be left to bargain for themselves in individual transactions—subject to the proviso that if, in this new state of affairs, new abuses of power crop up, as they well may, new decisions will have to be made as to which aspects of trade regulation should be handled at the world level and which could be decentralized.

But the basic, general decisions must be made by world society as a whole, under the presumption that decision making and policy implementation should be decentralized as far as is consistent with the maximization of world-wide well-being.

Eternal vigilance is the price of freedom. Continuing appreciation of the problems involved in deciding what should be centralized and what may be decentralized is the price of the most desirable level of living and of genuine, effective individual freedom.

PART V

Money, Short-term Funds, and the Business Cycle Problem

Chapter 16

THE FOREIGN EXCHANGE MARKET

❧ ❧ ❧

Description of the process by which payment for an international ship-
ment of goods is made indicates the necessary connection between
the goods transaction and the international movement of short-term
funds. This knowledge is useful for understanding of the relation-
ship indicated in the balance of payments statement between goods
movements and international lending (unilateral transfers or gold
shipments).
An international financial center is likely to be a net debtor at short term.
Being an international debtor at short term is probably evidence of finan-
cial strength rather than financial weakness.
London was the chief center for financing commodity trade during the
nineteenth century and continues to play a more important role than
New York. London finances almost half of the world's trade.
Both London and New York are major debtors at short term.

❧ ❧ ❧

INTERNATIONAL trade, like domestic trade, essentially involves
the exchange of things of value—i.e., of goods and services. The
financial juggling connected with monetary transfers has no
intrinsic usefulness in isolation. Part IV was concerned with measures directly influencing the quantities of goods and services exchanged.
The present part deals with short-term financing. This topic, while it is
one degree removed from the basically important movements of goods,
can nevertheless be of great importance either in stimulating or in
frustrating the goods movements, especially when either speculators or
exchange controls enter the field.

Although there is a certain similarity between the internal and the
international function of money, there are also important differences.
Money in the form of dollars or francs or pounds sterling does not
move internationally, as dollars may move in a person's pocket from
New York to Texas. Despite the fact that we are prone to speak of
the international movement of funds or of credit, the currency of one
country does not move freely to other countries. One national currency

is generally not acceptable as payment in ordinary transactions in another country; it is not legal tender in the other country. The paper franc cannot be used to finance ordinary business transactions in the United States, and the same is true of most currencies. Of course, there is no hard-and-fast rule that one country's paper money (or its gold coins, if it has any) shall never be shipped to another country. A paper currency such as the dollar, when it is the money of the country which is financially strongest at the moment, may be acceptable or even desirable in other countries so that it would not be correct to say that the foreigners have no desire to possess dollars as such. They may want them to hold. In addition, there are the coin collectors and paper-money collectors to be considered. But basically national monies do not move from one country to another.

MECHANICS

Mechanics Proper (*An Individual Transaction*)

The international short-term financial problem, then, essentially involves explaining how payments are made by people in one country, who have that country's currency at the start of the process, to people in another country, who want to end up with the currency of their own country. In order to pose this problem satisfactorily, it should be useful to describe how a shipment of goods may be financed. It is probably unnecessary for present purposes to describe the different ways in which international payments can be made and the types of documents (bills of exchange and letters of credit) that may be used under different circumstances, but it is extremely important to understand what is fundamentally involved in the process. Such understanding may be obtained by studying any one of the different financing methods.

In Chart 8 it is assumed that a private United States exporter has sold some goods to an importer in England. Naturally, before the shipment occurs, the exporter and importer have agreed by contract as to what goods are to be shipped and what the price shall be.[1] They are both satisfied with the terms of the sale and with the implications of those terms at the prevailing rate of exchange between their respective national currencies. They will also have agreed upon the identity of the currency in which payment is to be made. In this example it is assumed that the British importer has permitted the United States exporter to draw a

[1] In these days of government controls over trade, they will probably have been forced to obtain export and import licenses as well as permits to buy and sell each other's currencies. Also, the importer may have obtained a letter of credit from his bank stating that the bank has available certain funds to pay off the bill of exchange that the exporter will draw up. Actually if the latter were the case the example which follows might end with step 4.

CHART 8

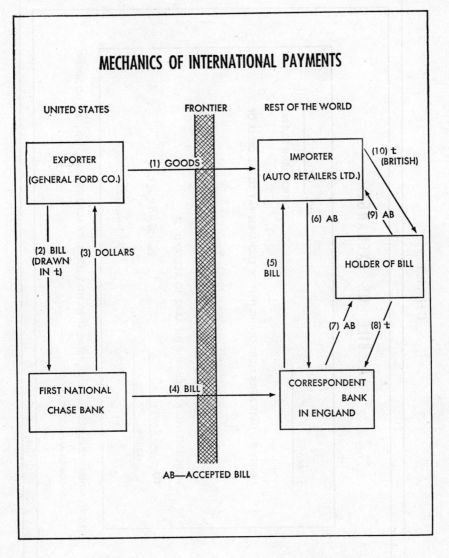

MECHANICS OF INTERNATIONAL PAYMENTS

UNITED STATES   FRONTIER   REST OF THE WORLD

EXPORTER
(GENERAL FORD CO.)

(1) GOODS

IMPORTER
(AUTO RETAILERS LTD.)

(10) £
(BRITISH)

(2) BILL
(DRAWN
IN £)

(3) DOLLARS

(6) AB

(9) AB

HOLDER OF BILL

(5)
BILL

(7) AB   (8) £

FIRST NATIONAL
CHASE BANK

(4) BILL

CORRESPONDENT
BANK
IN ENGLAND

AB—ACCEPTED BILL

CHART 9

A BILL OF EXCHANGE

£ 1,000

NO. 101

DETROIT, JUNE 30, 1953

NINETY (90) DAYS AFTER SIGHT OF THIS FIRST OF EXCHANGE PAY TO THE ORDER OF

The First National Chase Bank of New York   THE SUM OF

****One thousand pounds sterling****

VALUE RECEIVED AND CHARGE THE SAME TO ACCOUNT OF

TO: Auto Retailers, Ltd.

London

The General Ford Co.

(signed)
John Doe, Treasurer

NOTE: WHEN "ACCEPTED" (BY ENDORSEMENT TO THAT EFFECT) BY AUTO RETAILERS, LTD., THIS DOCUMENT
BECOMES AN ACCEPTANCE.

ninety-day bill of exchange against him in terms of pounds sterling to cover the agreed-upon price of a General Ford car. This means that the United States exporter (the General Ford Company) may write on a sheet of paper that he orders the importer in England (Auto Retailers, Ltd.) to pay within ninety days the sum of £1,000 to an appropriate recipient (perhaps the First National Chase Bank of New York—see Chart 9). In this case the American exporter (or bank) will gain if the pound sterling appreciates or gains in value in terms of the dollar while the transaction is going on; he will lose if it depreciates or declines in value. But the British participant will not be directly affected by appreciation or depreciation—because the number of pounds he pays remains unchanged.

The exporter may take the bill of exchange (the document he has drawn up demanding payment from the British importer) to his bank (the First National Chase Bank of New York) in the United States. The bank incurs little risk of loss, for it can, in the event of default, have recourse against the United States exporter of whose credit standing it is aware. Moreover, the shipping papers, enabling the holder to claim the goods at the customs, are probably attached to the bill of exchange. It is at this point that a foreign-exchange rate (on ninety-day bills) is established. And in this example it is established by negotiation between the United States exporter and the United States bank. The British importer is not involved, since he has done nothing more than promise to pay in pounds. The United States bank has to decide how many dollars it will give the United States exporter in exchange for his claim on £1,000. Perhaps it is decided that at the current rate £1 equals $2.80; accordingly, the American bank gives the United States exporter $2,800.[2]

At this point the exporter is paid in dollars, so that from his point of view the transaction has been completed, and completed in the proper currency. Of course, the United States bank might call on him to "make good" in the event that the bill "went sour" somewhat further along the line. But that does not generally occur.

The United States bank may then send the bill to a correspondent bank in England—perhaps the London and Southminster Bank. The correspondent bank will submit the bill to the importer, who must accept it (perhaps promising to pay in ninety days) in order to obtain the attached documents which he needs to get the goods out of customs. The

---

[2] Probably at this stage in the operation the United States bank will sell its pounds. It may draw a banker's sight draft against the pounds it is about to acquire in England. Banker's sight drafts, because the bank's credit is better than the exporter's credit and also because the time involved is shorter, sell for somewhat more than ninety-day bills—perhaps for $2.84 to the pound. The profit of the United States bank in connection with the transaction is likely to be made from the difference between the rate of exchange applied to the ninety-day bill and the rate applied to the banker's sight draft.

correspondent bank will probably discount the acceptance on the money market, receiving a quantity of pounds sterling, perhaps £1,000 less a discount of £10 (if the discount rate is 4 per cent a year). The correspondent bank will then make an entry in its books crediting the United States bank with £990 of deposits, the New York bank's short-term assets in the importing country thereby being increased by this amount.[3]

At this point the short-term loan by the United States to England which is financing the goods exports takes the form of an increase in the deposits of the United States bank in the English bank to the amount of £990.[4] Such a transaction would appear in the international balance of payments statement as a movement of short-term funds from the United States to England. And the movement has financed the goods trade. In Table 12 this figure of £990 would be part of the total of $194 million (item 36) in private United States short-term capital flowing out from the United States.

The transaction from this point onward loses its international flavor. The importer is the debtor of the other Englishman, who holds the bill during the ninety-day period. After the ninety days, the importer will pay to the holder in his country the sum of £1,000. The importer thus pays in his own currency, pounds sterling; the exporter is paid in the currency of his country, dollars; there has been no international movement of currency; but there has been an international movement of goods, and the international payment has been effected. In the process, however, there has been what is generally called an international movement of short-term funds. The United States bank (or some United States speculator) has increased the amount of money it has on deposit in the bank in England; and the movement of goods has occurred as tangible evidence that "something worth having" has moved from one country to the other as an aspect of the lending process.

Relation of Funds Movement to Goods Movement

It is extremely important to understand the nature of the relationship between the international shipment of goods and international lending.

---

[3] If the United States bank has already sold these pounds via a banker's sight draft, it is worth noting that for the United States bank to make any money the foreign-exchange rate on banker's sight drafts has to be enough higher than the rate on ninety-day bills to allow for the £10 pound discount. If the rate on ninety-day bills was $2.80 to the pound, the United States bank paid out $2800 to the United States exporter. If the rate on banker's sight drafts was $2.84 to the pound, he received $2811.60 for his £990 and consequently netted $11.60. Some such relation between the rates must exist to make the transaction profitable for the United States bank.

[4] The situation is not changed fundamentally if the United States bank has meanwhile sold its £990 pounds to a United States speculator. It is merely the United States speculator rather than the United States bank who has the deposit in pounds in England. The national identity of the owner of the deposit remains the same.

It is not in the nature of some vague, indefinable relationship between goods movement and lending. In this isolated case the international loan in an amount equal to the value of the goods shipment was an automatic corollary of the goods shipment.[5] And in all cases the international shipment of goods must be financed in some way or other. There is simply no such thing as an export of goods and a favorable balance of trade in some kind of a vacuum that has no relation to financing arrangements. As is repeated over and over in this book, an export or import balance on goods and services must have as a counterpart either lending, giving, or gold movement.

To return to the example under consideration, it is conceivable, and even likely, that a goods movement going from Britain to the United States may be financed by a transaction which is substantially the reverse of this one, and that as a consequence a British bank acquires a dollar deposit in a correspondent United States bank. In Table 12 this would appear as part of entry 44, short-term foreign capital inflow into the United States, a figure which was a net $700 million in 1955.

Let us say that, as a result of many such transactions, British banks have on deposit in the United States $751 million and United States banks have on deposit in British banks the equivalent (at $2.80 to the pound) of $35 million in pounds sterling.[6] Perhaps a British bank decides it does not wish to hold quite so many dollars and wishes to sell $28,000 for pounds sterling. If $2.80 to the pound is a workable foreign-exchange rate, it will be possible to find a United States bank with some pound sterling deposits which it will be willing to convert into dollars at that figure. If the United States bank and the British bank can agree on a foreign-exchange rate (e.g., the ever-recurring $2.80 equals £1), then the British bank can turn its $28,000, held in the United States, over to the United States bank and the United States bank can turn £10,-000 of its deposits in Britain over to the British bank.[7]

In this example there has been a repatriation of capital by *both* parties. Both the British and the Americans have reduced their foreign investments by $28,000 (or £10,000). This transaction, in terms of Table 12, would mean a reduction of both entry 36 and entry 44 by $28,000.

---

[5] Granted there is a difference between £990 and £1,000. But the difference represents payment for a service—not some unknown magical factor making inequality possible.

[6] Figures for February 28, 1953. See: *Federal Reserve Bulletin,* May, 1953, p. 560.

[7] Actually, in this situation, one should not take the foreign-exchange rate as given. We are, in fact, right at the heart of the analysis of the forces that set the rate. If British banks are more anxious to sell dollars for pounds than American banks are to buy dollars with the pounds they have, the foreign-exchange rate is likely to change, perhaps to $2.90 per pound.

Aggregate Mechanics (Financing of Exports and Money Flows)

It is desirable to consider how the international trade-financing mechanism may work in the aggregate—as well as how it works in the case of an individual transaction. This is important for analyzing the relationship between national income and international trade. Assume that at the beginning of a year United States banks have $1 billion in balances in foreign banks and foreign banks have $1 billion in balances in United States banks.[8] The situation might be represented as follows:

BASIC SITUATION   As of January 1st

United States	*Rest of World*
United States Banks:	Foreign Banks:
Have $1 billion in deposits to credit of foreign banks	Have $1 billion in deposits to credit of United States banks

Actually, in terms of the *net* position, neither banking system is in debt to the other. Each system has assets and liabilities of $1 billion in terms of its relation internationally to the other.

If during the year trade valued at $10 billion moves both ways—exports equaling imports—the net position of the two areas will remain unchanged. But, depending on the nature of the financing arrangements, various things might have happened to the gross positions. Either of the two following results would be possible:

CHANGE I   As of December 31st

United States Banks:	Foreign Banks:
Have $500 million in deposits to credit of foreign banks	Have $500 million in deposits to credit of United States banks

CHANGE II   or

United States Banks:	Foreign Banks:
Have $2 billion in deposits to credit of foreign banks	Have $2 billion in deposits to credit of United States banks

Exports in effect have paid for imports. Various changes in the size of gross balances occur. But the net creditor-debtor relation internationally remains the same.

Let us assume, on the other hand, that United States exports during the year exceed United States imports by $500 million. Then the re-

[8] Assume a "one-to-one" foreign exchange rate so that it is possible to speak of dollars or of units of the foreign currency indifferently.

lationship between the sizes of the balances would change. The relationship might change in a setting involving decline in the combined balances:

CHANGE III	As of December 31st	
United States Banks: Have $250 million in deposits to credit of foreign banks		Foreign Banks: Have $750 million in deposits to credit of United States banks

Or it might change in a setting involving increase in the combined balances:

CHANGE IV	As of December 31st	
United States Banks: Have $1,500 million in deposits to credit of foreign banks		Foreign Banks: Have $2 billion in deposits to credit of United States banks

In analyzing the effect of these developments on money flows, it has been customary to assume that Changes I and II (that is, no change in the balance) would have similar effects and that Changes III and IV (increase in United States exports by $500 million) would have similar effects. But in actuality it is going to make considerable difference to internal activities in the United States whether the export balance is financed as in Change III or as in IV. This is true in spite of the fact that exporter income relative to importer expenditures has in both cases risen by $500 million. In Change IV United States banks have deposits $1,250 million larger than in Change III. This circumstance is likely to make considerable difference in their lending practices.

This is merely further evidence that in connection with analysis of the relation between national income and international trade, it is at least as important to identify the method of financing and the channels through which financing occurs as it is to identify that there has been a change in the balance of trade—at least in the short run.

In the foreign-trade operations an increase in imports actually could carry with it an increase in loanable funds in the country experiencing the import increase. Assume that United States imports, relative to exports, rise by $500 million. The banking relations could change to become:

CHANGE V	As of December 31st	
United States Banks: Have $750 million in deposits to credit of foreign banks		Foreign Banks: Have $250 million in deposits to credit of United States banks

Or they could change to become:

CHANGE VI   As of December 31st

United States Banks: Foreign Banks:
Have $2 billion in deposits   Have $1.5 billion in deposits
  to credit of foreign banks   to credit of United States
                                                    banks

Change VI is a far from impossible development; if it occurs, deposits in United States banks are substantially increased—in spite of the import balance. And the proclivity of United States banks for lending may be substantially increased—in spite of the import balance. All too little is known about how bankers actually react in their lending policies to these various situations. In the short run there is very considerable latitude for banker option, and for borrower option as well.

The financing of foreign trade may change the amount of money and credit in circulation in various directions. It all depends on the nature of the financing; and if exports are financed by a process that does not put new money in the hands of spenders, there is no necessary reason why an export boost should have a stimulating effect.

Depending on the way trade is financed, an import increase might, with about as much probability as an export increase, cause a rise in money and credit in circulation.[9]

If a foreign importer buys some dollars (which are already in circulation) with some francs and pays the American exporter with the dollars, this is just one transaction in the history of some old money and credit as it turns over and over. It is not new funds in the money-flow stream. It is no more likely to be spent again than it was in any case. True, as a corollary of the process, some American has acquired some francs in France; but that does not per se have anything to do with money flows in this country.

As for imports into this country, they might be financed by American banks lending new funds to the American importer. Admittedly, the American importer would turn them over to the foreign exporter. But they are new funds in the money-flow stream in the United States, and the foreigner "gets something out of them" only if he uses them for purchases in the United States or sells them to someone who does. Depending upon the method of financing, imports as well as exports could function to increase the supply of funds in the money-flow stream.

[9] In the short run; and depending on banker reactions. Bankers, in fact, may well react to the export balance by greater willingness to lend. But they need not. Of course, in a somewhat longer run the reserve position of the banks will influence their behavior and will affect the relation between trade financing and internal credit creation.

Role of Interest Rates

Most goods movements between countries are financed by the use of bills of exchange or some similar type of commercial paper. The *total* amount of short-term funds moving internationally during a given year could be a figure very substantially larger than the *net* figures shown in Table 12. But the balance of payments statements generally indicate the movement of short-term funds in net rather than gross figures. The net movement of short-term funds partly explains the financing of the difference between goods exports and goods imports in the first instance, although it still does not identify cause and effect. It does not establish for certain whether the funds moved in the first place because of an interest-rate attraction or because of a price attraction. In 1952, United States bankers (irrespective of what was happening in connection with goods movements) might have wanted to sell dollars and hold pounds in order to take advantage of the higher money rates prevailing in England (as exemplified by the 3 per cent rate on bank acceptances in England in contrast with the 1.75 per cent rate in New York).[10]

MEANING OF A FAVORABLE BALANCE OF PAYMENTS

As if the difference in meaning between *favorable terms of trade* and *favorable balance of trade* did not make for confusion enough, there is also the concept of *favorable balance of payments*. This expression more properly should be *balance of payments on current account,* since the balance of payments statement itself obviously balances out and has to do so—with the help of an errors and omissions entry.

What is involved in the concept of the unfavorable balance of payments? It indicates that circumstances are developing which will make for insufficient resources in short-term balances to finance the goods-and-services trade which prevails or is likely to prevail at the current rate of exchange. Perhaps the combination of entries 36, 40, 44, 45, and 46 (short-term balances and gold) in Table 12 is the crucial grouping for this purpose. If a country runs out of such short-term balances, it may not be able to provide foreign funds (at the present rate of exchange) to its importers who need to make payments abroad.

Consequently, a favorable balance of payments position involves the possession of "large enough" gold and foreign-exchange reserves (or the existence of conditions calculated to make adequate gold and foreign-

---

[10] The effort by United States bankers to sell dollars for pounds, and the reluctance of the British to sell pounds for dollars, in this case might well lead to a slight rise in the value of the pound in terms of the dollar—a change in the foreign-exchange rate. The effect of interest-rate differences on the international movement of short-term funds is discussed more at length in Chapter 17.

exchange reserves available to a country). And an unfavorable balance of payments position on current account means insufficient (or the threat of insufficient) gold and foreign-exchange reserves to meet the requirements at the prevailing rate of exchange.

But what is "large enough"? Is the figure that matters the gross or the net figure? There is no final answer to these questions. For Mexico gold and foreign-exchange reserves of $28 million (U.S.) were adequate in 1939 and reserves of $78 million (U.S.) were inadequate in 1948. At all events, the *trend* of gold and foreign-exchange reserves matters as well as the absolute size.

As for the relative importance of the gross and the net figure, in one sense it can be said that United States citizens control the use of their balances in foreign banks, and foreigners control the use of their balances in United States banks. Hence it might be concluded that the United States has freedom of action only with respect to its own foreign balances, so that it is change in the total rather than change in the net figure that matters. But what if the balances are "blocked"—that is to say, what if the foreign government says that United States citizens cannot freely use their foreign balances? Because a sizeable proportion of all foreign balances is blocked or can only be used under conditions carefully regulated by the foreign government, it is not always feasible to count gross foreign balances as freely usable reserves. Furthermore, the process by which foreigners repatriate the funds they have on deposit in this country may, almost automatically, reduce the foreign balances of Americans— if the Americans are willing to sell their foreign balances at the foreign-exchange rate offered. All of this means that there is no definitive criterion as to what constitutes adequate foreign-exchange reserves for the purpose of financing goods trade.

Moreover, from the brief history that follows, it is not even certain that being a net creditor at short term—having what ostensibly is a strong balance-of-payments position on current account—is a particularly advantageous position. A favorable balance of payments is a luxury that the financially strong does not need to pay for. The United States, for example, is a major *debtor* at short term.

HISTORY AND DEBTOR STATUS OF FINANCIAL CENTERS

Certain aspects of the history of foreign-exchange markets are well known; other aspects are obscure. While some of the historical statistics are readily available, a great deal of essential information concerning international financial operations of the past can never be obtained. The transactions cleared through banks that kept regular data are a rich source of information. But the unreported buying and selling of great quantities of bills of exchange leaves a gap in the picture. Nevertheless, it is possible to hazard some guesses as to the history of the short-term financing of foreign trade.

In the Middle Ages, it was the Italian commercial cities such as Venice and Genoa and Florence and the northern cities of the Hanseatic League which handled the financing of international trade. Also, bills of exchange were used between the traders at the great fairs in Champagne, Antwerp, Bruges, Lyons, and so on. Trade centers have been financial centers; financial centers, in turn, not only have been trade centers but also centers of culture—therefore places where the human being stood a better chance of getting more out of life. Commercial activity and hegemony over the whole trading process tends to concentrate in the centers willing to assume the responsibility for the financing of trade, or vice versa. This concentration has important implications for political and economic leadership in the world. Such was the case in the Italian and Hanseatic cities of the Middle Ages and early modern times.

During the period of the Commercial Revolution of the sixteenth and seventeenth centuries, Amsterdam moved into a place of pre-eminence in the financing of trade. Strangely, it has probably been true of each great financial center—Amsterdam during those years, London in the nineteenth century, and New York more recently—that it has been a debtor, at least at short term.[11]

This is worth mulling over. We are prone to associate British hegemony in the nineteenth century with her position as a great creditor country, but she was a creditor at long term only. And we are prone to associate the recent United States hegemony with a creditor's role, yet the United States is now a major debtor at short term, as Table 22 indicates. The idea that financial strength invariably associates with a creditor status can be extremely misleading as an indication of what is going on in the everyday give-and-take of buying and selling.

There may be some intangible, hard-to-appraise factors helping to make the financially strong country a debtor at short term. But there are also some obvious practical reasons for it. The financial center is the safe place to hold balances. That has to be part of the combination of circumstances that makes it a financial center. In the nineteenth century it was a real convenience to an Argentine bank to have a working balance in a financial center like London. Why not have your liquid funds in the most useful place, too? It should be noted, in this connection, that such funds are not immobilized when on deposit in a safe bank in a financial

[11] Actually in some respects London may still be more of a financial center than New York. Sterling still finances 50 per cent of the world's trade. (*International Financial News Survey,* October 28, 1955, p. 141).

center. They can be used at any time. Even in a transaction such as that shown in Chart 8, it is not the foreign bank with a deposit in London whose funds are tied up pending the maturity of the bill of exchange; it is the "holder of the bill," an Englishman, creditor of another English-

TABLE 22

SHORT-TERM FOREIGN ASSETS AND LIABILITIES OF THE UNITED STATES

	A UNITED STATES SHORT-TERM INVESTMENT ABROAD [1] ($1,000,000)	B FOREIGN SHORT- TERM INVEST- MENT IN U.S.[1] ($1,000,000)	C SHORT-TERM CLAIMS ON FOR- EIGNERS REPORTED BY BANKS IN U.S. ($1,000,000)	D SHORT-TERM LIABILITIES TO FOREIGNERS RE- PORTED BY BANKS IN U.S. ($1,000,000)
1869	Negligible	150		
1897	Negligible	250		
1914	Negligible	500		
1919	500	800		
1924	900	1,000		
1927	1,300	2,900		
1930	2,000	2,700		
1931	1,300	1,500		
1934			1,140	670
1935	900	1,301	779	1,301
1936			673	1,623
1937			655	1,893
1938			594	2,158
1939	1,060	3,975	509	3,221
1940	885	5,300	384	3,938
1941			368	3,678
1942			247	4,205
1943	975	6,375	258	5,374
1944			330	5,597
1945	1,516	9,076	393	6,883
1946	1,514	8,542	708	6,007
1947	1,782	8,824	949	4,854
1948	1,801	9,319	1,019	5,854
1949	1,599	9,229	828	5,960
1950	1,838	10,245	898	6,923
1951	1,989	11,289	968	7,661
1952	2,076	12,485	1,049	8,961
1953	1,893	13,437	905	10,019
1954	2,636	14,684	1,387	11,153
1955			1,549	11,722
1956			1,834 (Octo- ber)	13,096 (No- vem- ber)

[1] Private plus U.S. Government.

Sources: *Historical Statistics.. . . ,* p. 242; *Statistical Abstract; Banking and Monetary Statistics,* pp. 574–95; *Federal Reserve Bulletin.*

man, the importer, whose funds are tied up. The English money market is providing the liquid funds to see the transaction through to maturity, in spite of the fact that England is a debtor to the foreign country in connection with the international aspect of the transaction.[12]

The situation is somewhat different, and somewhat more awkward, when a country with an export trade balance is trying to be a financial center, yet foreigners at the same time are insisting on holding balances there. This is the situation in the United States and New York today, as Table 22 indicates. In such a case, if we accept the fact that foreigners insist on having large balances in the safe, liquid financial center and also that the country has favorable trade balances, then either long-term lending or giving by the financial center must be proportionately larger or the gold inflow must be considerable.

The funds which the foreign country has loaned to the financial center, and which take the form of bank deposits there, are liquid funds which may be used as part of the reserves (foreign-exchange reserves) behind the money and credit structure in the foreign country. Consequently, such lending from the financially weak country to the financial center need involve no credit contraction in the peripheral country. The latter goes ahead and counts the deposits which it has in the financial center as part of its reserves, and considers itself financially stronger for having them. But the United States is presently almost the only country in the world that does not carry freely convertible foreign-exchange holdings as part of the legal reserve behind its money and credit structure. Consequently an increase in foreign balances held by United States banks as a result of an export increase does not in this case have a tendency to increase the internal money and credit supply—unless some other things happen. Thus, you might say that the financial center is in the enviable or unenviable position of being the depository of the financial reserves of other countries, and is a debtor at short-term, as a consequence of the safe, convenient facilities it provides.

Table 22 gives some relevant figures for the United States. Columns A and B indicate that at the end of 1953, for example, the United States had foreign short-term assets to the extent of only $1,893 million, whereas foreigners had short-term investments (bank deposits, etc.) in the United States six times as large—$13,437 million. Similar figures for United States banks alone indicate that at the end of 1955, United States banks had on deposit abroad only $1,549 million as compared with foreign deposits of $11,722 million in banks in the United States.

It is a fair guess that a great deal of this discrepancy represents the feeling of foreigners that the United States is a good, safe place to have

[12] For an up-to-date description of the London market see: N. Macrae, *The London Capital Market—Its Structure, Strains, and Management* (London: Staples, 1955).

their money. A Latin American dictator or an Egyptian king would like some liquid assets abroad when he is no longer the power in his home country. When the current role of New York is compared with the role of London in the nineteenth century, it may well be concluded that London owed its role as debtor at short term somewhat more to the functions it performed as an international clearing house, profiting from its situation by having an import trade balance, whereas New York, which has never been as adept as London at handling the mechanics of financing trade, owes its possession of large foreign balances somewhat more to its being a safe city of refuge. Obviously the position cannot be attributed to the fact that an import trade balance is being financed for the New York market by foreigners.

In any event, it should be repeated that financial strength is not a necessary corollary of the creditor role. It is a commonplace in private business that an active, expanding enterprise is likely to be going into debt. Perhaps what is involved in a nation's being a debtor at short term is somewhat similar. The fact that a nation is a debtor at short term may well be a better criterion of financial strength than being a net creditor or a creditor at long term only. But the proposition should be slightly qualified. All this is no law of nature but rather a circumstance that results from the nature of the institutional-financial organization of society.

FINANCING OF INTERNATIONAL TRADE IN THE UNITED STATES

A General Appraisal

It is generally agreed among American bankers that the private American banking system has never developed adequate facilities for financing foreign trade. This inadequacy results in part from the nature of United States exports. To a marked extent American banks are oriented to the financing of short-term (perhaps ninety-day) credit—internally. But much international trade, and this is particularly true of the typical exports of the United States, consists of heavy equipment, machinery, tractors, other farm machinery, and other vehicles. If the export of these items is to be facilitated, the credits have to be for two or three years— as a practical matter.

More than this, in their foreign sales American exporters tend to demand cash on the barrelhead. The following exchange occurred between Senator Homer Capehart of Indiana and August Maffry, vice-president of the Irving Trust Company of New York, in 1954: [18]

[18] United States Congress, Senate, Committee on Banking and Currency, *Study of Export-Import Bank and World Bank,* Hearings before the . . . , 83rd Congress, 2nd Sess. (Washington: Government Printing Office, 1954), part 1, p. 177.

The Chairman. Why, if you handle their domestic requirements [speaking of the bank's customers], can't you handle their foreign requirements?

Mr. Maffry. It is partly a matter of banking law. It is partly a matter of banking supervision. It is even more, I should say, a matter of banking practice. . . .

The Chairman. Then, if we are going to have an expanded world trade, or export business, and do business other than on a cash basis, are you saying that our banking system in the United States is just not geared to the point of handling it at the moment?

Mr. Maffry. I do say this, sir, because there is a great gap in our banking system. Unfortunately, we do not have in the United States a type of banking which exists in Europe, known as merchant banking. It has never developed in the United States. It is the type of banking that would undertake to finance transactions of this sort. . . . There is a type of export, particularly exports of equipment, which requires in many instances financing at extended term. This is a type of financing which is not available in the United States at this time from private sources.

Bankers and traders are concerned that, as a result of these practices, the United States may be losing ground in the export markets of the world, although the trade figures do not yet indicate this. Chester R. Dewey, president of the Grace National Bank of New York, testified to the Capehart Committee: [14] "Germany has reverted to her old policy of selling credit rather than merchandise. Four years to pay is almost standard. Contrast this with the cash on the barrelhead irrevocable New York letter of credit policy of most of our manufacturers." During the hearings, examples were multiplied almost without end of situations where American exporters lost orders not because of price or quality considerations but because Europeans were willing to offer more favorable credit terms.

An impressive array of American bankers testified before the Capehart Committee that the Export-Import Bank (a United States government agency) was doing a fine job in helping with the financing of exports. Especially they commended the Export-Import Bank for its loan-guarantee program, and they expressed a desire to see the system continued and expanded. (Essentially what is involved is the guarantee by the Export-Import Bank of such loans, chiefly term loans of two or three years, as private United States banks might make to finance certain United States exports.)

[14] *Ibid.*, p. 252.

At the hearings it was a rare witness that urged American banks or American exporters to shoulder their own financial burdens without leaning on the government. But Herbert F. Boettler, vice-president of the First National Bank of St. Louis, was such a witness. He condemned the Export-Import Bank's $300,000,000 loan of 1952 to Brazil to bail out frozen United States balances there: "I do not feel it is good policy for the Federal Government to bail out businessmen who make mistakes." [15] He also said: "To the extent that foreign trade is encouraged by such means [credit assistance by the Export-Import Bank], it is an indirect subsidy to special interests at the taxpayers' expense."

But so far as credit facilities are concerned, the United States importer is in some ways in worse shape than the exporter. After all, United States exports are large, even if United States banks are not providing the financial facilities. With regard to the financing of imports, Lewis N. Dembitz of the Federal Reserve System testified: [16]

> It may be well here to review some of the characteristics of the importing business that make financing [especially for smaller or more specialized importing firms that deal in manufactured or other non-standard goods] more of a problem for such firms than for firms dealing in domestic goods.
>
> In the first place, because of the time required for physical shipment of most imports, the aggregate amount of goods that the importer has in his inventory, plus in transit at any given time, is likely to be relatively large in relation to his volume of business. . . .
>
> And, secondly, whereas a dealer in domestic goods may be able to receive lines of credit from his suppliers, the importer is likely to need a letter of credit arrangement whereby a bank or other financial institution guarantees payment to the foreign seller. . . .
>
> For whatever reasons, a considerable number of importers told the Commerce Department in its 1950 survey that they were unable to get adequate credit from their banks, and that this caused them to forego many import propositions that they considered safe and profitable.

This on top of all the other trials and tribulations importers have! [17]

To revert to the relationship between trade financing and money flows, which was discussed earlier in this chapter: It may be that the

---

[15] *Ibid.*, p. 229.

[16] *Ibid.*, p. 163.

[17] One may hope that if and when Congress gives extended loan and loan-guarantee powers to the Export-Import Bank, it will provide somehow that the bank must give at least as much assistance to imports as to exports.

process by which exports are financed injects more money and credit into the stream than does the process by which imports are financed. But this depends, in large measure, on the nature of the institutional arrangements. It is a result of the fact that banks have defaulted on their obligations in connection with import financing—even more than in the case of export financing. It is not a result of an inherent tendency for the trading process to increase money supply if exports are involved and to decrease it if imports are involved.

In general, with regard to the financing of international trade in the United States, it may be concluded (and many bankers concur in this view) that the American banking system, up to now, has been unwilling to take the risks and develop the techniques needed if the United States is to assume leadership (or even do a good job) in financing international trade.

Role of the Export-Import Bank

This agency of the United States government currently handles the financing of a considerable portion of United States exports—$500 million to $1 billion in financing each year. It is also empowered to finance imports, as its name implies, but actually it does relatively little along that line. In its export-financing operations, the Export-Import Bank has been active chiefly in connection with heavy equipment—thus partially filling a major gap in the range of services provided by the private banks.

Bankers are not averse to financing international trade if they can be guaranteed against loss. Consequently, there has been very considerable pressure to work out arrangements that would permit private bankers to participate in Export-Import Bank loans. New arrangements to facilitate this were placed in effect in 1954.[18] One arrangement provides that on an "approved" sale in connection with which the foreign importer makes a down payment of at least 20 per cent, the Export-Import Bank will underwrite 60 per cent of the purchase price. The exporter, probably using funds borrowed from a commercial bank, will assume the remaining 20 per cent. Private bankers would like a government guarantee of the share of the purchase price they advance in connection with such export sales. As a result of their efforts, a program permitting Export-Import Bank guarantees in such cases has been adopted.

FINANCING ELSEWHERE

Foreign governments in general seem to be at least as interested as the United States government in aiding their national traders with their export-financing problems. In the Capehart Committee hearings on the

[18] *New York Times,* November 10, 1954, p. 51.

Export-Import Bank, American bankers frequently complained of the financial assistance that British, German, and French exporters are getting from their governments. Even the Mexican government, operating through the Banco Nacional de Comercio Exterior, has a program for aiding Mexican exporters with their financing problems.

But the fact that most governments have programs for aiding exporters with their financing problems does not mean that the mechanism for financing trade is, in general, efficient and effective. International trade used to be financed in the money markets of a few great centers, such as London, Amsterdam, Antwerp, and Paris, where the documents were efficiently handled and processed. At present, with much trade being conducted on a bilateral basis, the financing of trade is much more widely diffused over the world in many more financial centers; clearing occurs in considerable part between pairs of countries; and the complexity of the documents (including not only bills of exchange, bills of lading, and consular invoices, but also import and export licenses, and exchange permits) makes for an unprecedentedly complicated process. And the increasing complexity of documents is less effectively handled by less efficient processes in these heterogeneous centers. The paper work of the domestic manufacturer is as nothing to that required of the foreign trader—whose grief the typical domestic manufacturer is probably trying to increase at this very moment with some new and ingenious barrier to imports.

SUPPLEMENTARY NOTE: ARBITRAGE AND FORWARD EXCHANGE

The discussion of the mechanics of foreign exchange markets should not be left without mention of two procedures.

(1) ARBITRAGE involves the buying and selling of currencies in an effort to profit from non-conformity in the exchange-rate patterns in different markets. Thus if the following rate structure existed:

In New York	*In Paris*
£1 equals $5	1 franc equals 20¢
1 franc equals 20¢	£1 equals 24 francs

it would pay an alert arbitrager to sell francs for pounds in Paris. He would get £1 for 24 francs. Then he could sell his pounds for dollars in New York and get $5. He could then sell his dollars for francs in New York and get 25 francs. This is a neat profit rate for two minutes' work. In the good old days of the gold standard and free foreign-exchange markets, the banks that did a large international business kept professional arbitragers to engage in transactions of this sort literally on a second's notice. The result was the maintenance of comparability in the pattern of exchange rates in the different financial centers. Discrepancies of the sort indicated above were short-lived. Anyone who can see this is qualified to start work at once as a junior executive in a bank.

Governments may establish exchange controls that prohibit arbitragers from freely plying their trade. In such a situation it is possible for a "disorderly cross rate," such as £1 equal 25 francs in New York (by contrast with £1 equals 24 francs in Paris), to continue to exist, although the number of transactions that may occur at that rate will be affected by the nature of the controls.

(2) FORWARD EXCHANGE: An operation in forward exchange occurs on the assumption either that (a) the trader wants to avoid the effects of a possible exchange-rate change, or that (b) he wants to profit from a change in foreign-exchange rates.

Assume that an American bank which holds funds in London expects the pound to be devalued. It needs to keep its deposits in London in order to have a working balance there, but it wants to protect itself against the possibility of devaluation. The American bank may sell its pounds for dollars "now" at the prevailing rate of exchange (for such transactions— i.e., the forward-exchange rate) with the understanding that it will not give delivery until possibly three months hence. The buyer might be an American importer who is going to have to make a payment in London three months hence. The importer is not interested in speculating on a possible fall in the value of sterling (which would make it possible for him to profit by waiting to buy his sterling later) nor is he interested in taking a chance that the price of sterling will rise. He is satisfied with his contract; the bank is also satisfied with the current forward rate— which, of course, may differ slightly from the current spot or cable rate that will apply if the money is to change hands at once. He does not want to speculate; the bank does not want to speculate. Everybody avoids speculation by this particular operation.

But perhaps someone thinks that the pound is going to be devalued and wants to profit on that hunch. He has no pounds, but he does have dollars. He says to the American importer mentioned in the previous paragraph (catching him before he has time to dicker with the bank), "I will deliver to you pounds sterling three months from now at the pound-dollar (forward-exchange) rate prevailing now." It is a matter of indifference to the importer whether he deals with the bank or the speculator. If the speculator is correct and the value of the pound falls on the foreign-exchange market, the speculator steps out three months hence and buys the pounds with far fewer dollars than the American importer turns over to him in exchange for those pounds. If the pound should be appreciated instead of depreciating, he would lose heavily.

Forward-exchange operations, if allowed by the government to occur, do not necessarily have a stabilizing effect comparable to the consistent tendency of arbitrage to bring the rates in the different markets into harmony. Forward-exchange speculation may force a currency devaluation which otherwise might not have occurred. If speculators as a group have convinced themselves that the pound sterling is likely to be devalued, the falling rates which they quote on the pound actually are the devaluation—at least they are after the spot rate follows the forward rate down in response to the alarms.

However, it should also be noted (and this is frequently pointed out as a useful service of speculators in forward exchange) that if the foreign-exchange rate is reasonably sound, but there is a temporary shortage of one of the currencies in one of the markets, short-term violent rate fluctuations can be ameliorated by the operation of dealers in forward exchange, since these dealers may promise now to give future delivery of the scarce currency at fairly reasonable prices and thus assuage everybody's fears.

Chapter 17

THE RELATIVE VALUES OF CURRENCIES: THE BASIC FORCES

❧ ❧ ❧

A foreign-exchange rate is the price of one currency in terms of another.
The tenability of a given foreign-exchange rate is influenced by certain
long-run, basic forces and by certain short-run, ostensible factors.
The basic forces are (1) prices and the underlying demand and supply
conditions that influence prices, (2) institutional and technological
factors and developments, (3) money supply, national income, and
price levels, and the policy decisions that influence these economic
variables, (4) the actual quantity of exports and imports, and (5) the
foreign-exchange rate itself—since, also, the actual quantities of ex-
ports and imports are not determined till the rate is set.
These basic forces are mutually interdependent.
The chief immediate, ostensible influence, which was not included in
the basic forces listed above, is the adequacy of gold and foreign-
exchange reserves.

❧ ❧ ❧

THE ANALYSIS[1] of the role of money in international trade
could be handled in much the same terms in which it is handled
internally if it were not for the fact that the values of different
currencies may change in relation to each other. A monetary
unit common to the whole world would be a fine simplifying factor
in the face of our current confusion and complexity. But, even though
a common monetary unit is not possible, it remains true that some degree of certainty and order in the behavior of the prices of one currency in terms of another would facilitate foreign trade immensely.

The price of one currency in terms of another is the foreign-exchange
rate—see Table 23.[2] What determines the value of one currency in terms

[1] The chief purpose of this chapter is to list the basic forces at work and to identify certain relationships which are supposed to prevail.
[2] R. Sedillot, *Toutes les Monnaies du Monde—Dictionnaire des Changes* (Paris:
Sirey, 1955).

TABLE 23
FOREIGN EXCHANGE RATES
(AS OF NOVEMBER, 1956, OR APPROXIMATELY THAT DATE)

	CURRENCY UNIT	UNITED STATES DOLLARS PER FOREIGN CURRENCY UNIT
Argentina	Peso	$ .055 [3] [5]
Australia	Pound	2.240 [5]
Brazil	Cruzeiro	.054 [3] [5]
Canada	Dollar	.960 [1]
Chile	Peso	.0091 [3] [5]
France	Franc	.0028 [2]
Germany, Western	Deutsche mark	.238 [5]
India	Rupee	.21 [5]
Italy	Lira	.0016 [2]
Japan	Yen	.0028 [5]
Mexico	Peso	.08 [5]
United Kingdom	Pound sterling	2.80 [5]
U.S.S.R.	Ruble	.25 [4]

[1] Canadian dollar not held at this figure but allowed to fluctuate; [2] market rate, not an International Monetary Fund par; [3] country actually has a multiple rate structure; [4] Russian official; [5] International Monetary Fund par.

Source: *International Financial Statistics*, February, 1957, *passim*.

of another? May it be fixed by a comparison of legally determined gold contents of the monetary units? Or may it be determined by government fiat? Or may the rate be allowed to fluctuate like any other price? If it is allowed to fluctuate like other prices, what determines where it will settle: demand and supply, or comparative purchasing power, or government meddling, or the dickering of private monopolies?

RATE SETTING METHODS

The possible methods by which exchange rates are set may be catalogued as follows (bearing in mind that, for the most part but not entirely, these are mutually exclusive alternatives and that only one of the methods may be operative at a given time):

I. Gold standard (or any standard involving money with intrinsic value or redeemable in a set amount of something with intrinsic value) involving either:
   A. A specie-flow adjustment mechanism, or
   B. A transfer of purchasing power adjustment mechanism;
II. Freely fluctuating paper involving either:
   A. A purchasing power parity adjustment mechanism, or

      B. A demand and supply adjustment mechanism, or

      C. An institutionally oriented adjustment mechanism;

III. Government rate-setting involving either:

      A. Government intervention in the market process to influence the rate, or

      B. Rate-setting by decree, the discussion of which is broken down into:

          (1) Theoretical implications,

          (2) Multiple rates,

          (3) Bilateral trade treaties;

IV. State trading; and

V. The International Monetary Fund

The listing of the above possibilities does not prove that any of them is either a satisfactory or an unsatisfactory method for determining exchange rates. In fact, the fixed rates of the gold standard are untenable if the price levels in the two countries diverge too far from the relationship indicated by the rates. The constantly fluctuating rates, resulting if free market forces are allowed to operate, may be undesirable if they inject an element of instability into the picture. If a government sets rates (either by buying and selling in the market or by government fiat) which diverge too far from the price relationships prevailing in the two countries, it may not have the resources with which to maintain the rates for long without exchange control as well; and even if there is exchange control, the volume of trade may be drastically reduced. In state trading an implicit rate is set, whether or not an explicit one is expressed. The International Monetary Fund may not be able to work satisfactorily until it has the power to regulate the supply of money and credit internally in the different countries.

It is literally true that there are conceivable circumstances in which any of these rate-setting techniques would be satisfactory and conceivable circumstances in which any one of them would be unsatisfactory. The following chapters on the adjustment process are intended to indicate the conditions under which the various rate-setting devices may and may not work.

But throughout this discussion it should be remembered that a monetary system, such as the gold standard, is not an end in itself. It is a tool, at best, and how desirable it is as a tool depends on how well it works.

INTERNAL VS. EXTERNAL STABILITY

The statement frequently was made during the 1930's—and it sounded very reasonable—that no country can be expected to sacrifice internal

CHART 10

FOREIGN EXCHANGE RATES

(UNITED STATES-MEXICAN AND UNITED STATES-BRITISH)

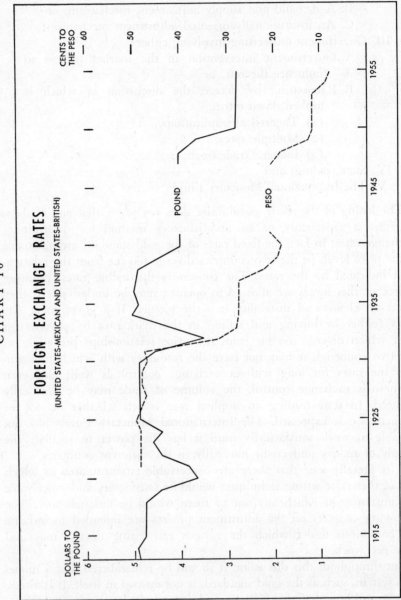

Sources: *Banking and Monetary Statistics; Federal Reserve Bulletin.*

stability (internal prosperity) on the altar of external stability, meaning presumably stable foreign-exchange rates (or equilibrium in the balance of payments on current account). A country could not be expected to undergo an internal depression merely in order to maintain gold standard pars. Stated that way, probably, no one should take exception to the proposition. Anybody would be foolish to support gold pars if their maintenance caused a depression. And certainly if a tangible gain from devaluation can be seen, there is nothing sacrosanct about exchange stability. On the other hand, devaluation is not an automatic cure for all ills, whatever they may be. The cause-and-effect relationship is all too frequently not established in this saying about sacrificing external for internal stability. A country is all too likely to sacrifice the one without gaining the other.

We now have a far better basic concept to use in evaluating policies than the internal vs. external stability dichotomy. It is that countries must co-ordinate their economic policies. They must not engage in policies that will make matters worse for other countries. This is true because: "Prosperity is indivisible."[3] Essentially, all nations are going to be prosperous or depressed together. Real growth in any one country must involve growth for all. And all must be reasonably well satisfied with their economic lot for any one to be sure of its own continued prosperity.

THE BASIC FORCES

A listing of the basic forces affecting foreign-exchange rates and the adequacy of foreign-exchange reserves seems worth-while as a basis for operations.[4]

The basic forces that enter into determining the pattern of international economic exchange are: (1) price (cost and demand) conditions at home and abroad, (2) institutional and technological forces (including autonomous policy decisions and untoward events), (3) the quantity of money and credit and national income considerations, (4)

[3] International Monetary Fund, *Summary Proceedings, Annual Meeting, 1956*, p. 43. The quotation is from Harold Macmillan.
[4] George Joachim Goschen Viscount Goschen, *Theory of the Foreign Exchanges* (Fourth edition; London: Pitman, 1932); Alfred E. Kahn, *Great Britain in the World Economy* (New York: Columbia University Press, 1946); Ragnar Nurkse, "Conditions of International Monetary Equilibrium," *Essays in International Finance* No. 4 (Spring, 1945); F. W. Paish, "Banking Policy and the Balance of International Payments," *Economica,* III-New Series (November, 1936), 404–22; Joan Robinson, "The Foreign Exchanges," *Essays in the Theory of Employment* (2nd ed.; Oxford: Blackwell, 1947), Part III, Chap. 1; Gottfried von Haberler, *The Theory of International Trade with its Applications to Commercial Policy,* translated by Alfred Stonier and Frederic Benham (London: Hodge, 1936), pp. 13–62; F. W. Taussig, *International Trade,* pp. 197–221, 337–408.

the relationship between exports and imports and the quantity of goods being traded, and (5) the foreign-exchange rate. An important feature of these relationships is that they are mutually interdependent. No one is determined until all the others are determined. Or better put, as each changes, all the others are affected.

Price Conditions

These are the factors on which Ohlin centered his analysis. In a rather general way, prices (and the cost and demand conditions that lie behind them) are fundamental. But none of the overt manifestations of price—prices themselves, interest rates, profit rates, rents, wage scales, and foreign-exchange rates—are finally set until all of the others are set. Ohlin is right to emphasize the interdependence of these forces.

Once all the forces have interacted, price comparisons play a significant role in determining the identity of the goods actually moving in international trade. But it is price comparisons made in a certain institutional setting, not absolute price differences, that matter.

Institutional and Technological Forces [5]

It seems clear that the dynamic force of technical change is the important positive force and institutional barriers are the negative force influencing (a) the evolution of the price (cost-demand) patterns over long periods of time, and (b) the short-run reaction to a sudden change in those same patterns—such as is likely to be precipitated by currency devaluation, war, conniving dictators, or pressure-group-inspired Senators. In (a) the technological factors are probably more important, in (b) the institutional.

How an institution will react to suddenly changed circumstances has to be ascertained by study of that institution. Take a currency-devaluation type of situation. Institutional reaction to the devaluation intervenes, even in an instant of time, to become an important factor affecting the quantity of goods trade that will follow the devaluation. There are the practical problems of opening new marketing channels under these changed conditions. All the attitudes of long-term investors (and their attitudes do affect goods movements) are subject to reappraisal. Is the devaluing country a poor risk with a shaky currency? Let us not commit any money there. Consequence: less imports but not necessarily more exports! Is it a country which has just solved a problem by its devaluation (instead of making a new one) and which will be a good

[5] C. E. Ayres, *Theory of Economic Progress* (Chapel Hill: University of North Carolina Press, 1944).

place to do business in the future? Consequence: more imports but not necessarily more exports (even in this very short-run type of situation)! Any number of other attitudes may affect exports and imports in various ways.

Countries tend to use devaluation as the answer to every problem. They devalue when they have a goods shortage at home in the hopes of exporting more in order to be able to import more (the British case in 1949). They devalue when they have goods surpluses at home—in the hope of being able to export more with no attendant desire to import more (the United States case in 1933). Thus devaluation and the assumed resultant increase in exports are supposed to solve those most opposite of problems: scarcity and glut. Amazing, is it not, that people can convince themselves that the same measure is a cure for both conditions! In fact, the predilection for devaluation itself might be looked on as an institution. How else can one account for the fact that devaluation is not just a response to a difficult situation in a setting where there is no other choice. It is a step engaged in frequently, with evident relish, by those who think they are putting something over on their neighbors.

The assumption that each institution will act in a predictable manner so as to change its buying or selling habits in a certain way in response to various price changes is simply not tenable. The circumstances that occasioned the price change make too much difference in determining how different institutions will react to them. The more-or-less intangible forces of the institutional, cultural, and social setting lie behind costs and prices, influencing the rate at which adjustments will occur and also determining whether equilibrium or orderly change can occur, whether it be on an instant's notice or for the long run.

The attraction that potential foreign investors feel, or fail to feel, for foreign climes influences the availability of the financing that is necessary if there is to be a discrepancy between exports and imports. Adam Smith and Ricardo recognized, to the point of overemphasizing, this possibility. Major price differences can exist; when they do, they may permit differences in the real price level and the real cost of living in different countries, and such differences may continue indefinitely. Smith and Ricardo can hardly be condemned for claiming that capital and labor were immobile internationally. But Ohlin has been somewhat more realistic in using a more sophisticated concept—the *costs of transfer*. But costs of transfer are something more than insurance and freight, tariffs and quotas. They include a whole complex of attitudes, prejudices, and desires.

In the longer run, the positive influence of technological change seems to be far more important than the inhibitory force of certain institutional lags. It has been the inventions of the wheel, iron, the horse collar, the keeled ship, the blast furnace, gunpowder, the printing press, the steam engine, and the atom bomb that have changed fundamentally man's conditions of life and his relation to his environment. In the long run, technological changes move the whole cost curve in a sense that is far more important for price theory than the concept of cost elasticities at an instant of time. In fact the whole cost, demand, and pricing pattern evolves as technological change occurs.

To summarize, development is influenced (1) by the possession of as much technical knowledge as possible, by the dynamic, expanding nature of the technical process, and by the difference in the impact of such change on different countries and regions; (2) by the extent to which institutions inhibit (or encourage) technical development; and (3) by the possession of raw materials appropriate to the stage of technical development.

And developments of this sort interact with the other forces to determine the trading pattern.

The Money Supply, National Income, and Price Levels

We come now to somewhat more superficial forces—but nevertheless forces which are capable of influencing whether that also superficial phenomenon, the foreign-exchange rate, will be changed.

A government may, as a matter of policy (perhaps influenced by Keynesian theory), decide to expand the domestic supply of money and credit in order to stimulate domestic investment in an effort to raise internal income and level of living. If these policies are pursued at a judicious rate (or rather if the implementation of the development program is well done), and the production of goods expands proportionately with the expansion in the supply of money, there need be no inflation, no significant rise in the price level.

The chief present concern however, is with the repercussions which follow if there is a substantial change (either way) in money and credit or in money national income without a corresponding change in goods production. With domestic prices rising, if the exchange rate continues the same, local citizens tend to buy relatively more abroad and relatively less at home. This uses up the gold and foreign-exchange reserves (the freely available means of financing) and cannot continue indefinitely in the absence of some international lending or giving. But, unless some more intelligent developments occur, what will happen is very simple. When the foreign-exchange reserves give out, trade will cease. But the more intelligent developments involve adequate reckoning with the whole complex of basic forces—not just struggling with a problem in elasticities or constants.

Relationship Between Exports and Imports

The superficial price-level changes cause *changes in the relationship between exports and imports (and in the total amount of trade)*. Changes in the quantities of goods traded will change the whole cost-price pattern in each country and involve changes which may use up the foreign-exchange reserves and make a given foreign-exchange rate unconducive to trade.

This proposition, in spite of its abstruse sound, is an elementary proposition in general equilibrium analysis. If the United States domestic price level, let us say, should rise, the United States export of certain items would no doubt be reduced. There would consequently be a primary effect on foreign-exchange reserves and on the tenability of the exchange rate. In addition, production in those lines of endeavor affected by the primary decline in exports would be reduced. There would be repercussions in one direction on various raw materials and in another direction on labor and labor wages. The ultimate effects would spread with varying degrees of impact through the whole economy. And the second round of impacts would affect again the identity and quantity of exports. The effect on exports would, this second time also, affect foreign-exchange reserves and the tenability of the foreign-exchange rate.

The Rate Itself

The identity of the goods which will be traded is not determined till the foreign-exchange rate itself is set. Consequently nothing is determined—cost patterns, prices, or income—until the rate is set.

It is these superficial forces (3, 4, and 5) that for the most part are responsible for creating the situation we call balance of payments disequilibrium, which necessitates foreign-exchange rate changes. But fundamental cost and demand changes, or technological and institutional changes, also could create a disequilibrium necessitating a rate change. It is not so certain, however, that they need do so. The growth and developmental changes, the changes in production patterns and consequently in cost relationships, the changes in institutional arrangements and consequently in cost and demand conditions—all those changes occur slowly. The economy can adjust to slow change, unless people and institutional attitudes prevent adjustment. In the latter case, the medicine which is called for is a strong purgative, administered to certain people or institutional attitudes, and not an artificial sedative—like currency devaluation—that rarely succeeds in putting the patient to sleep.

A major effort to prevent normal long-run adjustment is now being made in the United States. Those in the United States who are trying to prevent normal adjustment are the special-interest-pleaders for keeping out imports that may by some stretch of the imagination compete with their domestic product. There is every reason to believe that normal development in the next few years calls for the shifting over by the United States to an import trade balance.

THE TOOLS

The planning tools which are available for dealing with balance of payments difficulties have been listed by Professor Meade as follows:

(1) Fiscal policy measures (changes in taxes or in government spending);
(2) Monetary policy measures (to expand or contract the supply of money and credit, perhaps via gold movements and interest-rate changes);
(3) Measures affecting money wage rates;
(4) Change in the foreign-exchange rate; and
(5) Commercial policy measures (changes in the tariff, quota, or licensing arrangements affecting international trade).

BASIC SITUATIONS

We need to identify the basic types of situations to which the foregoing may be relevant. In fact, analysis of disequilibrium in the balance of payments does not make much sense except in terms of the types of situations in which trouble is likely to occur. Several such situations are: (1) short-run (speculative, flight of capital, and catastrophic) difficulties, (2) business cycles, and (3) economic growth and chronic difficulty.

CERTAIN OSTENSIBLE RELATIONS

The existence of balance of payments disequilibrium, such as might occasion a variation in the foreign-exchange rate, has customarily been analyzed in terms of the relationships among the balance of trade, gold stocks, interest rates, short-term balances, money supply, price levels, and national income.

The Rate and Reserves

The most relevant and immediate relation is that between the prevailing foreign-exchange rate and gold and foreign-exchange reserves. A given rate (such as $2.80 equals £1) can be maintained, for example, as long as somebody will sell sterling for dollars at that rate. Looking at the situation from the viewpoint of the British government, as long as it has reserves of dollars (or gold) it can continue to offer dollars for pounds at that rate. After its supply of dollar reserves (chiefly short-term dollar balances and gold) is exhausted, it is no longer possible for the British government to make dollars available for pounds at $2.80 to £1.

For such purposes as these, a country's reserves are essentially gold plus short-term balances (including chiefly bank deposits) standing to the country's credit in other countries. (The United States is almost the only country which does not formally count its reserves as gold plus freely convertible foreign exchange.)

In arguing the necessity or desirability of currency devaluation, the information most frequently taken into account is the size of these reserves. Britain, for example, is said to be experiencing a dollar shortage that may require devaluation if the British are short of dollar exchange or dollar balances.[6]

The Balance of Trade and Gold Stocks

Gold stocks are an important element in a country's reserves. What developments may increase or decrease gold reserves? The most obvious possibility is that increased exports may lead to a gold inflow (in payment for the exports) and increased imports may lead to a gold outflow.

Balance of Trade and Short-term Balances

The other chief element in reserves is short-term balances or foreign-exchange reserves. Normally if there is an export trade balance, short-term claims on foreign currencies should increase; if there is an import balance, short-term claims against foreigners should decrease. Of course, the change in gold stocks could be of such magnitude as to cause the short-term balances to change in the wrong direction; and the change in short-term balances could equally be of such magnitude as to cause the gold reserves to change in the wrong direction.

There may also be other factors influencing short-term balances.

Interest Rates and Short-term Balances

Interest-rate variations have frequently been indicated as causing the movement of short-term funds and consequently influencing foreign-exchange rates. In order to analyze the effect of interest rates, it is not change in the domestic rate alone, but change in the relationship between the domestic rates and the rest-of-the-world rates, which is sig-

[6] Some statistical material directly related to this relationship is presented in connection with the discussion of currency devaluation in Chapter 19.

nificant. If rest-of-the-world rates were falling faster than domestic rates, the development conceivably might be analyzed in terms of a *relative rise* in domestic rates even though these rates were actually falling.

Table 24 shows the change in two important sets of rates in different countries between May, 1952, and May, 1954. In terms of an absolute comparison of rates, it would seem that short-term funds should be flowing from the United States (and Switzerland) to the rest of the world—attracted by the higher interest rates elsewhere. And yet it is common knowledge that the United States and Switzerland in recent years have

TABLE 24
INTEREST RATE COMPARISONS

| | BANK RATE | | THREE-MONTH TRADE BILLS | |
	May 1952	*May 1954*	*May 1952*	*May 1954*
Belgium	3.25	2.75	3.25	2.75
France	4	3.25	5.6	4.85
Western Germany	6	3	7	4
Netherlands	3.5	2.5	4–5.5	3–4.5
Sweden	3	2.75	3	2.75
Switzerland	1.5	1.5	1.5	1.5
United Kingdom	4	3	4–5	2.5–3.5
Canada	2	2	4.5–6	4.5–6
United States	1.75	1.5	2.25–2.875	1.5–1.875
Japan	5.84	5.84	5.5–14.5	7.75–12

Source: *International Financial News Survey,* June 18, 1954, p. 389.

been the havens of refuge for short-term funds. One might almost conclude that the common interpretation of the process should be reversed. In that case, the financially and politically strong countries attract short-term funds and can therefore afford to pay lower interest rates.

As to the implications of the changes between May, 1952, and May, 1954, the situation is not clear-cut. It should be noted that various government controls and subsidies affect the impact of such changes in relationships as have occurred. But, in the absence of these artificial restraints, it seems reasonable to say that the really significant factor in the short run, which will influence the direction of movement of short-term funds, is a change in the relationship among the rates—rather than absolute differences in the rates.

In the United States in 1930 interest rates were falling and funds, on the balance, were moving out. But one may suspect that the real explanation was as much political as economic. Right about 1930 was *the* period in recent years when capitalism and the American economic system looked the weakest. Perhaps funds flowed out of the United States in response to the feeling that the United States was not the safest place to hold balances. But, as early as 1934, the inflow of funds was resumed in spite of the continuance of extremely low interest rates in the United States.[7] And the persistent inflow of funds for the last two decades has been more certainly due to the desire to hold funds in the safest place than to an apparently nonexistent interest-rate attraction.

Nevertheless, in literature on this subject, it is generally stated with some confidence that "things were different" before 1914. Thus Arthur I. Bloomfield has said:[8] "Under the pre-1914 gold standard, with exchange stability taken for granted, fluctuations in exchange rates within the narrow limits of the gold points had, as is well known, characteristically set into motion speculative short-term capital movements of the stabilizing or equilibrating type." One may hazard the guess that this was true of the relation between the London market and three or four other well-established financial centers, such as Amsterdam, Paris, and New York, and still believe that an important set of relations worked differently even then. Merchants in Buenos Aires, Rio de Janeiro, and Calcutta kept balances in London in spite of the fact that the ostensible interest rates were far higher in Buenos Aires, Rio, and Calcutta than in London. And probably those people, in deciding whether to increase or decrease their balances slightly, were at least as sensitive to minor changes in the political climate as they were to minor changes in the interest-rate relations.

Reserves and Money Supply

The obvious generalization is that, with an expansion of reserves, the money supply should expand, and with a contraction in reserves the money supply should contract.

In Chapter 16 the allegation was made that, depending on the place where international trade is financed, either *exports or imports* may increase the supply of money in the domestic spending-saving stream. Two further observations may be hazarded. In the first place, given the prevailing attitude that exports are to be encouraged and imports discouraged, countries and their banking systems are more likely to go out of their way to provide the financing for exports than for imports. In the second place, given legally established gold-reserve requirements in the long run, the gold stocks will have at least a limiting influence on the supply of money and credit—unless the legal reserve requirements are changed. (It should be added, however, that change in the

[7] How low, by comparison with foreign rates, is a relevant consideration that might alter these evaluations somewhat—but could not change the basic evaluation that it has been the widespread belief that the United States is the safe place to hold funds that really accounts for the inflow.

[8] Arthur I. Bloomfield, *Speculative and Flight Movements of Capital in Post-war International Finance,* International Finance Section (Princeton: Princeton University Press, 1954), p. 14.

legal reserve requirements is a not unlikely development.) However, given a certain set of reserve requirements, given a certain trade balance on goods and services, and given the appropriate response in terms of gold movements, the ability to finance will be increased by exports and decreased by imports. And the tendency to use the financing ability to finance exports rather than imports may well be determined by the institutional attitude which is more favorable to exports than to imports.

In view of these ostensible, natural, and even legally established relationships, it is amazing that there is so little relationship between fluctuations in reserves and fluctuations in the money supply.

To digress slightly from the foregoing comments, there is one sort of institutional difference between types of countries (developed and underdeveloped) which may make for different types of difficulties in different phases of the business cycle. Underdeveloped countries, which are largely raw material exporting, enjoy large foreign-exchange proceeds in good times, miserable proceeds in bad times. The large proceeds of foreign exchange during good times probably lead to credit expansion. But the contraction of foreign-exchange reserves during bad times is generally not followed by a corresponding contraction of money and credit. In fact, in bad times it is not unlikely that yet more money and credit will be, or should be, pumped into circulation in an effort to fight the depression. The situation is made difficult by the fact that imports remain relatively high priced (while export prices fall relatively) and, since internal money supply does not contract, the tendency to try to import holds up. Exhaustion of foreign-exchange reserves, and resultant exchange control or foreign-exchange rate change, are almost inevitable consequences. But underdeveloped countries get into this particular type of difficulty only *after* depression has begun elsewhere.

In any event, if a country cannot or will not conquer its own depression, other countries cannot be expected to sit idly by and watch declining exports react on them in the form of declining income.

Money Supply, Price Levels, and the Trade Balance

The price level should rise in response to an expansion in the money supply, and the size of the export balance should drop as the prices rise and the country becomes a less attractive place in which to buy.

National Income and the Balance of Trade

The relationship between income and trade was discussed at some length in Chapter 8. Presumably the causal sequence would be that an increase in income increases imports; and an increase in exports raises income. As was observed in Chapter 8, these relationships are not clear-cut, precise, and reliable. And the relation between exports and national income may not hold frequently enough to be important. The relation between national income and imports also is not completely reliable and predictable; but it probably operates with somewhat more reliability than does the relation between exports and income.

The more meaningful relation is that income, exports, and imports rise and fall together without much regard for what is happening to the balance of trade.

General Evaluation

Of course, the reliability with which these variables change in relation to each other in the way they should is a major factor influencing exchange-rate viability.

Chapter 18

THE RELATIVE VALUES OF
CURRENCIES: THE GOLD
STANDARD

❧ ❧ ❧

There is a precisely set quantity of gold in the monetary unit of a country on the gold standard.

The par rates of exchange for countries on the gold standard are determined by a comparison of the gold content of the monetary units.

Actual foreign-exchange rates between countries on the gold standard may vary slightly from par because of the cost of shipping gold. The so-called gold points are the limits of rate fluctuation permitted by the cost of shipping gold.

Gold standard pars represent a sort of price control—the rate being maintained by the government's willingness to redeem its own currency in gold in the set quantity.

The system breaks down if the government exhausts its gold reserves.

The specie-flow adjustment mechanism and the transfer of purchasing power adjustment mechanism have been presented as explanations of processes contributing to the viability of a gold standard.

The adjustment mechanisms may work; but they cannot be counted on to work in all possible situations.

The specie-flow adjustment mechanism may not work either because prices do not adjust fast enough or because central banks fail to play by the "rules of the game."

The transfer of purchasing power mechanism may fail to work because of the perverse behavior of demand.

❧ ❧ ❧

HISTORICAL SUMMARY

EFORE considering how well the various monetary standards have worked in practice, it may be helpful to present a brief history.

The Gold Standard

Many of the rules and procedures assuring the redeemability of paper money in a precious metal of a certain weight and fineness were evolved in western Europe, and especially in England, in the period between the discovery of America and the Napoleonic wars. David Hume described the specie-flow adjustment mechanism, which became a cornerstone of the international gold standard structure, in the 1740's. Then, during the Napoleonic wars, England went off her modified gold standard. (The gold standard never seems to function through a major war.) With peace restored, England went back on the gold standard in 1816 and proceeded, during the rest of the nineteenth century, to set an example of financial leadership for the world. But it was actually not until the 1840's that the rules of the gold standard became formalized in what came to be generally considered their proper form. There followed the years of London's financial and commercial hegemony in the world. Having an orderly and understandable monetary standard (whatever that standard may be) undoubtedly does contribute to leadership. Those were also the years of Britain's greatest political ascendancy. Cause and effect? The British then carried the "white man's burden" from Suez to Singapore and back to the Transvaal in time for the Boer War. Although Britain in those years probably owed her position to the fact that the Industrial Revolution had begun in England, and had raised English productivity and level of living to an outstanding degree, it is understandable that some observers attributed a certain omnipotence to the particular monetary standard that Britain happened to have.

Despite the fact that we have been taught to think of the gold standard as an institution whose respectability and reliability have stood the test of time, the standard actually was in general use for a rather short period of time. England might be said to have been on the gold standard by the early nineteenth century. But most other countries were still on a bimetallic standard or a silver standard until almost the end of the nineteenth century. Not until 1873 did the United States go on a *de facto* gold standard by making the gold dollar rather than the silver dollar the monetary unit, and not until 1900 was the Gold Standard Act actually passed. Then it was in the decade following 1900 that Mexico and many smaller countries of the so-called underdeveloped areas went off their silver or bimetallic standards onto some rough approximation of the gold standard. Thus the gold standard really flourished for only a very brief time before World War I. It is amazing that such a system (which was in existence for such a short time, which has never been able to withstand hard times) should have obtained such a dominant hold on the minds of some people and become the symbol of financial soundness and respectability.

At all events, the World War started in 1914. England abandoned this fair-weather friend and went off the gold standard, as did virtually all other countries. After the war, England returned to the gold standard at the old gold par—but not until 1925, and then only over the strong opposition of many who pointed out that that par did not accurately reflect the purchasing power of the pound sterling. Keynes at that time alleged that going back on the gold standard at the old par was a mistake and that British industry would suffer. But "perfidious Albion," in order to maintain her financial respectability and hegemony, insisted on doing the honorable thing.

France returned to the gold standard in 1928, but not at the pre-war par, which had been 19.3¢ (U.S.) to the franc. In fact, the franc was devalued by about four-fifths to 3.9¢ (U.S.) to correspond with the decline in purchasing power of the franc relative to the dollar which had already occurred. It has been alleged that this devaluation gave French exports enough of a competitive advantage over British exports in the late twenties (especially after England appreciated in 1925) so that, although England was suffering seriously from the depression by 1930, the depression did not really hit the French until the wave of devaluations of the early thirties had brought the value of the pound and other currencies down, thereby causing the French to lose their advantage. It was 1936 before the French finally went off the gold standard—but when they did they were in "horrible shape."

England and the United States were about the only large countries on bona fide (more or less) gold standards during the middle and late twenties. But quite a few countries at the end of World War I went onto modified gold standards called "gold-exchange standards." The paper currency of a country on the gold-exchange standard was redeemable either in gold or in foreign exchange drawn against deposits in a gold-standard country; for instance, the currency of the Philippines was redeemable in United States currency, and the currencies of India and Austria were redeemable in British sterling. Since it was desirable from the viewpoint of the gold-standard country thus to tie the other countries financially to its coattails, such a country was not averse to giving guarantees that it would honor, in gold if need be, the foreign-exchange claims which the gold-exchange standard countries might have against it.[1]

---

[1] One of the arguments (originally offered in the early twenties) for the use of the gold-exchange standard was that gold was in short supply in the world and the gold-exchange standard would result in economy in its use, since paper currency might be issued in more than one country on the basis of the same gold reserves. It did not actually work out in that way, however, since the gold-standard country, to play safe, was likely to set aside and earmark gold to be used to support the gold-exchange standard currencies that it was obligated to support.

It may be noted here that the idea of using foreign exchange as part of the re-

At any rate, during the 1920's various countries were returning to modified gold standards under varying conditions; but they were having their troubles in doing so, and international trade was no longer quite as free and unrestricted as it had been before the war. Governments were nastier about requiring people to have passports. Other barriers to trade were increasing in severity. The split-up of the Austro-Hungarian and Russian empires resulted in the creation of many new countries, each with its own trade barriers. England's first protective tariff law in almost a hundred years was passed during World War I.

Short-term funds also became a chronic and difficult problem in the twenties. Before World War I, short-term credit had been largely used to finance goods trade, and it performed this function in a relatively orderly fashion. But during the 1920's a much larger proportion of the short-term credit in existence had nothing to do with financing goods trade. A Balkan or Latin American ruler might keep a large balance in a British or United States bank for use if he lost power in his own country. There was considerable uncertainty in the world in the 1920's in spite of the ostensible prosperity; and the movements of funds were increasingly uncertain and highly erratic.

Another characteristic of the 1920's, foreshadowing the action that would be taken in the troubled thirties, was the growing conviction, indicated over and over again in central bank reports that, if there was a choice between internal stability and external stability (that is, a choice between internal prosperity and the gold standard), the proper course would be to try to solve the internal problem even at the cost of international stability (that is, at the cost of the gold standard). That attitude represented a major change in governmental and central bank

---

serves behind a currency is still common in countries no longer on the gold-exchange standard. In fact, the United States is about the only country where "gold only," instead of "gold and foreign exchange," is carried by the central bank as reserves behind the currency. In the United States, of course, the Treasury Department holds the gold at Fort Knox, Kentucky, as trustee for the Federal Reserve Banks which are the actual owners. The Federal Reserve Banks are issued gold certificates by the Treasury as evidence of their claim. The Federal Reserve Banks, in turn, are required to have a gold certificate reserve of at least 25 per cent behind the Federal Reserve Notes they issue or the loans they make to commercial banks. In most countries the law requires that the central bank maintain reserves in gold, perhaps silver, and foreign exchange as a certain percentage (perhaps 30 per cent) or within a certain range (perhaps between 25 per cent to 50 per cent) of the value of the currency outstanding or of the central bank credit outstanding. The exact formulae and the identity of "what is related to what" vary. This is likely to be the case even in countries where the citizen within the country cannot, of his own volition, convert his currency into gold and may be greatly restricted in his freedom to convert into foreign exchange.

Governments with monetary arrangements of this sort may provide that only foreign exchange of countries where the currency is freely convertible can be counted as reserve behind the currency. The United States dollar is most in demand for this purpose—whereas so-called blocked balances in countries that do not allow free convertibility cannot generally be counted as reserves.

thinking, in contrast with the nineteenth century emphasis on abiding by certain rules of the international gold standard.

The Crisis of 1929–1933

Hard on the heels of France's return to the gold standard in 1928 came world-wide depression in 1929. The general depression was already well advanced when, in May, 1931, the Credit Anstalt, the big Rothschild bank in Vienna, failed (partly because a country as small as Austria had no business having a city as large as Vienna). As a by-product of the failure of that bank, there was an increase in the international movement of short-term funds, "hot money," that was quite unrelated to goods movement. For example, before its failure, the bank tried desperately to save itself by withdrawing funds (gold) from Germany, England, and France. The impact of the Credit Anstalt failure was especially felt by the German banking system. Germany was in a state of general unrest during those days anyway: Hitler was ranting; the brownshirts were throwing rocks. And one of the six big German banks, the Darmstaedter und National Bank, failed. The German banking system in its turn resorted to extensive withdrawals of funds, particularly gold from England, in an effort to deal with its difficulties. There was a run on England's gold reserves. Britain, as was pointed out in Chapter 16, was a debtor at short term, the natural position for a financial center; and she was vulnerable to this sort of action. By July of 1931 British gold reserves were reduced to $642,500,000 (at $20.67 a fine ounce); England then went off the gold standard, with the loss of gold serving at least as partial justification. A group of countries, including the British dominions and several of the smaller countries of northern Europe, which became known as the sterling bloc, also devalued at the same time. The merry-go-round of devaluation was whirling. And the United States climbed on in 1933.

Recent Policies

Following the general abandonment of the gold standard in the early 1930's, various policies were adopted by the different governments. None, however, seriously experimented with freely fluctuating rates. Several, led by the United States and Britain, attempted to control the foreign-exchange rate by extensive government trading on the foreign-exchange markets through the instrumentality of stabilization funds. Others, led by Germany, attempted to control rates by more positive exchange control based on the police power. These control methods will be discussed in Chapter 20.

During World War II, the governments which previously had relied chiefly on stabilization funds also made extensive use of exchange control. And virtually all international traffic in currencies was under the control of governments—except for black market operations.

At the close of World War II, the International Monetary Fund was established; the governments which joined (and that included most governments) agreed to permit the Fund to control foreign-exchange rates. Rate changes of any importance now have to be approved by the Fund; and the Fund has reserves of various currencies which it may make available to the different governments to aid them in supporting a given rate. The articles of agreement establishing the Fund also called for close restriction of the conditions under which exchange controls could be used by governments. But ten years after the end of World War II governments are still making extensive use of exchange controls—although perhaps not quite as extensive as in 1945.

DEFINITION OF THE GOLD STANDARD

Under the gold standard, the gold content of the monetary units of the various countries sets limits to the fluctuation of exchange rates. Before everyone went off the gold standard in the early 1930's, there were 113.0016 grains of fine gold in the British pound sterling and 23.22 grains of fine gold in the dollar. By dividing one figure into the other, the *par rate of exchange* could be computed. The pound-dollar par in the old days, fairly accurately worked out, was $4.86656 (U.S.) equals one British pound sterling.

Some of the more important characteristics of the monetary system of a country on the gold standard were:

(1) That its paper currency be freely convertible into a given amount of gold and that gold be freely convertible into an equivalent amount of paper currency;

(2) That gold be legal tender;

(3) That gold be freely imported and exported (no tariffs on gold); and

(4) That credit be expanded internally if there was a gold inflow and contracted if there was a gold outflow. This latter procedure has been called "playing by the rules of the game."

But even under the gold standard a comparison of gold contents did not fix the foreign exchange rate, unalterably and permanently, exactly at the par figure. This was because of the cost of shipping gold. The so-called "gold points" (gold export point and gold import point), determined by the cost of shipping gold, established high and low figures beyond which the exchange rate could not fluctuate. The elements of cost involved in shipping gold that would account for the range between the gold points included (1) freight, (2) insurance, and (3) loss of interest on the money during the time it took to ship the gold. If a person who had to make a foreign payment took advantage of the redeemability of his paper money in gold to obtain the gold to ship abroad and settle his obligation, he incurred the cost of shipping the gold in addition to the actual sum of money involved in the payment. Consequently, an importer would be willing to pay slightly more than the par of exchange (but less than the par of exchange plus the cost of shipping the gold) to buy the foreign currency from some agency such as a bank which happened to have some foreign currency, perhaps in the form of deposits in a foreign bank. (This procedure, which more likely would involve a somewhat more complicated transaction using a bill of exchange, was discussed in Chapter 16.) Much trouble—going to the mint, getting the gold, and shipping it—is avoided if you can buy or sell a piece of paper on the foreign-exchange market.

The distance between the gold points could vary as the shipping charges, insurance premiums, and interest rates varied. But during the latter years under the gold standard, the gold points (establishing the range of possible fluctuation of the pound-dollar rate) were generally from $4.887 to $4.847 to the pound.

ALTERNATIVE ADJUSTMENT PROCESSES

From time to time, disturbing influences may place pressure on the foreign-exchange rate. Such a disturbance might be a large foreign loan, a substantial change in the amount of money in circulation in one country, or a change in buying habits, such as a decision by foreigners that they wanted United States automobiles above all things that they could think of, instead of the bicycles they had previously been buying from France. These are examples of the autonomous changes mentioned in the discussion of the balance of payments in Chapter 7. There have been two chief explanations of how the adjustment process may work under the gold standard following a disturbance: (1) the specie-flow explanation and (2) the transfer-of-purchasing-power explanation. And, in retrospect, one may also speculate as to how (3) national-income theory would explain gold-standard adjustments.

Specie-flow Mechanism

According to one explanation, the specie-flow mechanism is the process which might make it possible for the gold standard to continue operating indefinitely, maintaining the foreign-exchange rates set within narrow limits by the gold points. This explanation originally obtained wide acceptance as the result of an essay entitled "Of the Balance of Trade," which was written, probably in the 1740's, by David Hume.[2] It continued until the 1930's to be the "orthodox" explanation of how the adjustment process works out under the gold standard.

The argument runs somewhat as follows: Let us assume that there are only two countries in the world, the United States and the "rest of the world," and that both areas are on the gold standard. An autonomous disturbance then occurs which results in the rest of the world buying more goods in the United States than it had previously bought there—step 1 in Chart 11. This might occur because the United States had developed an attractive new product, or for one of the other reasons mentioned above. If the possibilities of lending and giving are ruled out, gold has to flow from the rest of the world to the United States to effect payment for these goods, and there is consequently more gold in the United States and less gold in the rest of the world than there was before—step 2.[3]

In Hume's example, he merely assumed that gold circulated as money, but during the nineteenth century, because of the increased use of paper money, the analysis was refined to allow for paper money and credit—paper money being convertible into gold, of course, if the country was on a gold standard. But the addition of paper money calls for a very important additional assumption—that the banking system will play by the "rules of the game." It is not necessarily true that the banking system will expand the amount of money and credit in existence following an inflow of gold—steps 2 and 3. But the successful operation of the specie-flow mechanism required this to happen.[4] And banking ethics in the nineteenth century came to require that the proper action be taken. So, strangely enough, before World War I, a system operated which required that a nation subject its own "selfish interests" to certain international rules. Although there was no international law or international police force to contend with, the banks (and Grover Cleveland) played by the rules, trying to contract the supply of money and credit when

[2] David Hume, *Political Discourses* (London: Walter Scott, 1906 [?]), pp. 51–6. The *Political Discourses* was originally published in 1752.

[3] A somewhat more polished version of this process allows for the probability that the first step would involve payment with a bill of exchange and an international movement of short-term funds rather than the actual gold movement. Presumably the gold movement occurs as a result of the building up of excessive short-term balances.

[4] The inflow of gold and expansion of reserves means that there is a tendency to money and credit expansion and to lower interest rates, but it is a tendency that can easily be nullified by prevailing business conditions or by government action.

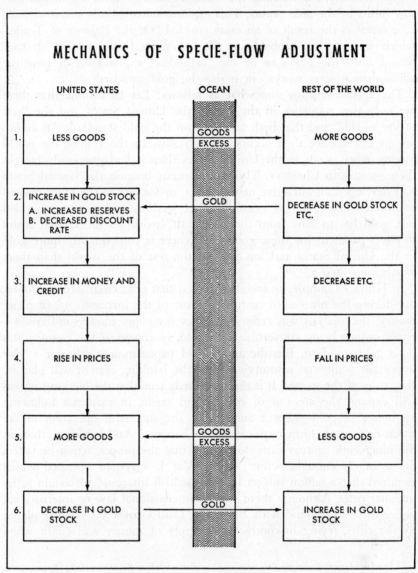

CHART 11

MECHANICS OF SPECIE-FLOW ADJUSTMENT

UNITED STATES	OCEAN	REST OF THE WORLD
1. LESS GOODS	GOODS EXCESS	MORE GOODS
2. INCREASE IN GOLD STOCK A. INCREASED RESERVES B. DECREASED DISCOUNT RATE	GOLD	DECREASE IN GOLD STOCK ETC.
3. INCREASE IN MONEY AND CREDIT		DECREASE ETC.
4. RISE IN PRICES		FALL IN PRICES
5. MORE GOODS	GOODS EXCESS	LESS GOODS
6. DECREASE IN GOLD STOCK	GOLD	INCREASE IN GOLD STOCK

there was a gold outflow, and to expand the supply when there was a gold inflow.

A somewhat more detailed explanation of stages 2 and 3 in the process would also consider the expansion in the supply of gold, and the consequent increase in bank reserves, which would lead to a reduction in the interest (or discount) rate. This development, it was thought, would encourage people to borrow and thus would increase the actual amount of credit being used.

As a consequence of the increase in money and credit, prices would rise—step 4. At least they would rise if yet another assumption is correct. This is the quantity theory of money, which states that as a result of an expansion in the amount of money and credit there will be a rise in prices. Much has been said pro and con with regard to the quantity theory of money and just how precise it is in operation. As a crude evaluation of that debate, it would appear that the price level is almost certainly affected by major changes in the quantity of money and credit, but does not vary in direct proportion to the changes in the supply of money and credit and may not respond at all to minor changes in such supply. However, the working out of the specie-flow adjustment is not dependent upon an exactly proportional relation between money and credit supply on the one hand and prices on the other. The working out of the process is merely dependent upon a substantial rise in prices consequent on a substantial increase in the supply of money and credit.

Meanwhile, in the rest of the world, on the basis of the same assumptions, less gold has meant less paper money, less credit, and lower prices. Consequently, prices are higher in the United States than they were; prices are lower in the rest of the world than they were. Thus the United States has become a relatively less attractive place in which to buy; and the rest of the world has become a relatively more attractive place in which to buy. At some stage in this process, when buying in the rest of the world becomes attractive enough and buying in the United States unattractive enough, there will be a shift in the direction of movement of the trade and an excess of goods will begin to move from the rest of the world to the United States—step 5. Thus an adjustment process has worked out to counterbalance (more or less—or enough for viability) the original disturbance. No change in the exchange rate was necessary; but a change in relative price levels was necessary in the process of working out the adjustment.

If these developments occur as described, certain implications for terms of trade follow. During the adjustment process the unit terms of trade moved against the rest of the world and in a direction favorable to the United States—this being by definition the meaning of a situation in which foreigners have to pay a higher price for goods bought in the

United States and United States citizens a lower price for foreign goods. But, in the end, things are back more or less where they started: the goods trade balanced out (more or less), the gold is back where it started from (more or less), and prices are back where they started (more or less).

In evaluation of the specie-flow explanation, it may be said that things *might* work out in this way if the adjustment process were given enough time. But there are difficulties. What if there is not much time allowed; and the gold is moving fast out of the rest of the world at step 2; and the mere fact that it is moving fast alarms people; and they lose confidence in the currency of the country that is losing gold? As a result of this loss of confidence, the gold moves out even faster as people try to get dollars for francs (and in so doing sell their francs for gold and ship the gold to the United States to buy dollars). A country may well lose so much gold so quickly that it is forced to suspend redemption of the currency in gold before the specie-flow adjustment process has time to work itself out. There is no clear indication that the cause-and-effect relationships posited by the specie-flow explanation are operating. In fact for the period before 1933, while the United States was still on the gold standard, prices seem to have jumped around with little regard for what was happening to the gold reserves and only slightly more respect for what was happening to currency and demand deposits in circulation.

If time is important, the specie-flow mechanism may not be able to solve the problem of adjustment. And the specie-flow mechanism is a process which requires time in a setting where there literally may not be the time—in which case another adjustment process (going off the gold standard) may assert itself.

Another difficulty may result from the unwillingness of a government to play by the rules of the game. A government may not want the adjustment mechanism to work in the manner described. Following 1933, there was an inflow of gold into the United States as described in steps 1 and 2 of Chart 12. By the "rules of the game" the rest of the world, which was losing gold to the United States, should have contracted the amount of paper money and credit in circulation. But the world was afflicted with depression. Hence it is not strange that the rest of the world did not desire to play by the rules. Other countries tried to avoid contracting money and credit—stage 4 of Chart 12 —to correspond with the outflow of gold. And many countries succeeded in expanding money and credit, in spite of the gold outflow, in an effort to fight their depression.

Another possible difficulty may be suggested by the tools of price analysis discussed in Chapter 6. Even though prices change, and change

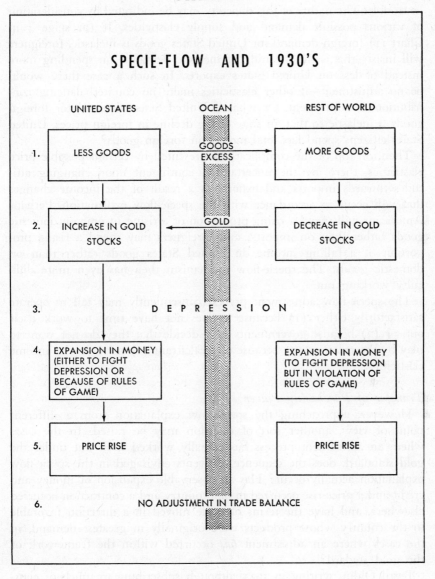

CHART 12

SPECIE-FLOW AND 1930'S

UNITED STATES	OCEAN	REST OF WORLD

1. LESS GOODS — GOODS EXCESS → MORE GOODS

2. INCREASE IN GOLD STOCKS ← GOLD — DECREASE IN GOLD STOCKS

3. D E P R E S S I O N

4. EXPANSION IN MONEY (EITHER TO FIGHT DEPRESSION OR BECAUSE OF RULES OF GAME) — EXPANSION IN MONEY (TO FIGHT DEPRESSION BUT IN VIOLATION OF RULES OF GAME)

5. PRICE RISE — PRICE RISE

6. NO ADJUSTMENT IN TRADE BALANCE

with speed, as implied in the specie-flow explanation, there still may be trouble. The nature of this difficulty may be indicated by consideration of various possible demand and supply elasticities. If (at stage 4 in Chart 11) foreign demand for United States goods is inelastic, foreigners will insist—this is the meaning of inelastic demand—on spending more instead of less on United States exports. In such a case there would be no adjustment—if other elasticities make no counterbalancing contribution to adjustment. Or what if United States demand for foreign goods is inelastic so that, in spite of the decline in foreign prices, United States citizens spend less total money on foreign goods?

Then, on top of the complications presented by certain possible price elasticities, there are the uncertainties contingent upon changing attitudes towards imports and exports as a result of the income changes that will occur in accordance with the specie-flow explanation. Perhaps Americans will spend a rising proportion of a rising income on domestic goods rather than on imports; and foreigners may spend a rising proportion of a falling income on United States goods rather than on domestic goods. The specie-flow mechanism then has even more difficulty working out.

The specie-flow adjustment process consequently may fail to operate satisfactorily either (1) because it does not have time to work itself out, or (2) because governments may decide that they do not want to play by the rules, or (3) because of recalcitrant (a) price or (b) income elasticities.

Transfer of Purchasing Power

However, approaching the specie-flow explanation from a different point of view, another sort of question may be raised. In the cases where an adjustment process has actually worked itself out under the gold standard, does the sequence of events envisaged in the specie-flow explanation actually occur? Has an observable expansion of money and credit and a price rise occurred in one country and a contraction occurred elsewhere, and have the terms of trade moved in a direction favorable to the country whose products were originally in greatest demand, in the cases where an adjustment *has* occurred within the framework of the gold stadard?

Bertil Ohlin, writing in 1933, although subscribing to much of classical and neo-classical economic analysis (in spite of his own allegation to the contrary), still believed that the adjustment process under the gold standard was different, simpler, and capable of working faster than that envisaged in the specie-flow explanation.[5] Ohlin's argument, somewhat simplified, might run as indicated in Chart 13. Again, some

---

[5] Ohlin, *Interregional and International Trade, passim.*

CHART 13

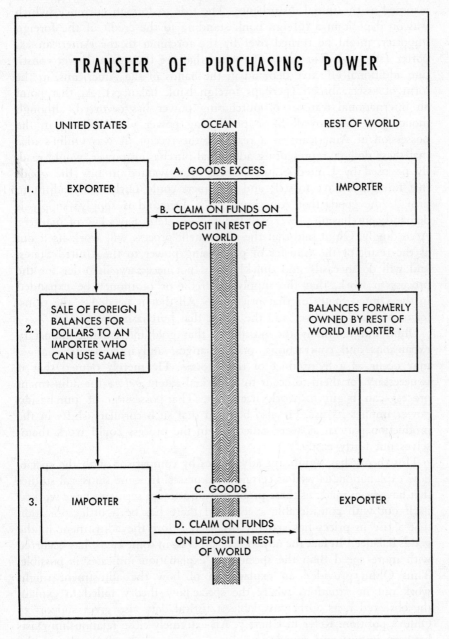

TRANSFER OF PURCHASING POWER

UNITED STATES	OCEAN	REST OF WORLD
1. EXPORTER	A. GOODS EXCESS →	IMPORTER
	← B. CLAIM ON FUNDS ON DEPOSIT IN REST OF WORLD	
2. SALE OF FOREIGN BALANCES FOR DOLLARS TO AN IMPORTER WHO CAN USE SAME		BALANCES FORMERLY OWNED BY REST OF WORLD IMPORTER
3. IMPORTER	← C. GOODS	EXPORTER
	D. CLAIM ON FUNDS ON DEPOSIT IN REST OF WORLD →	

"rest of the world" increase in demand for United States goods is assumed as the initial disturbance. The title to foreign currency, which was on deposit in a foreign bank standing to the credit of the foreign importer, might be turned over by the foreigner to the American exporter (step 1b). The sums of money that are thus turned over constitute additional effective demand in the hands of the Americans, in the form of assets abroad (perhaps foreign bank balances). At that point an international transfer of purchasing power has occurred, although money has not moved. More purchasing power was built up in the possession of Americans as a result of the receipt. It was Ohlin's idea that these dollars, representing additional purchasing power, would readily be used by United States citizens who wanted to buy the goods that foreigners have to sell; and foreigners could fairly easily adjust to provide the goods that Americans want. Demand is supply; supply is demand; purchasing power will be used—so states Say's law of markets. Accordingly, Ohlin said that the adjustment process will work itself out as the result of the transfer of purchasing power to the United States, and will do so easily and quickly. It is not necessary, in order for the process to work, that the supply of credit or of money be expanded in the United States or that prices rise. All that is needed is the transfer of purchasing power and the use of that purchasing power.

Ohlin did not deny the possibility that gold movements, monetary expansions and contractions, price changes, and interest-rate changes may occur as a by-product of this process. He merely denied that it is necessary for them to occur to a marked extent *before* the adjustment process can begin to work itself out. The possession of purchasing power implies its use. He also believed that such corollary shifts in the production pattern as were called for in the process could work themselves out fairly easily.[6]

This theory has significant advantages by comparison with the specie-flow explanation, as well as certain weaknesses. In some statistical studies that have been made of these problems, adjustment seems to have worked itself out with considerable speed, and there has been little indication that a rise in prices has actually occurred *before* the adjustment in the goods balance.[7] In fact the adjustment process, in some cases, has occurred with more speed than the specie-flow explanation indicates is possible. Thus Ohlin provided an explanation of how the adjustment might work out in situations where the specie-flow theory failed to explain the observed facts. Other available statistical data also gives support to Ohlin's position. Refer to Chart 7. An extremely close relationship exists between import and export variations—an amazingly close relationship, in fact. The existence of the close relationship in the movement of

[6] See Chapters 6 and 24 for further ramifications of Ohlin's theory.

[7] Iversen, *Aspects of the Theory of International Capital Movements, passim.*

exports and imports does support the possibility of a connection closer than that via gold movements, interest rate changes, etc.

Since all Ohlin essentially did was to point out that price theorists in analyzing international trade had forgotten to apply one of their own tools (Say's law of markets), he was in a sense completing the logical picture that orthodox theory called for anyway, rather than developing a new theory—as he has been fond of claiming.

But difficulties exist, and have existed, that Ohlin does not take into account. The close relationship in export and import movement has not always been close enough to prevent payment difficulties from existing. The existence of frequently recurring payment difficulties is also a readily observable phenomenon. On top of that, Ohlin's theory did not clearly explain the relationship between the purchasing power derived from exports and the use of that purchasing power—by other people— in financing imports. The application of national-income theory to international trade represents an effort to fill this gap.

National Income Theory

Ohlin in 1933 (and earlier in 1929 in an argument with Keynes, which was carried in the *Economic Journal*) identified the increased purchasing power that the exporter derived from the sale of his export as the factor which would be used to increase imports correspondingly. Keynes, at that time, would have none of it. Later, in 1936, Keynes formalized what has come to be called national-income theory in his now classic work: *The General Theory of Employment, Interest and Money*. But, strangely enough, when national-income theory is applied to international trade it has some remarkable similarities with Ohlin's transfer of purchasing power theory—in spite of the Keynes-Ohlin argument of 1929 to 1933.

The national-income application runs somewhat as follows: As a consequence of increased exports the income of exporters in, say, the United States is increased. The increased income is partly spent on domestic goods, partly spent on imports, and partly saved. But if, in any given expenditure of income, Americans spend only 5 per cent, 10 per cent, or even 30 per cent of their additional income on imports, it will take thirty (more or less), fifteen, or five turnovers to make the import increase roughly correspond with the export increase. And if there is any domestic saving in the United States, the adjustment of imports to an amount equal to the export change may never occur (see Table 14). But even if adjustment may occur through the working of forces posited in national-income theory, the process is going to take time. Thus national-income theory does not describe a process that is theoretically any speedier than the specie-flow explanation. A reasonable conclusion would seem to be that sometimes the process has worked with speed as described by Ohlin; sometimes it has not worked at all. And maybe it takes a direct tie between the possession of purchasing power and desire for foreign goods to make a truly speedy and sure adjustment.[8]

In any event, the manner in which a sudden increase in income will be spent is one of the most uncertain things in this world. Demands and supplies may be generally elastic and predictable in the long run; but they are not in the short run. This element of uncertainty affects both the specie-flow and the transfer of purchasing power explanations. It also affects national-income theory as applied to international trade.

But, in general appraisal of these theories, it may be said that in combination they describe forces that may operate under gold-standard conditions to make the fixed exchange rates of the standard workable. There is no assurance, however, that those adjustment forces will automatically work in time to save the standard in a particularly difficult situation.

Comment on Relationships

It would be a great help in analyzing the problem of balance of payments adjustment if the various factors would interrelate in some regular and predictable pattern. Unfortunately, they do not. The problem of the researcher, then, is not to allege a lot of relationships which logically ought to exist but in fact do not. It is rather to understand what is going on.

Businessmen, international traders, foreign-exchange dealers, and government officials concerned with trade problems—not to forget the population at large—behave in a certain way during one crisis. They carry certain recollections of the previous crisis into the next. Some of those recollections may inspire them to act the same way next time. But a great many of the recollections will inspire them to act differently.

It is very ticklish procedure to try to set up a theory as to how adjustment will work, since one cannot safely assume it will work the same way twice in succession. To reduce the uncertainties just a fraction, maybe someone should distribute a questionnaire asking how people would respond to certain conditions in the next depression.

[8] See Chapter 24.

Chapter 19

THE RELATIVE VALUES OF
CURRENCIES: FLUCTUATING
EXCHANGE RATES

❦ ❦ ❦

*Purchasing power parities and demand and supply forces have been
advanced as explanations of the forces determining foreign-exchange
rates if the rates are allowed to fluctuate freely.*

*The purchasing power parity explanation states that change in the com-
parative purchasing power of currencies controls the natural fluctuation of the rates.*

*The demand and supply theory states that all of the factors affecting
the demand for and the supply of the various currencies on the
foreign-exchange market must be taken into account in explaining
rate determination.*

*The demand and supply approach is more adequate theoretically; but
it is not usable as a guide to actual policy because of the impossibility of taking all of the factors into account.*

*The purchasing power parity concept can be a useful guide to policy
in spite of its theoretical inadequacy.*

*Currency devaluation may occur as a matter of deliberate policy; or
it may occur as a result of circumstances more or less beyond the
control of the devaluing country.*

*Currency devaluation which is intended to increase exports in an effort
to increase national income is of doubtful merit because there are
better ways to increase national income.*

*Currency devaluation which is expected to increase exports enough to
increase the foreign-exchange receipts obtained from exports is likely
to be ineffective.*

❦ ❦ ❦

THE VALUE of one currency unit in terms of another may
be more or less pegged by relating the value of each to a set
amount of gold. At least the values may be pegged within
narrow limits for as long as each country has gold. This sort

of government interference with the free market process is considered quite respectable. Other methods for setting the rates by controls involving stabilization funds and government fiat are not generally considered so respectable.

This chapter is not, however, concerned primarily with the foregoing possibilities but rather represents an attempt to identify the forces which would be at work if the price of one currency were allowed to fluctuate in terms of other currencies—like other prices. In this setting there are two chief possibilities: (1) freely fluctuating rates and (2) planned and sporadic currency devaluation. These possibilities are discussed below.

FREELY FLUCTUATING RATES

Rates may be allowed to fluctuate as they will. There have been two chief explanations as to the forces which would control the manner of fluctuation in that eventuality: (1) the purchasing power parity relation and (2) the forces of demand and supply.

Purchasing Power Parity

The purchasing power parity theory is a venerable doctrine going back at least to Malynes about 1600. But in its recent and much discussed form it owes its formulation to Gustav Cassel, who developed the theory, or re-developed it during World War I, as a suggested means for dealing with the then existing exchange-rate problem.[1] In 1914 most of the warring governments went off the gold standard; and exchange rates were subject to arbitrary government control during the ensuing war years. At the end of the war, when the controls were removed, the purchasing power of the pound sterling was revealed to have fallen relative to the dollar. England then had the problem of deciding whether to go back on the gold standard and, if it did, whether to go back at the old gold par or some other par.

Cassel's purchasing power parity theory was developed in part as a guide to the governments in determining what to do in this type of situation. And specifically, according to the doctrine, what they were to do was to let the relative change in the purchasing power of their currencies since 1914 serve as a guide in fixing the new exchange rates.

A *too crude* statement of the doctrine would be that the value of the currency (the foreign-exchange rate) would be determined by its purchasing power. If the purchasing power of a unit of the national money

[1] Gustav Cassel, *Money and Foreign Exchange after 1914* (New York: Macmillan, 1922).

is twice as much in one country as in another—if the pound, for example, would buy twice as much in England as the dollar would buy in the United States—then the rate of exchange would be two to one, $2 equals £1. But there is the legitimate question whether exchange rates could be expected to correspond in the absolute sense with price-level differences, even if such differences could be measured absolutely rather than via index-number comparisons. First, with regard to the possibility of making absolute comparisons, this may be said: Although there exists no accurate measuring device for comparing price levels in a direct way, nevertheless certain rough general impressions as to differences in price levels can be obtained by travelers. A tourist may have a somewhat warped conception of the nature of these differences because of his somewhat atypical points of contact—hotels, restaurants, curio shops, and the like. But still and all, on the basis of a considerable contact with other countries, it is possible to make allowance for the exchange rate and still be pretty sure that there is a substantial difference in price levels. For most of Latin America in the late 1930's, one could say with assurance that the price level was substantially lower than in the United States, and had been for many years. More generally, it may be said, though it is rather difficult to prove, that there have been discrepancies in price levels between countries over long periods of time even after proper allowance is made for the rate of exchange. For that matter, two areas within the same country (the South and the Northeast in the United States) can have substantially different price levels; or two areas, such as the United States and Puerto Rico, with the same monetary unit can have substantially different price levels almost indefinitely.[2]

Cassel was probably well enough aware of this; in fact, his theory is more properly viewed as a means of accounting for change in the rate rather than a theory alleging that a workable rate can be obtained by comparing absolute differences in price levels.

Cassel's theory, then, is not a theory of absolutes; it is intended only to serve as a guide to change. The technique would not be useful "at the beginning of the world" to set up *de novo* exchange rates. In order to apply the theory, it is necessary to assume that the prevailing exchange rates during some earlier year were viable. Then index-number changes in prices in subsequent years are compared to arrive at a clue as to how the exchange rate should be changing. Thus in analyzing British–United States relations it might be assumed that the exchange rate in existence in 1910, £1 equaling $4.86, was a part of a viable situation. With 1910 as the base year, the exchange rates that ought to prevail after the war, say in 1921, might be computed somewhat as follows, using hypothetical figures:

[2] The existence of absolute price differences was discussed more fully in Chapter 6.

	PRICE LEVEL INDEX NUMBERS		EXCHANGE RATE
	United Kingdom	United States	*(Number of dollars to £1)*
1910	100	100	$4.86
1921	200	100	$2.43

The actual formula for computing the new rate would be:

$$\frac{\text{New U.S. price level} \times \text{Original par (number of \$ in £)}}{\text{New British price level}} = \text{New par}$$

$$\frac{100 \times \$4.86}{200} = \$2.43$$

Such a computation, if accurate, according to Cassel, would be the basis for saying that, at the end of World War I, the British pound should have been devalued from $4.86 to $2.43 to the pound sterling.

Parenthetically it might be pointed out at this stage that, according to the specie-flow adjustment mechanism operating under gold-standard conditions, such a change would be unnecessary because in 1921 at the $4.86 rate people would buy more in the United States and less in England. Gold would flow to the United States. Prices would adjust in both countries, and perhaps come together at 150, more or less. Under these circumstances, the type of adjustment indicated by the purchasing power parity theory would not be necessary. Such adjustment is possible, it is true, if gold reserves are not exhausted too quickly; but this leaves unanswered the question as to which type of adjustment is least painful.

The purchasing power parity theory is an explanation of the identifiable, measurable forces that may be used as a guide in the direct setting of changed, workable exchange rates. But even as a guide in making changes, this theory presents some difficulties. What index number should be used in making a computation of this sort: the index number of internal wholesale price, or the index number for the price level of goods that enter international trade, or some other? One might be tempted to say that the goods that are involved are the goods that move internationally, so that the index covering the goods that are bought and sold internationally would be the proper one to use. The trouble with using the index number for the price level of these goods is that the identity of the goods which will move internationally is not determined until the exchange rate has been set, but the whole idea of the operation is to obtain data that will be usable in setting the rate. Thus the problem becomes a circular one. Granted there will be some goods that will be traded under almost any conditions. Nevertheless, there is a group of goods that may or may not move internationally, depending on the foreign-exchange rate. Thus it is impossible to use this index number covering fluctuations in the price of internationally traded goods; and one is left with the internal wholesale price index which, although not entirely satisfactory, does not represent a logical impossibility. It is not entirely satisfactory because the prices of many articles which will never enter international trade are included. But the fact that there are elements in the internal wholesale price index that do not enter international trade means only that that index is not an entirely accurate guide as to what a workable exchange rate would be, not that it is completely unusable. It might, however, be better to devise a third index-number series covering the prices of goods that are "typically part of the exports" and use it instead of either of the others. But governments do not commonly construct such index numbers as yet.

The problem of selecting a suitable index number does not refute the argument that the purchasing power parity approach may provide a useful guide in setting rates. Nor does the fact that price levels are probably never precisely comparable in an absolute sense. Possibly a Latin American government, by applying Cassel's purchasing power parity theory, could make a fair estimate of the extent to which its currency should be devalued, even though the exchange rate did not accurately compare purchasing powers in an absolute sense either before or afterward. In other words, if the price levels in a country should double over a rather short period of time, the value of the currency might well be cut in half on the foreign-exchange market, irrespective of whether the foreign-exchange rate made exact allowance for international price-level differences either before or after.

But the purchasing power parity theory still leaves something to be desired as a theoretically complete explanation even of the forces influencing change, and consequently it falls short as a general theory of exchange-rate determination.

As a general propositon, if there is a significant change in the institutional organization of a society so that things are done differently than before, that alone would be enough to explain the possibility of changes of varying degrees in the price levels in different countries. In a setting where there are costs of transfer, trade barriers, and other institutional barriers to the costless transfer of goods through space, the circumstances permit substantial differences in price levels between different countries. In fact, it would only be in two societies whose institutional organizations were exactly similar and between which there were no transfer costs that one would expect the price levels to correspond exactly and involve the same commodity composition; and it would require parallel change in institutional organization to cause price levels to change to the same degree.

It is all very well thus to refute the purchasing power parity theory as a general theory of exchange-rate determination. But let us turn now to a more satisfactory theoretical formulation and a less satisfactory practical theory.

Demand and Supply

One objection to the purchasing power parity theory is that the theory simply does not take enough into account. The theory assumes that the only factors that influence individuals in buying and selling currencies are the market forces affecting the buying and selling of goods. But there are other reasons for going onto the foreign exchanges to buy and sell currencies; the demand and supply theory attempts to take these into account. One such factor, which may be important in influencing people to buy and sell currencies on the foreign exchanges, is "flight of capital," perhaps motivated by the desire of a German Jew to escape his country during the 1930's. Or an individual may go onto the foreign-exchange market to take advantage of a difference in interest rates abroad. Or he may want to speculate on the possibility of currency devaluation. Or he may not know exactly what he is doing but be an "inside-dopester" who thinks the foreign-exchange market is a good place to operate.[3]

The demand and supply theory states that all the factors which influence the demand for foreign currency and all the factors which influence the supply of the home currency on the foreign-exchange market should be taken into account.[4] Thence, the procedure is, as in ordinary price analysis, to use a supply curve for the one currency and a demand curve to show how much of the first currency will be bought with the second at various possible prices. And the exchange rate is the figure that will equate the demand for and the supply of these currencies. To be theoretically acceptable the demand and supply theory must take into account all the factors that lie behind these demands for and supplies of currencies. Both Ohlin and Haberler emphasize the need for such inquiry. If it does not delve into these fundamental issues, the demand and supply theory is little more than a truism which skims the surface. The background demand and supply factors involved are the factors discussed in Chapter 6 in connection with Ohlin's mutual interdependence theory.

It may be that a demand and supply theory has or could have a real usefulness as a theory in explaining how rates are set, if the foreign-exchange markets were free of control.

It may also be true that the operations of demand and supply in a free market do not necessarily lead to an equilibrium exchange rate. This might happen because the foreign-exchange market is a center of speculation rather similar to the stock exchanges. And when there are many "inside-dopesters" added to the other interested parties operating in the market, and a psychological situation arises in which a lot of the parties

---

[3] The term "inside-dopester" is borrowed from David Riesman, Nathan Glazer, and Reuel Denny, *The Lonely Crowd* (Abridged; New York: Doubleday Anchor, 1955), pp. 210–17.

[4] Ohlin, *Interregional and International Trade;* Haberler, *Theory of International Trade with its Application to Commercial Policy.*

trading on the exchange think that the exchange rate is going to go down still farther, when it has already gone down to some extent, there may develop a perverse relationship resulting in unmotivated, continuing devaluation. The fact that the rate goes down a little may convince enough people that it is going down yet farther to insure that it does. Consequently, out of the interaction of these forces there may be a tendency away from equilibrium instead of a tendency toward equilibrium.

This phenomenon is hardly susceptible of analysis with demand and supply curves, or rather the curves may not remain stable long enough to effect an equilibrium. In the early part of the 1930's the trouble seems to have been just about this. When a country devalued its currency slightly, people concluded that it was a weak currency (and a weak government) and that the value of the currency would go down farther; and before they got through selling it short, it would go down again. Since this sequence of events occurred repeatedly during the 1930's, it was easy for governments to convince themselves that they should not entrust their currencies to a free foreign-exchange market and allow supply and demand to regulate the rates.

But the 1930's were unusual times; and it is doubtful if the workability of freely fluctuating rates can actually be appraised by reference to the developments of that era—when the devaluations that did occur were only partially a result of speculation and much more a result of major domestic money supply expansion and connived devaluations, intended, by the governments which connived them, to increase exports.

If enough factors are taken into account and if it is understood that equilibrium is not a necessary result of the process, if free competition is not assumed and if enough frictions and institutional barriers are taken into account, demand and supply does become the most correct, theoretically, of the various explanations as to what is going on. But this conception of demand and supply analysis is different and broader than is usually implied by the term.

In this new and more general setting, however, there are some intriguing possibilities. Freely fluctuating rates never really had a chance in the chaotic conditions of the early 1930's. Of course the possibility exists that they will fluctuate in a perverse direction—down and down—if given the chance. But the possibility also exists that any given money supply internally—however small—may be turned over so rapidly as to create a runaway inflation. But we do not let that possibility keep us from desiring fairly free internal markets.[5]

[5] In more ordered times, if governments are reasonably judicious about the amount of money they allow to come into existence, and if everyone—including all the "inside-dopesters"—knows that the rates are going to be allowed to fluctuate freely and that there is no chance of making money at the expense of some government agency by anticipating one of the devaluations "by fits and starts" that have characterized our times, then freely fluctuating rates set by demand and supply in

Comparison

But if one looks at the problem, not in terms of the most workable institutional setting for the foreign-exchange market but rather in search of a formula that will tell what foreign-exchange rate is likely to be most workable, it is necessary to revert to the purchasing power parity approach. Obviously, as a practical matter, not all of the factors affecting demand and supply can be evaluated quantitatively and added together to serve as a guide in setting exchange rates. The purchasing power parity concept then emerges, not as a theory of the foreign exchanges, but as the most useful available guide in decision making when the practical problem of setting a foreign-exchange rate arises under circumstances where people are convinced that they have to *set* a rate.

It is interesting to note that Professor Haberler, who made a searching theoretical criticism of the purchasing power parity theory in 1936, was saying in 1952:[6]

> . . . in most cases where there occurred a deterioration in the balance of payments, it can be easily traced to inflationary excesses. In this connection, I should like to mention that I have been impressed by the fact that the old-fashioned purchasing power parity works so well. . . . Almost without exception, in countries whose balance-of-payments situation has deteriorated in 1951, prices and wages have risen sharply (since 1950) as compared with the United States, whilst no such pronounced rise occurred in those whose balance of payments improved or remained stationary.

Major disequilibrium in the foreign-exchange markets occurs in troubled times. Substantial internal money and credit expansion, if it causes prices to rise excessively, is likely to be the main source of trouble. This may mean that the purchasing power parity concept is the most workable approach if it is desired to set rates. But it may also mean that it is better not to try to set them by fiat.

PLANNED AND SPORADIC CURRENCY DEVALUATION

In the years that followed the British devaluation of 1931, most countries did not choose to allow the working of demand and supply to

---

the broad sense may well represent a more satisfactory situation than gold standard specie-flows or government controls—albeit a less satisfactory situation than a uniform international currency. This question is discussed further in Chapter 23.

[6] Gottfried Haberler, *Theory of International Trade with its Application to Commercial Policy*, pp. 30–40; and "Reflections of the Future of the Bretton Woods System," *American Economic Review, Papers and Proceedings*, XLIII (May, 1953), p. 83. Reprinted with the permission of the *American Economic Review*.

determine the new exchange rate, nor did they make any very scientific use of purchasing power parities, nor did they elect to re-establish the gold standard at new pars. Instead, two major new systems of controls were set up involving the use of (1) stabilization funds and (2) exchange controls. Then within the setting established by these controls, currency devaluations, sometimes planned but always sporadic, took place. Currency devaluation may occur as a result of the force of circumstance (e.g., going off the gold standard because of lack of gold); it may also occur as the result of a governmental policy decision to the effect that it is desirable for some reason or other to devalue, probably in order to try to increase exports. When a country decides to use fluctuating foreign-exchange rates as a matter of policy, it is almost always currency devaluation rather than currency appreciation which is involved. This is a one-way street running downhill. Rare exceptions were the British appreciation of 1925 and the Russian appreciation of the late 1940's.

Mechanics

A loose general statement that is frequently made is that the devaluation of a currency increases exports. But is this true—and would it be a good thing if it were true?

If we take the United States devaluation of 1933–34 as an example, the line of argument runs somewhat as follows: The United States cut the gold content of the dollar to 59 per cent of what it had been. This had the effect of changing the value of the dollar on the foreign-exchange markets by a corresponding amount to 59 per cent of its former value. This change occurred immediately. And the franc-dollar rate, for example, promptly changed from 3.9¢ to the franc to 6.6¢ to the franc. Frenchmen could obtain the same number of dollars after devaluation with only 59 per cent as many francs; or with the same number of francs they could obtain 69 per cent more dollars.[7] But the price level in the United States did not rise immediately to correspond with the abrupt decline in the international value of the dollar. In fact, it took roughly eight years—and World War II had begun—before United States prices rose by an amount which corresponded with the devaluation.

The argument for currency devaluation as a stimulus to exports is, at best, only valid for the period before the internal price level has changed sufficiently to counterbalance the devaluation (foreign prices remaining the same); after that, there is no stimulation to exports to be expected from the devaluation. This period may be quite long, as it was for the United States following the 1933 devaluation; but a devaluing country

[7] Sixty-nine per cent involves computation of the rate of increase in a devalued figure that will bring the devalued figure back to the original figure. The devaluation amounted to 41 per cent of the original value of the currency. But to bring the new value, which is 59 per cent of the old, back to the old par, its value must be increased by 69 per cent (or 41/59).

cannot count on this. The period may be very brief—as it is especially likely to be for the underdeveloped countries which are experiencing rapid internal inflation.

At any rate, for the period before prices have risen significantly internally, the argument runs that the Frenchman will be stimulated to make more purchases in the United States, where his francs will go farther than they would before devaluation. Since Americans will have to offer many more dollars for the same sum of francs, they will be discouraged from buying in France. If the value of the trade is measured in the currency of the country from which the goods are going—that is, dollars—the argument is valid enough. There is almost certain to be some increase in the amount of United States exports relative to imports (measured in dollars) as a result of devaluation. One may generalize that the amount of exports measured in the currency of the devaluing country, as well as the physical volume of exports, is almost certain to be increased.[8] But is this necessarily good?

For purposes of the Keynesian multiplier type of analysis, discussed in Chapter 8, an increase in the dollar value of exports was significant in itself. It may represent additional income to the exporter, which may then have a multiplier effect in increasing national income as it diffuses through the economy. But by this operation the devaluing country gains nothing that it could not have gained better by additional domestic investment or that it could not have gained more surely by dumping the goods in the ocean.

On the other hand, the purpose of the devaluation may be to make increased purchases of foreign goods possible. But that will require a substantial increase in the physical quantity of exports—because of the decline in the international value of the devaluing country's money. In the case of the United States devaluation of 1933, dollar sales by the United States needed to be increased by 69 per cent for the foreign purchasing power of the United States to be increased at all. That is to say, the expenditures of Frenchmen in dollars on United States exports must increase at least 69 per cent for the quantity of francs which United States exporters will receive to increase at all—other things being equal.

Table 25 represents an effort to analyze a group of the more significant recent currency devaluations to determine their effect. There are sixteen case studies. Entry (a) under each heading represents the percentage that exports (measured in the currency of the devaluing country) need to increase to give an increase in foreign-exchange receipts. Entry (b) indicates the percentage which exports actually increased the year after devaluation by comparison with the year before devaluation (or the year of devaluation, whichever will give the greatest increase).

For the United States devaluation of 1933, Table 25 indicates that United

---

[8] For qualification of this statement, see the discussion below of "elasticity."

States exports increased by only 32 per cent between 1932 and 1934. In fact, Table 25 suggests that it is the exception for exports to increase enough in consequence of devaluation to increase the foreign purchasing power of the devaluing country.

TABLE 25

CHANGE IN TRADE PATTERNS AS A RESULT OF DEVALUATION

		EXPORTS	TRADE BALANCE(C)	NET TERMS OF TRADE(D)
		(MILLIONS OF LOCAL CURRENCY)		(INDEX NUMBERS)
(1) United States devaluation of 1933 (a) 69% (b) 32% (1932 to 34)	1932 *1933* 1934 1935	1,625 *1,694* 2,149 2,302	283 184 391 −100	115 121 127 126
(2) British devaluation of 1931 (a) 43% (b) 8.5% decline (1931 to 32)	1930 *1931* 1932 1933	666 *461* 422 422	−386 −409 −287 −263	99 109 110 114
(3) British devaluation of 1949 (a) 44% (b) 37% (1948 to 50)	1948 *1949* 1950 1951	1,646 *1,851* 2,262 2,713	−432 −429 −352 −1,198	100 102 94 83
(4) Mexican devaluation of 1932 (a) 23% (b) 27% (1932 to 33)	1931 *1932* 1933 1934	334 256 324 529	127 77 86 192	
(5) Mexican devaluation of 1938 (a) 39% (b) 9.5% (1938 to 39)	1937 *1938* 1939 1940	790 710 777 760	177 216 150 91	
(6) Mexican devaluation of 1948 (a) 76% (b) 71% (1935 to 38)	1947 1948 1949 1950	1,989 2,595 3,389 4,027	−1,218 −355 −135 −375	
(7) French devaluation of 1936–37 (a) 94% (b) 97% (1935 to 38)	1935 1936 1937 1938 1939	15,575 15,514 24,010 30,806 31,763	−5,484 −9,947 −18,457 −15,476 −12,287	
(8) French devaluation of 1948 (a) 193% (b) 252% (1947 to 49)	1947 1948 1949 1950	223(bil.) 434 785 1,078	−174(bil.) −239 −143 4	107 100 91
(9) Argentine devaluation of 1930–31 (a) 56% (b) 7.7% decline (1930 to 32)	1930 *1931* 1932 1933	1,396 1,456 1,288 1,121	−284 282 452 224	89 ⎫ Base 67 ⎪ year: 65 ⎬ 1937 66 ⎭

TABLE 25 (*continued*)

		EXPORTS	TRADE BALANCE(c)	NET TERMS OF TRADE(d)
		(MILLIONS OF LOCAL CURRENCY)		(INDEX NUMBERS)
(10) Argentine devaluation	1932	1,286	452	65
of 1933–34	*1933*	1,121	224	66
(a) 78%	*1934*	1,438	328	68
(b) 22% (1932 to 35)	1935	1,569	394	72
	1936	1,656	539	93
(11) Argentine devaluation	1948	5,542	−648	
of 1949	*1949*	3,719	−923	
(a) 111% (curb rate)	1950	5,427	600	
(b) 46% (1949 to 50)	1951	6,711	−3,781	
(12) Brazil devaluation	1930	2,888	544	
of 1931	*1931*	3,358	1,477	
(a) 46%	1932	2,501	982	
(b) 13.5% decline	1933	2,780	615	
(1930 to 32)				
(13) Italy devaluation	1935	5,238	−2,554	
of 1936	*1936*	5,542	−497	
(a) 53%	1937	10,444	−3,499	
(b) 99% (1935 to 37)	1938	10,502	−771	
(14) Japan devaluation	1930	1,864	−133	
of 1931–32	*1931*	1,474	−205	
(a) 139%	1932	1,793	−131	
(b) 59% (1931 to 33)	1933	2,342	−110	
	1934	2,777	−174	
(15) Australia devaluation	1930	98.1	−20.8	
of 1931–32	*1931*	90.6	28.4	
(a) 43%	1932	97.1	46.1	
(b) 8.6% (1931 to 33)	1933	98.4	33.6	
	1934	114.4	46.6	
(16) Australia devaluation	1948	406.1	68.0	100
of 1949	*1949*	542.7	128.6	112
(a) 44%	1950	613.7	77.6	118
(b) 51% (1948 to 50)	1951	981.8	240.4	170

Notes: (a) The percentages represent the amount that exports need to increase to give the same amount of foreign exchange that accrued from exports before devaluation. (b) The percentage which exports actually increase the year after devaluation as compared with the year before devaluation (or the year of devaluation, whichever is lower). (c) Export balance, no sign: import balance, (−) sign. (d) The base years for the index numbers are 1948, unless otherwise indicated.

Sources: Data on the extent of devaluation is from *Banking and Monetary Statistics* or from *International Financial Statistics*. The trade data and index numbers are from the United Nations, Statistical Office, *Yearbook of International Trade Statistics, 1952.*

Elasticity

It has recently become customary to attempt to analyze the effect of currency devaluation on the balance of trade by taking into account foreign and domestic demand elasticities and foreign and domestic supply elasticities. What are the likely or possible situations so far as elasticity patterns are concerned?

The country that can be fairly sure that the demand for its product is elastic, and consequently that it is likely to expand exports by devaluation, is the little country that is producing something which many other countries are also producing. In addition, such a country is less likely to stir up the cycle of competitive devaluation that devaluation by a larger country such as the United States is almost certain to arouse.[9]

A country which is a monopolistic supplier (South Africa for diamonds), on the other hand, is not well advised to use currency devaluation at all. With due regard to the foreign-exchange rate—which can be anything—the problem of the producer in the exporting country in this case is the monopoly price problem. And he may well hope that the government does not keep changing the foreign-exchange rate, thus confusing his calculations.

On the supply side an inelastic condition would mean that production volume shows a lack of responsiveness to price changes. Coffee is a good example. It takes perhaps five or six years for additional coffee trees to come into production. If the weather and other circumstances have reduced Brazilian ability to produce coffee, and if the price happens to rise, it will be a long time before the prevailing high prices can substantially increase the supply. Under such conditions currency devaluation intended to increase foreign-exchange reserves would be a silly maneuver for Brazil. It would amount to reducing prices to foreigners, selling about the same physical quantity of coffee as before, and realizing far less foreign-exchange receipts.

If a country imports a large number of commodities which cannot be produced at home, the elasticity of demand for imports tends to be low. The demand for imports tends to hold up in spite of devaluation. In such a case, devaluation is relatively less likely to improve the balance.

In slump conditions, such as prevail when the game of beggar-my-neighbour is most in vogue, the elasticity of supply of commodities is likely to be high. Or better put, there is much unused capacity in manufacturing, and there may well be large agricultural surpluses, in all ex-

---

[9] Guy H. Orcutt has argued that devaluation is also likely to be effective for a large country or bloc. Guy H. Orcutt, "Exchange Rate Adjustment and Relative Size of the Depreciating Bloc," *Review of Economics and Statistics,* XXXVII (February, 1955), pp. 1–11. The reader may be interested in studying Orcutt's views, which are essentially contrary to those expressed in the text.

porting countries. In such a case the elasticity of demand for the exports of any one country is likely to be high. At first thought, this suggests that devaluation will be effective in improving the balance. But under such circumstances, the competing exporting countries are certain to engage in competitive devaluation—and the end result of the whole operation is likely to be that all of the exporting countries have the same share of the market as before—they are merely all selling for less.

Demand for the exports of virtually all countries is probably elastic in the long run, especially if we assume that income tends to rise in the long run, since people tend to buy more and more as that happens. But it is not the long run that matters in currency devaluation situations. A country devalues in order to increase its exports or improve its balance substantially and with some speed. The implications of this situation are perhaps better analyzed with the study of certain institutional attitudes than with assumptions of mathematically determinable elasticities. In what way are foreign countries likely to retaliate? What will competing exporting countries do? What are the marketing arrangements and channels through which goods will have to move? In the short run, all this is most uncertain and much dependent on perverse and unpredictable human impulses.

Some of the possibilities can be tested by reference to the case studies of Table 25. Amazingly, in three of the sixteen cases of devaluation there was an absolute decline in the value of exports, measured in the currency of the exporting country. This is something worse than 100 per cent inelastic demand. If fact, it indicates how misleading can be analysis of a rigid, mathematical nature, which does not consider time, human nature, and the retaliatory give-and-take of international economic relations.

Even more amazingly, in only five of the sixteen cases did the value of the exports rise by enough to increase the supply of foreign exchange available to the devaluing country. The speed with which business men react to devaluation of their currency by raising their prices is probably part of the explanation of this, and it raises the question whether devaluation is even temporarily effective in encouraging exports.

The effect on the trade balance (computed in terms of the currency of the devaluing country) is better. In eleven of the sixteen cases the balance of trade improved following devaluation. In fact, this performance is amazingly "good" by comparison with the performance of exports alone. All of which indicates, perhaps, that the performance of imports is somewhat more predictable than the performance of exports. Imports can really be reduced by devaluation (and other trade restrictions). After all, a government has its thumb on them, whereas it may have a little more trouble coercing foreign importers and preventing foreign retaliation. But even in connection with the effect on the balance, it might be questioned whether improvement in eleven out of sixteen cases is a very good record.

The statistical studies which have been made in an effort to compute elasticities leave matters in a confused and unsatisfactory state. The elasticities frequently seem to be in the neighborhood of unity or even negative.[10]

Actually, one might guess that whether or not a country increases its foreign-exchange holdings as a result of devaluation depends on the attitude of people toward the fact of devaluation as much as on goods prices and the various elasticities. If devaluation causes people to lose confidence in their currency, in spite of high prices they will buy more abroad. But if—and this is rather unlikely—currency devaluation causes people to think that at last the devaluing country's currency is valued properly to encourage internal economic activity, funds would flow in (more foreign exchange would be available) as foreigners took advantage of that situation. The more favorable pricing of the country's exports might be a factor, but a minor one.

The Terms of Trade

There are several different theoretical arguments that might be used to explain the effect of currency devaluation on the terms of trade of the devaluing country. One might be termed the Haberler argument, another the Robinson argument, and a third the "immediate-effect" argument.

Haberler argues that currency devaluation will not automatically affect the terms of trade.[11] In a free-trade world in the long run, he might well be substantially correct. If the prices of individual commodities are all set on a world market and if the devaluing country is too small to influence the world price, the prices of all commodities in all countries must bear the same relationship to each other after devaluation as they did before. In such a situation, if the composition of the exports and imports of the devaluing country is the same after devaluation as before, its terms of trade must be unchanged.

Looking more closely at the process of adjustments than at the long-run results and considering that the composition of trade may change, Joan Robinson says that the unit (or net barter) terms of trade will turn

[10] C. P. Kindleberger, *The Dollar Shortage*, pp. 44–8; T. C. Chang, "International Comparison of Demand for Imports," *Review of Economic Studies*, XIII (1945–46), p. 67; J. H. Adler, "United States Import Demand during the Interwar Period," *American Economic Review*, XXXV (June, 1945), pp. 418–30; Guy Orcutt, "Measurement of Price Elasticities in International Trade," *Review of Economics and Statistics*, XXXII (May, 1950), pp. 117–32; J. J. Polak, *An International Economic System*, p. 160.

[11] Gottfried Haberler, *A Survey of International Trade Theory* (Princeton: International Finance Section, Princeton University, 1955), p. 42.

against the devaluing country if

$$\frac{\eta_h}{\epsilon_h} > \frac{\epsilon_f}{\eta_f}$$

where:

> η_h is the elasticity of home-country supply of exports;
> ϵ_h is the elasticity of home-country demand for imports;
> ϵ_f is the elasticity of foreign demand for home-country exports; and
> η_f is the elasticity of foreign supply of imports.[12]

Mrs. Robinson argues that rest-of-the-world demand for the exports of a country (ϵ_f) is less elastic than is the rest-of-the-world supply (η_f) of the goods the country imports. She says that this is true because specialization is more pronounced, so far as any one country is concerned, in production than in consumption. Chile, for example, concentrates on the production and export of copper and nitrates but imports a much greater variety of items. Consequently,

$$\frac{?}{?} ? \frac{1}{2}$$

is a likely situation so far as rest-of-the-world demand and supply are concerned in relation to the devaluing country. Mrs. Robinson also argues that the home elasticity of demand is not likely to exceed the home elasticity of supply by enough to compensate for the foreign pattern. This is true, she says, because imports are likely to involve a wide variety of goods that cannot be produced at home. Consequently the demand for imports by one nation is relatively low:

$$\frac{?}{.8} ? \frac{1}{2}$$

It is unlikely that home elasticity of supply will be enough lower than home elasticity of demand to make the relation between the two expressions anything other than one in which the left term is larger than the right term, as in the following example:

$$\frac{.7}{.8} > \frac{1}{2}$$

Consequently, Mrs. Robinson says that the terms of trade probably will turn against the devaluing country.

A third possibility, the "immediate-effect" argument, would run somewhat as follows: The commodities involved in trade are not homogeneous nor are they uniformly priced on a world market. Following devaluation the prices of a country's export items may not change immediately to allow for the devaluation and the influence of some nonexisting world

[12] Joan Robinson, "Beggar-My-Neighbour Remedies for Unemployment," in *Readings in the Theory of International Trade* (Philadelphia: Blakiston, 1949), pp. 399–400.

price. Combining these elements with the thought that the important effect of devaluation is in the very short run, one may well conclude that there is an immediate and automatic tendency for devaluation to worsen a country's terms of trade in the only sense that can be significant. Temporarily a country's exports keep more or less the same prices in domestic currency that they had before. Import prices measured in foreign currencies also remain the same. But the foreigner can get more of the devaluing country's currency for a given amount of his own than he could before. And the citizen of the devaluing country can get less of foreign currencies with a given amount of his own than he could before. In any meaningful definition of terms of trade, this has to mean a worsening situation so far as the devaluing country is concerned.

What has actually happened to terms of trade following devaluation? The statistical data seem to be inadequate to give an entirely satisfactory answer. Table 25 gives net or unit terms of trade data for only seven cases. However, the terms improved in four of these cases and worsened in three. It makes one wonder if there is anything as perverse as trade data in failing to do what they are supposed to do.

How should countries that are considering the possibility of devaluation be influenced by such knowledge as we have with regard to what will probably happen to their terms of trade? In the effort to answer this question it should be remembered that (1) devaluation may occur in a setting of goods glut where the devaluing country is trying to increase its exports (the United States in 1933) and (2) it may occur in a setting of goods scarcity where the devaluing country is trying to build up its foreign-exchange reserves (Britain in 1949).

Most countries in the 1930's were showing a singular disregard for terms of trade in their desperate attempt to get an export increase. At that time the basic difficulties involved unemployed resources, surpluses, and a distribution system that was failing to get available goods to consumers. Therefore, whatever happened to the terms of trade was apparently not considered to be particularly important. But the situation was different after World War II. Goods were scarce, especially by comparison with what the population in western Europe was used to.

It is most doubtful that a postwar shortage of goods calls for currency devaluation to stimulate exports, in the vague hope that reserves can be protected or a microscopic increase in imports can be obtained at a terrific sacrifice in goods. And if the devaluation is intended to replenish depleted foreign-exchange reserves, the planner has a heavy responsibility to be certain that it will accomplish that purpose. It is very questionable that the British situation called for devaluation in 1949. By comparison with 1939, British prices had not risen as much as American. The kind of difficulties the British were in called for controls until such time as there was reason to believe the free foreign-exchange market could work. Devaluation may have been appropriate, however, in such countries as France and Italy which, unlike Britain, had experienced major inflation.

The behavior of the terms of trade in Table 25 now takes on more meaning. In important cases where it did not matter whether the terms of trade improved or not (the United States in 1933 or Britain in 1931), they improved. In important cases where improving terms were highly desirable (Britain in 1949 and France in 1948), they worsened. This seems to be rather alarming evidence of the unreliability of currency devaluation as a policy tool.

Intentional and Forced Devaluations

But denouncing currency devaluation does not prove that it cannot or should not occur. One might be tempted to say that, if a country loses all its gold and foreign-exchange reserves, devaluation is inevitable. This line of thinking may be analyzed from two points of view. (1) Is it certain that devaluation will increase foreign-exchange reserves? (The possibility that it will not has been discussed above.) And (2) how were the conditions which led to the loss of reserves brought about? Substantial domestic price rises force either import restriction or currency devaluation. But what forces the price rises?

The Mexican devaluation of 1948–49 may be cited as an example of this process. The Mexican foreign-exchange rate remained substantially the same, at 4.86 pesos to the dollar, from 1938 to 1948. But during those years certain forces operated which necessitated change in the foreign-exchange rate—or some other adjustment—by 1948. During the years that preceded devaluation the supply of money and credit in circulation was increased tremendously and at a faster rate than in the United States—see Table 26. This development, although partly unintentional, was also part of a planned effort to stimulate development by increasing the supply of money and credit. National governments control, insofar as there is control, the supply of money and credit in their countries at their own best (or worst) discretion. The Mexican government chose to reason on the basis of a crude (but not necessarily inaccurate) sort of Keynesian analysis that new money and credit would stimulate the industrial development that was desired. And as a by-product of that policy there seems to have been a certain amount of industrialization and a tremendous amount of price inflation in recent years. Mexican prices were rising in relation to United States prices: the former almost tripled between 1938 and 1948; United States prices barely doubled in the same period. The peso would buy less and less in Mexico, but its purchasing power, if converted into dollars at 4.86 pesos to the dollar, was holding up better. There was a consequent increase in Mexican imports relative to exports during those years, and this development was especially marked as the wartime restrictions were lifted following 1945. With imports rising

TABLE 26

MEXICAN GOLD STOCK, FOREIGN EXCHANGE RESERVES,
MONEY SUPPLY, AND PRICE LEVELS

	1939	1948	PER CENT RISE
MEXICO:			
Gold Stock (million U.S. dollars)	27	42	56
Gold and Foreign Exchange Reserves of Bank of Mexico (million U.S. dollars)	28	78	178
Money Supply (currency in circulation plus deposit money in million pesos)	887	4,035	356
Wholesale Price Index, Mexico City (1948 equals 100)	38	100	168
UNITED STATES:			
Money Supply (currency in circulation plus deposit money in billion dollars)	36.2	111.6	121
Wholesale Price Index (1948 equals 100)	48	100	108

Sources: *Statistical Yearbook; International Financial Statistics; Banking and Monetary Statistics; Historical Statistics; Statistical Yearbook of the League of Nations.*

relative to exports, Mexico naturally was using up her reserves of gold and foreign exchange between 1945 and 1948. To what extent is it justified to call a government-made phenomenon such as this a "fundamental disequilibrium"? There was no mysterious development of unknown cause to occasion the loss of gold and exchange. It was a result of actions that it was within the power of the Mexican government to take or not to take.

But this is not the whole story. At the time when Mexico devalued, it is all too true that some change was inevitable. The Bank of Mexico scarcely could supply dollars to those who wanted to buy them at one peso to 21¢ (U.S.). For that matter, who is to say with certainty that the industrialization of Mexico is not more important than the maintenance of the exchange rate or that the expansion of money and credit did not make a sufficiently valuable contribution to that end to justify itself? [13]

[13] On the other hand, the financing of development in Mexico by these very inflationary means has been a major factor in contributing to a very undesirable result. A large proportion of the gain has gone to increased profits and much, if not all, of the improvement in living standards in Mexico has gone to a very few. If this were a necessary price for a moderate rise in the living standards of all, it would be worth the cost. But is it necessary? Could not more intelligent planning eliminate the price inflation and the warped distribution of income as well—accomplish the same industrial expansion with less money and credit expansion? According to the Combined Mexican Working Party, *Economic Development of Mexico* (Baltimore: Johns Hopkins Press, 1953), p. 147: "In the past, imports were curtailed by drastic measures such as import embargoes and devaluation of the monetary unit which sometimes created much economic disturbance. Mexico's economic development has now reached a stage where the same ends could be

The analysis offered by Celso Furtado implies an even more devastating condemnation of currency devaluation as sporadically practiced in Latin America.[14] He interprets currency devaluation by underdeveloped countries as a method of socializing losses that would otherwise be carried by the wealthy, upper-class exporter group. The argument is that, whatever else devaluation may do, it increases the monetary income of the exporters in the domestic currency relative to the income of the rest of the population.

Business cycle fluctuations may affect different countries in different ways. If the prices of the raw commodity exports of an underdeveloped country should fall drastically in a depression relative to the prices of imports, its foreign exchange accruals would fall. If it chose not to contract its internal money and credit supply (and this seems to be the usual situation), its foreign purchases would tend to hold up; and it would soon give out of gold and foreign-exchange reserves. Rising internal prices which result from strictly internal credit-expansion policies may make a given foreign-exchange rate untenable. Domestic citizens, in possession of greatly increased blocs of purchasing power as the result of the credit expansion, and finding internal prices high, will find it increasingly attractive to buy abroad, while the exchange rate remains the same. This process will eventually use up the foreign-exchange reserves (especially since foreigners are at the same time finding this country a less and less attractive place in which to buy). Then something has to change. The purchasing power parity theory would indicate that the rate in question is no longer appropriate. But one might equally well question whether it was not rather the original internal credit expansion which was inappropriate or poorly handled. (Some of the implications of development financing by underdeveloped countries by means of skyrocketing credit expansion are discussed in Part VII.)

The *Economic Survey of Latin America, 1953*[15] cites Argentina, Brazil, Bolivia, Chile, Colombia, Mexico, Paraguay, and Peru as countries which have had a considerable amount of domestic monetary inflation in recent years. Among the Latin American countries, those with more stable price levels have been Costa Rica, Cuba, the Dominican Republic, Ecuador, El Salvador, Guatemala, Honduras, Nicaragua, Uruguay, and Venezuela. The countries in the first group have, almost without exception, had difficulties with foreign-exchange reserves and have utilized either ex-

---

achieved by methods which would cause a minimum of disturbance. By means of a progressive tax on incomes which, without impairing incentive, *siphoned off excess purchasing power from the income groups which exert the greatest demand for imports,* imports of consumer goods could be restricted while, at the same time, the Government would obtain funds for investments."

[14] Celso Furtado, *A Economia Brasileira* (Rio de Janeiro: Editora a Noite, 1954), p. 103.

[15] P. 69.

change restrictions of a rigorous sort or currency devaluation or both. The countries with more stable price levels have, with few exceptions, been able to maintain their foreign-exchange rates with little difficulty in a setting of relative freedom in foreign-exchange operations.

Before leaving the Mexican case study, a further point should be made. The Mexican example provides excellent evidence of a situation in which money supply and consequent price changes affect gold and foreign-exchange reserves—rather than the other way around as was the assumption in connection with the gold standard—specie-flow explanation. In Mexico the contraction of reserves after 1945 did not cause a contraction of the money supply. Rather it was the expansion of the money supply (relative to what was going on in the United States) that was causing the loss of reserves. It turns out to make considerable difference whether the hen or the egg came first.

The Mexican example is not intended to indicate the only possible line of development from credit expansion to devaluation. Credit expansion accompanied by sufficient expansion of goods production might not raise prices, cause a loss of reserves, or lead to devaluation. Nevertheless it does suggest that there is a relationship among volume of credit, prices, exports and imports, foreign-exchange reserves, and devaluation that has to be watched. Certain internal credit policies *may* lead to developments which must occasion adjustment of some sort. Whether devaluation is the proper cure is another matter.

In conclusion, with regard to the usefulness of sporadic currency devaluation, it is tempting to say that currency devaluation, instead of being a panacea for all ills, is rather a cure for none. There are, in fact, economists who believe that, if raising the level of living is the goal, currency appreciation would be better than currency depreciation—a proposition which might well be true if intentional policy measures in this area could do any good at all.[16]

Dollar Shortage

The possibility of "chronic shortage of a currency" over many years—shortage which continues irrespective of the exchange rate and independently of money-supply changes—has been raised in recent years.[17] Those who say that there is a permanent dollar shortage are likely to attribute the present shortage to factors of longer duration than (1) the postwar lack of goods and capital equipment in Europe which gave Europeans a desire for more United States goods, and (2) the unrealistic exchange rates which (when related to the price levels in Europe and America) made American goods extremely attractive to Europeans.

[16] Warren L. Smith, "Effects of Exchange Rate Adjustments on the Standard of Living," *American Economic Review*, XLIV (December, 1954), 808–25.

[17] C. P. Kindleberger, *The Dollar Shortage* (New York: John Wiley, 1950).

If there is a permanent dollar shortage which will crop up regardless of the exchange rate, how could that be possible? [18] It seems to this writer that if there is any such phenomenon as the dollar shortage, it is a consequence of the present institutional setting—as such it could be fairly long-lived, but would not necessarily be permanent. The heart of the cause would be (1) an institutionalized tendency to inflation in other countries relative to the United States combined with (2) the implications of the difference in level of living in the United States in relation to the rest of the world.

(1) The tendency to inflation would operate through purchasing power parity forces.

(2) The implications of the difference in level of living need to be examined further.

It is rather well known from the statistical research on national income which has been done of late years that the lowest segment of the population, in terms of money income, year after year spends more than its money income. This is possible because institutional arrangements are permissive—that is, because of continuing pressure on plantation owners, shopkeepers, landlords, and loan sharks for credit, credit which is doled out to underpaid individuals in rather substantial total amounts, and in connection with which there is either ultimate default or permanent debt. It is this growing debt, which is being continually defaulted, that makes possible continual buying beyond income by those at the bottom of the income scale.

One should not conclude from this that the storekeepers, loan sharks, and plantation owners are being exploited by the poor. They would

[18] A variety of explanations in addition to those discussed in the text have been mentioned at various times. Kindleberger in his book *The Dollar Shortage* has been especially suggestive.

Some of the reasons, which really are more suggestive of the possibility of exchange disequilibrium in general or of export promotion rather than of dollar shortage proper, include (1) the technical superiority of the United States, (2) the tendency of most countries to push their own exports artificially, (3) the desire to use idle capacity, and (4) increasing inelasticity of supply and demand generally.

One or two fairly plausible reasons have been advanced by others but have been rejected or found unproven by Kindleberger: (1) the idea that the United States has an inherent tendency to underimport, (2) the idea that the United States has a chronic tendency to stagnate relative to the rest of the world.

The argument that the United States has a chronic tendency to underinvest abroad is hardly one that the Marxists or Hobson would accept. The argument that a country in the stage of rapid growth is likely to have an export balance is rendered suspect by the case history of England in the nineteenth century.

Kindleberger also suggests the possibility that the United States may tend to reduce incomes excessively in the face of a balance of payments deficit and to fail to expand incomes sufficiently in the face of a balance of payments surplus; and he says that if "the rest of the world were to operate in a contrary fashion," then the United States would tend to have an export balance and the rest of the world an import balance (p. 100). Kindleberger does not indicate that he is convinced this is the case.

consciously or unconsciously (probably the latter) rather pay low salaries or charge high interest rates and then experience some defaults than pay higher salaries or charge lower interest to begin with. The system of debt peonage in underdeveloped countries, that functions to tie the agricultural laborer to the plantation, is well known. Something similar has been known in the American South. The storekeeper may be price gouging, the loan shark collecting exorbitant interest, and the *hacendado* binding the peons to him in a system of debt peonage that is much to his advantage. Nevertheless, the poor are ostensibly living beyond their meager income and the rich are ostensibly being generous or being victimized by a lot of unrepaid debt.

Internationally somewhat the same thing may happen. United States per capita productivity is increasing relative to the rest of the world. Ragnar Nurkse has suggested an explanation which, to be comprehensible, depends on the institutional setting. The argument runs somewhat as follows:[19] People in the underdeveloped areas of the globe have been tremendously enticed by what they know of the level of living in the United States and western Europe. The role of the movies has been not unimportant in this connection. As a result, when they are blessed with a slight increase in income, they are much more likely to buy a Buick car than were the Scotsmen who were the prime movers in the early days of the Industrial Revolution in England; after all, the Scotch Presbyterians did not have the example of a race of Buick-car-users anywhere in the world around them—at least not in 1800. This line of argument is needed to explain why Brazil, for example, spends a high proportion of an increase in income on luxury imports.

The rest of the world desires to share more fully in the fruits thereof—Nurkse's emulation or demonstration effect. There tends to be, as a continuing proposition, increasing desire for United States goods on the part of foreigners relative to the desire of United States citizens for foreign goods.[20] The country which is better and better off relative to the rest of the world feels occasional twinges of conscience (somewhat like some millionaires in their latter days). To the extent that the United States (government or private citizens) yields to this pressure, an excess of United States currency, and consequently of United States exports, is made available to foreigners.

Certain results may follow from the increasing intensity of foreign demand for United States goods and decreasing intensity of United States

[19] Ragnar Nurkse, *Problems in Capital Formation in Underdeveloped Countries* (Oxford: Blackwell, 1953), pp. 57–81.

[20] There is some statistical evidence to support the proposition that the income elasticity of demand for imports is relatively high in the agricultural and underdeveloped countries relative to the industrialized countries such as the United States. (J. J. Polak, *An International Economic System*, p. 160; Kindleberger, *op. cit.,* pp. 14–15).

demand for foreign goods—if there is any such phenomenon. At a given foreign-exchange rate, foreigners may buy more and more American goods relative to the amount of foreign goods Americans are buying. Dollar-exchange reserves are ultimately exhausted and the standard next step is devaluation of the foreign currency. This temporarily (perhaps) increases foreign exports to the United States and decreases United States shipments to foreigners. Then the foreigners' ever increasing desire for United States goods begins to be felt all over again and the process is repeated. This would seem to be a process that *could* explain repeated devaluation, even though it is a futile process in the sense that foreigners do not actually get more United States goods (relative to what they sell to the United States) out of it. Whether it is a process that is actually going on, someone other than this writer will have to judge.

Of course, to the extent that foreign desires and United States responses to those pressures are continuing, permanent United States foreign investment must be continually growing, or there may be periodic defaults and cancellations, or continuing gifts and grants, as a by-product of a permanent export balance.

A dollar shortage in the sense that millions of people would like more dollars, or more money of any sort, undoubtedly exists and has always existed, internally and internationally. But this is the type of shortage which in the past has given concern to idealistic reformers, not to economists. Everybody would like more money, whether it is foreign exchange or domestic currency. But, as the elementary economics texts say, it is demand—not desire—that counts.

United States willingness, institutionally determined (by the threat of Communism), to cater to these foreign needs and desires may create a phenomenon which might be called a dollar shortage but which could better be called something like "hush money." Institutionally determined unwillingness to cater to the poor under such conditions in the nineteenth century gave Britons the time to ride to hounds in red jackets to the accompaniment of the loud yapping of a lot of hounds and an unfavorable balance of trade. There was no pound shortage in the nineteenth century.

But to look at this matter a little differently, in the post-World War II discussion of the dollar shortage, some of the discussants have undoubtedly mistaken the chicken for the egg. Continuing willingness of the United States to provide dollars to foreigners, because of the desire to have an export balance of trade, would show many of the superficial attributes of a dollar shortage and yet might well be called a dollar surplus.

At all events, a disturbance of the magnitude of World War II caused such tremendous changes in the economic structure of the world that it could not be otherwise than true that time and experimentation would be required to work out a new milieu for stable growth; and along with all the other maladjustments there has been disequilibrium in the balance of payments. The existence of a great demand for dollars during the last ten years is certainly a result of World War II. Whether it is also the result of a chronic, long-run dollar shortage is uncertain.

Chapter 20

THE RELATIVE VALUES OF CURRENCIES: STABILIZATION FUNDS AND EXCHANGE CONTROL

After going off the gold standard in the early 1930's most countries, instead of permitting freely fluctuating rates, resorted either to stabilization funds or to exchange control.

The stabilization fund approach involves the existence of a free foreign-exchange market. But the government's stabilization fund, which possesses reserves of its own currency and of various foreign currencies, stands ready to buy or sell one currency for the other at the rate it is trying to maintain.

If stabilization funds are to operate successfully in maintaining certain rates between the currencies of their respective countries, the countries need to be in agreement as to what those rates are.

A stabilization fund is limited in its ability to support a certain rate by the adequacy of its reserves of foreign currencies. There need be no limit to its resources in its own currency.

Exchange control involves government establishment of the exchange rate by fiat.

The exchange control agency may require exporters to sell at a set rate to the agency the foreign currencies they receive in payment for their exports.

The agency may sell to importers at a set price the foreign currencies which they need in order to pay for their imports.

If the enforcement is effective, the government may impose any rate it chooses; but there may be much or little trade at that rate.

The government may complicate matters further by enforcing different foreign-exchange rates depending on the type of transaction; such an arrangement is called "multiple exchange rates."

The effect of multiple exchange rates is virtually the same as the effect of a tariff rate structure involving the same pattern of differences.

WHATEVER the merits of freely fluctuating exchange rates guided by purchasing power parities or demand and supply, governments decided in the early 1930's that they wanted no part of them. Therefore, after going off the gold standard, they did not in most cases change over to freely fluctuating rates but rather to a scheme of things involving various types of government controls (and sporadic government-planned or permitted devaluations). The two chief types of measures were (1) stabilization funds and (2) direct government controls (foreign-exchange controls).

STABILIZATION FUNDS

The first such fund, called the Exchange Equalisation Account, was set up by the British following their abandonment of the gold standard in 1931. The United States set up its Stabilization Fund, also after going off the gold standard, in 1933.

A stabilization fund works like this: The government turns over to the fund a large sum of money—in the case of the United States in 1933 it was $2,000,000,000 in gold, valued at $35 a fine ounce. Some of the fund's resources will be held in the national currency, some in various foreign currencies. The fund is then in a position to enter the foreign-exchange market to buy and sell the various currencies with or for its own currency in order to maintain the rate on which the government has decided. The government is then merely an additional demand and supply factor in an otherwise free foreign-exchange market, albeit a large factor possessing considerable power to influence the market.

The funds are used somewhat as follows: If the value of the national currency is falling relative to the values of foreign currencies, the fund may go onto the foreign-exchange market and buy its own currency with the foreign currencies it possesses and thus bid the price back up to the desired level. The fund could also sell its national currency for additional supplies of foreign currencies, thus increasing the supply of its currency on the market and bringing down its price.

For an arrangement of this sort to last any length of time it cannot be unilateral. The various governments involved have to be in agreement as to what the exchange rate should be. If the British fund were trying to maintain a different pound-dollar rate from that which the United States fund was trying to maintain, one of the funds would soon lose its reserves of the other's currencies. A kind of Gresham's law would operate. For example, if the British were maintaining a $4 equals £1 rate and the United States was maintaining a $5 equals £1 rate, an enterprising foreign-exchange dealer could arbitrage the situation to death, selling pounds for dollars in the United States and dollars for pounds in Britain. It would be an untenable situation for stabilization funds to operate on free markets without an agreement, overt or tacit, as to rates. There seems to have been a sort of tacit understanding between 1934 and 1936 vis-à-vis British relations with the American Stabilization Fund. And in 1936 the formal Tripartite Agreement was concluded among the Americans, British, and French to control the actions and interactions of their respective funds. In fact, also in the later 1930's, several smaller countries adhered to this so-called three-way agreement—Belgium, the Netherlands, and Switzerland.

A group of countries that has come to be called the sterling bloc devalued at the same time the British did in 1931. These countries tend to keep their foreign-exchange reserves in London and to depend on the British to protect their foreign-exchange rates. The composition of the group has varied. Argentina, the Scandinavian countries, Portugal, Iraq, and Thailand once were members but are no longer. Chiefly the members are the British Commonwealth countries, except for Canada.

Other countries (the term *dollar bloc* might be used) have maintained a similar relation to the United States. Dollars have constituted much of their reserves. And the United States Treasury has occasionally advanced them dollars to help defend the value of their currencies. Countries in this group would include many of those in the Central American and Caribbean area. And the United States Treasury has made several advances of the type mentioned to aid Mexico.

How does the adjustment process work when stabilization funds are used? The process is very similar to that at work under the gold standard. A stabilization fund can maintain a rate if the disequilibrating forces are of relatively minor importance so that the fund's resources are large enough to bring the value back into line, but if one of the two governments involved is engaged in a permanent program of inflating money, credit, and prices, and the other government is not, there will come a time when even the biggest stabilization fund will not have the resources necessary to maintain the par. To cite one example (see Table 26), Mexico in the 1940's was continuing to engage in inflation to a greater extent than the United States. Mexico tended to increase its imports from the United States more and more at the prevailing exchange rate because of price considerations, and Mexico became a less attractive place in which to buy because of the rising prices which were a by-product of the Mexican inflation. As the situation continued, the Mexican stabilization fund (the Bank of Mexico) tended to lose the United States dollars it had in its stabilization fund.

A government cannot engage in extensive monetary inflation and maintain indefinitely the par value of its currency using the stabilization fund method. For a stabilization fund to work satisfactorily in maintaining an exchange rate without exchange controls, the internal money-credit-price picture must be in reasonable harmony with similar structures in other countries. The situation is thus substantially the same as under the gold standard. Under the gold standard a government uses its gold reserves, as long as they last, to keep the foreign-exchange rate at the par it has decided to maintain. And if it loses all of its gold, it can no longer maintain the par. Stabilization funds are merely a slightly different device for maintaining fixed rates at least temporarily. They involve the use of the fund's foreign-exchange reserves for as long as they last (or as long as the government chooses to use them) to maintain the exchange rate at a certain figure. If a government runs out of reserves and can no longer maintain the rate at that figure on a free market, it must either turn to direct control or alter the exchange rate.

Of course, a government may like the idea of devaluing its currency every now and then; and the real role of the stabilization fund may merely be to keep the exchange rates stable for short periods of time between devaluations; and long before the danger point is reached in losing reserves, the government may use such loss of reserves as an excuse for devaluation.

In Chapter 16 it was alleged that, depending on the particular financing arrangements, exports or imports may have the result of expanding or contracting the money supply internally. These divergent possibilities are illustrated by the difference in British and United States procedure in handling the operation of their stabilization funds. The British Exchange Equalisation Account has sometimes been called a credit type of fund. Actually, the Account has rather typically operated in a manner designed to insulate the internal money supply from the effects of rising and falling international short-term balances. When an "inflow" of funds occurs—when the supply of short-term balances held by foreigners in London increases—the Account may sell Treasury bills to the public, thereby taking out of circulation a supply of money corresponding to the increased size of the London balances.

The procedure of the United States Stabilization Fund is different. Its procedure has led to its being called a gold type of fund. If gold flows into the United States, the importing agency (probably the Federal Reserve Bank of New York) turns the gold over to the United States Treasury, which gives the bank gold certificates in exchange. These gold certificates are then the legal basis (given the 25 per cent reserve requirement currently prevailing) for a fourfold increase in Federal Reserve Notes or Federal Reserve credit to commercial banks. Similarly in the United States, the export of gold might necessitate a considerably larger contraction in the domestic money supply—again given the prevailing 25 per cent reserve requirement.

One might almost say that, in respect to these operations, the United

States is even now ostensibly playing by the rules of the gold standard, but Britain is not.

DIRECT GOVERNMENT CONTROL
(EXCHANGE CONTROL) [1]

Instead of relying on foreign-exchange reserves, which may soon be exhausted, to support the value of its currency on a free foreign-exchange market, a government may merely say that the exchange rate will be such and such, and that anyone who deals at any other rate will go to jail— or be fined. This was the policy which was followed in Germany, Italy, and many other countries in the 1930's and which is still used in many places.

Adjustment Theory

Let us assume a certain type of situation: The foreign-exchange rate between the dollar and some country's peso is being maintained at 40¢ (U.S.) to the peso. To further oversimplify, assume for the moment that the peso-country has only one foreign-exchange rate and is engaged in a major amount of internal money and credit expansion which is significantly raising the internal price level. In this situation, at the 40¢ rate, the peso-country's imports will be greatly stimulated as a result of the preference of local citizens for buying abroad; and exports would be virtually non-existent. Americans would not want to pay 40¢ for pesos and then get virtually nothing for them when they use them to purchase goods in the peso-country. But since it is also possible for the government of the peso-country to maintain the 40¢ rate indefinitely by fiat, what happens? After its government has exhausted the supply of dollars available to it to sell to its citizens at the 40¢ rate (and since it is not renewing its supply of dollars because of the falling off of United States purchases of its exports), there comes a point when it no longer has the dollars to sell to its citizens to finance the imports; and the amount of imports falls to a low level (to match the low level of exports).[2] Thus it is possible to maintain an unrealistic rate, which does not correspond to the purchasing power parities (and the other criteria which contribute to an equilibrium rate); and it is possible to maintain it indefinitely; but it is not possible to effect a large volume of trade under such conditions. (This is also the

[1] Raymond F. Mikesell, *Foreign Exchange in the Postwar World* (New York: The Twentieth Century Fund, 1954).

[2] This illustrates again the basic proposition that, except for the ability to finance a discrepancy, the money value of exports must equal the money value of imports—whether there is free trade or government control.

position of the private monopolist, who can set price or volume but not both.) The impact of the adjustment, then, in the case of exchange control falls squarely on the quantity of goods traded.[3]

Control of the exchange rate has generally been implemented by government regulation of the conditions under which foreign exchange may be bought and sold. Table 27 summarizes the situation as of January 1, 1956, and indicates whether the trader had to go to his government to get an exchange permit to make an international payment. The coordinating of the issuance of exchange permits with the issuance of import licenses and the setting of import quotas has been worked out with varying degrees of efficacy in different countries.

There are many variations in the mechanics of these schemes. One such variation involves the provision that exporters have to turn over to a government agency—commercial banks may operate as the agents of the exchange-control authorities for purposes of conducting such transactions—the foreign exchange they receive from their exports. Their own government may recompense them in local currency then or later at whatever foreign-exchange rate it chooses. A variation on this theme is a "currency retention scheme" which permits the exporter to dispose of a certain percentage of his foreign exchange on a free market as he sees fit, while turning the rest of it over to his government at the rate set by the government.[4]

The counterpart of the exporter's turning his foreign exchange over to his government would be an importer's obtaining the foreign exchange he needs to pay foreign exporters by making payment in his national currency to his own government and securing title from his government to some of that foreign exchange which the government derived from its own exporter. Of course, if the foreign government is, in its turn, controlling the disposition of the aforementioned foreign exchange (handling it as a "blocked balance") the two governments may have to do a little arranging between them. This sort of situation provides the basis for the bilateral agreements which are discussed later.

[3] At this point it may be well to identify explicitly an implicit assumption that has been made in connection with this analysis. There is direct government control of certain facets of the trading process, true enough; but the decision on whether to trade is still in the hands of free private businessmen. This was a more-or-less valid assumption even for the Germany of the late 1930's, for Germany was a private enterprise economy, albeit a closely regulated one. However, to the extent that Germany was a "patriotic economy" full of patriotic businessmen, more interested in national power and glory than in monetary profits, German businessmen, perhaps, did not behave quite like American businessmen. (In any event it is not the case of state trading, or of government trading for its own account, which is being discussed here.)

[4] Germany, France, Holland, Denmark, Norway, Austria, and many other countries have such mixed arrangements in effect, or have had them in effect. See the *Economist* (London), September 27, 1952, p. 770; also see Table 29.

TABLE 27

*EXCHANGE CONTROL REGULATIONS IN PRINCIPAL FOREIGN
COUNTRIES APPLYING TO IMPORTS FROM THE UNITED
STATES (JANUARY 1, 1956)*

COUNTRY	IS EXCHANGE PERMIT REQUIRED?
Argentina	Yes, for goods contained in lists of imports granted official rate of exchange. No, for goods contained in free-market lists.
Australia	No; import license carries right to foreign exchange.
Brazil	No; exchange for most imports is sold at auction.
Bulgaria	Import license automatically assures foreign exchange.
Canada	No.
Chile	Yes; in form of notation on import license.
Colombia	Payment for imports requires exchange registration (registro), which is normally granted upon submission of the import registration and evidence (customs manifests) that the goods have entered the country.
Cuba	No.
France	No separate permit required; import license carries right to foreign exchange.
Germany, Federal Republic	Yes; import and payments license combined in one document.
Germany, Soviet-occupied Zone	Yes.
India	Yes; however, foreign exchange is automatically released upon presentation of validated import license to exchange bank.
Italy	No separate permit required.
Japan	Some commodities, announced by Japanese government from time to time, require allocation certificate; for others, import license carries right to foreign exchange.
Mexico	No.
Switzerland	No.
United Kingdom	Yes; granted automatically following issuance of import license.
U.S.S.R.	Yes; all exchange is allocated by U.S.S.R. State Bank upon receipt of import license.

Source: *Foreign Commerce Weekly*, February 13, 1956, pp. 8–13.

The Foreign Exchange Budget

A country, in order to administer a comprehensive system of exchange controls, may work out a rather complicated budget ahead of time. It must guess what foreign-exchange receipts it is going to derive from exports and other sources during the period ahead. Then it must plan the allocation of the foreign exchange available to it among importers and other claimants on the foreign-exchange reserves.

Table 28 is a statement of Chile's "ordinary" foreign-exchange budget for 1955. A comprehensive system of foreign-exchange controls can, indeed, be a very comprehensive thing.

TABLE 28
CHILE'S ORDINARY 1955 FOREIGN EXCHANGE BUDGET

RECEIPTS (million U.S. dollars)

Major export receipts	201.7
Exports under agreement with Argentina	57.2
Other exports	23.3
Total exports	282.2
Government receipts	5.0
Services and other private receipts	5.1
Total "ordinary" receipts	292.3

EXPENDITURES (million U.S. dollars)

Essential imports	114.8
Imports under agreement with Argentina	57.2
Other imports	23.3
Services and other private expenditures	6.3
Government payments	7.5
Defense expenditures	9.5
Capital repayment and servicing	53.7
Repayment of arrears (25% of total)	20.0
Total "ordinary" expenditures	292.3

Source: *International Financial News Survey,* April 22, 1955, p. 332.

Variations in Mechanics

(STERLING BLOC CASE STUDY): The Sterling Area includes most of the British Commonwealth countries, except Canada. It also includes Burma, Iraq, Jordan, Libya, and Ireland. In many respects the area centers its international financial relations in London. The International Monetary Fund summarizes certain features of the British exchange-control system as follows: [5]

> Exchange control is not imposed on transfers to other countries in the Sterling Area, but all payments to non-Sterling Area countries require exchange control approval, which, upon verification of the amount and provided the method of payment is in accordance with the general prescription of currency requirements, is granted automatically for licensed imports, contractual payments (except films), and many types of noncontractual payments. Some types of noncontractual payments are subject to monetary limitations and, in some instances, to discrimination according to the country of receipt. Export proceeds must be received in the manner prescribed in the regulations, and certain currencies must be sold to an authorized bank. . . .

[5] International Monetary Fund, *Sixth Annual Report: Exchange Restrictions,* (Washington, 1955), pp. 301–4.

The sterling accounts (other than Blocked Accounts . . .) of nonresidents, i.e., those resident outside the Sterling Area, are available for payments in the Sterling Area and for transfers to other nonresidents, according to the groups described below. Additional transferability is achieved by granting licenses to effect payments outside the prescribed arrangements.

1. *American Accounts* (Bolivia, Colombia, Costa Rica, Cuba, Dominican Republic, Ecuador, El Salvador, Guatemala, Haiti, Honduras, Liberia, Mexico, Nicaragua, Panama, Philippine Republic, United States and possessions, and Venezuela) and Canadian Accounts. These accounts may be debited freely for payments to any sterling account (other than a Turkish Account or a Blocked Account). Balances on American Accounts and Canadian Accounts may be converted freely into Canadian or U.S. dollars, or used to purchase gold through the London market.

2. *Transferable Accounts* (all other countries outside the Area except Turkey, payments with which are on a bilateral basis). Payments from Transferable Accounts may be made freely to any account related to the Transferable Account Area (other than a Blocked Account).

3. *Registered Accounts* (all countries outside the Sterling Area except Group 1). These accounts are intended primarily for entries related to the purchase and sale of gold in the London market. In addition, Registered Accounts are freely convertible into Canadian or U.S. dollars. They may be credited with the proceeds of the sale of Canadian or U.S. dollars to an authorized bank in the United Kingdom, and are available for transfers to any sterling account, including payments to residents in settlement of U.K. exports to any destination.

4. *Blocked Accounts* (all countries outside the Sterling Area; however, these arrangements do not apply to residents of Denmark (including Greenland), the Faroe Islands, Norway, and Sweden, who may transfer all their sterling assets to their respective countries). The purpose of these accounts is to receive funds which are not placed at the free disposal of nonresidents, e.g., capital proceeds. Such funds are available for transfers to other Blocked Accounts, except that transfers may not be made to Blocked Accounts of residents of American Account countries or Canada if the transferor is resident outside those countries. Funds held in Blocked Accounts are available for the purchase of certain securities payable in a currency of the Scheduled Territories and not redeemable within ten years from the date of acquisition. (The income on such securities can, however, be remitted to the country of the account holder.)

The British discriminate as among nations and as among types of transactions in determining whether payments may be transferred. But the Sterling area itself has few restrictions on payments as among the countries within the area.

(BRAZILIAN CASE STUDY): A recent problem in the operation of exchange controls involves Brazil and the United States. Brazil makes extensive use of exchange control, the United States does not. United States traders have made substantial exports to Brazil in recent years for which Brazilians have not had the dollar exchange to make payment. (Why might seem a mystery in view of the price of coffee.) But the difficulty can be explained by the fact that the internal price level has been rising far faster in Brazil than in the United States (it rose in Brazil from 27 in 1938 to 178 in January, 1953; in the United States, from 49 in 1937 to only 105 in January, 1953). Brazilian prices have risen six times over during a period of time when United States prices have about doubled. And the change in the exchange rate has not been enough to make up this difference. The curb rate was 20.15 cruzeiros to the dollar in 1938 and 38.30 to the dollar in January, 1953.[6]

Be that as it may, the Brazilian government, which is running a system of exchange control, simply did not have the dollar exchange to sell to Brazilian importers to pay off United States exporters in dollars in the United States for shipments which the United States exporters had, perhaps injudiciously, made. In terms of the foreign-exchange mechanics described in Chart 8, either of two things could have happened. The American exporter, instead of being paid off in dollars by an American bank, might have been the one who ended up with a cruzeiro account in Brazil, which the Brazilian control authorities would not or could not allow him to convert into dollars. Or conceivably the United States exporter might have been paid off by an injudicious United States bank, which then would be left with the cruzeiros in Brazil. Or conceivably Brazilian importers just owe United States exporters as a result of open-account transactions. At any rate injudicious Americans have cruzeiros in Brazil which the Brazilian exchange controls kept them from selling for dollars, in this case apparently because Brazil really did not have the dollars to meet the demand at the prevailing foreign-exchange rate.

The lot of these American traders and bankers had not been a happy one before 1953. They wanted to get their money out of Brazil. And they can thank the United States government for bailing them out in 1953 to the tune of $300,000,000 (U.S.), a tidy sum.[7] "Under the procedure adopted [in the agreement between the United States and Brazilian gov-

---

[6] Thus the purchasing power parity theory actually can explain why United States exporters are having trouble collecting on their shipments to Brazil—in spite of the high price of coffee.

[7] *Foreign Commerce Weekly*, July 13, 1953, p. 3.

ernments], drafts against which cruzeiro deposits were made are being liquidated first, to be followed by the liquidation of drafts without cruzeiro deposits and finally the backlog of payments covering shipments made on open account."

Certain general observations about the significance of direct government controls and blocked balances may be based on this Brazilian–United States experience. There has been much complaint, for example by United States exporters, about the difficulties and hardships they are forced to undergo as the result of the "improper" action of foreign governments in blocking their balances and refusing to allow them to bring home the receipts from their exports. Such was the case in the Brazilian example just cited—United States-owned balances were blocked in Brazil. The United States exporters, to hear their story, were being much mistreated by the Brazilian government which was not honoring all of its obligations at the going rate of exchange, but rather was forcing them to leave their hard-earned profits blocked south-of-the-border, where no one in his right mind would want to leave his money.

Somewhat more sophisticated commentators on this type of situation analyze it as a balance of payments difficulty (which it certainly is) with obtuse ramifications centering around the forces which increase and decrease the supply of foreign exchange available to the Brazilian or such other government as may find itself in a similar fix. The meaning of balance of payments disequilibrium is discussed elsewhere, but it cannot hurt to inject some common sense into the metaphysics at this point. The United States exporters to Brazil were selling to a "bankrupt" buyer. How much sympathy would a merchant get in this country, if he sold goods to someone who, he knew, was a poor credit risk, who was in fact already in default? And yet in the twenty years since Germany set the fashion of direct government controls, blocked balances, and aski marks, exporters have insisted on continuing to sell to countries which were not honoring their short-term obligations, and which obviously would not have the foreign exchange to do so in the ascertainable future.

Brazilians, of course, are going to want to buy in the United States, if that is the attractive source of goods, given the ostensible foreign-exchange rate in effect. And as Brazil uses up its dollar reserves, the Brazilian government is going to begin to think in terms of rationing dollars and using them to buy items, such as industrial equipment, which the government thinks important, rather than using them to pay off those United States traders who already have balances in Brazil. There are smarter ways for the government of the exporting country to deal with this problem than by paying off its own exporters and holding the sackful of blocked balances itself—this being, apparently, what the United States government did in 1953.

If the United States government were really and intelligently concerned about the situation, a reasonable thing for it to do would be to let the United States exporters and bankers "sweat it out." But since we are a nation which insists on "doing something" about difficult situations, we might inaugurate a counterbalancing set of exchange controls ourselves and require all importers of goods from Brazil to make payment to the United States government—which would then owe a certain sum of blocked dollars to the Brazilian exporters. The United States government could then pay off United States exporters with these dollars, which were received from the United States importers. The Brazilian government, in turn, could pay off its own exporters with the blocked cruzeiros that it had owed the United States exporters. Everybody is satisfied; and substantially the situation described in Chart 14—the payments agreement—has resulted.

But, you say, there is nothing new about a proposal like that; most governments, if not the United States, were retaliating more or less in that manner by the middle 1930's; and the next step for both governments would be the signing of a bilateral agreement—to keep each other informed about the balances on each side, perhaps assign an agency in one country or the other to clear the transactions, and regulate a little more effectively the identity of the goods being traded, so that whatever plans the governments might have at home could be more effectively implemented. Later in this chapter the working of bilateral agreements will be discussed further.

As has been repeatedly said, the money value of exports can diverge from the money value of imports only to the extent that financing can be arranged. Exporters, who sell to countries currently engaged in blocking short-term balances, are financing the excess of exports to those countries; as long as they are willing to do it, and only that long, the blocked balances will grow and the balance of payments disequilibrium persist. The blocked balances would not grow and what we call "balance of payments disequilibrium" would not develop in cases of this sort if the exporters and the bankers financing exports used ordinary business acumen with regard to the credit rating of the nation to which they make sales.

But the implication of carelessness or stupidity on the part of the exporters needs to be qualified. Such an implication may be very misleading as to what is actually going on. The exporters in most cases are well aware of the risks they are running. And the importers in the countries that are blocking balances may pay heavily in the form of discriminatory prices; consequently, if the exporter in some way can get his money out of the blocking country, he really has a good thing. But if he runs into difficulties, what could be more natural than that he should turn to his

CHART 14

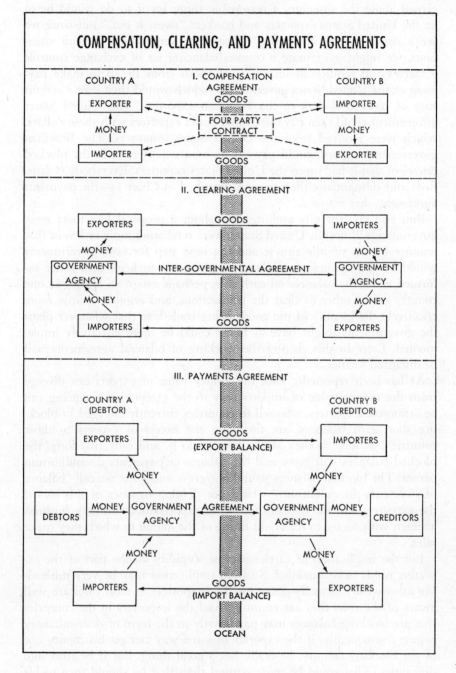

COMPENSATION, CLEARING, AND PAYMENTS AGREEMENTS

I. COMPENSATION AGREEMENT

COUNTRY A   COUNTRY B

EXPORTER   →→→ GOODS →→→   IMPORTER

MONEY   FOUR PARTY   MONEY
                     CONTRACT

IMPORTER   ←←← GOODS ←←←   EXPORTER

II. CLEARING AGREEMENT

EXPORTERS   → GOODS →   IMPORTERS

MONEY   MONEY

GOVERNMENT   ← INTER-GOVERNMENTAL AGREEMENT →   GOVERNMENT
AGENCY   AGENCY

MONEY   MONEY

IMPORTERS   ← GOODS ←   EXPORTERS

III. PAYMENTS AGREEMENT

COUNTRY A   COUNTRY B
(DEBTOR)   (CREDITOR)

EXPORTERS   → GOODS →   IMPORTERS
                 (EXPORT BALANCE)

MONEY   MONEY

DEBTORS   → MONEY →   GOVERNMENT   ← AGREEMENT →   GOVERNMENT   → MONEY →   CREDITORS
                     AGENCY   AGENCY

MONEY   MONEY

IMPORTERS   ← GOODS ←   EXPORTERS
                 (IMPORT BALANCE)

OCEAN

government, howl about the discrimination to which he is subjected abroad, and get the United States taxpayers to bail him out and recover his profits to the tune of $300,000,000? It is a good trick if you can do it.

Multiple Rates

(ARGENTINE CASE STUDY): To further complicate the situation, a government which has experimented with setting a foreign-exchange rate by fiat is likely to say to itself: "If I can set one rate by decree, why can't I set several and have a different rate apply depending on how much I approve of the transaction that a particular trader has in mind?"[8] Countries as far apart as Germany and Argentina have set up complicated multiple exchange-rate systems.

Such a system might work as follows: A more favorable exchange rate may be given to an importer bringing in something that the government favors than would be given to the importer of a non-favored item —with the same impact that a comparable tariff-rate discrimination would have. The same policy would apply to exporters. For example, if the government wished to encourage the export of a certain item, the exporter of that commodity would receive more domestic currency per unit of the foreign currency he received in payment for his exports than would the exporter of items the government desired to keep at home—the same thing as a discriminatory export tariff pattern. Or it might be that an extremely unfavorable rate would be given to discourage foreign investors from trying to take their capital home. In line with such thinking, the Germans during the 1930's gave a relatively large number of marks for the dollar to American tourists to encourage trips to Germany, but gave a relatively small amount of dollar exchange per mark to United States investors trying to take their money out of Germany.

Table 29 describes the Argentine exchange-rate structure as of December 31, 1955. The details have, no doubt, been changed several times since than; but the rate pattern may still illustrate the range of possibilities. In foreign-exchange transactions, the foreign currency is handled as though it were a commodity. The foreign currency is the thing being bought and sold; and the domestic currency is the money. Thus, Table 29 is set up from the Argentine point of view; the buying rate is the rate at which dollars are bought with pesos (perhaps by the Argentine Central Bank) and the selling rate is the rate at which dollars are sold for pesos. Under the buying rate column, the first entry states that the Argentine Central Bank will give 13.5 pesos in Argentina for one dollar (which is

---

[8] The fact that exactly the same thing, with exactly the same impact on all parties, could be done with a pattern of import and export tariffs, does not even slow the government down. Here is a new toy to play with, a new complication for an already too complicated world.

perhaps on deposit in a bank in New York) to an exporter of greasy wool.

Obviously, so far as exporters are concerned, the rate of 13.5 pesos to the dollar is the least favorable rate; and it is only the law which keeps them from transferring all of their dollars to pesos at the free rate of 35.5 pesos to the dollar. Argentina seems to be discriminating most against the least highly processed products of the livestock and timber industries.

Yankee tourists in Argentina are probably entitled to get pesos at 35.50 to the dollar.[9]

If it is true that governments are the willing partners of domestic

TABLE 29

ARGENTINE EXCHANGE RATES (AS OF DECEMBER 31, 1955)
(PESOS PER U.S. DOLLAR)

BUYING RATE [1]	SELLING RATE [2]
13.50 (Official Rate less 25% Levy) Exports of greasy wool, dry and salted hides, timber. Re-exports.	
14.40 (Official Rate less 20% Levy) Exports of scoured wool.	
15.30 (Official Rate less 15% Levy) Exports of meat, most dairy produce, combed wool and tops, etc.	
16.20 (Official Rate less 10% Levy) Exports of grains, oilseeds, other farm products, yerba mate, etc.	
18.00 (Official Rate) Exports of ores and other mining products, tanned hides, yarns and threads, etc.	18.00 (Official Rate) Imports of goods and commercial invisibles entitled to the official rate.
35.50 (approx.) (Free Market Rate) Proceeds of all other exports. Invisibles. Capital.	36.50 (approx.) (Free Market Rate)— Imports of goods permitted at the free rate. Income from foreign investments accruing since June 30, 1955. Other invisibles. Capital.
	56.50 (Free Market Rate plus 20 peso Surcharge)—Imports of motor bicycles and spares for motor vehicles and for industrial and other machinery.

[1] The rate the exporter receives from the Argentine Central Bank (the buyer) for his foreign exchange. [2] The rate the importer must pay to the Argentine Central Bank (the seller) in order to obtain the foreign exchange necessary to pay for imports.

Source: International Monetary Fund, *Seventh Annual Report, Exchange Restrictions, 1956* (Washington, 1956), p. 347.

[9] In some foreign cities (Paris) if they step around the corner (as tourists have a predilection for doing) and take a chance on getting put in jail and causing their consul no end of trouble, they can possibly get a rate somewhat more favorable than that to which they are legally entitled.

producers in a continuing effort to stimulate exports, the reader may wonder why the government is at such pains to deny the attractive rate of 35.5 pesos to the dollar to many of its exporters. Instead, for the most part, it makes them take the relatively unattractive rate of 18 or fewer pesos to the dollar.

The explanation is that even the 13.50 pesos to the dollar rate is a devaluation and represents more pesos to the dollar than Argentine exporters formerly got. In part what is involved is the group of forces tending to make a weak currency that has been devalued fall yet farther. Currency speculators are selling it short in all the alleys and at the Jockey Club. Thus the actual position of the government is ambiguous. The basic rate is a devalued rate designed to encourage exports. But at the same time the government is fighting against the yet more devalued rates that threaten to discredit the currency completely.

On the import side (selling rate: rate at which the Central Bank sells dollars to its citizens) the situation is reversed. The rate of 18 pesos to the dollar is the more attractive rate to the importer, who wants to buy the dollars he needs to pay for his imports at as low a rate as possible. Preferred imports get the more desirable rate, since the Argentine government discriminates in their favor. The reason for the discrimination against spare parts (the 56.5 rate) is not clear.

Whether the exchange-control agency makes a profit on its operations or loses money depends on the pattern of activities. If it gave all exporters the 35.5 peso rate and all importers the 18 peso rate, it might soon be out of foreign exchange and have to curtail imports drastically. If it gave most exporters the 13.5 rate and made most importers pay the 56.5 rate, it might well find itself accumulating ever larger foreign-exchange reserves.

On the whole, the basis for discrimination in applying the multiple exchange-rate structure is the same as the basis for discrimination in granting quotas and licenses; and the impact of the discriminations is the same as that which tariffs could give.

In appraisal of the usefulness of a system of multiple rates, even for a country which thinks it is using the system to raise the level of living within its own country, it may still be said that systems of multiple exchange rates, as practiced, are guaranteed to muddy the water to such a degree that the would-be government planner cannot possibly tell what he is doing or whether his country is being helped or hurt by what he is doing. In this confusing world, well-meaning people who are trying to raise levels of living will do well to keep their operational framework as simple as possible if they wish really to be able to appraise the effect of their actions. Multiple exchange rates (like tariffs) make it quite impossible to appraise the cost of a development encouraged by them. They warp the price structure out of all rhyme and reason.

Types of Bilateral International Agreements

Countries practicing exchange control have frequently found it desirable to enter into agreements with other countries with regard to the trade between them.[10] They got into all sorts of difficulties while practicing their restrictions unilaterally—witness the difficulties involved in the United States–Brazilian case cited earlier in this chapter. Treaties implementing systems of exchange control, if they do not contain most-favored-nation clauses, have generally been called bilateral treaties. Treaties containing most-favored-nation clauses, even though they are concluded between two countries, are not generally called bilateral treaties.

Bilateral agreements have been classified as (a) compensation agreements, (b) clearing agreements, and (c) payments agreements.[11] Although it is generally difficult to classify an agreement as being precisely of one type or the other, and even difficult to guarantee that these terms are used uniformly, the making of a distinction among them may help to clarify the nature and operation of such agreements.

The compensation agreement does not involve the governments, but the private traders. In a typical example involving country A and country B, four traders (two in each country) have decided among themselves to engage in the transaction—see Chart 14. The arrangement involves an exporter in country A shipping goods to an importer in country B, and an exporter in B sending goods to an importer in A. The importer in A pays the exporter in A, and the importer in B pays the exporter in B. There is no foreign-exchange transaction, yet everyone is paid off and presumably satisfied. This type of agreement involves the difficulties of four people getting together in a transaction where the value of the goods going one direction must equal the value of the goods going in the other direction, unless someone is willing to incur some debt. Some governments, using exchange control, have allowed private traders to engage in compensation agreements, some have not. In general, however, private compensation agreements are becoming increasingly prevalent.[12]

The next degree of complication is the clearing agreement. A government agency enters into the process described in the compensation agreement in such wise that, although the value of the goods going each way

[10] Merlyn N. Trued and Raymond F. Mikesell, *Postwar Bilateral Payments Agreements,* Princeton Studies in International Finance, No. 4 (Princeton University Press, 1955); Johan H. C. de Looper, "Current Usage of Payments Agreements and Trade Agreements," *International Monetary Fund Staff Papers,* IV (August, 1955), 339–97. The General Agreement on Tariffs and Trade publishes an *Index of Trade Agreements* with the January and July issues of the *International Trade News Bulletin.* The Index contains a brief summary of the provisions of the agreements.

[11] A somewhat more refined classification is presented in Meade, *Balance of Payments,* pp. 386–96.

[12] *Economic Survey of Latin America, 1954,* p. 71.

between the two countries is still equal, the value of the goods involved would not have to be equal so far as any small group of traders is concerned. The individual trader does not need to concern himself with the equality; all he needs to consider is whether or not he can get an export or an import license and a desirable foreign-exchange rate from the government. In this simplified version of the clearing agreement, the importer pays the government agency and the government agency pays the exporter in each country.[13] All is well as long as shipments occur on schedule. But such an arrangement may result in a bitter argument when one country gets ahead of the other in goods shipments and the other country, instead of hurrying to catch up in its shipments, lets them lag yet farther. Depending on how the government which is overexporting handles the case, either the government agency or the exporter has become an international creditor in spite of himself. The nature of the institutional arrangement (the clearing agreement) may thus make possible, temporarily, the spontaneous generation of the financing of a discrepancy between exports and imports. In fact, the clearing agreement itself is not unlikely to provide for the possibility of short-term credits to finance temporary disparities in goods shipments to and fro.

All this must be done within the framework of a complicated treaty arrangement between the two governments, which probably tries to specify ahead of time varying amounts or values of different types of goods which shall be exchanged during a given time period. The chances are that such an agreement, however, leaves the setting of the price in the individual transaction to be determined in each case, while the setting of the exchange rate (which may be implicit or explicit) rests with the governments. Under such circumstances, neither government can really guarantee fulfillment of the quotas set in the agreement. Compliance depends in large part on whether businessmen will perform as expected in the setting provided. More often than not, there are difficulties; and as was indicated above, instead of the values imputed to exports equaling the values imputed to imports, there is a discrepancy, and one government ends up owing the other.

The payments agreement is generally broader in coverage than the clearing agreement and makes provision for the settlement of old debt within the framework of the bilateral agreement—as well as for the possibility of short-term debt created in connection with the operation of the agreement itself. Assume that individuals in country A have been in debt to individuals in country B before the payments agreement is signed and that the two governments agree to arrange the financing of some

---

[13] Actually the agreement may designate the government clearing agency of one of the countries to handle the accounts for both. In that case one of the two agencies would be handling far more of the transaction than the other. See Meade, *Balance of Payments,* Chap. 29.

debt repayment in connection with the operation of the agreement. (It is equally likely that new debt, even long-term debt, could be incurred, perhaps involving only the government agencies, perhaps also involving private citizens.) This would involve basically the shipment in one direction of goods of greater value than the goods shipped in the other direction. In the debtor country the payments made by the individual debtors are used to pay the exporters responsible for the export balance of trade. In the creditor country the sums received from the importers which are not needed to pay exporters (because exports are less than imports) may be used to pay off the creditors. This example is yet another illustration of the close relationship between the balance of trade and the international lending or repayment of capital.

These simplified (perhaps oversimplified) examples of the mechanics of compensation, clearing, and payments agreements hardly do justice to the beautiful array of complications which characterize the typical "clearing and payments" agreement. No two agreements are alike; with each new agreement the parties think of new facets and subtle overtones and undertones intended to accomplish some new bit of skulduggery or to get back at the other country for something it has previously done —like failing to deliver the promised quantity of goods, or the foisting off of a lot of goods that turn out to be "lemons"—barbed wire, phonographs, typewriters, etc. (these being notorious examples of things Germany foisted off in the 1930's).

In connection with bilateral negotiations, the advantage has generally rested, at least in the short run, with the debtor, with the country with the import trade balance, and with the less scrupulous—that is, with those whose bargaining position was stronger. A few examples may illustrate the diversity of the possibilities. Douglas Miller has described some of the maneuvers connected with various German bilateral agreements: [14]

> . . . the South African government, under pressure from domestic wool growers, sold its entire wool clip to Germany against the future delivery of German locomotives, automotive equipment, and similar commodities. Unfortunately, as time elapsed, the South Africans were unable to get deliveries of German automobiles at prices which were at all in line with the cars offered from the United States and other countries. German locomotive plants seemed unable to deliver equipment which would suit the South African railroads, and the export of different types of electrical equipment, machinery and tools was prohibited, as those products were needed for the German army. . . .

[14] Douglas Miller, *You Can't Do Business with Hitler* (Boston: Little, Brown, 1941), pp. 74-5, 76-7. Reprinted with the kind permission of the author.

It was not long before most of my commercial attaché colleagues in Berlin, whose countries were working under clearings, spent a great part of their efforts in preventing shipments from their own countries to Germany, since they were fearful of running up too big a credit and finally being forced to take a loss. The Minister from Nicaragua in Berlin proudly explained that he had succeeded in stopping Nicaraguan shipments to Germany before they exceeded German goods sent to Nicaragua, and his government even went so far as to make sure that German goods entering Nicaraguan ports should actually be unloaded from the ships and placed in warehouses on the docks under Nicaraguan control before they allowed compensating products to be loaded. In that way, the little country managed to keep on the debtor side and could avoid the high-pressure tactics of the German debtor. Other countries were less cautious. They swallowed the German bait, hook and all, enthusiastically shipping commodities with little thought of how they were eventually to be paid.

War-minded Germany in the late 1930's was apparently looking at international trade like a state trading country, trying to give few exports for as much import as possible. This made it especially hard for the countries that were obsessed with maintaining an export balance to deal with her. They could get their export balance all right, all too easily. Then they were creditors in spite of themselves.

International payments by the end of the 1930's were strait-jacketed in a group of controls that were calculated not so much to facilitate trade, commerce, and interchange as to further some narrow conception of national interest. Business groups were either complaining about the restrictions of other governments or trying to make their own government establish yet more drastic trade impediments. The result was not felicitous in the pre-World War II era.

And bilateral clearing and payments agreements are still with us.

A group of experts evaluated some of Mexico's postwar bilateral agreements as follows: [15]

> Although Mexico has been able by these means to dispose of some commodities, for which it had no other readily available market, or for prices above those which it could have obtained in hard currency areas, it could take in return only what its

[15] Combined Mexican Working Party (Raul Ortiz Mena of Nacional Financiera, Victor L. Urquidi of the Banco de Mexico, and Albert Waterston and Jonas H. Haralz of the International Bank for Reconstruction and Development), *The Economic Development of Mexico* (Baltimore: Johns Hopkins Press, 1953), p. 122.

European customers were prepared to give, whenever they decided to give it, at prices that Mexico might not have been willing
to pay in all instances for similar goods in a free market.

The Economic Commission for Latin America has made a general evaluation to the effect that the prices resulting from bilateral agreements
are likely to be higher (going both ways) than the prices which would
prevail in the course of ordinary trade.[16]

Some of the most important bilateral agreements of the postwar era
have involved Britain and the Argentine, two countries which have meanwhile been growling at each other because of political disputes over the
Falkland Islands, sovereignty in the Antarctic, and the illustrations on
Argentine postage stamps. When the postwar negotiations began, there
were large balances in London built up by the Argentine as the result
of large World War II shipments of beef and wheat to Britain. During
the war the British government blocked the use of these balances. At
the end of the war, the Argentine government was interested in the purchase of the British-owned railways in that country. In the agreement
which was arrived at, Argentina contracted to pay a rather attractive
sum to the British investors. The Argentine blocked balances in London
in large part provided the funds actually used to pay the former owners
of the railroads.

England, in turn, was interested in obtaining additional large shipments of wheat and meat from the Argentine, because food was scarce
in England at the end of the war. And Argentina, for her part, was
interested in obtaining machinery to assist with domestic industrial development. The Argentine government held out for all it could get for
its wheat and meat, a procedure which has seemed to the British (and
other Europeans) like kicking a fellow when he was down. At the other
end of the process, the Argentine estancieros have been unhappy because
the peso prices paid them by the Argentine government for their products
were far less than the prices in foreign exchange which the Argentine
government was receiving for the exports. Much of these exports was
actually for the account of the Argentine government, and much was for
the account of the British government also—a case of state trading. The
Argentine government, for its part, could not get all the equipment it
desired from England. No one was entirely happy about the arrangements, and they were not well and effectively implemented by the parties.

Evaluation

In evaluation of the role of bilateral agreements and direct government
control it may be said that, in the theoretical discussions which have

---

[16] United Nations, Economic Commission for Latin America, *Study of the Prospects of Inter-Latin-American Trade* (New York, 1954), p. 27.

occurred, the emphasis has been at the wrong place. The problem has been discussed as though it is theoretically abstruse and practically difficult. Granted that balance of payments difficulties may have inspired the inception of some of the exchange-control programs, it does not follow that balance of payments difficulties and the ramifications of balance of payments problems are of the essence in explaining the working of bilateral agreements.

A government, let us say Brazil, is maintaining the cruzeiro foreign-exchange rate at a certain figure. At this figure Brazilian price relations with the rest of the world are such that Brazilians choose to buy substantial supplies of goods abroad and foreigners choose to buy little in Brazil. Consequently, after a time, Brazilians run out of foreign exchange and cannot effect payment for their imports. That is to say, they have cruzeiros; but ultimate payment must be effected in dollars. If the Brazilian government chooses to stand by its exchange rate and also to stand by the internal money and credit policies that have raised the Brazilian price level relative to that of the rest of the world, one of two things must happen. Unless there is lending (the creation of larger blocked balances in Brazil) by the foreigners, the volume of foreign shipments to Brazil must be reduced. The balance of trade will adjust to the financing, have no fear—with or without bilateral agreements.

There is a real problem involved in the determination of the institutional arrangements which will regulate this adjustment process. But the alternatives, fundamentally, are rather simple. If foreign exporters or foreign bankers are unwilling to make additional loans to Brazil (or hold blocked balances in Brazil), they must stop selling to Brazil or financing the trade to Brazil. Government controls and bilateral agreements offer no magic route around the basic proposition that a discrepancy between imports and exports must be financed.

Moreover, the agreements tend to strait-jacket trade in an inhibitory way. The tendency toward "bilateral balancing" is a tendency toward the reduction of total trade. As two governments haggle about the value of shipments between them, the one with the import balance is likely to demand that the other increase its purchases or the country with the import balance will decrease its own. Since it is easier arbitrarily to cut purchases by fiat than to conjure up buyers by fiat, the trade between the two countries will tend to balance—or balance with the agreed-on allowance for lending—at a figure for total trade that will be smaller than that which previously prevailed.

The price of looking at trade as a bilateral balancing proposition instead of as a system of multilateral interchange is less total trade.

However, it may be well to end the discussion of exchange control and bilateral agreements on a less negative note. On the whole, Trued and Mikesell seem to believe, if I interpret them correctly, that bilateral agreements are now working better than they did before World War II.[17] And it stands to reason that as governments become more experienced with the use of the tool—they were certainly inexperienced in the negotiation of bilateral agreements in the 1930's—the tool will work better. On top of this it may well be that *bilateral* agreements are better than unilateral exchange control. It is just that multilateral arrangements would be even better. In any event, as late as 1953, "less than half the trade of the free world was on a convertible currency basis." [18]

[17] Trued and Mikesell, *op. cit., passim*. They claim, for example, that bilateral agreements no longer imply bilateral balancing (p. 3).
[18] *International Financial News Survey,* October 1, 1954, p. 109.

Chapter 21

THE RELATIVE VALUES OF
CURRENCIES: STATE TRADING

❧ ❧ ❧

*When governments trade with each other for their own account, there
must be an implicit foreign-exchange rate even though one is not
overtly expressed.*

*The U.S.S.R. apparently handles the bookkeeping of her foreign trade
on the assumption that the ruble-dollar rate is an overt four rubles to
the dollar (ten rubles to the dollar since 1957).*

*The U.S.S.R., as a major gold-producing country, has an interest in the
continued use of gold as a monetary metal; however, the U.S.S.R. has
no major concern with the gold standard as such.*

❧ ❧ ❧

AS WAS pointed out in Chapter 14, state trading, unlike private
trade under government control, involves the government
as an actual contracting party in the trading process. In such
a case there need be no foreign-exchange rate expressed as
such, although there may well be an overt rate, and there will always be
one or more implicit rates.

THE FOREIGN EXCHANGE RATE

A socialistic country need not have a foreign-exchange rate on its currency—it need not have a currency. The same thing is true of any society,
whether socialistic or not. But a monetary system is a desirable working
tool, and there is little doubt that socialistic countries are well advised
to have monetary systems and overt and meaningful foreign-exchange
rates. But they could have monetary systems and still not allow any foreign-exchange transactions, so that there would be no explicit foreign-
exchange rate. In such a case, there would be an implicit rate that could
be computed for any given international transaction, but the rate might
well vary from transaction to transaction. The socialistic country also

can have an explicit rate; and that explicit rate may be either fairly meaningful or fairly meaningless.

From the viewpoint of intelligent planning, the more meaningful the rate the better. It will aid in giving the planners useful information only insofar as it is meaningful. Also, a meaningful rate would make it possible to buy and sell foreign exchange at this rate from and to ordinary private citizens (Russians and others) who want to come and go. The existence of such a rate could tremendously increase individual freedom of action. Russia seems to have an explicit but fairly meaningless foreign-exchange rate set on the ruble. That rate has been four rubles to the dollar since 1950. Before that it was 5.30 rubles to the dollar. It may be noted that the 1950 change was an appreciation and not a depreciation of the ostensible value of the ruble.

It seems that the Gosbank (the Russian State Bank) is ready to purchase foreign currencies in unlimited amounts at this rate. A foreigner owning rubles would be substantially free to make purchases in Russia with the rubles, but not free to export the goods except with a government permit which he would not be likely to get—unless the transaction fits into the government's over-all economic plan. But the Russian government is not willing to sell such foreign currencies as it owns in exchange for rubles in unlimited amounts at four rubles to the dollar. The only transactions of this sort involving individuals are carefully controlled. It is said that a Soviet diplomat coming to a United Nations session in New York may be sold dollars by the Gosbank at the rate of four rubles to the dollar. But there are not very many other types of situations where this would happen.

BARTER

There are several possibilities as to the mechanics by which the state trading process might be financed. One possibility would be simple barter. In this case each government might be assumed to have in mind a value which it sets on the goods which it is offering and which it is obtaining, possibly a value which is influenced by the money price at which those items are selling in its own country. There also may be value criteria of a somewhat different sort—some subjective value determined by the government officials on the basis of criteria such as a democratic vote, input-output coefficients established by planning under the materials-balance system, or a dictator's estimate as to what is important for industrialization, or important for war, or "good for the people." The relationship among these opinions and prices establishes an implicit exchange rate, although it is a rate that may not be the same in the next transaction. The terms of trade in such cases also are determined by subjective evaluation and may not be the same for both countries. But the same thing is true of subjective terms of trade as distinct from the terms of trade computed in money for the trade between economies, however organized.

From the point of view of the adjustment process, however, what is involved is quite simple. There will be trade every time the governments agree on a transaction. And the government will be influenced, in deciding whether to trade, by its estimation of the values of what it is giving and what it is getting. There is no financing problem, unless both parties agree that the value of goods going one way is not equal to the value going the other way and that they will make up the difference later. In this case the parties are taking about the same kind of a chance they would take in the case of a monetary loan.

King Solomon did some bartering with King Hiram of Tyre according to I Kings, and there are occasional true barter transactions even today. But most of the agreements called barter transactions in the newspapers are not quite that simple and involve some monetary adjustments. And Russian trade generally cannot be described as an example of simple barter.[1]

TRADE WITH UNITED STATES

Trade between the United States and Russia may be used as an example of the process when Russia is dealing with a country engaged primarily in private trading. But the details probably differ substantially in the trading arrangements between Russia and each other country—and the accuracy of specific details in the description may be open to question.

Russia has set up and controls a corporation called Amtorg (Amerikanskaia Torgovlia), which is chartered in this country and has offices in New York City. Trading is financed somewhat as follows—see Chart 15. (a) Russia (a Russian producing agency or export combine selling through the Ministry of Foreign Trade) may sell some furs to United States importers who will pay Amtorg with dollars; (b) Amtorg

[1] Information on the mechanics of the financing of Russian trade may be obtained from: Nicolas Spulber, "Economic Thinking and its Application and Methodology in Eastern Europe Outside of Soviet Russia," *American Economic Review, Papers . . . ,* XLVI (May, 1956), pp. 367–79; Edward Ames, "The Exchange Rate in Soviet-Type Economies," *Review of Economics and Statistics,* XXXV (November, 1953), 337–42; Edward Ames, "International Trade without Markets—the Soviet Bloc Case," *American Economic Review,* XLIV (December, 1954), 791–807; and Mikhail V. Condoide, *Soviet Financial System* (Columbus: Ohio State University [Bureau of Business Research], 1951), pp. 108–56. But it should be confessed that the factual basis for the descriptive material of this chapter is sketchy. I have been "reading" *Voprosi Ekonomiki* for several years without coming on an article giving useful, factual information on questions of this sort.

CHART 15

FINANCING OF RUSSIAN–AMERICAN TRADE

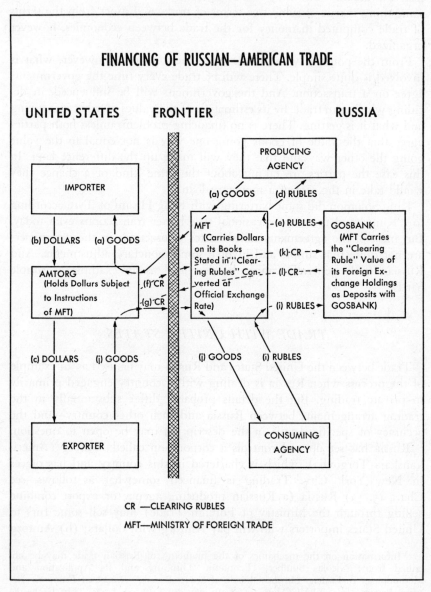

| UNITED STATES | FRONTIER | RUSSIA |

CR —CLEARING RUBLES

MFT—MINISTRY OF FOREIGN TRADE

thus ends this part of the transaction with dollars to its credit in the United States. Russia might want airplane engines (in the days before the "cold war" they might have been able to get them), or whatever, and could use those dollars to purchase them. There has been no foreign-exchange transaction in the ordinary sense involved. But this is not to say that it makes no difference to the mechanics of the transaction in Russia that the ruble-dollar rate is four to one, or some other implicit figure— even though Russia has sold her goods in the United States for dollars and turned around and spent those same dollars in the United States for United States goods.

This meant Russian agreeableness to the relationship between two sets of dollar prices in the United States: the price at which her exports were sold (step b) and the price she paid for her imports (step c). But in addition it is an oversimplification to speak of the Russian foreign trade monopoly as a homogeneous unit which has only "foreign relations" and no adjustment problems within itself.

The Russian government, in drawing up its plan of operations for the year, must try to relate the value of the goods it may export (step a) to the value of the imports it may obtain in exchange (step j). This should involve evaluating the total supply of goods which will be available domestically as the result of the interaction of these foreign trade activities on domestic production. Under the materials-balance system, the Russians are said to be guided chiefly by engineering estimates as to quantities of imports needed and exports available—quantities that are based on assumptions that the proportions of various raw materials used in production are constant. Nevertheless, the values received and paid by the export and import combines are surely expressed in money. And from their point of view, as well as from that of the capitalist, the more meaningful money prices are, the better for planning purposes.

The foreign trade activities are merely a part of the larger area of Russian planning, which covers many different agencies that produce, buy, and sell goods. The over-all plan will require some of those agencies to export some of their product and will permit other agencies to import goods from abroad. These various agencies keep accounts in rubles. Ruble costs are incurred in production; and the goods, once produced, are sold for rubles to Russian consumers and to other agencies of the Russian government, or they are exported. If they are exported as indicated in step "a," the export combine is probably paid in rubles by the Ministry of Foreign Trade. These goods are then sold abroad for dollars (the dollars mentioned earlier as coming into the possession of Amtorg in New York), but it seems that the Ministry of Foreign Trade, in recording on its books the value of these dollars to which it has a claim, does so in rubles ("clearing rubles" they might be called) converted from dollars at the official rate of exchange of four rubles to the dollar (step f). Thus at this point a foreign-exchange rate (even if no foreign-exchange transaction) appears to play a part in the procedure. But apparently the ruble value of the exports obtained by converting the dollar receipts to rubles at the official rate of exchange does not determine the ruble price which was paid by the Ministry of Foreign Trade to the producing agency—the amount of clearing rubles (step f) does not necessarily equal the amount of domestic rubles (step d). You might say that this difference is the equivalent of an export duty or subsidy— depending on which way the difference is. The Ministry of Foreign Trade then deposits with the Gosbank (turning over to the Gosbank its claim on) the dollars. But again, the value set up on the Gosbank books is the figure in rubles (clearing rubles) which has been converted from dollars at the official rate.

Thus the foreign-exchange rate ends up by influencing the amount of total ruble deposits (foreign-exchange reserves) with the Gosbank (step k). The Russian government might be influenced in its decisions on the quantity of money to be kept in circulation by considering the size of these reserves. But apparently it is not. Presumably the Russian government does not allow the size of Gosbank reserves to have a significant effect on the internal money and credit structure. But domestic production is "financed," even in Russia. Wages are paid. Raw materials are bought from other agencies. Goods are sold for a price. It can probably be said that the Gosbank's reserve situation affects bookkeeping and planning procedures, but that the government attempts to see to it that an adverse reserve position does not inhibit the full employment of resources. This is not fundamentally different from the procedure of a "western" government pursuing internal money and credit and planning policies (which are independent of the reserve position) in an effort to get full employment.

In connection with the financing of imports, the process works in reverse. The Ministry of Foreign Trade reduces its deposits at the Gosbank (step l) and authorizes Amtorg to write a check against the dollars which have all the while been standing to Amtorg's credit in a bank in New York (steps g and c). The dollars are paid to the exporter and the goods are shipped (step j), possibly care of the Ministry of Foreign Trade, to Russia. They are then "sold" by that Ministry (or possibly the Ministry never has title in any clear-cut meaning of the word) to the interested consuming agency or import combine for a price in rubles (step i) that may not be equal to the dollar price (of step c) converted to rubles at one to four.

The Ministry of Foreign Trade could make a profit or sustain a loss in the end in terms of domestic rubles (the relation of step i to step d) after all of these transactions are over, even though the dollars spent on the imports equaled the dollars obtained from the exports (even though step b equaled step c). This is possible because the ruble price paid to the producing agency and obtained from the consuming agency is not necessarily related to the dollar price relations prevailing between those goods in the United States. But exports equal imports—whether measured in dollars or in clearing rubles. There is no favorable or unfavorable balance of trade in the usual sense. And a discrepancy between the domestic ruble price paid by the Ministry for the exports and the domestic ruble price at which the imports are sold does not disturb the balance of trade. Nor would a difference between the price at which the manufacturer sold to the exporter and the price at which the importer sold to the consumer establish the existence of inequality between exports and imports for the United States. When we speak of the necessity that exports equal imports, we are speaking of the values imputed to them for international trading purposes by traders. We are not speaking of the eternal verities—or of the way either party will appraise the real terms of trade involved, or of subsequent or previous resale prices.

To illustrate with money figures what is involved here, let us say that some furs were sold by the producing agency to the Ministry for 10,000 rubles (step d). They were sold to the United States importer for $5,000 (step b), and consequently the dollar receipts were carried on the books of the Ministry and the Gosbank as 20,000 rubles (steps f and k), an ostensible 10,000 ruble export tariff. Later the $5,000 was spent for Fords (step c), which were sold to the consuming agency for 25,000 rubles (step i). Exports equal imports. For the United States both figures are $5,000. For Russia exports and imports are both 20,000 rubles. The Ministry has gained 10,000 rubles (20,000 minus 10,000) from the producing agency and 5,000 rubles (25,000 minus 20,000) from the consuming agency. If the Ministry were a private exporting-importing house in a capitalistic country, this would be a desirable result and, it might be added, quite the ordinary thing. As things are in Russia, it is probably no part of the intention of the Ministry to make a ruble profit out of deals of this sort. Nonetheless, at any given time the Ministry is operating at what might be called a profit or a loss in domestic rubles—and undoubtedly these agencies keep—or should keep—records indicating which is the case. How far an agency can go in either direction is up to the Russian government. And the decision making is not greatly dissimilar in kind from that involved in the United States in a decision as to whether any particular agency of the government shall be allowed to operate at a loss or be required to show a surplus.

So far as internal price differences between the United States and Russia are concerned and so far as differences in the price patterns are concerned, the same comment may be repeated which has been made many times before. Transfer costs are so great as to make tremendous price differences permissive. The institutional differences between the two economies are sufficiently great to make for actual differences in price relations within each country by comparison with other countries. This does not tell us whether the real price level (as an average) is higher or lower in Russia. But it may be that one institutional difference can indicate that, from the United States point of view, the terms of trade with Russia are unfavorable, or would be if there were much trade. We would be willing to dump in Russia (and were in the twenties and thirties) if it were not for the "cold war." And the Russians would be willing to take our dumped goods at bargain prices—even now. But the same is not true in reverse. The Russians are not going to dump just for the sake of dumping.

But whether this would make internal United States prices higher or lower than internal Russian prices is not established a priori. One argument might be that the handling of the terms of trade makes for relatively greater goods availability in Russia than in the United States; therefore Russia ought to have a lower price level. But we also suspect that goods are actually more readily available in the United States than in Russia (in spite of the attitudes toward the terms of trade); and that should make for relatively lower prices in the United States. In fact, travelers to Russia these days frequently report that Russian prices (at four rubles to the dollar) are extremely high.[2] This impression may in some measure be misleading, because of the sort of things foreigners insist on buying. But lacking better evidence, it seems justified to say that the Russian price level is relatively high.

The tremendous Russian emphasis on capital equipment production and armaments may tend to contribute to higher price levels on consumer goods. However, this would not necessarily make Russian prices relatively high, a development that requires a certain credit policy, in addition. The indicated price relationship would exist if Russia insists on maintaining the four ruble to the dollar rate and engages in more internal money and credit expansion (relative to production and population growth) than does the United States. Perhaps Russia is engaged in a rather considerable amount of money-supply expansion to finance her development. Maybe in Russia—just as in the Latin American countries—it is easier to use newly created credit to finance development than to tax. There is some contrary evidence to the effect that the Russian government in the last few years has come to grips with the problem of price inflation and that prices have fallen quite substantially. The Russian government's price-level index numbers indicate as much. At all events, the last word is far from being spoken on the nature and influence of price level differences between the United States and Russia.

---

[2] *New York Times*, September 3, 1954, p. 3; N. M. Kaplan, "A Comparison of Soviet and American Retail Prices in 1950," *Journal of Political Economy*, LXIV (December, 1956), pp. 470–91.

In many ways the Russian situation corresponds to that already described as applying to international trade in general. Differences between the prices paid by the Ministry to the producing agency and the price received abroad can be considered the equivalent of an export tariff or subsidy. The same is true on the import side, the price difference being the equivalent of an import tariff or subsidy. Russian financing of international differences between exports and imports can be arranged only by international lending, gifts, or gold movements, the socialist economy being no different in this respect than any other. But because of the present political situation, the Russians are roughly in a position where they have to pay cash—consequently, the actual trade financing procedures used by them involve keeping short-term balances in the United States. Russia is a creditor in relation to the United States in terms of short-term balances—although possibly not a net creditor if outstanding lend-lease accounts and Czarist debts are added to the picture. And a final point of similarity, internal financing of discrepancies between values assigned internally to exports and imports is dependent on internal credit policies—that is, dependent on which producers and consumers have access to credit and which do not, on which get relatively more or less favorable treatment from the Ministry of Foreign Trade.

BILATERAL AGREEMENTS WITH COUNTRIES OUTSIDE THE SOVIET BLOC

The sort of trading arrangement described or hypothesized between the Soviet Union and the United States is not dependent upon agreement between the two governments. Or rather, there merely needs to be governmental permission in the United States for the trade to proceed in this way. (As is well-known, the United States currently restricts but does not prohibit such trade.)

It is also possible that the trade framework may be established by a rather comprehensive bilateral agreement between the Russian government and the government of some country on this side of the "iron curtain": Great Britain, Sweden, or India. The Soviet Union and India, for example, concluded a bilateral agreement in December, 1953. The agreement provided that the trade would be based on the rupee with any differences to be adjusted in sterling.[3] Presumably this meant that Russian-owned sterling balances in London could be used to pay Indians in case Indian shipments to Russia exceeded Russian shipments to India, and vice versa. Rupee prices for the goods exchanged were probably determined by contract between Russian government foreign-trade agencies (possibly acting through the Ministry of Foreign Trade)

[3] *New York Times,* December 3, 1953, p. 2.

and private Indian traders. Such contracts can determine rupee prices all right, but they leave the willingness of private Indians actually to trade in the quantities provided for in the agreement dependent upon the forces of the market. Moreover, the provision that import and export goals would have to be agreed upon between the two governments on a yearly basis may effectively establish maximum figures for the amount of trade in different categories (such as heavy machinery from Russia and jute from India), but it does not assure that private Indian traders will demand or supply to that extent at prices that are agreeable to them and to the Soviet Union.

The statement that trade would be based on the rupee also probably meant that Indian importers would pay in rupees into an agreed-on banking account (perhaps clearing would be through the Reserve Bank of India). The Russians then could use these funds to pay private Indian exporters. If this is the procedure followed, it amounts to much the same thing as the procedure followed in trade with the United States, except for the additional feature that the government of India has a hand in planning the quantities and types of goods which should move.

So far as the bookkeeping in Russia is concerned, it seems to be substantially the same as that described in connection with Russian-United States trade. The Ministry of Foreign Trade and the Gosbank probably carry entries based on some assumed ruble-rupee rate.

TRADE WITHIN SOVIET BLOC

Another possibility (and something approximating this procedure has been used in the trade between Russia and the countries of eastern Europe) is a sort of modified barter arrangement. The participating governments, in writing up a bilateral agreement, may express the value of what they are willing to offer and receive in physical terms or in money terms; in some cases, values have been expressed in terms of United States dollars (strangely enough), but more recently Russian rubles have generally been used. This means that a money price is likely to be attached to the goods involved in the agreement. In these terms exports must equal imports.[4] Also it seems that in the Soviet bloc some attention is paid to the desirability of price comparability and price stability as a working tool.

Again in this situation, the problem involved in the adjustment process is relatively simple. There will be trade if an agreement can be made; there will not be trade if there is no agreement. The agreement will be implemented if the governments go through with it. There will be

[4] Spulber, *loc. cit.,* p. 376.

an international loan or gift to the extent that one government gets ahead on its shipments. There is no balance of payments problem. The determining factor is each party's conception as to whether it is getting its money's worth. They surely bargain in an effort to get relatively more goods in exchange for relatively less. (Note that this is the exact reverse of what a country does when it specializes in import tariffs, devalues its currency, and worsens its terms of trade in order to increase its exports.)

MULTILATERAL TRADE

State trading is not necessarily bilateral—as the foregoing might seem to imply. In fact, trade could be multilateral instead of bilateral with little additional complication. Russia might sell furs in the United States for dollars, exchange the dollars for Brazilian cruzeiros, and the cruzeiros for coffee. Or Russia could set up a clearing arrangement in rubles and have a system of multilateral clearing through Moscow. One of the stated purposes of the eastern European Council for Mutual Economic Aid, which was set up in 1949 to counter the Marshall Plan, was the development of such a system of multilateral clearing among the member countries. Russia could, and probably does, have an export balance with Poland; Poland could, and probably does, have an export balance with Czechoslovakia; Czechoslovakia could, and probably does, have an export balance with Russia.

Both Ames and Spulber believe that most Russian trade in fact is still conducted on a bilateral basis. And perhaps there is a tendency for socialist planners to operate on a bilateral basis in the interest of simplicity in the negotiations. Nevertheless, there is nothing inherent in socialism or in state trading that prevents the trade and clearing from being on a multilateral basis.

ROLE OF FOREIGN EXCHANGE RESERVES AND GOLD

Foreign Exchange Reserves

The problem of the adequacy of foreign-exchange reserves is solved by the socialist government's knowledge of how much in foreign-exchange reserves it has to operate with. Unless it can borrow, it simply cannot trade any more after it gives out of reserves. There is some reason to believe that the Russian government does have a conception of how large adequate foreign-exchange reserves need to be. "Generally speaking, the gold and foreign exchange reserves of the Soviet Union must not fall below a certain minimum in order to be able to maintain freedom of action in foreign trade." [5]

This is not far from being fundamentally the same situation which confronts economies characterized by private trading.

Gold

The situation so far as gold itself is concerned, however, calls for special comment. Russia is a major gold-producing country. On the one hand, in spite of all the Russian scorn for things capitalistic, of which the gold standard is the epitome, one finds Russia extremely desirous that gold maintain its value as an international medium of exchange. On the other hand, in view of our scorn for the Russian scale of values, it is rather strange to observe that the Russians seem to have a more rational attitude toward the role of gold than we do.

There is a distinction to be made between the desire not to have gold demonetized and the desire to have fixed par gold standards. These two attitudes are not the same thing. To illustrate with the United States devaluation back in 1933, which raised the price of gold in the United States, what the United States did was to change the price of gold from $20.67 a fine ounce before devaluation to $35 after. As far as the Russians were concerned, that was a desirable development. They could obtain $35 afterward, compared with $20.67 before, for an ounce of their gold. They could consequently buy more goods in the United States with a given amount of their gold after devaluation than they could before. They were not in favor of the gold standard fixed pars. They did not lament the United States going off the gold standard, for the manner in which the United States did this made gold a relatively more desirable thing. The United States went off the gold standard, raised the value of gold, increased the command of gold over goods, and did not demonetize gold for the purpose of financing international trade. Russia, being a gold-producing nation and being interested in using gold to buy the maximum amount of goods, was benefited. Whatever we may find to argue about with the Russians, it would seem that the argument will not take the form of competitive devaluations of the currencies, for, unlike most countries, the Russians find the other nation's devaluation desirable. This situation is comparable to the "absence of conflict" arising from the difference in attitudes toward the balance of trade.

CONCLUSION

The techniques for financing trade by the state trading countries have not been adequately described by those who really know what is

[5] *International Financial News Survey,* February 10, 1956, p. 245; Oleg Hoeffding, "Recent Trends in Soviet Foreign Trade," *Annals of the American Academy of Political and Social Science,* CCCIII (January, 1956), pp. 75–88.

going on. Consequently, this evaluation of the process must leave something to be desired. On the one hand, a description such as this might become theoretical, leave out of account the likely errors that will be injected into the arrangement by human failing, and reach an oversimplified solution that the Russians are intelligently using international trade to improve their level of living. (The material in this chapter might be criticized on just that score.) Or the whole process could be condemned without discrimination because of the vices which have been so obviously a characteristic of one part of the Communist regime— the concentration camps, regimentation, and intellectual intolerance.

What is really called for is not a sharp drawing of the line between how pure free private enterprise and competition would work (if we had them) and how complete government ownership and centralized planning would work (if the Russians could achieve that humanely and intelligently). Neither country fits this description, nor is either ever likely to. The real problem is the problem of continual adjustment of the borderline between private and public activity, and continual effort to decentralize governmental activity, as far as it can be decentralized, in a setting where the desirable result is a combination of as high as possible a level of living and as much as possible individual security and freedom of action.

Consequently, the really important questions involve the "mixed" situation and how it can be made to work most effectively. The argument over absolutes (pure free private enterprise and pure socialism) is one of the most sterile intellectual projects the race is engaged in; and it is working on some sterile ones.[6]

As for what the Russian position ought to be with regard to the policy suggestions to come in Chapter 23, something can be said here. What is good for the goose may also be good for the gander. For example, Russian internal planning could probably be more intelligently done if Russia had a more homogeneous measure of value than that which is involved in the present system—which so carefully insulates the domestic from the international. There is nothing about the socialistic or Russian type of economy that would keep it from being able to participate in an effectively working, homogeneous world-wide system of clearing or in a world-wide uniform currency. Russia's credit creation and rate of development would have to be subject to international control, the same as everybody else's. But, as will be alleged in Part VI, these are not controls which will be or should be calculated to hold anybody back in terms of the real rate of development and the full use of resources.[7]

[6] Adolf A. Berle, Jr., *The 20th Century Capitalist Revolution* (New York: Harcourt, Brace, 1954), p. 109.

[7] In 1957 the U.S.S.R. modified the ruble foreign exchange rate in a manner that makes the rate actually ten rubles to the dollar.

Chapter 22

THE INTERNATIONAL MONETARY FUND AND THE CURRENT PAYMENTS SITUATION

❦ ❦ ❦

The foreign-exchange rates applicable to most currencies cannot be changed without the approval of the International Monetary Fund.

The Fund has reserves of the currencies of various countries, which it may make available to assist the stabilization funds of countries whose currencies are under pressure, in order to support the rate they are obligated to maintain.

Since the Fund does not have effective control over the internal credit policies of member countries, any given country can create a situation which will make a given rate untenable.

The desperate post-World War II need for goods in Europe, which was largely responsible for the "dollar shortage," is now virtually a thing of the past; the nature of the next major international financial crisis can at present only be a matter of speculation.

❦ ❦ ❦

IN MANY quarters there was concern in the latter part of the 1930's and during the war years with regard to the unsatisfactory working of the international payments process. The random and miscellaneous bilateral agreements, exchange controls, and other barriers which characterized the trading world were hardly conducive to making that world a coherent economic unit.

The Bretton Woods conference of 1944 was intended to work out a solution to the foreign-exchange rate and international payments problems. All of the United Nations, including Russia, participated in this conference in the small town in the White Mountains of New Hampshire. And articles of agreement were drawn up, which were subsequently ratified by enough of the participating countries to go into effect, although the Russians did not adhere to the organization which resulted. The Fund went into actual operation by gradual stages during the winter of 1946–47.

It might be said now, if one likes a "term" to describe a "situation," that the monetary standard of many countries is not the gold standard or the gold exchange standard, but rather the International Monetary Fund standard—a comment which would not mean much, however, without an understanding of the operations of the Fund.

ORGANIZATION OF THE FUND

The Fund has its general headquarters at 1818 "H" Street, N.W., in Washington, and is headed by a Swede, Per Jacobsson.

Quotas, Voting, and Subscriptions

The basis for the financial and administrative participation of members in the Fund's work is found in the *quotas*. The so-called quota of each member country is set up as a money figure. The quotas which were originally provided for totaled $8,800,000,000, of which the United States quota was $2,750,000,000. The Russian quota would have been $1,200,000,000. The current quotas are indicated in Table 30. The quota figures were used in somewhat modified form to determine what voting power the members should have on the one hand and what monetary subscriptions the countries should make on the other; but the quota itself did not represent a sum of money that any government paid to the Fund. That was referred to as the subscription. However, since the voting strength and subscription were computed on the basis of the quotas, it was an important concept; and the fact that the United States quota is about 31 per cent of the total of the countries which actually joined has been controlling in determining the location of effective power within the Fund.

Apparently at the Bretton Woods conference there was not any specific criterion used for determining quotas. The quotas were stated precisely in the articles of agreement, but not the formula for determining what they should be. That was determined by haggling at the conference. And in this haggling process, governments on the one hand were influenced by their desire to have a large vote (and therefore a large quota) and on the other hand by their desire to make a small monetary subscription (and consequently have a small quota).

The vote that was granted to a country was based on the quota relationship, essentially, and in fact was exactly in proportion to the quota except in certain specific eventualities. There was provision that a country which was doing considerable borrowing from the Fund should lose votes, and the creditor, or the country from which the Fund was borrowing, should obtain an increase in its vote—in connection with the voting on a limited number of important questions such as (a) whether in a certain case the

TABLE 30

INTERNATIONAL MONETARY FUND: QUOTAS AND FUND HOLDINGS

(AS OF NOVEMBER 30, 1956)—(MILLIONS OF U.S. DOLLARS)

	QUOTA	SUBSCRIPTION		REPURCHASES ON SUBSCRIPTION ACCOUNT	NET MEMBER DRAWINGS	FUND HOLDINGS OF MEMBER CURRENCIES	
		Gold Tranche	Member Currency			(U.S. Dollars)	(In % of Quota)
1. Afghanistan	10	2.5	—	—	—	—	—
2. Argentina	150	37.5	—	—	—	—	—
3. Australia	200	8.4	191.6	—	—	191.6	96
4. Austria	50	5.0	45.0	-7.5	—	37.5	75
5. Belgium	225	56.3	168.7	—	—	168.7	75
6. Bolivia	10	2.5	7.5	—	2.5	10.0	100
7. Brazil	150	37.5	112.5	—	65.5	178.0	119
8. Burma	15	.5	14.5	-3.2	15.0	26.3	175
9. Canada	300	75.0	225.0	—	-15.0	210.0	70
10. Ceylon	15	.8	14.2	-1.0	—	13.2	88
11. Chile	50	8.8	41.2	-3.7	12.3	49.8	100
12. China	550	.1	—	—	—	—	—
13. Colombia	50	12.5	37.5	—	25.0	62.5	125
14. Costa Rica	5	.4	4.6	-.9	—	3.7	75
15. Cuba	50	12.5	37.5	—	—	37.5	75
16. Denmark	68	5.9	62.1	-.8	—	61.3	90
17. Dominican Republic	10	2.5	7.5	—	—	7.5	75
18. Ecuador	10	2.5	7.5	—	—	7.5	75
19. Egypt	60	9.5	50.5	-5.5	15.0	60.0	100
20. El Salvador	2.5	.6	1.9	—	2.5	4.4	175
21. Ethiopia	6	.1	5.9	-1.4	—	4.5	75
22. Finland	38	.8	37.2	-5.4	—	31.8	84
23. France	525	108.1	416.9	-22.9	—	393.7	75

TABLE 30 (continued)

INTERNATIONAL MONETARY FUND: QUOTAS AND FUND HOLDINGS

(AS OF NOVEMBER 30, 1956)—(MILLIONS OF U.S. DOLLARS)

	QUOTA	SUBSCRIPTION		REPURCHASES ON SUBSCRIPTION ACCOUNT	NET MEMBER DRAWINGS	FUND HOLDINGS OF MEMBER CURRENCIES	
		Gold Tranche	Member Currency			(U.S. Dollars)	(In % of Quota)
24. Germany (F.R.)	330	33.0	297.0	−45.1	−4.4	247.5	75
25. Greece	40	—	—	—	—	—	—
26. Guatemala	5	1.3	3.7	—	—	3.7	75
27. Haiti	2	.5	1.5	—	—	1.5	75
28. Honduras	2.5	.6	1.9	—	—	1.9	75
29. Iceland	1	.2	.8	—	—	.8	75
30. India	400	27.5	372.5	—	—	372.5	93
31. Indonesia	110	15.5	94.5	−12.0	55.0	137.5	125
32. Iran	35	8.8	26.2	—	25.3	51.5	147
33. Iraq	8	—	8.0	—	—	8.0	100
34. Israel	4.5	1.1	3.4	—	—	3.4	75
35. Italy	180	—	—	—	—	—	—
36. Japan	250	62.5	187.5	—	—	187.5	75
37. Jordan	3	.1	2.9	—	—	2.9	97
38. Korea, Rep. of	12.5	3.1	—	—	—	—	—
39. Lebanon	4.5	.2	4.3	−.9	—	3.4	75
40. Luxembourg	10	.5	9.5	—	—	9.5	95
41. Mexico	90	22.5	67.5	—	—	67.5	75
42. Netherlands	275	68.8	206.2	—	—	206.2	75
43. Nicaragua	7.5	1.9	5.6	—	—	5.6	75
44. Norway	50	12.5	37.5	—	—	37.5	75
45. Pakistan	100	3.5	96.5	—	—	96.5	96
46. Panama	.5	.1	.4	—	—	.4	75

TABLE 30 (continued)

INTERNATIONAL MONETARY FUND: QUOTAS AND FUND HOLDINGS

(AS OF NOVEMBER 30, 1956)—(MILLIONS OF U.S. DOLLARS)

	QUOTA	SUBSCRIPTION Gold Tranche	SUBSCRIPTION Member Currency	REPURCHASES ON SUBSCRIPTION ACCOUNT	NET MEMBER DRAWINGS	FUND HOLDINGS OF MEMBER CURRENCIES (U.S. Dollars)	FUND HOLDINGS OF MEMBER CURRENCIES (In % of Quota)
47. Paraguay	3.5	.9	2.6	—	2.0	4.6	132
48. Peru	25	3.2	21.8	-3.1	—	18.7	75
49. Philippines	15	3.8	11.2	—	15.0	26.2	175
50. Sweden	100	17.0	83.0	-8.0	—	75.0	75
51. Syria	6.5	.2	6.3	-1.4	—	4.9	75
52. Thailand	12.5	3.1	—	—	—	—	—
53. Turkey	43	10.8	32.2	—	15.0	47.1	110
54. Union of South Africa	100	25.0	75.0	—	—	75.0	75
55. United Kingdom	1,300	236.3	1,063.7	-3.7	—	1,063.5	82
56. United States	2,750	687.5	2,062.5	90.0	-418.0	1,693.4	62
57. Uruguay	15	—	—	—	—	—	—
58. Venezuela	15	3.8	11.2	—	—	11.2	75
59. Viet-Nam	12.5	3.1	—	—	—	—	—
60. Yugoslavia	60	7.9	52.1	—	9.0	61.2	102
Total	8,928.5	1,656.8	6,335.3(a)	-36.5	-178.1	6,082.4(a)	

Note: (a) An additional "Income and Expenditures" entry of − $38.3 is necessary to account for the balance of the difference between $6,335.3 and $6,082.4.

Source: *International Financial Statistics*, February, 1957, p. 4.

Fund should waive its rule limiting the amount of borrowing possible on the part of one of the members, and also (b) whether the Fund should limit the borrowing of a member on the ground that it "is using the resources of the Fund in a manner contrary to the purposes of the Fund." Thus the Fund agreement did provide for a certain favoritism to creditors and for some moderate fluctuation in the vote of different countries.

If one is something of a nationalist and worries about the ability of the United States to control or influence the operation of the Fund, there is reason for complacency about all this. If one is rather more interested in making the Fund a viable instrument in a troubled world and desirous of having it acquire stature as a genuinely impartial international agency, there is cause for concern that the Fund should carry the stigma of United States domination.

There was much arguing, and certainly a lot of misgiving, at the time of the conference with regard to this United States dominance. But, one might say, the other counties were beggars, and beggars could not be choosers. (They wanted to make small contributions.) The United States was willing to pay one third of the money in exchange for one third of the vote. Fair enough, one might say; the Fund needed the money. But if the United States and the rest of the world really wanted the Fund to work as a genuine international agency, power should have been more dispersed. The population of the world is something like 2,400,000,000, and the population of the United States, 160,000,000. The rest of the world cannot be expected to regard the Fund as genuinely serving world interests when it is effectively dominated by 7 per cent of the world population. Nor can the rest of the world expect anything else unless it is willing to carry a far larger proportion of the financial burden of the organization.

Whether the foregoing considerations were an important influence on the Russian decision not to participate in the Fund is uncertain. Surely there was another important element present influencing her decision. The reluctance of the countries in the Russian orbit to participate in the Fund[1] is indicated in part by the following statement by the Czech Klement Gottwald:[2] ". . . the direction that our foreign trade will take ought to be determined in a way that will assure us as large permanent markets for our goods as possible at the same time that they assure us of permanent sources for our essential imports in order that we may be independent of the effects of economic fluctuations and of crises." Russia,

[1] Poland and Czechoslovakia did adhere to the Fund originally. Poland withdrew from the Fund when she finally withdrew from the International Bank in a huff over her failure to obtain a loan—see Chapter 28. Czechoslovakia was expelled from the Fund, December 31, 1954.

[2] Guy Braibant, *La Planification en Tchecoslovaquie*, p. 97.

for her part, has also objected to having her monetary system tied to the "unpredictable" and "unstable" dollar and to having her economic system tied to the "unstable," capitalistic economic system of the United States. Thus the Russians seem to have had two different sorts of qualms about the Fund. From the political angle, they did not relish United States domination; and from the economic angle, they did not wish to tie the Soviet economic system in any way to that of the United States.

The term subscription is applied to the actual sums of money which are paid in by the member countries. Part of the subscription is in gold (the gold tranche), and part is in the currency of the paying country. Each country pays in gold either 25 per cent of its subscription or 10 per cent of its net official holdings of gold and United States dollars, whichever is smaller. As a result the Fund has received, paid in gold, a sum considerably less than 25 per cent of the subscriptions, $1,657 million out of $7,992 million as of November 30, 1956. The balance of the subscription is paid in by the member government in its own currency; there is consequently no problem of ability to pay so far as over three fourths of the subscription is concerned. In effect what the Fund actually obtains is drawing rights or the right "to write checks" against francs in France, or pounds sterling in England, or dollar balances in the United States, to the amount of the balance of the subscriptions. The Fund has then in its coffers something over a billion and a half in gold plus slightly over $6 billion in a combination of francs, pesos, and other currencies. Of this latter sum, the $2 billion in United States dollars is currently useful. Most of the rest is not.

These subscriptions would correspond exactly with the quotas except for the provision that there may be a "little" delay in paying the money. A country is not obligated to pay in its subscription until its exchange rate is fixed, and there has been some delay in fixing the currency par values of several of the members. Consequently, the total of the subscriptions in 1956 was not identical with the total of the quotas for Afghanistan, Argentina, China, Greece, Israel, Italy, Korea, Thailand, Uruguay, and Viet-Nam.

"Borrowing" and "Lending"

The resources derived from the subscriptions provide much of the working capital of the Fund; but it was not envisaged that the Fund would be able to conduct all of its operations with the resources derived from the original subscriptions.

Let us say that the European countries are all interested in making use of the Fund's resources in order to finance the purchase of goods in the United States, and that the Fund exhausts its supply of dollars. (This would have been the situation in the immediate post-World War II period, if free currency convertibility at Fund pars had been immediately established.) The question then becomes what can the Fund do to obtain more dollars, the currency in demand? The Fund may (a) seek to borrow dollars from the United States or (b) it may sell some of its billion-and-a-half in gold for dollars. The country in question (the United States) may or may not co-operate in lending its currency to the Fund; but it is required by the articles of agreement to sell its currency for gold. It is probable that the lack of power to force a loan is far more important than the power to buy with gold. The latter power is not in doubt, anyway.

If it fails to obtain a loan and does not have enough gold, what does the Fund do if it is exhausting its supply of a currency? When the situation becomes acute enough, it may declare the currency "scarce." This is a technical process. A currency is not necessarily a "scarce" one merely because everyone is out of it; it is a scarce currency because the Fund has declared it so. For example, the United States dollar has not been a scarce currency in this technical sense in the post-World War II period. The declaration that a currency is scarce means that the available supply may be rationed or allotted by the Fund among the countries that want it. At the same time, if the Fund declares the currency scarce and rations what is available, the Fund may also permit the countries that want the scarce currency to establish internal exchange control. If these developments should occur the Fund has failed, at least temporarily, to fulfill part of its stated purpose: the avoidance of exchange control and currency rationing affecting transactions on current account. But such problems are a concern of the future. At present countries cannot "get back into" this condition because they have never gotten out of it. The period of post-World War II transition, which was originally provided for in the articles of agreement and which permitted the continuance of the then-existing exchange controls, has become somewhat prolonged. In 1956, forty-seven of the fifty-nine members of the Fund were still availing themselves of the right to use such "transitional" arrangements.[3]

Nevertheless, it is probably better to have an international agency supervising the exchange controls that are in operation and continually pressuring governments to ameliorate them. This is better than the situation of the 1930's, when governments were trying to serve selfish national interests as selfishly as they could in a setting where there was no voice of conscience whispering in their ear.

In the process of trying to maintain the par value of its currency, and before any of the above-mentioned Draconian measures have been used, the government whose currency needs support may borrow, under certain conditions, from the Fund.

To get a little ahead of the story, the individual nation is instructed

[3] International Monetary Fund, *Seventh Annual Report, Exchange Restrictions,* p. 1.

by the articles of agreement of the Fund to maintain the value of the currency within 1 per cent of par. This is an obligation of the member government and not of the Fund. In doing this, governments essentially operate now with stablization funds, a procedure that was discussed in Chapter 20. The Bank of France or the Bank of England, or whatever agency is in charge of the process in the different countries, has a stabilization fund; and if the exchange rate is threatening to change more than 1 per cent from par, that agency is obligated to go on to the foreign-exchange market and buy or sell to keep the value near par.[4] But to do this, its own resources may not be sufficient. In that case, it may borrow from the International Monetary Fund to obtain the foreign exchange it needs to sell to its own citizens in exchange for its own currency, in order to maintain the rate within the limits specified. This operation is the heart of the Fund's functions.

The Fund, then, may provide the foreign exchange that the individual nation needs to keep the exchange rate near par. The Fund has almost $8 billion in gold and a variety of currencies (the subscriptions) which it may use for this purpose. It has not yet supplemented these resources by extensive borrowing of its own. Dollars now are the major currency in demand. The Fund has about $2 billion in dollars and a billion-and-a-half in gold, making working resources of over $3.5 billion, given present conditions, instead of $8 billion. The Fund might use its resources of dollars and lend them to the French, if France were the country running short of dollars. And the Fund has loaned $65.5 million to Brazil—that is, the fund bought $65.5 million worth of cruzeiros with dollars. This operation is designated by a plus sign under "Net Member Drawings" in Table 30 to indicate that the Fund is "purchasing" cruzeiros. That same transaction is entered again and is probably part of the minus $418 million entered opposite the United States. The Fund uses the minus to designate that it is "selling" the dollars.

As a deterrent to a country's borrowing more than is necessary (larger purchases of other currencies than the Fund feels is desirable), the Fund has a system of fees, and if a government borrows (sells its currency for some other currency) more and more, the rates of the fees that the Fund charges get higher and higher. The rates also get higher as the length of time that the loans are outstanding gets longer. Such charges vary from virtually nothing up to a current maximum of 5 per cent.

The articles of agreement also established quantitative limitations on the total amount of borrowing which a single country can do.[5] The over-all limitation on this type of operation is that the Fund's holdings of a

---

[4] Or it would be if the Fund actually were operating in the conditions envisaged by the articles of agreement.

[5] Unless a special vote, in which the representatives of creditor countries would have an enlarged voice, permitted increased borrowing.

member country's currency may not exceed 200 per cent of its quota. According to Table 30, in November, 1956, the Fund held 175 per cent of the Philippine, Burmese, and El Salvadorean quotas. Those were the largest figures. It may be recalled that the Fund already holds a quantity of each member's currency somewhere between 75 per cent and 100 per cent of its quota as a result of the original subscriptions. In consequence, the total amount of "lending" permitted to an individual member is roughly, or slightly less than, 125 per cent of the quota.

Also within the framework of the over-all 200 per cent limitation there is an additional limitation on how much borrowing a country may do in a given year. Such borrowing is limited, under ordinary circumstances, to 25 per cent of the country's quota.

Whether this approach is good is doubtful. A country will have sudden need of considerable foreign exchange, if it needs any, to meet an exchange crisis. It does not need a little dribble this year and a little dribble the next. Crises do not get 20 per cent worse every year for five years (assuming total borrowing permitted is 125 per cent of the quota, at 25 per cent a year the process can go on for five years). It is probably a mistake to restrict the judgment of the Fund officials with this limitation and the over-all 200 per cent limitation, even though those ceilings could be lifted in a vote somewhat stacked with creditor country representation—and in several cases the 25 per cent limitation on the annual drawing rights has been waived.

On the whole, since the end of World War II, lending by the Fund has been limited. This limitation seemingly has been justified by Fund officials on the theory that the Fund simply did not have the resources to deal with the terrific postwar maladjustments and would do better not to try—but rather to allow extensive currency devaluations and a temporary continuation of the exchange restrictions. Then it was hoped that if and when a reasonably stable set of conditions had come into existence, the Fund could thereafter use its resources more freely.

Exchange Rates

World War II, added to the exchange controls of the 1930's, had made the exchange rates of 1945 quite artificial as an expression of the relative values of the currencies. Yet the International Monetary Fund was, immediately upon its organization, faced with the problem of determining what the new par rates of exchange should be. The articles of agreement, subject to certain limitations, have given the Fund power to determine what foreign-exchange rates should be. But what kind of criterion should the Fund use? Certain vocal groups alleged that, imperfect as it might be, the only usable formula was the purchasing power parity criterion. But if the Fund were to use this approach, it would have to wait a year or two or three to set the rates, until such time as the countries had removed their rationing systems and price controls and allowed internal prices to seek their levels. Only after that would it be possible to set the foreign-exchange rates that would represent the change in relative purchasing power that had occurred since 1939 (or perhaps since 1929). The Fund apparently decided that it was better not to wait, that it was desirable to have precisely determined exchange rates immediately. Having reached that decision, they could not use the purchasing power parity criterion; and, on the whole, the exchange rates were confirmed at the artificial levels then prevailing. The process worked somewhat as follows: The Fund, after consultation with the government concerned, in most cases set the rate at the level prevailing sixty days before the entry into force of the agreement. Consequently, the rates which went into effect initially were, for the most part, the rates which were prevailing on October 28, 1945.

The Fund was well enough aware that these rates were artificial and would have to be changed. In its subsequent annual reports, it expressed repeatedly its willingness to consider requests for changes in exchange rates.

Handling by the Fund of the problem of exchange-rate changes takes place in the framework of certain rules laid down in the articles of agreement. Those articles obligate member governments to consult with the Fund before undertaking any devaluation. The old unilateral devaluations of the 1930's were presumably outlawed. For a devaluation of any magnitude to be legal under the articles of agreement, the government desiring to devalue must allege a "fundamental disequilibrium." The Fund then studies the situation, decides whether to allow the devaluation, and if so, how much it may be.[6] If a member changes the par value of its currency despite the objection of the Fund, the member shall subsequently be ineligible to use the resources of the Fund, unless the Fund decides otherwise.

If the Fund is to be at all effective in the long run, of course, the countries must abide by the articles of agreement and devalue only with the permission of the Fund. But some poor precedents have already been set. France and Mexico have flaunted the Fund by devaluing without previous permission; and the Fund has approved their devaluations ex post facto.

[6] The provisions of the Articles of Agreement actually read:

"If the proposed change, together with all previous changes, whether increases or decreases,

(i) does not exceed ten percent of the initial par value, the Fund shall raise no objection;

(ii) does not exceed a further ten percent of the initial par value, the Fund may either concur or object, but shall declare its attitude within seventy-two hours if the member so requests;

(iii) is not within (i) or (ii) above, the Fund may either concur or object, but shall be entitled to a longer period in which to declare its attitude."

The crux of the theoretical question as to whether this kind of an arrangement ever could work centers around the meaning of "fundamental disequilibrium." The articles of agreement merely state that a fundamental disequilibrium is to be taken as the justification for devaluation, but the term itself is not defined in the articles of agreement. What can the expression mean, or what must the Fund take it to mean, when the question arises whether devaluation will be allowed? One likely criterion is to look at the gold and foreign-exchange reserves, and if the country is losing them rapidly or is about to run out of them, to say that is evidence of fundamental disequilibrium and allow devaluation.[7] But this involves an assumption that the balance of trade will be improved by devaluation and that the reserves of gold and foreign exchange consequently will be built up again. The validity of that argument is dependent on factors discussed in Chapter 19. Suffice it to say here that this is not a result that can be counted on with certainty. Therefore, even if a condition exists which the Fund will agree to call a fundamental disequilibrium, it does not necessarily follow that devaluation is the nostrum called for. But by and large, governments seem to assume that devaluation is the cure for loss of gold and foreign-exchange reserves, fundamental disequilibrium, and all other ills; and the Fund, upon occasion at least (in the British case), has also subscribed to this viewpoint.

It is also important to consider whether the loss of gold and foreign-exchange reserves is in any sense a valid criterion of fundamental disequilibrium. Loss of such reserves is a rather superficial phenomenon. What is the cause of such loss; what forces lie in the background to bring it about? Loss of reserves may occur as a result of conditions (1) that a government has caused by its own positive action, (2) that a government could have prevented but did not, or (3) that it could not control at all. Could one properly describe as fundamental disequilibrium any but the third of these possibilities?

To explore the nature of the problem: what developments might cause the loss of gold and foreign exchange?[8] Over and over situations develop where it is obvious that expansion of the amount of money and credit internally is a result of more-or-less conscious government policy; and that such policy lies at the root of an internal price rise of considerable magnitude, which has surely been an important factor in causing the loss of gold and foreign exchange because it has made foreign countries a relatively more attractive place in which to buy. Without the power to control the quantity of money and credit internally the Fund cannot control such situations; at the same time it seems, as a practical matter,

[7] These are the same questions that arose in connection with the meaning of a favorable and an unfavorable balance of payments on current account—questions which have been discussed in Chapters 16, 17, 18, and 19.

[8] See also the Mexican case study in Chapter 19.

that any government by its own action can create a situation which the Fund will be forced to call a fundamental disequilibrium.

The reasonableness of exchange rates has to be a function of the supply of money and credit in the different countries. And an agency that cannot control the supply of money and credit, in the final analysis, can have only a nominal power over exchange rates.

EUROPEAN PAYMENTS UNION

Some of the foregoing comments raise the prospect of long-run difficulties which will almost certainly confront the International Monetary Fund. But there were also certain problems in the years just after the war, of a more immediate nature, which the Fund was not equipped to handle. The Fund was supposed to supervise the removal of exchange restrictions on a world-wide basis. But in the late 1940's this process was delayed by the magnitude of the world maladjustment. Meanwhile, action was proposed on a more limited European basis, and the European Payments Union was the result. It was set up in 1950, with the approval of the Fund, to implement less restrictive measures among a limited group of European countries.

The Union is the creation of the Council of the Organization for European Economic Co-operation (the organization of the governments of western Europe which implements their side of the Marshall plan program). It is administered by the Bank for International Settlements of Basel. The members are the countries participating in the Marshall plan program.

The Union sets up the machinery for relative freedom of payments in connection with current transactions among the countries of western Europe. At least payment follows automatically if a goods transaction is licensed. It also makes provision for liquidating long-term debt under certain circumstances.

The European Payments Union keeps books and functions somewhat as a clearing house, although it does not handle the financing of individual transactions. In this role it goes farther in facilitating international payments than does the Fund. Operations, under the revised European Payments Union agreement, beginning August 1, 1955, may be summarized as follows: [9]

(1) At the end of the month each member reports the bilateral end-of-month balances of its monetary area with other members and their monetary areas to the Agent (Bank for International Settlements). The Agent establishes a net surplus or deficit for

[9] *International Financial Statistics*, November, 1955, p. 13.

each member. (2) These net surpluses or deficits are settled three quarters by gold payments and one quarter by credit extended to or by the EPU. Debtors, however, may if they wish, settle fully in gold. Maximum limits have been established to which any member's claim on EPU, or its debt to EPU can rise. . . . The amount that a creditor country will, in case of need, make available to EPU, is equal to that country's maximum credit limit as a creditor minus the amount of credit already outstanding. Similarly, the amount of credit available to a debtor country is equal to that country's maximum credit limit as a debtor minus its already outstanding debt to EPU. (3) Deficits falling outside the established limits are settled fully in gold, and surpluses in excess of the established limits are settled in accordance with *ad hoc* arrangements between the Union and the country concerned.

The unused borrowing rights, etc., are indicated in Table 31.

At first Germany was the country doing considerable importing and making extensive use of her drawing rights. Then England rather than

TABLE 31

EUROPEAN PAYMENTS UNION SETTLEMENTS

(IN MILLIONS OF U.S. DOLLARS)

	NET SURPLUS OR DEFICIT OF EPU COUNTRIES' TRANS- ACTIONS WITH EACH OTHER DURING 1955	POSITION AFTER NOVEMBER, 1956, SETTLEMENT	
		Member's Claim on (+) or Debt to (−) the Union	Unused Borrowing Rights to Debtors
Austria	−78.8	2.8	—
Belgium-Luxembourg	162.0	187.3	—
Denmark	−41.9	−92.1	34.0
France	131.9	−209.3	140.5
Germany	360.8	688.1	—
Greece	52.8	—	—
Iceland	−3.4	−5.4	4.4
Italy	−190.6	−154.3	50.7
Netherlands	64.8	112.5	—
Norway	−46.1	−90.7	36.7
Portugal	−44.0	—	42.0
Sweden	−16.4	9.5	—
Switzerland	−67.6	76.1	—
Turkey	−41.0	−30.0	nil
United Kingdom and Ireland	−231.1	−350.0	324.8
Totals	+772.3 −760.9	+1,076.4 −931.7	

Source: *International Financial Statistics,* February, 1957, p. 13.

Germany became the problem child. England is a special problem in the Union anyway because of her position as a large short-term debtor. More recently France has become a major borrower and Germany the most important creditor. All in all, it may be a good sign that the identity of the problem children has changed from time to time.

Be that as it may, there does exist a European Payments Union, which presumably is relatively temporary, which operates with a modified gold standard technique, which serves to some extent as a clearing house, and which has no control over the internal credit policies of the member countries. Thus the European Payments Union, even in its limited area of operations, does not face up to the basic weaknesses which are likely to cause trouble for the International Monetary Fund. These difficulties, as is so frequently the case, are likely to be insurmountable in a world of nations still insistent on defending all their sovereign rights. They would likely prove to be of very minor importance in a more stable and orderly world where each nation of its own volition, and because of its desire to make the international economy work, took appropriate domestic action.

CURRENT PAYMENTS SITUATION

It is difficult to do justice to the complexity of the current world payments situation in a few paragraphs.

The United States has, since the end of World War II, financed a large export trade balance with a combination of grants and loans, chiefly grants. The war-damaged countries of western Europe have been desperate for consumer goods and capital equipment. They have obtained much from the United States and would have liked to obtain more. This circumstance is largely responsible for the prevalence of the term *dollar shortage* during the last ten years.

British financial relations involve several facets: (1) relations with the United States, (2) relations with the rest of the Sterling Area, and (3) relations with the rest of the European Payments Union. Financial relations with the rest of the world have not evolved in an entirely satisfactory manner since the end of the war. In terms of relations with the United States, Britain has shown almost continual alarm over lack of reserves. One aim in the devaluation of 1949 was to build up dollar reserves. There are still sporadic alarms with regard to the adequacy of Britain's dollar reserves, which totaled $543 million on December 31, 1955, by comparison with $818 million on December 31, 1952.[10] Britain continues to import substantially more from the United States than she

[10] These are the short-term liabilities to foreigners reported by banks in the United States in the *Federal Reserve Bulletin*.

exports to the United States. Some of the discrepancy has been financed by the United States aid program. But the explanation of most of the financing involves the relation of Britain and the United States to the Sterling Area. Britain has an export balance with the rest of the Sterling Area. And the rest of the Sterling Area has an export balance (cacao, tin, rubber, wool) with the United States. In the early days of the European Payments Union, the British were in a fairly strong financial position by comparison with the other members. But more recently, as was mentioned above, Britain has become one of the chief deficit countries in relation to the Union.

But in spite of various problems the British financial position could be much worse. True, Britain has been under pressure to make major structural adjustments because of the considerable liquidation of her foreign investments which occurred during and after World War II and the consequent loss of income. She has also suffered some loss in earnings on services, and her terms of trade have worsened since the war. But in spite of this, there has not been substantial price inflation in England; and the balance of payments has not been under the impossible pressure that has affected certain other countries.

France, for example, has been under greater pressure than Britain. There has been a major amount of internal price inflation in France; and this pressure added to the basic goods scarcity in the country after the war has led to a depreciation of the French franc from 29 to the dollar in 1937 to 350 to the dollar in 1956. France is still in difficulty; the financing of the wars in Indo-China and North Africa has contributed mightily to the continuing monetary inflation. And France in 1956 is a major deficit country in relation to the European Payments Union.

By contrast with Britain and France, the victors of World War II, the defeated country of Germany has enjoyed a positive economic resurgence. In 1946 and 1947, Germany was in ruins. The United States has aided Germany to the extent of some $4 billion since the war. Having undergone an effective monetary reform in 1948, Germany has had no marked price inflation since. German industry has developed apace. Germany (perhaps aided by the "surplus army" of unemployed refugees) has succeeded in holding the wage level down. German costs continue low in consequence. And German exports are competing effectively in world markets. There is no balance of payments pressure on Germany; on the contrary, she is the largest creditor of the European Payments Union.

Grouping the countries of western Europe, it may be generalized that production has revived swiftly and is at levels far higher than those of pre-World War II days. "Industrial production in Europe is at present 70 per cent, and the volume of European exports more than 70 per cent, above prewar." [11] The desperate situation that characterized the immedi-

[11] *International Financial News Survey,* November 25, 1955, p. 173.

ate postwar years is over. Countries can expect to have occasional balance of payments crises in the future because of sporadic difficulties. But the only countries in real, chronic difficulty are those that are experiencing major price inflation at home. A phase, the postwar phase, of balance of payments history, which might be called the dollar shortage phase, is coming to a close—or has already come to a close.

By contrast with Europe, most of the underdeveloped countries of the world suffered little or no wartime damage. In fact, they built up large foreign-exchange reserves during the war, chiefly by sales to the United States and Britain. But since the war, almost to a man, they have financed extensive development programs by financial measures that have led to major amounts of price inflation. They have used up their large backlogs of foreign-exchange reserves, and many of them have engaged in extensive currency devaluations and foreign-exchange control arrangements in recent years.

The countries in the Soviet sphere do not have overt balance of payments difficulties. But trade and production patterns have been dislocated by the reduction in trade between eastern and western Europe. Part of the "dollar shortage" has really been a Ukrainian wheat shortage; and the Russian trade pattern is not what it would be if she could buy more machinery in the West.

But, on the whole, conditions have improved to the point where a major effort to establish currency convertibility and price comparability may well be worth trying.

Chapter 23

POLICIES: TENABLE INTERNATIONAL ARRANGEMENTS IN THE FIELD OF MONEY

🐦 🐦 🐦

There needs to be international agreement as to which policies will be used to deal with which problems.

If nations continue to adopt policies at the random pleasure of each independent nation, they will continue to create problems which are incapable of solution with the policies available to other nations.

Various possible policy combinations might be workable; but it is necessary to select one by agreement and stick with it.

It is suggested that countries deal with the problem of internal depression with the tools of financial policy and that they deal with the problem of international disequilibrium with flexible exchange rates or with an international currency.

An international currency would not solve all problems, but it could work in a fashion that would suppress the overt manifestation of various of the international balance of payments problems.

There are problems in the financial relations between New York and New Jersey, but they do not operate to require devaluation of the New Jersey dollar in relation to the New York dollar.

The problems that emerge in this changed situation are the far more important problems (more important than exchange disequilibrium) —for example, the problem of facing up to the financial and credit policies that influence the differential rate of growth as between different areas.

🐦 🐦 🐦

THE PURPOSE of this chapter is to draw together some of the arguments developed in preceding chapters and to attempt to obtain a comprehensive picture of the factors affecting the tenability of exchange rates. In conclusion, certain utopian recommendations as to policy are made. The chapter is a continuation of the effort which was begun in Chapter 15 to develop a combination of policies which would contribute to a viable, growing world economy. Description of this pattern of policies is concluded in Chapter 36.

TOOLS

In Chapter 15, certain policy tools were considered:

    I. Fiscal policies,
    II. Prices (not including exchange-rate change), and
    III. Commercial policy measures (including the use of discrimination).

The present discussion assumes that a somewhat greater range of tools is available:

    I. Financial policies
        A. Fiscal policies
        B. Monetary policies
    II. Price Policies
        A. Subsidy to ameliorate price fluctuations
        B. Wage rates
        C. Foreign-exchange rates
    III. Commercial policies (including use of discrimination)
        A. Tariffs and subsidies on exports and imports
        B. Quotas, licenses, and other quantitative controls.

Presumably (and with suitable qualifications for special circumstances), decrease in taxes (accompanied by no change in government spending) would increase national income and consequently increase imports relative to exports; also, an increase in government spending (taxes remaining the same) would increase income and imports relative to exports. Expansion in the supply of money and credit would increase imports relative to exports. Higher money wage rates would increase imports relative to exports. And commercial policy measures will tend to affect the balance of trade, one way or the other, directly. Thus, lower tariffs would tend to increase imports.

SELECTION OF POLICIES

It was concluded in Chapter 15: (1) that if deviation from the competitive situation is desirable it should involve chiefly use of the production subsidy; (2) that price comparability is desirable in the interest of intelligent planning; and (3) that the use of commercial measures, such as tariffs and quotas, is undesirable and that discrimination in general is undesirable.

The chief new facet added to the situation in Part V is the possibility of conflict between stable foreign-exchange rates and economic prosperity in all countries simultaneously. The chief new tool is the possibility of fluctuating foreign-exchange rates.

Several tables which were developed by J. E. Meade are used to illustrate the nature of the difficulties involved in policy selection. Table 32

TABLE 32

CONFLICTS OF CRITERIA FOR INFLATIONARY AND DEFLATIONARY FINANCIAL POLICIES

NATIONAL IN-COME IN THE SURPLUS (EXPORT BALANCE) COUNTRY	NATIONAL IN-COME IN THE DEFICIT (IMPORT BALANCE) COUNTRY	IN THE INTERESTS OF		
		EXTERNAL BALANCE	INTERNAL BALANCE IN THE SURPLUS COUNTRY	INTERNAL BALANCE IN THE DEFICIT COUNTRY
Is too low (L) or *too high (H)*		*There should be an inflation (S+) or deflation (S−) of domestic expenditure in the surplus country and an inflation (D+) or deflation (D−) of domestic expenditure in the deficit country.*		
(a)	(b)	(c)	(d)	(e)
L	L	S+ D−	S+ D+	S+ D+
	H	S+ D−	S+ D+	S− D−
H	L	S+ D−	S− D−	S+ D+
	H	S+ D−	S− D−	S− D−

Source: J. E. Meade, *The Balance of Payments*, p. 117. Reprinted with the kind permission of the Oxford University Press and the Royal Institute of International Affairs.

summarizes the financial policy situation. The table indicates the effect on the balance of trade of expansionary (Meade uses the term inflationary) and contractive (deflationary) financial measures in the surplus and deficit countries. It is evident that financial measures alone cannot solve all of the various problems.

Table 33 indicates by similar means the impact of price adjustment policies—which may include foreign-exchange rate changes. Again, it is clear that price adjustments alone cannot be counted on to solve all of the various problems.

TABLE 33
CONFLICTS OF CRITERIA FOR PRICE-ADJUSTMENT POLICIES

NATIONAL IN-COME IN THE SURPLUS COUNTRY	NATIONAL IN-COME IN THE DEFICIT COUNTRY	EXTERNAL BALANCE	INTERNAL BALANCE IN THE SURPLUS COUNTRY	INTERNAL BALANCE IN THE DEFICIT COUNTRY
Is too low (L) *or* *too high (H)*		*There should be a rise ($S'+$) or fall ($S'-$) of money costs in the surplus country and a rise ($D'+$) or fall ($D'-$) of money costs in the deficit country.*		
(a)	(b)	(c)	(d)	(e)
L	L	$S'+$ $D'-$	$S'-$ $D'+$	$S'+$ $D'-$
	H	$S'+$ $D'-$	$S'-$ $D'+$	$S'-$ $D'+$
H	L	$S'+$ $D'-$	$S'+$ $D'-$	$S'+$ $D'-$
	H	$S'+$ $D'-$	$S'+$ $D'-$	$S'-$ $D'+$

Source: J. E. Meade, *Balance of Payments*, p. 154. Reprinted with the kind permission of the Oxford University Press and the Royal Institute of International Affairs.

Table 34, however, is intended to show how a judicious combination of financial and price policies may be used to solve all the problems. One clear-cut decision has to be made at the international level and cannot be left to the individual nations to make haphazardly. It is the decision as to whether (1) financial policy will be used for the preservation of internal balance, and price adjustment for the preservation of external balance, or (2) price adjustment will be used for the preservation of internal balance, and financial policy for the preservation of external balance. Once one or the other procedure is generally agreed upon, the individual nations may proceed independently (and as much decentralized initiative as possible is desirable) to take a variety of measures to fight domestic depression or rectify disequilibrium in the balance of payments. The use of financial policy to effect internal balance and of price adjustment to effect external balance is the more desirable of the alternatives.

The use of financial policy to effect internal balance means that fiscal policy measures, such as deficit financing and monetary policy measures that will expand credit, will be used to fight an internal depression. It

TABLE 34

RECONCILIATION OF CRITERIA FOR FINANCIAL AND
PRICE-ADJUSTMENT POLICIES

NATIONAL IN- COME IN THE SURPLUS COUNTRY *Is too low (L) or too high (H)*	NATIONAL IN- COME IN THE DEFICIT COUNTRY	THE SYMBOLS s$+$, s$'+$, s$-$, s$'-$, D$+$, D$'+$, D$-$ AND D$'-$ HAVE THE SAME MEANINGS AS IN THE PRECEDING ILLUSTRATIONS. *Only those instances are marked in this illustration in which the authorities in the country concerned should take the action indicated in the interests of both the internal and the external balance of that country.*		
(a)	(b)	(c)	(d)	(e)
L	L	S$+$ D$'-$	S$+$	D$'-$
	H	S$+$ D$-$	S$+$	D$-$
H	L	S$'+$ D$'-$	S$'+$	D$'-$
	H	S$'+$ D$-$	S$'+$	D$-$

Source: J. E. Meade, *Balance of Payments,* p. 156. Reprinted with the kind permission of the Oxford University Press and the Royal Institute of International Affairs.

also means that commercial policy measures, such as tariffs, quotas, and licenses, will not be used for this purpose. In the face of an internal depression, there is going to be much less institutional resistance to policies which expand the amount of money and credit and income than there would be to policies which emphasized price and wage cutting.

The use of price adjustment to effect external balance may require somewhat more justification. It is not intended here to defend all possible types of price adjustment. For example, it is not desirable to use wage reductions as a device for lowering production costs applicable to exports and for improving the competitive position of a country's exports. It is not desirable, if it is at all avoidable, to fight a depression with a policy which makes sacrifice by the working man the instrument of recovery. But since there are alternative price adjustment policies, one is not limited to wage adjustment. When price adjustment is used to effect external balance, the alternative of shifting foreign-exchange rates is added to the alternative of price and wage adjustment. And (at least in the absence of an international currency) it is freely fluctuating foreign-exchange rates which are the desirable solution to the problem of external balance.

BASIC SITUATIONS

This sweeping generalization, however, should be qualified somewhat by consideration of special conditions that may exist under various circumstances. The basic situations in which balance of payments difficulties may arise were identified in Chapter 17 as being: (1) short-run (speculative, flight of capital, and catastrophic) difficulties, (2) business cycles, and (3) economic growth, which involves also the possibility of chronic shortage of one currency.

Short-run (*Speculative, Flight of Capital, and Catastrophic*) Difficulties

Short-run difficulties present a real threat to balance of payments stability. Speculators influenced by a little "inside dope" (which is all too likely to be inaccurate), may, in a very short space of time, buy or sell so much of a currency as to cause a real problem. Legitimate, but non-economically motivated, flights of capital may also pose a real problem. Catastrophes, such as crop failures, earthquakes, and wars, may pose multitudinous problems on short notice.

As long as the foreign-exchange field offers a picture of set foreign-exchange rates or of "devaluations by fits and starts," it will offer a lush field for speculation. In order to control the speculators in such cases, monetary authorities need the power to deal directly (by police action if the power of suggestion does not work) with these people. The circumlocution involved in dealing with them by expensive countervailing exchange operations or fiscal or monetary policy measures is a lot of nonsense. If a speculator is selling a currency short in a manner that threatens to force devaluation under uncalled-for circumstances, thereby injuring many legitimate traders, the government should be able to prevent such behavior by direct action. It should not have to act indirectly by using its resources in an effort to buy up the currency the speculator is selling.

The problem posed by the flight of capital is more serious. It is a gross infringement of freedom of action to say that a Jewish refugee from Hitler cannot transfer his marks into dollars or pounds, even if it puts the mark under some strain. An international monetary authority must have the power to distinguish between this latter type of situation and the speculative type of situation. And yet, a realist may say with some justice that, at such time as it is possible to give such power to an international agency, dictatorships like that of Hitler will no longer be a menace to the freedom of people. I somehow do not believe this is quite true. An agency such as the International Monetary Fund, now, with very minor extension of authority, could be authorized to recognize such situations (when the United Nations officially declares—as it ought to do occasionally—that some government is not respecting human liberty) and the Fund could then sell to refugees from that country as much of any currency as they wanted in exchange for their home currency. The Fund might be stuck with some of the currency of a dictatorial government. But what of it? This type of action represents demand for the currencies of the "free" countries; so, there is no real problem on that side of the operation.

Probably war, as man has known it until now, calls for complete exchange controls, comprehensive direct controls and comprehensive discrimination, complete production guidance, complete distribution control, and a "ripsnorting" profits tax. Whether the great atomic war will call for anything besides weeping, wailing, and gnashing of teeth remains to be seen.

Lesser catastrophes, such as earthquakes and crop failures, undoubtedly call for a lot of short-lived controls—of which exchange control, direct trade controls, and discrimination might well be examples—and call for them promptly.

Business Cycles

The temptation is great to brush aside the business cycle problem rather cavalierly as a problem calling for the maintenance of full employment in the country where the depression begins. This is more or less what is meant when it is recommended that the problem of internal balance should be dealt with by the financial tools. If this approach is adopted, the other troubles that come and go as business cycles evolve will not be critical. (The remaining real problems would then be long-run change and catastrophes.)

Actually, in the initial stages of a depression the problem is rather simple. There is a tendency for declining income, unemployment, and declining imports to go together. For the most part, the policy tools a government is likely to use to build up income and employment will also build up imports. Deficit financing and the injection of additional money supply into the economy will do both. At this stage, planned currency devaluation should certainly be "verboten." But freely fluctuating rates should ease the difficulty if a legitimate balance of payments problem arises.

It is possible that a balance of payments disequilibrium may develop in spite of one country's best efforts. However, one may suspect that in a setting where the internal policies of most governments are successfully calculated to increase real income, the possibility of balance of payments difficulties resulting from business cycle fluctuations is minimized. In fact, as long as the expansionary policies are successful, there will not be depressions of a magnitude to occasion concern.[1]

[1] But given an institutional setting that permits depression and assuming that, if there is a real choice, a government ought to pick domestic expansion and full

Structural Change Related to Economic Growth
(Chronic Dollar Shortage)

For the most part, the problems in this area are slow in evolving; therefore, there is ample time for balance of payments adjustment. Certain possibilities connected with the "chronic shortage of a currency" were discussed in Chapter 19, but for the moment let us let the proposition rest with the allegation that slow change should not pose balance of payments problems—except in one case.

This case involves the effort arbitrarily to speed up slow change by substantial currency and credit inflation in the country that wants to develop. Such action, with the resulting substantial discrepancy in the purchasing power of different currencies, can create an impossible foreign-exchange situation. It is easy to say that development should not be financed this way (and the point will be discussed at greater length in Part VII). But if it has been done (in either a gold-standard or a stabilization-fund setting), the result may have to be exchange-rate change or exchange control and less trade.

FIXED VS. VARIABLE RATES

The chief advantage of fixed rates is rather obvious—the exporter or the importer would like to know ahead of time at what exchange rate a payment will be made. The trader will feel much more secure about engaging in international trade if he has such information and consequently knows how much he will actually pay or be paid in his own currency. The same is true of investors in foreign bonds.

But a person engaging in goods trade may protect himself against fluctuations in the foreign-exchange rate by forward exchange operations (if forward exchange operations are permitted). And a genuinely free foreign-exchange market and freely fluctuating rates would be infinitely preferable to the present system of "devaluation by fits and starts." Genuinely stable rates are desirable; but freely fluctuating rates are better than rates which are stable for a while and then subject to violent and unannounced change.

Under the gold standard in the days before World War I, without being forced by any treaty to do so, the countries of the world did submit themselves to far more objectionable outside controls than would be involved in making the international money and credit system viable. The gold

employment over balance of payments equilibrium: then, in a world that sets foreign-exchange rates by the use of the gold standard, stabilization funds, exchange control, or the present powers of the International Monetary Fund, balance of payments disequilibrium is possible—and either changed foreign-exchange rates or exchange control may be necessary.

standard, in some cases, obligated a country which was afflicted with a depression to take measures calculated to make the depression worse (i.e., contract credit), in the interest of maintaining the gold standard pars. And countries did it—shades of President Grover Cleveland! If nations were capable of such self-discipline fifty or seventy-five years ago, is it unrealistic now to expect nations to accept any abridgment of sovereignty in order to make the international monetary system work? We have come to a time when the world, to function satisfactorily, must function as an organic whole. No country is going to be allowed any longer to try to solve its own problems in a way calculated to leave the rest of the world in a worse situation. Hereafter, consideration must be given to the impact of each country's problems and their attempted solution on the rest of the world.

The gold standard is not and will not be again a satisfactory instrument. Under nineteenth-century conditions, in a setting involving the bankers of only five or six countries, it had a chance. Given present attitudes and forty or fifty separate monetary systems to reckon with, it could only be the instrument of a series of devaluations "by fits and starts." The same is true of the stabilization-fund approach. Exchange controls, on the other hand, are workable enough in a certain sense. But they tend to be the complicated, cumbersome instruments of poor planning.

FREELY FLUCTUATING RATES AND AN INTERNATIONAL CURRENCY

The important alternatives are freely fluctuating rates and an international currency. The nationalist who wants no world planning of his country's affairs should endorse the idea of freely fluctuating rates. They represent the only tenable arrangement in a setting where different countries are pursuing different credit policies and consequently experiencing marked differences in their price-level changes. If self-styled realists are correct in believing that nations will not tolerate international interference with their internal money-supply arrangements, freely fluctuating rates are the desirable alternative to devaluations "by fits and starts" and the attendant monetary chaos and sporadic balance-of-payments disequilibriums. J. E. Meade endorses the idea of a free foreign-exchange market very seriously, following his devastating criticism of rate setting via the adjustable pegs of stabilization funds.[2] He believes a workable arrangement would combine a free exchange market, a well-organized forward exchange market, and an internationally controlled exchange equalization fund. But this fund, instead of holding exchange rates at a predetermined

[2] Meade, *Balance of Payments,* p. 231.

figure by buying and selling currencies, would function chiefly to provide short-term funds in the emergency type of situation discussed earlier. The fund would not be a necessary feature of a system of freely fluctuating rates, but it would probably be a very desirable one.

Now I shall briefly plead more seriously the case for an international currency. Since a workable international currency will necessarily involve general control over money supply in different countries, I must first attempt to justify an arrangement involving international control—to some extent—of money-supply creation in the different countries.[3]

Access to the goods of the world cannot permanently be entrusted to the backhanded operation of internal, autarchic credit creation, which temporarily may increase imports but soon leads to exhaustion of foreign-exchange reserves and to either devaluation or the reduction of the quantity of trade. This is not to say that all credit extension, down to $10 consumer loans, should be subject to direct and specific control by an international agency. We have and shall continue to have with us the complex and everchanging problem of using judgment in deciding which specific decisions should be made centrally and which ones need not be.

One failure of the gold standard was that it did not make any allowance for special situations. Consequent on a gold outflow, the supply of money and credit should be contracted. Period! But what is needed is a flexible control that can make allowance for special problems in different regions, and such a control must perforce be international. It is the rough general decision as to the total amount of credit to be made available in different regions (or, even more especially, the enforcement of high standards in determining who gets it and for what purposes) which needs to be internationally made—and, very likely, that is all.

But if this much can be done, it is also possible to go one step farther and make a purely technical and administrative change, which will make life on this planet far simpler and automatically eliminate a broad area of pseudo-problems which have represented major headaches. If there were a central world bank and one currency, much of the "horseplay" about exchange rates and foreign-exchange reserves would be unnecessary.

The existence of such a currency unit would leave as the central problem what actually is the real problem: the relative availability of effective usable credit in one area by comparison with another. It becomes then

---

[3] It may also be pointed out that the advocacy of an international currency goes back at least a hundred years to Cournot. (Augustin Cournot, *Recherches sur les Principes Mathématiques de la Théorie des Richesses*, p. 29.) For more recent discussion of the possibility of freely fluctuating rates or of an international currency, see: J. E. Meade, *Problems of Economic Union* (Chicago: University of Chicago Press, 1953); and Milton Friedman, "The Case for Flexible Exchange Rates," *Essays in Positive Economics* (Chicago: University of Chicago Press, 1953), pp. 157–203.

the same problem that exists in the United States, in financial dealings between the Southwest and New York. What determines the relative availability of credit and command over goods in the Southwest by comparison with New York? The important decision in the United States is how accessible credit is going to be in certain areas, and that depends upon the interest rate, the reserve requirements, the size of the reserves, and a whole range of institutionally determined attitudes which very markedly influence bankers in different areas in their lending decisions. The fact that the United States has a uniform currency has not made it possible for the cotton sharecropper to "take" the New Yorker for a cleaning nor has it occasioned devaluation of the Mississippi dollar relative to the New York dollar.

Incidentally, it should be noted that central (Federal Reserve) banking in the United States has not really "faced up" to the differences in the problems and credit needs of different regions in the United States. It seems to think that security and willingness to pay interest should determine who gets a loan—rather than the desirability of a particular type of project and the qualifications of the borrower to do that kind of work. To recall the arguments concerning infant-industry tariffs, it is in access to credit that certain industries should be favored by government, rather than with tariffs, discriminatory quotas, and exchange control. If it is decided that the producers of filbert nuts deserve help, they should receive it in the form of easier access to money, not in the form of a tariff. If the world central bank should fail, as domestic banks in the United States have failed, to grapple with the problem of qualitative credit control and regional discrimination in making credit available, it might not last long. But the prospect that a decision may be poorly made does not mean that it is undesirable to come to grips with a problem.

Probably the most important decisions that are made in the business community are those which determine who has access to credit. Why should not the international problem be posed in those terms? Is it not strange that in the international field the chief questions argued should be currency devaluation and tariffs, though we generally do not and cannot have an accurate idea as to what the effect of the tariff or the devaluation will be? We argue about tariffs, justifying them, perhaps, as being of some help to an individual, poor, struggling businessman; and we do not concern ourselves with total impact. It is amazing how the great issues (tariffs and devaluations) have been analyzed and decisions have been made to take certain actions—actions which will obviously have a tremendous impact on people and on production—without regard to the fact that there is signal ignorance of the likely important effects. One is reminded of the horseman who "mounted and galloped off in all directions."

To deal with the real problems intelligently calls for an international currency and an international agency which can determine at least in rough, general terms the total amount of credit that will be available in different regions. And the criterion in deciding how much credit there is to be should not be financial but technological. What development is technically feasible and desirable? Financing should be made available for all such projects. The qualitative determination as to exactly which individuals will get the credit might well remain decentralized to a considerable degree, subject to the maintenance of certain high standards in appraising the character of the people who get the loans and the nature of the project which is to receive impetus from the loan. Incidentally, we are perhaps not so far from this partial millennium as one might think. The function of the International Bank for Reconstruction and Development is to decide whether certain countries (Colombia, Chile, or any other) have prospects for development and to grant them loans if their projects seem worth-while. This agency is discussed more fully in Part VI.

What is being talked about here as credit represents the effective power over goods. The credit that the International Bank makes available to some little country is effective purchasing power for buying goods. In a world of nation states, when a country like Mexico decides to make more money and credit available (and solves this problem unilaterally by manufacturing the money and credit itself), it can create nothing except its own currency (pesos). It may be able to speed up the industrialization process a little by this means, but not very much. When the credit is created too fast, it merely goes into inflation. This increases imports only until such time as the reserves are exhausted. If credit is made available by an international banking agency, it will not change the purchasing power of the money (the price level) in any given country by very much. However, a loan of $100,000,000 (U.S.) to Mexico today will mean pretty nearly $100,000,000 (U.S.) of additional goods available in Mexico as imports. The creation by the Mexican government of the equivalent of $100,000,000 (U.S.) of new pesos would have an effect chiefly inflationary, without much doubt, and could only temporarily increase imports till the foreign-exchange reserves were exhausted.

But what would be the effect of centralized control of the total amount of credit available to the great regions of the world? Initially in this book, it was stated that the desirable goals are improvement in the level of living, an increase in individual freedom of action, and security. This kind of centralization is therefore desirable only if it contributes to the specified goals. Whether it will or not depends on how it is handled. Properly handled, it would mean the extension to each region of the world of as much credit as the region can and will use to expand production at the rate which, in the view of society, involves the most desirable combination of productive effort and leisure time. Centralization of credit, if properly handled, thus conforms to the objectives of improving the level of living and permitting increased individual freedom of action and security.

Nonparticipation by a few countries need not prevent the establishment of an international currency. It could still be a tremendously useful and simplifying thing. Tourists, foreign traders, and foreign investors would all breathe one long, loud sigh of relief if there were one currency, usable in any country.

PART VI

Capital Movements

Chapter 24

DEFINITIONS AND TRANSFER
MECHANICS

🎵 🎵 🎵

A net export of goods and services (disregarding gifts and gold move-
ments) automatically has international lending as a counterpart.

But the total size of a nation's foreign investment may grow not only as
a counterpart to an export balance but also as the result of reinvest-
ing profits and as a result of an increase in the value of the property
in which the earlier investment was made.

There is not likely to be a transfer problem in connection with a new
investment, because the new investment occurs in a setting where it
is natural for the borrowing country to be willing to buy more from
the lending country (or from some third country which will buy
more from the lending country).

A transfer problem is more likely to occur in connection with repayment,
especially if the creditor resists repayment by raising barriers against
goods imports.

🎵 🎵 🎵

WE COME now to the discussion of certain long-run forces
which can make possible inequality between exports and
imports over considerable periods of years. But even
more important, they are forces which can profoundly
affect the evolution of some countries in relation to others. The subject,
of course, is long-run capital movements.

CLASSIFICATION

There is, in the analysis of long-term capital movements, much material
that complements, if not duplicates, the material on short-term capital
movements. The obvious difference between long-term and short-term
lending is the period of time for which the investor commits his money.
A commitment for less than a year is frequently said to be short-term; and

for more than a year, long-term. A medium-term category of one to five years may be added, however.

But there are several other practical differences that verge on being fundamental. The documents involved in the two cases (for example, bonds by comparison with bills of exchange) come into existence by different processes and are handled by different people who are affected by different sorts of institutional attitudes. But more important, long-term lending is likely to move in one direction for an extended period of time and is thus more likely to co-ordinate with a significant pattern of inequality between imports and exports. By and large, short-term lending functions as money or medium of exchange to facilitate goods trade and involves somewhat the same type of activity we are accustomed to associate with commercial banks. It is likely to take the form of foreign bank balances and of bills of exchange discounted in some money market such as London for a short period of time, such as three months. By contrast, long-term investment is overtly associated with property ownership, the financing of the international shipment of capital equipment (machinery and factories), operation of a business abroad, or bond issues which may be outstanding for ten or twenty years, although indirectly the long-term investment may eventuate in the financing of consumer goods trade. Long-term investments may be handled by investment bankers or by the corporations or individuals making the investment themselves. It is not generally considered a proper function for a commercial banker, although, as was mentioned in Chapter 16, there is increasing support for the idea that commercial banks should finance more medium-term transactions in machinery and heavy equipment.

It is reasonable to expect that the movement of long-term investments will be in one direction for a considerable period of time. A country may be a consistent exporter of capital for fifty years. It is also reasonable to expect that the capital funds will stay put for a long period of time. Obviously capital equipment itself, once produced and put in place, is substantially committed for as long as it lasts. By and large, repatriation of capital must refer to a financial operation rather than to the bringing home of the equipment which constituted the original investment. There is much misunderstanding on this score. It is not only the government of the underdeveloped country that resists the repatriation of capital. The capital itself resists.

In terms of *form,* a distinction may be made among (1) direct investments, (2) portfolio investments, (3) government investments, (4) investments by international institutions, and (5) short-term equalizing capital movements.

Direct Investments

In the case of direct investments, the creditor or lender ends up with ownership and control of the manner of use of the property in which the investment has been made in the debtor country. Domestically he would not be spoken of as a creditor or lender in such a case, but as an owner or investor. Perhaps he even ends up physically in the foreign country operating the property—although, if he changes his citizenship, it ceases to be a foreign investment. Thus, Standard Oil's investment in Venezuelan oil is a direct investment. Ownership of real estate abroad is, or at least for purposes of theoretical discussion in this section will be, classified as a direct investment.[1] A Ford assembly plant in Brazil, in a case where Ford still controls the operation of the plant, would be a direct investment, but would probably be carried as such only to the extent of the book equity, even though Ford controls the operation of the entire plant.

How should minority stock (not bond) ownership in a foreign enterprise be classified? Legal ownership and consequently—in theory, and perhaps in practice, too—the right to exercise some control is involved. Let us say that the General Ford Motor Company actually owns only 40 per cent of a plant in Brazil and Brazilians own the other 60 per cent. What kind of investment is this? From the percentage of ownership one does not know whether General Ford controls the operation or not. The Bureau of the Census handles this situation by classifying as direct investments:[2]

> The value of the United States equity in foreign business organizations owned to the extent of 25 per cent or more of the voting securities of the foreign corporations, by persons, or groups of affiliated persons, ordinarily resident of the United States, and analogous interests in partnerships and other organizations. . . . [and]
>
> The United States equity in foreign corporations whose voting stock is publicly held within the United States to an aggregate extent of 50 percent or more but distributed among stockholders so that no one investor or affiliated group of investors owns as much as 25 percent.

In evaluating the role of direct investments, an observation or two may be made. For one thing, direct investments involve no contractual, automatic burden on the economy of the debtor. Profits are made and are available for international transfer only if they are earned.

Direct investments may have impacts of varying sorts, depending on the nature of the enterprise in which the investment is made. It may be (1) export substituting, or it may be (2) import increasing, or (3) neither. The building of a plant in Latin America by International Harvester

[1] But the Bureau of the Census excludes from direct investment real property held solely for the personal use of the owner, or of a sole proprietor type of business enterprise. See *Survey of Current Business,* December, 1952, p. 19, for the text of the government's definition of a direct investment.
[2] *Ibid.,* p. 19.

to produce farm machinery is export substituting, since it will probably tend to decrease farm machinery exports from the United States. An investment by American Smelting and Refining in copper, lead, and zinc production in Mexico is probably import increasing, since more Mexican copper, lead, and zinc will come to the United States in consequence. But an investment by United States meat-packing companies in the frigoríficos of Argentina, which sell beef to England, has little effect on either United States exports to or imports from Argentina—although it might tend to cut beef shipments from the United States to England. (The reader should not impute from these comments any conclusions with regard to the effect of direct investments on total trade or on production in either country.) [3]

Portfolio Investments

A portfolio investment, on the other hand, is an investment in connection with which the lender does not control the use of the loaned funds. A typical example would be a bond issue. In fact, bond issues are sometimes carried in statistical summaries as the only type of portfolio investment. An example would be the flotation by the Peruvian government of a bond issue in the United States through the investment banking branch of the National City Bank. All that the real creditors who buy the bonds (for example, Illinois farmers) get is a claim to interest and a right to repayment when the maturity date arrives. They have no authority as to how the money is being used while the loan is outstanding—generally. They may not even know where Peru is. Thus the portfolio investment is likely to involve less interference by the investor in the internal affairs of the country where he has his investment than is the case with direct investment.

An important point to note in connection with a bond issue is whether it is to be paid off in the currency of the borrower or the lender. It is going to make a considerable difference to one or the other—the lender or the borrower—if the foreign-exchange rates change meanwhile. But regardless of which currency the obligation is stated in, portfolio investments (unlike direct investment) involve a definite annual obligation on the debtor's part—whether the investment is a money-maker or not.

Needless to say, there is a lot of middle ground between direct and portfolio investments. With regard to the distinction in the matter of control, there are many cases where the investment bankers (who have handled the flotation of portfolio investment) may have a lot to say about what is being done in the debtor country. An example would be the lending to Nicaragua of several years ago. One provision of the loan agreement was that, if Nicaragua should default on the bonds and cease to

[3] Or, if he must impute an effect, it is that trade both ways and production in both places will probably be increased.

pay interest to the creditors, then representatives of the creditors could step in and take over collection of the customs and pay themselves. In fact, the collector of the customs in Nicaragua for many years was named by the bondholders and was Colonel, later General, Irving A. Lindberg. The process may also work the other way; a direct investor may lose effective control of the operation of a plant, as was the case, apparently, with General Motors' Opel Works in Germany during the Hitler regime.

Government Investments and Borrowing

Government investments and borrowing abroad may or may not involve a substantial amount of government control of the use of the money. The lending procedure may be very similar to that involved in the case of portfolio investments, except for the actual engraving and issuance of the bonds. Or it may closely resemble the direct transfers of capital equipment which are sometimes a feature of direct investments.

A government may lend to a foreign government or to foreign private citizens or corporations. The latter procedure is rather uncommon, however, unless the loan carries a guarantee signed by the government of the private borrower. But government borrowing from foreign private lenders has been one of the chief forms that the phenomenon of international lending has taken since the beginning of such lending. Private lending to governments was one of the standard procedures in the portfolio investments of the United States in the 1920's.

This range of possibilities confuses the statistics considerably. But generally, in a government's own statistics, classification of a loan as public or private depends on whether that government or its citizens are one of the parties, without regard to whether the foreign party is a government or private citizen.

International Agencies

Participation in the process by international agencies is likely to involve two aspects. The agency, such as the International Bank for Reconstruction and Development, is likely to be the debtor of some government. You might say that it is the debtor of all the governments that own it. It also may be a sort of portfolio debtor to private citizens in various creditor countries as the result of floating bond issues there. But in its turn it may be the creditor of other governments and of private corporations (if the corporations can get a guarantee from their government). The International Bank generally reserves to itself substantial power to check on whether the borrowed money is being spent in the manner agreed upon.

Equalizing Short-Term Capital Movements

Somewhat non-homogeneous with the foregoing are equalizing short-term capital movements. Perhaps dollars are borrowed at long-term by

Peruvians. But the borrowed dollars are not used at once and remain on deposit in a bank in New York. The Peruvians have made an effective short-term loan to (deposit in) the New York bank. The long-term loan in one direction is canceled out, at least temporarily, by the short-term loan in the other direction. A rather substantial amount of lending, including a considerable amount of Marshall Plan aid, has been canceled out in this way—as perusal again of Table 12 will indicate. Generally the short-term balance is later used to buy goods which constitute the effective foreign investment. But it is conceivable that the short-term balance may never be used. In that case, in a certain sense, there has been no foreign loan.

DISTRIBUTION OF UNITED STATES INVESTMENTS

Table 35 indicates that at the end of 1955 the United States was a gross creditor to the extent of $45 billion and a net long-term creditor to the extent of $29 billion. Direct investments abroad (gross) amounted to $19 billion; portfolio investments amounted to over $5 billion, divided about half and half between bonds, in connection with which the debtor was obligated to effect repayment in dollars (dollar bonds), and securities payable in local currencies, in connection with which the repaid creditor could repatriate his money as best he might be able; and United States government investments amounted to almost $16 billion. It should be noted that the United States was a short-term debtor to the extent of a very large figure, $14 billion, a circumstance which reduced the net creditor position considerably. The implications of that phenomenon were discussed in Part V.

Direct private investment is distributed as follows among industries: [4]

Manufacturing	$6,322 million
Petroleum	5,792
Mining and Smelting	2,195
Public utilities	1,588
Trade	1,289
Other	2,000

The percentage of United States foreign investment which is direct rather than portfolio has been rising of recent years; it is now three fourths of the total.

Geographically, United States foreign investment is concentrated in Canada, Latin America, and western Europe, with an additional significant direct investment, not clearly differentiated in Table 35, on the hot sands of the southwestern shore of the Persian Gulf. The example

[4] *Survey of Current Business,* August, 1956, p. 19.

TABLE 35

INTERNATIONAL INVESTMENT POSITION OF THE UNITED STATES
BY TYPE OF INVESTMENT AND BY AREA, YEAR END 1955

(MILLIONS OF DOLLARS)

	TOTAL	WESTERN EUROPE	CANADA	LATIN AMERICA
I. United States Investments				
Abroad, Total	44,888	14,953	10,655	9,237
A. Private Investments	28,994	5,362	10,648	8,224
1. Long-term	26,605	4,623	10,344	7,293
a. Direct	19,185	2,986	6,464	6,556
b. Foreign Dollar Bonds	2,646	194	1,476	148
c. Other Foreign Securities	2,900	598	2,153	39
d. Other	1,874	845	251	550
2. Short-term	2,389	739	304	931
a. Deposits	447	229	127	53
b. Other	1,942	510	177	878
B. United States Government Credits and Claims	15,894	9,591	7	1,013
1. Long-term	15,162	9,128	5	983
2. Short-term	732	463	2	30
II. Foreign Assets and Investments in the United States, Total	29,575	15,643	4,137	3,289
A. Long-term Investments	12,606	8,468	2,601	924
1. Direct	4,274	2,707	1,365	134
2. Corporate Stocks	6,575	4,643	1,091	524
3. Corporate, State and Municipal Bonds	259	165	6	48
4. Other	1,498	953	139	218
B. Short-term Assets and United States Government Obligations	16,969	7,175	1,536	2,365
1. Private Obligations	8,471	3,359	687	2,023
a. Deposits	7,402	2,657	623	1,885
b. Other	1,069	702	64	138
2. United States Government Obligations	8,498	3,816	849	342
a. Long-term	1,636	623	351	264
b. Short-term	6,862	3,193	498	78
III. United States Net Creditor Position	15,300			
A. Net Long-term	29,200			
B. Net Short-term	−13,900			

Source: *Survey of Current Business,* August, 1956, pp. 15, 18.

of the oil investment in the Middle East emphasizes the need to maintain mental reservations in interpreting these statistical estimates. Geologists have recently increased very markedly the estimates of crude-oil reserves in the area. In fact, in all seriousness, the estimates are so fabulous that there is reasonable basis for saying that the estimate of the net long-term creditor position of the United States instead of being $28 billion, should be $100 to $200 billion.[5]

PARTIES INVOLVED

The parties to the arrangements in the different types of foreign investment situations might be classified as follows:

(1) DIRECT INVESTMENTS: The direct investor is the same person or institution in both countries. Governments play a part in laying down the rules under which direct investments are made. But they need not be parties to the actual lending-borrowing process.

(2) PORTFOLIO INVESTMENTS: The parties in the lending country are (a) the bondholder and (b) the investment banker. The parties in the borrowing country may include (c) a negotiator, who is a separate individual from the borrower, and (d) the borrower. The investment banker and the negotiator are likely to take a small cut as the money goes by (the investment banker's cut is considered a legitimate commission, provided it is not too large; the cut of the negotiator in the borrowing country is a little more likely to contain an element of graft, especially if he is a government official). But the role of the investment banker and of the negotiator is basically that of middlemen. They do not put up or receive the money themselves. However, this is not a hard and fast rule, and the investment banker is likely to become an important figure in the transaction in the event of default, if he takes the lead in representing creditor interest—as he is likely to do.

(3) GOVERNMENTS: Governments may be the actual lenders or the actual borrowers. In cases where governments are the lenders they generally lend to governments, and there are only the two parties. In cases where a government borrows from private citizens in the lending country, there is probably an investment banker intermediary in the lending country.

(4) INTERNATIONAL AGENCIES: An international agency, such as the International Bank for Reconstruction and Development, may borrow from private citizens (or governments) in one country and lend to governments (or private citizens) in another.

[5] Of course, Saudi Arabia may expropriate. . . . The serious estimates of proven oil reserves in the ground in the Middle East are now of the order of magnitude of 150 billion barrels. A skeptic should try valuing that at $2.75 a barrel, discount the future generously, allow the Middle Eastern governments 50 per cent of the profits, make some generous allowance like $5 billion dollars for development cost, remember that each well will produce several thousand barrels a day—this is not Texas with its 5 to 10 barrel a day recovery—and see what he has left. Large allowances for current operating costs are not going to keep the result from being a substantial figure.

(5) Equalizing Short-term Capital Movements: These transactions involve two separate operations. The original long-term loan might be as described under portfolio investments. The equalizing short-term capital movement, however, would involve investment by the long-term debtor of his money in the capital exporting country. The long-term debtor is then the short-term creditor of a bank or some such institution in the capital exporting country.

PROCESS OF TRANSFER

It is all very well to talk about the form which an investment eventually takes and to talk about the parties to the lending. But, what is it that moves when we talk about capital movement? Or need anything move, necessarily, for a change in the value of investment to occur?

If anything worth having is being transferred from creditor nation to debtor nation, it has to take the form of an international "shipment" of goods or services. But the value of a foreign investment (the extent of the creditor's claim on the debtor) can change without this being the case and without anything of value being exchanged. The explanations of the manner of operation of the transfer process when something of value is actually transferred from creditor to debtor parallel the explanations of the adjustment processes which may operate in connection with short-term funds—recall Part V. The basic possibilities are: (1) specie-flow, (2) transfer of purchasing power, (3) national-income theory, and (4) borrowing to buy.[6] These possibilities will be discussed below.

But first it is desirable to emphasize that the value of foreign investments may change *without international movement of any goods or services*. But, if such changes occur, they will not be reflected in the international balance of payments statement. Both (1) reinvestment of earning and what amounts to (2) capital gains and losses can change the value of a foreign investment without any international transfer of funds taking place. Also a foreign investment could come into being as the result of (3) a straight gift of property located in one country to nationals of a foreign country or (4) the change of country of residence by the owner of a piece of property. Thus, in a certain sense, this is not a symmetrical relationship. And the value of foreign investment by no means necessarily coincides with the value of the capital funds which

---

[6] For detailed discussion of the various theories of the adjustment process see: Carl Iversen, *Aspects of the Theory of International Capital Movements* (Copenhagen: Levin and Munksgaard, 1936). John Stuart Mill in the *Principles of Political Economy* (Book III, Chap. XX) makes what seems to have been the first comprehensive application of the price-specie-flow explanation to capital transfers.

have moved internationally. The United States Bureau of Foreign and Domestic Commerce in the *Balance of Payments of the United States, 1949–1951* (p. 164) published a table reconciling the changes in the value of foreign investments indicated by the balance of payments statement with the changes in the value of investments shown in Table 35. The chief elements in the reconciliation were changes in the value of direct investments and changes in the market value of portfolio investments during the year. It is to be regretted that the Department of Commerce has not continued to publish the "Reconciliation."

Data on changes in the value of foreign investment which involve the international transfer of funds are contained each year in the balance of payments statement. See Table 12.

Specie-flow

The explanation of the adjustment process in connection with long-term investments, which would correlate with the gold standard specie-flow explanation, might run somewhat as follows—see Chart 16. As a consequence of higher interest rates in Argentina than in England, Englishmen are induced to lend to Argentina, and Argentines to borrow in England (steps 1 and 2). Six per cent might be an attractive interest rate to both. The lender in England, who has paper pounds, might obtain for them gold to ship to the borrower in Argentina (if the price of Argentine pesos on the foreign-exchange market has risen to the gold export point—as it will if the lending operation is of any size). The Argentine could then obtain his national currency for the gold. The English lender is out of pocket paper pounds. The Argentine borrower has paper pesos and the power to buy Argentine (not English) goods. (Note here the "possibly unnecessary" assumption that the borrower is not himself interested in obtaining goods from the lending country.) England has lost gold and Argentina has gained gold; consequently, if the banks in the two countries play according to the "rules of the game" of the old gold standard, the supply of money and credit will be contracted in England and expanded in Argentina (step 4). If the quantity theory of money operates, prices will rise in Argentina and fall in England. England becomes a relatively more attractive, Argentina a relatively less attractive, place in which to buy. Argentines now buy more in England. England consequently has an export (favorable) balance of trade with Argentina to correspond with the "export of capital." The gold returns to England to pay for the goods shipment (step 6). England can again expand money and credit and have a price rise to somewhere near the earlier level. Argentina can do the reverse. They are both back near where they started so far as the monetary phenomenon is concerned. But England has increased her long-term foreign investment, and there has been a net export of goods from England to correspond roughly in

CHART 16

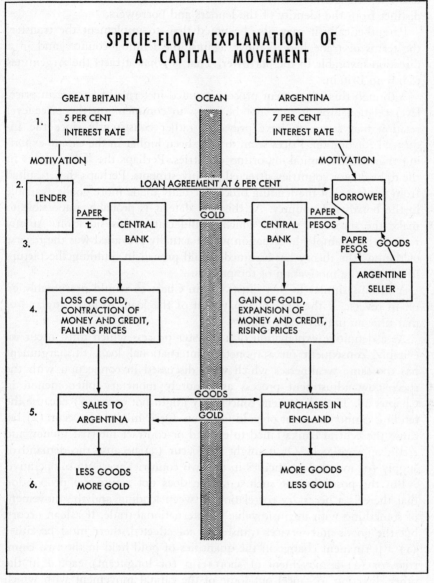

SPECIE-FLOW EXPLANATION OF A CAPITAL MOVEMENT

| GREAT BRITAIN | OCEAN | ARGENTINA |

1.
| 5 PER CENT INTEREST RATE | | 7 PER CENT INTEREST RATE |

MOTIVATION .... MOTIVATION

2. LENDER — LOAN AGREEMENT AT 6 PER CENT → BORROWER

3. LENDER → PAPER t → CENTRAL BANK → GOLD → CENTRAL BANK → PAPER PESOS → BORROWER

PAPER PESOS / GOODS → ARGENTINE SELLER

4.
| LOSS OF GOLD, CONTRACTION OF MONEY AND CREDIT, FALLING PRICES | | GAIN OF GOLD, EXPANSION OF MONEY AND CREDIT, RISING PRICES |

5.
| SALES TO ARGENTINA | GOODS →   ← GOLD | PURCHASES IN ENGLAND |

6.
| LESS GOODS MORE GOLD | | MORE GOODS LESS GOLD |

value with the foreign investment. However, the identity of the individuals who engaged in the international trade in goods may have been quite distinct from the identity of the lenders and borrowers.

Parenthetically it may also be noted that, to implement the transfer, the terms of trade had to move against the lending country and in a direction favorable to the borrower. That is what attracts the Argentines to buy in Britain.

Although this adjustment process is stated in terms of change in price-level relationships, it may not be amiss to comment on the price-level relation that seems to have prevailed rather consistently since the Industrial Revolution. Prices seem to have been higher in the capital-exporting than in the capital-importing countries. Perhaps the lower prices in the to-be-debtor countries attracted the investments. Perhaps they resulted from the fact that the lending process actually made more goods available in the borrowing country. At this late date it is probably impossible to make the statistical studies which would clarify this situation. At any rate, in this example the situation which actually prevailed was the reverse of the one the theory has assumed would prevail in building the picture to explain the motivation of the process.

A process similar to that illustrated in Chart 16 would presumably go on in reverse at the time of repayment of the loan, to give England at that time an import trade balance.

As a definitive explanation of a transfer process which must occur inevitably, consequent on a monetary international loan, this argument has the same weaknesses which were discussed in connection with the specie-flow adjustment process as a purely monetary phenomenon in Chapter 18. The adjustment conceivably might not occur (1) because the lending country ran out of gold too soon. Or it might not occur (2) because the central banks failed to expand or contract internal money and credit appropriately. Or it might not occur (3) because the demand or supply (or income) elasticities in the two countries were un-co-operative.

But the possibility of such a failure does not refute the proposition that there is a necessary correlation between lending and the movement of something with intrinsic value in international trade. If a loan occurs, but the goods and services transfer is not effected, there must be either (1) a permanent change in the quantities of gold held in the two countries, or (2) a movement of short-term (or long-term) capital in the other direction to cancel out some of the capital movement with which the process started out.

Somewhat more comprehensive statements of the specie-flow theory as applied to international capital movements take into account the possibility that these adjustments may be multilateral rather than bilateral. A. P. Winston has shown that the Argentine railroads bought a very

CHART 17

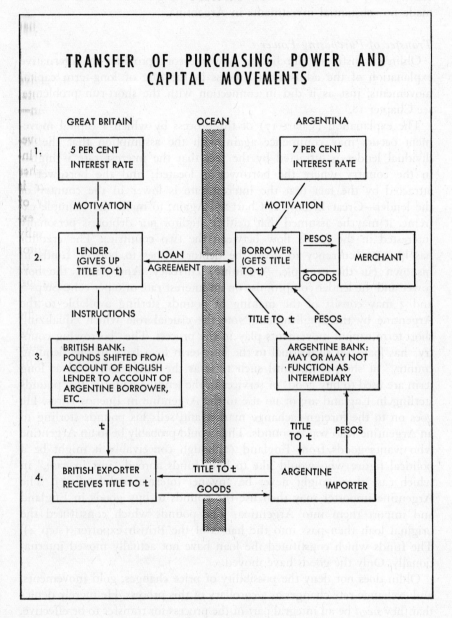

TRANSFER OF PURCHASING POWER AND CAPITAL MOVEMENTS

GREAT BRITAIN   OCEAN   ARGENTINA

1. 5 PER CENT INTEREST RATE | 7 PER CENT INTEREST RATE

MOTIVATION | MOTIVATION

2. LENDER (GIVES UP TITLE TO t) — LOAN AGREEMENT — BORROWER (GETS TITLE TO t) — PESOS → MERCHANT ← GOODS

INSTRUCTIONS

TITLE TO t   PESOS

3. BRITISH BANK: POUNDS SHIFTED FROM ACCOUNT OF ENGLISH LENDER TO ACCOUNT OF ARGENTINE BORROWER, ETC. | ARGENTINE BANK: MAY OR MAY NOT FUNCTION AS INTERMEDIARY

t

TITLE TO t   PESOS

4. BRITISH EXPORTER RECEIVES TITLE TO t — TITLE TO t — GOODS — ARGENTINE IMPORTER

substantial proportion of their rails and rolling stock in countries that made no substantial investments in Argentina.[7]

Transfer of Purchasing Power

Ohlin's transfer of purchasing power theory provides an alternative explanation of the adjustment process in the case of long-term capital movements, just as it did in connection with the short-run problem—see Chapter 18.[8]

The explanation (Chart 17) of the process by which a capital movement occurs may commence again with the assumption that the individual lender is attracted by the fact that the interest rate is higher in the country where the borrower is located; and the borrower is attracted by the fact that the interest rate is lower in the country of the lender—Great Britain in Chart 17. Again, to make the example extreme, it may be assumed that neither creditor nor debtor is personally interested in the goods flow between the two countries. The creditor has his own currency to give; the debtor wishes to borrow funds in his own (in the example, Argentine) currency. And again, the borrower and the lender compromise on an interest rate of 6 per cent. Steps 2 and 3 may consist of the making of pounds sterling available to the Argentine by the Englishman. Note the crucial role which equalizing short-term capital movements play in the process. The "borrowing country" has loaned a sum equal to the long-term loan back to the "lending country" at short-term, until such time as the funds borrowed at long term are used to buy goods or services in the lending country. But pounds sterling in England are of no use to the Argentine in Buenos Aires. He goes on to the foreign-exchange market and sells his pounds sterling to an Argentine who wants pounds. That would probably be to an Argentine who wants goods from England (although conceivably it might be a political figure who would like to hold funds abroad "just in case," in which case there might never be any net international lending). The Argentine importer may then use the pounds to buy goods in England and import them into Argentina. The pounds which constituted the original loan then pass into the hands of the British exporter (step 4). The funds which constituted the loan have not actually moved internationally. Only the goods have moved.

Ohlin does not deny the possibility of price changes, gold movements, and exchange-rate changes as a corollary of this process. He merely denies that they *need* be an integral part of the process for transfer to be effective.

---

[7] A. P. Winston, "Does Trade Follow the Dollar?" *American Economic Review,* XVII (September, 1927), 458–77.

[8] Bertil Ohlin, *Interregional and International Trade,* pp. 406–8. See also Iversen, *op. cit.;* and C. F. Bastable, "On Some Applications of the Theory of International Trade," *Quarterly Journal of Economics,* IV (October, 1899), 1–17.

And he denies that the terms of trade must necessarily move against the lending country if transfer is to be effected. He says the price movements in the two countries may be either way.

But the description of the train of events in Chart 17 may not convince the observer that such a development is likely to occur. What are the chances and what are the reasons stimulating the Argentine importer to buy the goods? Ohlin's explanation lies in the argument that the purchasing power which has been transferred from Britishers to Argentines will be used—as was stated in Chapter 18. It is fundamentally a proposition based on Say's law of markets,[9] which, like most such arguments, contains overtones of Mallory's explanation as to why he wanted to climb Mount Everest: "It is there." Ergo, the purchasing power is there; it will be used—and it will eventually be used to purchase goods in the lending country. It would seem reasonable that this process as described might or might not work faster than specie-flow; the purchasing power may have to change hands several times in Argentina before it finds its way into the hands of someone interested in buying British goods.

If it still may sound a little mystifying that purchasing power, which has been transferred internationally, must eventually be used to buy goods in the country from which it came, it may bear repeating why this must be so. If the purchases do not occur, there is an automatic movement of short-term funds in the other direction. There is no net international investment.

It may be noted that when the transfer of purchasing power is used to explain a long-run capital movement, speed is no longer of the essence as it was in the short-run disequilibrium problem. But the question still remains whether the process, however slowly, necessarily or generally works this way. Ohlin's version does not describe an adjustment process which must work, any more than does the specie-flow explanation. And history has given abundant evidence that Say's law of markets does not work automatically to eliminate market surplus. It may work and it may not.

National Income Theory

At this point Ohlin's theory logically should be restated in terms of the marginal propensities of national-income theory—as was done in a similar situation in Chapter 18. I do not, however, believe that this will serve a particularly useful purpose in elucidating the transfer process. It

---

[9] The purchasing power necessary to take goods off the market is derived from the remuneration paid to the factors of production who produced them and it will be used. If the goods wanted by the Argentines—who now have the purchasing power—are slightly different from those which the Britishers who previously had the purchasing power would have bought, according to Ohlin, the required change in the production pattern will be easily made.

will probably be better, for the present, to turn to a discussion of what is realistically involved in the transfer process.

Borrowing to Buy

Yet another explanation of the transfer process is probably more relevant in most cases than the specie-flow, or the Ohlin, or the national-income explanation. The borrower borrows because he actually wants goods from the country where he is borrowing the money. Or, in terms of the pattern, people in the type of country interested in borrowing want goods from the type of country interested in lending. An example would be the actual shipment of a drilling rig by an oil company to Venezuela. The decision to make the investment and the decision to move the equipment are part of the same process. And the value of the rig is subsequently United States investment in Venezuela.

This is not to say, of course, that all foreign investments involve "borrowing to buy" relations. In the case of bond issues there is clearly no direct connection between the borrowers and lenders on the one hand and the buyers and sellers of goods on the other. Nevertheless, many of the important situations have involved such a direct connection.

Several examples may be cited. Much international lending of recent years has been handled by the Export-Import Bank, an agency of the United States government. There is no real transfer problem in connection with its loans, although sometimes credits which it extends are not used. By and large, the United States now is the country where goods, and particularly capital equipment, can be obtained. A foreign government may borrow from the Export-Import Bank and actually obtain the power to write checks against a dollar balance in a New York bank. It may write a check to pay for some machinery (perhaps farm machinery from International Harvester). There is thus no actual foreign-exchange transaction, in most cases, and what the borrower gets is the equipment —straight and to the point. And the whole business occurred because the borrower wanted the machinery.

Fairly similar are the mechanics of Marshall plan aid. Obviously the reason for being of the Marshall plan is that the European countries in the late 1940's wanted and needed goods, and food, and equipment for reconstruction. The United States was willing to supply them, partly out of compassion for former allies in difficulties, partly because it seemed like a good way to build up support against the Russians. At any rate, the goods movement was a direct and immediate result of the expression by the United States government of willingness to finance a particular shipment of goods—see Chart 18.

The Organization for European Economic Cooperation (O.E.E.C.), an organization of the European governments participating in Marshall plan aid, and the International Cooperation Administration, which is

CHART 18

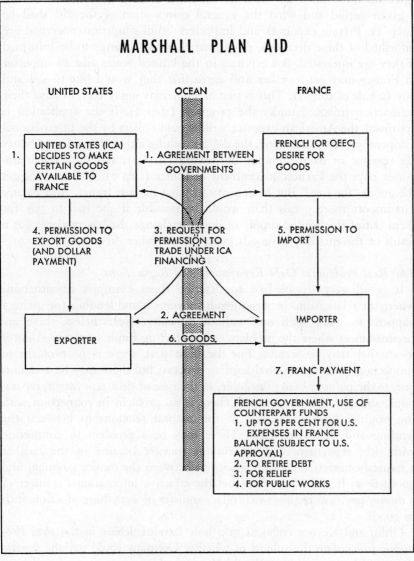

MARSHALL PLAN AID

UNITED STATES	OCEAN	FRANCE

1.
UNITED STATES (ICA) DECIDES TO MAKE CERTAIN GOODS AVAILABLE TO FRANCE

1. AGREEMENT BETWEEN GOVERNMENTS

FRENCH (OR OEEC) DESIRE FOR GOODS

4. PERMISSION TO EXPORT GOODS (AND DOLLAR PAYMENT)

3. REQUEST FOR PERMISSION TO TRADE UNDER ICA FINANCING

5. PERMISSION TO IMPORT

EXPORTER

2. AGREEMENT

6. GOODS.

IMPORTER

7. FRANC PAYMENT

FRENCH GOVERNMENT, USE OF COUNTERPART FUNDS
1. UP TO 5 PER CENT FOR U.S. EXPENSES IN FRANCE BALANCE (SUBJECT TO U.S. APPROVAL)
2. TO RETIRE DEBT
3. FOR RELIEF
4. FOR PUBLIC WORKS

currently implementing the program for the United States government, agree on how much aid shall be extended to each government during a given period and what the general composition of the aid shall be (step 1). Private exporters and importers in all countries concerned are informed of these decisions, or at least they can arrange to be informed if they are interested. An exporter in the United States and an importer in France may get together and agree that they would like to sell and buy (a bale of cotton). This is step 2. They may apply then to have their transaction financed under the program (step 3). If the application is approved, the American exporter will be paid dollars by the International Cooperation Administration, the dollars coming either from United States tax revenue or from domestic borrowing (step 4), and the French importer pays the French government in francs (step 7). He does not get the goods "for free." But he can pay in what he has: francs. And France can import more goods than would be possible if she had to pay for them out of the limited supply of dollar exchange she has available (as a result of the quantity of goods going in the other direction).[10]

The Real Problems: Debt Repayment and Reparations

It is all very trouble-free to describe these examples of situations where the relationship between goods movement and lending (or giving) happens to work itself out without difficulty. Nevertheless, there are circumstances where the problem of transferring funds from one country to another may be serious. For the most part, there is no problem in connection with the original lending process; but there may be a serious one, to the point of being insoluble, in the case of debt repayment, reparations, and war-debt repayment. There is no problem in connection with the original lending because of the natural relationship between the lending and the goods flow. There may be a problem in connection with debt repayment and reparations transfer because of the lack of a natural connection in such situations between the money payment and goods flow. It will be recalled that the effective international transfer of a money payment requires a corollary transfer of something of value, such as goods.

Ohlin and Keynes engaged in a now famous debate in the 1929 *Economic Journal* on the subject of whether Germany could pay the reparations which the victors in World War I had assessed against her.[11] It is,

[10] It is not that there will necessarily be a dollar shortage and a foreign-exchange crisis in the absence of Marshall plan aid. Whether there would be or not would depend on forces discussed in Part V. The European countries might merely have to do without and suffer, like any poor man.

[11] J. M. Keynes, "The German Transfer Problem," *Economic Journal,* XXXIX (March, 1929), 1–7; Bertil Ohlin, "The Reparation Problem: A Discussion," *Economic Journal,* XXXIX (June, 1929), 172–8; also see: J. M. Keynes, *The Economic Consequences of the Peace* (New York: Harcourt, Brace and Howe, 1920).

of course, rather notorious now that Germany did not try, and such reparations as she did pay in the 1920's were largely financed by United States lending to her. Thus the debate was academic rather than practical. But it was dealing with the important problem-type of situation, rather than trying to make a problem out of no problem as has been the case with most of the theoretical analysis concerned with the original transfer of new loans.

Keynes argued that German reparations could not be transferred internationally, even though the marks could be raised in Germany, because the sums involved were too large. He thought that the necessary combination of (1) elasticity in the foreign demand for German goods and (2) the possibility of lowering production costs and export prices by Germany sufficiently to stimulate a large increase in foreign purchases of German goods, simply did not exist.

Ohlin argued that the reparations could be transferred, since Frenchmen in possession of the marks could not resist spending them. Even though the recipients of reparations had in mind at the beginning of the process no specific German goods that they wanted, still they would spend the money (Say's law)—and eventually a recipient of the funds would spend them on German goods and the German trade balance would consequently adjust to make the international transfer possible. Effective demand would be increased in the countries receiving the reparations; the purchasing power would be used. Moreover, the nature of the goods being produced in Germany could be changed sufficiently to service the export market.

By means of a simplified case, Keynes pointed out very logically, if not very realistically, that, if all Germany had to export was caviar, it would take an impossibly great decline in the price of caviar to increase foreign sales of caviar sufficiently for them to serve as the basis for the reparations payment. His conclusion was that Germany therefore could not pay. It can hardly be said that Germany's failure to pay proved Keynes's theory. Lending to Germany in the 1920's effectively counterbalanced such reparations as Germany did pay, so that reparations never were a real burden to the German economy. It is probably no exaggeration to say that Germany never really tried to pay. And by the early 1930's her power was again great enough so that she could get away with a refusal to pay.

Or again, there were the "great defaults" of the early 1930's which soured United States investors on foreign bonds. Were there elements in the international financial picture that forced those defaults or were they economically unnecessary, but precipitated by political "gripes" and anti-foreign sentiment, or some such thing? This also is a real-problem type of situation.

In the case of reparations and debt repayment, it is not automatic that the country which is supposed to receive the payment wants goods at current prices from the paying country, or from anybody (via multilateral trade) in sufficient quantities to effect the transfer. Both the specie-flow and the transfer of purchasing power explanations might work to resolve the difficulty. They simply have not always done so. And the test of an adjustment process lies in whether it will solve a problem-type situation, not whether it will effect adjustment in a situation where there is no problem in the first place. Probably the correct explanation is rather simple. If the critical situation develops quickly, or if it is produced in a situation where there is political animosity, or if it develops in a situation where there are already a lot of trade barriers, there is likely to be trouble. If the necessity for the changed payments pattern evolves slowly, some almost invisible combination of specie-flow, transfer of purchasing power, and institutional adjustment will make for a manageable set of new relations.

The changing of tariff rates is an example of an institutional adjustment that may help or hinder with the transfer problem—depending on which way the rates are changed. For example, the Smoot-Hawley tariff of 1930, which raised United States tariff rates to an all-time high, undoubtedly increased the difficulties of debtors who tried to honor their obligations in the early thirties. Such a measure would not make payment impossible. It might merely make it more expensive. The new, higher rates would tend to decrease the amount of dollar exchange foreigners got from their shipments to the United States. The higher tariffs were also disadvantageous to United States exporters; since these developments would limit further the supply of dollar exchange available to would-be importers in the debtor country, they would decrease purchases from the United States.

People in the United States were not happy about the defaults of the 1930's. "Where there is a will there is a way," we told the debtors in the early thirties; but we probably would not have liked the way, if they had tried to pay. Maybe things could have been worse. But to repeat a statement made earlier, in working out the transfer process it is loan repayment and reparations payments which pose the difficulties, not new lending. The adjustment necessary to effect the transfer of the original sum of net new lending does not pose and never has posed real problems.

Chapter 25

HISTORY THROUGH WORLD WAR II

❦ ❦ ❦

By and large, the foreign investment of the major creditor countries has grown as the result of reinvested earnings and accretions in land values and not as the result of an export balance of trade.

Foreign lending will support an export balance of trade, net of interest and profits, only very briefly.

Foreign investment did not support an export balance for Britain at the time when the growth of British foreign investment reached its peak, in the latter nineteenth century.

The current United States export balance is for the most part supported by unilateral transfers and not by net new lending.

Underdeveloped countries are, even now, not the recipients of any significant net amount of resources from the already developed countries.

❦ ❦ ❦

THIS chapter is intended to provide some historical background as to the manner in which the debtor and creditor status of certain countries has evolved. But it is also intended to do something more. It is intended to cast doubt on the belief that seems to be widely held at present that foreign investments are built up in a process that involves a large outflow of tangible goods and services from the lending to the borrowing country.

SCHEMATIZATION OF "LENDING-BALANCE OF TRADE" RELATIONSHIP

The relationship (between lending and the balance of trade) may be outlined somewhat as follows:

(a) The immature borrower will tend to have an import trade balance;

(b) The mature borrower will tend to have an export trade balance;

(c) The immature lender will tend to have an export trade balance; and

(d) The mature lender will tend to have an import trade balance.

A debtor country engaged in net new borrowing is an immature borrower; a debtor country engaged in debt repayment to an amount in excess of its new borrowing is a mature borrower; a creditor country engaged in net new lending is an immature lender; a creditor country in the process of receiving repayment in excess of its new lending is a mature lender.[1]

The possibility of a country's having an export trade balance is dependent on whether it is engaging in net new lending (or giving, or whether it is experiencing a gold movement)—not on whether it is a net debtor or a net creditor. And the effort to encourage exports relative to imports will be successful if the country is engaging in lending (or debt repayment); it will be unsuccessful if it is not. No matter how many pages are used in writing laws or how much effort is spent on devaluing currencies, or raising tariffs, or establishing embargoes, no matter how extensively corporations engage in dumping, the possibility of having a favorable balance of trade is dependent on whether net lending (or giving) is going on (if gold movements are neutral). Whatever one may think about the desirability of a favorable balance of trade (that it is desirable because it stimulates business or that it is undesirable and amounts to giving one's substance to foreigners), it is quite impossible of realization in the absence of some device for financing the export surplus. Other control devices such as tariffs and quotas, to the extent that they accomplish anything, merely reduce the total volume of trade and leave the balance unaffected.

The possibility of an export balance depends to a marked extent on whether lending is going on. But, as was pointed out in Chapter 24, change in the size of debt is not entirely dependent on the balance of trade. The size of debt may change by accretion, by plowing back earnings, etc. In the following discussion of the investment history of various countries the chief point to note is whether the change in their debt position resulted chiefly from balance of payments forces or not.

INVESTMENTS—HISTORICAL BACKGROUND

Great Britain—Growth by Accretion

Probably in the late Middle Ages (fourteenth and fifteenth centuries) England was a debtor country with an export balance of trade.[2] England seems to have been the underdeveloped, raw-commodity (wool)

---

[1] Of course, the net lending being done by debtors and the net borrowing being done by creditors needs to be allowed for as well.

[2] M. Postan and E. E. Rich (eds.), *Trade and Industry in the Middle Ages*, pp. 212, 240–1.

supplying country of the Middle Ages. The Low Countries, Flanders, and Brabant, and perhaps Italy, further away, were the manufacturing and financial centers. A major change in the English position occurred in the fifteenth and sixteenth centuries. In the fifteenth century wool manufacture in England experienced a spurt in importance. And English industrial power was increasing rapidly by Tudor times. Perhaps one could make something of the proposition that English development was stimulated by foreign investments in England. Perhaps, also, one could develop the proposition that the significant change over from debtor to creditor status for England was facilitated by the activities of the English privateers of Queen Elizabeth's time.

Keynes observed with regard to these activities: [3]

> Indeed, the booty brought back by Drake in the Golden Hind may fairly be considered the fountain and origin of British Foreign Investment. Elizabeth paid off out of the proceeds the whole of her foreign debt and invested a part of the balance (about £42,000) in the Levant Company; largely out of the profits of the Levant Company there was formed the East India Company, the profits of which during the seventeenth and eighteenth centuries were the main foundation of England's foreign connections; and so on. In view of this, the following calculation may amuse the curious. At the present time (in round figures) our foreign investments probably yield us about 6½ per cent net after allowing for losses, of which we reinvest abroad about half—say 3¼ per cent. If this is, on the average, a fair sample of what has been going on since 1580, the £42,000 invested by Elizabeth out of Drake's booty in 1580 would have accumulated by 1930 to approximately the actual aggregate of our present foreign investments, namely £4,200,000,000—or, say 100,000 times greater than the original investment. We can, indeed, check the accuracy of this assumed rate of accumulation about 120 years later. For at the end of the seventeenth century the three great trading companies—the East India Company, the Royal African and the Hudson's Bay—which constituted the bulk of the country's foreign investment, had a capital of about £2,150,000; and if we take £2,500,000 for our aggregate foreign investments at that date, this is of the order of magnitude to which £42,000 would grow at 3¼ per cent in 120 years.

Whether or not the Golden Hind booty directly accounts for so much, other obvious developments of the sixteenth and eighteenth centuries indicate that the basis for the British foreign investment has not rested

[3] John Maynard Keynes, *A Treatise on Money* (London: Macmillan, 1930), II, 156–7. Quoted with the kind permission of Macmillan & Co. and of Harcourt, Brace and Company.

on a significant amount of goods and services export from England. It was not built up by a large export trade balance extending over a substantial period of time.

One large bloc of the British foreign investment (or colonial investment) in the early days was the investment in the plantations of Virginia and the West Indies. The expeditions which established these colonies were undoubtedly expensive, by contemporary standards; but they were hardly requested by the Indians and they hardly represented a capital-goods contribution to the colonies. The chief British contribution was people and technical knowledge—the technical knowledge to operate tobacco and sugar plantations and find a market for the output. But none of these items would have appeared in the balance of payments statement, if there had been one in those days.

Even more significant events occurred meanwhile in India. Queen Elizabeth had chartered the East India Company in 1600. With the passage of the years it acquired some land in India, and the trade between Britain and India grew. How much Britains were really out of pocket for the original Indian lands is not certain—but it probably was not much. Then, in 1757, Robert Clive won a battle at Plassey over the nawab of Bengal and installed his own nawab Mir Jafar, obtaining from Mir Jafar at the time a large present and the quit-rent of the company's territory. And about 1765 the company obtained territorial sovereignty in India jointly with the British crown.[4] Apparently the large British investment in India grew chiefly by accretion from these beginnings and did not evolve to any marked extent out of an export trade balance on goods and services.

The statistics will probably never be available to establish clearly the evolution of the British balance of trade between 1500 and 1800. Nor will they be available to establish clearly when England became a creditor country. Keynes' statement that the Golden Hind loot enabled Elizabeth to pay off her foreign debt should be taken in a somewhat more limited sense.

Holland was still a creditor country engaged in some lending to the British as late as the 1750's,[5] although England was probably a net creditor by then. One might be tempted to guess that the Napoleonic wars served the same role in strengthening England's creditor position which World War II was later to serve for the United States. But there are some elements in the picture which are not entirely comprehensible on the basis of this interpretation. Chart 19 indicates that England had an import merchandise balance seemingly during most of the Napoleonic wars. Perhaps the data is mistaken.

[4] It was deprived of its governing powers in 1858 and dissolved in 1873.
[5] Alice Carter, "Dutch Foreign Investments, 1738–1800," *Economica,* New Series, XXII (November, 1953), 322–40.

Did England really export great material aid during those years, which she was not as careful to record in the data as the United States was a hundred years later? Or is it really a myth that England was the island arsenal supplying the Continent for the war against Napoleon? Maybe English armies, after they got over to the Continent, just lived off the countryside.

At any rate, English foreign investment expanded steadily during the nineteenth century, and up until World War I, in the face of an import trade balance. The expansion seems to have been chiefly due to the reinvestment of earnings—at least indirectly. There is quite good data for the period 1870 to 1911.[6]

Cumulative data for 1870 through 1911 indicates the following:

Growth of Foreign Investment by:	£2,715 million
(This may well be an incomplete figure)	
Cumulative Interest Received on Foreign	
Investment:	3,681
In spite of which	
Cumulative Import Trade Balance (Goods	
only) was:	5,168

The inclusion of goods and services instead of goods only in computing the trade balance would alter the data, but not by enough to change the nature of the basic relations. It was the receipt of interest, dividends, and capital gains (and the plowing-back, either directly or indirectly, of these gains) that made available to England substantial foreign funds with which to enlarge British foreign investment during those years. The financing of foreign investment growth clearly did not come from an export trade balance; the growth was by accretion.

How long had this been going on? All the time since the Napoleonic wars? Possibly. Was the whole great British foreign investment built, in a sense, on plowed-back earnings and increment in the value of land? Did Britain never go through a period of substantial export balance on goods as concrete transfer of something of value to foreigners in exchange for the tremendous investment that evolved? Maybe all the net capital export England ever made was "Clive of India," and England has been living on the interest ever since—and expanding the capital investment on the strength of the interest as well.

British behavior during those years from Clive to Disraeli, however lacking in charity it may have been, was not very good evidence for the Marxist thesis that capitalist countries are searching for foreign markets with increasing desperation. Winston has pointed out that Eng-

[6] C. K. Hobson, *The Export of Capital* (New York: Macmillan, 1914); A. K. Cairncross, *Home and Foreign Investment, 1870–1913,* (Cambridge, Eng.: University Press, 1953), pp. 180–6; Iversen, *op. cit.,* pp. 360–9; Herbert Feis, *Europe the World's Banker, 1870–1914* (New Haven: Yale University Press, 1930).

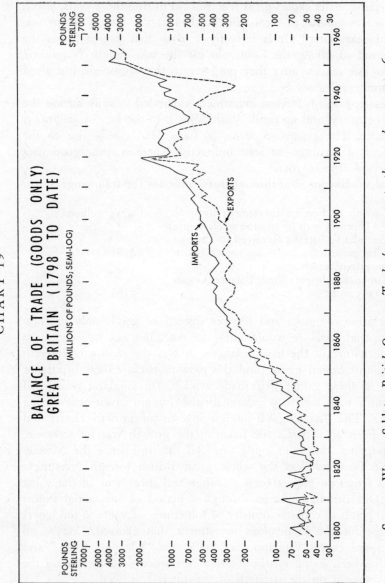

CHART 19

BALANCE OF TRADE (GOODS ONLY)
GREAT BRITAIN (1798 TO DATE)

(MILLIONS OF POUNDS; SEMI-LOG)

Sources: Werner Schlote, *British Overseas Trade from 1700 to the 1930's*, pp. 121–26;
Leone Levi, *History of British Commerce, 1763–1870*, pp. 491–93; *Yearbook of International Trade Statistics*; Albert H. Imlah, "Real Values in British Foreign Trade, 1798–1853," *Journal of Economic History VIII* (November, 1948), pp. 148–49; *International Financial Statistics*.

land did not even provide the rails and rolling stock for the Argentine railways.

One point that may be noted about the pattern of British trade relates to the impact of the Industrial Revolution. It is reasonable to say that the typical British trading pattern, following the Industrial Revolution, involved the import of raw materials and the export of manufactured goods. But this circumstance establishes nothing with regard to the direction of net lending and the state of the balance of trade. This is a point that was originally made in Chapter 2.

At any rate England, during the period of her great affluence and influence from 1800 to World War I, was a mature creditor with an import trade balance. She was uncontested as a leader until the 1870's and not really challenged till World War I. And the great increase in her foreign investment in the nineteenth century was financed from plowed-back earnings and reinvested profits, not from an export balance on goods and services.

Continental Countries—More Growth by Accretion

The other important creditor countries before World War I were the countries of western Europe: France, Germany, the Netherlands, and Belgium. And the creditor position of all of these countries was built up rather rapidly after 1871.

The transition of several of these countries (including certainly France and Holland) to the position of mature creditor is lost in the dim past, much as was the case with England. Probably the transition was made at a time when the investment was quite small. And the tremendous growth of the thirty-five years preceding World War I was, in terms of the over-all impact, financed out of earnings and by accretion. Harry D. White has estimated that between 1880 and 1913 net capital export from France was 30,245 million francs and net French revenues from foreign investments were 30,150 million francs.[7] The tremendous growth in investment was no real drain on the French economy, any more than it had been on the English.

United States—Evolution via the Balance of Trade

In the early part of its history the United States pretty clearly was in the immature borrower stage with the corresponding import trade balance. Thus large sums borrowed in England figured in the building of the railroads across the western part of the country.

This situation continued until the 1870's or 1880's. The data on balance on goods only indicates that 1874 was the year of transition—see Table 10. The goods and services balance, as distinguished from that on goods only, calls for a date probably in the 1880's—see Table 36.

[7] Iversen, *op. cit.*, p. 344.

TABLE 36
BALANCE OF TRADE (GOODS PLUS SERVICES) FOR THE UNITED STATES
(IN MILLIONS OF DOLLARS)
EXPORT BALANCE: NO SIGN; IMPORT BALANCE: (−)

	Balance on Goods and Services	Income on Investments (Net)	Balance on Goods and Services (Income on Investments Excluded)
Annual average 1850–1873	−115	−38	−77
Annual average 1874–1895	−32	−85	53
Annual average 1896–1914	96	−164	260
Annual average 1914–1918	2,394	80	2,314
1919	4,867	589	4,278
1920	3,522	476	3,046
1921	2,121	340	1,781
1922	989	565	424
1923	826	710	116
1924	1,342	622	720
1925	1,076	742	334
1926	817	753	64
1927	1,064	741	323
1928	1,367	805	562
1929	1,138	809	329
1930	1,022	745	277
1931	504	546	−42
1932	395	392	3
1933	346	322	24
1934	591	302	289
1935	108	366	−258
1936	84	299	−215
1937	285	282	3
1938	1,280	385	895
1939	1,055	311	744
1940	1,719	354	1,365
1941	2,410	357	2,053
1942	6,413	355	6,058
1943	11,038	353	10,685
1944	12,452	411	12,041
1945	6,041	358	5,683
1946	7,704	594	7,110
1947	11,592	857	10,735
1948	6,763	1,060	5,703
1949	6,372	1,062	5,310
1950	2,343	1,248	1,095
1951	5,214	1,527	3,687
1952	4,973	1,438	3,535
1953	4,748	1,416	3,332
1954	5,024	1,747	3,277
1955	4,126	2,000	2,126
1956	6,170	2,015	4,155

Source: *Historical Statistics*, pp. 242–3; *Statistical Abstract; Survey of Current Business.*

Between that time—whenever it was—and 1914, the United States continued as a net debtor country but with a substantial export trade balance. The country was engaged in a considerable amount of debt repayment, as well as interest payment, especially to England. At the same time the United States was engaged in some new lending on its own account, especially in Latin America, where United States mining companies were becoming active, such as the American Smelting and Refining Company in Mexico and the Cerro de Pasco Mining Company in Peru. United States-owned banana companies also were already active in Central America before World War I. Thus the United States was, during those years immediately preceding World War I, a clear-cut example of the net debtor country engaged in debt repayment (plus a limited amount of new lending on its own account) to an amount in excess of its new borrowing.

Estimates of the change in United States foreign investments through

TABLE 37

EVOLUTION OF UNITED STATES FOREIGN INVESTMENTS
(IN BILLIONS OF DOLLARS)

	NET POSITION			GROSS FOREIGN INVESTMENT				FOREIGN INVESTMENT IN U.S.
	CREDITOR (+), DEBTOR (−)				Long-	Long-	Long-	(Total long-plus short-term)
		Long-term	Short-term		term	term	term	
	Total	term	term	Total	total	Direct	Portfolio	
1843	−0.2	(n.a.)	(n.a.)	(neg.)	(n.a.)	(n.a.)	(n.a.)	0.2
1869	−1.46	−1.31	−0.15	0.08	0.08	(n.a.)	(n.a.)	1.54
1897	−2.71	−2.46	−0.25	0.69	0.69(sic)	0.64(sic)	0.5(sic)	3.4
1908	−3.9	(n.a.)	(n.a.)	2.5	2.5	1.6	0.9	6.4
1914	−3.7	−3.2	−0.5	3.5	3.5	2.6	0.9	7.2
1919	3.7	4.0	−0.3	7.0	6.5	3.9	2.6	*Long-* 3.3
1924	7.0	7.1	−0.1	10.9	10.0	5.4	4.6	*term* 3.9
1927	7.2	8.8	−1.6	13.8	12.5	6.6	5.9	*U.S.* 6.6
1930	8.8	9.5	−0.7	17.2	15.2	8.0	7.2	*Gov't* 8.4
1931	12.1	12.3	−0.2	15.9	14.6	8.1	6.5	3.8
1935	7.1	7.5	−0.4	13.5	12.6	7.8	4.8	6.4
1940	−1.3	3.1	−4.4	12.3	11.4	7.3	4.0	0.08 13.6
1945	−0.8	6.8	−7.6	16.8	15.3	8.4	5.3	1.6 17.6
1950	13.4	21.8	−8.4	32.8	31.0	11.8	5.7	13.5 19.5
1951	14.4	23.7	−9.3	35.0	33.0	13.1	6.2	13.8 20.6
1952	14.7	25.1	−10.4	37.3	35.2	14.8	6.3	14.1 22.5
1953	15.8	27.4	−11.6	39.5	37.5	16.2	5.9	15.4 23.6
1954	15.5	27.4	−11.9	42.2	39.6	17.7	6.6	15.2 26.8
1955	15.3	29.2	−13.9	44.9	41.8	19.2	7.4	15.2 29.6

(n.a.), not available; (neg.) negligible.

Source: *Historical Statistics*, p. 242; *Statistical Abstract, 1955*, p. 885; United States, Bureau of Foreign and Domestic Commerce, *Balance of Payments of the United States, 1949–1951*, p. 162; *Survey of Current Business*, August, 1955, p. 12.

the years are made in Table 37. A comparison of the data for 1897 and for 1914 indicates that a country may be a net debtor in the mature borrower stage engaged in more debt repayment (plus lending on its own account) than new borrowing, and yet the size of its debt may grow nonetheless. Between 1897 and 1914 the net United States debt seems to have increased from $2.71 billion to $3.7 billion. Perhaps a little of the power of accretion (or something) has slipped in—even in the United States case. At any rate, at the beginning of World War I the United States was a net debtor to the extent of $3.7 billion—in spite of having a foreign investment of its own of $3.5 billion. This meant that investment of foreigners in the United States was $7.2 billion at that time.

The Debtor Countries—the Transfer Problem

The underdeveloped countries in the nineteenth century went through several cycles of borrowing and default in connection with their portfolio borrowing. It was estimated not so many years ago that the Caribbean countries had been in default 403 years out of a collective existence of 955. Much of this undoubtedly was due to poor management, as the creditors have claimed. But some of it was inevitable. Meanwhile, through the course of the nineteenth century there was considerable accretion in the value of the direct investments. How much, it would be impossible to say exactly.

Accurate balance of trade figures for the underdeveloped countries are sketchy for the nineteenth century. But by about 1900, when data begins to give a rough picture of the situation, the countries were, as a group, already mature borrowers with export trade balances. And it seems probable that they had been in this condition for many years. This would be the corollary to be expected from the import trade balances of Britain, France, and Germany.

This situation was already established firmly enough in the 1920's so that the Latin American countries maintained export trade balances in the face of large new import of capital, especially portfolio lending from the United States. Latin America in those years furnished an example, then, of a mature borrower engaged in more debt repayment than new borrowing, yet the size of the debt was nevertheless increasing.

Probably most people are under the impression that a great deal of private investment is now flowing from the United States to the various underdeveloped countries and assisting in their development. Surely, one would think, this aid considerably overshadows the amount of interest that is being taken out of the underdeveloped countries. Yet a study by the Economic Commission for Latin America indicates that during the years 1948 through 1952 only $1,472 million (U.S.) of net new investment has been made in Latin America, while $3,971 million

(U.S.) of earning and interest on foreign investments have accrued to the investors.[8]

If only the investment of United States capital in Latin America and the actual international remittances for repatriation, amortization, and financial services on the United States investment in Latin America are taken into account (reinvested earnings being excluded from the computation), the developments for 1950 to 1953, in millions of dollars, look as follows:[9]

| | TOTAL INVESTMENTS OF PUBLIC RESOURCES AND PRIVATE CAPITAL | REMITTANCES | | | EXCESS OF REMITTANCES OVER INVESTMENT |
		Repatriations and Amortizations	*Financial Services*	*Total*	
1950	265	87	554	641	376
1951	671	82	685	767	96
1952	797	93	637	730	−67
1953	714	96	648	744	30

It seems that actual remittances of interest and profits and repatriations exceed new investments by the United States in Latin America. And if one adds reinvested earnings to the picture, the discrepancy between earnings and new investments gets even larger.

It is easy to overemphasize the contribution that foreign investments make to an economy. Apparently very soon after the initial investment is made, the "power of compound interest" is such that all further investments accomplish is the offsetting of interest payments. One might seriously question whether the underdeveloped countries are well advised to expect much net real contribution to their development from an inflow of such investments. The self-financing of capital goods imports by means of an export balance of trade might make for more of a real net contribution.

It is complete misrepresentation of the situation to say with W. Arthur Lewis:[10]

> Nearly every developed state has had the assistance of foreign finance to supplement its own meagre savings during the early stages of its development. England borrowed from Holland in the seventeenth and eighteenth centuries, and in turn came to

[8] United Nations, Economic Commission for Latin America, *Economic Survey of Latin America, 1953*, p. 29. The figure of $3,971 does include the reinvested earnings of subsidiaries.

[9] United Nations, Economic Commission for Latin America, *International Cooperation in a Latin American Development Policy* (New York, 1954), p. 17.

[10] W. Arthur Lewis, *The Theory of Economic Growth*, p. 244. Reprinted with the permission of George Allen and Unwin and of Richard D. Irwin.

lend to almost every other country in the world in the nineteenth and twentieth centuries. The United States of America, now the richest country in the world, borrowed heavily in the nineteenth century, and is in turn called upon to become the major lender of the twentieth.

A developing country would find difficulty in supporting its capital programme exclusively from domestic savings even if it wanted to, in so far as development programmes usually involve importing some capital goods from abroad.

WORLD WAR I AND THE 1920'S

During World War I there was a drastic and rather sudden change in the position of the United States from that of a net long-term debtor to that of a large net creditor. The United States was in debt (net long-term), chiefly to Europe, to the extent of $3.2 billion at the start of the war and was the creditor to the extent of some $18 billion (gross) at the close, if the so-called "war debts" were included. They are not included in Table 37, where the relevant net figure of $4 billion includes only long-term investments exclusive of about $11 billion of war debts.

Early in World War I, the house of Morgan began to make large loans to the British and French governments; and during the later war years, the United States government also made loans to those same governments. Much of the bitterness that followed the war, and especially the bitterness that the people of several European countries felt toward the United States during the early 1930's, involved the war debts which the British, French, and Belgian governments owed to the United States government. The Europeans felt, perhaps with considerable justice, that during the war they had suffered the casualties, and there was no way they could get back their dead; whereas the United States, which had suffered the loss merely of matériel and loans, was insisting on getting the loans repaid. This is a rather powerful type of argument; and it is little wonder that "Uncle Shylock" was attacked with some bitterness in the Continental press during the early depression years. These so-called war debts, long since defaulted, still exist and now total about $11 billion of unpaid principal plus a substantial, ever-growing sum of back interest. They are no longer generally carried in tables of the foreign investment of the United States, such as Table 37.

At any rate, at the beginning of the 1920's the United States might well have switched over to the status of mature creditor with an import trade balance, but did not. Through the 1920's private lending continued in large quantities, and with it the export balance. The United States was thus still an immature creditor during the 1920's. The increased

United States foreign investment in those years was not financed out of earnings. There was a substantial export balance on goods and services, even if interest and profit receipts are excluded from the data.

GERMAN REPARATIONS

Following World War I, the so-called war debts mentioned above were owed by the Allies among themselves, chiefly by England, France, Italy, and Belgium to the United States. Reparations were owed by Germany, in compensation for war damage, chiefly to France, Belgium, Italy, and England.

Following the Treaty of Versailles, in the London settlement of 1921, the Allies set the German reparations obligation at a figure of 132 billion gold marks. The Germans were most vociferous in the 1920's in complaining about the heavy burden of reparations. In 1923 they failed to make deliveries of certain reparations in kind which were due to the French and Belgians; and Franco-Belgian troops occupied the industrialized Ruhr. The Germans were non-co-operative; industry was at a standstill; and the British and United States governments were not overly sympathetic with the French-Belgian position.

Eventually an adjustment called the Dawes plan (after Charles G. Dawes) was worked out and put into operation in 1924. It called, among many things, for payments which, from the fifth year on, were to settle at 2.5 billion gold marks a year (about $595 million in United States dollars), which were guaranteed by a sort of mortgage on German industries and railroads, a claim against a so-called transport tax, and a general claim against the German budget. No total figure for reparations was specified. The French and Belgians withdrew from the Ruhr. And the Germans continued to complain about the amount of foreign meddling and influence in the internal operation of the German economy, the size of the debt payments, and the fact that the total amount of their obligation had not been set—all this in spite of the fact that they paid only 11 billion marks on reparations account between 1924 and 1931 and during the same period borrowed abroad 18 billion, of which roughly half came from the United States.[11] It seems that reparations actually were never any net burden on the German economy.

Partly as a result of the continued complaints, a revised plan, the Young plan (after Owen D. Young), was drawn up and put into operation in 1929. It fixed the total amount of German reparations at a figure equivalent to $7.83 billion (U.S.) by contrast with the Dawes plan which had set no total figure. It provided for the payment of

[11] Harold G. Moulton and Leo Pasvolsky, *War Debts and World Prosperity* (New York: Century, 1932), p. 300. This was a Brookings Institution study.

annuities for 59 years. The annual payments, which for the first thirty-seven years were to average 1.99 billion reichsmarks, were thus substantially smaller than the Dawes plan annuities. The Young plan also freed Germany from foreign financial supervision. The Bank for International Settlements was established at Basel to receive the payments in marks in Germany and worry about the international transfer problem. All Germany had to do was raise the marks. She did not have to worry about the transfer problem. Under these conditions reparations should not have been a great headache to Germany, even though they might have been a headache to the Bank. Then came the great depression, the Smoot-Hawley tariff, default on the war debts, default on reparations, and the Hoover moratorium, Adolf Hitler, and permanent default. Permanent default seems to have occurred more because it was a "point of honor" with the Hitler government to show they could get away with defaulting than because there was any necessary economic reason for it.

THE DEPRESSION YEARS

In 1929, United States foreign lending dried up. It virtually ceased during the spring of that year, perceptibly before the depression began, apparently as a result of the large profits that could be made by speculating on Wall Street, rather than because a depression was to begin in the fall. Capital consequently flowed to the United States, to take advantage of profit-making possibilities on Wall Street. After the onset of the depression, foreign lending continued at a low ebb, except for a brief spurt of lending in 1930.

Nevertheless, the United States continued to make extensive efforts to protect its export trade balance in the face of this cessation of lending. Two of the most conspicuous examples of this tactic were the Smoot-Hawley tariff of 1930 and the currency devaluation of 1933. A country can maintain an export trade balance under certain conditions; but it is well to recall what the conditions are; and neither tariffs nor currency devaluation are among the fundamental conditions. The consequences in this case were (1) defaults, (2) a large gold inflow, and (3) considerable reduction in the size of the export balance. In fact, as Table 36 indicates, the balance on goods and services (income on investments omitted) was actually an import balance in 1931, 1935, and 1936.

Foreigners justified their defaults on several bases. They could point out that the continuing effort of the United States to maintain an export trade balance made payment difficult. The French, Belgians, and British could wax morally indignant over United States insistence that the war debts be repaid. And the debtors, especially the Latin Americans who had borrowed in the New York money market during the 1920's, could point out how onerous were the terms under which they had borrowed.

One as well placed to know as Thomas Lamont had said in 1927: [12]

> I have in mind the reports that I have recently heard of American bankers and firms competing on almost a violent scale for the purpose of obtaining loans in various foreign money markets overseas. Naturally it is a tempting thing for certain of the European Governments to find a horde of American bankers sitting on their doorsteps offering them money. . . . That sort of competition tends to insecurity and unsound practice.

In the flotation of an international bond issue there are perhaps four parties directly concerned: (1) lender, (2) investment banker, (3) representatives of the borrower, and (4) the borrower.[13] The investment banker has a direct interest in the volume of bond flotations as distinct from the quality, because his remuneration is a more or less fixed percentage of the face value. Thus the investment banker (not the lender) may find it profitable to bribe the nephew of the president of Peru or the brother-in-law of the president of Cuba to encourage those governments to borrow for dubious projects. In such cases, one can say that the conduct of the investment banker in the lending country and the conduct of the representatives of the borrower in the borrowing country were both highly dubious. But does there remain a moral obligation on the part of the borrowers (who may be the taxpayers of the debtor country), who did not get their money's worth, to repay the lenders, who actually were out of pocket the sums of money that were loaned? It has been argued that the taxpayers of the debtor country are responsible for their government and must reap the consequences of their own poor government by paying off these debts. Conversely, it has been argued that in many cases the investment bankers and the foreign corporations (for example, the banana or mining companies) have meddled in the internal politics of the debtor countries and perhaps have had more influence on the formation of the government than the local citizenry itself.[14]

Perhaps the individual creditors in the lending countries had an

---

[12] United States Congress, Committee on Finance (Hearings, 72–1), *Sale of Foreign Bonds or Securities in the United States* (Washington: Government Printing Office, 1932), p. 25.

[13] See Chapter 24.

[14] Who would care to evaluate the relative responsibilities of the State Department (John Foster Dulles and John Peurifoy), of the United Fruit Company, and of the Guatemalan people for the present government of Guatemala? Let us say that the United States makes a loan to the Castillo Armas government which is in large

obligation to inform themselves better about the nature of the loans they were making and the purposes to which the money was to be put (whether it was to pay for an extravagant public monument or to pay the back salaries of the soldiers who had placed the current, but perhaps very transient, dictator in power). And since the creditors did not so inform themselves, perhaps they should lose their money. Or one might say that, given the misleading nature of the prospectuses issued by the investment bankers during the 1920's, it was impossible for the individual Illinois farmer, who was deceived thereby, to inform himself adequately of conditions in faraway Peru. He could not judge the merit of the "spread" between the price he paid for the bonds, the sum turned over to the borrower, and the face value. He had no conception of the propriety or lack of it of the taking over of the customs (of Nicaragua) in case of default, the reasonableness of provisions freezing the tax structure in the borrowing country, or other refinements of the flotation agreement. And he scarcely understood that in his loans to Germany, he was in effect providing much of what reparations Germany actually paid in the 1920's.

Thus it was in a setting ideally adapted to mutual recrimination that the depression began and the defaults of the early 1930's occurred. It may be argued that debtors who really wanted to pay could have done so. The prices of their exports might have been lowered. The terms of trade would have been increasingly unfavorable to them; but they could have paid the price necessary to get the necessary dollars and effect an import trade balance for the United States. Or could they have paid the price? Was the called-for change in the payment pattern in the early thirties so drastic that debtor countries could not have worked out the payments problem with the foreign-exchange reserves they had, no matter how willing they might have been to tolerate a worsening of their terms of trade? Maybe, even though this adjustment could have worked itself out, given a little time, it could not have worked itself out in the short time available following the change in the United States lending pattern and before reserves were exhausted.

Various short-sighted, selfish, and strange things were done by the people and governments of various countries as a result of the difficulties engendered by the depression. In the United States there were the Smoot-Hawley Tariff of 1930 and the currency devaluation of 1933, calculated to increase United States exports and decrease imports at a time when the reverse had to occur if debt repayment was to be effected. But this is not to say that the debtors paid as much as they could have

part used to pay off the troops who fought that rebellion. Then let us stretch our imaginations yet farther and say that the Castillo Armas government is forced from office in a democratic election and the new government refuses to honor his debts. Who should lose his money?

in the then prevailing state of the foreign-exchange market. Not only did the dictators, who came to power or established stronger controls over their economies in the early 1930's, choose to default on many of their obligations, regardless of ability to pay; but also many individuals who were persecuted by those dictatorships found it desirable to transfer funds to the United States. So there were forces motivating a capital flow to the United States, which involved an extensive inflow of gold. The gold reserves of the United States were built up from $4,000,000,000 (at $20.67 a fine ounce) in 1930 to $22,000,000,000 (at $35 a fine ounce) by 1940.

This combination of developments, and in particular the gold flow, thus financed the continuation of the small export trade balance of the United States and a capital inflow into the United States at the same time. But the gold inflow financed little or no debt repayment. Here is an example of a situation where extensive gold movement, during a period of ten years, made it possible for the trade balance of an important country not to correspond with the direction of capital movement. It may be noted, however, that gold did about as much as it could along this line during the 1930's; most of the gold reserves of the world were in the United States by the start of World War II.

At all events, by 1935 Latin America was in default on about 80 per cent of her portfolio borrowing in the United States and the whole world was in default on about 37.5 per cent.[15] There can be no default on direct investments, although the government of the country where the investment exists may embargo the transfer of profits or repatriation of capital by means of exchange controls, or it may even expropriate the property.

Table 38 indicates that the "great defaults" of the 1930's resulted in no over-all loss to the United States investors. They probably did involve real loss in individual cases, however; and they certainly resulted in the investors getting less return than they expected to get.

About 1937, the United States government decided that foreign lending ought to be resumed. The reasons were various. Germany was engaged in a trade drive for the Latin American market, a drive which the United States government wished to combat. President Roosevelt had assumed a strong anti-German position with the Chicago "quarantine the aggressor" speech of 1937. Also the United States wished to build up the supply of raw materials in the western hemisphere in order to be less dependent on Asia and Africa. That same year, 1937, the Export-Import Bank of Washington, an agency which had been created in 1934 to finance trade with Cuba and Russia, was authorized

[15] J. T. Madden, Marcus Nadler, and Harry C. Sauvain, *America's Experience as a Creditor Nation* (New York: Prentice-Hall, 1937), p. 126.

to make loans for development and other purposes to foreign governments or to other agencies (subject to government guarantee).

Thus a new major factor entered the foreign investment field. The
United States government moved onto the scene as the chief factor
in the world of international investments, and has continued to occupy
that position, if anything with increasing influence, since that time. This
was a major reversal of policy so far as the United States was concerned,
and it has effected a major change in the institutional setting in which
foreign lending is occurring. But it followed the failure of a strong
appeal by the government to private investors to step into the breach
and make loans. In justification for their failure to respond to the
government appeal, lenders could and did point out the losses due to
default after 1929, and they expressed the fear of expropriation. Be
that as it may, it was only after the failure of an appeal to private
enterprise to resume lending that the government stepped into the field.
And the Export-Import Bank, which has become the chief agent of
the United States government in its international lending activities, had
authorized $1,269,800,000 of lending by 1945.

LEND-LEASE

With the outbreak of World War II, it seemed desirable for the United
States to provide large amounts of equipment and supplies to Great
Britain, Russia, and the other United Nations. Bearing in mind the
sad history of the war debts of World War I, the Roosevelt administration
decided on the "lend-lease" formula. In this formula a distinction was
made between equipment that was primarily and obviously of a military nature, and machinery that could be used for ordinary industrial
purposes after the war. Military equipment, such as tanks, was considered expendable. If the tank which England received from the United
States was destroyed on the battlefield, there was no payment to be expected. If the tank happened to survive the war, the United States could
reclaim it if it desired. Thus the great amount of equipment that was
used and destroyed during the war was written off. However, if the
equipment had a postwar usefulness in the country to which it was
sent, the United States after the war negotiated with the possessing
country concerning value. The European government then assumed the
obligation of paying for such equipment.

Lend-lease aid between 1941 and 1948 (there being very little such
aid after 1946) totaled $49,100,000,000.[16] In the postwar settlements, the

[16] United States, Bureau of Foreign and Domestic Commerce, *Foreign Aid of the
United States Government, 1949-1951* (Washington: Government Printing Office,
1952), p. 34.

TABLE 38

PRIVATE FOREIGN INVESTMENT EXPERIENCE OF THE UNITED STATES, 1920–48

(MILLIONS OF DOLLARS)

	FOR THE PERIOD, 1920–40			FOR THE PERIOD, 1920–48		
	Direct Investments	Portfolio Securities (market value)	Total	Direct Investments	Portfolio Securities (market value)	Total
Value, beginning of period	3,880	2,576	6,456	3,880	2,576	6,456
Net additional investment during period	3,554	3,609	7,163	7,271	4,022	11,293
Total	7,434	6,185	13,619	11,151	6,598	17,749
Value at end of period	7,340	2,725	10,065	11,379	3,904	15,283
Net capital loss (−) or gain (+)	−94	−3,460	−3,554	228	−2,694	−2,466
Income received	7,391	4,950	12,341	11,892	6,103	17,995
Income received plus capital gain or loss	7,297	1,490	8,787	12,120	3,409	15,529

Source: *Survey of Current Business*, November, 1949, p. 20.

United Kingdom has assumed the obligation of repaying $622,000,000 (total lend-lease aid to the United Kingdom: $31,000,000,000, against which should be offset $7,000,000,000 of reverse lend-lease). Settlements with other countries have provided for repayment of $1,134,000,000. As of June 30, 1951, the remaining (unpaid-off) recognized foreign debt arising out of lend-lease totaled $1,575,582,000. The United States has not yet worked out a satisfactory general lend-lease settlement with Russia or with China, but the Russians have returned a small amount of the equipment which remained in their possession at the end of the war.

CONCLUSION

International investment ostensibly exists as a manifestation of the movement of capital, goods, and technical knowledge out from the centers where such things are concentrated, a movement which is quickly countered by the growth of interest payments going the other way. But growth of foreign investment also may occur by accretion without any movement of goods or capital.

Chapter 26

POST-WORLD WAR II GRANTS
AND AID

⩗ ⩗ ⩗

*Partly motivated by a willingness to aid in postwar reconstruction, partly
to gain support against the U.S.S.R., partly to further economic
development in the underdeveloped countries, the United States has
in recent years engaged in an extensive program of international
grants and aid.*

⩗ ⩗ ⩗

IN THE latter part of World War II, the United States and Russia were, at least superficially, co-operating. And the United States gave to the Russians a substantial amount of lend-lease assistance, about $11 billion worth, one fourth of the total extended during the war.

YALTA (AND GERMAN REPARATIONS)

Then, at the Yalta Conference in February, 1945, it seems that President Roosevelt agreed that Russia should regain the southern half of Sakhalin (lost in 1904), should acquire the Kurile islands, should have the right to participate in the operation of the Chinese Eastern Railroad jointly with China, and should have the wish implemented that the commercial port of Dairen be internationalized. (Russia's pre-eminent interest in Dairen was recognized.) A tentative working basis for reparations settlement anticipated that Russia would get half of $20 billion of total reparations from Germany. This reparations figure was a rather modest sum on the whole, considering the destruction and casualties that Germany had caused—not to mention that the figure was well under half of the figure for wartime lend-lease aid and also less than half of the gross foreign aid the United States has provided since the end of the war. Just as was the case in the 1920's, such reparations as Germany has paid since the end of World War II in effect has been financed largely by United States aid. The United States has provided Germany since the end of the war with $3.8 billion of aid.

In terms of the discussion in Chapter 24, there can hardly be any doubt that it is possible for Germany to transfer at least $20 billion of reparations, given any time at all. If an export balance of $5 billion is possible in one year for the United States, with no perceptible strain on the economy, an export balance of, say, $1 billion a year for twenty years is possible for Germany. The recent success of Germany's export trade drive is additional evidence on this score. But again, as was the case in the 1920's, there is the question of German willingness as well as of German ability.

However, these comments are now largely dated. The issue of German reparations is thoroughly subservient to the issue of Russian–United States friction.

THE TRUMAN DOCTRINE

The wartime co-operation between the United States and Russia was never much more than skin-deep. There had been a background of friction and mistrust between the two countries since 1917. The Communist Russians have always feared a capitalistic conspiracy to destroy their government. This is a fear for which there would seem, from their point of view, to have been some basis, if one recalls that in 1918–19 the United States, Great Britain, and France put several divisions of troops into Russia at Archangel and Vladivostok and actively fought against the Reds. Thomas W. Lamont has described it as [1] "the 1918 invasion of Russia by the Allies which, ever since that time, has been the greatest source of suspicion to the Soviet Government and to the Russian people, and is today one of the chief factors that continues to make relations difficult." In fact, the United States government did not grant diplomatic recognition to the Communist government of Russia until 1933.

Perhaps contributing to the change in United States attitude in 1933 was the change in the conviction of the Russians that their revolution must be world-wide to be successful. The position of Lenin and of Trotsky in the early twenties had been that a Communist revolution could not succeed in just one country. They believed that the non-Communist countries would not allow it to succeed. To be successful, they thought such a revolution had to be world-wide in the first place. This attitude could hardly be comforting to the non-Communist govern-

[1] Thomas W. Lamont, *Across World Frontiers* (New York: Harcourt, Brace, 1951), p. 96.

ments of the world. But after the advent of Stalin to power (1924-27), the official position was changed; and it was affirmed that Communism could be successfully established in Russia without the necessity that the rest of the world be Communist first. Then began the series of Five-year Plans that was intended to make Communism a success in Russia.

But, in spite of these developments, all did not become harmony and understanding between the Communist and non-Communist worlds. Communist parties continued to be active in most countries; and the Comintern, with headquarters in Moscow and an Italian, Palmiro Togliatti, as the secretary-general, continued to agitate for the overthrow of non-Communist governments. This policy was only partially de-emphasized in the late thirties as Russian Foreign Minister Litvinov made a show of co-operating with other countries, especially through the League of Nations machinery. During the 1930's, the Communist parties in the various countries were quite intransigent in refusing to co-operate with non-Communist parties of the left in running governments. Communist parties were especially antagonistic to the parties with reform ideas quite close to, although not quite as far to the "left" as, their own, such as the Second International Marxian Socialists—the Social Democrats in Germany and the Socialist Party of Leon Blum in France. They were, in fact, more likely to co-operate with the extreme right than with the parties of the moderate left. One such instance was their co-operation with the Nazi party in Prussia in 1932, just before the Nazis maneuvered themselves into power. This instance ranks with the hindrance by the French Communist Party of French armaments production in 1939 and 1940, when the Nazi menace was overshadowing.

At all events, between December, 1941, and the fall of 1945 the United States and Russia were both fighting against the Axis, and considerable assistance was extended back and forth, especially in the form of the United States lend-lease aid to Russia. But the two governments were never on intimate terms. The Russians were not informed of the dates of significant Western operations, such as the Normandy invasion. And they were not a party to the atomic bomb project. For their part, the Russians also seem to have refused Americans free access to virtually all confidential military information. And they were most restrictive in their control of the actions of such American troops as found their way into Russia during the war.

Despite the fact that the Yalta conference of February, 1945, ostensibly settled the differences between Russia and the West, relations were beginning to be strained by the time the war was over in Europe in May. In the inter-Allied agreement that specified which sections of Germany the different Allied armies would occupy, Saxony was included in the Russian zone; but it had been occupied, during the fighting, by the American Third Army, which was slow to withdraw. A period of time elapsed, and a certain amount of Russian verbal insistence occurred, before the Americans withdrew.[2] A very similar incident, with the shoe on the other foot, involved the Russians, who were slow in withdrawing from Iran in 1946. Winston Churchill's Fulton, Missouri, speech of March 5, 1946, calling for a military alliance between the United States and Britain against Russia and coining the expression "iron curtain," brought into common use a term to describe the cleavage, and perhaps contributed to making the cleavage worse.[3]

At the end of the war the Russians seem to have thought they could take over the governments of western Europe (France, Germany, Italy, etc.) through the democratic process. Their "party line" called for active effort to win votes in elections and for participation in governmental cabinets, in the process of trying to obtain control of the governments. But the Russians were not particularly successful in taking over governments by this process, except in countries which were already occupied by Russian troops. Nevertheless, by 1947 Communist-controlled governments existed in Poland, Bulgaria, Rumania, Yugoslavia, and Hungary (Russia having absorbed the Baltic countries of Estonia, Latvia, and Lithuania), and by 1948 the Communists were in complete control in Czechoslovakia. Yugoslavia was probably the only one of these countries where the Communist success was not facilitated by the presence of Russian troops. And that is the country where Russia has not succeeded in retaining dominance and subservience.

By early 1947, if not sooner, the United States government was active in trying to counteract the spread of Communism. The Truman doctrine, calling for $400 million in economic and military aid to Greece and Turkey, was approved by Congress in May of that year. The aid included food, machinery, and equipment to aid industrial development, as well as military equipment and military advice and advisers.[4]

It may be worth-while to attempt an appraisal of this Greek-Turkish

[2] Strangely enough, the occupation has proceeded most harmoniously where it has been joint and where no geographical lines have been drawn—that is, in Vienna; but there has been continuing friction where precise geographical boundaries have been maintained. This may be an argument for as free international movement of people and as few frontier barriers as possible.

[3] Who can say for certain that there was not the possibility at that time of a postwar world in which a major conflict was avoided between Russia and the West, although perhaps the Russians should have appreciated that Churchill was not at that time prime minister of England?

[4] The Russians said that this showed there was some substance to their fear of capitalistic encirclement and the charge that there is a capitalistic conspiracy against them. Moreover, what would Americans think if Russia were to do in Mexico what the United States was doing in Greece and Turkey?

loan in the light of the problem of transfer mechanics. The motivation in this case was fairly clear-cut and had nothing to do with the difference in interest rates in Greece and the United States. The United States government was willing to make the loan for political reasons, to build up allies who were threatened by Russian expansion. Greece and Turkey, for their part, wanted goods, supplies, capital equipment, military equipment, foreign balances just-in-case, and what have you, from the one country which was in a position to supply such things. Given motivation of this sort, there is no transfer problem in connection with the original loan; but repayment may be something else again.

Repayment of interest and principal in the case of these Greek and Turkish loans may represent a serious problem for two reasons: one economic, the other political. Repayment of such a sum will require a certain adjustment in the trade balances which will not occur as naturally as the adjustments connected with the original lending. But probably the sum involved is not of such magnitude as to present a major difficulty to payment—unless, at the time of attempted repayment, an inflationary credit policy in Greece and Turkey coincides with a deflationary policy in the United States; and the appropriate foreign exchange rates changes do not occur. In such a case there could be transfer difficulty. But in that case there would be balance of payments trouble among these countries anyway.

The political aspect of the problem cannot be so easily disposed of. Any new Greek or Turkish government is bound not to be too happy about the repayment of such loans. If a Communist government were to gain power in either country, such a government almost certainly would default. But it is a fair guess that any government except a monarchist government in Greece and a Republican People's Party government in Turkey would be tempted to do the same. Such governments are likely to say to themselves that the United States has bought $400 millions-worth of alliance and friendship and gotten what it paid for—why should it get its money back as well? A genuinely democratic (non-Communist) government of the center or left-center might say as well that the United States loan had tended to prop up the "no-good" right-wing governments of kings George II and Paul in Greece.

At any rate, the Communist coup d'état in Czechoslovakia in 1948, the Berlin blockade which began April 1, 1948, and continued Communist agitation in France and Italy convinced the United States Congress that the type of thing being done for Greece and Turkey would have to be done on a far larger scale—on a scale so large as to make repayment economically difficult and politically impossible. Furthermore, we should aid our former allies to recover from the war's desolation, should we not?

THE MARSHALL PLAN

The Proposal

In fact, on June 5, 1947, the Secretary of State and former Army Chief of Staff, George C. Marshall, in an address made at the Harvard University commencement exercises, proposed what has since become known as the Marshall plan. This was only a month after Congress had approved the Greek-Turkish loan and almost a year before the Czech coup and the Berlin air lift.

And it may legitimately be claimed by the United States that the Marshall plan was something more than just an anti-Russian move. It followed the terrible storms of the winter of 1946–47 and the crop failures of that year which, on top of the wartime suffering and destruction, meant desperate conditions in Europe in 1947. The United States could well have had a somewhat guilty conscience as a result of suddenly cutting off most aid to Europe (notably lend-lease) immediately after the war was over and before even a start had been made at repairing the wartime damage. Then, too, on May 30 (less than a week before the Harvard speech) the moderate regime of Ferenc Nagy was overthrown in Hungary by the Communists; and concern about Communist successes was not wanting in the United States.

George Marshall's proposal was for a "European-sponsored program embodying foreign aid, self-help, and mutual assistance, designed to place Europe on its feet economically." [5] The U.S.S.R. and the Russian-dominated countries were invited to associate with most of the other countries of Europe in the project. This was before the cold war was crystallized by the Czech coup and the Berlin air lift; and the inclusion of the U.S.S.R. and the satellite countries in the invitations was undoubtedly the statesmanlike thing to do. With the exercise of just a little imagination at that time, the Russians could have participated and received a substantial amount of aid, and the climate of international relations might have been considerably improved.

The Russian Position

Instead the Russians chose to take the position that their inclusion in the invitation was just a sham and that they would not receive really worth-while aid under the program; probably also they did not dare allow their satellites to participate because the aid might tend to draw them away from their subservience to Russia. Russia's next moves in Czechoslovakia and Berlin were calculated to convince the United States

[5] United States, Bureau of Foreign and Domestic Commerce, *Foreign Aid by the United States Government 1949–1951*, p. 56.

Senate that there was real need for the Marshall plan. The Russian procedure in 1947 and 1948 was truly one of history's tragic démarches —one which cannot be explained either on the basis of Marxian logic or of common sense, although it offers one more bit of evidence that the judgment of dictators, even in the area of short-run conniving, is not always good.

Marxian logic would indicate that if Russia wished the overthrow of the United States government, she should not have intensified the difficulties of 1947 into the "cold war" of 1948 and the "hot war" of 1950. Marx said in the *Communist Manifesto:* "The need of a constantly expanding market for its products chases the bourgeoisie over the whole surface of the globe." But the Russian-inspired war scares and wars provided the United States economy with just the markets which otherwise, according to the Marxist view, would have failed. In terms of Marxist logic the result of the cold war was to shore up the United States economy rather than to foster its collapse. If Russia wanted the United States economy to disintegrate, in accordance with the Marxian theory, she should have ended the cold war, talked much of peace, and waited for overproduction, market failure, and depression to do her work for her. In depression times Communist ideas might be expected (by the Russians) to have the sympathy of many Americans who presently see Communism as a political and military menace and as little more.

Given the terrible implications of atomic war, the only possible approach the United States can take to the Russian problem—saving the possibility that the Russian regime will fall from within—is the assumption of the long-drawn-out stalemate. We have to live in the world with the Russians, and the possibility remains that we can live under improving conditions. The circumstances of the world may force this evolution on the Russians (in spite of their Marxist philosophy) just as circumstances forced it on Catholics and Protestants after the Thirty Years War.

But despite their alleged Marxian background, the Russians seem to think, in the age-old way, that military measures (perhaps through the instrumentality of subversion), and geographical expansion, and constant attrition of one's foes are the ways to conquest. Man has learned little in all the thousands of years of his history; the Russians do not seem to have learned much from Marx or from history. And the United States, according to Communist theory, has Russia to thank for full employment and rising national income.

Or does the somewhat conciliatory attitude of the Russians at the Geneva "Summit" conference of 1955 indicate that they are finally doing as their theory indicates they should do?

At all events, in 1947 the Russians refused to participate, and refused to allow their associated countries to participate, in the Marshall plan. What the Russians did do was to set up a somewhat similar aid program themselves. The program is under the jurisdiction of the Council for Mutual Economic Aid and seems to be assigned the general responsibility for control and co-ordination of economic activities in the Soviet bloc, China included.[6] How much real Russian generosity there has been in connection with all this is uncertain. After all, significant grants to foreign countries would represent something more of a sacrifice for Russia than they represent for the United States. Nevertheless, as a result of all this the Communist sphere is becoming ever more deeply committed to the proposition of pulling itself up by its own bootstraps.

Mechanics of the Marshall Plan

Whatever the Russian position, the countries of western Europe were interested in the Marshall plan because they needed United States goods. They were suffering from the physical destruction of the war, from the hardships of the winter of 1946–47, and from the crop failures; and, after the war, they wanted to rebuild and to eat.

Thus the Marshall plan was no more interest-rate motivated than the Truman doctrine had been. The recipient countries wanted goods where they could get them, and the United States had a mixed anti-Russian and humanitarian motive for supplying them.

The plan went into operation with the Economic Cooperation Administration (ECA)—Paul Hoffman, director—functioning as the responsible United States government agency and the Organization for European Economic Cooperation (OEEC) functioning as the responsible intergovernmental agency for the participating European governments (Austria, Belgium, Denmark, France, Greece, Iceland, Ireland, Italy, Luxembourg, Netherlands, Norway, Portugal, Sweden, Switzerland, Turkey, and the United Kingdom). The name of the Economic Cooperation Administration was changed in 1951 to the Mutual Security Agency to emphasize the increased importance of military and security matters by comparison with the economic. And in 1953 a new over-all organization was set up, the Foreign Operations Administration (FOA), with Harold E. Stassen as director. The Republicans were apparently willing to continue the Truman program, but only under a new name.

Further reorganization of the administration of the program was effected July 1, 1955. At that time most of the functions of the program were transferred to an again renamed International Cooperation Administration within the Department of State. Certain military aspects of the program were transferred to the Department of Defense. The head of the new International Cooperation Administration is John B. Hollister,

---

[6] The Council for Mutual Economic Aid is briefly discussed in Chapter 14.

a former law partner of Senator Robert Taft. Meanwhile Harold Stassen became a special assistant to President Eisenhower—in charge of working out a disarmament program.

Table 39 is a summary of all the foreign aid, not just Marshall plan aid, which the United States has extended since 1945. It will be noted that

TABLE 39

UNITED STATES GOVERNMENT FOREIGN GRANTS AND CREDITS, TOTAL POSTWAR PERIOD, 1945 THROUGH 1955

(IN MILLIONS OF DOLLARS)

Net Grants and Credits		53,151
Net Grants	42,283	
(Gross New Grants)	(46,142)	
Net Credits	10,868	
(New Credits)	(12,290)	
* * * * *		
Military Grants (Net)	15,788	
Other Grants and Credits (Net)	37,363	
Western Europe (Excluding		
Greece and Turkey) and		
Dependent Areas		24,474
(United Kingdom)	6,898	
(France)	5,502	
(Germany)	3,877	
(Italy-Trieste)	2,758	
(Spain)	98	
(Yugoslavia)	758	
Eastern Europe		1,098
(U.S.S.R.)	426	
Near East and Africa		2,589
South Asia		588
Other Asia and Pacific		6,584
American Republics		1,048
Canada		−1
International Organizations		
and Unspecified Areas		982

Source: *Statistical Abstract, 1956*, pp. 891–4.

grants represent about four fifths of the total and credits (calling for repayment) one fifth.

Of the ICA expenditures, about three dollars out of four are spent for the purchase of goods and services in the United States. About one fourth is "offshore procurement"—the purchase of goods or the financing of plant construction abroad. The evolution of the spending program since 1948 is indicated by the following tabulation.[7]

Foreign aid appropriations under the Truman administration:

[7] *New York Times*, August 1, 1956, p. 10.

Fiscal Years

    1948–49........$6,386,800,000. Includes no military aid
    1950...........$5,173,200,000, including $1,314,000,000 military assistance
    1951...........$7,339,400,000, including $5,223,000,000 military assistance
    1952...........$7,282,300,000, including $5,267,000,000 military assistance
    1953...........$6,011,900,000, including $4,098,000,000 military assistance

Foreign aid appropriations under the Eisenhower administration:

Fiscal Years

    1954...........$4,724,000,000, including $3,219,000,000 military assistance
    1955...........$2,799,300,000, including $1,193,000,000 military assistance
    1956...........$2,703,000,000, including $1,100,000,000 military assistance
    1957...........$3,766,570,000, including $2,017,500,000 military assistance

The importance of the economic and technical co-operation parts of the program actually has slipped even more in recent years, relative to the military, than this tabulation indicates. There is a category of so-called "defense support" expenditures, described as having both a military and an economic facet and therefore not included in the military part of the above tabulation. Defense support expenditures were scheduled to amount to over $1 billion in fiscal 1956. The combination of military assistance and defense support currently runs well over four fifths of the total. Technical co-operation and genuine development assistance combined total only $300 to $400 million dollars.

For 1956, assistance under the foreign-aid program was scheduled to be divided by regions as follows:

Asia	52 per cent
Near East and Africa	14
Europe	13
Latin America	3
Non-regional	18

The mechanics of the Marshall plan grants were described in Chart 18. As the chart indicated, the fundamentals are simple. But essentially there is no international movement of funds in the ordinary meaning of the term. The United States government pays the United States exporter in dollars for the goods covered. The European importer pays his government in his local currency for the goods imported. This is not difficult. There is no shortage of francs in France or of pounds sterling in England. There is no transfer problem inasmuch as the United States is willing to provide the goods and the European countries desire them.

But the disposition of the money (francs) which the recipient (French) government then possesses has presented one of the most delicate problems in connection with the plan. These are the "counterpart funds." The difficulty derives not so much from the "up to" 5 per cent of the funds ($722 million by June 30, 1956) that may be used to meet United States government expenses in Europe (although that sum may permit United States government personnel to ensconce themselves rather comfortably abroad), as from the other 95 per cent. In effect, the United States government is in a position to tell the European governments how a sum which amounted to $13,752 million by June 30, 1956, should be spent within their borders.[8]

Of course, the European governments may well consider a little United States meddling in their internal affairs preferable to having to repay the money. Nevertheless, the situation does permit a considerable amount of meddling by some rather irresponsible individual Americans in the internal affairs of certain European countries. The Economic Cooperation Administration had to recruit a rather large staff on rather short notice in 1948. Some business executives in government service under such circumstances just do not seem to be able to forget the interests of the private corporation with which their basic affiliation is. It is perhaps not strange that a businessman, on leave temporarily from an oil company and working for the ECA in Rome, would find it difficult to resist the temptation to suggest to certain Italian officials that it might be appropriate for the Italian legislature to change its law on oil concessions so that United States oil companies could acquire certain properties in the Po valley. Or to cite another example, according to Francis Biddle:[9] "Yet on May 12, 1948, Paul G. Hoffman, economic co-operation administrator, testified before the Senate Appropriations Committee that he would probably refuse to assist the United Kingdom to develop an industry which the British government had determined to nationalize."

There is the classic example of double entendre from the Economic Cooperation Administration itself:[10] "In the case of France, the E.C.A. agreed to the release of counterpart funds at the same time as the French Government undertook on its own initiative to work out plans

---

[8] The disposition of the actual withdrawals made from European program counterpart funds through June 30, 1956, was as follows (International Cooperation Administration, *Counterpart Funds and ICA Foreign Currency Accounts, Data as of June 30, 1956*):

Military purposes	$1,786 million
Debt retirement	2,511
Promotion of production	4,394
Productivity projects	73
Other	1,079
Total	$9,843 million

These figures do not include the $722 million reserved for actual use by the United States.

[9] Francis Biddle, *The World's Best Hope* (Chicago: University of Chicago Press, 1949), p. 114.

[10] United States, Economic Cooperation Administration, *A Report on Recovery Progress and United States Aid* (Washington, 1949), p. 14.

to reform its tax structure and to keep governmental expenditures within non-inflationary limits." Alex L. Hillman in his report on the *Foreign-Aid Program in Europe* said:[11] "Too often the technicians sent from the United States are arrogant, domineering, and contemptuous of the Europeans." In addition, various United States Senators can be counted on to give ill-timed speeches saying that if various European countries don't do so-and-so their aid had better be cut off.

To return to certain theoretical considerations of an economic nature: In view of the fact that most Marshall plan aid has taken the form of grants, the liquidation of the plan will not pose serious problems of repayment and balance of payments adjustment. The relatively small proportion of the aid which has been in the form of loans or credits should present no great repayment problem—if there is any will at all to pay or be paid on the part of borrower or lender.

A slightly different issue connected with the end of the program of assistance may be worth mentioning, however. One will look a long way among countries organized on a free private enterprise basis before finding any that are interested in the encouragement of imports relative to exports. The typical attitude, of course, has been to push exports and cut off imports insofar as possible. One might guess, in consequence, that Marshall plan aid is likely to come to an end, not so much when the United States decides to cut off the assistance, as when the countries in Europe decide that they do not want the net inflow of goods any longer. It will be interesting to note how those in the United States who are continually complaining that the United States has to prop up the rest of the world will explain this development—of the not-too-distant future.

THE PROBLEM OF FRIENDSHIP

Speculation on the nature and usefulness of the Marshall plan can give rise to some strange thoughts. The United States is trying to use the program to win friends and allies against Russia. How do you win real friends? One would think generous giving would help. But a moment's reflection back over one's own life may serve to raise a doubt. How often does the person to whom something is given feel resentment against the giver? Mark Twain once wrote:[12] "If you pick up a starving dog and make him prosperous, he will not bite you. This is the principal difference between a dog and a man."

[11] United States Congress, Senate, Committee on Appropriations, Investigations Division, *Foreign-Aid Program in Europe* (Washington: Government Printing Office, 1953), p. 27.

[12] Mark Twain, *Pudd'nhead Wilson* (New York: Harper, 1893), p. 158. An entry in Pudd'nhead Wilson's Calendar.

How often does the giver feel that he is entitled to patronize the mendicant to whom he has given something? The result of the charity is consequently bitterness and animosity instead of friendship. I believe that most soldiers who went through either World War I or World War II in the American army in Europe felt the essential friendliness of the people. The fact that there was no significant sabotage behind the Allied lines in World War II made life far easier for the Allied armies than it had been for the German armies earlier in the same areas. We had a backlog of good will at the end of World War II. The United States has spent a tremendous sum of money in recent years to maintain and increase that backlog, and yet has largely lost it.[13]

Actually the United States, since World War II, has engaged in a program of genuine, sincere charity which is unprecedented in history. Millions of kind-hearted people have generously given of their substance to foreigners: flood relief in Piedras Negras, an earthquake in Chile, Care packages to Europe, support of UNRRA, teaching in the back-country of Paraguay, the United Appeal for Overseas Relief, Rehabilitation, and Reconstruction. And yet one gets the feeling that we are losing ground—in terms of genuine friendliness felt all over the world toward the United States.

That it should be so is perhaps not strange, but it is certainly very regrettable. It has given a look of authenticity to the Russian charge that the United States has been buying Europe for the American style of free private enterprise by means of the Marshall plan, and that American enterprises were going to end up with the property titles also if they could. And the officials who have taken it on themselves to engage in this sort of activity in addition to their proper ECA functions would have done better to have stayed at home. The stakes involved in the Russian-American game today are far too important to allow this crude sort of private-enterprise self-seeking to interfere with the larger American interest in peace, democracy, and stable world order. Let the British decide whether they want socialized medicine or not. It is their business! American strength in the world rests as much on disinterested democratic leadership as on industrial might. If we are to have the real heartfelt support of most people against the Russians, we need to keep our record for humanity and a certain selfless promotion of the general well-being reasonably unsullied. Pressuring for special privilege cannot help this cause, nor can insistence that every other country do just as we say, under threat that we will cut their aid off.

But we have lost a great deal, and here in the United States our concern must be more for our own conduct than for that of the foreigners—we will go to heaven on the strength of our good deeds, not

[13] *New York Times,* June 12, 1956, p. 19.

on the strength of foreign misdeeds. We will be well advised to speculate as to why all this has happened. And the cause, of course, goes a good deal beyond the behavior of certain Marshall plan officials. Perhaps some of the factors may have been: our failure to back popular governments in the countries we occupied during and after the war (our not enviable record including support of the King and Badoglio in Italy, Fritz Schaeffer in Bavaria, and the most conservative non-Nazi element in almost every town where Military Government set up an administration); our repudiation (never overt but none the less definite) of the non-Communist parties of the left in Italy, France, Germany, etc.; our affiliation with and propinquity to unconstructive governments in the under-developed countries;[14] the Russian exploitation of the argument that they (not we) are interested in peace and human welfare (whether they are or not); our energetic pushing for "security and incentives" for American investment everywhere; our energetic repetition of the statement that the greatest pearl of all we have to offer them is free and unadulterated private enterprise.

Some facets of the psychological difficulties growing out of postwar United States aid to France are indicated by the following quotation from Bernard Lavergne (describing a condition which antedates Mendes-France and the Indo-China armistice by two years):[15]

> . . . we remain, it seems, in Indo-China—although it is folly for us to do so—in order not to displease the Americans. . . .
> We are, of course, very grateful to the Americans for providing us with arms and dollars even though we ought to find the means to do without them. . . . [translation by the author]

But perhaps some comfort is to be gained from the fact that Russian troops seem to be just about as unsuccessful in coercing people into alliance as American money is in buying true friends.

[14] There are, for example, Franco and the King of Greece. Till recently, there were Bao Dai and King Farouk. There are twenty "republics" in Latin America. The governments of perhaps three of them are genuinely decent—Mexico, Costa Rica, and Uruguay. The governments of three or four more are perhaps entitled to the benefit of the doubt. The rest are intolerable. (See: German Arciniegas, *The State of Latin America* [New York: Knopf, 1952]). At this point I cannot resist inserting one quotation from *Hispanic American Report*, August (September), 1954, p. 10, on the subject of Guatemala: "Castillo Armas picked José Bernabé Linares, who ran the secret police under the late dictator Ubico, to perform this service for him. Linares was known to have submerged political enemies in electric-shock baths, and perfected a head-shrinking steel skull cap to pry loose secrets and crush improper thoughts." That the United States government has a considerable responsibility for the existence of the Castillo Armas regime seems fairly obvious. That the United States government has given the regime none of the really tangible aid and support which it needs if it is going to be a success also seems fairly obvious.

[15] Bernard Lavergne, "Le Redressement de l'Ordre Politique Intérieur," *L'Année Politique et Economique,* April, 1952, p. 135.

If "good can come of evil," perhaps Ernest T. Weir is correct in saying: [16]

> And to assume that Russian leaders would attempt to take the unwilling citizenry of their own and other countries into a war of such magnitude is to ascribe to those leaders a degree of stupidity that they have not yet shown. . . . In short, for these and other reasons, Europeans believe that Russia would not engage in war unless actually attacked or unless the people could be convinced that attack was unavoidable.

Perhaps, with a little statesmanship on our part, there may not be an atomic war after all. The *Boston Globe* has commented: "Man's apparent decision not to have an atomic war is the most sensational triumph of common sense since he first decided to come in out of the rain."

[16] Ernest T. Weir, *Notes on the Foreign Situation Based on a Trip Abroad* (Grant Building, Pittsburgh, Penn., 1953), p. 11.

Chapter 27

POST-WORLD WAR II ATTITUDES
TOWARD INVESTMENTS

ⱶ ⱶ ⱶ

*Developed countries desire to expand their foreign investments because
of the profit to be made from them, because they are thought to
support an export balance of trade, and because of the prestige
and influence gained from having large investments.*

*Developed countries are reluctant to make foreign investments because
of the defaults and expropriations of the past. They also are concerned about exchange controls and taxes.*

*Underdeveloped countries are desirous of obtaining investments because
of the belief that they make a net contribution to development.*

*The desire of underdeveloped countries to receive investments is tempered
by their recollections of the measure of foreign dominance and
intervention which has frequently been a by-product of investment
in the past.*

*There probably cannot be an entirely satisfactory solution to these prob-
lems short of an international court with effective jurisdiction over
disputes involving foreign investments and short of an effective
international taxing authority.*

*Meanwhile, nondiscrimination and reasonable tolerance on both sides
can help a good deal.*

ⱶ ⱶ ⱶ

LET us turn from these sweeping generalizations about matters of
high policy to more mundane questions concerning the foreign
investment picture in the postwar world as it looks to private
investors and to borrowers.

PRESENT DEBT STATUS

With regard to United States portfolio loans, interest payments have
been resumed on much of what was defaulted during the 1930's. Less

than one fourth of the total is in default; 89 per cent of the defaults are in Europe and about 10 per cent in Latin America. True, the agreements providing for resumption of service frequently have provided for some writing down of the principal or reduction of the interest. But if one recalls the power of interest to compound, something along this line may well have been appropriate. Service was resumed partly because funds derived from United States aid, especially Export-Import Bank loans, facilitated such resumption; partly because of the implied (at least) threat that a country might not get Export-Import Bank or International Bank aid unless it worked out a settlement on its defaulted obligations.

Since World War II, private portfolio lending, for example to Canada, has been resumed on a small scale by the United States. But, on the whole, portfolio investment has continued to be of minor importance.

The United States has been, by all odds, the chief creditor-lender country in the world in these times. But most of the private investments going out from the United States since the end of World War II have been direct: chiefly in oil, but to a lesser extent in manufacturing. On the whole, the rate of return on these direct investments is substantially higher than the rate of return on the old portfolio investments.

By contrast with the United States situation, much of the British foreign investment (especially in Argentina, Iran, and India) has been lost. The process has gone on in various ways. Much of the funds required to repurchase the Argentine railways was derived from the surplus of Argentine shipments to England during World War II. The government of Iran moved directly to take over the property of the Anglo-Iranian Oil Company in that country. A settlement of the dispute left the Iranian government with formal title to the properties and most of the responsibility for production and marketing in the hands of a consortium which included several United States companies as well as Anglo-Iranian (which had meanwhile changed its name to the British Petroleum Company). In India, as in Argentina, the large amount of wartime aid by India to Britain provided the resources for repatriating a good deal of the British investment in India. England has not completely abdicated her role as a creditor-lender country and is making an effort to provide new investment funds in the colonies and dominions. Nevertheless, whether England is a net creditor or a net debtor at present is anybody's guess. The United States government, since the end of World War II, has loaned the British government almost $4 billion.

Whether or not Britain is still a net creditor, the interest rate and profit rate remittance pattern is still such that Britain is netting some gain from the foreign investment situation. Britain's balance of payments statement for 1954 showed that she netted as interest, profits, and dividends in that year £35 million.[1] However, this figure compares with a typical

[1] *Economist,* April 9, 1955, p. 135.

£200 million in the period between World War I and World War II.

France, the Netherlands, Japan and other countries which formerly had substantial foreign investments have lost a large part of them. And it is still too early after World War II to guess how much of their position they will be able to regain.

A new factor has emerged on the scene, however—the International Bank for Reconstruction and Development. Immediately after World War II it made some reconstruction loans in western Europe. During the last few years it has been lending more and more in the underdeveloped areas of the world.[2]

PRIVATE INVESTMENT CLIMATE

Important in this postwar investment picture are certain political and institutional considerations, especially government regulations, which influence the attitudes of (1) potential lenders and (2) potential borrowers.

Attitude of Potential Lenders

As to the foreign investment climate, potential investors say it is bad for a variety of reasons: the conditions of capital entry are frequently controlled; there is danger of expropriation or confiscation; foreign-exchange controls may establish the conditions under which principal and interest can be transferred home; internal regulations may hamstring them in their operations; investors are subject to an onerous tax burden; and investors are discriminated against.[3]

CONDITIONS OF ENTRY. Debtor countries are prone to regulate closely the conditions under which foreign investments may enter the country. Registration of a new foreign investment with some designated government bureau or with some agency of the central bank is frequently required. In Brazil it is the Council of the Superintendency of Money and Credit; in Cuba, the Stabilization Fund; in France, the Exchange Office; in Turkey, the Ministry of Finance. By and large, the registration requirement is not used as a device for keeping investment out—although it may be so used. Chiefly the purpose is to identify the investment in order to establish the conditions under which repatriation or transfer home of profits will be permitted. For example, at this stage the investment may by classified as "productive" or "unproductive," and this classification

---

[2] The International Bank is discussed more fully in the next chapter.

[3] United States, Department of Commerce, *Factors Limiting U.S. Investment Abroad,* Part 2, *Business Views on the U.S. Government's Role* (Washington: Government Printing Office, 1954). Part 1 was a *Survey of Factors in Foreign Countries;* International Monetary Fund, *Sixth Annual Report: Exchange Restrictions 1955* (Washington, 1955).

may determine whether profits can freely be taken home or whether a maximum of, say, 8 per cent a year may be taken home.

The conditions imposed on foreign investors in mining and oil properties have generally involved a good deal more than simple registration. In most countries the right to produce minerals is obtained by concession from the government rather than by lease from the surface owner. The surface owner does not own the minerals under his land. A mining company may pay the land owner some surface rental for the use of the land on which the installations are placed, but it does not pay the surface owner for the minerals. On this point the rest of the world is generally out of step with the United States, a country where the quickest, if not the only, way for a farmer to get rich is to have oil discovered on his land.

In Venezuela, for example, the foreign oil companies are all operating under concessions obtained from the Venezuelan government. These concessions were necessary as a preliminary to any operation at all. And they established many of the conditions under which operations have continued. Of recent years, countries have become more restrictive as to the conditions under which concessions can be obtained. Foreigners, for example, are virtually prohibited from obtaining new mining concessions in Brazil at all. In Mexico oil development may be pursued under certain circumstances by foreigners subject to contract terms which leave title and operation, after oil is discovered, to the government—but which give foreigners a certain percentage of the oil.

It is a clear advantage to the foreigner to know ahead of time the conditions under which his investment is made: If the rules are changed later, that is something else again. Investors can and do protest such changes. Some of the implications of such changes are discussed below. But the possibility of later difficulties is no argument against the desirability of having a clear understanding of the situation in the beginning.

Of course, to the extent that the registration law is unnecessarily complicated or to the extent that it provides for conditions that the investor does not wish to live under, he will not make the investment—or should not. On the positive side, it may be said that countries with simple registration formalities—or no registration formalities at all—may attract more foreign investment. Be that as it may, the registration formalities give the investor some appreciation of the kind of setting he is entering. They are thus notice and warning so far as he is concerned. Depending on the nature of the warning, he may be deterred from investing. Nevertheless, it must be recognized that the procedure itself is a legitimate one—except to the extent that the underdeveloped country penalizes itself by the use of unnecessarily complicated regulations.

EXPROPRIATION. That the loss of foreign-owned property is a real possibility is evidenced by Mexican oil (1938), Iranian oil (1951), Mexican agricultural land (1917–40), Bolivian tin (1952), and Russian government bonds (1917).[4] In most such cases, more or less adequate compensation has finally been paid; so the cases really involved expropriation rather than confiscation. But several cases have involved virtual confiscation; and more possibly would have involved confiscation but for assiduous pressure applied to the would-be confiscator by the home governments of the expropriated.

Loss of investment is a possibility which the foreign investor should take into account. How may that be done without a crystal ball? The answer must be that the possibility of expropriation or confiscation cannot be anticipated with certainty. The investor may know that he is somewhat less likely to lose his property if he conscientiously observes local laws and resists the temptation to meddle in local politics. Also, if he shows some appreciation of his social responsibilities he will be more secure.

In the past, upon occasion, the home governments of foreign investors have used force or coercion in an effort to protect their people against loss. Examples include the Maximilian episode in Mexico in the 1860's, German naval action against Venezuela at the turn of the century, United States intervention in Haiti, the Dominican Republic, and Nicaragua during the first two decades of this century. Britain's withdrawal of her diplomatic representative from Mexico following the oil expropriation in 1938 is a milder example of the same sort of thing. Latin American countries have thought to protect themselves against foreign intervention by the inclusion of Calvo Clauses in the original agreements with such foreign concessionaires. But in several cases the foreign investors, in spite of the Calvo Clause, have appealed to their governments and been supported by them.

The right and wrong of this type of situation is not entirely clear. Perhaps there is no satisfactory solution, short of an international court to which litigants can appeal from national supreme courts. But probably the United States is more opposed to this procedure than are most other countries.

TRANSFER CONTROLS. Foreign investors run into difficulties from another quarter. Foreign-exchange controls in the debtor country may establish the conditions under which principal, interest, and profit can be transferred home. Such controls may prohibit transfer, provide for discriminatory foreign-exchange rates in the event of transfer, or specify the percentage of interest, profit, or principal that may be transferred in a given period.

The outright prohibition of transfer was common in the 1930's. But since the end of World War II many of the flat prohibitions have been lifted. Many still apply, however, to unregistered investments and to investments that were made before the war. Argentina, for example, on

---

[4] Wendell Gordon, *Expropriation of Foreign-Owned Property in Mexico* (Washington: American Council on Public Affairs, 1941).

and off since the end of the war has blocked the transfer of principal and earnings on "old" investments. The rule established in November, 1955, is that such transfer is permitted only with special authorization from the Central Bank.

Another possibility is direct discrimination in terms of the foreign-exchange rate granted the foreign investor who wants to repatriate some principal or interest. Thus in Bolivia (at least at one time) there were two chief foreign-exchange rates: 60 bolivianos to the dollar and 101 bolivianos to the dollar. The holder of non-registered capital, who wished to transfer it home from Bolivia to the United States, had to buy his dollars at the less favorable rate of 101 bolivianos to the dollar.[5] It is not unusual for the law, in a multiple exchange rate situation, to permit the foreign investor to transfer his capital home at the free, or freest, rate. Since the free rate is generally the most devalued rate, it is the least desirable so far as the investor is concerned.

A distinction should be made between the impact of such a procedure on an investment in manufacturing and its impact on an investment in public utilities. If a country is experiencing considerable inflation (a common state in the underdeveloped countries), manufacturing profits will probably rise proportionately with, if not faster than, the inflation. Consequently, the investor in manufacturing may not be adversely affected to any considerable degree by having to transfer his profits home at the less favorable exchange rates. But public utilities, with rates set in terms of the local currencies, will find themselves at a marked disadvantage when they try to transfer their profits home at devalued and falling foreign-exchange rates.

Provisions are common regulating how much interest, profit, or principal may be transferred home in a given year. Such regulations are generally stated in terms of a percentage of the original investment. The new Italian law (January, 1956) provides that, in the case of capital invested by foreigners in enterprises classified as "nonproductive," dividend transfer is limited to 8 per cent of the invested capital. In the case of enterprises classified as "productive," there is no limit on the percentage of dividends and earnings that may be transferred abroad.[6] Other countries have discriminated on the basis of a distinction between new and old (or prior) investment. Thus, under Peron, Argentina at one stage allowed a higher return to be transferred in connection with new investments (8 per cent) than was allowed in connection with prior investments (5 per cent), such as those of the United States meat-packing companies.

---

[5] International Monetary Fund, *Second Annual Report on Exchange Restrictions, April 1951* (Washington, 1951), p. 51. Other restrictions of this sort are discussed in: United Nations, Department of Economic and Social Affairs, *Foreign Capital in Latin America*, p. 21.

[6] *International Financial News Survey*, February 10, 1956, p. 247.

Something should be said by way of comment on regulations that distinguish between old and new investments simply on the basis of timing and not on the basis of contribution to the economy. The potential investor may well be suspicious of a regime that is promising new investments better terms than old investors are enjoying.

Freeing the foreign exchanges from complicated discriminatory regulations of this sort would probably do more to facilitate foreign investments than any other step that is relatively feasible in the immediate future. But keeping the exchanges free is going to depend upon conquering the business cycle—much more than on opposing the inclination of the governments of underdeveloped countries to be nasty to foreign investors.

INVESTMENT GUARANTY. In an effort to deal with the problems of expropriation and transfer controls, Congress in 1948 gave the original Economic Cooperation Administration the power, for a fee, to guarantee certain new foreign investments against expropriation (and foreign-exchange transfer difficulties). The broader extension of such a guaranty program was much discussed in subsequent years. And the Mutual Security Act of 1954 provided that the successor organization, the International Cooperation Administration, should have the power to guarantee certain foreign investments against either (1) difficulty in transferring their profits home, or (2) expropriation or confiscation. The claim to the investment becomes the property of the United States government, if the government makes good on its guaranty.

To implement this legislation, the State Department has proceeded with the negotiation of a series of international agreements under which the government of the country where the investment is made agrees to recognize a transfer of title from the United States private investor to the United States government. Thus an agreement which was concluded with Guatemala in March, 1955, read in part:

> (2) The Government of the United States agrees that it will issue no guaranty with regard to any project unless the project is approved by the Government of Guatemala.
> (3) . . . , the Government of Guatemala agrees:
> a. That if the Government of the United States of America makes payment in the United States dollars to any person under any such guaranty the Government of Guatemala will recognize the transfer to the United States of America of any right, title, or interest of such person. . . .

The agreement goes on to provide for direct negotiation at the governmental level and for the possibility of arbitration.

August Maffry advocates such a system of guarantees [7] "It should be made clear to Congress that it is entirely feasible to establish a government investment guaranty system which would effectively stimulate private investment abroad and at the same time be fully self-supporting." Elsewhere, for example from former Secretary of Commerce Charles Sawyer, one finds an evaluation that is not so commendatory: [8] "The much discussed investment guarantee proposals are not an answer nor a wise expedient. Guarantees offered by the United States against occurrences which are the result of policies pursued in other countries would tend to encourage rather than discourage unsound policies, and to promote the very thing which the businessman is afraid of. Realization of this fact here and abroad will stimulate and not retard the processes required to persuade private American capital to invest in other countries." It may well be true that an artificial device, such as a government guaranty, is a coward's device to protect the American investor at the expense of the American public and offers no solution to the fundamental problem. Of course, if the scheme actually was self-supporting, as August Maffry says, it would not be at the public expense; the more successful and competent investors would merely be supporting those who showed poor judgment. But one may well suspect that such a scheme would be self-supporting only until a wave of difficulties, similar to those of the 1930's, occurred; and thereafter the burden would be on the public.

A change in attitude in the underdeveloped countries may solve this problem without the need for any artificial devices; this is what happened in the United States when it went through a similar evolution from "poor credit risk" to "sterling credit risk" during the last half of the nineteenth century. In the 1840's, various state governments were in wholesale default on bonds; in the 1860's, the United States government confiscated the property right in slaves without compensation; but shortly thereafter it was again considered a fine place to invest money.

Actually, there is no solution to this problem until the attitudes of both investor and debtor countries change to such an extent that expropriation becomes uncommon. These changes involve all the other conditions under which foreign investments occur. Meanwhile, to the extent that the danger of confiscation remains real, the legal claims can be settled fairly only by an international court of justice to which appeal can be taken from national courts and an international police force which can enforce the decisions of the court. Guarantees can be nothing more than a superficial palliative for this disease. The use of force by the

[7] August Maffry, "Increasing Private Investment in Foreign Countries," *Comments on Argentine Trade,* July, 1953, p. 29.

[8] Charles Sawyer, "Secretary Sawyer's Survey of Europe," *Foreign Commerce Weekly,* December 22, 1952, p. 17.

creditor country cannot be trusted to give justice any more than the creditor can really trust the local courts to give justice. But probably the only common basis for appeal from national courts to international courts should be on the ground that there has been discrimination against foreigners. Possibly, however, the violation of some minimum standard of justice might also be grounds for appeal, even though there was no overt discrimination against foreigners. Should foreigners have some special protection that domestic citizens do not enjoy in the case of property confiscation to implement a program which will promote the general welfare? The Mexican government, between 1920 and 1940, argued that the land redistribution program was in the general interest. Perhaps the property of foreigners was confiscated, but so was the property of Mexicans. Why should Americans be paid and Mexicans not? The program was of such importance that it should occur, whether compensation could be paid or not. After all, in another program involving somewhat similar considerations (the Mexicans argued), the United States had confiscated the property rights in slaves without compensating British and French citizens who owned slaves in the United States. On the other hand, perhaps some minimum standard of justice, enforced by an international court, would be a good thing in protecting oppressed citizens against their own government.

In terms of the purpose (oft-repeated in this book) of expanding human freedom of action, resort to the international court of justice as a court of appeal in cases of this sort is a good example of central control (power moved from the national to the world level) which would tremendously increase freedom of action at the individual level.[9]

INTERNAL REGULATIONS. Another possibility is that internal regulations hamstring the foreign investor in the operation of his investment. In 1937 and 1938 the oil companies in Mexico thought that the regulations on paid vacations and salaries which the Mexican government was trying to impose on their operations would have made those operations prohibitively expensive. Consequently they resisted and were expropriated in the spring of 1938. Whether the regulations were genuinely onerous remains a question. But at least the oil companies thought so or said so.

Foreign investors commonly inveigh against the social welfare legislation in the countries where they are operators. The law may provide for a tax to support unemployment insurance. It may provide for the payment of three months wages in the event of the discharge of an employee (severance pay). It may provide for numerous paid holidays and for longer paid vacations than investors consider reasonable. Exten-

[9] The right of appeal by an individual against arbitrary arrest could be a major blow at the oppressive power of dictatorship from Caracas to Moscow. American diplomats might spend their time to better advantage arguing for a few rights of this sort.

sive health and old-age benefits may be provided for. There may even be provision to the effect that, if operations are discontinued (even temporarily), the workers may take over the plant. By and large, the laws on these matters are general laws which do not discriminate against foreigners. However, foreign investors frequently argue that such legislation is more effectively enforced against them than against their domestic competitors. And such may well be the case in many instances.

Most of the Latin American governments provide by law that a certain proportion of the employees or a certain proportion of the payroll (the figures varying from about 50 per cent to 95 per cent) must be or must go to nationals. This, too, is sometimes considered a burdensome restriction by foreign investors—even by some who are attracted to foreign parts by "cheap foreign labor." One might think that the investor who goes abroad to take advantage of cheap foreign labor would expect to hire a rather high proportion of such people and that consequently these percentage hiring requirements should not, on the whole, be significant deterrents.

At any rate many such restrictions exist. To what extent, in the general picture, they are a deterrent to investment would be difficult to say. Perhaps anything is a deterrent that somebody is deterred by—however rational or irrational the mental processes by which the person decided to be deterred. The meaning of this is apparent to someone who will think awhile about how high (in an absolute sense) profit expectations would theoretically need to be to draw out investment.

Taxes. There are at least two distinct issues in the tax argument. There is the question whether the over-all tax burden of the foreign investor is unduly high. And there is the question of discrimination in rates as between domestic and foreign investors.

The chief source for the belief that foreign investors may be subject to an unduly high over-all tax burden results from the circumstance that more than one taxing jurisdiction is involved—the possibility of double taxation. Of course, the simpler the tax structure the better; but, since everybody is subject to "quintuple taxation" now, it would seem that the mere fact that foreign investors are subject to double taxation is no ground for special complaint on their part. It is going to happen almost automatically to anybody operating in more than one legal jurisdiction.

The possibility, however, that the total American tax burden falling on Americans investing abroad is heavier than ordinary is a ground for concern, if true. And examples to show that it is true have been cited. Franz Schneider of Newmont Mining Corporation has pointed out that his company pays only a 7.8 per cent tax on dividends it receives on stock of domestic corporations which it owns (the basic law being that dividends received by one domestic corporation from another are 85 per cent tax-exempt), whereas it pays 52 per cent on the same proportionate holding of a foreign stock.[10] There is an inequity here. But part of the rectification might well take the form of a higher rate on the domestic dividend.[11]

On the whole, except in that one special sort of situation, it seems that the tax position of foreign investors is rather good. A recent United Nations report of this subject [12] indicates that in spite of the possibility of double taxation, the tax burden on United States business operating abroad is as low as or lower than the tax burden on domestic business in the United States. The basic burden (if not the complication) of double taxation is eliminated by the provision in the United States law to the effect that in the case of a branch plant the foreign income tax paid on the operation of the branch may constitute a deduction from the United States income tax (not a deduction from income before computing the United States tax). Thus, for the most part, corporations pay their foreign income tax, then compute their United States tax on the base of their whole income, deduct the foreign tax from the United States tax figure, and pay the balance.

Price, Waterhouse, Peat and Company has prepared the following comparison of the impact of the 1954 United States tax law on a branch and on a subsidiary operating abroad, on the basis of certain assumptions: [13]

	Branch	Subsidiary
Income before tax	$100	$100
Foreign income tax, say 40%	40	40
Accumulated Profits		
U.S. tax 52% on 100	52	
U.S. tax 52% on 60		31
Foreign tax credit		
Tax imposed on recipient	40	
Deemed to have been paid tax of		
40% of 60		24
U.S. tax payable	12	7
Total income tax	52	47

The burden of the branch operation turns out, after both foreign and United States taxes have been paid, to be the same as the burden of the United States tax; for the subsidiary it turns out to be less. Actually, in the case of the subsidiary, if the dividends were not transferred back to the

[10] Mr. Schneider's article is reproduced in International Bank for Reconstruction and Development, *Summary Proceedings, Eighth Annual Meeting of the Board* . . . , September 9–12, 1953 (Washington, 1953), p. 31.

[11] The justification for tax favoritism to holding-company arrangements is by no means established.

[12] United Nations, Department of Economic Affairs, *United States Income Taxation of Private United States Investment in Latin America* (New York, 1953).

[13] *Comments on Argentine Trade*, March, 1955, p. 19. Reprinted with the permission of the publisher.

parent corporation in the United States, there would be no tax burden at all.[14]

Not only is the chief burden of double taxation avoided in this way, but in addition there are in existence several "tax dodges," and intentional provisions as well, that enable the foreign investor to reduce his taxes. The fact that movie stars (and other people as well) who will work abroad for at least seventeen out of eighteen months can exclude from taxation their income earned outside the United States is well known to those who have observed the exodus of American movie actors.

Also, legal provision for so-called Western Hemisphere Trade Corporations permits to "domestic corporations [and the term includes manufacturing, mining, and oil companies] which derive substantially all of their gross income from sources within the Western Hemisphere outside the United States . . . [considerable] exemption from corporate income taxes through a rate pegged at fourteen percentage points below the regular corporate rate." [15] This procedure has clear advantages to eligible companies and will help to explain the tendency for a United States company planning to operate in Latin America to incorporate a subsidiary for that purpose in the United States (not in the Latin American country). (In this case the nature of the foreign operation is that of a branch—a branch of a subsidiary incorporated in the United States.)

A study made by the Harvard Law School, International Program in Taxation, indicates that for 1950 on income (profits) of $905 million derived from direct investments in Latin America, the net United States tax liability was only $16.4 million.[16] There does not seem to be available a comparable estimate of total taxes paid on the $905 million in Latin America. But the income taxes alone paid by United States enterprises in Latin America represented 28 per cent of profits as an over-all average. The combination of these two figures is still a long way from the domestic United States figure of 52%.

The actual tax burden on foreign investments seems to be no higher than that on domestic profits, and in many cases substantially lower. However, such comments on comparative rates do not dispose of the complexities involved in making happy the tax collectors in several countries. That is bound to be more difficult than making them happy

[14] Ira T. Wender, "Taxation of Foreign Trade and Investment," in U.S. Congress, Joint Committee on the Economic Report, *Federal Tax Policy for Economic Growth and Stability* (Papers, 84th Cong., 1st Sess. [Washington: Government Printing Office, 1955]), pp. 713–24. The general rule in the case of branches is that profits are taxable whether repatriated or not. However, this rule does not apply in the case of blocked balances.

[15] United Nations, Department of Economic Affairs, *United States Income Taxation . . .* , pp. 3–4.

[16] United Nations, Department of Economic and Social Affairs, *Foreign Capital in Latin America*, p. 14.

in only one. But, for the most part, it seems that the tax burden on foreign investors is not onerous because it works out to be high; it is onerous chiefly because it is uncertain, or because the rate *may* be raised, or because it is complicated, or because any tax is too high if there is any chance of getting it reduced.

As matters stand, however, the power to tax is both the power to destroy and also a proper power vested in government that will not be abdicated to ease the minds of foreign investors. Since the United States government has used taxes as devices for putting certain organizations out of business or for curtailing their activities (for example, the taxation of state bank notes out of existence), it can hardly complain that the procedure is improper per se. The only sanction, as matters stand, against governments that do this sort of thing is and should be (pending a higher authority) that they get no more investments. Foreign investment is not a right; it is a privilege—to both parties.

One suggestion for improvement of this situation might be to reframe the tax law pertaining to Americans with foreign investments so that the United States resident (or resident corporation) with foreign invest-ments will declare to the United States government his whole income from all sources foreign and domestic. The amount of tax should then be computed at the full domestic rate for the total amount. Then the individual or corporation should actually pay in tax to the United States government the proportion of this figure which his income from domestic sources is of his total income. Income derived from international trade and commercial operations could be taxed as though half of the income pertained to the United States.

Such a proposal would have several advantages over the present ar-rangements. It lends itself to unilateral adoption by one country and to later unilateral adoption by others. It relates the rate of taxation (on income derived from domestic sources) to the individual's total income—which is as it should be if we are agreed on the desirability of a progressive system of taxation. But it does not involve taxing the income derived from foreign sources at all. This avoids the complication of trying to take the foreign tax law into account. Probably it is a desirable general principle that taxes—even income taxes—should be paid to the government of the geographical area in which the income is earned. At least this should be true until such time as we delegate to a world authority the power of collection of such taxes as can be more equitably and efficiently collected by a world authority.

But since, in fact, tax burdens are not onerous on foreign investments, one may well wonder why such a fuss has been made over this matter of late. And it turns out that what the potential investors really are after is positive tax incentives (favoritism the other way). One finds such statements as the following by Jay E. Crane: [17] "I favor a much stronger statement in support of tax incentives to encourage foreign investment. While I agree that there are many obstacles to American investment abroad, it is clear that tax relief would offer a positive encouragement to such investment." Gordon H. Barrows says that there is "an encouraging trend toward the healthy realization that fiscal incentives must be given the explorer and/or developer, together with a satisfactory political climate. In this trend is involved a greater appreciation abroad of the part that such incentives have played in areas of major petroleum development." [18]

Even if the problem of the over-all tax burden to which foreign investors are subjected is resolved, there remains the discrimination question. Governments have a tendency to tax foreign investments at a rate higher than that at which they tax domestic investments. Even the United States government has been known to do this. Apparently United States corporate income taxes work out to be somewhat higher as applied to profits going to non-resident shareholders than is the case with profits held in this country. Examples of tax discrimination by other countries against foreign investments could be cited almost without end. Chile has had an extra profits tax of 10 per cent on copper companies with over two-hundred employees. In effect this seems to have applied exclusively to the foreign companies. In Argentina, foreign-owned land companies have paid a surcharge of 30 per cent on the ordinary profits tax.

DISCRIMINATION. Discussion of several of the above points has indicated situations in which the foreigner, by comparison with the native, is the victim of discrimination. He may pay higher taxes, or he may be prohibited from engaging in certain types of business, or something of the sort.

The State Department has attempted to deal with the discrimination issue by a new series of treaties. The crux of the model treaty is the provision that "nationals and companies of either Party shall be accorded, within the territories of the other Party, national treatment and also most-favored-nation treatment." [19] Actually, not very many countries have signed these treaties. The chief examples are Italy and Uruguay. Such treaties might do some good, especially if enough of them were concluded. But the problem is more likely to be resolved in the less formal area of changing attitudes.

[17] Committee for Economic Development, *Taxes, National Security and Economic Growth* (New York, 1954), p. 32.

[18] Gordon H. Barrows, "Private Capital on Road to Getting 'Fair Shake' Abroad," *World Oil*, August 15, 1953, p. 85. August Maffry, *loc. cit.*, p. 29, also pleads for special tax incentives. And George Humphrey seems interested: *New York Times*, December 13, 1953.

[19] *Department of State Bulletin*, December 5, 1949, p. 867a. The clause is Article IV of the 1949 treaty with Uruguay.

It might be reasonable for foreign investors as individuals to insist on a nondiscrimination rule. Foreign investors could abstain from investing in any country except those that agree to levy taxes in such a way that there is no discrimination between domestic and foreign capital. It may reasonably be expected that most governments would abide by such a promise—whether made in domestic law, or by verbal understanding—if that was the way most other countries were behaving. But if they did not, it must be confessed that the investors would have little redress short of an international court and an international police force and the ultimate sanction of abstaining from further investment.

The underdeveloped country which wishes to encourage industrialization might well levy taxes on industrial development at a lower rate than the taxes in the United States. In this setting, probably little would be gained by discrimination between domestic investors and foreign investors within the underdeveloped country. This type of tax reduction or governmental subsidy to new industrial projects is in line with the general argument urged at various points in the book. Some discriminatory aid to new industrialization probably is necessary. But such aid arrangements should be simple, direct, and to the point.

SUMMARY. After this inconclusive discussion of investment climate from the viewpoint of the investor, it may not be amiss to discuss the same subject from the viewpoint of the country where the investment occurs—and leave unanswered a question which is suggested by some of the foregoing discussion: How venturesome is venture capital?

Attitude of Potential Borrowers

The underdeveloped countries complain about much in connection with foreign investments: (1) fantastic monetary profits, (2) the draining of raw materials (goods), (3) meddling with internal politics.

MONETARY PROFITS. Some enterprises have made fantastic monetary profits (see Table 46); but whether the average profits have been fantastic is not so certain. Even if the monetary profits of the past have been fantastic, this need not be a major problem of the future. The individual, sovereign nation can (and is derelict in its responsibilities if it does not) establish the degree of progressiveness in its tax laws which its people think desirable. This could well be done by the procedures suggested above: after the total over-all profits were computed, the government would apply its tax rate to the total profits, but collect as tax only that percentage of the potential tax which corresponded with the percentage of the over-all operation which was in that particular country.

DRAINING RAW MATERIALS. Actually, the making of monetary profit by foreigners has little meaning in national terms (however much indignation against individuals may be called for). At the national level exploitation cannot be a matter of money; it must be a matter of goods. So the important questions become: what is happening to the balance of trade and the terms of trade (and, more fundamentally, what is the effect of the existence of the investment on the supply of goods available for domestic internal consumption)?

The charge, frequently made, that foreign investors are draining debtor countries of their wealth in goods has a peculiar relationship to the facts. The reverse is nearer the truth: the process of exploitation does not involve an overt effort by the foreign investors to get more goods out and back to their own country—over the strenuous objection of the debtor country. In spite of the talk about drainage, the laws of the under-developed countries are frequently worded to speed up production. This is accomplished, for example, in connection with Venezuelan oil, by legislation which provides for increasing certain taxes and rentals as the production period is prolonged. That makes it sound as though they want the production and export of oil accelerated. In Chile, new legislation in 1955 applicable to the copper industry provided for tax reductions as production rises.[20] But the clincher in the argument that foreign investors are not out to drain the wealth is to be found in the fact that they do not seem to care where the materials go. As Standard of New Jersey said: It bought into the Arabian-American Oil Company (Aramco) in order "to meet expected increases in demand for petroleum products in the Eastern Hemisphere. . . ."[21] And obviously the United States is not engaged in any conspiracy to drain (net) resources from the under-developed areas. The efforts of the United States to have an export balance of trade are adequate refutation of that.

This does not refute the proposition that the investors are interested in maximizing money profit. But it does mean that in terms of the relationship between the nations, there is no organized effort to get as much goods out of the underdeveloped area in exchange for as little going the other way as can be managed. Quite the contrary, it means that there is a tendency to resist receiving the real gain (increased imports) in the capital-exporting country and that the monetary transfer of profits has a rather different effect than is generally assumed.

If, in the creditor country, the inflow of goods is resisted but the monetary mechanism works so that the individual investors end up with their monetary profit, what then? It means that, in the capital-exporting country, there is a tendency for a relatively larger proportion of the real national income to pass into the hands of those who have investments abroad. This happens because there is a shift within the investing country, as interest and dividends are received from abroad, of the identity of the groups with the greatest command over what goods there are. This shift benefits the foreign investors and hurts the rest of

[20] *Hispanic American Report,* September (October), 1955, p. 428.
[21] *Lamp,* March, 1947.

the population—if a monetary transfer of the profits from foreign invest-ments has been (or rather could be) effected without a corresponding import of goods.

In the country where the investment is made there is a similar shift in the identity of the groups with relatively greater command over what goods there are. This change benefits especially the laboring group in the industry in which the investment has been made (oil-field workers), although the relative position of certain other groups (e.g., Venezuelan lawyers) may also be improved—at the expense of other Venezuelans.

It should be noted that in both the creditor and the debtor country the primary impact of the profit-making process is a redistribution of income within a country and not an international transfer of real profit. There is a real gain to the debtor country if, as a result of the investment, internal production and consumption expand.[22] (To the extent that for-eign investment has been in raw material extraction and in "mine to port" transportation, it has not made much contribution along this line.)

There is a real gain to the creditor country if the industrial leadership—which explains why it was the lending country in the first place—is fur-thered by the whole process so that the expansion of domestic goods pro-duction proceeds apace.

The preceding comments are chiefly applicable to the behavior of the United States in relation to debtor countries. The British case history indicates that the capitalistic country will sooner or later—perhaps you might say in spite of itself—take its gain in the form of an import trade balance. Britain in the nineteenth century was a major creditor country with an import balance of trade. The United States is resisting with all its power the tendencies leading in that direction.

MEDDLING IN LOCAL AFFAIRS. The chief valid basis for unhappiness with foreign investors is probably on the political-social side. Foreign investors do not seem to be able to resist trying to influence the composi-tion of the governments and the manners and morals in countries where they operate. Examples of such incidents, in connection with which the information is always a little confused, are legion. Did Henry Lane Wilson, the United States ambassador, connive in the overthrow and murder of Francisco Madero in Mexico in 1913 because of a mistaken impression that Huerta would favor the American oil companies over the British? How many Central American revolutions has United Fruit participated in? In the 1920's, the United States agreed to pay an indem-nity to Colombia as hush money for the Roosevelt-staged revolution that had made Panamanian independence possible in 1903. At substantially the same time that the United States government agreed to pay the in-

[22] Of course, this statement is subject to the qualifications stated in the Introduc-tion.

demnity, the government of Colombia granted the Barco concession to Andrew Mellon's—he was the Secretary of the Treasury—Gulf Oil Company.

It seems that the French government, desiring to build up the French-Russian alliance, was active for political reasons in the period from 1880 to World War I in encouraging misinformed French investors to speculate heavily in Czarist bonds. In 1908, by threatening to refuse listing on the Bourse to Danish securities, France forced a reduction in Denmark's duties on French wines. In 1909, France refused to permit the flotation of a Serbian loan in Paris unless Serbia agreed to buy arms from Schneider (French) rather than from Krupp (German). Serbia objected, pointing out that Krupp's prices were cheaper. The French government forced Schneider to lower his prices.

The United States ambassador in Iran, Loy Henderson, seems to think he had some hand in the overthrow of Mossadegh—with oil in the background.[23] Obviously a lot of crude and ill-advised meddling in local politics may accompany every government that is overthrown. This sort of thing has tremendously important implications in the sphere of freedom of action—whatever the effect on level of living may be.

Moreover, a foreign colony, if it is on the average wealthier than the national citizenry, is not going to be very popular anywhere. And colonies of American citizens in foreign capitals seem to be no exception to the rule. Some of the members do not always behave with tolerant consideration toward the local citizenry with whom they come into contact. All of this makes for difficulties, some of which are nobody's fault. People of all races, creeds, and pocketbook sizes show poor judgment and are capable of being rude and inconsiderate. If that were the worst part of this picture, the importance would be small in a sense —although large in the sense that man irritating his fellow man is responsible for a substantial proportion of the misery of this life. That foreign colonies in underdeveloped areas are a major reactionary force preventing development and social progress is a proposition to which Gilbert Grandval, resident-general of Morocco, no doubt, adhered in 1955.[24]

Important in terms of the problems of international relations are the straight power implications of the existence of the large business unit that is responsible for most foreign investment. And these corporations are chiefly run by self-perpetuating oligarchies. Although the implications in some ways are much the same whether the enterprise is foreign or domestic and regardless of country, in the underdeveloped countries a disproportionate proportion of large enterprises is foreign.

[23] Houston *Post,* August 22, 1953, p. 1.
[24] Houston *Post,* July 16, 1955, p. 1.

J. Peter Grace, Jr., president of W. R. Grace and Company, in an address before the Investment Bankers Association in March, 1955, advised foreign investors as follows: [25]

> Stay out of local politics. This doesn't mean stay partially out, it means stay out! If you do this you will be able to get along with whatever government is in power.
>
> Employ as managers of your business able and outstanding nationals wherever this is practical, and keep them out of politics, too.
>
> Have your management, and particularly the Americans in your management, closely identify themselves with local community life, and become part of the countries in which they live.

But, to be constructive, the question becomes one of taking from the foreign investor the power to meddle effectively in the domestic politics of the country where he is a guest. Here again, as was the case when the shoe was on the other foot in the event of expropriation, the only real solution is an international court of justice to which such cases can be taken (involving, perhaps, the punishment on criminal charges of anyone who stirs up a revolution—but punishment by an international court, not by the aggrieved incumbent government).

Shortly after the turn of the century, various Latin American governments began a notable effort to deal with the problem by the use of the Calvo Clause. This provision called for jurisdiction of local courts in cases involving losses by foreigners. The statement of the clause as it appeared on the stock of the Aguila (the Dutch-Shell subsidiary in Mexico before 1938) read: [26]

> Any alien at any time by whatever title acquiring any interest or participation in this company shall, by so doing, consider himself a Mexican with respect to either, and shall be understood as agreeing not to invoke the protection of his government with regard to said interest or participation, under penalty, should he violate this agreement, of forfeiting them for the benefit of the Mexican nation.

The validity of the Calvo Clause was an issue in the dispute over Mexican oil expropriation following 1938. By and large, the foreign offices in capital-exporting countries deny that the signing of the clause by one of their citizens debars them from intervening if they choose.

---

[25] *New York Times*, March 17, 1955, p. 33. Reprinted by permission of the *New York Times*.

[26] Gordon, *op. cit.*, p. 165.

According to this line of argument, the investor cannot appeal to his foreign office for protection, but the foreign office can give it without being appealed to. This interpretation tends to increase the use of the back door. The wording of the Calvo Clause is reasonably clear, and by and large investors are not under duress when they sign it. One might think this would bind the investors. But, after losing their property, they have nothing further to lose by an appeal. And so it goes.

Certain other measures may make a contribution to creating a healthier general situation. A new pattern in manufacturing investments, used in many cases in Latin America, involves a small monetary commitment on the part of the United States company plus the providing of technical and managerial personnel. In such cases much of the monetary investment and a majority of the stock ownership is local. An example of this arrangement is the Mexican company Industria Eléctrica de Mexico, which manufactures electrical equipment. Westinghouse of the United States has, approximately, a 10 per cent interest in Industria Eléctrica and has provided that firm with technical and managerial personnel. The stock of the company is quoted on the New York Stock Exchange. A jointly owned company of this sort does not present the clear-cut cleavage of interest along national lines that has been the source of a good deal of the trouble in the past.

Another procedure that might help would involve the division of the eggs among a few more baskets. Why are concessions made to one oil company or to so few? Saudi Arabia is asking for trouble by dealing only with Aramco, just as Iran's trouble resulted to some extent from dealing only with Anglo-Iranian. Various measures might improve such a situation considerably: (1) increasing the number of foreign concessionaires, (2) some effective prohibition against producing companies which are jointly owned by many, if not all, of the major oil companies, (3) the provision that producing companies cannot monopolize transportation facilities, and (4) requiring transportation companies to stick to transportation.

The climate might be ever so much healthier in Central America if United Fruit only transported bananas, instead of producing them as well. Peru and Chile might be a little more autonomous if the Grace Line stuck to shipping.[27]

Many of the difficulties described above could be resolved by the international incorporation of businesses with international operations. This is a proposal which was made by Eugene Staley in *War and the Private*

[27] All the world's ills cannot be cured by breaking up monopolies, nor by subdividing into three where there was one before. But there are some situations where a little activity along this line will not hurt a bit. If the real danger of the monopolies adheres in their power and size, rather than in their high profit rates (which certainly do not in all cases exist, anyway), well-calculated measures breaking them up are all to the good.

Investor some twenty years ago.[28] There is a good deal to be said for the proposition that incorporation should be granted by a level of government that has jurisdiction over the company's whole operation. Presumably, for such a situation to exist satisfactorily, there would also need to be a court with commensurate jurisdiction to handle the disputes involving the company.

In addition, taxes would probably need to be imposed by the level of government having jurisdiction over the whole operation. Grants-in-aid could be prorated back to the lower levels of government in proportion to the investment in each jurisdiction (or the volume of business done in each jurisdiction). In this setting, the corporation would be more likely to give accurate data on the value of its investment as between different legal jurisdictions. At present, corporations operating internationally are inclined to make their profits show up in the jurisdiction with the lowest tax rates. International incorporation could obviate the desirability of using these subterfuges—and also simplify the solution of the tax problem which was discussed earlier.

Any corporation that tries to get around the requirement of international incorporation by holding-company-type operations that involve separate incorporated units in different countries should, at least, have to pay the full income tax on all dividends (instead of having intercorporate dividends 85 per cent tax-exempt—as in the United States). At most, it might be desirable to prohibit holding-company-type operations entirely.

Centralized responsibility for the behavior of a business organization which is itself centrally controlled is desirable. Efforts to decentralize responsibility while centralizing power should be penalized.

It would probably turn out that such international incorporation would be a factor freeing the corporation of some of the taint of close political ties with its home government. It would have no home government to appeal to in the case it is wronged. At the same time, appeal to the protection of the international court would be quite legitimate and perhaps provide for more effective protection for legitimate interests.

International operations are going to be on an unsatisfactory basis until some such thing is done. Real freedom of action in local operations can only be obtained at the cost of a more comprehensive, if less pressing, control such as this in the background.

United States Government Position

The attitude of the United States government has varied through the years. In the "big stick" days of dollar diplomacy before World War I,

[28] Eugene Staley, *War and the Private Investor* (Garden City: Doubleday, Doran, 1935). It is a proposal that would also have considerable merit within the United States—that any corporation operating across state lines should have to have a federal charter.

the government seemed to feel that support, by force if need be, was proper. In those days the State Department energetically supported potential foreign investors in their negotiations. Secretary of State Philander Knox, the Chinese Consortium, and the Harriman scheme for a round-the-world, railroad-steamship transportation system are examples.

In the early twenties the State Department announced that it would like to have new foreign dollar bond issues submitted to it for disapproval. It emphasized that it was not positively endorsing anything; but it wanted the chance to suggest that a certain flotation should not occur. During the 1920's, the State Department rejected a Brazilian loan on the grounds that it was to be used to finance a scheme to prop up the price of coffee —and such a scheme in the United States would be illegal under the Sherman Antitrust Act. In 1927, it also rejected a loan to finance a Czech brewery—on the grounds that making alcoholic beverages would be illegal in the United States under the Eighteenth Amendment. Meddling can take a variety of strange forms, when the principles that can reasonably justify meddling are not established by proper procedures.

In 1934, by the Johnson Act, the United States forbade new private loans to governments in default on their obligations to the United States government. Then in the Neutrality Acts of the late thirties the government attempted to avoid entanglement in the threatening war in Europe by prohibiting commercial intercourse (including lending of the sort it was then thought had helped to embroil the United States in World War I) with belligerents. At the same time that the Neutrality Acts were passed, the lending power of the Export-Import Bank was extended, in part at least as an anti-German move, to finance development in Latin America, especially in the production of certain raw materials, and to finance exports to Latin America in competition with the Germans.

Meanwhile, the principle of nonintervention had been accepted by the Pan American countries. Under Secretary of State Webb described the results:[29]

> I should like to state for the record as forcefully as I can that whatever may have been our mistakes in the past, it is the policy of this Government not to intervene in the domestic affairs of foreign countries. . . . The particular form of government in any country and the particular persons who constitute that government are a matter of domestic concern to the peoples of that country. The fact that there may be American investments abroad in no way alters the fact that this Government will not intervene in the affairs of other nations.

[29] United States Congress, House of Representatives, Committee on Banking and Currency, *Export-Import Bank Loan Guaranty Authority* (Washington: Government Printing Office, 1949), p. 56.

The treaty between the United States of America and other American Republics relative to nonintervention, signed at Buenos Aires on December 23, 1936, and ratified by the President of the United States on July 15, 1937, provides in article 1 that "The high contracting parties declare inadmissible the intervention of any one of them, directly or indirectly, and for whatever reason, in the internal or external affairs of any other of the parties." This treaty is the law of the land.

EVALUATION

I cannot resist including in this discussion of investment climate a comment about an article in the Houston *Post,* which was written by James S. Keat:[30] "Americans here [Bogota] who are familiar with Colombia laws and practices governing foreign investment say this nation has the 'healthiest climate' for foreign investment of any South American country, and probably one of the best in the world." The type of thinking that would lead to an observation of this sort, seriously made, leaves one wondering. At the time this statement was made (1953), chronic civil war had been going on in Colombia since the Pan American conference of 1948.[31] Because of bitter political differences involving the Colombian president and his own party, the Congress had not functioned for a long time after November 9, 1949. And the president, Laureano Gomez, had not actually served as president, except for a period of a day or two before he was unseated by the revolution led by General Gustavo Rojas Pinilla in June, 1953. To make people talk about a favorable investment climate does it merely take an extremely conservative, anti-labor government, which suppresses freedom of the press, but which has some laws on the books which sound favorable to investment? How much protection could investment, made under the aegis of such a government, reasonably expect if the Colombian Liberal Party came back into power (much less the Communist)?

Perhaps this leads to the conclusion that a whole lot could be done toward improving the "investment climate" if investors would appreciate that they must operate under labor, social security, and health laws that give reasonable protection to the workers, and under a general

---

[30] "Colombia Business Climate Is 'Healthy,'" Houston *Post,* September 3, 1953, sec. 5, p. 9.

[31] German Arciniegas, *The State of Latin America,* pp. 153–86. Arciniegas said (p. xiii): "The precarious balance in Latin America is recognized most clearly by those who maintain order by force. The very people who invite foreign investments deposit their own fortunes in the banks of New York or Switzerland. The meaning of this two-way street seems to us Latin Americans like that of a roadside warning: Proceed at your own risk!"

pattern of local laws (especially those affecting business organization) which are a matter for local determination [32] without the studied assistance of the lawyers of the foreign companies. The American who cannot accept the internal institutional organization of a foreign country as he finds it, or as the local citizenry want to make it, should stay home.

As a corollary, local governments should stand on their own feet, pass laws that are really intended to raise the level of living and increase the freedom of action of their people, but which are in general nondiscriminatory against foreigners and foreign investors, and then insist on observance of the laws.

[32] Subject to world society approval but not to investor approval.

Chapter 28

THE EXPORT-IMPORT BANK,
THE INTERNATIONAL BANK, AND
THE INTERNATIONAL
FINANCE CORPORATION

ⅶ ⅶ ⅶ

*The Export-Import Bank is a creation of the United States government.
Its chief activity is to aid in the financing of United States exports
of capital equipment. The operation frequently aids a development
project in an underdeveloped country.*

*The International Bank for Reconstruction and Development is an in-
ternational institution which participates in the planning and
financing of development projects.*

*The International Bank obtains funds from the subscriptions of the mem-
ber governments and by direct borrowing in the various capital
markets.*

*It requires a government guarantee before it will make a loan; and it
attempts to avoid competition with private lenders. Its interest charges
now run about 4½ or 5 per cent.*

*The International Finance Corporation is closely associated with the
International Bank. It can make loans without government guarantee; but it cannot provide equity capital or participate in the management of the projects which it helps to finance.*

ⅶ ⅶ ⅶ

ONE national government agency and two international agencies have emerged since World War II as the chief factors
in the international investment picture. They are the Export-
Import Bank, an agency of the United States government,
the International Bank for Reconstruction and Development, which is
affiliated with the United Nations, and the International Finance Corporation, which is affiliated with the International Bank. This chapter
describes the work of the three organizations.

EXPORT-IMPORT BANK[1]

Something was said of the formation and work of the Export-Import Bank (Eximbank) in Chapters 16 and 25. The institution was given the power in 1937 to make sizable long-term loans to other countries. And in the latter 1930's these loans played a role in building fences against the Nazi menace. Since 1945 they have played a similar role in relation to the Russians. They also have been intended to foster development in other countries and to stimulate United States exports—chiefly the latter. Export-Import Bank loans, almost without exception, either have financed the export of United States-made equipment or have been

TABLE 40

EXPORT-IMPORT BANK LOANS

(MILLIONS OF DOLLARS)

	TOTAL CREDITS AUTHORIZED FROM FEB. 12, 1934 TO JUNE 30, 1956	BALANCE OUTSTANDING AS OF JUNE 30, 1956	
		Undisbursed Authorization	*Outstanding Loans*
To:			
Latin America	2,633	415	869
Asia	1,278	200	343
Europe	2,870	58	1,283
Canada	375	0	0
Africa	229	63	133
Oceania	23	3	18
Other	12	0	0
Total	7,423	740	2,648

Source: Export-Import Bank of Washington, *Report to Congress for the Period January–June 1956*, (Washington: Government Printing Office, 1956), pp. 94–7.

made to enterprises in which United States corporations have a substantial interest.[2] The Bank has engaged in very little import financing.

The magnitude of Export-Import Bank operations is indicated in Table 40. The most important loan made since the preparation of the table is probably the $151 million loan of July, 1956, to Brazil to finance economic development in general, and in particular the purchase in the United States of equipment for the rehabilitation of Brazilian railroads.

[1] Hawthorne Arey, *History of Operations and Policies of Export-Import Bank of Washington* (Washington: Government Printing Office, 1953). Glen E. Edgerton is (1956) the president of the Bank.

[2] United States Congress, Senate, Committee on Banking and Currency (83:2), *Study of Latin American Countries*, Report (Washington: Government Printing Office, 1954).

The Bank may have loans, guaranties, and insurance to a maximum of $5 billion outstanding at any one time.

The Bank engages in the direct financing of exports. It does this frequently by paying United States exporters and by taking over from them their claim against the foreign importer. It may also make a loan, either to a United States exporter or to a foreign importer (governmental or private) to finance the purchase of United States materials, equipment, or services destined for a project abroad. Similarly, but infrequently, the Bank directly finances imports when it pays off the debts of United States importers and waits then upon payment by the United States importer.

The Bank also may provide guaranties to United States exporters that they will be paid or, rarely, to foreign shippers to the United States that they will be paid. In such cases the Bank would not advance any money, but its willingness to provide guaranties presumably facilitates the transactions.[3]

Loans made by the Bank may be broadly classified as either credits to exporters or as development loans. "Applicants may be divided into three general types, as follows: (1) United States exporters or importers, (2) private firms, whether domiciled in the United States or abroad, that desire to purchase United States materials, equipment, or services for utilization in a project abroad, and (3) foreign governments or their agencies that wish to purchase United States materials, equipment, or services for utilization in a project abroad."[4]

"The Bank ordinarily requires that a United States exporter who desires financial assistance from it shall have contracted to receive a cash payment of not less than 20 per cent of the invoice value not later than delivery of the goods, and that the exporter shall participate in the financing to the extent of not less than 25 per cent of the financed portion. Similarly if the applicant is the foreign buyer he should, wherever possible, arrange participation in the financing by the proposed United States exporter."[5]

"The Bank seeks to supplement and encourage the use of private capital. Accordingly, the Bank endeavors to obtain the maximum participation by commercial banks or other financial institutions in credit arrangements to which it is a party. The Bank also uses the facilities of private financial institutions for making funds available to borrowers under its guarantee, for receiving payment of interest and principal, and for handling other matters in connection with the extension and collection of credits."[6]

[3] Export-Import Bank, *General Policy Statement, July 1, 1955* (Washington, 1955), p. 5.
[4] *Ibid.*, p. 6.
[5] *Ibid.*, p. 11.
[6] *Ibid.*, p. 12.

The Export-Import Bank is an important, active organization in 1956. The Bank is an effective and adaptable instrument of United States foreign policy in the economic sphere; and in the nature of things Bank lending has, undoubtedly, been tied to current considerations as to foreign policy. Up to this time the repayment record in connection with Bank loans has been excellent. What the likelihood of repayment may be under changed political conditions is not certain. Conceivably anti-United States governments would engage in extensive defaults.

INTERNATIONAL BANK

Factors Influencing Establishment [7]

The organization of the International Bank for Reconstruction and Development was planned, along with the International Monetary Fund, at the Bretton Woods conference in 1944.

An important factor leading to the establishment of the International Bank for Reconstruction and Development was (1) the desire to filter the politics out of the international lending process and place the process on a genuine economic quid pro quo basis which would ensure that the borrower could use his money freely and that the lender was really entitled to repayment. Other factors were (2) the desire to assist with post-World War II reconstruction, and (3) the desire to help plan and finance the economic development of underdeveloped areas.

Organization of the Bank

The Bank began operations June 26, 1946. Its home office is in Washington, D.C., in the same building in which the International Monetary Fund is housed; and Eugene R. Black (United States) is the incumbent president. The Bank now has fifty-eight members.

(a) CONTROL AND VOTING: Control in the Bank is apportioned in about the same fashion as in the Fund. The United States has, again, almost one third of the vote, much as is the case with the Fund:

(b) SOURCES OF FUNDS: By June, 1956, subscriptions to the capital stock of the Bank totaled $9.05 billion in terms of United States dollars. The articles of agreement provide that each of the members should actually turn over to the bank at least 2 per cent of its subscription in gold or United States dollars at once, and the balance necessary to make 20 per cent (therefore generally 18 per cent) in non-interest bearing non-negotiable demand notes which the Bank, on call, could request the member to honor in its national currency.

[7] International Bank for Reconstruction and Development, *International Bank for Reconstruction and Development, 1946–1953* (Baltimore: Johns Hopkins Press, 1954). The Bank also publishes an *Annual Report* and periodic *Press Releases*.

As a consequence of these various provisions the Bank actually has $749 million "paid in" in United States dollars ($635 million by the United States government). The $7.24 billion of the subscriptions which has not been paid in at all is subject to call to meet the obligations of the Bank if at some time in the future the Bank's borrowers default and the Bank finds itself in difficulty so far as paying off its own creditors is concerned.

The Bank also has available to it such funds as it can borrow, against its own bonds, in the various money markets. From this source it has obtained about $850 million, chiefly in the New York market but some also from Canada, the Netherlands, Switzerland, and the United Kingdom.

TABLE 41

INTERNATIONAL BANK FOR RECONSTRUCTION AND DEVELOPMENT: STATEMENT OF SUBSCRIPTION TO CAPITAL STOCK AND VOTING POWER, JUNE 30, 1956

($1,000 U.S.)

	SUBSCRIPTIONS	AMOUNTS PAID IN			SUBJECT TO CALL TO MEET OBLIGATIONS OF BANK	NUMBER OF VOTES
	Amount	U.S. *Dollars*	Currency of Member Other Than U.S. *Dollars*	Non-Interest-Bearing, Non-Negotiable Demand Notes		
1. Afghanistan	10,000	200	1,800	—	8,000	350
2. Australia	200,000	4,000	360	35,640	160,000	2,250
3. Austria	50,000	1,000	1,837	7,163	40,000	750
4. Belgium	225,000	4,500	6,344	34,156	180,000	2,500
5. Bolivia	7,000	140	13	1,247	5,600	320
6. Brazil	105,000	2,100	18,900	—	84,000	1,300
7. Burma	15,000	300	52	2,648	12,000	400
8. Canada	325,000	6,500	53,201	5,299	260,000	3,500
9. Ceylon	15,000	300	33	2,667	12,000	400
10. Chile	35,000	700	6,300	—	28,000	600
11. China	600,000	9,340	1,080	106,920 [1]	480,000	6,250
12. Colombia	35,000	700	6,300	—	28,000	600
13. Costa Rica	2,000	40	360	—	1,600	270
14. Cuba	35,000	700	63	6,237	28,000	600
15. Denmark	68,000	1,360	2,728	9,512	54,400	930
16. Dominican Republic	2,000	40	4	356	1,600	270
17. Ecuador	3,200	64	576	—	2,560	282
18. Egypt	53,300	1,066	96	9,498	42,640	783
19. El Salvador	1,000	20	180	—	800	260
20. Ethiopia	3,000	60	540	—	2,400	280
21. Finland	38,000	760	6,840	—	30,400	630
22. France	525,000	10,500	27,938	66,562	420,000	5,500
23. Germany	330,000	6,600	14,874	44,526	264,000	3,550

TABLE 41 (*continued*)

	SUBSCRIP- TIONS	AMOUNTS PAID IN			SUBJECT TO CALL TO MEET OBLIGA- TIONS OF BANK	NUMBER OF VOTES
	Amount	*Currency* *of Mem-* *ber Other* *Than* *U.S.* *Dollars*	*Non-Inter-* *est-Bear-* *ing, Non-* *Negotiable* *U.S.* *Dollars*	*Non-Inter-* *est-Bear-* *ing, Non-* *Negotiable* *Demand* *Notes*		
24. Greece	25,000	500	4,500	—	20,000	500
25. Guatemala	2,000	40	360	—	1,600	270
26. Haiti	2,000	40	11	349	1,600	270
27. Honduras	1,000	20	180	—	800	260
28. Iceland	1,000	20	180	—	800	260
29. India	400,000	8,000	722	71,278	320,000	4,250
30. Indonesia	110,000	2,200	198	19,602	88,000	1,350
31. Iran	33,600	672	60	5,988	26,880	586
32. Iraq	6,000	120	21	1,059	4,800	310
33. Israel	4,500	90	8	802	3,600	295
34. Italy	180,000	3,600	9,971	22,429	144,000	2,050
35. Japan	250,000	5,000	2,672	42,328	200,000	2,750
36. Jordan	3,000	60	15	525	2,400	280
37. Korea	12,500	250	2,250	—	10,000	375
38. Lebanon	4,500	90	810	—	3,600	295
39. Luxembourg	10,000	200	118	1,682	8,000	350
40. Mexico	65,000	1,300	11,700	—	52,000	900
41. Netherlands	275,000	5,500	9,500	40,000	220,000	3,000
42. Nicaragua	800	16	144	—	640	258
43. Norway	50,000	1,000	370	8,630	40,000	750
44. Pakistan	100,000	2,000	180	17,820	80,000	1,250
45. Panama	200	4	36	—	160	252
46. Paraguay	1,400	28	252	—	1,120	264
47. Peru	17,500	350	262	2,888	14,000	425
48. Philippines	15,000	300	1,200	1,500	12,000	400
49. Sweden	100,000	2,000	18,000	—	80,000	1,250
50. Syria	6,500	130	44	1,126	5,200	315
51. Thailand	12,500	250	53	2,198	10,000	375
52. Turkey	43,000	860	363	7,377	34,400	680
53. Union of South Africa	100,000	2,000	6,060	11,940	80,000	1,250
54. United Kingdom	1,300,000	26,000	33,170	200,830	1,040,000	13,250
55. United States	3,175,000	635,000	—	—	2,540,000	32,000
56. Uruguay	10,500	210	1,890	—	8,400	355
57. Venezuela	10,500	210	1,365	525	8,400	355
58. Yugoslavia	40,000	800	7,200	—	32,000	650
Total	$9,050,500	$749,850	$264,287	$793,303	$7,240,400	105,005

[1] Amount past due: China, $2,660,000.

Source: International Bank for Reconstruction and Development, *Press Release No. 454*, August 7, 1956, Appendix D.

The Bank also can serve as an intermediary, guaranteeing a bond issue that one government might float in a foreign bond market. As of June 30, 1956, the Bank was the guarantor of only $26 million of loans to which it was not directly a party. This procedure has considerable unrealized potential.

Despite the fact that it is called a bank, the International Bank for Reconstruction and Development has no power to create additional funds in connection with the lending process, no power to operate against fractional reserves. In fact, it does not now have loans outstanding to a sum anywhere nearly as large as its ostensible capital, an unusual situation for a bank. Conceivably the magnitude of its operations could be substantially increased by large new bond issues. But at present the Bank is not much more than a moderately large investment trust which also performs certain underwriting functions.

(c) BORROWING FROM THE BANK: The Bank is rather closely circumscribed in its lending powers. The articles of agreement provide, for example, that the Bank is not to compete with private lenders; and if the borrower can borrow on reasonable terms in the private money markets of the world, the Bank is to refuse to deal with him. That the Bank has been conservative in enforcing this precept is attested by statements made by Bank officials. In a January, 1955, brochure the first statement (and almost the only statement) made under "Lending Policies" was: "The Bank is intended to promote private investment, not to compete with it, and does not undertake business which private investors are willing to transact on a reasonable basis." The Bank has been generous to private international banking groups in its concept of a "reasonable basis."

Governments (or corporations which can induce their government to guarantee their project) which would like to borrow from or through the Bank present their request. The Bank then makes a study of the project. Full-scale studies of whole economies—those already published cover Colombia, Cuba, Guatemala, Jamaica, Mexico, and several other countries —represent significant contributions to the descriptive economic literature on those countries.

The Bank may, then, on the basis of one of these studies, make a loan to a country that wishes to borrow. The loan will either be to the government, to some semi-official government entity, or to some corporation for which the government will act as guarantor. The projects have ranged from electric power development in Mexico, to equipment for timber production in Finland, to railway rehabilitation in India, to equipment and materials for reconstruction and development in France. In effect, what the Bank generally does is to make available to the borrower a sum of foreign exchange in the currency of the country in which the borrower needs to buy some equipment. The Bank does not generally lend to help a country obtain funds with which to pay for

TABLE 42

INTERNATIONAL BANK FOR RECONSTRUCTION AND DEVELOPMENT: LOANS GRANTED AND DISBURSED, OUTSTANDING
SEPTEMBER 30, 1956

(MILLIONS OF U.S. DOLLARS)

	PRINCIPAL TOTAL	DISBURSED PORTION
Australia	233.0	230.7
Austria	21.8	14.1
Belgium	78.0	72.7
Brazil	182.3	147.8
Burma	5.4	—
Ceylon	19.1	4.1
Chile	31.1	19.5
Colombia	96.7	54.2
Denmark	35.8	35.8
Ecuador	8.5	2.2
El Salvador	22.4	15.1
Ethiopia	8.1	7.2
Finland	52.3	33.3
France	235.8	231.5
Guatemala	17.6	5.4
Haiti	2.2	—
Honduras	3.3	—
Iceland	5.7	5.7
India	94.3	51.0
Italy	73.6	41.0
Japan	44.0	33.3
Lebanon	27.0	.2
Luxembourg	8.5	8.5
Mexico	124.4	101.5
Netherlands	65.0	65.0
Nicaragua	14.6	5.7
Norway	73.0	48.2
Pakistan	66.6	38.5
Panama	4.9	.9
Paraguay	4.5	2.6
Peru	31.8	16.5
South Africa	107.8	86.4
Thailand	33.9	24.6
Turkey	60.3	47.9
United Kingdom	118.9	49.2
Uruguay	32.7	30.1
Yugoslavia	56.4	53.8
Totals	$2,101.4	$1,584.1

Source: International Bank for Reconstruction and Development, *Press Release No. 464,* November 7, 1956, Appendix C.

equipment and labor that can be obtained domestically. The currency in which the Bank has chiefly trafficked of late years has been United States dollars, the United States being the country which, since World War II, has had the machinery, equipment, and grain that other countries have needed.

After the loan has been made, representatives of the Bank have extensive power to supervise the manner in which the debtor handles the development project which is being financed. Indeed, the Bank may cut off further funds during the work on the project if it does not approve of the fashion in which the development is going on. In the articles of agreement, the countries which are members of the Bank have agreed that the Bank may "make arrangements to ensure that the proceeds of any loan are used only for the purposes for which the loan was granted, with due attention to considerations of economy and efficiency and without regard to political or other non-economic influences or considerations." [8]

The Bank thus has a rather significant amount of power to intervene in purely internal activities in the borrowing country, a power which the International Monetary Fund does not have. When France tried to make an issue of this provision and deny the Bank representatives effective power of supervision following a 1947 loan, France was forced to back down. This is one of the few minor victories for international order which has occurred since the end of World War II.

Activities of the Bank

It was originally planned that the International Bank for Reconstruction and Development, as its name implied, should give reconstruction and development aid. And there was hope that a genuine international agency, to which the taint of making loans on the basis of political considerations could not be attached, would be at the heart of the reconstruction and development lending of the postwar years. In the nature of things, of course, much of what it would make available initially would be United States dollars, but they would be United States dollars the disposition of which would be controlled by an international agency and the repayment of which would be guaranteed by an international agency. Thus the political taint would be taken out of the international lending process. The loans then would presumably stand on their economic merit, and repayment could be insisted on with a far clearer conscience than was the case during the 1930's.

But things have not worked out this way. The United States government and its Export-Import Bank have remained in the field as active participants in the lending process, instead of abdicating that function to the International Bank. The desire of the United States to make politi-

[8] *Articles of Agreement*, article III, section 5 (b).

cal loans to Greece and Turkey in 1947 was undoubtedly a major factor in causing the United States government to remain active in the field.

Countries associated with Russia have complained of some political bias against them on the part of the Bank. Russia, although participating in the Bretton Woods conference, did not choose to join the Bank when it was actually established and can therefore hardly complain of failure to obtain a loan. But Poland and Czechoslovakia, for example, are another story. Poland had been ravaged by war perhaps more than any other single country and in 1946 had great need of a loan. Poland joined the Bank and more or less continually was requesting a loan from 1946 on, but failed to obtain one. She finally resigned from the Bank in a burst of righteous indignation in 1950. No country on the other side of the "curtain" has obtained a loan from the Bank. But Yugoslavia and Finland, doubtful borderline countries which the United States has been active in trying to win over from the Russian orbit, have obtained loans. Poland thus, in resigning, could present some evidence in accusing the Bank of playing politics. And *Fortune* in August, 1954, stated that the Bank is playing the United States game in the field of international politics.[9]

A distinction should be made between an agency which can and should legitimately serve the political needs of its country (the Export-Import Bank and the International Cooperation Administration) and an agency that claims to be genuinely international, such as the International Bank. If an agency is going to claim to be international and above national political considerations, then it should so be. A loan to Poland in 1946 or 1947 might have done a great deal to disprove the Russian claim of an encirclement conspiracy and to prove that international agencies, even agencies in which the United States has had a major influence, were not discriminating against Communist countries. But as matters stand, the United States is actually in a position to prevent the Bank from lending to Poland funds which the Bank has raised in Switzerland.

A loan to Czechoslovakia, during the years between 1946 and 1948, might have been an important factor in keeping Czechoslovakia from slipping into the Communist camp in 1948. According to Guy Braibant, although Czechoslovakia, along with Poland, applied for a loan in 1946, she was refused because of "the ill will of the American officials of the bank toward the measures of nationalization and over-all planning, and even more because of the pro-Soviet attitude taken by the Czech delegation at the Luxembourg conference several months earlier. From then

[9] The Bank's articles of agreement say that neither the Bank nor its officers shall "be influenced in their decisions by the political character of the member or members concerned. Only economic considerations shall be relevant. . . ."

on, Czechoslovakia thought that she could not obtain foreign loans except at the price of her independence, from which in certain quarters an explanation has been deduced for one of the most controversial developments of our time: Czech hostility to the Marshall plan." [10]

More recently American officers in the Bank have been accused of using their position to prevent the socialization of certain industries in Austria.[11]

> Dr. Fritz Bock, State Secretary in the Ministry of Trade, who belongs to the People's party, implied last week that Austria need not expect a loan from the International Bank for Reconstruction and Development if she nationalized the enterprises returned by the Soviet Union.
>
> Dr. Bock contended that a warning to this effect had been given to him by Robert L. Garner of the United States, vice president of the world bank who was here recently on an inspection trip.
>
> The quarrel over nationalization is the most serious threat yet to the preservation of the coalition Government.

A Russian indictment of the Bank runs as follows: [12]

> The International Monetary Fund and the International Bank for Reconstruction and Development are not international institutions but instruments of United States policy. The purpose of credit operations of the International Bank, particularly in the underdeveloped countries, is not the economic development of those countries; the credits are designed to assist the infiltration of American capital, to develop the branches of the country's economy that benefit American capitalists, and to finance the stock-piling of strategic materials by the United States of America (for example, the loans to Ethiopia, Brazil, Iran and the Belgian Congo). The Bank encourages private investments, with a view to their yielding large returns. The high rate of interest on its loans enriches American financiers on the international money market, and the many conditions attached to its loans allow unwarranted interference by the United States of America in the underdeveloped countries. The Bank also promotes the large-scale export of American goods: 73.1 per cent of credits pro-

[10] Guy Braibant, *La Planification en Tchecoslovaquie*, p. 83. (The author is responsible for the translation.) It will be recalled that the Marshall plan was proposed before Czechoslovakia moved into the Communist sphere.

[11] *New York Times*, October 7, 1955, p. 5. Reprinted with the permission of the *New York Times*.

[12] *International Social Science Bulletin*, V (no. 1, 1953), p. 218. The statement is part of the paraphrase of an article: G. Rybalko, "Rol Mezhdunarodnovo Valiutnovo Fonda i Mezhdunarodnovo Banka Rekonstruktsii i Razvitiia v Agressivnikh Planakh S.S.A.," *Vneshniaia Torgovlia*, July, 1952, pp. 29–35.

vided by it between 1947 and 1951 were used for the purchase of these goods.

There is much exaggeration and misinterpretation in this statement. Loans such as the Brazilian loans, which were largely for electric power development, can hardly be disposed of in this cavalier fashion. And the last sentence is repetition of the overworked Soviet thesis that somehow or other everything the United States does can be related to the desperate search for markets. Pretty obviously, since the end of World War II, other countries have desperately wanted goods that only the United States could supply. And even the Russians should be willing to admit that is a large part of the reason for the substantial share of United States exports in world trade. Nevertheless, there is enough merit in the charge that this Bank, which is ostensibly international, is in fact influenced by considerations of United States foreign policy to give pause for thought—as to what the role of the Bank really is and should be.

One may hope that the Bank's difficulties with becoming a genuine international agency are temporary and will disappear as the "cold war" passes from its acute to its chronic phase.

Other problems, however, remain. Some bank lending has been at rates as low as $3\frac{1}{2}$ per cent (commission included); but for the most part (and increasingly) the rates are higher, having risen to about $4\frac{3}{4}$ per cent for loans up through fifteen years and 5 per cent for longer periods. Perhaps it could be argued that this is a reasonable rate—it is certainly lower than the rates most of the underdeveloped countries had to pay on their borrowing of the 1920's. But it is well above the rates which the governments of the United States and the United Kingdom have to pay for borrowed money. Might it not be a good idea, especially if the facilitating of development is really the purpose behind all this, to lend the money at rates that economies can really afford to pay?

The project being financed should be a genuinely constructive project, and the Bank should supervise its progress to see that the money is well spent. Repayment can then be insisted on with a clear conscience, and the lower interest rate will be justified by the fact that repayment is assured. A genuine international agency can do this kind of thing effectively, where a single nation state could not.

Other questions pertain to the actual significance of the volume of the Bank's activities and to the nature of the projects in which the Bank has put its money. The Bank's disbursed loans amount to approximately $1.6 billion. By comparison, United States investments abroad (public and private) amounted to $45 billion at the end of 1955 and United States government grants and aid between 1945 and 1955 totaled $53 billion. Loans by the Export-Import Bank alone have substantially exceeded the International Bank total.

A breakdown of International Bank lending by purpose, cumulative through June 30, 1956, is as follows: [13]

Reconstruction	$497 million
Electric Power	789
Transportation	656
Communications	26
Agriculture and Forestry	228
Industry	331
General Development	140
Total Cumulative Lending	$2,667 million

Virtually all of the reconstruction loans were made immediately after the close of the war.

The Bank, soon after it began operations in 1946, made desperately needed reconstruction loans to Holland and France and a few other countries, but not to any of the Russian satellite countries. Then came the Marshall plan, and the Bank decided to get out of the business of granting reconstruction loans altogether. The idea was to leave reconstruction aid to the Marshall plan organization and concentrate thenceforth on carefully planned, long-run development aid. The latter activity is all very well. But the effect of the sequence of events was to leave the immediately important reconstruction aid to purely political forces. The United States reconstructed its "friends"; and Russia reconstructed its "satellites."

The other types of loans have been made at a slower tempo since. As may be seen, the development loans have been chiefly in basic areas which for one reason or another are not too attractive to private capital. They have been made in electric power, transportation, and improvement projects in agriculture. The Bank has made a positive effort to stay out of the standard branches of manufacturing which offer profitable prospects for private entrepreneurs.

Bank officials have been aware that their institution has been failing to provide a substantial volume of aid to the industrialization programs of the underdeveloped countries. In partial justification for this dereliction, Bank officials have argued that the articles of agreement do not give the Bank adequate powers to finance development. And they have sponsored the establishment of an auxiliary organization, the International Finance Corporation.

INTERNATIONAL FINANCE CORPORATION

The articles of agreement of this organization (which came into formal existence July 25, 1956) emphasize the purpose of "encouraging the

[13] International Bank for Reconstruction and Development, *Eleventh Annual Report, 1955–1956* (Washington, 1956), p. 58.

growth of productive private enterprise in member countries, particularly in the less developed areas." But the Corporation is debarred from assuming any "responsibility for managing an enterprise" in which it has invested. The chief feature of the Corporation's operations, which distinguishes it from the Bank, is its power to make loans "without guarantee of repayment by the member government concerned." But its activities also are circumscribed by the provision that it is not to make loans in cases where sufficient private capital is available on reasonable terms.

The authorized capital stock of the Corporation is $100 million (U.S.). The full value of the subscription to the stock, which is assigned to each member, must be paid in gold or United States dollars. (The reader may recall that the Bank was less fortunate in terms of the proportion of the value of its capitalization which was actually "paid in" in usable funds.)

The Corporation may also acquire additional operating funds by borrowing. On this point Robert L. Garner has said: [14]

> IFC will have authority to borrow funds and in that connection to issue its own securities, but it is not expected that it will do so in the early years of its operations. Until it proves itself, IFC will have to operate solely with the funds subscribed by its members. Through revolving those funds by portfolio sales, however, and through securing the association of private capital, the effective contribution of IFC will, we hope, be many times the size of its own capital. In this connection, we have been encouraged by a number of recent indications that substantial amounts of investment capital will be available to help finance projects in which IFC participates.

Provisions similar to those in the articles of agreement of the Bank debar the Corporation and its officers from interfering "in the political affairs of any member; nor shall they be influenced in their decisions by the political character of the member or members concerned. Only economic considerations shall be relevant." But the Corporation, unlike the Bank, is going to be saved much embarrassment on this score because none of the countries associated with Russia are going to be members.

[14] Robert L. Garner, *Statement on the International Finance Corporation, Tenth Annual Meeting of the Board of Governors, Istanbul, September 15, 1955,* p. 9.

Chapter 29

MOTIVATION AND CAUSE

⌇ ⌇ ⌇

It has frequently been alleged that foreign investments occur because of the attraction of higher profits in the country where the investment is made. But this explanation falls considerably short of providing a satisfactory basic explanation of the process.

It is doubtful that average profits are higher in debtor countries than in creditor countries.

Chronic inflation seems to be the chief explanation of higher interest rates on monetary loans in underdeveloped countries. But much of the meaningful, real lending in such countries is interest free.

Assuming that the actual projects in which foreigners make investments yield a higher profit than the general profit rate in the debtor country, this is not enough in itself to explain why the foreigner has the opportunity to make this desirable investment rather than a citizen of the underdeveloped country.

It is probably the advantage conferred by greater technical progress and managerial knowledge which determines whose nationals will be debtors and whose will be creditors.

Also, entirely apart from a comparison of the profit rates in the two countries, a particular enterprise in the developed country may be more profitable as a result of adding a foreign facet to its operation than would be the case if it remained entirely domestic. The fact that the international operation is thus rendered more profitable does not establish the greater profitability of the foreign operation taken in isolation.

⌇ ⌇ ⌇

THE QUESTION as to the identity of the forces motivating foreign investments brings us back to fundamentals again. Why does an individual make a foreign rather than a domestic investment? Perhaps he wishes to be different. Perhaps he wishes to stay at home with his kith and kin. Perhaps he is content with the religion of his fathers. Perhaps, to practice a new religion of his choice, he must go somewhere else. Perhaps his father's business is good enough for him. Perhaps the fabulous wealth of the Spice Islands lures him on—or the tales of El Dorado. If he has capital to lend, perhaps the domestic interest rate seems to provide a high enough return. Perhaps a higher foreign interest rate is an attraction. If he is enterprising, perhaps the profit prospects of a particular domestic enterprise are lure enough. Perhaps the thought of higher profits from some particular enterprise abroad entices him to foreign lands.

Much of economic theory, including Marxian theory, is built on the assumption that the individual is a profit-seeking unit and that monetary profit maximization is the objective that he seeks. This book has been written on the assumption as to motive that it is some sort of subjectively additive combination of material level of living, individual freedom of action, and security. To a nation or to the world the maximization of the sum of individual monetary profits means nothing. Nations can create or destroy money as the whim dictates. This is additional reason for feeling considerable reservation in accepting the assumption of a monetary-profit-maximization motive.

RATE POSSIBILITIES

In the discussion which follows (1) the short-term interest rate, (2) the long-term interest rate, (3) the profit rate, (4) the unique and different interest and profit rates applicable to particular transactions and particular enterprises, have been singled out as the important concepts. (Of course, there is a whole complex of rates applicable to different types of transactions under each heading.)

Two rather different considerations are intermingled in the discussion which follows. One is whether interest and profit rate differences between nations are necessary to motivate the international lending process, and the other consideration is whether capital movements are especially sensitive to such differences even when they exist.

In this discussion the purpose is not so much to prove that there is no international difference in interest rates on investments of comparable quality as to show that lending has not been primarily motivated by such differences.

DIFFERENCES IN THE RATE OF RETURN

Such theoretical discussion as there is in this chapter is not concerned with the important debate now going on as to the fundamental forces determining interest rates. Rather such theory as is here discussed involves merely the analysis of the forces determining the relationship between interest rates in different countries and the question as to whether those differences affect capital movements.

An explanation of the motive behind a capital movement in economic literature is not unlikely to start with an assumption of an interest-rate or profit-rate differential. Even Iversen, whose "modern theory" is trying to de-emphasize price differences as prerequisite to a change in the pattern of goods movement, must say in a dozen places something like this:[1] "the immediate 'cause' which calls forth an international capital movement is usually a difference between interest rates of two countries, which is large enough to outweigh the costs of transfer occasioned by the obstacles to such capital flows."

But the Marxist, Paul Sweezy, much like Iversen, says:[2] "Clearly the capitalists in low-profit countries—generally speaking the countries in which accumulation has already gone farthest—will export capital to the higher-profit countries." It seems all shades of opinion, neo-classical, "modern," and Marxist, agree that the significant motivation behind foreign investments is interest-rate and profit-rate difference— actual differences, not just underlying differences. If the interest rate is 4 per cent in your country and 6 per cent abroad, you will make more money by investing abroad, and are likely to do so.

The international comparison of profit rates and interest rates needs to be conducted on several levels. (1) Both classical (Ricardian) and Marxist theory indicate the existence of a falling rate of profit in the developed countries relative to the underdeveloped countries. (2) And from this it should follow that profit rates in general should be lower in the developed countries than in the underdeveloped countries. (3) But capital movements may be caused by profit and interest rate differences without there being a general rule that such rates are regularly higher in underdeveloped than developed countries. (4) Capital movements may occur when no such rate differences exist. If capital movements frequently occur, when no significant rate differences exist, then some modification of the theory that makes such movements primarily depend on rate differences is called for.

Short-term Rates

It is probable that an interest-rate comparison of a direct sort motivates (or did motivate before 1929) considerable international movement of short-term funds. If the rate on short-term funds was enough higher in the London market than in the New York market to cover the

[1] Carl Iversen, *Aspects of the Theory of International Capital Movements*, p. 93.
[2] Paul M. Sweezy, *Theory of Capitalist Development*, pp. 291–2.

cost of two foreign-exchange transactions, and something more, an individual in New York with some temporarily idle funds would be tempted to invest them in London.[3]

But the various descriptions of the working of this process in connection with short-term funds (assuming it worked) do not imply a significant net movement of capital one way or the other. They merely imply that the movement back and forth tends to equalize interest rates in the two countries.

In the more stable days (were they really?) of the pre-World War I period, such minor interest-rate differences may have been fairly significant in attracting short-term funds from one country to another. And they may be so again. But they are not now, and very likely they never were except between such highly developed money markets as London, New York, and the Continental centers. It seems rather doubtful that it was common practice in the 1870's for short-term funds to flow from London to Rio for a 0.5 per cent difference in the overt interest rate.

Joan Robinson says the interest rate is "30 per cent in an Indian village and 3 per cent in London."[4] And presumably a scholar of the quality of Joan Robinson is talking about comparable rates. No doubt, if that is the interest-rate difference now, it has also been the difference, more or less, for many years. Why has not English short-term money gone to India to equalize the rates? Miss Robinson says the difference is possible because of "social, legal, and institutional" factors. (And they are, no doubt, a large part of the explanation of the rate differential. But more of that later. . . .)

If interest-rate differences, today, were really functioning to motivate short-term capital movements, such funds would surely be flowing from the United States in large quantities to virtually every country in the world except Switzerland and Canada—see Table 24. The fact that they are not doing so (Canada and Switzerland being, on the contrary, about the only countries to which United States short-term funds would venture) suggests that other considerations outweigh the direct interest-rate comparison. Such considerations include: (1) transfer difficulties which result from the fact that many currencies are not freely convertible, (2) political considerations and uncertainties, (3) the fear of inflation in the short run, and (4) something more—connected with the proposition that this type of thinking has cause and effect all mixed up.

Some comment should be made at this stage regarding some of the problems involved in comparing interest rates. There is a large element of non-comparability in the nature of ostensibly similar interest

---

[3] See Chapters 16 and 18 for qualifications.

[4] Joan Robinson, *The Rate of Interest and Other Essays* (London: Macmillan, 1953), p. 3.

rates in different countries. For example, it may be that many short-term commercial loans, as made by Latin American banks, should be compared with consumption loans as made by small loan companies in the United States. To delve into ancient history, the Mexican banking system was insolvent in 1914 because the loans which had been made ostensibly as self-liquidating, commercial loans, many to large hacendados and political figures, were really consumption loans. The interest rate on consumption loans as made by small loans companies in the United States is still an effective 12 to 40 per cent. If this latter figure is compared with the pseudo-commercial (actually consumption) loans of the Latin American bank to the hacendado-politico, it looks high; if it is compared with what the Mexican poor would have to pay a loan shark for a consumption loan, it looks low. Many Latin American countries are only now getting away from the hacienda store (tienda de raya) arrangement under which the peon virtually sold his soul and that of his children for generations to come in exchange for a consumption loan.

Also it might, with considerable justice, be argued that the interest rate in underdeveloped countries, far from being 30 per cent by comparison with 3 per cent in the center of civilization—London—is actually zero by comparison with 3 per cent in London. The meaningful borrowing that occurs in many underdeveloped countries consists of a man's helping his neighbor free of charge in clearing his land or building his house, in exchange for the tacit understanding that the aid will be reciprocated under similar circumstances.

Also, for discussion of this sort, the ostensible short-term interest-rate comparisons between nations need to be corrected for differences in the rate of inflation in different countries to be more nearly comparable as "true" interest rates. Let us say that price levels remain the same in the United States and rise 5 per cent a year in Chile, a not implausible statement of the relationship. Let us also say that the interest rate is an ostensible 5 per cent in the United States and 10 per cent in Chile. This is the order of magnitude of interest-rate difference that has frequently been alleged as typical of the relationship between England and the United States on the one hand and underdeveloped countries on the other.[5] But the 5 per cent a year inflation is also not untypical; it may even be conservative. And yet the real interest rate (the purchasing power which the investor gets back as the price for lending his money) is the same in both countries. It is also an effective 5 per cent, approximately, in Chile because the rest of the ostensible 10 per cent is neutralized by the price rise. These are real forces that need to be taken into account. David L. Grove has estimated that as a result of inflation the "real"

---

[5] Senator Homer Capehart says 8 to 16 or 18 per cent. United States Congress, Senate, Committee on Banking and Currency (Hearings, 83:2), *Study of Export-Import Bank and World Bank,* Part 1, p. 172.

interest rate in Chile in recent years actually has been negative.[6]

But in any event, and even if it were demonstrable that short-term interest rates have been higher in underdeveloped countries, that would not explain foreign investments in underdeveloped countries, because short-term balances have in general moved from the underdeveloped to the developed countries and not in the other direction.

Long-term Interest Rates

Keynesian theory has pointed up the differences in nature between the profit rate and the interest rate. Profit is what the businessman-promoter-entrepreneur gets—or hopes to get. Interest is the price he has to pay for the money he borrows to engage in the activities that will give him a profit. Consequently he is motivated by the difference between the profit rate and the interest rate. A high interest rate is a deterrent to investment and production, whereas a high profit rate encourages them.

But the discussion up to this point has implied that international differences in the interest rate seem to act in much the same way as international differences in the profit rate in affecting the likelihood of foreign investment. And so they do. The businessman-entrepreneur-promoter goes where he can get, or hopes he can get, the highest profit (again assuming a profit motive); the saver goes where he can get the most interest. The essence of the international distinction is between profit rates in the two countries or interest rates in the two countries. It is not a distinction between profit rates and interest rates. Thus the concern, in this chapter, is not essentially with Keynes' interest rate–profit rate relation. Rather it involves a relation between different interest rates in one setting and between different profit rates in another.

First, then, turning to the interest-rate comparison, are long-term interest rates actually higher in underdeveloped countries than in developed countries? In the important theoretical treatises on the subject of foreign investments, the authors have been likely to assume such a difference and to proceed from there.[7] But the authors also may cite isolated examples. Ohlin gave several specific examples of higher interest rates in the countries on the eastern side of the Baltic than in Sweden. He said:[8] "In northern and western Europe industry is paying about 5 per cent for borrowed capital in 1930, whereas not further away than in the

---

[6] David L. Grove, "Role of the Banking System in the Chilean Inflation," *Staff Papers, II* (September, 1951), 33–59. Allowance for inflation in the borrowing country is also necessary in connection with long-term bond issues repayable in the currency of the borrowing country, but not necessary in the case of bond issues repayable in the currency of the lending country or in the case of direct investments. The shoe would be on the other foot in the case of long-term portfolio investments repayable in the currency of the lending country, if it was the currency of the lending country which fell in purchasing power.

[7] Iversen, *Aspects . . . , passim.*

[8] Ohlin, *Interregional and International Trade,* p. 275.

Baltic nations the level is four or five times as high." And he alleged instances of corporations in Esthonia, Latvia, or Lithuania borrowing money for capital improvements and paying 25 per cent. Presumably these were cited as typical examples, although interest rates substantially lower than these might still be higher than those prevailing in more developed countries, and prove Ohlin's argument.

With regard to the proposition that such conditions motivate investment, this may be said: Capital improvement cannot afford to pay the charges cited by Ohlin. Bankruptcy would be inevitable, automatic, and quick. Therefore Ohlin was not describing a setting in which a significant, continuing amount of investment was going on. Now it may be true that not much borrowing of capital funds was going on in the Baltic countries at any figure (and particularly at these figures), and that not much industrialization was going on at any price for borrowed funds. In that case there is no special point in talking about a market charging 25 per cent as though the market actually existed. If and when the combination of technological and institutional factors in those countries permits industrialization, the interest rates will be lower.

TABLE 43
INTEREST RATES ON LONG-TERM SECURITIES
(VARIOUS COUNTRIES)
(PER CENT)

	DEBENTURE ISSUES (MAY, 1954)	LONG-TERM GOVERNMENT BONDS (FEB., 1956)
Europe:		
Belgium	4–4.4	4.19
Denmark	—	5.65
France	6.5	5.12
Italy	—	6.36
(Western) Germany	4–4.5	—
Netherlands	4.25	3.39
Norway	—	3.14
Portugal	—	3.49
Sweden	3.75–4	3.66
Switzerland	3	2.96
United Kingdom	4.5	4.61
North America:		
Canada	4.25	3.27
United States	3.125	2.82
Other:		
Australia	—	4.57
Japan	9	—
New Zealand	—	4.38
Union of South Africa	—	4.68

Source: *International Financial News Survey*, June 18, 1954, p. 389.

In Table 43 perhaps one would be justified in identifying as underdeveloped Italy, Portugal, Australia, New Zealand, and the Union of South Africa. But it would be difficult to demonstrate that interest rates in those countries are appreciably higher than the norm. This is relevant to the argument of classical and Marxist theory to the effect that the rates should be higher in the underdeveloped countries. But since relatively little portfolio capital has been moving to those countries since World War II, it is not relevant to the other and simpler proposition (the third level among the levels on which this problem may be discussed) that investment moves merely in response to interest-rate differences—without bothering to explain the interest-rate differences.

Since the countries which are currently attracting capital are not necessarily the underdeveloped countries, it becomes pertinent to try to distinguish them and inquire whether their interest rates are high or low. But again there is the same ambiguity. High interest rates in France and Italy are not as successful as lower rates in Germany and Switzerland in attracting funds.

Of course, current conditions are chaotic; they are not a fair test of the relationship between interest rates and the direction of movement of funds. You might say that such differences would be more meaningful in more normal times—say, the 1920's. A comparison of the average yields in the United States on newly issued domestic bonds with the yields on newly issued foreign bonds gives fairly clear evidence of a slight difference in yield—see Table 44. Through the 1920's the yield on

TABLE 44

AVERAGE PRICE OF NEW CAPITAL
(UNITED STATES)

	I MOODY'S WEIGHTED AVERAGES OF YIELDS ON NEWLY ISSUED DOMESTIC BONDS (ALL CORPORATIONS)	II WEIGHTED AVERAGE YIELD INDEX OF NEW FOREIGN DOLLAR BONDS
1920	—	7.69
1921	7.23	7.54
1922	6.28	6.63
1923	6.09	6.42
1924	5.96	6.56
1925	5.75	6.51
1926	5.61	6.51
1927	5.34	6.14
1928	5.24	6.09
1929	5.34	5.81

Source: United States, Department of Commerce, *Handbook on American Underwriting of Foreign Securities* (Washington: Government Printing Office, 1930), p. 44.

the new foreign issues averaged about 10 per cent (or 0.5 per cent depending on how you choose to look at it) higher than the yield on new domestic issues. Whether the additional complications and risks that are part of the international transaction are fully compensated by this 0.5 per cent difference remains a question. It looks suspiciously from that data as though the "real" foreign interest rate was lower than the real domestic rate in the 1920's, during the period of major United States portfolio lending abroad.

The bond interest rate comparisons of Table 45 (for example, the 1955 comparison of the domestic 3.25 per cent and the foreign 3.5 per cent) can hardly do much more than explain why there is only a modest amount of portfolio lending now out from the United States. They certainly do not indicate a substantially higher rate of return on the foreign issues.

TABLE 45
FOREIGN AND DOMESTIC (UNITED STATES) PROFIT AND INTEREST RATES

	1950	1955
I. Profit Rates		
A. Domestic (United States)		
1. Per cent return (after taxes) on net assets for a sample of over 3,000 corporations (1)	13.3	12.0
2. Per cent return (after taxes) on net assets for a sample of over 1,500 manufacturing corporations (1)	17.1	15.0
B. Private United States Direct Investments Abroad		
1. Value of investment at end of year ($1,000,000) (2)	11,800	19,200
2. Earnings (balance of payments income plus undistributed earnings of direct investment subsidiaries) ($1,000,000) (2)	1,769	2,846
3. Per cent return (before U.S. taxes)	15	15
II. Interest Rates		
A. Domestic (United States)		
1. Per cent return on domestic corporate bonds (yield) (3)	2.86	3.25
2. Per cent yield on long-term U.S. governments (3)	2.32	2.80
B. Return on Foreign Lending		
1. Yield on private portfolio investment (2)	3.5	3.5
2. U.S. government lending (2)	0.7	1.7
III. Condensed Totals for Direct, Portfolio, and U.S. Government Foreign Investment		
A. Value of investment ($1,000,000) (2)	32,800	44,888
B. Return ($1,000,000) (2)	2,068	3,380
C. Per cent rate of return	6.3	7.5

Sources: (1) First National City Bank, *Monthly Letter;* (2) *Survey of Current Business;* (3) *Statistical Abstract.*

A study of new public issues in England for the significant period 1888–1913 by R. A. Lehfeldt, similarly failed to reveal that "foreign share investments were more profitable than domestic ones." [9] However, Cairncross presents some spotty evidence to support the contention that British foreign investment returned 5 per cent in the period 1870 to 1913, while home investment returned only 3.5 per cent.

The foregoing must be deemed inconclusive. It does *not* establish that interest rates are lower in the countries to which capital migrates or that they are higher there. But it is amazing, in view of all the discussion there has been on the subject, that it is not certain that there has been a meaningful difference in long-term interest rates even during the periods when a major amount of foreign lending has occurred.

Profit Rates

The conclusions to be drawn from the discussion of long-term interest rates are uncertain. But the more important questions can be analyzed to better advantage in a discussion of profits than in a discussion of interest. In the following discussion the chief point to note is the nebulousness of the "average rate" concept.

Professor J. Fred Rippy, of the University of Chicago, has been assembling miscellaneous empirical data on the profits which have actually been made by a great number of British investors in foreign lands. Some of the profits made have been high—see Table 46. But many an enterprise has gone bankrupt as well. The data establishes that some enterprises have made consistently high profits. But there is wide variation from one enterprise to the next. And the truth or falsity of the proposition that foreign profits average higher than domestic profits is not established by random high profit figures such as these, even if they were especially high on the whole, which they are not. Domestic corporations such as Texas Gulf Sulphur have high profit rates also.

Table 45 also hardly establishes the existence of any significant difference in the profit rates on domestic and foreign investment in the postwar period. Yet a considerable amount of direct foreign investment has occurred during this period, direct investment being the one area (oil and manufacturing) where significant amounts of private foreign investment have occurred.[10]

[9] Iversen, *op. cit.*, pp. 103–5. Iversen cites R. A. Lehfeldt, "Rate of Interest on British and Foreign Investments," *Journal of the Royal Statistical Society,* LXXVI (January, 1913), 196–207; and 1913–14, pp. 432 et seq.; A. K. Cairncross, *Home and Foreign Investment, 1870–1913,* pp. 22–35.

[10] The reader may have noted that in Table 46 the profit rates are given as a percentage of nominal capitalization. He may also have wondered as to the basis for establishing the capitalizations used for computing the average profit rates of Table 45. About all that can be said is that probably in manufacturing and mining (but probably not in public utilities), there is a tendency to show capitalization as less than it really is. It is standard, conservative accounting practice to depreciate

TABLE 46

SOME PROFITABLE BRITISH FOREIGN INVESTMENTS

(DIVIDENDS AS A PERCENTAGE OF NOMINAL CAPITALIZATION)

COMPANY	PERIOD COVERED	ANNUAL AVERAGE
Sao Paulo Railway	1876–1931	11.2%
Cie. Aramayo	1910–1950	15.5
Sao Joao d'El Rei Mining (Brazil)	1875–1951	9.2
Venezuelan Oil Concessions	1926–1949	27.4
Alianza Nitrate	1903–1929	20.4
Lobitos Oil Co. (Peru)	1912–1950	18.2
London and River Plate Bank	1876–1924	14.7
Liebig's Extract of Meat (Uruguay)	1874–1951	16.1
Rio de Janeiro Flour Mills	1893–1951	13.5
Linggi Plantations	1906–1919	107.4
Burmah Oil	1906–1950	24.0
Anglo-Iranian Oil	1920–1950	17.1

Source: J. Fred Rippy, "British Investments in Latin America: A Sample of Profitable Enterprises," *Inter-American Economic Affairs,* Spring, 1953, pp. 10, 12.

An observant reader will question the propriety of comparing "per cent return (after taxes) on net assets" in the case of the domestic corporations with "per cent return (before U.S. taxes)" in the case of the private United States direct investments abroad. Of course it would be better to have a figure on the return from the foreign investments after United States taxes; but, so far as I know, such data is not available. Such information, if it were to be had, however, could only make the return on the foreign investments look yet lower.

I should like to hazard the guess that, if data could be obtained for the average return on all business activity (including agriculture) in the less developed countries, the figure would be substantially lower than the average rate of return in the industrially more developed countries.[11] And I should also like to hazard the opinion that this has

---

assets as rapidly as possible. Whether the understatement of capital value, and consequently the overstatement of the profit rate, is greater in connection with foreign than with domestic investment is difficult to say. Possibly foreign investors are successfully concealing a relatively high profit rate behind a relatively high capitalization; but it is by no means established that they are doing so. Lacking, for the present, better data, we must use what we have.

[11] There is some support for statements of this sort in the United Nations study of the *Processes and Problems of Industrialization in Under-Developed Countries* (p. 11): "It is not generally true, for example, that the return on a unit of industrial capital invested in an under-developed (capital-poor) country is likely to be greater than that on a unit invested in an advanced (capital-rich) country. Nor is it generally true that the early investment of capital in an under-developed country is more productive than the later investment."

been true as a general pattern at least since the Industrial Revolution.[12]

Reflection will indicate the likelihood that profits (real profits), along with real wages and various other "real" things, are in greater abundance and rising faster in the country experiencing the fastest rate of growth. The wealthy, prosperous, profitable "countries of opportunity" are the countries which are showing the greatest relative development. And, as long as we speak in terms of averages, average profits (and average real, effective interest rates probably as well) are not going to be as high in the underdeveloped and lagging country as they are in the developed and developing country. Ohlin, Iversen, Sweezy, and others, who seem to predicate the motivation for the international lending of years gone by on the basis of such differences in average interest and profit rates as were thought to exist (the existence of which is allegedly established by isolated examples) are simply wrong. Such differences as may have existed were peripheral and incidental to the important forces at work.

It is amazing that neo-classical economists, especially those of the "modern" school, like Ohlin and Iversen, saddled themselves with the interest rate–profit rate differential as the motivation explaining whether investment will occur; after all, they had been most careful to deny that the evolution of price differences is a necessary preliminary to effecting international transfers in the case of balance-of-payments maladjustments. It is not so strange that the Marxists erred in the same way, since the argument that the differential exists is a logical result of their fundamental line of thought. In any event, both groups made the assumption of uniform interest and profit rates within a country but higher rates in the borrowing than in the lending countries—and claimed that, if such differences exist, investment will occur.

The Marxist argument requires that in recent years—and especially during the depression years of the 1930's—the capitalist countries should have been desperately trying to expand their foreign markets and should have been engaged in large-scale capital exports to do it. But the rate of capital export from Europe has fallen off as a general pattern, at least since World War I. And in the United States, the capitalists reacted to the depression by suspending capital export rather than by increasing it.

The Marxist would say that the present aid program of the United States government—the Marshall plan, and so on—is a reflection of this desperate search for markets. But even including such aid in the computation, the industrialized countries are not now investing as large a proportion of their income abroad as they did before World War I.

[12] However, this need not have been the case. And the basic argument on motivation which will be developed later is largely independent of comparison of average profit rates as between countries.

And it may well be that even the pre-World War I developments were not a very good demonstration of the Marxist argument because the foreign investment growth of England, France, etc., was financed out of earnings on the foreign investments and consequently did not provide the basis for an export balance of trade.

Unique and Different Rates of Return

It is simply not correct to say that one can invest in the "average rate of return" at long term. At long term the investment has to be in a specific project, mine, or manufacturing plant, or in a specific bond issue. And profit rates and interest rates vary from one project to the next. At long term one cannot make a foreign investment on the simple basis that the foreign interest rate is 6 per cent and the domestic rate is 4 per cent without further inquiry into the nature of the particular bond or piece of property that is being bought.

Perhaps the answer to the dilemma is that investment decisions must be made *project by project*. The individual investor is not concerned with the average rate of profit abroad nor with the average rate of profit at home. He is not going to invest in subsistence agriculture in the underdeveloped areas, a sector where the profit rate, if there is any profit at all, is so very low. He is going to invest in a particular enterprise which has, he guesses, the most likely prospects for making the most profits of any of the alternatives, foreign and domestic, which are open to him.

The profit rates on foreign direct investments indicated in Table 45 are probably held down by low returns on investments made long ago in public utilities. This does not prevent Arabian oil from offering lucrative prospects for the future. Typically low returns on subsistence agriculture in Latin America do not keep the banana business from being profitable, or sugar, or coffee, or Argentine wheat and beef. The rate of return among different foreign investments, in fact, varies more than the alleged average interest-rate discrepancies of Table 43 that were supposed to motivate investments. In 1952 the rate of return on United States direct investment in Latin America averaged 16 per cent (before United States taxes, which might reduce the figure slightly), distributed as follows: [13]

Agriculture	15%
Mining	12
Petroleum	29
Manufacturing	14
Public Utilities	3
Trade	17

[13] *Latin-American Business Highlights,* March, 1954, p. 9.

The crux of the matter in individual decision-making has to be future expectations regarding particular projects, not knowledge of past over-all averages. And knowledge of the sad current state of public utility investments may well discourage investment in public utilities.

The average profit being realized on existing investment may well be lower than the profit expectation in connection with investments now being made. Foreign investment may occur, then, because of the profit prospects on a series of individual deals, irrespective of what the average profit rates are in the two countries. Investment will be made in the property with the most profitable prospects, wherever it may be.[14] But at this point a difficulty from another direction besets the analysis. What insures that the foreign investor will be the one privileged to make this prospectively profitable investment? One would expect farsighted businessmen in the country where the opportunity exists also to be interested. What determines the nationality of the investor?

INSTITUTIONAL THEORY

The answer is in part institutionally determined and in part technologically determined by the differential rate of industrial development in the different countries. In the past it has also been determined in large part by the realities of power politics.

Institutional Factors

Certain institutional attitudes have affected the willingness of people with money in underdeveloped countries to put their money in the most profitable lines of business. It would seem that for many years manufacturing and commerce have been extremely profitable branches of activity in the underdeveloped countries. At least one hears tale after tale of high unit profits realized on a small volume of business in such lines of activity in the Latin American countries. The virtual certainty of a return of 30 or 40 per cent, it is frequently stated, is necessary to call out any domestic investment in such lines. Nevertheless domestic capital has typically gone into land or mortgages, in spite of the low return in those areas; and it has gone there because of the social prestige connected with land ownership. Or it has gone into foreign bank balances because of the danger of domestic upheaval and the desirability of having funds abroad to fall back on (or out on). The return from holding short-term foreign balances was not high relative to the profits on commerce and industry. The preference

---

[14] The prospects with regard to risk, expropriation, the transfer of profit, and the climate for investment obviously qualify the real profit prospects.

for investment in land was there all right, but it was determined by traditional attitudes, not by the interest rate. Again this is evidence that you have to look to something more fundamental than the rates of return themselves, even in limited lines of activity, for an explanation of broad patterns of development. In the so-called underdeveloped countries, in the past, institutional and social and political considerations have had a far more important influence than profit maximization in determining into what channels domestic funds would go. And one of the significant institutional differences in the past has been that domestic investors have not been interested in the same types of investments as foreigners.

Unique and different rates of return and institutional differences may explain why particular investments occur or do not occur. But they do not explain why it is, or was, a foreigner rather than a domestic investor who makes the particular, attractive-looking investment. Differences in institutionally determined attitudes must be looked to for explanation in this area.

It has frequently been remarked—by Keynes and Macmillan, among others—that Britain was institutionally biased in favor of foreign investment before World War I. And Day, writing about more recent conditions, says: [15] "It is an odd situation where British savings cannot be used to build milk bars and luxury flats in London, but can easily be used to build them in Sydney and Johannesburg. (In the seven years following the Second World War, capital movements to the outer Sterling Area exceeded Britain's total receipts under Marshall Aid and American Defence Aid combined.)"

Other situations may be cited where institutionally determined attitudes are more important than interest-rate differences. The flight of capital from high interest-rate to low interest-rate countries may well be a by-product of the movement of refugees. Also, it is very apparent that wealthy people and political figures in underdeveloped countries find it convenient to keep large sums in centers like New York and London. And they prefer to keep them liquid rather than to get as high a return as possible. Consequently, the rate of return on foreign investments in the United States and England is extremely low, lower than the average return on domestic investments in the United States.

The Relative State of Development Itself as Cause

Also basic in explaining why foreign investment occurs is the stage of technical and industrial development of the countries involved.

For example, Britain in the first half of the nineteenth century had developed manufacturing techniques considerably in advance of those

[15] A. C. L. Day, *The Future of Sterling* (Oxford: Clarendon Press, 1954), p. 105; see also A. E. Kahn, *Great Britain in the World Economy,* pp. 71–8.

in use in the rest of the world. British investment in Mexican mining (which occurred in the 1820's) was, from the viewpoint of the British, an only moderately important by-product of a development, the crux of which was the fortunate juxtaposition within England of (1) a certain stage of technical knowledge, (2) an institutional arrangement that permitted industrial development, and (3) possession in reasonable abundance of the raw materials which were most important for development at that stage (coal and iron, and the humid climate of Lancashire). The level of living was probably rising more rapidly in England than anywhere else in the world during those years (although income distribution apparently left something to be desired). And it is a fair guess that profits were extremely high in England—grind them any way you will: monetary profit, real profit, real capital accumulation. England acquired the Mexican mines because she had the knowledge needed to run the Mexican mines—the pumps to pump the water out from the shafts. As Barbara Ward said: [16] "It did not take much more than a couple of decades to provide the country [England in the early nineteenth century] with a very adequate network of railways— that first and most typical enterprise of the Industrial Revolution—and once Britain was supplied, the enterprising railwaymen went abroad."

England had the goods and the productive capacity and the technical skill. Hence, if those things were going to flow one way or the other, they had to flow out from England. She also had the political and military power, primarily because of her early industrialization. Consequently, foreign investment could flow out from the country where profits may well have been high and rising. And she had the power and prestige to make weaker countries respect her claim to property titles.

The Englishmen of the nineteenth century were in a better position than other people to seek out and exploit the opportunities for profit that the Industrial Revolution, which had developed in England, had itself created. This is, in part, because a foreign investment (especially a direct investment) is not likely to be a separate and independent profit-making unit—sufficient unto itself. It is rather more likely to be a facet of a far larger pattern of activity which centers in the more developed country. The operation centering in the more developed country is likely to be more profitable as a result of the foreign investment than it otherwise would be. But it would be rather difficult to measure and assign a certain percentage of profitableness to the part of the activity which is foreign by comparison with the part which is domestic. They are complementary!

Of course, accountants can and do perform the feat of assigning costs and profits to various phases of an integrated operation—but al-

[16] Barbara Ward, *The West at Bay* (New York: Norton, 1948), p. 24.

ways with the aid of a few "rules of thumb" and a slight tendency
to make profits show up in the jurisdiction with the lowest tax rates.
The problem of the accountant, is a real one—how to handle joint
products and how to appraise "profit" and "value added" at different
stages in an integrated productive process—and it is a problem to which
there is no theoretically satisfactory solution.

It is also worth noting that, in this situation, it would be difficult
for non-Englishmen to take advantage of the investment possibility
at all, since they do not have their finger in the far more important
part of the pie back in the developed country.

In a great many important situations—and perhaps this is almost
the basic situation—there is no meaningful comparison of the profit
on a potential foreign investment with the profit on a potential domestic
investment. But the estimate which is actually made is whether the
profit on the over-all operation will be greater if the over-all operation
is supplemented by some particular foreign investment or some particular domestic investment. Operations in a frame of reference such as
this are pretty clearly more feasible for the industrialists in the already
developed countries than for a national of an underdeveloped country
starting *de novo*. The oil industry is a good example of the pattern
of relations described here. Standard Oil of New Jersey is a more profitable operation because of its investment in Saudi Arabia. But individual
Saudi Arabians did not have the technical background to develop the
oil industry initially in their country—and it is lack of technical knowledge and lack of participation in an integrated company already active
in that type of production which is the important factor, *not lack of
monetary capital*.

The country that leads in development is capable of absorbing goods,
including raw material, technical knowledge, and people from all directions. It is also capable of spewing goods, capital equipment, knowledge, and people in all directions. Of course, the shape, form, quality,
or nature of the goods and people coming will be different from that
of the goods and people going (but it is just as likely that it will be
one type of manufactured goods for another as that it will be finished
goods for raw materials).

This does not necessarily mean that the price level of goods in general—or even of capital equipment in particular—is necessarily lower
in the more developed countries, as the Marxists imply. It is not unlikely that if the goods are available at all in the underdeveloped area,
they will be cheaper than in the country from which they come (see
the discussion of dumping in Chapter 13), but the goods are literally
not to be had at all from local manufacture in the underdeveloped
areas. They have to be bought from the high-priced source. And yet
the high-priced source may make them available to the underdeveloped,

low-priced area at reduced prices. The existence of these counteracting forces goes a long way toward explaining why the discussion of the relationship between the secular movement of the terms of trade for developed and underdeveloped countries has been largely sterile.[17]

But the tendency of things to flow from where they are to where they are not is conditioned by the necessity for financing an export balance of trade. The burden of incoming interest payments and repayment of principal can soon become so large as to make impossible a net flow of capital funds (net of interest) out from the creditor country. The possibility of financing, as has been said over and over, is a necessary condition of a discrepancy between exports and imports. And as the financing becomes available in increasing amounts to finance imports, there comes a time (and fairly soon in the absence of gifts) when net outflow of goods and services ceases. However, the foreign investment may continue to grow via accretion of plowed-back earnings; that seems to have been the process by which the British investment actually grew in the nineteenth century.

I am tempted to conclude that most of the growth of foreign investment is dependent on relative national power (which in turn is dependent on relative technological advancement). If the relative power position is maintained, the foreign investment will grow by accretion. If the relative power position is lost (because of a relative loss of technological and industrial position), the foreign investment will be lost by default, expropriation, or liquidation by agreement—such as happened to the British investment in Argentine railroads in the late 1940's.

A distinction must be made between the factors that will contribute to an export balance and the factors that will contribute to an export of capital equipment. However, this does not mean that it is impossible for capital equipment to move from a developed to an underdeveloped country in the absence of an export trade balance on the part of the developed country; capital equipment may flow out and be paid for by raw commodity imports in a setting which does not involve foreign investment. But it does mean that the country that wants to engage in continuing capital export and have a permanent export balance of trade had better charge an extremely low rate of interest.

CONCLUSION

The conclusion to be drawn from this discussion is that interest rate and profit rate differences may or may not exist as a superficial explanation as to why foreign investments occur. The more important conclusion as to the cause underlying foreign investments is that their

[17] See Chapters 5 and 13.

growth is largely the result of the relative development stages of the various countries. The nationals of the stronger country are, by and large, the creditors of the nationals of the weaker country. And, by and large, their investments have grown as the result of accretions in the value of earlier investments and not as the result of an export balance of trade. But, even if growing foreign investment did occur superficially as the result of the attraction of higher profits abroad, the more fundamental explanation would be that they grew as the counterpart of the spread of industrial power and technical knowledge out from their center. Also, the relative power positions are a result of the relative technical and industrial development.

PART VII

Growth

Chapter 30

MOTIVATION—POVERTY
AND MATURITY

ᛃ ᛃ ᛃ

The growth problem involves two chief facets: (1) raising the level of
well-being in the underdeveloped countries, and (2) avoiding the
undesirable aspects of stagnation in the more developed countries.
Well-being is a combination of level of living, freedom of action, and
security.

ᛃ ᛃ ᛃ

P OSITIVE measures to improve the lot of men are highly desirable. The human race should be capable of the modicum of co-
operation that is required to provide plenty for all. But we are
still a long way from this "promised land."

POVERTY IN UNDERDEVELOPED COUNTRIES

Level of Living Data

Two thirds of the population of the world is in an endemic state of
starvation.[1] Table 47 offers data indicative of the great differences in level
of living over the world.[2] The Food and Agriculture Organization of the
United Nations has stated that a per capita intake per day of 2,550 to
2,650 calories represents a minimum.[3] The illustration indicates that all

---

[1] American Geographical Society, Medical Geographical Department, *Study in
Human Starvation* (New York, 1953).

[2] The ambiguity of the Venezuelan position in the table calls for comment.
National-income data makes Venezuela rank quite high; but on the basis of
calory food consumption the country is low. This is merely another example of the
ambiguity of national-income data that is computed in such a way that exports are
an addition to income and imports are a deduction. Venezuela has a very large
export trade balance because of the oil industry. And a substantial part of the payment for the excess of exports accrues as profit to the foreign oil companies.

[3] Food and Agriculture Organization, *Proposals for a World Food Board and
World Food Survey* (Washington, 1946), Part II, p. 11. A group of experts assembled
by the Food and Agriculture Organization decided that: "A per caput calorie intake

of the countries on the bottom right fall below this figure. Without much doubt, China and many other countries could appropriately be added to that list.

TABLE 47

INTERNATIONAL COMPARISON OF PER CAPITA INCOME

1949—BY CONTINENTS (U.S. DOLLARS)		1954—MISCELLANEOUS COUNTRIES (U.S. DOLLARS)	
Africa	75	United States	1,850
North America	1,100		
South America	170	Australia	990
Asia	50	Argentina	224
Europe	380	Canada	1,235
U.S.S.R.	310	France	762
Oceania	560	Germany (Fed. Rep.)	541
		United Kingdom	831
World Average	230		
		Brazil	154
		Burma	43
		Colombia	135
		India	59
		Italy	327
		Pakistan	48
		Venezuela	494

PER CAPITA CALORY FOOD CONSUMPTION PER DAY

(CC. 1949–1953)

HIGH COUNTRIES		REASONABLE MINIMUM	LOW COUNTRIES	
United States	3,120		Brazil	2,350
			Burma	1,990
Australia	3,290	2,550	Colombia	2,370
Argentina	3,190	to	India	1,590
Canada	3,130	2,650	Italy	2,580
France	2,850		Pakistan	2,030
Germany (Fed. Rep.)	2,840		Venezuela	2,280
United Kingdom	3,060			

Sources: United Nations, Statistical Office, *National Income and Its Distribution in Under-developed Countries,* Statistical Papers series E, no. 3, p. 3; *Statistical Yearbook, 1955; International Financial Statistics; Statistical Abstract, 1955.*

The top of Table 47 contains data comparing average per capita money income in various countries. The significance of these figures may be roughly indicated by the statement that the average Asian has the purchasing power to buy in a whole year what the American could buy with $50.00. The average African can buy in a year the quantity of goods that

of 2,550–2,650 should be taken as the minimum level to which intake should be raised in the low-calorie countries, and the quantities of additional foods required should be estimated on this basis."

an American could buy with $75.00—and the Union of South Africa raises this African average considerably. Even allowing for a considerable element of error in these figures, the comparison should be disturbing.

Of course, this is not to say that two thirds of the race is hungry all the time and will be dead of starvation in two weeks. Great masses of people can live in a rather dull, unhappy stupor, making the best of their lot for years on end. They may even manage to be more pleasant and agreeable while doing it than many of their more fortunate brethren. But this does not prove it is better and more satisfying to be hungry and unhealthy.[4]

Eugene Staley says:[5]

> The poverty of underdeveloped countries means that their people, on a broad average, have a life expectancy only about half that of the people of the highly developed countries. They suffer much of the time from malaria, dysentery, tuberculosis, trachoma, or other ills. They have the services of less than one-sixth as many doctors in proportion to population. Their food supply is about one-third less, measured in calories, than that of developed countries, and when account is taken of the needs of the human body for the relatively expensive "protective" foods, such as milk and meat, the extent of malnutrition is found to be very great indeed. The opportunity to attend school is limited to a small minority in most underdeveloped countries, even for the lower grades. High school, college, and professional training is even less available. Only one person in four or five, again on a broad average of underdeveloped countries, knows how to read and write. The supply of cloth for clothing, home furnishing, and other purposes is about one-fourth as great per person in underdeveloped as in highly developed countries. Non-human energy to supplement the labor of human beings in industry, agriculture, transport, and household tasks is less than one-twentieth as plentiful, measured in horsepower-hours per person. Incomes, on the average, are less than one-tenth as high.
>
> These disparities in living levels between underdeveloped and highly developed countries appear to have been growing wider, rather than narrowing, in recent years.

Data and incidents without end might be cited to prove that the lot of much of the population of the world is unhappy. And there would be some point in a considerable recitation of such detail. The population of

[4] Try to find someone who believes that poor people are as happy as rich people who is willing to be poor.

[5] Eugene Staley, *The Future of Underdeveloped Countries* (New York: Harper, for the Council on Foreign Relations, 1954), p. 15. Reprinted with the kind permission of the Council on Foreign Relations.

the United States is, these days, all too complacent about this sort of thing. A stuffed stomach is conducive to complacency. The Randall Commission reported: [6] "Although the United States has only about 5 percent of the world's population, we produce well over 40 percent of the world's total output of goods and services." Such a situation may be a source of pride to the ardent nationalist; but it can occasion considerable concern to anyone who thinks in terms of a viable world.

Viewpoint of Underdeveloped Country

Do the people of the underdeveloped regions want to do something about their condition? Or are they content?

B. R. Sen of India has said that "the common man especially in underdeveloped areas had become increasingly aware of his right to a better and a fuller life. His dissatisfaction was increasing with the ever-widening gap between food production and population growth. Unless speedy action was taken to meet his claims, a far greater menace to mankind than the present world tension would arise." [7] Mr. Sen is surely uttering a great truth when he states that the menace of great discrepancies in level of living is a far greater threat to world peace and order in the long run than the United States–Russian friction ever thought of being.

That the people of the underdeveloped areas are restless and wish a higher level of living, industrialization, freedom of action, social security, and, in general, the good things of this world is far from enough to insure improvement in these respects. The institutional organization, the mores, and the folkways of people may constitute a considerable force inhibiting efficient development. The role of institutions in this setting will be discussed more at length in Chapter 31. Here we will say only that there is a mounting clamor for such growth from Colombo to Port-au-Prince, and add a quotation from Ralph Linton answering the charge that American Indians living on reservations have been a slovenly lot who did not wish to improve: [8]

[6] United States, Commission on Foreign Economic Policy, *Staff Papers,* p. 1.

[7] A paraphrase appearing in the *United Nations Bulletin,* August 15, 1953, p. 144. Mr. Sen is wrong when he says that the people of the under-developed areas have a "right" and a "claim" to have their lot improved by action which, by implication, is from the outside. The real work of effecting the improvement has to be done by the people themselves. Anyway, for them to obtain real satisfaction from the evolving process, they have to be carrying the real burden themselves. Outside help can be and should be only a minor factor—but it should be freely and generously given when it can serve a useful purpose, not because it is a right but because the community of nations has decided it will be a better world if things are done that way.

[8] Ralph Linton, "Cultural and Personality Factors Affecting Economic Growth," *The Progress of Underdeveloped Areas,* ed. Bert F. Hoselitz (Chicago: University of Chicago Press, 1952), p. 76. Reprinted with the kind permission of the publisher.

One often hears that our own reservation Indians have no desire to improve their economic condition. Government experts will tell them how to breed cattle or get better crops by scientific methods, but they will go on as they are. If one follows back the history of the dealings of our Indians with the United States government, it is easy to understand the reason for such apathy. Tribe after tribe made a real effort to copy white ways when they were placed on reservations. They saw that the old life was ended and did their best to adapt. However, whenever a tribe got a communally owned cattle herd which could be a valuable source of income, stockmen who wanted the range brought pressure in Washington, and the tribe suddenly found its herd sold and the money "put in trust." If a tribe developed an irrigation project and brought new land under cultivation, presently an excuse would be found for expropriating this and moving the tribe to a still more submarginal territory. The Indians were frustrated and puzzled by changing government policies, in which the only consistent feature was that they always lost, and finally settled back into apathy and pauperism.

Viewpoint of Developed Country

Some consideration of reverse motivation in the already developed countries may not be amiss.

One line of argument, suggesting caution in aiding the development of other areas, arises from the thought that a program calling for industrial and agricultural development and for raising the level of living in another area is not beneficial to the areas from which the assistance comes. In some quarters it seems to be assumed that such a development implies in some sense a loss to the aiding country.

Particular industries in the previously developed areas of course may lose markets—e.g., International Harvester may lose export markets if the manufacture of agricultural machinery is developed in Latin America (or it may profit, but in a different way, by moving to Latin America and participating in the development there). But so far as the interests of United States exporters in general are concerned, they can expect an expanding market as a result of the expanding incomes in Latin America that result from the development of manufacturing there (although it would take a brave soul to estimate the exact amount of such increase). They can expect this result, that is to say, unless trade barriers are imposed on an increasing scale in the developing countries.

Exports back to the developed countries from the underdeveloped countries should also increase because of the increase in production. This is good in that it contributes to more total trade, greater range of goods selection everywhere, and more goods everywhere—rather than because increasing export has any merit per se to the nation from which it comes.

But we still must deal with the charge frequently made in Communist quarters, and justified by the argument derived from the assumption of a falling rate of profit (to which Keynesian analysis based on an assumption of a constant multiplier gives some credence), that the United States and countries like her have to strive desperately for such an export surplus or their economies will collapse. On the basis of these arguments, it is alleged that there is nothing charitable about current United States aid. Now it may be granted that a free private enterprise economy in which no planning (or very poor and inadequate planning) exists can work itself into a position where a boost in exports will give a desirable lift to business. But this possibility does not need to rest on the assumption that the various multipliers are constants (see the discussions of Chapter 8). And it does not provide a motivation for long-run, artificial promotion of exports; at best it merely is an argument for occasional short-run export promotion.[9] Even then, it is valid only if various self-imposed institutional barriers make impossible the taking of more intelligent measures—such as internal investment and direct increase of internal purchasing power.

The interest of the developed country in development in the underdeveloped country must rest on the two-fold proposition that (1) there cannot be great inequality in income distribution if the world is to be free of bitterness among people and free of wars, and (2) income in the United States can still rise, even though it is rising at a somewhat more rapid rate in other areas. This can happen if American ingenuity and resourcefulness even approach the claims made for them, and probably even if they do not.

Development in the low-level-of-living countries is desirable. That is certain. But how it is to be effected is another matter.

STAGNATION IN MATURE COUNTRIES

The problem of development in the backward areas of the world is crucial today. But the problem of stagnation in the mature countries is potentially as great a problem. In this context two related questions arise: (1) Is there a tendency toward slowing down in the rate of growth in developed economies, and (2) if there is, is that a bad thing?

Alvin Hansen contended in the 1930's that the United States was moving into a period of secular stagnation. And in connection with

[9] The argument in Keynesian terms for export stimulation can really have a measure of validity only for the short run—while foreign-exchange reserves last. It consequently is not relevant to the problem of growth—which occurs in the long run in a setting where exports must equal imports.

European agriculture Ingvar Svennilson has written more recently: [10] "These statistical indicators show that European agriculture as a whole has progressed very little in the last forty years. As will be seen later, there are great divergences between individual countries, but the over-all picture is almost one of stagnation."

Moses Abramovitz has averred that the net national product of the United States, between 1869 and 1953, grew at the average rate of 3.5 per cent per year and the net product per capita grew at the rate of 1.9 per cent per year. He says, with that background, that he is not certain whether the rate of growth is slowing down or not—but he thinks probably it is in the United States.[11]

In the broader picture, the possibility exists of a declining rate of increase in real per capita income. Such a development could occur in a setting where the institutional arrangements fail to adjust properly; and it could involve chronic or erratic unemployment and other hardships. But it need not! Growth and improvement may still be going on in a setting where the rate of growth has slowed down.

In any case, major problems certainly exist in connection with adjustment to this situation.

THE GROWTH CURVE

It may help to consider several graphs which illustrate the possibilities growing out of the preceding discussion.

The basic Gompertz growth curve is shown in Chart 20 (I). It does not rise ever more steeply forever. It rises more and more steeply for a while, and then rises less and less steeply for a while.

But conceivably the process is not limited to one phase of increasing and then decreasing rate of growth. Several such phases may occur in sequence, as indicated in II. Growth does not necessarily taper off to virtually nothing forever—after one "cycle" of rapid growth.

It is sometimes said that production is rising continually at an increasing rate, or that the accumulation of capital is doing the same thing, or that the accumulation of technical knowledge is doing the same thing— possibility III. I must confess to an inability to conceive of the possibility of such a process. And thinking about growth as a series of recurrent growth curves (possibility II) seems an easier, less strained conception.

However, another possibility (IV) is growth along a curve which has violent short-run fluctuations up and down. Granted—this is a practical possibility and in fact may be the more accurate description as to

[10] Ingvar Svennilson, *Growth and Stagnation in the European Economy* (Geneva: United Nations Economic Commission for Europe, 1954), p. 96.

[11] Moses Abramovitz, "Resource and Output Trends in the United States Since 1870," *American Economic Review, Papers . . .* , XLVI (May, 1956), pp. 7, 14.

CHART 20

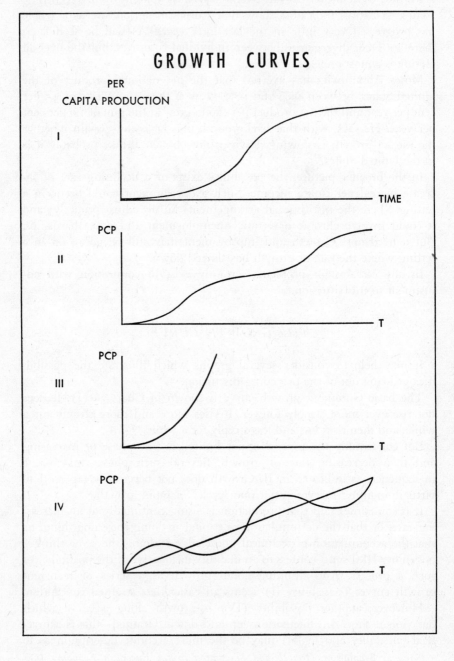

GROWTH CURVES

what the economy has actually been doing in the medium run. But it leaves the problem of long-run trend unattacked.

Possibility II is really most heartening to consider. It offers an alternative to the impossible implications of III and is somewhat more encouraging than I in its pure form. It also suggests that even though business cycle fluctuations (IV) cannot be entirely eliminated, they may be tempered into a pattern of evolution that does not involve periods of suffering and unrest—if intelligent institutional adjustments are made.

A world growing now faster, now slower, but continually growing, sounds like a better process than either the upward moving cycle or the steadily rising curve. The ever-faster-rising curve is impossible. The rising secular trend with alternate periods of prosperity and depression is undesirable. A straight-line rising trend would be dull.

Writers have sometimes alleged that in the history of many countries there have been decades or centuries of fairly vigorous growth, succeeded by decades or centuries of relative stagnation.[12]

Statistical evidence as to the actual long-run growth pattern is rather scanty. Chart 21 graphs what is probably the most significant series available—British total industrial production since 1700. And, if one may speak broadly, it looks more like possibility II, several growth curves occurring in sequence, than any of the other possibilities.

CONCLUSION

The raising of the level of living in the underdeveloped two thirds of the world is the great economic problem of our time. The great disparities in living standards that now exist cannot continue. Starvation and want cannot continue to be endemic in many places while plenty prevails elsewhere. The world cannot continue a pleasant place in which the wealthy can enjoy their plenty in a paradise surrounded by slums. There must be substantial equality in general living levels among the great regions of the world if peace and order and well-being are to prevail over any period of time, although the equality cannot be, perhaps should not be, exact.

The truth of this contention is not established by past history. There have been great inequalities in the level of living and in the power status of different regions in the civilizations of the past. And yet the human race has evolved to this point. What is involved is the supposition that a democratic type of civilization, in which the people of the world are freely intermingling, will not be viable if there are large groups of people who are socially, politically, or economically worse off than other large groups. The underprivileged, kicked-around masses of the world

[12] W. Arthur Lewis, *The Theory of Economic Growth,* p. 292.

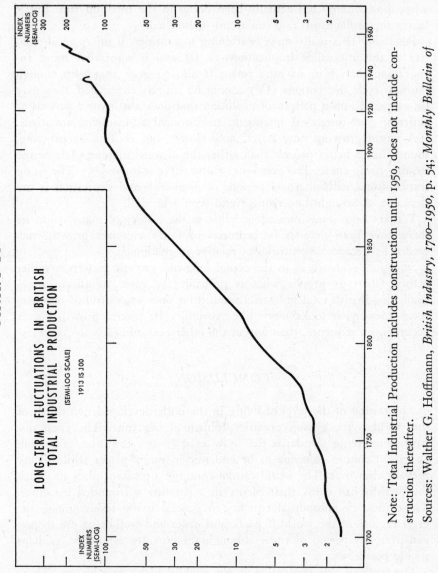

CHART 21

LONG-TERM FLUCTUATIONS IN BRITISH
TOTAL INDUSTRIAL PRODUCTION

(SEMI-LOG SCALE)
1913 IS 100

Note: Total Industrial Production includes construction until 1950, does not include construction thereafter.

Sources: Walther G. Hoffmann, *British Industry, 1700–1950*, p. 54; *Monthly Bulletin of Statistics.*

have already seen enough of the better life and been told often enough that they are as entitled to it as the next man. They will no longer (if they ever did) rest content with social servility or economic want.

No country need have a falling level of living as a result of the development of other countries, although there may be a tapering off in the rate of growth. If the level of living in the United States fifty years from today is not higher than it is today, in a setting where the rest of the world is much better off, then we have failed to show that initiative for which we are so widely self-acclaimed.

The overriding consideration remains that the world has to be a reasonably satisfactory place for all people to live in to be a satisfactory place for anyone.[13]

[13] Recent books on the growth problem—in addition to those by Veblen and Ayres cited in the next chapter—include Harold F. Williamson and John A. Buttrick, *Economic Development: Principles and Patterns* (New York: Prentice-Hall, 1954); Lewis, *op. cit.*: Simon Kuznets, Wilbert E. Moore, and Joseph J. Spengler (eds.), *Economic Growth: Brazil, India, Japan* (Durham: Duke University Press, 1955); Eugene Staley, *Future of Underdeveloped Countries;* Bert F. Hoselitz, *The Progress of Underdeveloped Areas* (Chicago: University of Chicago Press, 1952).

Chapter 31

THEORY OF DEVELOPMENT

彡 彡 彡

The formulation of theories of development is currently the vogue in economics.

The national-income application and the institutionalist theory are probably the two most important.

The national-income approach emphasizes the relationship among the rate of growth in output, the capital coefficient, and the percentage of income saved. In the setting established by these concepts the crucial relations are between actual, warranted, and natural rates of growth. The warranted rate of growth is a rate of growth which, if continued, will leave businessmen satisfied with what they are doing. The natural rate of growth is the maximum rate which, given the resources available, is possible.

The institutionalist theory emphasizes the relationship between technology and institutions. Technology is thought to be the dynamic force in the growth process. Prevailing institutional arrangements operate as something of a drag on the development process. The availability of resources appropriate to a given stage of technical development also needs to be taken into account.

The underdeveloped countries must undergo major institutional reorganization to permit the process of growth to go on.

However, the copying by the underdeveloped countries of the institutional organization of the already developed countries is probably neither possible nor desirable.

Primary responsibility for planning the process must rest with the native population.

彡 彡 彡

THE THEORY of economic development is the most important area of theoretical study in economics—from now until the next depression. Some theorizing along these lines goes back to the mercantilists and to Smith and Ricardo. But most of the "development" of the theory of development has been recent.

BACKGROUND (SMITH AND RICARDO)

The classical economists, notably Smith and Ricardo, were interested in the use that might be made of economics in dealing with the problems of public policy. And they were especially interested in economic change in relation to public policy. In Smith's conception—and this was the major change from the mercantilist view as to the nature of wealth—the thing to be maximized was goods. But Smith, and before him Sir Dudley North and David Hume, had already shown a perception of the proposition that growth occurs most effectively in a setting where all countries are growing. Smith wrote:[1] "A nation that would enrich itself by foreign trade, is certainly most likely to do so when its neighbours are all rich, industrious, and commercial nations."

Ricardo's analysis of the process of change was built around the ideas that, with the passage of time, wages would remain stationary, profits would fall, and rents would rise—as the existing land was more intensively utilized. The description of the process by which this would happen constituted an embryonic theory of change. But it was a theory of change which the history of economic thought could well have done without—unless of course it happened to be correct. Such statistical evidence as we have on these trends hardly indicates that they have evolved as Ricardo suggested.

Little work was done on the theory of change and development by economists in the last half of the nineteenth and early twentieth centuries. Until very recently, the emphasis was on price theory, and on the concepts of demand and supply and the way they would interact to produce equilibrium in a static society. There are two notable exceptions to this generalization, of course: Marx and Veblen.

Recently, however, the study of the process of economic growth and change has become quite the vogue among economists. In formulating their theories, they now have to draw on: (1) the ideas of Smith and Ricardo, (2) certain price-theory concepts, (3) a modification of Keynesian concepts, (4) Marx, and (5) Veblen.

PRICE THEORY CONCEPTS

Price theory, in the ordinary formulations of the past seventy-five years, has done little with the concepts of growth and change. It has been chiefly concerned with the problem of arriving at static equilibrium. Nevertheless, some of the concepts can be and have been used to deal

[1] Smith, *Wealth of Nations,* p. 462.

with the problems of growth and change. Chief among the possibilities along this line are: (1) Schumpeter's innovator, (2) Leontief's input-output analysis, and (3) Meade's indifference curves.

Schumpeter's Innovator

Schumpeter, working from an assumption that the profit rate tends to settle at zero, placed the innovator in the crucial role.[2] The innovator is the farsighted one who sees profit possibilities in a new invention or method. He is thereby stimulated to make the innovation, and his reward is profit for a time. But as other businessmen observe this situation, they turn to the same activity; and soon the profit rate drops to zero in that line as well. At all events, in Schumpeter's view, growth and change would be an outcome of a sequence of events that is set in motion by a businessman's desire for profit.

It has sometimes been said that the lack of growth in the underde-veloped countries has been due to a lack of Schumpeter's innovators. It has been said that the United States and western Europe have been richly endowed with citizens of this sort, but the rest of the world has not. However, stated this way, the problem becomes an institutional one which can better be handled with the tools of institutional theory than price theory. This is true even if the facts are correct (that countries lag because of lack of innovators); and the correctness of that view has hardly been proven. They may lag; and they may lack and need inno-vators—without that lack being the cause of the lag.

Input-Output[3]

Input-output analysis encompasses linear programing. And to date it has involved a tremendous amount of statistical work. Data is gathered on the quantities of buying and selling between different sectors (in-dustries) in the economy. How much raw material comes from where; how much investment is used; how much import is used, etc.? It is then assumed that a given industry will use in the future the same proportions of various resources (inputs) which it has used in the past. This data is used as a basis for forecasting "what of what" it will take to implement a certain expansion of production in a certain industry.

This approach represents an effort to appraise the meaning of general equilibrium for the whole economy, not just partial equilibrium for one industry. Data on the whole mutually interacting system—including

[2] Joseph Schumpeter, *Theory of Economic Development* (Cambridge: Harvard University Press, 1934).

[3] Wassily W. Leontief, *Studies in the Structure of the American Economy* . . . (New York: Oxford, 1953); Hollis B. Chenery, "The Role of Industrialization in Development Programs," *American Economic Review, Papers and Proceedings,* XLV (May, 1955), 40–57.

exports and imports—is evaluated. However, at this stage in the development of input-output analysis, there are some real difficulties in using the knowledge of the known relationships to plan growth. The procedure used involves the assumption that certain relationships will remain the same. For example, Chenery's assumptions include the following:[4]

1. The division of national income between consumption and investment is taken as fixed. Consumption is assumed to be a function of per capita income only, as described below. All elements in final demand are therefore determined by the assumed increase in national income.

2. Total investment must equal savings plus the excess of imports over exports, summed over the time period involved (ten years). . . .

3. The excess of imports over exports must correspond to the required amount of external investment funds determined by the solution. Solutions must be determined for several possible levels of the trade deficit to meet this condition.

4. The price of labor must be such that total demand does not exceed the total supply.

These assumptions debar consideration of some of the most important conditions affecting growth. But these are problems involved in the "growth of a theory of growth."

Meade

Meade has speculated on the role of free competition by comparison with government intervention in planning and orienting the growth process. As was indicated in Chapter 6, he alleges that there are various circumstances in which uncontrolled free competition will not get the best results. One of his arguments, that having to do with structural change, is particularly relevant for the theory of growth.

Meade's position on this point is aptly indicated by an analogy he draws with mountain climbing. The adjustments by marginal increments, which are posited in competitive price analysis, may lead to one mountain peak. As Meade says:[5]

If, then, whenever he finds an upward slope he moves up it, he must eventually reach a peak. But he may not be on the highest peak of the mountain range; he might be able to get still higher if he came down again and went up the next mountain. The structural changes in the economy which we propose to discuss in this chapter concern the rules, not for climbing a mountain,

[4] Chenery, *loc. cit.*, p. 42.
[5] Meade, *Trade and Welfare*, p. 119. Reprinted with the kind permission of the Oxford University Press and the Royal Institute of International Affairs.

but for choosing the right mountain to climb. This choice cannot be made simply by making small marginal excursions in every direction from the particular point from which one happens to start.

The decision as to which mountain to climb may well be one that the individual entrepreneur is simply not in a position to make. Governments must take the initiative by indicating in a broad way the direction of development—perhaps by supporting the construction of a basic steel mill; perhaps by a highway and dam building program. After this is done, a major amount of the subsequent development may occur in the natural course of events as the result of planning in terms of "marginal increments" by individual entrepreneurs.

KEYNESIAN CONCEPTS (HARROD)

Keynesian theory uses investment, consumption, saving, and the interest rate as the chief tools of analysis. Roy Harrod in developing a concept of growth has chiefly used these and similar macroeconomic concepts.[6]

Harrod's basic formula, in the arrangement relevant for international trade, is:

$$GC = s - b$$

where:

(1) G (growth) "is the increment of total production in any unit period expressed as a fraction of total production";

(2) C (capital coefficient) "is the increase in the volume of goods of all kinds outstanding at the end over that outstanding at the beginning of the period divided by the increment of production in that same period";

(3) "s" is the fraction of income saved; and

(4) "b" is "the balance of trade expressed as a fraction of income."

To illustrate, (1) assume a 3 per cent rate of growth in production, (2) also assume that the increase in the stock of capital needs to be double the annual production increase in order to make possible such a rate of production increase, (3) and also assume that exports exceed imports by 1 per cent of national income, (4) then savings must represent 7 per cent of national income:

$$.03 \times \frac{2}{1} = .07 - .01.$$

[6] R. F. Harrod, *Towards a Dynamic Economics*, pp. 77–8, 105.

Other things ("C" and "b") being equal, the greater the rate of rise in production, the greater the rate of saving required. This is true because it takes more savings to support more investment (savings equal investment); and investment must rise if the 2:1 ratio is to be maintained between capital stock and annual production.

Also, if a certain net amount of the national product is exported, it is going to require a higher rate of saving (abstinence from domestic consumption) to support the maintenance of a 2:1 (domestic capital stock to total domestic production) ratio than would be the case if more of the production stayed at home—without being consumed at home.

The equation as it stands is more or less a truism. But it is a truism standing astride some difficult problems. For example, there is the question as to why the capital coefficient need remain a constant such as 2:1. It reduces the usefulness of this formula as a guide to the amount of saving and investment required to finance a given amount of production growth if the capital coefficient is not a constant. And it is not a constant if, with the passage of time, technical improvements work to require less and less capital per unit of output. As will be mentioned later, recent studies by the National Bureau of Economic Research indicate that this is probably the case.[7]

Harrod's actual analysis of the growth process is done by consideration of the relationship among three kinds of G's:

(1) G: representing the actual growth occurring;

(2) Gw (warranted rate of growth): representing "the condition in which producers will be content with what they are doing"; and

(3) Gn (natural rate of growth): representing the "rate of advance which the increase in population and technological improvements allows."

Harrod argues that it is divergence among these various growth concepts that leads to the difficulties that beset the growth process. When G exceeds Gw, growth is actually booming along at a rate faster than the business community thinks proper. This condition will likely lead to trouble. If Gw exceeds Gn (if businessmen want to expand faster than conditions permit), there is also likely to be trouble—a tendency toward depression according to Harrod.[8]

---

[7] Harrod allows for this possibility with a not very satisfactory technique that involves putting another term ("d" for deepening) on the right-hand side of the equation.

[8] Harrod, *op. cit.,* p. 88. Harrod argues that one might think that it is wholesome for businessmen to want to expand their activities faster than conditions permit. But he says that the real effect of business effort to expand faster than conditions permit is that departures from the trend have to be "in a downward direction." And this, then, is an influence in an undesirable direction.

Gn, it may seem, has a close relationship to Keynesian full employment. And additional spending tends to be non-inflationary below the full employment level and inflationary above.

The role that "b" (the balance of trade) plays in the system is somewhat as follows. Given the capital coefficient, then, the larger the export balance the larger must be the rate of saving to support a given rate of increase in G. Keynesian theorists in recent years have chosen to be alarmed on the ground that in a highly developed economy the rate of saving tends to be too high. Harrod's equation suggests that, if this is true, a large export balance will help to solve the problem.

With regard to the growth equation, and the concept of growth, several things may be said. The analysis is all true enough, given the assumptions. But what is the true meaning of Gw? In a significant theory of growth should Gw be taken as given data? Perhaps the businessman's conception of the "condition in which he will be content with what he is doing" is one of the very crucial changing elements in the picture, or had better be. There is good reason to believe changing concepts along this line are extremely important for understanding the impact of development on Latin America and Southeast Asia, the Middle East, and central Africa. The weakest part of Harrod's analysis is the assumption of the unchanging nature of Gw.

For its part, Gn is a function of technological change (and population growth), so that a formulation which clearly identifies technological change as a major variable might be preferable. Veblen's theory more clearly singles out technology and institutions for analysis. The Harrod analysis half hides them in the concept of G and singles out the formalized concept of the interrelationship among G, Gw, and Gn to belabor.

MARX

Logically or illogically, the Marxian theory has been discussed elsewhere—especially in Chapter 10. In brief summary: the capitalistic system tends to accumulate greater and greater productive capacity. The output of this capacity can be marketed domestically only at lower and lower profit rates. This leads the capitalists to a desperate program of export and foreign investment promotion. The argument is based on the proposition that it is the particular institutional arrangements of capitalism that make for this untenable result.

Thus both the Harrod and Marxist theories seem to lead to the conclusion that it would be better to set up the basic growth theory in terms that can indicate the crucial roles of technological and institutional changes.

INSTITUTIONAL THEORY (VEBLEN-AYRES) [9]

Since World War II, the development of a theory of economic growth has become all the rage among economists. Various schools of economists have proceeded apace to formulate their own theory of growth using the tools—many of them rather rusty—with which they were familiar. Institutional theory, at the end of World War II, was probably a more satisfactory vehicle for describing the growth process than any of the theories mentioned earlier in this chapter.

According to the institutional theory, growth, the rate of growth, the changing pattern of production, the changing quantities of goods available for domestic consumption, the changing stocks of capital and equipment are determined by:

(1) The dynamic forces inherent in the process of accumulation of technical knowledge;

(2) The more or less static resistances to such change which exist because of the institutional organization in the society; and

(3) The appropriateness of the available raw material resources to the state of the technical knowledge.[10]

In this theory the dynamic force is technical change. Knowledge of the nature of matter and of the physical processes, the development of new tools and new production methods—these are cumulative processes. One bit of knowledge is acquired and then it is possible to acquire another bit—which could not have been acquired without the background of the earlier knowledge. By and large then, the acquisition of technical knowledge is a process that builds on itself. And chiefly it is motivated by the nature of the inquiring mind of man, with little regard for the profit motive or the interest rate—at least in the long run. And in discussing the growth process we are concerned with the long run.

The automobile is possible because the internal-combustion engine went before. It is also possible because the vulcanization of rubber went before. Rumor has it that the atom bomb was possible because of earlier work of Einstein on the relationship between energy and matter. The radio and television did not descend full blown upon us. Much background work in electricity, wave theory, and so on, had to go before.

In this process development will go on faster, the larger the reservoir of technical knowledge to be drawn on. Or, to change the simile, cross-

---

[9] Thorstein Veblen, *The Theory of the Leisure Class* (New York: Modern Library, 1934); Thorstein Veblen, *Theory of Business Enterprise* (New York, Scribner's, 1927); C. E. Ayres, *Theory of Economic Progress* (Chapel Hill: University of North Carolina Press, 1944). *The Theory of the Leisure Class* was first published in 1899; *Theory of Business Enterprise,* in 1904.

[10] The factors which Ayres and Veblen have emphasized are technology and institutions.

fertilization leads to the discovery of new types of plants. Broader-scale interchange of ideas leads to more discoveries of new processes and techniques for doing new things. This means that many countries co-operating closely in such a process will develop faster than one country trying to develop in isolation.

Appreciation of the importance of technology suggests that a more meaningful conception is obtained of the problems involved in accumulating capital equipment if one looks at such accumulation as a facet of the growth of technical knowledge. More benefit derives from this view than from looking at the accumulation of capital equipment as dependent on saving and the interest rate.

This modified outlook on the role of capital accumulation has important international implications. It means that foreign investments and the financing of the international movement of capital equipment are not the crux of the matter. Rather the ability to construct and use the capital equipment is far more important. Of course, this proposition does not gainsay the desirability of occasional foreign investments nor the usefulness of the international movement of much capital equipment.

To turn to the relationship between technology and institutions, the speed with which the technical knowledge can be accumulated is controlled by the institutional setting. A society, to get the maximum accumulation, has to be willing to facilitate a considerable amount of basic theoretical research, which has no direct connection with the immediate marketing of a product like television sets which will make a lot of money. And it has to be willing to change features of its way of life to facilitate the development.

The institutions of some societies are so organized that they almost completely inhibit technical progress and the use of new technical knowledge in the society. The rigid institutional setting, the set way of doing things, prevented any progress to speak of in the Eastern Roman Empire between the sixth and the fifteenth centuries. At the time when China was "opened" in the mid-nineteenth century, it had been stagnating for many centuries in a rigid institutional setting. But these are extreme examples. For present purposes the far less pronounced institutional differences between Britain and the United States on the one hand and, say, Latin America on the other are the important conditions explaining why the first two countries have grown faster in the past two centuries (or perhaps, better said, since 1600) than has Latin America. R. H. Tawney has written a classic work arguing that the Protestant Reformation broke down a variety of institutional barriers that Catholicism offered to inhibit the growth of what has become modern industrial society.[11] For example, Catholicism frowned on the taking of interest, whereas the new

[11] R. H. Tawney, *Religion and the Rise of Capitalism* (New York: Penguin, 1947 [first published, 1926]).

Protestant religions made saving into a cardinal virtue, and encouraged it by permitting interest taking. These were important considerations at the inception of the Industrial Revolution; whether they are necessary characteristics of the continuance of growth past 1960 is not so certain.

To illustrate the meaning of institutional barriers with a somewhat more modern example: Commercial bankers, at a particular time, are, it would seem, mentally adjusted to favor loans for one type of project and not for another, not always on the basis of which project will make the most significant contribution to expanding production. Or, to be still more definite, for many years in Latin America custom has dictated that people with money should invest in real estate and not in manufacturing. This state of mind has been an "institutional barrier" to the development of manufacturing in Latin America. A change in this attitude is important to the development of manufacturing in that region.

It is frequently said, with reason, that technology is dynamic and institutions are a drag on development. But this much, alone, does not give one a criterion for knowing how to handle any particular institution which is functioning as a "drag." Nor is it enough to say that engineers, taking technical considerations alone into account, could satisfactorily guide production if the institutional barriers could be eliminated. What criteria are *they* going to use in deciding whether a certain development should or should not occur? It is not enough to say that a dietitian can work out the proper diet, and the engineer-planner-farmer can provide it. We are not dealing with an economic order which can or should think in terms of providing bare minima (or even bare luxury) of "this and that" to people—out of a spoon. We are dealing with an economy of increasing abundance, and with circumstances which make it possible that each unique individual may be free to express his own creative instincts more effectively. To revert to the earlier discussion of the issue between decentralization and control, centralized planning and control (by engineers or anyone else) is desirable only—and even then subject to democratic control—as it contributes to the maximum social well-being.

Technical change tends to change institutions. But when the impact comes, it makes a great deal of difference whether the institution is one which is cherished by the people or one whose demise they can view with indifference. One might almost have thought in the 1930's that American businessmen were prepared to destroy the country rather than lose their right to relatively free and unrestricted pursuit of profits. On the other hand, a development like the automobile may destroy all the patterns of action that went with the horse and buggy with scarcely a regret being felt by anybody.

A culture which is institutionally adjusted to prize the scientific method of study and research is going to permit more technical progress than is a culture committed to deductive logic as the only method of inquiry.[12] One reason England progressed more rapidly than did Spain during the seventeenth and eighteenth centuries was that England had gone over to emphasis on scientific research—following the precepts of Francis Bacon, whereas Spain was committed by the Jesuits and the Inquisition to the suppression of such inquiry as was not in the tradition of Thomas Aquinas, deductive logic, and the syllogism. Consequently, in the 1820's, the mines at Pachuca in Mexico, which had been abandoned by the Spaniards because of water deep in the shafts, could be reopened "as British investments in Mexico" because the British had developed pumps which could get the water out. In this case, surely, the British investment in terms of a net movement of goods to Mexico was nominal—if such a net movement existed at all. But the British contribution was a bit of technical knowledge which the scientific method had permitted them to acquire.

Aside from the issue of the scientific method versus deductive reasoning—that is to say, aside from the question of how good the research methods of a society are—increasing cultural contact between one society and another makes it possible to select and assimilate the more desirable traits of other cultures. Such interchange necessarily makes a contribution to the fuller life, whether or not it improves any country's technology. But it will probably improve the technology as well because, when institutional patterns are in a state of flux, there is less resistance to the implementation and spread of the technical knowledge being accumulated.

THE GENERAL ROLE OF INSTITUTIONS

Different countries are now endowed with widely differing institutional organizations.[13] Some of these institutional organizations are rather set and stable. But most of them lately have been in a state of considerable flux.

The nature of the institutional organization in a country at any given time has a considerable influence on what technical changes will be introduced, how fast they will be introduced, and the special direction they will take.

[12] Deductive logic involves reasoning from already accepted general principles to concrete applications; it is in contrast with inductive logic, which involves arguing on the basis of empirical data in order to establish general principles.

[13] United Nations, Department of Economic and Social Affairs, *Processes and Problems of Industrialization in Under-Developed Countries* (New York, 1955), pp. 15–25; United Nations Educational, Scientific and Cultural Organization, *Cultural Patterns and Technical Change* (Paris, 1953); S. Herbert Frankel, *The Economic Impact on Under-Developed Societies; Essays on International Investment and Social Change* (Oxford: Blackwell, 1953).

Some institutions, at a given time, may be treasured by a people (as the Pilgrims treasured their religion); some institutions may be highly expendable (dope peddling). Some institutions may be active in trying to inhibit desirable technical progress (the Inquisition of the sixteenth century); some may be rather indifferent with regard to a particular bit of change; some may provide a very fertile milieu for the introduction of a given bit of technical progress (the American family and television).

Wilbert E. Moore says:[14] "Whether for the individual or for the system as a whole continuity and not change is likely to be the major value." And probably it is true that there is this tendency for individuals to adhere to the customary ways of doing things. In fact, this is the reason for emphasizing the role of institutions in the study of the process of change. But it is doubtful that a sweeping generalization should be made to the effect that "continuity and not change is . . . the major value." The raising of the level of living in the underdeveloped areas of the world is precisely a major problem now because those people are dissatisfied with their lot.

The introduction of the technical processes that will make a significant contribution to raising the level of living in the underdeveloped countries clearly calls for significant institutional changes. A considerable proportion of the population will have to orient their lives around factories instead of around agriculture.[15] These changes call for consideration of two propositions: (1) Is laissez-faire-free-competition-free-private-enterprise called for? (2) Who determines the nature of the institutional changes?

Free Private Enterprise (Similarity of Institutions)

Walter Williams, the Under Secretary of Commerce, said at an address to the Washington State Fourth International Trade Fair, March 11, 1955:[16]

> Free enterprise promotes economic progress. . . .
>
> Moreover, these policies are no more than a translation into worldwide terms of the policies followed at home. As such, they represent an attempt to apply on a global basis the economic truths learned from our domestic experience. The principles of dynamic capitalism which have made our free-enterprise system so eminently successful will be equally effective in creating a progressive and dynamic world economy if the world is willing to give it half a chance. Standards of living through the world can

[14] Wilbert E. Moore, "Labor Attitudes toward Industrialization in Underdeveloped Countries," *American Economic Review, Papers and Proceedings,* XLV (May, 1955), 162.

[15] Bert F. Hoselitz, "The City, the Factory, and Economic Growth," *American Economic Review, Papers and Proceedings,* XLV (May, 1955), 166–184.

[16] *Foreign Commerce Weekly,* March 11, 1955, p. 17.

> be raised if the expansive forces of enterprise are liberated from
> restraint and regimentation. . . .
>
> We have not done, however, a good job of selling our kind of
> free-enterprise system abroad. And yet this system and our demo-
> cratic way of life are our two most distinctive and original con-
> tributions to civilization's progress.
>
> The Commerce Department, through its expanded trade-fair
> program, is trying to apply American sales techniques to the job
> of selling the free-enterprise system abroad.

The spurt of Japanese development during the late nineteenth and early
twentieth centuries indicates that, for an economy to expand industrially,
its crucial need is technical knowledge. This the Japanese acquired in
an energetic program sponsored by the government following the "opening" of the country by Matthew Perry in 1854. The important initiative
was Japanese. The Japanese determined the manner of assimilation of
the technical knowledge and the nature of the institutional changes that
perforce occurred in response to these developments. Institutional changes
occurred in Japan all right, but not the establishment of either a free
private enterprise system or a system similar to that in the United
States.[17] It is simply not correct that a program of successful industrialization and improvement of the level of living requires copying either
the free enterprise system or the American system or any other set of
institutional arrangements.

In fact, there are identifiable, specific circumstances where it can be
seen that the copying of American business methods—transplanted to
the environment of the underdeveloped country—has a deleterious effect.
Students come from the underdeveloped countries to study in the United
States and acquire knowledge as to industrial techniques and business
practices that will be useful in the industrialization of their own country.
But one of the bits of indoctrination they are likely to pick up is the idea
that profit-making is the desirable goal—and anything within the law is
legitimate. Especially, for some reason, they are likely to take a keen
interest in the application of this knowledge in the sphere of commodity speculation. Then they go back to their own country and make
a fortune in commodity speculation and make no contribution to the
genuine development of the country.

To turn to the positive rather than the negative aspect: An institutional
climate sympathetic to development is necessary if development is to
occur. But the necessity for a sympathetic institutional climate does not
imply the necessity for the same institutional organization as exists in
the areas which experienced the development first. India does not need
to have a type of free private enterprise organization exactly similar to

---

[17] It is not certain that the American economic system is exactly the same thing
as a free private enterprise economic system.

that in the United States to experience a very satisfactory and satisfying improvement in the level of living and expansion of the freedom of action and range of choice and security of the people.

Indeed, the world will be a far more stimulating place in which to live if the institutional organizations are different in different places. Who really wants everybody to look alike and behave alike? Probably not even the most rabid advocate of free private enterprise for Turks, if the truth be known.

Similarity of institutions may not be called for, but Latin America and other underdeveloped regions do need to give consideration to drastic changes in the institutional arrangements and attitudes that they are using to implement their development programs for, as Jose Figueres, president of Costa Rica, has pointed out:[18] "The situation of the moment is such that the advanced countries . . . are growing at a faster rate than are the underdeveloped countries. That is to say that the United States and Canada, advanced as they already are relative to Latin America, are drawing farther ahead each day."

Identity of Decision Maker

(a) WHICH NATION? The other question was, who determines the nature of the institutional change? On this point, I believe, it is justified to be quite dogmatic.

No race of people will appreciate the imposition of a way of life from outside. The people making the change must possess the initiative in determining which customs and practices brought in from outside they will assimilate and which they will not.[19] Much of the richness of life is involved in this process. Experimentation, acceptance, rejection is a process out of which comes a new richer whole, not just a parrotlike copy of a system of free enterprise that actually does not exist even in the United States.

Knowledge as to the way of doing things in the United States can be, and should be, made available to the people of the underdeveloped areas. Then it is up to them to pick and choose, adopt and reject. There is reasonable chance of contentment with the new order of things if it comes about in this way. And, incidentally, the new way of life will almost certainly contain a goodly proportion of American ways. But it will be something more as well.

(b) GOVERNMENT OR PRIVATE ENTERPRISE? Meade's "which mountain to climb" analogy goes a long way toward indicating the role of govern-

---

[18] Jose Figueres, "Mensaje Inaugural . . . , 8 de Noviembre de 1953," *Trimestre Económico,* XXI (January, 1954), 104.

[19] A Javanese example of the unsatisfactory results obtained if new institutional arrangements are imposed from outside is cited in the *International Social Science Bulletin,* no. 3, 1954, p. 424; see also, Wendell Gordon, *Economy of Latin America* (New York: Columbia, 1950), chap. 1.

ment and the role of private enterprise in the implementation of economic development. The individual, private entrepreneur is simply not in a position to make a basic decision as to what the main line of development is going to be. No one private enterpriser could have taken a decision to embark on an atomic bomb project in 1942. Nor can he determine the broad outlines of a transportation or power development program. The governments must do certain basic things. After that, a good deal of the development can, no doubt, be left to the private entrepreneur, and the sort of limited decision making of which he is capable.

It has been argued earlier in this book that, when the government interferes with the economic process, it should not do so with a complicated variety of tools such as will make appraisal of the results of any one measure difficult or impossible. Rather government interference with the economic process should be simple and direct when it occurs. Let us now look at the range of possibility of such government action.

Direct government action to build and provide basic facilities like highways and dams is the extreme example of government use of funds directly to implement production. A second possibility is the money payment of a subsidy to a private producer to aid him in initiating production of something the government believes to be desirable. A third possibility is qualitative credit control. This latter would involve action by the government through its general power over the banking system to facilitate access to credit on the part of private businesses in those lines of production which the government believes to be most important. By way of comfort to those who worry about such things, it may be safely alleged that action in terms of qualitative credit control should be and probably will be more important than the direct production subsidy. But in the nature of things, much of the basic expenditure for major new service facilities, such as highways, is going to be made by the governments.

SOME PARTICULAR INSTITUTIONS

For present purposes, several institutional arrangements that affect the relative rate of institutional development in different countries may be singled out.

Size of Country

One such factor is the size of a great number of countries. At the present time, great effort is being expended in many of the underdeveloped countries of the world to develop manufacturing and to expand the variety of commodities produced. Thus, in Cuba, diversification is much discussed as a measure to gain protection against the drastic effects of change in the price of sugar.

But for a small country to push this line of argument to the point of trying to produce everything would be most unsatisfactory. If El Salvador were to try to build a continuous wide-strip steel mill of anything like optimum size, she would have neither the raw materials nor the market —unless she could be the producer for other Latin American countries as well. If she adds to the steel mill the heavy chemical plants of economical size, the oil refineries, the shops to build railway locomotives, and all the other plants required to enable El Salvador to produce everything, the objective becomes impossible of attainment. If El Salvador should try to set up one of each of these plants of a size to be reasonably efficient, there would not be enough workers in the country, literally, to start the project, let alone finish it. The International Bank mission to Colombia reported: [20] "The capacity of the smallest mechanized [light bulb] plant is such that three months' operation would fulfill Colombia's present demands for a year."

The problem is of greater range and complexity than merely the difficulty of a very small country in establishing one plant of optimal size. There is also the problem in timing of the middle-sized country which wishes an expansion from say three plants to four. If the fourth plant is built when the market is only a little larger than the capacity of three, a bitter, competitive price war is likely to result. The alternative in the middle-sized countries is strong trade-association control of industry expansion—and a consequent tendency not to expand. Stagnation in England and France in the period between World War I and World War II seems to have been to a marked extent a result of this type of behavior.

Even if the expansion is planned, there are still problems. Several years may pass before a country develops from the demand to absorb the product of three plants to the demand to absorb the product of four of efficient size. Meanwhile, would it be better to establish a smaller plant of less than optimum efficiency, but which would cost less and be of about the right size to supply the market? Or should the optimum-sized plant be built and allowed to stand largely idle for several years? Or should all action be postponed until demand has increased to the point where it can completely absorb the product of four optimum-sized plants? [21]

The retarding influence of a small market is much more effective than is suggested merely by the question of whether total demand will

[20] International Bank for Reconstruction and Development, *The Basis of a Development Program for Colombia* (Washington, 1950), p. 93.

[21] Tibor Scitovsky, "Economies of Scale, Competition, and European Integration," *American Economic Review*, XLVI (March, 1956), pp. 73-4.

support one optimum-sized plant. But in addition to the problems already suggested, there are others. Not only must the amount of growth that can be achieved in a limited period of time be sufficient to support an optimum-sized plant; it must also be sufficient to support the technology needed to create an optimum-sized plant. Manufacturing plants do not just grow like Topsy. Great quantities of technical knowledge and managerial skill are required to initiate and operate them. Such skills develop further and faster in a setting where there is a lot of similar activity going on and ideas can be exchanged in a broader setting.

Svennilson seems to believe that Danish development would have worked out better if the Scandinavian countries had been one country:[22] "A change of frontiers would have completely changed the conditions for growth. It is, for example, likely that the development of Danish manufacturing industry would have been more favourable if it had come within the same frontiers as the expanding Scandinavian pulp industries and had not been associated only with a depressed agriculture."

In a larger setting, he seems also to believe that general European agricultural development has been hamstrung by too many frontiers.[23]

> In no other field was economic nationalism such a striking success to the detriment of general European efficiency. Yet in no other field of comparable importance to Europe as a whole were natural conditions so different and the potential advantages of trade over national frontiers so great; not the least of these advantages could have been derived from increased exports from the east towards the west, and from the south towards the north of Europe. In a period when transport by road and the technique of canning and freezing were great innovations, the advantages of intra-European trade in agricultural products were increasing. . . . The contrast with the enormous cross-country transport of grain, dairy products, fruit and vegetables within the wide United States market is striking.

Haiti, El Salvador, Nicaragua, and various other countries are too small. They are too small to command respect in the community of nations. They are too small to develop satisfactory, diversified production patterns. They are too small to provide (in a world of trade barriers) a satisfactory market for goods produced by plants of optimum size. In fact, the opinion may be hazarded that any country that has a real monoculture and diversification problem is *too small*. It is too small for the good of its citizenry (although perhaps about the right size to provide a private domain to gratify the ego of some dictator and about

---

[22] Ingvar Svennilson, *Growth and Stagnation in the European Economy*, p. 37.
[23] Svennilson, *op. cit.*, p. 90.

the right size for foreign corporations trading in bananas to have things much their own way).

There are too many too small countries. In Latin America, for example, if a good many of the countries joined together they would acquire the advantage of larger markets and larger and more diversified resources— automatically. They would also be in a stronger position for talking back to Uncle Sam. Fusion would seem to have numerous advantages on all scores. Eastin Nelson has written that: "The effectiveness of the bid of Latin Americans for a place in the modern industrial world depends very largely on the degree to which those people can develop mass markets over which to distribute the large overhead costs which are a feature of modern industry." [24] This process can be facilitated by a reduction in the number of countries.

There is a relationship between the size of a reasonably workable economic unit and the nature of the technology of an age. And the technology of these times calls for economic units larger than most of those now existing in the underdeveloped areas—larger populations (save India and China), larger resources and more diversified resources, larger markets. (The fact that markets grow *pari passu* with production does not negate the even more basic proposition that neither development will occur unless there is reasonable potential for both.) There are too many countries. The circumstances, discussed above, which make it difficult for El Salvador to develop many, if any, basic industries would become unimportant if all the countries of the Caribbean region were united in one great country. Enough basic industries to give effective diversification could be established in this larger area.

Some may wish to argue that the importance of diversification is overemphasized and point out that the United States has violent business-cycle fluctuations in spite of diversification. But the United States has also enjoyed a tremendous material development; and the guess may be hazarded that the large size of the domestic market and the possibility of extensive diversification and specialization (note that El Salvador could do neither) has contributed tremendously to the development of the United States.

The little country is at a great disadvantage merely because it is little. It must have easy access to international markets to flourish. If the United Nations cannot effectively and quickly lower trade barriers over the world, these little countries had better do some fusing, even at the terrific cost of having one president where there were formerly two.[25]

[24] Eastin Nelson, "Revolution in Economic Policy in Latin America," *Southwestern Social Science Quarterly*, XXXIV (December, 1953), 15.

[25] Seventy of the eighty-five states now distinguished by United Nations statistics have barely 20 per cent of the total population of independent states.

One of the striking results of the inception of the European Community for Coal and Steel has been the appreciation of the need for larger markets. French industry has been one of the most restrictive in Europe. Yet one now finds a man like Georges Villiers, president of the Conseil National du Patronat Français saying:[26] "The French market is too restricted, even if one thinks of it in terms of the enormous development possibilities in the whole French Union. Our market cannot develop in isolation from our European neighbors. It can only develop in close unison with those of other West European countries."

Absence of Entrepreneurs

It has been said that in most of the underdeveloped countries there exists no free private enterpriser-entrepreneur-promoter type of individual of the sort which is so common in the United States and which is sometimes alleged to provide the spark that keeps the economy going and growing.

Some related types abound in the underdeveloped countries. There is a speculator type that traffics in inventories and may attempt to corner the market at the wholesale level; but that is a different breed of man. James Baster says:[27] "Western visitors who have any anxieties about business enterprise in the Levant would be well advised to visit these cities and to spend some time—but not too much money—in the bazaars, where the force of dynamic self-interest may be seen operating daily in almost classical simplicity."

It is true that the type of talent that can run a production and distribution organization, as well as the type of talent that can get a productive enterprise set up in the first place, is essential to the development process. But probably the skills that the underdeveloped countries really lack are the skills of the plant manager and production engineer rather than the promotional skill per se. For the most part, developmental planning in the underdeveloped countries is going to be handled differently than has been the case in the United States, anyway. In the United States, at least according to the mythology, initiative has rested with a private promoter handling his financing through a private investment banker. In the growth of the underdeveloped countries, it is, and will continue to be, exercised by a kind of co-operative process involving the governments, the new public international lending institutions, and private interests. But, pretty clearly, if private interests chiefly function to operate corporations already planned and financed by such a public

---

[26] *France Actuelle,* March 15, 1956, p. 1.

[27] Henry G. Aubrey, "Industrial Investment Decisions: A Comparative Analysis," *Journal of Economic History,* XV (December, 1955), p. 353. The statement occurs in Baster's comments on the Aubrey discussion.

process, the role of private enterprise is to provide efficient operation rather than imaginative risk taking.[28]

Tariffs and the Balance of Trade

The prevailing attitude (it does prevail widely in Latin America, too) that there is something inherently good about barriers to imports and about an export balance of trade is not genuinely helpful of development.

An export balance, in and of itself, does not contribute to increasing the nation's welfare. Venezuela's goods balance is heavily "favorable." Exports are double the value of imports. And yet that discrepancy is almost exactly the same as the value of foreign exchange derived from Venezuelan exports that never passes into the possession of anyone domiciled in Venezuela! Venezuela may be benefited by the oil industry. But she is not benefited by the export balance which is a by-product of oil industry operations. As for the United States, the mere fact that it was a large tariff-free area in the nineteenth century played a major role in facilitating development. Individual states in the Union did not direct their attention from more important matters to a calculated (however futile it might have been) effort to have export balances of trade with each other.

Miscellaneous Customs

Examples of customs that may be inhibitory of industrialization may be multiplied almost without end. One report on these problems says:[29]

> The iron plough has sometimes been resisted as an assault upon the land. In villages of the United Provinces of India, it threatens established human relationships. A man inherits a relationship to a carpenter family whose task it is to make and repair the plough. The family is always invited to the farmer's feasts, and the women are given *saris*. The relationship, the

[28] There is another type of worker present in goodly store in the United States but almost entirely absent in the underdeveloped countries. This is the "willing worker" who is prepared to sink his or her personality into that of the boss and perform a major responsible role in holding the organization together. The competent female secretary is a prime example of this species. And yet the female secretary cannot perform such a role and be "handled like dirt"—as is the common practice in the underdeveloped countries. I do not believe it is real exaggeration to say that, as a pattern in the underdeveloped areas—whatever the relation of the male may be to the female who is his social equal—the male looks upon his stenographer as a drudge to do his bidding at the snap of a finger. The bidding is likely to involve much poorly organized minutiae, petty and frequently unnecessary errands, and a proper demonstration of servility.

[29] United Nations Educational, Scientific and Cultural Organization, *Cultural Patterns and Technical Change*, p. 209.

"pay," the gifts continue whether ploughs are made or not. It is part of a pattern of interdependencies, and of the structuring of responsibility, so that it is not direct self-responsibility, but circular. Perhaps the farmer can be taught to repair his own plough, but it would mean personal reorientation as well as a change in the valued relationship structure.

With regard to such a situation this may be said: Whether the custom in question is a real barrier and should be dispensed with is a decision that should be locally made. Foreign efforts, however well meant, to force a change in customs can only result in resentment on the part of the people being meddled with. On the other hand, there will be no major problem in connection with the cultural change if the people involved are allowed to accept or reject freely and of their own volition.

CONCLUSION

In this book the assumption is made that genuine growth must be defined as the rate of increase in the combination of level of living, freedom of action, and security which the people as a whole, acting through the democratic process, determine to be most desirable. The quantity of growth that will be effected and the conditions under which it will occur are determined by the interaction of resources, technology, and institutions.

Growth becomes a problem only because people want economic growth and development. To the extent that they want it, the chief institutional hurdle has already been overcome. But so far as the minor institutional inhibitions are concerned, their change must primarily be controlled from within. Officious aid by foreigners, no matter how well meant, cannot help but have an unfortunate outcome.

Chapter 32

THE MOVEMENT OF PEOPLE

Ⅺ Ⅺ Ⅺ

The free international movement of people is a highly desirable part of
the goal of maximum freedom of action.
In addition, the international movement of people is one of the best
ways of transmitting technical knowledge.
At present, however, there are innumerable restrictions of the free move-
ment of people.
During the last thirty years the United States has permitted annual
immigration only about one tenth as large as the volume that pre-
vailed at the immigration peak before World War I.

Ⅺ Ⅺ Ⅺ

THIS chapter deals with the greatest of all institutional barriers:
restrictions of migration.

ROLE OF PEOPLE

Motivation

The role of people in the growth process is complex. They are the
society. Their well-being is the end, purpose, and goal of economic
activity. At the same time they are factors in the productive process. Their
income depends on their contribution to the productive process, their
family background, and their aptitude in the sorts of business practices
that prevail in the economy.[1]

The international movement of people not only should be a right,
implementing freedom of action, but it is also a process influencing goods
production. Much of the international movement of people, but by no
means all of it, is motivated by a sort of profit and loss consideration.
Thus much migration has been from low (real) wage countries to higher

---

[1] Nurkse has discussed these matters. In some respects his views concur with,
in some respects they are quite opposed to, those expressed here. He does, however, emphasize the role of migration in the nineteenth century: See Ragnar
Nurkse, "International Investment Today in the Light of Nineteenth-Century Experience," *Economic Journal,* LXIV (December, 1954), 744–58.

(real) wage countries, or to countries with a higher level of living, or to countries in which the immigrant hopes he can live better. Such motivation seems clearly to have been present in the Irish migration to the United States occasioned by the potato famine (1845–55) and the immigration of south Europeans between 1890 and World War I. They were coming to the promised lands: the United States, Canada, Argentina, etc. It was somebody else's profit that brought the Negro slaves from Africa, although the direction of movement was also from a "low wage rate"—in a manner of speaking—to a high wage rate country. But immigration may also be from the high wage country to take advantage of specific opportunities in the low wage country, for reasons very similar to those alleged to be the actual motivation behind foreign investment in Chapter 29.

Leaving home, moving into a different society, finding out about opportunities (even inaccurately) is not accomplished easily. The fact that there has been so much migration in search of better things is evidence of considerable difference in levels of living as well as being evidence that men, or at least many men, have a considerable wanderlust and are a long way from being "of all things the most difficult to move." Compare the mobility of people with that of capital. It is easy to say that capital is more mobile than labor. It just takes a moment for an individual with some liquid capital funds to be attracted by a higher interest rate and make a foreign investment by buying a foreign bond. But this is a rather superficial transaction, as anyone can appreciate who thinks in terms of the mobility of capital equipment. When you speak of a movement of capital, you do not commonly mean that a factory is torn down in the lending country. The international movement of capital almost never means a reduction in the amount of established capital equipment in operation in the lending country. It is only new capital equipment, not yet in operation, which (with rare exceptions like Russia's taking German equipment as reparations after World War II) moves internationally. Thus in terms of mobility it is literally true that, by comparison with land (nature and raw material deposits) and capital (if we mean real capital in being), people are highly mobile.

Population may move internationally in response to the attraction of a higher level of living, or in response to other motives: the escape from the tyranny of autocratic governments and from the enforced servility of rigid class systems to the freedom of the New World. Non-economic, religious factors were important in causing the movement of the Pilgrims from England to New England in the seventeenth century and the movement of many Huguenots from France to the Low Countries and England in the same century. Several of these population movements were extremely important in effecting the movement of technical knowledge. The expulsion of the Jews from Spain was important to the development of industry in the Low Countries and England, as was the movement of the Huguenots from France. The revocation of the Edict of Nantes in 1685 by Louis XIV, and the consequent exile of thousands of skilled Huguenot craftsmen, was probably a not inconsiderable influence in the industrial rise of England, the Low Countries, and Germany relative to France. The technical knowledge brought by the English colonists to the United States was, in its turn, important to the economic development of the United States. In fact the technical knowledge of the colonists was *the* important contribution of England to United States industrialization, not money capital investment.

This argument leads to a proposition similar to that expressed in connection with capital movements. Wage differences in different countries may well exist and motivate some migration; but they are not necessary as an explanation of migration. Many other factors of an institutional sort operate.

Contribution

In the past, population movements have been more important than the foreign investment of capital funds and the movement of capital equipment in facilitating development in the areas to which the movement was directed. It will be recalled that it is questionable whether England provided other countries with much if any net real value of goods in the process of building up her foreign investment. But the movement of population has been another thing. The movement of population seems generally to have been a gain to the receiving region. The chief export contribution England has made has been Englishmen. But by and large the emigrants have been no loss to the country they left. In England second sons were no loss. And migrants were certainly no loss to famine-swept Ireland in the mid-nineteenth century or to southern Europe about 1900. Many years ago the Argentine Alberdi recognized the contribution that European immigrants might make to the development of his country with a policy admonition to his government: "To govern is to populate."

In the United States, of course, it is impossible to conceive what pattern the development of this country might have taken if no substantial immigration had been permitted after 1783. Population would certainly be far smaller; industrial production would certainly be far smaller; and very likely the United States would not now be the most powerful country in the world. It is even a fair guess that the reader of this book would not be here if such restrictive practices had been followed. There is very great likelihood that at least one of his ancestors migrated to this country since that time.

Right

The motivation behind the decision of individuals to move internationally is thus susceptible of analysis in terms of motive and contribution. But in another sense the analysis of the movement of people must be handled in an entirely different way from the movement of goods and investments. People have an inherent right to be able to move. It means nothing to the goods whether they move or not. The difference is due to the fact that people are ends as well as means in the economic process. In addition, they may choose to move to fulfill their freedom of action rather than their money-making aspirations. There is no "entry" covering the movement of people in any international balance of payments statement. No value is placed on the people moving, and they are not bought and paid for like merchandise. And yet their movement is a far more important phenomenon in terms of contribution to development than is the movement of the goods.

To be sure, the remuneration of a technician, living temporarily abroad, may be transferred home and thus find its way into the balance of payments. Immigrant remittances back to the "old country" may also find their way into the balance of payments statement. And in a sense this is partial refutation of the categorical statement made in the preceding paragraph—but only partial and not fundamental. Neither of these types of payment needs to find its way into the balance of payments statement merely as a result of the international migration of those people. It only finds its way there because those people, after they have made the money, choose to transfer it internationally. There is no necessary entry in the balance of payments statements to correspond with the actual movement of people or to correspond with the technical knowledge that they provide.

And yet the people are the most important thing moving internationally, not only because they are the end of the economic process but also because of the effect of their movement on goods production. Therefore the international balance of payments statement, which leaves them out, must give a very imperfect picture of the international economic process. The movement of people cannot be subsumed in a system of double-entry bookkeeping and *quid pro quo* payments (somewhat adulterated by gifts), such as is described in the balance of payments statement.

Before leaving the issue of the right of the individual to freedom of movement, another sort of question needs to be dealt with. Has the individual no responsibility to the community in which he is born, that supports him and educates him in youth, and that will be penalized if he leaves it as soon as he becomes mature and productive? The answer is that of course he has such responsibilities. Effort is made in

Chapter 33 to suggest one way these responsibilities may be met. But, at all events, the problem is not dealt with by restricting movement. And it is worthy of note that in a country such as the United States, which gives the best opportunities possible to its youth, there is no feeling that the young man is defaulting on an obligation to the United States if he goes abroad to be, for example, a technical assistance expert in an underdeveloped country.

Role in Growth

The preceding paragraphs, for the most part, have looked at international migration in terms of individual motivation and the right to freedom of action. But such movement also must be considered when we think in terms of the role of people in raising the level of living. The contribution of migration to the spread of technical knowledge is more appropriately discussed in Chapter 33, however, in relation to the technological process.

FREEDOM OF MOVEMENT

Whenever and wherever it occurs, restriction of the freedom of movement of people represents a significant curtailment of one of the important and meaningful freedoms. Powerful and well-substantiated arguments, showing that freedom of movement in a certain case would reduce level of living or security, would be necessary to overweigh the presumption in favor of freedom of movement. There are many interesting ideas to be exchanged, ideas which will enrich both ourselves and others. Much of the significant development in human history has resulted from the catalytic action involved in the international movement of people and ideas. In spite of this, there are innumerable hindrances to the freedom of movement of people.

Travel and Passports

According to Myrdal:[2] "The institution of passports is important as an indication of a totally new regulative and restrictive attitude towards people's movements. There was in old Russia a saying that men consisted of three parts—soul, body, and passport; we might be moving in that direction."

The would-be tourist is met with many and formidable administrative barriers to his travel. And the nature of the pattern of hurdles that must be surmounted is not the same for any two countries. But the miscellany of hurdles that must be surmounted in a particular case is

[2] Gunnar Myrdal, *An International Economy: Problems and Prospects,* p. 90.

likely to include passports, visas, tourist cards, entry permits, photographs, birth certificates (or witnesses that one was born), postal money orders, letters certifying to credit standing, return tickets, police letters, various medical shots, inoculations, and injections, plus various customs formalities. The order in which these formalities are attended to may make a considerable difference in the smoothness of the process. Never is it possible to get all of the formalities worked out satisfactorily the first time around. One may even run into the complication that the transportation agency wants to be sure all of the official papers are in order before it will sell a ticket. And the foreign counsul may insist that the would-be tourist have a return-trip ticket already purchased before he will issue a visa.

The genuine usefulness of several of these documents is subject to question. It is doubtful if the passport serves any useful purpose in connection with the operation of actually crossing an international frontier. So far as the United States is concerned, the possession of a United States passport is not a necessary prerequisite for either entering or leaving the country, say to visit Mexico. However, one is legally required to have a passport to travel outside the Western Hemisphere. Nor does the present procedure which is involved in issuing passports to United States citizens even provide accurate information as to where abroad United States citizens are going. Since passports may be used for many different trips abroad, the statement on the original application for the passport as to where and how one is planning to travel on one's first trip has little more than a nuisance value—especially if one has not decided where or how he is going to travel at the time of making the application. It should be conceded that the document may be of some use if the traveler gets into trouble abroad and wishes to prove quickly to local government officials that he is a bona fide American entitled to all the special privileges to which Americans are now entitled, or think they are entitled, over the surface of the globe. But the passport could serve this minor purpose without being nearly as thick as it is.

The visa (stamped into a passport by the consul of the country the traveler wishes to visit) and the tourist card (which is the same sort of permit stated on a card rather than as a stamp in a passport) are among the more meaningful of the various documents. They represent the permission by the foreign government to the traveler to enter. Physical possession of the visa or tourist card is generally necessary at the port of entry to get in. The obtaining of a visa, however, may be a terrible nuisance to anyone who does not live in a large city where there are many consuls. And they are a fair nuisance there, involving very likely the prior obtaining of photo, police letter, shots, vaccination, and passport.

Americans have troubles getting visas to travel abroad. Foreigners have troubles getting visas to visit this country. The *Bulletin of the Atomic Scientists* has described the difficulties involved in visits by foreign scientists to this country:[3]

> Six cases of international organizations who have refused to hold meetings in the United States because of past experiences are discussed in the next section. The loss of these scientific meetings for this country is our greatest concern.
>
> Our survey also indicated that there were two main types of visa difficulties for foreign scientific visitors. In the first class, prospective visitors experienced a long and uncertain delay in their visa applications, making it impossible for them to meet deadlines for meetings, lecture courses, etc. In the second class, visas were refused (before or after deadlines) apparently because of political affiliations or associations of the applicant.

The application form for a visa which the non-immigrant, temporary visitor has to fill out to visit the United States is fantastically long and involved.

To turn to the subject of shots, vaccinations, and inoculations: there may be real disease problems. If there is danger of a disease being transmitted across an international frontier, shots or some sort of preventive action obviously are called for. For the most part, international travelers, especially if they are United States tourists, should want to take the shots that are required because they are going to the area where the danger lies. Government action in the country where the disease exists, however, should emphasize inoculation of the domestic population—in whose welfare the government ought to be more interested than in that of the foreigners. At all events, health regulations are not at present very well co-ordinated. For example, Guatemala requires all travelers coming from Bolivia to have been inoculated for yellow fever. Honduras, however, has no such requirement, and passage from Honduras to Guatemala is relatively free of restrictions.[4]

Perhaps the statesmanlike position to take in this matter is that an informed medical opinion at either the world or the national level could adequately deal with the medical question, if only people who want to restrict international freedom of movement for other reasons would not insist on using quarantine regulations for this purpose. A considerable amount of international co-operation to integrate the inoculation and quarantine procedures of different countries is urgently called for.

[3] "American Visa Policy: A Report," *Bulletin of the Atomic Scientists*, XI (December, 1955), pp. 367–75. Reprinted with permission. The *Bulletin* is published by the Educational Foundation for Nuclear Science, Inc., 5734 University Ave., Chicago 37, Illinois.

[4] United Nations Educational, Scientific, and Cultural Organization, *Travel Abroad* (Paris, 1953, et seq.), sections on Guatemala and Honduras.

As for the "police letters,"[5] one may wish the police departments the best of luck in catching criminals, and perhaps believe that the F.B.I. fingerprint file should include everyone in the country, and even that there should be a similar world-wide file, and still not believe in police letters. Most Americans would probably agree as to the undesirability of requiring each tourist driving into California to have with him a letter from the chief of police in his home town certifying that he is an upstanding citizen. Of course, it might help keep criminals out of California; and there are possibly more criminals in California than there should be. But we have chosen not to introduce this additional bit of paper work domestically in the United States. Criminals are caught in other ways, if they are caught. Perhaps a criminal was once deterred from traveling because of the difficulty of getting a police letter, but it is doubtful. Police letters at the international level make for a lot of paper work and do little good. Any police department that is really alert will want to pass its unsavory types off on some other jurisdiction. But some rather unpleasant situations may be created for bashful and retiring citizens, not used to police stations, who may be handled temporarily like criminals by police who think the police letter should mean something—the officers are frequently not quite sure what.

One of the odder things about police letters is the prevalent ignorance of the police as to the purpose of the letter. They seem to be under the impression that the letters are submitted to the State Department in connection with the passport application and that it is useful for that department to know whether the applicant is a Communist. Consequently, the letters generally deal at some length with the police department's knowledge, or lack of it, as to the Communist affiliations, or lack of them, of the applicant. But the letters do not go to the United States government; they go to the consul of the country to which one plans to travel, and they are used in connection with the visa application. And if one is planning to go to Russia then information that one is a Communist, contained in the police letter signed by a Texas police chief, would presumably be favorable information instead of adverse, so far as the Russian consul is concerned.

Passports, visas, and many of the auxiliary papers should be largely dispensed with—or else standardized into an intelligible, simple pattern. With regard to the suggestion that passports and visas be dispensed

[5] The police letter is a statement, signed by the chief of police, or similar official, in the city where the would-be traveler is resident, stating that the person has or has not a police record and what known connection he has with subversive organizations. It is submitted as a supporting document in getting a visa from the foreign country. Police letters are not used in connection with getting a passport from the traveler's own government, at least not under the United States procedure.

with, some will say: "But what about the Communists who may filter in as tourists." Are they as great a menace as Senator McCarran seemed to feel? Some spies and potential saboteurs might find their way in—probably would—if the restrictions on tourist entry were virtually removed. But the gain in understanding of the American system, on the part of the foreigners who come and see it, ought to more than offset this relatively minor danger of sabotage. Sabotage is effective and prevalent anyway only against a rotten society with which the population is basically disaffected. The people who are afraid to let foreigners enter our country and who fear it can be successfully attacked by a few subversives are showing about as little confidence in our system as the Russians are showing in theirs by pursuing the same methods. Probably in the long run little compromise should be made with the proposition that most of these documents are undesirable. Passports, visas, and similar restrictions should be eliminated. But given the current state of the world, it may be that we should practice reciprocity —give tourists from beyond the iron curtain as much or as little freedom to move into and around in our country as they give our tourists in theirs. But, even now, freedom of egress and ingress for students and tourists from other than iron curtain countries should be complete— that is, free of administration annoyance beyond that necessary to give governments a record of who is coming and going to and from where, the barest formalities.

This, however, does not entirely dispose of the question of passports. Each person should carry some form of identification (tourists and natives alike). Most foreign countries require identification cards of one kind or another. The United States might well do the same, and some international standard form of identification card could substitute for the passport. On this point it might be said that we now are supposed to carry on our person (or nearby): driver's license, social security card, one or two selective service cards, one or two credit cards, medical and hospitalization insurance papers, the title to the car; and if we are traveling abroad: passport, police letters, health certificates, photographs, various entry cards, etc. In fact, it takes so much space for the papers that there is hardly any left for the curios.

The international identification card, if it could substitute for three or four of these documents, could render a true service to harassed mankind. The fewer controls the better, but if a government insists on having controls they should be clear, definite, enforced, and known to all travel agencies. Also, it would be helpful if various countries had uniform requirements—except perhaps for a pattern of vaccinations and inoculations that might be planned by an international agency and vary depending on where the traveler is going and where he has been.

Migration

The foregoing was primarily related to travel documents and to the troubles of tourists. Working abroad and permanent immigration pose additional problems.[6]

Probably Americans, if polled, would express general agreement that there should be few if any artificial barriers to their working abroad. Typically, to enter a country to work or reside more or less permanently there, the alien must meet the passport, visa and other requirements which the tourist must meet. In addition, there are special hurdles. In Indonesia, according to the United States Department of Commerce, the "applications of all such persons [those desiring permanent stay visas] are carefully screened by the Immigration Service and the interested government agencies (e.g., Ministry of Economic Affairs for the businessmen and the National Police for former residents or visitors). This process usually takes about four months."[7] It is the individualized screening of the would-be permanent immigrants that makes for the greatest uncertainty. The person trying to obtain the permanent entry visa may be made to wait varying lengths of time under conditions where he has no idea what is going on or how long the wait may be. After he finally gets into the country where he desires to work, his administrative troubles are far from over. He is likely to be required to report at regular intervals to the police. He is liable to be deported rather summarily. An American who has worked for an oil company in Venezuela can generally tell quite a tale of petty administrative harassment.

But the troubles of the American working abroad are as nothing to the troubles of the foreigner who wishes to come to the United States.

The United States began a quantitative limitation of immigration during the World War I period. Acts passed by Congress in 1917, 1921, 1924, and 1929 finally limited immigration to a total of approximately 150,000 persons a year. This figure compares with high immigration figures of 1,285,000 in 1907 and 1,218,000 in 1914. Of the total of 150,000 immigrants per year permitted in recent years, a quota of roughly 65,000 has been assigned to Great Britain, 26,000 to Germany, and 18,000 to Ireland. This has not left much for the rest of the world. The quota allotted to most of the countries of Asia and Africa has been 100. The quota allotted to a typical southern European country has been under 1,000. Italy, in fact, with a quota of 5,600, is the only country in southern Europe with a quota over 1,000. The actual mechanics by

[6] A good general work on this subject is Brinley Thomas, *Migration and Economic Growth* (London: Cambridge University Press, 1954).

[7] United States, Bureau of Foreign Commerce, *Indonesia—Regulations and Procedures Affecting Tourists and Temporary Visitors,* Business Information Service, World Trade Series, No. 600 (Washington, 1954), p. 2.

which these quotas are allotted among the different countries is rather complicated. The Immigration and Nationality (McCarran-Walter) Act of June 27, 1952, reads that "the annual quota of any quota area shall be one-sixth of 1 per centum of the number of inhabitants in the continental United States in 1920." It also provides that "the minimum quota for any quota area shall be one hundred." [8]

At the end of World War II, there were literally millions of displaced persons in Europe and Asia—people who did not dare or could not return to their homes and people who had no homes to return to. Thousands and thousands of such people, ten years after the end of World War II, are still living under wretched conditions. Many are living in former German concentration camps and in prisoner of war stockades, many are in the Gaza strip, and many are in south Viet-Nam.

Congress has been reluctant to let any very large number of these people enter the United States. But finally, August 7, 1953, President Eisenhower signed the Refugee Relief Act authorizing admittance of about 200,000 emergency refugees, and in signing the bill into law he said: "We are giving a new chance in life to 214,000 fellow humans. . . . This action demonstrates again America's traditional concern for the homeless, the persecuted and the less fortunate of other lands." But apparently the directive did not get through to Scott McLeod, the government official responsible for the administration of the Act. Nor had the members of the House and Senate who were responsible for the drafting of the law themselves been especially sympathetic to the idea that large numbers of the displaced of Europe and small numbers of the displaced of Asia should come into the United States. Cabell Phillips, a *New York Times* reporter, wrote of the Act: [9]

> For an alien to avail himself of the benefits of the act, these hurdles must be cleared:
>
> (1) He must have a United States citizen personally sponsor his immigration and guarantee to the Government that he will not become a public charge.
>
> (2) He must be assured of a particular job with a particular employer at the going rate of pay, with a guarantee that taking such a job does not displace an American workman.
>
> (3) He must have made specific and final arrangements for the housing of himself and family, with a guarantee that his occupancy of such housing does not displace an American family.
>
> (4) He must be able to prove that he has never been a Communist or advocated Communist principles.

[8] *United States Code* (1952), title 8, par. 1151.
[9] *New York Times,* September 12, 1954, sec. 4, p. 4. Reprinted by permission of the *New York Times.*

(5) He must be able to withstand a security check of his activities and associations for the two years preceding his entry into this country.

(6) He must pass the rigid health requirements of the Immigration and Naturalization Service.

(7) He must offer documentary proof that the country from which he is emigrating will take him back at any time in the future that he may be expelled from the United States.

It should not take much imagination to surmise that a Russian displaced person living in straightened circumstances in a former German concentration camp in the Vosges mountains is going to have trouble establishing the necessary preliminary contacts in the United States. Or again, what happens to the displaced person who has tuberculosis—a not uncommon disease among the DP's? Also, it stands to reason that France is not going to be very enthusiastic about promising to take a Russian back who has briefly sojourned in France if, after two years, we decide to deport him.

Congressman Emanuel Celler is reported to have said of the law that it should not have been called a Refugee Relief Act but rather a Relatives Relief Act—because perhaps 16,600 relatives of United States citizens came in under its terms during a period when only about 1,000 genuine refugees came in.[10]

In early 1955, a New York Republican named Edward J. Corsi was appointed as a State Department adviser to expedite the immigration program. In April he was politely fired from his job—seemingly because he showed some interest in implementing the law. In a letter to Secretary of State Dulles, Mr. Corsi then wrote:[11]

I am sure you agree that the admission to date of less than 1,000 refugees in sixteen months does no credit to the Administration and injured severely American prestige in the world. It casts serious doubt upon the good faith of those who are responsible for the administration of the act.

In my recent report to you I made recommendations for the salvaging of the program which I hope will be put through. The recommendations call for new and vigorous administrative leadership in the field, particularly in Germany and Italy, and here in Washington; priority for the program all along the way; reaffirmation of its emergency character by you and the President, and a tightening of the whole administrative machinery to eliminate excessive security checks, red tape and bureaucratic

[10] Drew Pearson, "Washington Merry-Go-Round," *Austin American,* March 27, 1955, p. D-2.

[11] *New York Times,* April 12, 1955, p. 20. Reprinted by permission of the *New York Times.*

control which are basically responsible for the scandalous failure of the past seventeen months.

But more than this, Mr. Secretary, more than administrative energy and leadership, the program needs heart. It needs to be entrusted in the hands of men who have faith in humanity, who honestly believe that America has a responsibility toward the victims of war and persecution in the world. I am not convinced that [it] is now in the hands of such men.

Apart from the misnamed Refugee Relief Act, the United States has recently dabbled with the problem of displaced persons in another area. It may be recalled that in the latter days of the Korean War we held prisoner in South Korea substantial numbers of Chinese and North Koreans who did not wish to return to China and North Korea. In the course of the armistice negotiations, we firmly and righteously took the position that such prisoners should not be forced to return to Communist lands in the prisoner exchange which was being negotiated. We were even willing to continue the war for an indeterminate period in support of this principle. On this point Secretary of State Dulles said in a statement made on the occasion of the Korean armistice, July 26, 1953: [12]

In this hour, we welcome also the triumph of the principle of political asylum. Many of the North Korean and Chinese prisoners of war want hereafter to live in freedom. The Communists stubbornly insisted that these prisoners must be forcibly returned. Now that demand is abandoned. No prisoners will be returned against their will. They may choose freedom. The consequences of this decision run far beyond Korea. The Communist rulers now know that if they wage another war of aggression, those who unwillingly serve in their Red armies can escape to freedom, confident that they will never be handed back. Thus the Red armies become less dependable as instruments of aggression and the chance of aggression is correspondingly reduced.

What then happened to these ex-Communist prisoners of war? A. M. Rosenthal has this to say, as of February, 1955, with regard to the disposition of these persons: [13]

For almost a year the Government of India has been host to about fifty almost-forgotten men of the Korean war.

Once prisoners and now living in a kind of legal no man's land, they want to leave India and the Government is eager to wish them godspeed. But no other country has made a move

[12] *Department of State Bulletin*, XXIX (August 3, 1953), p. 132.
[13] *New York Times*, February 25, 1955, p. 2. Reprinted by permission of the *New York Times*.

to take them and it looks as if the reluctant guests and the reluctant hosts will be together for a long time.

There is more in the article about the morale of these men and their
bitterness. It seems that several have even, on their own recognizance,
been permitted to return to Communist lands. Apparently the prospect
of spending the rest of their lives in a barracks does not appeal to all of
them—life in Red China, bad as it is, looks better to some.[14]

Free immigration might result in a flood of immigration to the United
States. What is to be done?[15]

An American cannot properly object to immigration—permanently—
on the ground that the influx of cheap labor would lower the American
level of living. More important than the consideration that an increase
in population might lower the level is the consideration that the world
as a whole is not going to be a stable, peaceful place in which to live
as long as there are substantial differences in well-being as between
regions. There will be unrest in the less privileged regions as long as
there are other regions where the population is substantially more privileged. And no single individual in the more privileged area is entitled
to say that his privileges are the result of his own merit. The people
of the more privileged regions must recognize that all the people of the
world are equally entitled to live and work in the more desirable places.
America, the land of second and third generation immigrants, has
turned against the immigrant and seems to be trying to protect an
island of good living in a world of misery and unrest by keeping other
people out of this Garden of Eden. This, in spite of the inscription
on the Statue of Liberty:[16]

> Give me your tired, your poor,
>   Your huddled masses yearning to breathe free,
> The wretched refuse of your teeming shore.
> Send these, the homeless, tempest-tost to me.
> I lift my lamp beside the golden door!

If there were effective freedom to migrate from one country to another,
many of the fighting issues in the world today would lose their importance. Much of the harsh feeling of people in the underdeveloped
areas of the world toward the United States would lose its reason for
being. The United States would no longer be an artificially isolated
island of plenty in a sea of misery.

[14] Substantial numbers of the Korean ex-P.O.W.'s have since gone to Brazil. See
the *New York Times,* February 15, 1956, p. 3.

[15] The present organization for dealing with the problem is supposed to be the
Intergovernmental Committee for European Migration, which was provided for
in an international convention signed at Venice in 1953. The United States and
various Latin American governments are parties to the agreement along with
most of the countries of western Europe. Neither the U.S.S.R. nor any of her
associated countries belong.

[16] The verse was by Emma Lazarus.

But even if there were agreement as to the desirability of removing the barriers to the free movement of people over the surface of the globe, it would probably not be desirable to remove them all at once. Population movement to the United States might be so large as to create an unmanageable mess if it were suddenly allowed on an unrestricted basis; at least that must be recognized as a possibility. Some formula for gradually eliminating the barriers to migration might well be workable, however. Formulas to permit gradual (not violent) change in the desirable direction seem to represent the best approach to most problems.

Immigration represents a special problem. An immediate large increase in permitted immigration to the United States is called for if the United States is even to begin to do its duty in helping to solve this greatest of the World War II tragedies—the tale of the displaced person. But a permanent change in policy is also called for. Perhaps the long-run problem could be dealt with by the raising of immigration quotas 20 per cent each year. In addition, some special adjustments are probably called for in connection with the countries which have the very small quotas currently set at one hundred. Perhaps this formula can be improved upon, but some sort of a "percentage increase" formula would avoid a sudden disruptive movement of population and yet open the prospect of complete freedom of movement.[17] There would come a point in this process, and it might come sooner than some Americans might fear, when other countries would no longer fill their quotas. The British were not consistently filling their quotas in the years before World War II. The greater the rise in the real level of living in other countries, the less the tendency to migrate to the United States. Other things being equal, the scenery in the United States is not calculated to attract anyone from Naples or Rio de Janeiro, anyway.

CONCLUSION

Freedom of movement, freedom to go into any line of business anywhere, equality before the law, the right to live anywhere—all these things are essential to real freedom of action. It is not argued here that freedom of movement will solve the world's problems; but it is argued that the world's problems will not be solved without freedom of movement.

It does not follow that one has to associate socially with just anybody. We personally pick our friends, and the right to do so is one of the

[17] Meade (*Trade and Welfare*, p. 569) has expressed misgivings about permitting free movement of population if one area permits its population to increase rapidly and others do not. But in reply it might be urged that this is more of a plea for selective birth control than for limitation on international migration.

freedoms of action we should most cherish. But if there are some people whose physical proximity we cannot stand in an elevator, we ought not to use them for elevator operators. Of course, a lot of this is controversial and involves issues on which some people are extremely sensitive. But it would be a help to intelligent discussion of the issues if some people would realize that it cannot be true both that United States progress and material welfare are the result of some inherent superiority of the American people (perhaps the spirit of enterprise) and that the present day American has something to fear from the competition of the immigrants. A lot of immigrants would be just additional hands for Americans to direct, if we are what we pretend to be. If not, can it be true that we owe our world dominance to geographical and institutional accident and not to our own merit? As to the freedom of movement of people, that can make a major contribution to growth; but even more important, it is called for as a matter of right.

Chapter 33

TECHNOLOGY AND KNOWLEDGE

☙ ☙ ☙

The international spread of technical knowledge can make, and probably will make, a far greater contribution to the growth of the under-developed countries than foreign investments can or will.

The United States Point Four program and the United Nations Technical Assistance program are major efforts along this line.

Such technical exchange might be entirely financed by the recipient country. Actually, at present, costs are generally shared between the aiding agency and the recipient government.

☙ ☙ ☙

EVOLUTION OF TECHNICAL KNOWLEDGE

TECHNICAL knowledge grows on itself, although, depending on the institutional climate, the rate of accumulation may be speeded up or slowed down. But it is the nature of the knowledge possessed at any one time which determines what the next bit of knowledge to become part of man's store will be. The relative genius of inventors and scientists may determine who gets the Nobel prize for making the discovery, but not what the discovery will be.

In olden times, because of transportation difficulties, knowledge acquired in one culture such as China might be very slow in becoming part of the store of technical knowledge of another culture such as western Europe, and vice versa. However, tales such as the following even come out of the Dark Ages:[1] "It was, however, by this route that Nestorian monks travelled to Constantinople with the eggs of the silkworm hidden in their staffs, thus founding the silk-growing industry that later was to be the pride of Byzantium."

Then during the nineteenth century there was a period when anyone in any country, who had the necessary determination, had access with almost complete freedom to the knowledge of the world.[2] In con-

---

[1] *Cambridge Economic History of Europe*, II, p. 90.

[2] Whether an individual could or would take advantage of the opportunity, of course, was institutionally determined by his social background, his family's income, his own faculties, and so on.

sequence, the accumulation of technical knowledge proceeded at an unprecedented pace. By the end of the nineteenth century (this is the significant development of modern times—and it occurred fifty or seventy-five years ago, not in 1945 with the detonation of *the* bomb), man had become the master of his environment rather than the environment being the master of him. Man now has the technical knowledge to make of himself what he chooses; he can determine by his own will what his level of living will be. That he has made such a botch of the job up to now is a tribute, as much as anything, to the institutional attitude we have come to call nationalism. But also, perhaps, it would have been hoping for too much to expect the human animal to establish a satisfactory world social organization immediately, and without experimentation, after he acquired the technical knowledge to provide a decent level of living for all.

But to return to the evolution of the acquisition of technical knowledge, in the nineteenth century the existing knowledge was freely available to anybody whose institutional background permitted him to take advantage of it. And during the nineteenth century the impact of the institutions of different countries was such that the reservoir became larger in the countries where it was already relatively large, while the countries that were lagging initially lagged yet more.

Things are different, however, in mid-twentieth century. Some of the most considerable barriers which exist are those inhibiting the exchange of knowledge. Let me illustrate with a problem which the University of Texas Library encountered in 1955. A library order was placed for the *Bulletin* of the Institute of Economics and Law, a Bulgarian publication. The Library's final explanation as to why it could not obtain the *Bulletin* runs as follows:

> The Bulgarian Academy of Sciences will send their publications abroad only on an exchange basis. They will neither sell them nor send them free. We are not permitted to maintain exchange agreements with iron-curtain countries; therefore, we cannot acquire this publication. . . .

My preceding comments are based on the idea that technical knowledge should be freely available to all, and that we are not afraid of intellectual competition. Everybody's lot will be better and the general climate of the world economy will be more salubrious if development is encouraged to go on apace, stimulated by the exchange of ideas, which will make the sum total of knowledge grow faster as well. No matter how much knowledge a given nation may have at any one time, that nation may fail to make the next significant advance because of the lack of the catalytic effect which a certain bit of foreign knowledge might provide.

To quote L. V. Berkner:[3]

[3] *New Republic*, July 12, 1954, p. 6. Reprinted by permission.

We all know that such ideas as the laws of mechanics and the concepts of space and time derived from astronomy, together with the work of Planck on high-temperature radiation, led Einstein to postulate the equivalence of mass and energy through his concept of relativity. On this concept is based the discovery of nuclear energy. Yet today, any intelligent military organization, operating under the present rules and concepts, would certainly classify the equivalent of Planck's work so that it would be denied to a possible Einstein. . . .

Let me take the coward's way out and discuss the question of the usefulness of spreading technical knowledge, not in terms of atomic energy, but in terms of rubber and pretzels. Smuggling a *hevea brasiliensis* seedling out of Brazil in the latter part of the last century made the plantation rubber industry of the Far East possible. That made rubber available at a much lower price and in far greater quantities than would have been the case if Brazil had succeeded in protecting her monopoly and in maintaining the industry on the basis of tapping wild rubber trees. And what would we do without pretzels? The *World Almanac* of 1952 reports:[4]

Long popular with beer drinkers and at cocktail bars is the twisted pretzel, defined as a salted biscuit of German origin. On May 9, 1951, the town of Lititz, Pa., pop. about 5,500, won headline attention because it observed the 90th anniversary of the opening of the country's first pretzel factory. Sen. James H. Duff and Rep. Paul B. Dague, Republican Members of Congress from Pennsylvania, led a parade. The National Pretzel Bakers Institute provided a plaque to commemorate Julius Sturgis, said to have been the first to bake pretzels for commercial purposes. The United Press reported that he obtained the "secret" of the pretzel from a vagabond.

As to whether knowledge of all technical advance should be freely available to all who desire to try to assimilate it (if they are willing to pay for the patent rights),[5] the person assumes a tremendous social responsibility who says that one segment of the human race should have certain knowledge and profit thereby and another segment should not. Such a program also involves assuming a tremendous policing role, which the counter-intelligence agents may not be capable of performing. As long as our "enemies" are going to find out anyway, we might as well let our "friends" in on the secret graciously.

The most important single thing which the underdeveloped countries can do in the implementation of their programs of growth is to

[4] *World Almanac,* 1952, p. 637. Reprinted by permission.
[5] Parenthetically, it may be alleged in a rather cavalier fashion that change in the patent laws to provide for compulsory licensing is called for. But it is hardly possible to go into a detailed discussion of the patent laws here.

foster the acquisition, accumulation, and development of this technical knowledge within their own borders and by their own people.[6] This is immeasurably more important than foreign borrowing, than capital equipment imports, than aid in the form of gifts of goods. And it is also the sort of program that a self-reliant citizenry should prefer to emphasize. International begging by nations is no more dignified than individual begging by people called beggars.

But what can be done to facilitate the exchange of knowledge in general and the acquisition of useful technical knowledge in particular by the people of the underdeveloped countries?

STUDENT EXCHANGE

Some of the best young talent from the underdeveloped areas can be sent to centers of technical knowledge for training. A great deal of the groundwork for development can be laid in this way at what is very moderate expense by comparison with the total amount of money, time, and effort that is being put into development. One-hundred-million dollars would give between ten and twenty *thousand* reasonably economical men and women a complete college education in western Europe or in the United States. This is a lot of technicians. Of course, this is easy to say; and it sometimes happens that, after the scholar from the underdeveloped country has received the education (which should be so useful when he returns home), he either does not bother to go home or he goes home and engages in some really useless activity like commodity speculation. But even if this growing reservoir of technical knowledge is not used in the most effective way, there can be no doubt that increasing the size of the reservoir is one of the most constructive (and least expensive) ways of helping along the process of economic development in the underdeveloped areas. It has the additional advantage of placing the power to take initiative in the hands where it can most properly lie—domestic ones.

There is a growing group of young men and women receiving free

[6] There is not 100 per cent agreement with regard to the usefulness of foreigners as sources of technical knowledge. The Mexican Alfonso Cardoso has written (*Experiencias en Economía* [Mexico: EDIAPSA, 1953], p. 48) that: "Consulting with foreigners would give the well-known result of obtaining opinions as inadequate as those expressed in the books of Mosk and Tannenbaum, which have been so much commented upon." He adds that Mexico has enough "economists, engineers, and industrialists of indisputable capacity." If this is true there is no international problem. Technical assistance should not be forced on those who do not want it. On the other hand, a lot of poor advice has undoubtedly been given—and incidentally a lot poorer than that of Mosk and Tannenbaum. Sanford A. Mosk, *Industrial Revolution in Mexico* (Berkeley: University of California Press, 1950); Frank Tannenbaum, *Mexico, The Struggle for Peace and Bread* (New York: Knopf, 1950).

university education abroad. For them as individuals this is a golden opportunity denied to the great proportion of their countrymen. The funds to finance the education are provided by society—by their own government, by the United States government, or by any one of many private foundations and international agencies. Society in providing these funds believes it is making a contribution. It believes that the recipients of these educational grants will go back to their own countries and make a significant contribution.

Perhaps this is just the sort of situation where something similar to the Hippocratic Oath of doctors is called for. The student might affirm his intention to return to his own land and make use of the knowledge he has gained—either in a public or a private role—with primary concern for the increased production and effective distribution of goods and for the increase in the well-being of his countrymen. An *esprit de corps* might well develop, which does not now exist, among the students. The contribution they can make, if they will, is tremendous.

TRADE IN KNOWLEDGE

The overseas libraries, such as the United States government has maintained in large numbers since the end of the war, have been a fine thing. They are extensively patronized by young and old eager to learn. People are interested in how things are done in the United States. If anything, it adds to the prestige of the United States, in the eyes of these people, that these libraries may have material which is something other than 100 per cent crass and crude anti-Russian propaganda. Of the many disservices which the hyper-nationalists have done to the standing of this country abroad, the undermining of the respectability and scholarly integrity of the overseas libraries is one of the worst.

Technical knowledge may also be spread cheaply through the scholarly journals. However, scholarly journals, since they cannot completely substitute for actually working with equipment under the watchful eye of someone who knows how the thing is done, are probably chiefly useful as a supplement to the actual exchange of scholars. But the scholarly journals represent a way for someone who already has a technical background to keep up with recent developments.

TECHNICAL ASSISTANCE PROGRAMS

Very useful and inexpensive is the sending of technically trained people from the developed areas to the underdeveloped areas to get projects started and assist with the technical training of the nationals who will manage the projects in the long run. This was one of the special features enunciated by President Harry Truman as Point Four in the program announced in his 1949 inaugural address.

Fourth, we must embark on a bold new program for making the benefits of our scientific advances and industrial progress available for the improvement and growth of underdeveloped areas.

More than half the people of the world are living in conditions approaching misery. Their food is inadequate. They are victims of disease. Their economic life is primitive and stagnant. Their poverty is a handicap and a threat both to them and to more prosperous areas.

For the first time in history, humanity possesses the knowledge and the skill to relieve the suffering of these people.

The United States is preeminent among nations in the development of industrial and scientific techniques. The material resources which we can afford to use for the assistance of other peoples are limited. But our imponderable resources in technical knowledge are constantly growing and are inexhaustible.

I believe that we should make available to peace-loving peoples the benefits of our store of technical knowledge in order to help them realize their aspirations for a better life. And, in cooperation with other nations we should foster capital investment in areas needing development.

Our aim should be to help the free peoples of the world, through their own efforts, to produce more food, more clothing, more materials for housing, and more mechanical power to lighten their burdens.

We invite other countries to pool their technological resources in this undertaking. Their contributions will be warmly welcomed. This should be a cooperative enterprise in which all nations work together through the United Nations and its specialized agencies wherever practicable. It must be a world-wide effort for the achievement of peace, plenty, and freedom.

The "technical" details of the various programs of "technical" assistance which have resulted are the special province of scientific agriculture, medicine, engineering, etc., rather than of economics. Here only a very little will be said about the extent and financing of the programs.

United States Government Program

United States developmental aid is now provided by a curious hodgepodge of governmental agencies, whose activities seem to be sometimes co-ordinated and sometimes not.

The Institute of Inter-American Affairs was originally established in 1942, and thus actually antedates President Truman's 1949 enunciation of Point Four. The Institute may aid a Latin American country to establish a plan and help it to finance a group of technicians working in the fields of (1) public health and sanitation, (2) agriculture, and (3) education.[7]

President Truman's Point Four program proper was implemented by the Act for International Development of 1950—the Act was title II of the more general Foreign Assistance Act of the same year. It established the Technical Cooperation Administration specifically to implement the Point Four program. It was originally placed under the State Department. At that time the Institute of Inter-American Affairs was integrated into the Technical Cooperation Administration and assigned the Latin American field. Similar subunits in the TCA were called the Near East and African Development Service and the Asian Development Service.

In 1953, the incoming Eisenhower administration moved the Technical Cooperation Administration under the Foreign Operations Administration. This was a newly created over-all independent agency headed by Harold Stassen. As was mentioned in Chapter 26, it had jurisdiction over the general aid program that had grown out of the Marshall plan. The changes of the summer of 1955 returned the technical co-operation program to the State Department, the responsible semi-autonomous agency being the International Cooperation Administration, with a new administrator, John B. Hollister. This latter agency has general jurisdiction over the economic side of the whole foreign aid program as well as jurisdiction over the technical assistance program in particular. In this new framework, the Institute of Inter-American Affairs continues to have primary responsibility for the Latin American part of the program and is under the International Cooperation Administration.

Technical exchange activities are not primarily related to international lending. They may not involve any lending at all. Chiefly they involve the providing of technicians by the United States in a program jointly worked out with certain government agencies in the country receiving the aid. The expenses have been assumed by the United States and the recipient government in varying proportions. In some cases, the United States government has carried almost all of the expense of the program.

[7] For considerably more detail on the work of the various agencies see: Walter R. Sharp, *International Technical Assistance, Programs and Organization* (Chicago: Public Administration Service, 1952). The discussion of IIAA is on pp. 4–6 and *passim*. Also see: United States Congress, Senate, Committee on Foreign Relations, *Technical Assistance Programs* (Washington: Government Printing Office, 1955); and Howard M. Teaf, Jr., *Hands across Frontiers—Case Studies in Technical Cooperation* (Ithaca: Cornell University Press, 1955).

In other cases, the United States has carried little or none of the monetary expense. In 1956, in the Latin American part of the program,
the United States put up $29 million and the Latin American
governments, $50 million.[8] But in a somewhat different type of arrange-
ment, Liberia has "pledged 20 per cent of its total national revenue for
1950–51 to cover local technical assistance and economic development
costs."

The basic categories of technical exchange are (1) agriculture and
natural resources, (2) health and sanitation, (3) education, (4) industry
and transportation, (5) public administration, and (6) community development and housing. The assistance given has ranged from dusting
the natives with DDT in remote villages in Peru, to work at Santiago
de las Vegas to develop a one-man machine to process kenaf (and
make in Cuba a burlap-type bag to hold sugar). And it has included
aid to the Swynnerton plan in Kenya for the improvement of African
native agriculture. The plan called for sending nineteen American technical specialists to Kenya to work on the agricultural program. A few
programs of this sort may not be amiss in the land of the Mau Mau.

As of December 31, 1954, there was, in the general technical assistance
program, the following distribution of personnel as between the United
States and the other participating countries:[9]

TO OR FROM:	U.S. TECHNICIANS ABROAD	PARTICIPANTS TRAINING IN THE UNITED STATES
Far East	398	671
Latin America	553	371
Near East, Africa, and South Asia	868	422

In spite of an untoward incident at Saltillo, Mexico, in late 1955,
the inter-university contracts are one of the most promising aspects of
the technical assistance program. These are contracts, sponsored by the
International Cooperation Administration between an American and a
foreign university. They may provide that the American college will
send some of its professional staff to teach in the partner university
in the "host" country. Assistance in curriculum planning and extension
and demonstration programs are also likely to be provided for.[10] Among
the pairs of universities that have concluded such contracts are:

Purdue and the Rural University of the State of Minas Gerais
    (Brazil);
Michigan State and the National University (Colombia);

[8] *New York Times,* August 6, 1956, p. 1.
[9] United States . . . , *Technical Assistance Programs,* p. 8.
[10] The text of a contract is cited in United States . . . , *Technical Assistance
Programs,* p. 47.

University of Idaho and the Universities of Quito and Guaya-
quil;

University of Pennsylvania and the National University of Mexico;

University of North Carolina and the National School of Engineering (Peru);

University of Illinois and the Allahabad Agricultural Institute (India);

University of Southern California and the University of Tehran
(Iran);

New York University and the University of Ankara (Turkey);

University of California and the University of Indonesia;

University of Minnesota and the National University of Seoul
(Korea);

University of Texas and the Chulalongkorn University (Thailand).

Probably the American universities need to acquire experience in
order to co-operate as effectively as possible. More of the engineers and
agricultural experts sent out need to have better knowledge of the language of the countries to which they are going—and a better appreciation of the economic and social significance of some of the measures
they recommend. Nevertheless, the inter-university exchange program
has tremendous possibilities.

The United Nations Program

The United Nations also has developed a program of technical exchange, which is in many respects similar to that of the United States.
For the United Nations the co-ordinating agency, which answers to
UNESCO, is called the Technical Assistance Board. Total pledges for
the 1956 technical exchange program were about $28.9 million, of which
$10 thousand is from Afghanistan, $15.5 million from the United States,
$2 thousand from the Vatican, $125 thousand from the Ukrainian S.S.R.,
$1 million from the U.S.S.R., and $2 million from the United Kingdom,
not to forget $238 thousand from the German Federal Republic and
$1.4 million from France.[11] Seventy-three nations participate in support
of the program, which is making a genuine effort to emphasize international participation, even though at present most of the financing
is provided by the United States Government.

The exchange program is as diverse, but not as extensive, as that
of the United States. Not all the technicians have been Americans.
The program has involved sending a Haitian coffee specialist to

[11] United Nations, Technical Assistance Committee, *Eighth Report of the Technical Assistance Board* (New York, 1956).

Ethiopia, sending a Bolivian to help with the control of parasitic diseases in the Philippines, and sending an expert from Formosa to help introduce into Haiti the Asiatic practice of the pond culture of fish.

An additional facet of the United Nations program has been the sponsorship of co-operative regional arrangements. One such is a Central American center of technological research to be established in Guatemala. The share in the cost to be carried by the United Nations is $75,000 the first year, to decline to nothing the fifth year. Thenceforth, all of the cost will be carried by Guatemala, Honduras, El Salvador, Nicaragua, and Costa Rica.

Private Programs

Private manufacturing companies operating in the underdeveloped countries share a considerable amount of technical knowledge—some of it intentionally, some of it because they cannot help themselves. In the issue of July 5, 1955, the *New York Times* devoted a section to case studies of situations where United States corporations have contributed technical knowledge to the countries in which they operate. The individual examples cited (the activities of American and Foreign Power in Brazil or of Hershey in Cuba) do not sound epoch-making. But the cumulative impact of this sort of thing, in the end, may well be considerable.

Until fairly recently, foreign investments (aside from bond issues which are irrelevant for present purposes) were chiefly in mining, transportation, and public utilities, and to only a minor extent in manufacturing. But increasingly of recent years foreign direct investments have been in manufacturing plants. The workers cannot help acquiring a store of knowledge on manufacturing processes and plant management which will facilitate the establishment of domestically owned manufacturing plants.

Evaluation

Both the United States government and the United Nations now have active programs of technical assistance and send teams of technicians to the underdeveloped areas. Such aid has already been extended to many countries from Liberia to India in connection with many types of work ranging from agriculture to manufacturing. The range of activity has been great. But in terms of the desirable volume, the work is just beginning.

A characteristic of the program is that initiative with regard to the nature of projects needing technical aid comes from the country—from the culture—to be aided. The expense of such aid is generally divided between the United States government or the United Nations and the country receiving the aid in some "agreed-on" proportion, which might be fifty-fifty but can vary anywhere from free aid to 100 per cent payment of the technicians by the receiving country.

This program is one of the finest things going on, or that has ever gone on, in the history of the human race.

To that sort of businessman mentality which worries, in connection with this sort of development, about the loss of markets, it may be said that trade follows the technician more than it ever followed the flag or the investor. The technician will want to introduce the equipment he is used to. And once it is introduced, it calls for more (including the inevitable repair parts) of the same type from the same country.

In evaluating the program of technical exchange, a more important point should be made. It will be most constructive in the long run to look on these programs as involving essentially the exchange of technical knowledge among all nations. No good purpose will be served by emphasizing the idea that the heart of the process is the generous sharing by the United States of its store of technical knowledge in a one-way process leading out from this country. For one thing, this is inaccurate. A not inconsiderable part of the program already involves the sharing of the knowledge that one underdeveloped country has with another. And many of the technicians in the United Nations Program are persons from one underdeveloped country going to another.

But even so far as the United States itself is concerned, the program should not be a one-way street. Many of the so-called underdeveloped countries are possessed of quantities of technical knowledge which the United States could use to advantage. Texas oilmen recently discovered that the Soviet industry had a drilling method superior to the system in use in the United States, which has called for rotation of the whole drill stem even if it is four miles long. The Soviet method involves rotating merely the end of the drill stem.

The best way to look at the whole process is as one gigantic information-sharing operation that will benefit everybody.

SECULAR TERMS OF TRADE

A considerable amount of technical knowledge is now being exchanged internationally; and economic development has been going on at varying rates of speed in different countries. What does this process mean in terms of the division of the gain from the development process as between the different countries? There was some discussion of this point in Chapter 5. There it was alleged that the statistical evidence is inconclusive as to whether either the unit terms or the gross barter terms of trade show a regular pattern of movement which is identifiably more favorable to developed or underdeveloped countries.

The chief possible qualification to this would seem to derive from the improvement in the quality of manufactured goods which cannot be allowed for in the statistical data. If manufactured goods are of higher quality than formerly and if primary products (such as a pound of copper or a bushel of wheat) are not of higher quality than they were a hundred years ago, it might be argued that there has been improvement in the terms of trade of the raw commodity producing countries which the statistics do not show.

By and large, the terms of trade concepts represent an effort to describe who is getting a little more value and who is getting a little less value (in exchange for what he is giving up). But what is value? The various terms of trade concepts are limited, in terms of what they reveal, by the manner of their composition. It will be recalled that the double factoral terms of trade concept, which was also discussed in Chapter 5, represented an effort to take productivity changes into account. But if United States productivity increases, should that properly be looked on as anything that *should* be shared in a really fair evolution of the terms of trade?

If the statistical data properly took all the variables into account, what would determine the division of the gain from increased productivity as between the developed and the less developed countries? It is easy to say that it would depend on the patterns of demand and supply elasticities; but what do they depend on?

Several meaningful observations may be made. (1) If the benefit of growth is distributed as lower prices on the goods produced, the gain will be spread fairly indifferently over the world, since all nations can buy at the lower prices. (2) If the benefit is distributed in the form of higher real wages, it will tend to stay at home since the higher wages will only be paid to domestic workers; also the development process of the home country will be spurred because of the tendency of workers to spend most of the income and thus create a high domestic "multiplier." (3) If the benefit goes chiefly to higher profits and rent, it will also tend to stay at home if the enterprisers and the landowners are domestic citizens; but further growth will be somewhat inhibited because of the lower multiplier consequent on the tendency of the wealthy to save a large proportion of their income.[12]

Prebisch and Singer have expressed the view that the gain from increased productivity in the industrialized countries has chiefly been kept at home in the form of higher incomes. Without necessarily passing a moral judgment on the propriety of this, Prebisch is explicit that

[12] See the discussion of the double factoral terms of trade in Chapter 5.

what the underdeveloped countries need to do about it is to industrialize themselves. He does not place much reliance on gains from increased productivity in agriculture because of a belief that the institutional organization of the market is such that those gains will be spread to the whole world in the form of lowered prices.[13]

The statistics are simply not available to verify all of these relations. But the predilection of manufacturers for export dumping suggests one factor casting doubt on whether the international aspect of the relations is exactly as Prebisch and Singer suggest. Even if the situation is just as Prebisch describes, the underdeveloped countries need to beware of an additional element in the situation. The division of the gains of development among the classes within a country is perhaps a more important way of viewing the problem than the international division. There is now in the underdeveloped countries a marked tendency for the chief gain from the development process to go to profits and rent.[14] A reasonably large sharing with the working class of the gains from development is also a factor to be considered—on top of everything else, they are the group which will spend the money to make additional effective demand to keep the process of development going.

A simple cleavage that is established, however, is the rising level of living in the United States (and to a lesser extent in western Europe) relative to the rest of the world. This has been a long-run trend covering a hundred-and-fifty years. But it has yet to be established that there is a clear-cut relation between the development of this cleavage and any change in the terms of trade, or that there is a clear-cut connection between this development and the identification of which type of country or industry is hit harder by depressions.

Don Humphrey alleges, with regard to the business-cycle relationships, that the only one which is really clear-cut is the one between everybody's domestic prices and everybody's export prices. International prices (whether they are manufactured goods prices or raw commodity prices) fluctuate more violently than the domestic, internal prices of the same manufactured goods and raw commodities.[15]

The course of the price relationships between these two types of commodities, even if we knew what it has been, is a long way from being

[13] Other economists have developed a line of argument indicating that the developed countries are suffering or will suffer. Keynes, Colin Clark, and W. Arthur Lewis have developed such arguments. Chiefly they lean on the proposition of diminishing returns in agriculture which will, it is alleged, ultimately force agricultural prices up relative to manufactured goods prices. Keynes, in fact, alleged before World War I that the statistical data for the decade 1900–1910 showed that this process was already going on. (Joel W. Sailors, *Secular Terms of Trade: Theory and Measurement* [Unpublished Ph.D. dissertation, Department of Economics, University of Texas, 1956], pp. 76–142).

[14] See Chapter 19.

[15] Humphrey, *American Imports*, p. 45.

the whole story. There is an important quantitative element besides. The quantity of manufactured goods production has been rising relative to the quantity of raw commodity production since the Industrial Revolution. In addition, the demand for manufactured goods has been rising.[16] The relative importance of manufactured goods has been rising. What could these changes have been expected to do to the prices of manufactured goods? The increased supplies should have resulted in lower prices; the increased demand should have resulted in higher prices. Whether prices actually rise or fall depends on the relationship between the rate of growth of manufactured goods production and the rate of growth of demand for manufactured goods (both foreign and domestic), and upon the institutional organization of the merchandising process. Observation of the merchandising process suggests that producers more effectively exploit the consumers in their own country than the consumers abroad. Recall the predilections for dumping abroad! This would suggest that the underdeveloped countries are probably on weak ground in alleging a long-run worsening in their unit terms of trade as the heart of their difficulty.[17]

I feel some misgiving, in connection with the foregoing, to observe that it corresponds with the Marxist position, one feature of which is the argument that the capitalist countries are desperately searching for foreign markets, and will cut prices and do all manner of evil things to get them. But it may help the Latin American Marxist, who is inclined to attribute all kinds of evil to the United States, to recall that the United States cannot at the same time be guilty of exploiting Latin America by (a) causing a worsening of her unit terms of trade, and (b) distress selling of goods at lower and lower prices in the Latin American market.

All of this indicates, if it indicates anything, that the fact of development per se does not show which way the price relationships between the developed and the underdeveloped countries must go.

Also relevant, in an effort to evaluate the division of the gain from an evolving technological development, is an argument presented by Veblen. Veblen pointed out that there is a tendency for the country which experienced the earliest growth ultimately to fall behind technologically.[18] Veblen said with regard to the relative industrial backwardness of England: "All this does not mean that the British have sinned against the canons of technology. It is only that they are paying the penalty for hav-

[16] In fact, the quantitative changes may so completely overshadow the long-run terms of trade changes as to make rather trivial the current argument—which is of a somewhat moralistic nature—as to what is happening to the terms of trade.

[17] They may be on stronger ground in alleging that they are victimized by institutional forces that subject them to very violent price changes between the peak and the trough of the business cycle.

[18] Thorstein Veblen, *Imperial Germany and the Industrial Revolution* (New York: Macmillan, 1915), p. 128.

ing been thrown into the lead and so having shown the way." The British built their factories first and had a tendency to continue using them even after the knowledge was acquired which would permit building them better. This line of thinking offers encouragement as to the position of the underdeveloped countries twenty years hence—if they will only go in for advanced technology instead of second-hand textile equipment.

At all events, as the complex of forces works itself out over a long period of time, it is not simple to identify the person or country that is profiting most. Some of the most ostentatious living in the world is in the underdeveloped countries—recall the maharajah of Hyderabad.

A distinction needs to be made between absolute and relative gain. (Relative gain is less important than absolute gain and the preceding comments are chiefly pertinent to relative gain.) A developed country may share its technical knowledge; and some previously underdeveloped area may profit tremendously and gain ground relatively in terms of degree of industrialization and level of living. It may then be in a position to make a certain contribution to further technical advance—a contribution which will contribute to some further advance in the country that was industrialized first. In consequence, the latter may well experience some absolute gain itself, even though the underdeveloped countries have gained relatively. Amazingly, there seem to be some people so selfish that they are willing themselves to forego absolute gain in order to prevent relative gain by others. Whether people who think in such terms are capable of maintaining even their relative advantage was a point that was speculated on in Chapter 9.

CONCLUSION

A strong case for the modified free trade position can be built around the "catalytic effect of interchange" in stimulating intellectual and productive activity. Breaking away from monocultures and importing and exporting a wider range of commodities can, so far as any one nation is concerned, destroy many of the rigidities which have been a barrier to development. And the greater exchange of knowledge and experience which is part of the process will contribute greatly to a better life for all people.

Chapter 34

RESOURCES AND PRIORITIES

☙ ☙ ☙

The planning of development in terms of the priorities to be given to the different projects involves relating the technical knowledge available to the resources available, and relating these in turn to the likely demand situation.

Development can probably make an important contribution faster if a limited number of major areas are selected for development. Then, these areas and related industries should be concentrated on.

Attempts at simultaneous development along many major lines will make for a slow and wasteful process.

Since it is not possible to be 100 per cent clairvoyant about the future, some errors in assigning priorities will be made.

But a few errors in assigning priorities are preferable to such extreme caution that large quantities of resources remain idle—waiting on the absolute certainty that never comes.

Much more time and attention needs to be devoted to the problem of the technical preparation of specialists in the area of development planning.

☙ ☙ ☙

IN PLANNING economic development the technological and institutional factors are controlling, within rather broad limits, as to what may be done. But the immediate concern of the planners is to make estimates on four matters: (1) the total amount of feasible production, (2) the division of that production between consumer goods and capital goods, (3) the division between private and governmental, and (4) the selection of the particular industries to be encouraged. The problems of determining the amount of feasible production and the division of that production between consumer goods and capital goods and between private and governmental are discussed in Chapters 31 and 35.

The present problem is the selection of the particular industries to be encouraged. This is a problem in which resource availability plays a key role.

RESOURCES

Resources are the things with which man, conditioned by his institutional attitudes and technical knowledge, has to work in his effort to effect the rate of growth of that combination of level of living and freedom of action and security which he considers most desirable.

The identity of the resources which he will actually use is determined by the state of the technical knowledge. Many elements in the earth might become useful and, as we learn more, will become useful. But given such knowledge as we have at any given time, some of the earth is neutral stuff and some of it is valuable resource.

Knowledge of the availability of various resources is of the essence in identifying the industries whose development should be given priority in different countries at any given time. General coverage of the availability of resources and how they may be used is to be found in the classic work of Erich W. Zimmermann, *World Resources and Industries;* it is also to be found in Woytinsky and Woytinsky; in the *Commodity Yearbook,* and in good economic geographies.[1]

The planning of development priorities in any one country, of course, must involve comprehensive study of that particular nation's resources in the light of the general world pattern of resource availability. Much relevant information has been assembled by study groups sent out by the International Bank for Reconstruction and Development. Fairly comprehensive reports have already been prepared on many countries, including Colombia, Mexico, Cuba, and Turkey. But the surface has hardly been scratched, and such study must be continuing.

PRIORITIES

To a marked extent, new technical progress is continually changing neutral stuff into resources. In addition, from time to time new deposits of resources are discovered. Either of these two developments may completely change the resource picture of a country. To say this is to emphasize that resource availability is a dynamic concept—a point that was mentioned above. Professor Zimmermann is fond of pointing out that there has been a tendency among economic geographers to describe known resource deposits and then construct a definitive explanation as to

[1] Erich W. Zimmermann, *World Resources and Industries* (Revised edition; New York: Harper, 1951); W. S. Woytinsky and E. S. Woytinsky, *World Population and Production—Trends and Outlook* (New York: Twentieth Century Fund, 1953); *Commodity Yearbook* [annual] (New York: Commodity Research Bureau [various years]); United Nations, Department of Economic and Social Affairs, *Processes and Problems of Industrialization in Under-Developed Countries,* pp. 43–7.

what future development is possible on the basis of these known deposits. This is an essentially static approach which, in the past, has led to saying such things as that Russia does not have the resource base to be a great power.

Undoubtedly, present knowledge of known resources is important. But, for planning purposes, the approach should *not* be: Our future planning is controlled by the availability of this known stock of resources. And planning should not involve the drawing up of a long-run inflexible plan based on present knowledge of resources. Rigid long-run planning based on the knowledge of the past tends to make growth in the underdeveloped countries a mirror image of what it has been in the developed countries. Another approach is required if the underdeveloped countries are to be something more than swimmers against the current, never quite reaching their goal, and never quite catching up with the already industrialized countries. The heart of the planning needs to be the concept that the plan itself must be capable of continual adjustment to take account of new discoveries of deposits or of new technical progress which has turned what was neutral stuff into valuable resources.

Planners in the underdeveloped countries should make a fetish of taking only the qualitative best of the technology of the developed countries, and of establishing only the most advanced of industries. The importation of second-hand textile machinery and old railroad rolling stock would be a contrary case in point.

The foregoing comments suggest a general approach that the underdeveloped countries might follow in planning their development and in determining priorities. I make the prescription with some misgivings, but it is a viewpoint that merits consideration. There have been two conflicting views about the orientation of the development pattern as between emphasis on steel and on consumer goods. One runs to the effect that the steel industry is the basis of economic power in the United States and western Europe. And if the Latin American countries are ever going to catch up, they have to develop large steel industries. The other proposition is that expansion in agriculture and in the manufacture of consumer goods should have the highest priority because level of living is currently so desperately low.

But a third approach may provide a better basis around which to orient thinking in these matters. It would call for emphasis at one extreme on the significant *new* industries in connection with which the underdeveloped countries have a reasonable resource endowment and at the other extreme on relatively inexpensive improvements in agriculture. Instead of emphasizing steel plants, the Latin American countries should be emphasizing atomic power and aluminum and magnesium manufacture.

In the various countries which have emphasized the development of steel plants—Mexico, Colombia, Chile, Brazil, Argentina, and now Venezuela—there has been a real problem in terms of the adequacy of coal reserves. And Argentina does not have adequate iron, either. But several of the Latin American countries have adequate supplies of both bauxite and water power. The proposition suggested here is that emphasis would be better placed on aluminum than on steel production.[2]

Atomic power production for peaceful purposes offers even more important prospects—especially in a region short of coal. President Eisenhower's program for sharing such knowledge of atomic energy as may be used for peaceful purposes offers the prospect of making available the technical knowledge that is needed initially. At this stage in the knowledge of the geography of reserves of fissionable material, all that can be said is that Latin America is as likely to have adequate reserves as any other region. Latin America will have made a long stride toward catching up with the United States if she develops an adequate atomic power industry with rapidity. This is a stride which skips a lot of accumulation of capital equipment per se. It accelerates growth in Latin America relative to the United States in a significant sense that is not allowed for in general propositions that measure growth in terms of quantity of capital equipment alone—without regard to how efficient it is.

W. Arthur Lewis has observed (in a view somewhat similar to that taken by Veblen, which was discussed in the preceding chapter):[3]

> More plausible is the argument that the older country loses by its specialization; in 1850 and onwards it develops its facilities (banking, marketing, training, transport, engineering, etc.) to supply what is wanted in 1850; then it gets into a rut, or to use a finer phrase, it gets carried along by the momentum of its endeavors in the 1850's, and fails to adjust to the changing demands of the 1880's. So when new industries come along they go to newer countries not yet so heavily committed elsewhere. This rut may show itself also in loss of technological leadership; the best brains are engaged in solving the problems of the old industries. Meanwhile, the brains in the new countries not merely catch up with or copy the old country in the old industries, but also forge ahead in the new industries, and wrest technological leadership from the old country in the trades which are now expanding.

The underdeveloped countries, to take advantage of such possibilities,

[2] Which does not mean that some steel mills in Latin America are not highly desirable and appropriate, especially in Venezuela and Brazil.

[3] Lewis, *The Theory of Economic Growth*, p. 346. Reprinted by permission of George Allen & Unwin and of Richard D. Irwin.

need to emphasize the new industries—atomic power and the light metals—rather than steel and coal.

It is frequently pointed out, and quite properly, that one of the chief resources of the underdeveloped countries is a large reservoir of under-employed labor—chiefly unskilled labor. It is concluded that planners should therefore emphasize labor-intensive industries. Planners in under-developed country should, of course, still give attention to agriculture and to the fairly inexpensive capital improvements and simple tools which may make agriculture much more productive. Technical ex-change rather than expensive investment is of the essence in this area. And continuing development in the manufacture of consumer goods will certainly make an important contribution to raising the level of living. The improvement of marketing procedures in the large cities could well have a high priority also, especially as it would help in cutting the inci-dence of disease. Bogota is eliminating the old-style, unsanitary public markets which have been such a health blight and tourist attraction. All this is important and should be combined with a special emphasis on the use of new resources, newly discovered resources, and new tech-niques.

Another sort of priority based on function should also be taken into account. An integrated production pattern can contribute more, with more speed, to raising levels of living than can a production pattern which involves the promotion of miscellaneous industries without re-gard to the connection between the industries. In part, this is the prob-lem of complementary industries. Perhaps initially there would be an objective basis for saying that a meat-canning industry should have a high priority. Canning will preserve the meat better as it is merchandised in the unrefrigerated markets which have been so typical of underdevel-oped countries. But if a decision has already been made to spend a lot of money on refrigeration facilities, some of the premium is removed from meat canning. Or, to use a somewhat different sort of example, a de-cision to emphasize aluminum manufacture would call for emphasis on dam building and power production. Moreover, if dam building and power production are emphasized, aluminum production is then a fea-sible thing—where it was not before.

Development, to be most effective, calls for co-ordination among proj-ects. It most definitely does not call for a confusion of unrelated manu-facturing projects. The country wishing to develop should not try to have enterprises of all kinds. Growth will be faster and productivity will rise faster if development occurs as a pattern and industries complement each other.

Meade has called this phenomenon the "economies of conglomera-tion":[4] "There may be important economies to be derived from the fact

[4] Meade, *Trade and Welfare*, p. 258.

that a large number of firms in any one industry, and, indeed, a large number of industries, are all 'conglomerated' close together in the same locality."

In this setting, transportation and power loom large as high priority activities. Development in productivity—regardless of the special line of production emphasized—calls for improvement in the distribution processes by which the increased supplies of goods get from factory or farm to consumer. Therefore, highway, railroad, and air transport quite properly have a high priority in most development plans. An example would be the building of trans-South America transportation facilities from Santos in Brazil across Bolivia by way of Santa Cruz and down to the Pacific in northern Chile. The belt of territory across South America served by this railway will undoubtedly enjoy a phenomenal development in the next few years—development of "complementary" industries. In petroleum Latin America has a rich source of power. Dam building and the suggested atomic development are other sources.

In fact, a very considerable development in what has been called "social capital" might well precede extensive development in manufacturing. Transportation and power, which were mentioned above, along with school buildings and improved housing, can make a tremendous contribution to development and at a very early stage in the process. Because of the low, or non-existent, profit to be made on such activities, the original expense must almost certainly be carried by the government. Much development along these lines must go on as a preliminary to private-enterprise investment in profitable lines of manufacturing.

The espousal of development patterns and specialization is, however, a long way from the endorsement of monocultures.[5]

Specialization can be pushed so far in limited areas that the resulting dependence on one product results in very great vulnerability to business cycle fluctuations. Drastic fluctuations in the price of sugar have had a devastating impact on the Cuban economy at different times. The continuance of maximum total production in the world over long periods of time and at *steadily* expanding rates calls for the striking of a reasonable balance between the advantages of geographical specialization and the disadvantages of monocultures. To say this is to emphasize that our listing of the goals of economic activity includes maximum security as well as high levels of living and maximum freedom of action.

But the advantages of large-scale production do make considerable specialization desirable. As Adam Smith said, the degree to which di-

[5] Strictly speaking, a monoculture would be an economy which produced only one product. Actually the term is applied to countries in which the production of one product represents a substantial proportion of total production or the export of one product a substantial portion of total exports. Thus, in table 8, the various countries listed could well be considered monocultures because such a large percentage of total exports is one commodity, or two very similar commodities.

vision of labor can be pushed is limited by the extent of the market. Little countries can choose to do all things if they wish; but they cannot choose to do all things well. It is not desirable, and it is not going to be desirable in the ascertainable future, for all countries to produce everything, as long as there are so many countries.

It is oversimplified to speak of eight or ten large basic industries such as steel, chemicals, automobiles, and a few more, and state that a country is obviously large enough to provide a market for an efficient mill in each of those lines. No one of these industries is homogeneous. There are not only wool, cotton, and synthetic textile industries, but breaking these industries down yet further, there are for example in woolens: hard weaves and loose weaves, suits and blankets. One area or country may well specialize in woolens of one type and not produce other types at all.

To illustrate what is involved with the Swiss watch industry: That industry is not located in Switzerland because of a permanent inability to produce good watches in other places, and it is not located there because of superior Swiss endowment in the appropriate raw materials. Watches are light enough so that the raw materials could be shipped anywhere in the world without increasing the cost perceptibly. But watchmaking is a highly skilled industry, and there is a good deal to be said for having the labor supply concentrated so that the skills can be developed and exchanged. If this labor supply were spread evenly over the surface of the globe with production also spread evenly over the surface of the globe, to improve techniques might be something of a problem, with ten workers here and twenty there. A decade or two later, the quality of the product certainly would not have improved as much as would be possible in a situation which facilitated more effective interchange, where the workers complement each other. Where certain industries are concentrated in major centers, the problems of information exchange can surely be dealt with on a far more intelligent basis. The improvement of skills and techniques will go ahead much faster, more "cross fertilization" being possible.

TECHNIQUES

Models

What specific techniques are actually available to planners for assigning priorities to one project by comparison with another? Probably there is still no substitute for thoughtful mulling over of all the factual material available. However, several analytical methods are available which provide frameworks into which much of the data may be fitted.

Leontief's input-output analysis and linear programing give a range of information on an industry-by-industry basis which provides clues as to the priorities which might well be assigned to different industries. But the assumption of constant relations among the quantities of resources and labor going into the production of specific commodities (an assumption which is involved in linear programing) hardly permits this method of analysis, at least as yet, to provide useful clues to completely new directions of production.[6]

Formulas have been prepared, based on judgments as to the desirability of using domestic rather than imported raw materials, on an appraisal of value added in the manufacturing process, on capital-output ratios, on concentration vs. decentralization in location, on scale of plant, on a comparison of the availability of capital with the availability of labor—and other considerations. When the data is assembled, the use of the proper equation is supposed to identify which industry should be favored. Without doubt model processes such as these provide useful clues as to project priorities. But they are still just clues and indications. The models are not yet comprehensive enough to justify accepting the answers they give without further evaluation of more general and intangible factors.

Whatever the model, however, intelligent planning of the priorities to be assigned to projects is markedly dependent on price comparability. And the great disservice of the existing complicated patterns of foreign trade controls is precisely their destruction of price comparability. The trouble is not that there are controls. The trouble is that the controls are unnecessarily complex, so complex that their consequences cannot be determined.

The Planning Profession

Engineers are probably the best qualified professional group to make decisions with regard to industry priorities. However, there is probably place here for a new profession which would involve a liberal mixture of engineering and social-science training. This is the profession of development planning—which is now being performed over the world by a conglomeration of economists, businessmen, lawyers, and engineers, who by and large do not have a satisfactory general perspective as to what they are doing.

It is largely an engineering decision to determine the quantities of the various resources, other than people, available under various possible conditions and to appraise the industrial techniques which may be used. It is the province of the businessman to judge price-cost patterns and demand conditions. But neither the engineer nor the businessman can make a meaningful decision without regard to the social setting in which all this is going on. For instance, in the case of demand if there is a conflict between what the people say they will pay, through the price mecha-

[6] See Chapter 31.

nism, and what the people operating through the democratic process say they can have, it is clear which decision should prevail—although not entirely certain which will.

The Planning Agencies

At the beginning of this book a presumption was made in favor of the decentralization of decision making. Some of the broad aspects of the priorities must undoubtedly be determined at a center. But if the development planners in the centralized position are reasonably intelligent and thorough about describing the nature of the over-all problem as they see it so that such knowledge is widely diffused and available, a good deal of the implementation, project by project, will take care of itself.

The positive role of an international agency in planning should probably be more or less limited to supervision of the financial mechanism to make certain that the financing is available to permit full use of resources. But it may also provide technicians and technical knowledge; and it may suggest plans on request by the individual nations. The individual nation needs to do some over-all planning; it needs to implement certain major basic developments itself; and it needs to supervise a system of qualitative credit control calculated to aid private enterprise in expanding in the most desirable directions. Decisions on the relative roles of government and private enterprise and of different sizes of private enterprise should not be made on a dogmatic and final basis at the start of the development process. They are essentially the types of decisions which will need to be continually reappraised as the process goes on.

CONCLUSION

All this discussion of planning and priorities is at first glance rather indefinite. But, on second glance, some useful concepts may emerge. In planning development, it is roughly known that various resources (redundant labor in subsistence agriculture, iron ore in Venezuela, irrigable land, and rivers that can be dammed) are available at a given time. It is agreed that all resources should be used. The financing is made to conform to the resources. The problem is to assign an order of priority to what is probably a relatively small number of feasible large-scale projects at the moment. The range of possibility is also limited by the prerequisite that patterns of development be followed. It does not matter too much if the project that should have been ranked number four gets ranked number two (or if it does matter, the engineer responsible for the miscue had better be demoted); and it does not matter too much if a lot of small-scale projects are experimented with and succeed or fail under the aegis of private initiative; therefore, insistence on precisely accurate decision making is not necessary. It is not only unnecessary, it would be futile to insist on accurate planning beforehand. Nothing would ever be done—for lack of the unattainable assurance of success.

This chapter has, obviously, done nothing more than skim the surface of the broad question as to which companies or projects can and should come into being. And it has only suggested the nature of the decision-making precesses that may be involved.

Chapter 35

THE ROLE OF CAPITAL

If the development process is well planned, the limitation on the speed with which it goes on will be the physical limitation of technical knowledge and resources and not the financial limitation of capital funds.

Capital equipment and technical knowledge obtained from abroad can make a major contribution to the process; but it is not necessary, in order for them to make this contribution, that they be financed by foreign investment.

For the most part, it will be more desirable to pay for the capital equipment imports with exports.

IN THE discussion of growth, capital plays a special role. The accumulation of capital goods and the contribution of capital goods to the expansion of production are primarily technological problems. The behavior of capital funds in influencing the accumulation of capital goods is chiefly an institutional problem.

It may well be that the institutional arrangements which now exist in the world's capital markets and which control the availability of capital funds operate in a certain pattern. And this pattern of behavior needs to be allowed for in planning the availability of capital funds to finance the creation of capital equipment.

But it still remains the capital equipment which is important. If the institutional organization of the capital-funds market is adequate, there is no basic reason why the availability of capital funds should be a limiting factor in growth.

RATE OF ACCUMULATION

Decision Making

Rate of growth involves a decision by society as to how much effort it desires to put into capital equipment in relation to the effort it desires to put into consumer goods production. (It also involves a decision between productive activity and freedom of action and security.) These are the over-all decisions as to total production and total capital accumulation which are part of the decision-making process. Another sort of decision, which was discussed in the preceding chapter, is the decision as to priorities among the different industries.[1]

What is involved is not exactly the idea that rate of growth should be maximized in terms of any tangible meaning of the word maximization. Society as a whole is worrying about how to obtain the maximum well-being (in terms of level of living, freedom of action, and security), but the meaning of *maximization of the combination* can only be determined by a subjective decision expressed through the democratic voting process.

But is this maximization for today, tomorrow, or next year? This is the old problem of how much to discount the future—which has been expressed in many ways. More consumer goods may be available this year if the rate of growth in capital goods accumulation is a little less. More consumer goods may be available next year if the rate of growth in capital goods accumulation is a little more.

It seems to me that about all that can really be concluded on this point is that this decision for this year will be made this year. More aptly phrased, the decision as to the division of effort between capital goods and consumer goods production, which is basic in determining rate of growth, is a decision which is made currently. How that division will be made in connection with the work of this instant is made at this instant. It is made by people who have some stake in the future and some knowledge of the past. In fact, the latitude allowable in the decision making is limited by the decisions of the past and the conditions they have created. But so far as the men of the future are concerned, they are simply not there to speak for themselves.

Man at the moment makes the decision as to the distribution of effort between consumer goods production and capital goods production. There is no way to construct a democratic process that will let the future vote. But at least the decision as to this allocation of effort between leisure time and "work," and between consumer goods and capital goods, should be democratically made.

The Need for Capital

It has become commonplace to analyze the role of capital in the development process in terms of the capital/output ratio. This is substantially the capital coefficient term (C) in the Harrod formula of Chapter 31. It used to be assumed by economists that the process of economic growth would involve a rise in the quantity of capital relative to output, or that

[1] Yet another is the decision as to whether certain activity shall be engaged in by the government or by private enterprise.

at the least the ratio should be assumed to be a constant. Recent studies by the National Bureau of Economic Research, however, present the strong likelihood that the ratio of capital to output may be falling in the highly developed countries.

Simon Kuznets believes that the ratios of capital to output for various countries range from about 3 to 1 to 7 to 1. In the young, rapidly growing countries, such as the United States, Canada, and Australia, he believes the ratio to be the lower one, 3 to 1. Kuznets also says that the ratio rose during the late nineteenth century and until World War I for the developed countries such as the United States, Great Britain, and France. He thinks that the ratio for the United States rose from 2.8 to 1 in 1879 to 3.8 to 1 in 1919; for Great Britain, from 4.6 to 1 in 1865 to about 6.2 to 1 in 1895. Apparently the industrial development of the late nineteenth century was capital intensive. But, and this is the most important point, the rise stopped some time during the first two decades of this century. The thought that the low-standard-of-living countries may have quite high capital-to-output ratios is also quite a novel idea. It seems that, although such countries do not have much capital, what they have is poor and inefficient and the output is correspondingly low.[2]

Gross capital formation figures may be quite high, as evidenced by Table 48, and may be a substantial proportion of national income as well. But effective addition to genuine industrial plant and equipment may still be quite small. Much government expenditure does not increase industrial plant and equipment (especially in the United States today). Housing also is a major element in gross capital formation that does not increase productive capacity. Kuznets has estimated that for the United States the proportion of national product going to increase the stock of industrial plant and equipment may be no more than 5 to 7 per cent.[3]

How has the tremendous production increase of recent years in the United States then been possible? In answering this question, Kuznets takes a position quite comparable to that of Veblen and Ayres:[4]

> Two answers to this puzzle, if it be a puzzle, may be suggested. First, technical progress consists not only of inventions and innovations that require heavy capital investments but also of a stream of relatively cheap changes and improvements whose cumulative effect is a drastic reduction in input of resources accompanied by increases in output. The major capital stock of an

[2] Robert Lekachman (ed.), *National Policy for Economic Welfare at Home and Abroad,* p. 38.

[3] Lekachman, *op. cit.,* p. 39. Kuznets also has estimated that, defined in this way, the capital/output ratio may be only 1:1. He qualifies these arguments with the thought that a lot of true capital is hidden in consumer goods.

[4] Lekachman, *op. cit.,* p. 39–40. Quoted with the kind permission of the Trustees of Columbia University in the City of New York.

TABLE 48

GROSS DOMESTIC PRODUCT AND CAPITAL FORMATION,
SELECTED COUNTRIES, 1952

(IN MILLIONS OF NATIONAL CURRENCY)

		GROSS CAPITAL FORMATION	
COUNTRY AND CURRENCY UNIT	GROSS DOMESTIC PRODUCT	AMOUNT	PER CENT OF GDP
I. Developed Countries:			
Australia (pound)	3,853	1,581	41
France (franc)	13,412 (billion)	2,392 (billion)	18
Germany, West (deutschemark)	125,967	29,657	24
Japan (yen)	6,180 (billion)	2,387 (billion)	39
United Kingdom (pound)	15,376	2,060	13
United States (dollar)	346,500	130,100	38
II. Underdeveloped Countries:			
Brazil (cruzeiro)	306 (billion)	52 (billion)	17
Ceylon (rupee)	4,572	609	13
Chile (peso)	126,327	15,545	12
Colombia (peso)	6,124	1,163	19
Cuba (peso)	2,395	392	16
Guatemala (quetzal)	558	53	10
Israel (pound)	672	150	22
Mexico (peso)	43,299	5,937	14
Peru (sol)	20,866	5,550	27
Puerto Rico (dollar)	1,124	307	27
Southern Rhodesia (pound)	127	58	45

Source: United Nations, Department of Economic and Social Affairs, *Processes and Problems of Industrialization in Under-Developed Countries*, p. 16.

industrially advanced nation is not its physical equipment: it is the body of knowledge amassed from tested findings and discoveries of empirical science, and the capacity and training of its population to use this knowledge effectively. One can easily envisage a situation in which technological progress permits output to increase at a high rate without *any* additions to the stock of capital goods.

Second, if technological changes permit huge additions to output with only minor additions to reproducible physical capital, it may be that the essential investments are largely in human beings, the active agents in society, not in sticks, stones, and metal. Even if we disregard the social inventions that are necessary and consider only the purely material flows, the concept of capital used above is probably much too narrow for an analysis of economic growth.

. . . technological change may make it possible to produce much greater volumes of final product with the same or lesser

volumes of *all* resource input, or may minimize and reduce the
need for large stocks of physical capital. . . .

The proposition that most of the tremendous increase in goods production of recent years comes not so much from a great increase in capital as from an increase in output per unit of capital is increasingly commented upon.[5]

If there were some force tending to make this ratio a constant or making it desirable that the ratio should rise or fall, the ratio would be a
cause for some concern. Since this is not the case, the ratio merely provides significant information for analyzing the process that is going on.
But the ratio itself should be looked on merely as a creature of the evolving process.

The possibility of considerable production expansion on the basis
of relatively little investment is an encouraging thought and should tem-
per some of the rather discouraging appraisals of the growth problem
which have been made. For example, the United Nations has prepared
an estimate—see Table 49—of the financing needed if the underdeveloped countries of the world are to grow at a rate of 2 per cent a year in
terms of production expansion. This is a courageous and interesting statistical attempt. But it leaves a false impression of considerable importance. The implication is that the countries themselves can contribute
only $5.24 billion a year to their development and that, by subtraction,
foreigners must contribute $13.89 billion. The truth of the matter is that
the underdeveloped countries are going to grow by at least 2 per cent a
year, but the net contribution of the developed countries (after interest,
profits, and repatriation of principal are allowed for) is going to be nothing like $13.89 billion a year. And yet the figures are all probably accurate
enough—as rough estimates go. The difficulty, in a sense, is that the data
does not take into account the creation of funds by the banking system
(forced saving), and it also misses the impact of technological change
(especially of the capital-saving sort mentioned above), which may well
be extremely important in the next few years with the expansion in use
of atomic energy.

The contribution of foreign capital to the growth process should be
arrived at by a direct estimate of the amount of capital equipment to be
imported (which it would be inconvenient to purchase with proceeds
from exports). It is not justified to arrive at a figure for foreign contribution to the growth process by computing how much growth is desirable, how much domestic saving will volunteer, and then subtracting.

[5] Theodore W. Schultz, "Latin-American Economic Policy Lessons," *American
Economic Review, Papers and Proceedings,* XLVI (May, 1956), pp. 430–1; Valavanis-
Vail, "An Econometric Model . . . ," *loc. cit.,* p. 217; Evsey Domar, "Interre-
lation between Capital and Output in the American Economy," *International
Social Science Bulletin,* VI (no. 2, 1954), p. 243.

TABLE 49

CAPITAL REQUIRED BY UNDERDEVELOPED AREAS ANNUALLY IN INDUSTRY AND AGRICULTURE TO RAISE THEIR NATIONAL INCOME BY TWO PER CENT ANNUALLY

1	2	3	4	5	6	7	8	9
		EX-PECTED RATE OF AN-NUAL		NET DO-				
	POPU-	POPU-	NA-	MESTIC	NEEDED FOR			DEFICIT
	LATION	LATION	TIONAL	SAV-				(COL. 8
	(MID 1949) (MIL-	IN-CREASE 1950–	INCOME 1949	INGS 1949	Industri-alization	Agri-culture	TOTAL NEEDED	MINUS COL. 5
AREA	LIONS)	60 (%)			(Millions of U.S. Dollars)			
Latin America	158	2.25	24,000	1,990	1,580	960	2,540	550
Africa (excl. Egypt)	178	1.25	13,200	720	1,780	528	2,308	1,588
Middle East (incl. Egypt)	94	1.50	9,000	540	940	360	1,300	760
South Central Asia (a)	436	1.50	24,000	1,200	4,360	960	5,320	4,120
Far East (excl. Japan) (b)	661	0.75	26,400	790	6,610	1,056	7,666	6,876
Total	1,527	1.25	96,600	5,240	15,270	3,864	19,134	13,894

(a) Includes India, Pakistan, Ceylon, Maldive Islands, and the adjacent areas of Nepal and Bhutan.

(b) Includes Burma, China (including Formosa), Korea, Mongolia, Philippines, Thailand, British Borneo, Malaya, Hong Kong, Indonesia, Indo-China, Macao, Timor, Singapore, and New Guinea.

Source: United Nations, Department of Economic Affairs, *Measures for the Economic Development of Underdeveloped Countries*, p. 76.

Rate of Growth

Certain estimates have also been made as to the rate of growth in output in various countries:[6]

	REAL ANNUAL PER CAPITA RATE OF GROWTH	
Japan	3.26	
Germany	2.11	
Sweden	1.97	
Canada	1.59	
Australia	1.21	
New Zealand	0.99	
United States	1.9	(1869–1953)
Latin America	2.4	(1935–1953)

[6] United Nations, Department of Economic and Social Affairs, *Analyses and Projections of Economic Development, I. An Introduction to the Technique of*

These figures are not comparable as to the time period covered, although presumably a rather long period of years was involved in all of the examples except the Latin American.

Limiting Factors

(a) INTEREST RATE: It is sometimes alleged that the interest rate may function in a limiting capacity to check the rate of growth. In this connection it is frequently alleged that an attractively high interest rate is needed to bring out savings to finance development. A reply, based on Keynesian theory, to this argument would be that an attractively low interest rate is needed to make the enterprisers willing to borrow. What is the relative role of these influences? [7]

It is frequently pointed out that such limited saving as occurs privately in the underdeveloped countries goes into land (or land speculation or mortgages), or into foreign balances, or into inventory speculation—but not into goods production. Keynes attributed the lag in the rate of development in such countries to the high interest rate on mortgages. Keynes probably attributed the attraction to the wrong force. The attraction of mortgages and land ownership in underdeveloped countries is the institutionally determined result of the social status that goes with land ownership rather than the result of a relatively high interest rate on bonds. Be that as it may, the preference for mortgages and land ownership by comparison with investment in industry has probably existed; but it has been largely independent of the interest rate.

One reason domestic citizens shy away from bonds in underdeveloped countries is because of chronic inflation. A bond is not a very good way to hold money when price levels are rising. The attitude of the people in underdeveloped countries with regard to bond issues might be improved considerably if "constant purchasing power bonds" were issued.[8] Such bonds would provide for a correction in the face value of the bond to correspond with the change in some appropriate price level index. Because of the drastic inflation continuing at the present time in Latin America, only an idiot would buy bonds.

But this does not quite dispose of the question of the pure interest rate. What does it need to be? Perhaps the interest rate would have to be as low as is necessary to get the project implemented. But a government can always finance a project at a zero rate of interest if it chooses. Roy

Programming, p. 10; Moses Abramovitz, "Resource and Output Trends in the United States since 1870," *American Economic Review, Papers . . . ,* XLVI (May, 1956), p. 7.

[7] Keynesian theory indicates that, if a certain amount of investment has occurred, it will draw out an equivalent amount of saving. But that does not quite deal with the present problem, which is the acquisition of the funds necessary to get the development started.

[8] Javier Marquez, "Bonos de Poder Adquisitivo Constante," *Trimestre Economico,* XXI (January, 1954), pp. 6–43.

Harrod is a strong advocate of a zero rate of interest.[9] Meade thinks the tendency is toward such a zero rate of interest.

Perhaps it is impossible to answer the question as to interest rate directly except by saying that, if planning studies indicate the availability of real resources and competent labor to undertake a project which society thinks is desirable, lack of privately saved funds should not be permitted to act as a deterrent. The problem should be dealt with by either: (1) qualitative credit control, (2) government tax and spend, (3) government tax and subsidize, or (4) government tax and lend.

(*b*) WORTHWHILE PROJECTS: A more important limiting factor in this process is the availability of worthwhile projects. Wolf and Sufrin have observed this difficulty.[10] It is true, of course, that in an area where there has not been much development there do not exist many carefully thought-out projects. This should be obvious. And worthwhile, constructive projects are the crux of the matter. John Maynard Keynes wrote:[11]

> It has been usual to think of the accumulated wealth of the world as having been painfully built up out of that voluntary abstinence of individuals from the immediate enjoyment of consumption, which we call Thrift. But it should be obvious that mere abstinence is not enough by itself to build cities or drain fens.
>
> . . . It is enterprise which builds and improves the world's possessions. . . . If Enterprise is afoot, wealth accumulates whatever may be happening to Thrift; and if Enterprise is asleep, wealth decays whatever Thrift may be doing.

The commitment of resources to development must be conditioned by the availability of worthwhile projects in connection with which (a) the engineering planning has been competently done, (b) raw materials are reasonably available, (c) there is prospect of sufficient competent labor, (d) the management will be able and honest, (e) there is reasonable prospect of a market, (f) the appropriate auxiliary and associated industries are developing. The fancy projects and luxury housing which have received emphasis during the last ten years could well be postponed. Aldo Ferrer has estimated that 50 per cent of all the current investment in Latin America is unproductive.[12]

Capital funds are required only if, as, and when worthwhile projects

[9] Harrod, *Towards a Dynamic Economics,* pp. 129–59; Meade, *Trade and Welfare,* pp. 94–100.

[10] Charles Wolf, Jr., and Sidney C. Sufrin, *Capital Formation and Foreign Investment in Underdeveloped Areas* (Syracuse: Syracuse University Press, 1955), p. 56.

[11] John Maynard Keynes, *A Treatise on Money* (London: Macmillan, 1930), II, 148–9. Quoted with the kind permission of Macmillan & Co. and of Harcourt, Brace and Company.

[12] Aldo Ferrer, "Distribución del Ingreso y Desarrollo Económico," *Trimestre Económico,* XXI (April, 1954), p. 178.

are available. But when such projects are available, lack of funds should not impede their implementation. Unlimited credit creation will not do the job alone. Some of the most regrettable features of the Latin American development programs as they stand are the result of reliance on uncontrolled credit creation. If the process is largely uncontrolled (and graft and official favoritism are rampant), the bulk of the credit created and most of the command over the increasing store of goods slips into the hands of a relative few, and inequality in the distribution of income is increased. This seems to be what has been happening in many of the underdeveloped countries in recent years.

The chief role of the International Bank must be the providing of technical assistance and the making of economic studies which will be useful to the underdeveloped countries in planning their development. The calibre of these reports will no doubt improve as a group of competent technicians develops—a group which is really conversant with the problems involved in a nationwide survey of development potential.

(*c*) PROFIT RATE: Monetary profit making has nothing to do with the rate of growth, with this qualification: Certain institutionally determined (and consequently changeable) states of mind about profits will influence the way people behave. But, institutional preconceptions aside, we have no objective basis for saying that a society will develop in general (not one particular industry) because of the golden glow of 6 per cent when they would not develop because of the murky attraction of 3 per cent.

After all, 2.5 billion people have twenty-four hours a day on their hands. What are they going to do? Sleep and starve if the profit rate is 3 per cent instead of 6 per cent? They may sleep and starve because of an institutionally determined state of mind, as they tended to do in 1936 in the United States, for example, when businessmen chose to believe that the Roosevelt administration had made things so unsatisfactory that all that was left for them was hara-kiri. But it is not the profit rate at a time like this (and certainly not in real fact the difference between 6 per cent and 3 per cent, or between income taxes of 30 per cent and 60 per cent on the high income brackets) that really accounts for mass refusal to produce. The businessmen are reacting to a situation on the basis of certain institutionally determined preconceptions; the profit rate is largely incidental.

(*d*) DEMAND: It is probably true, however, that if potential promoters have the feeling that *demand* is increasing, they will be more likely to promote. In terms of the role of the private sector in this process, it may well be that too much concern has been paid to the role of saving and not enough to the building up of consumer purchasing power at the lower end of the scale.[13] The institutional arrangements that have pre-

[13] Aldo Ferrer, "Distribución del Ingreso y Desarrollo Económico," *Trimestre Económico*, XXI (April, 1954), 141–84.

vailed in the development programs of recent years seem to have increased inequality in income distribution. There might have been some justification for this if a considerable amount of constructive saving had resulted. But since it has not, maybe savings should come from other sources, and more emphasis should be placed on redistributing income downward.

INTERNATIONAL PROCESS

Let us turn now to the positive question of how international assistance to development should be handled. In this area there is bound to be a lot of trial and error.

Grants

Grants will become less and less important, as they should. They do not establish the right relation between giver and recipient. However, a certain amount of private charity should continue, and surely will continue, through such channels as the Red Cross and Care. When a catastrophe occurs, spontaneous aid from other countries is a fine thing. But government grants, if they occur at all, should be part of a carefully thought out world-wide tax system, in connection with which it might be desirable to hand grants-in-aid back to lower levels of government. Grants of the Marshall-plan United-States-controlled type cannot in the long run have a useful place in a well-organized world.

Role of Foreign Investment

As to international loans, the institutional arrangements orienting them must be changed. If matters take their course, it is a fair guess that the excess of net new lending (over principal repayment and interest), even for the United States, will be very small in the future. The usefulness of a lending process which does not provide anything to the debtors may well be questioned.

The reader may recall from Table 12 that the United States in 1955 was a net lender to the extent of only $22 million. Net income on United States foreign investments, after deducting the income foreigners received from their investments in this country, was $2 billion. The net income quite overshadowed the volume of net new investment. The United States export balance is currently financed by grants, not by loans. And there is every reason to believe that the net inflow of funds toward the United States will become larger in the next few years. To put the matter a bit differently, a little foreign investment can go a long way in giving the creditor a claim on income that eventually quite overshadows the original loan. The nineteenth century record of England, France, and Germany should be recalled—see Chapter 25. Underde-

veloped countries will do well to pay for capital goods with exports
where they can, instead of saddling themselves with interest charges.

The record of private foreign investment has not been so good in
facilitating manufacturing development in the underdeveloped countries,
anyway. Ragnar Nurkse cites the following figures as applicable to
United States foreign direct investment in 1948: [14]

	PERCENTAGES OF TOTAL	
INVESTMENT IN:	*Underdeveloped Countries*	*Developed Countries*
Extractive industries	59%	23%
Manufacturing and distribution	22	59
Public utilities	16	7
Miscellaneous	3	11
	100%	100%

He concludes:

> . . . private foreign investment in the past has not done much
> to spread industrial development to the backward agricultural
> countries, but has concentrated rather on primary production
> for export to the advanced countries. . . .
>
> The big markets in the past were in the industrial countries.
> Foreign capital in the underdeveloped areas found it profitable
> to work for these markets, rather than for the domestic con-
> sumers whose purchasing power in real terms was usually miser-
> ably low.

In a somewhat similar vein Sir Benegal Rama Rau has said: "Before
private capital can flow into an area certain basic economic developments must already have taken place." [15] If foreign investors wait until a
country is industrialized to invest in its industry, one may well wonder
whether they are going to make any great contribution to the industrialization program of the next few years. This is not to say that the contribution of private foreign direct investors to the industrialization of
the underdeveloped areas should be small—merely that it will be. The
importance of capital movements in the past has been much overemphasized. If a period of time of any length is taken into account, the
discrepancy between exports of goods and services and imports has been

[14] Ragnar Nurkse, *Problems . . .* , p. 84. The statistical data is from United
States, Bureau of Foreign and Domestic Commerce, *The Balance of International
Payments of the United States, 1946–1948* (Washington: Government Printing Office, 1950), pp. 162–5.
[15] International Bank for Reconstruction and Development, *Summary Proceedings—Eighth Annual Meeting of the Board of Governors* (Washington, 1953),
p. 35.

very small—even for the famous creditors of history during the periods of alleged net lending.

But imported machinery and capital equipment can make an important contribution in underdeveloped countries. These imports can be financed by either of two processes: (1) payment for capital imports with commodity exports, or (2) interest-free (or almost interest-free) lending and direct investments and qualitative credit control at the international level.

As to point one, it may be said that in such a case capital imports do not have to be paid for by lending. The raw commodity exports of the underdeveloped country can, should, and will pay for the bulk of the capital goods imports that can play a useful role.

One virtue of the direct investment is that profits which are not made pose no transfer problem. The profit rate is self-corrective in a sense that the interest rate is not. If the economy cannot pay it, it does not. Enterprise in a depression economy does not make profits. The same cannot be said for interest on portfolio investments, payable at set rates in foreign currencies. Probably it is not necessary or desirable for underdeveloped countries to count on private portfolio investments to play an important role. However, portfolio investments may surprise; and the long-run willingness of investors to take a very low rate of interest may surprise. Also, in the long-run the International Bank for Reconstruction and Development may prove willing to take something less than its current $4\frac{3}{4}$ per cent.

By way of precedent for the statement that underdeveloped countries may take long strides along the development road without incurring large foreign debts, the examples of Japan and the U.S.S.R. may be cited.[16]

Own Bootstraps

The main point is that each country should make the most effective contribution possible to its own development. In the international trade field, it is highly desirable that trade be reoriented so that exports and imports are as large as possible and equal, and so that a large proportion of the imports consists of capital goods and technical knowledge. But the guiding of imports into these desirable channels does not need to be and should not be through the extensive use of tariffs, quotas, licenses, exchange control, and multiple foreign-exchange rates—measures that have as a main effect the raising of domestic prices.

If qualitative credit control (and production subsidies and public works) are effectively used to place increased purchasing power in the hands of those actively participating in the industrial development proc-

[16] Simon Kuznets et al. (eds.), *Economic Growth: Brazil, India, Japan,* p. 183. The author of the article on Japan is Edwin P. Reubens.

ess, they will have the purchasing power to buy the foreign equipment they need. And they will be freer to exercise good judgment in making the purchases than is the case if they are hamstrung by a lot of trade controls. But the efficacy of this approach requires that the qualitative credit controls be operated in such a way that large blocks of funds do not go as profits to wealthy people who will use them largely to finance the import of consumer durables—such as television sets and Buick cars.

The financing of industrialization by promiscuous credit creation discourages (rather than encourages) the process. The sad case history of Spain between 1500 and 1800 is, perhaps, enough evidence of this.[17] The great wealth brought from the New World encouraged a price rise in Spain relative to the north of Europe. Spaniards preferred to buy from England and France rather than from Spanish producers because English and French prices were relatively lower. This relationship had a great deal to do with the encouragement of English industrialization relative to Spanish during the years of the Commercial Revolution. But it may also be worthy of comment that United States industrialization in the nineteenth and early twentieth centuries did not involve price inflation—and certainly did not involve a rise in United States prices relative to the rest of the world.[18]

If development planning emphasizes this approach instead of the import of capital goods financed by foreign borrowing, the longer run effects may be more salubrious. It is best to have goods exports financing capital goods imports rather than financing the transfer of interest and profits.

Assuming Independent Monetary Systems

The financing of international capital movements will involve quite different institutional arrangements, depending on whether nations continue to have independent monetary systems or whether a world central bank and an international currency are established.

Assume for the moment that independent monetary systems continue.[19] There are, then, the two basic possibilities discussed in Part V: fixed rates and fluctuating rates. If the rates are fixed, impossible situations may result for reasons discussed in Chapter 18. How much foreign investment can go on in this setting—or how much giving? Needless to

---

[17] Celso Furtado, *A Economia Brasileira*, p. 31.

[18] One may even wonder if the tremendous upsurge of industrialization in the United States would have occurred if the United States had been under-going chronic price inflation. And these thoughts may lead to some speculation as to the encouraging role political stability plays in encouraging industrialization.

[19] Much of the argument here is the same as in the preceding sections. It is repeated to clarify the contrast with the situation which would exist if there were an international currency.

say, as much giving can go on as people are willing to give or take. How much of a net real contribution foreign investments can make is severely limited by the interest rates and the power of compound interest.

If freely fluctuating foreign-exchange rates are allowed, the exchange rate situation itself becomes viable in a sense not true when the rates are set. But the implications of the lending and giving situation are much the same. As much giving can go on as people are willing to give and take. The net real contribution of foreign investment will still be limited by the interest rates and the power of compound interest; and it will be further complicated by the difficulty of the borrower and lender in reaching agreement on the interest rate and on the identity of the currency in which the loan will be repaid.

Assuming International Currency

The most desirable alternative involves the establishment of an international currency, such as was discussed in Chapter 23.

A viable world financial structure does require that the relative availability of credit in the different areas of the world be determined by an international agency. With regard to long-term credit, the basic rule would be that no constructive development, which there are the real resources to establish, should be held back because of lack of funds. Of course, if there is full and efficient employment of labor in a given country at a given time, there is not much latitude for new projects. But if a worthwhile project has been developed and the resources are available to implement it, the international agency should jockey its reserve requirements, etc. (this is the essence of qualitative credit control) to permit domestic private banks to advance the funds the project needs. Under an international currency and an international monetary unit, these funds would be freely usable anywhere in the world—just as $1000 borrowed from the Bank of the Southwest in Houston is now freely usable for purchases anywhere in the United States.

It may legitimately be alleged that this is a far better working basis for international finance than the old ones. The operation of the gold standard could necessitate credit contraction when all common sense called for credit expansion. Somewhat differently, but equally bad, the controls of the years since 1929 have had a strangling effect on trade, and the complicated foreign-exchange controls, quotas, and licenses have probably inhibited development because of their tendency to limit the size of the market. The use of all these restrictive devices involves an effort to bring about development by trickery instead of by work. And development in the underdeveloped areas calls for a lot of work and sweat; it calls for emphasis on the implementation of worthwhile projects.

One has to hope and trust that the decisions of the international agency will be intelligently made by giving priority to the industries and to the areas that have the best prospects of attaining relatively low-cost production. There is every reason to believe that decisions as to relative rate of development would be better made under these changed circumstances than they are now. And on the basis of these decisions it would actually be true that the relative rates of economic development in the different areas of the world would be controlled by some very broad and general international planning.

To those who worry about the alarming implications for national sovereignty it may be said: As matters now stand, do you know who or what controls the relative rate of development of different areas of the world, and are you sure you approve of who they are or what they are doing?

Under the gold standard the financing of development may be stymied merely because a country is experiencing an outflow of gold. Also, it would take a courageous soul to allege that there was any rhyme or reason to the relative growth rates that evolved from the quotas, licenses, exchange controls, and general international hard feeling of the 1930's. A pattern of freely fluctuating foreign-exchange rates would still leave different rates of credit expansion in different countries as an unplanned, disturbing influence.

If genuine international supervision of the process becomes possible, revised financial arrangements may facilitate development considerably. The International Bank and the Fund need to be substantially reorganized to effect the operation successfully. The international agencies need to be in a position to manufacture credit (probably a revised Fund, which would become the real central bank) which will be usable by the recipient for purchases in any country that the international agency may designate (the actual long-term loan planning being a function of a revised International Investment Bank). Such power is great, so great that it would give the international agencies the same sort of power possessed by an ordinary private commercial bank. In a way it is strange that we should so fear giving to an international agency the same type of power that is possessed by thousands of more-or-less irresponsible commercial bankers. But in reality it is merely evidence of the tremendous power actually possessed by bankers to control the rate of economic development in different areas, the types of activities which develop, and the identity of the individuals who end up in control of them. Possibly we do not worry about what the commercial bankers will do with this power merely because we are used to the idea of their having it.

But there are those who say that, regardless of the theoretical merit of having an international agency in a position to control to a certain extent the relative rate of internal credit extension in different countries, it is mere wishful thinking to conceive that it is possible. Strange, is it not, that this argument is being used in the world of the hydrogen bomb? Posterity is going to realize that the age of nationalism ended with World War I and went through its death struggle with the exaggerated nationalism of fascism; and yet here we are in the 1950's talking as though a little international control of the differential rate of economic growth were impossible, we who submitted before World War I to the tyranny that playing by the rules of the international gold standard involved for internal money and credit.

The only real barrier now to genuine international co-operation in these respects, at least on this side of the iron curtain, is centered mainly in the United States and in Texas.[20] We use our strength to inhibit international agreement on matters of obvious benefit to the whole world. How many Americans have now forgotten that the presence of the veto in the United Nations charter is largely the work of the United States? We now have the technical knowledge needed to effect a major improvement in the level of living all over the world, and such improvement would surely mean a more stable, more livable world for us. And the step of establishing an international currency is a minor one which would not have any effect on the day-to-day lives of individuals, any effect of which they would be really conscious—and it would have no adverse effect at all.

CONCLUSION

The American Geographical Society, in the report referred to in Chapter 30, states that there is sufficient food produced to feed everyone. And certainly, if there is not, there soon could be. Agricultural technology surely is far enough advanced to justify making this statement with confidence.

The financing of at least as much economic development as is needed to feed and clothe the world in a minimum sort of way is a *sine qua non* for the future peace and security of the world. After that is done, the experts can afford to be slower and more deliberate about the relative merit of different additional development projects. (This is not to deny that considerable industrial development may and should appropriately go on *pari passu* with the agricultural development.)

After all, the world is not going to be a healthy place for the United States to live in as long as there is great inequality in income as between geographical areas, and as long as there is consequent envy and jealousy. There is far more real danger to the peaceful progress of the world in the level-of-living gulf between the United States and two thirds of the world than in the United States—Russia cleavage. The political conflict

[20] Or are France, Britain, Germany, Italy, Spain, and Argentina just as bad?

between Russia and the United States can be neutralized—rendered impotent, left to simmer in its juice (like the Catholic-Protestant issue since the Thirty Years War)—if the rest of the world is developing, sees a bright future, and is not afraid of being caught in an atomic war between the United States and Russia.

PART VIII

Toward an Integrated Program

Chapter 36

CO-ORDINATION OF POLICIES

☙ ☙ ☙

As was stated in Chapter 23, there needs to be international agreement as to which policies will be used to deal with which problems.

Chiefly it is important that in each area of the world there be available enough internationally usable credit to finance as rapid a development as seems possible and desirable in the light of prevailing conditions.

Co-ordination of policies is desirable in order that the policies which improve matters for one nation may not worsen them for another.

☙ ☙ ☙

TAKEN in isolation, any one of the goals advocated in this book could be achieved by various conceivable policies. But the matter cannot satisfactorily be disposed of by dealing with one isolated goal at a time. The policy which satisfactorily solves one problem may worsen another. Also we live in a world of many nations. A policy which in one country may tend to implement a desirable goal may have undesirable repercussions on the efforts of other countries to reach other goals. We need to utilize a pattern of policies co-ordinated in such a way that they do not tend to offset or negate each other. The policies used will thereby have as much desirable effect as possible and as little undesirable effect as possible.[1]

THE PROBLEMS NEEDING SOLUTION

The goals, as alleged at various points in this book, are:

(1) Raising the level of living,
(2) Increasing security, and
(3) Increasing freedom of action.

[1] The orientation of this chapter was suggested by the method of treatment used by J. E. Meade in *The Balance of Payments* (London: Oxford, 1951); and in *Trade and Welfare* (London: Oxford, 1955).

The Tools

The basic types of policies which are available for solving the foregoing problems are:

    I. Financial policies.
        A. Fiscal policies—progressiveness of tax and spend structure, total volume of tax and spend (including the production subsidy and public works), and debt position.
        B. Monetary policies—including international capital movements, international grants, and qualitative credit control.
    II. Price policies.
        A. Subsidy to ameliorate price fluctuations.
        B. Wage rates.
        C. Foreign-exchange rates: (i) an international legal tender monetary unit, or (ii) freely fluctuating rates.
    III. Commercial policies (including use of discrimination).
        A. Tariffs and subsidies on exports and imports.
        B. Quotas, licenses, and other quantitative controls.
    IV. Freedom of movement.
        A. Of people.
        B. Of knowledge.
    V. Other institutional adjustments.
        A. Assured medical care.
        B. Decent provision for old age.
        C. Anti-unemployment "measures."
        D. Retraining aid.

THE PATTERN FOR CO-ORDINATING POLICIES

An example may serve to illustrate why these policies should not be used at random by various national governments to deal with the various problems in a hit-or-miss fashion. Assume a two-country world. Both nations are afflicted by depression; but the "home country" has an export balance vis-à-vis the "rest of the world." If policies are co-ordinated and if both countries use financial policies to the extent necessary to conquer the depressions and if they use price adjustments to solve the balance of payments problem, all of the difficulties may be solved— see Table 34. But if the "home country" tries to fight its depression by altering its foreign-exchange rate (devaluation to encourage exports) while the rest of the world tries to fight its depression by financial policy (perhaps domestic money and credit expansion, which might not only stimulate domestic production but also inflate domestic prices and thus attract even more imports), the depression may be somewhat ameliorated but the balance-of-payments disequilibrium will be made worse.

If there are policy patterns which will solve the various difficulties, it is surely better to use them than for un-co-ordinated policies to be used which, although they may well accomplish the primary goal of helping solve one problem, will have secondary effects that will inhibit the solution of other problems. There must be broad international agreement on policy patterns. That is the only way to avoid contradictory policies and mutual recriminations. This is not to say that there should be international control of the detailed operation of these policies. Far from it! This is, in fact, a good example of a situation where a modicum of international planning makes permissive a tremendous amount of decentralization of detailed programs.

Moreover, it seems clear that there will not be any major elimination of trade barriers unless the various countries can see such an international pattern in the making, which will protect them from sudden and harmful foreign policy measures.

It is not possible to realize "a liberal international economic order merely by free trade between sovereign nations; something more positive" by way of co-ordinated planning is also necessary.[2]

It may be that a quite different juxtaposition of policies and problems from that suggested in Table 50 would work as well. The main thing, however, is to agree as to which policies will be used in which situations and to be consistent in their use thereafter.

At all events, Table 50 catalogs the various important problem situations and sets up certain policies as appropriate for dealing with each problem. Taken in isolation, one of the policies might be used to solve a problem other than the one with which it is associated. But if this is done, it is likely that the solution of some other problem (perhaps by some other country) will be rendered more difficult.[3]

If a tool (say monetary policy) is assigned to the solution of a certain problem (say internal depression), the use of that tool may have an adverse effect on the solution of some other problem (say balance of payments disequilibrium). Therefore we must have another tool (say freely fluctuating exchange rates) that can be used to overshadow

---

[2] Meade, *Trade and Welfare,* p. 571.

[3] I am aware that the following material is greatly oversimplified. Also, in some instances the argument involves a value judgment as to which influence will be strongest. Nevertheless, the presentation of the argument is justified on the ground that we must face up to the fact that we are living in One World and co-ordination of policies is certainly desirable if it is possible. These are the terms in which we should be thinking.

TABLE 50
CO-ORDINATION OF POLICIES

PROBLEMS AND GOALS	POLICY TOOLS
	General Purpose Tools: (a) Price comparability, (b) A "do as you would be done by" attitude.

I. Level of Living
A. Short-run
  1. Internal
    a. Income distribution as among individuals — (a) Progressiveness of income tax and expenditure patterns.
    b. Internal depression — (a) Financial policy: (i) Fiscal policy—involving relation among total amount of tax, borrow, and spend (rather than progressiveness), and consumption subsidy; (ii) Monetary policy (control of total amount of credit).
  2. International
    a. Balance of payments disequilibrium — (a) An international legal tender monetary unit (and price and wage adjustments) *or*
       (b) Freely fluctuating exchange rates, *but not both*, and
       (c) Constructive free trade.
    b. Terms of trade — (a) Subsidy to ameliorate price fluctuations,
       (b) Measures in the area of economic growth (See B).
B. Economic Growth
    Increasing rate among underdeveloped countries — (a) (i) Foreign investment (minor factor), (ii) International grants (minor factor), (iii) Technical exchange, *and*
       (b) Financial policy: (i) Fiscal policy—public works and the production subsidy, (ii) Monetary policy (qualitative control and adequate credit for all worthwhile, technically feasible projects).
       (c) Institutional adjustment.
    2. Prevention of stagnation in developed countries — (a) Largely a problem in institutional adjustment and
       (b) Educational opportunities (including retraining aid).
    3. International income distribution — (a) Growth on low side, not retardation on high side,
       (b) Freedom of movement of people.
II. Security — (a) Policies that contribute to improved level of living, and more particularly,
       (b) Freedom of movement of people, and

TABLE 50 (*continued*)

(c) (i) Assured medical care, (ii) decent provision for old age, (iii) anti-un-employment measures, and
(d) No war.

III. Freedom of Action

(a) Freedom of movement of people, *and*
(b) Freedom of transmittal of technical knowledge, *and*
(c) The Bill of Rights.

Unused Tools: (1) Commercial policies (tariffs, quotas, licenses, embargoes [except for genuine health purposes], discrimination, export subsidies, dumping, and cartels); (2) Wage cutting.

completely the impact of monetary policy on the balance of payments situation. Tools are assigned to problems in a manner intended to have this effect.

Some explanation is no doubt in order as to the nature of the relationships alleged in Table 50. The basic relationship, in the area where there may be conflict among policies, is that suggested by Meade. *Financial* policies should be reserved for the effort to fight depression and raise income internally. Moreover, the governments need to commit themselves to use them. *Price* adjustments—as policy tools—should be used to deal with the problem of international balance of payments disequilibrium. However, the specific price adjustments suggested here are somewhat different from those considered by Meade; for example, wage cutting is not used.

In many of the practical situations which arise, the best measures are those that are designed to implement a gradual change in the direction indicated. Policy should also permit gradual change in the direction indicated without the violent ups and downs of cyclical fluctuation along the way. Thus, on tariffs, the policy recommended is gradual reduction; in agriculture, it is a policy designed to let individual prices in the long run move in the direction in which they are trying to move, but to reduce short-run price fluctuations; on the international movement of people, it is a policy which in a very few years would establish complete freedom for the individual to live anywhere in the world he chooses, but which would not provide for this tomorrow.

One might say that the two chief rules of thumb in appraising policies are (1) simplicity, and (2) the desirability of implementing gradual change in the proper direction.

In Table 50, the problems in the group first considered are those affecting internal level of living in the short run. In that area the basic problems are income distribution and depression unemployment. As has been repeatedly stressed earlier in this work, decisions concerning the degree of inequality in the distribution of income which is desirable should be made by the people speaking through the democratic process. Once such a decision is made, it can be implemented by a combination of fiscal policies designed to tax more heavily those whose incomes are to be reduced. Also, government expenditure policies can be calculated to benefit those people who, it has been decided, should have more income.

A more important aspect of the co-ordination of policies is the problem of depression unemployment. The salient feature of the co-ordination scheme here recommended is the decision to use financial policies, not price policies, to fight depressions. This means that a depression should be fought by a fiscal policy of tax, borrow, and spend—which involves increased spending. It may also be fought by a monetary policy which increases the supply of money and credit and consequently increases total spending. In expanding the supply of money and credit the traditional tools are available: (1) change in the reserve requirements, (2) change in the interest rate, (3) open market operations, (4) moral suasion, (5) change in margin requirements, and (6) the regulation of installment buying. In fact, for the pattern of policies to work, governments must be obligated in a positive sense to pursue such measures as these. Some governments may be reluctant. But since the whole process is in the interest of each nation as well as being in the interest of the whole world, there should not be too much reluctance.

Balance of payments disequilibrium should be resolved by quite different tools.

The really desirable policy would involve the establishment of an international monetary unit and a currency which would circulate as legal tender anywhere. Then let the individual "commodity by commodity" price adjustments occur as they will—except for the qualification noted below in connection with the terms of trade. But the "realists" claim that there is no practical possibility of an international currency. If that is true, the most desirable alternative is at the other extreme—freely fluctuating foreign-exchange rates. Probably such a system would function in a more orderly fashion if all countries let the values of their currencies fluctuate freely. But there is nothing in the nature of things to prevent one nation from taking such a step by itself.

Change in the terms of trade has frequently been pointed out as a circumstance placing one nation at a disadvantage relative to another. The statistical data for the long run does not establish the existence of significant trends. But over the period of the business cycle, there may be movements which are especially likely to involve more violent changes in raw commodity prices than in manufactured goods prices. Since the chief real problem in this area has to do with short-run violent fluctuations in certain prices, it may well be that the best policy tool is a sort of price subsidy calculated to ameliorate but not eliminate price fluctuations.

Inequity in income distribution as between countries probably should not be dealt with by means of tools intended to influence the terms of trade. International income distribution involves important and far-reaching questions as to the nature and impact of the growth process. The terms-of-trade question is important merely because violent price fluctuations have an undesirable, unsettling short-run influence. The international income-distribution problem is dealt with below.

Long-run change and the process of economic growth remain. Internationally, the process of economic growth can be aided by investments (provided the rate of return is modest), by grants, and by the international transmittal of technical knowledge, the last of which is by all odds the most important of these three processes. It is then up to the people of the receiving country and their institutional arrangements whether they make effective use of the knowledge.

Commercial policy measures, such as tariffs, quotas, licenses, exchange control, and discrimination, should be used with circumspection, if at all. Any measures to encourage growth which, during the transition period, make goods scarcer and higher priced in the developing country are suspect. So are measures which tend to increase international ill will.

Internally, the decision as to which industry should be encouraged relative to others can best be implemented by qualitative credit control (supplemented by the production subsidy and public works). Qualitative credit control, the production subsidy, and public works have the advantage over the tariff and kindred measures that, during the period of transition, they are compatible with more and lower priced goods for consumers.

A somewhat different type of growth problem is that presented by the possibility of stagnation in the developed countries. This would seem to be a complicated problem of institutional adjustment, the nature of which will vary from case to case depending upon the particular institutional arrangement theretofore prevailing. The most relevant aspect of this situation may well involve the tendency for a developed society to freeze into a customary way of doing things and stagnate. The standard example in past history has been the Byzantine Empire; maybe a modern example will be the British Empire. The problem is to resist the tendency for behavior to become rigidly set in certain institutional patterns. The chief aid that a government can give in avoiding this danger is to emphasize retraining assistance for people getting out of old and stagnating industries, rather than to emphasize assistance in maintaining the profits of such industries long after their contraction has become a natural development. In addition, the problem of stagnation in developed countries may be dealt with by the same policies used against internal depression.

Other growth problems arise from the differential rate of growth in different countries. The world will not be safe from major wars, and it will not become a healthy place to live in, as long as there are major differences in income as between countries—at least this is true in a setting where the people in the lagging countries have awakened to consciousness of their disadvantageous condition and do not like it. Increasing the relative rate of growth among the underdeveloped countries, at the same time that the already developed countries continue to grow, is the most important corrective. This is accomplished by the tools mentioned above (see Table 50) in connection with "increasing rate among underdeveloped countries." But in connection with international income distribution per se another tool needs to be added: freedom of movement of people. People should be free to go and try to make a living in those areas more blessed by nature, technology, or institutions, and characterized by a higher standard of living.

Our understanding of the process of economic growth is conditioned by the knowledge that the process occurs by jolts and not by marginal increments. Indicative of what is involved is the analogy (for which J. E. Meade is responsible) to the effect that you may climb a mountain by marginal increments. But after you get to the peak, you are not going to be able to proceed to the summit of the next and higher peak simply by means of further positive marginal increments. Great and significant changes are not introduced by entrepreneurs looking to their marginal profits. They are initiated by governments or by adventurers with freedom of action.

The realization of security is essentially dependent on a high level of living, but it also has an important freedom-of-movement aspect which is sometimes overlooked. People should know they will be able to move from an area of famine to an area of plenty if they are to feel secure where they are in their daily labors. But, more specifically, security is gained by a series of measures that are chiefly a matter of domestic policy and that are not necessarily dependent on the highest possible level of living. They are assured medical care, decent provision for old age, and anti-unemployment measures as well as retraining aid. Involved here must be a broadened concept of unemployment and of work guarantees which will see people through depressions. The other important aspect to the realization of security is the avoidance of war. One would think this would be easy of accomplishment for a species as advanced as mankind. But essentially the obtaining of security is a negative sort of thing. It is necessary to establish the setting in which the positive gains of freedom of action may be obtained.

Freedom of action is, in a sense, the highest of the goals. It rises above the mundane stuffing-the-stomach implications of the goal of raising the level of living. It is not largely negative, as is the case with the realization of security. It represents, on the contrary, the area where man expresses himself in a positive way. Satisfaction in life is largely gained from doing things we like to do or which we consider constructive—and doing them well. Freedom of movement and freedom to exchange knowledge make their tremendous contribution in facilitating such activity.

Bibliography

Abramovitz, Moses. "Resource and Output Trends in the United States since 1870," *American Economic Review, Papers. . . . ,* XLVI (May, 1956), 523.

Adler, J. H. "United States Import Demand During the 'Interwar Period,'" *American Economic Review,* XXV (June, 1945), 418–30.

Allen, R. G. D., and Ely, J. Edward (eds.). *International Trade Statistics.* New York: John Wiley, 1953.

American Geographical Society, Medical Georgraphical Department. *Study in Human Starvation.* New York, 1953.

American Tariff League. *Let's Not Import Depression.* New York, 1953.

American Tariff League. *What about the Wage Gap?* Publication No. 134. New York, 1954.

"American Visa Policy: A Report," *Bulletin of the Atomic Scientists,* XI (December, 1955), 367–75.

Ames, Edward. "The Exchange Rate in Soviet-Type Economies," *Review of Economics and Statistics,* XXV (November, 1953), 337–42.

Ames, Edward. "International Trade without Markets—the Soviet Bloc Case," *American Economic Review,* XLIV (December, 1954), 791–807.

Arciniegas, German. *The State of Latin America.* New York: Knopf, 1952.

Arey, Hawthorne. *History of Operations and Policies of Export-Import Bank of Washington.* Washington: Government Printing Office, 1953.

ATL Topics. New York. A serial publication of the American Tariff League.

Aubrey, Henry G. "Industrial Investment Decisions: A Comparative Analysis," *Journal of Economic History,* XV (December, 1955), 335–51.

Austin American (Statesman). Austin. Daily Newspaper.

Ayres, C. E. *Theory of Economic Progress.* Chapel Hill: University of North Carolina Press, 1944.

Balogh, T. "Some Theoretical Implications of International Aspects of the United States Recession, 1953/54," *Economic Journal,* LXV (December, 1955), 641–53.

Bank for International Settlements. *[Twenty-Third] Annual Report, [1st April 1952–31st March 1953].* Basle [1953].

Banking and Monetary Statistics. Washington: Board of Governors of the Federal Reserve System, 1943.

Barrows, Gordon H. "Private Capital on Road to Getting 'Fair Shake' Abroad," *World Oil,* August 15, 1953, 85–90.

Bastable, C. F. "On Some Applications of the Theory of International Trade," *Quarterly Journal of Economics,* IV (October, 1889), 1–17.

Bauer, P. T. *The Rubber Industry—A Study in Competition and Monopoly.* London: London School of Economics and Political Science, 1948.

Beer, Max. *Early British Economics.* London: George Allen and Unwin, 1938.

Bentham, Jeremy. *Introduction to the Principles of Morals and Legislation.* Oxford: Clarendon Press, 1907. First published: 1780–89.

Berle, Adolf A., Jr. *The 20th Century Capitalist Revolution.* New York: Harcourt, Brace, 1954.

Biddle, Francis. *The World's Best Hope.* Chicago: University of Chicago Press, 1949.

Bidwell, Percy W. *The Invisible Tariff*. New York: Council on Foreign Relations, 1939.

Blair, C. P. "Sequence of Events in the International Spread of Depressions." Unpublished Master's thesis, Department of Economics, University of Texas, 1952.

Bloomfield, Arthur I. *Speculative and Flight Movements of Capital in Postwar International Finance*. Princeton: Princeton University Press, 1954. The study was sponsored by the International Finance Section.

Board of Governors of the Federal Reserve System. *Flow of Funds in the United States, 1939–1953*. Washington, 1955.

Boyer, Frederic, and Salle, J. P. "The Liberalization of Intra-European Trade in the Framework of OEEC," *International Monetary Fund Staff Papers*, IV (February, 1955), 179–216.

Braibant, Guy. *La Planification en Tchecoslovaquie*. Paris: Colin, 1948.

British Record. New York. A periodical prepared by the British Information Services, an agency of the British government.

Buchanan, Norman S. *Rebuilding the World Economy*. New York: Twentieth Century Fund, 1947.

Bulletin of the Atomic Scientists. Published by the Educational Foundation for Nuclear Science, Inc., 5734 University Ave., Chicago 37, Illinois.

Cairncross, A. K. *Home and Foreign Investment, 1870–1913*. Cambridge, Eng.: University Press, 1953.

Cairnes, J. E. *Some Leading Principles of Political Economy*. London: Harper, 1900. First published 1874.

Cambridge Economic History of Europe. See: Postan.

Cantillon, Richard. *Essai sur la Nature du Commerce en Général*. Paris: Institut National d'Etudes Démographiques, 1952. Text of the 1755 edition.

Cardoso, Alfonso. *Experiencias en Economía*. Mexico: EDIAPSA, 1953.

Carman, Harry James, and McKee, Samuel, Jr. *A History of the United States*. Boston: Heath, 1931.

Carter, Alice. "Dutch Foreign Investments, 1738–1800," *Economica*, New Series, XXII (November, 1953), 322–40.

Cassel, Gustav. *Money and Foreign Exchange after 1914*. New York: Macmillan, 1922.

Chang, T. C. "International Comparison of Demand for Imports," *Review of Economic Studies*, XIII (1945–46), 53–67.

Chenery, Hollis B. "The Role of Industrialization in Development Programs," *American Economic Review, Papers and Proceedings*, XLV (May, 1955), 40–67.

Combined Mexican Working Party. *Economic Development of Mexico*. Baltimore: Johns Hopkins Press, 1953.

Comments on Argentine Trade. Buenos Aires. Monthly publication of the United States Chamber of Commerce in Argentina.

Committee for Economic Development. *Taxes, National Security and Economic Growth*. New York, 1954.

Commodity Yearbook. . . . New York. Published by the Commodity Research Bureau.

Condoide, Mikhail V. *Soviet Financial System*. Columbus: Ohio State University (Bureau of Business Research), 1951.

Considerations on the East-India Trade. London, 1701. Reproduced in J. R. McCulloch (ed.). *Early English Tracts on Commerce*. London: Political Economy Club, 1856.

Coulter, John Lee. *Public Opinion in the United States on Foreign Trade*. American Tariff League, Publication No. 117. New York, 1946.

Cournot, Augustin. *Recherches sur les Principes Mathématiques de la Théorie des Richesses.* Paris: Marcel Rivière, 1938. The work was originally published in 1838.

Cunynghame, H. *A Geometrical Political Economy.* Oxford: Clarendon Press, 1904.

Custom House Guide. . . . New York (Custom House): Custom House Guide. An annual publication.

Daily Texan. Austin. The daily University of Texas student newspaper.

Davis, Joseph S., Gibbs, H. M., and Taylor, E. B. *Wheat in the World Economy.* Stanford: Stanford University Press (Food Research Institute), 1945.

Day, A. C. L. *The Future of Sterling.* Oxford: Clarendon Press, 1954.

Department of State Bulletin: see United States, Department of State. *Department of State Bulletin.*

DeRoover, Raymond A. *L'Evolution de la Lettre de Change.* Paris: Colin, 1953.

Domar, Evsey. "Expansion and Employment," *American Economic Review,* XXXVII (March, 1947), 34–35.

Domar, Evsey. "Interrelation between Capital and Output in the American Economy," *International Social Science Bulletin,* VI (No. 2, 1954), 236–46.

Dorrance, G. S. "The Income Terms of Trade," *Review of Economic Studies,* XVI (1948–1949), 50–56.

Dunlop, Robert G. *The Challenge of Free Markets.* Philadelphia: Sun Oil Company, 1953.

East-West Trade Controversy. New York: United States Council of the International Chamber of Commerce, 1952.

Economic Survey of Latin America. . . . See: United Nations, Economic Commission for Latin America. *Economic Survey.* . . .

Economist. London. Weekly magazine.

Edgeworth, Francis Y. "Pure Theory of International Values," *Papers Relating to Political Economy.* London: Macmillan, 1925. Vol. II, 3–60. This work originally appeared in the *Economic Journal* in 1894.

Elliott, William Y., et al. *International Control in the Non-ferrous Metals.* New York: Macmillan, 1937.

Export-Import Bank. *General Policy Statement, July 1, 1955.* Washington, 1955.

Export-Import Bank. *Semiannual Report to Congress for the Period.* . . . Washington.

Federal Reserve Bulletin. Washington. Monthly Publication of the Board of Governors of the Federal Reserve System.

Feis, Herbert. *Europe the World's Banker, 1870–1914.* New Haven: Yale University Press, 1930.

Ferrer, Aldo. "Distribución del Ingreso y Desarrollo Económico," *Trimestre Económico,* XXI (April, 1954), 141–84.

Figueres, José. "Mensaje Inaugural . . . , 8 de Noviembre de 1953," *Trimestre Económico,* XXI (January, 1954), 93–105.

First National City Bank of New York. Mimeographed information on corporate profits.

Fitooni, L. "Ob Ekonomicheskoi Pomoschchi Slaborazvitim Stranam," *Voprosi Ekonomiki,* November, 1953, 80–95.

Food and Agriculture Organization. *Proposals for a World Food Board and World Food Survey.* Washington, 1946.

Ford, Henry, II. *Expanded Trade and World Peace.* Dearborn, Michigan: Ford Motor Company, 1953.

Ford, Henry, II. *The Free World Can't Trade on a One Way Street.* Detroit: Ford Motor Company, 1953.

Foreign Commerce Weekly: see United States, Department of Commerce. Foreign. . . .

Fortune. New York. Monthly magazine.

France Actuelle. Paris. Published by Comité France Actuelle, 31, Avenue Pierre 1er de Serbie, Paris (XVI), France.

Frankel, S. Herbert. *The Economic Impact on Under-Developed Societies; Essays on International Investment and Social Change.* Oxford: Blackwell, 1953.

Friedman, Milton. "The Case for Flexible Exchange Rates," *Essays in Positive Economics.* Chicago: University of Chicago Press, 1953, 157–203.

Frisch, Ragnar. "On the Need for Forecasting a Multilateral Balance of Payments," *American Economic Review,* XXXVII (September, 1947), 535–51.

Furniss, Edgar S. *The Position of the Laborer in a System of Nationalism.* Boston: Houghton Mifflin, 1920.

Furtado, Celso. *A Economia Brasileira.* Rio de Janeiro: Editora a Noite, 1954.

Garner, Robert L. *Statement on the International Finance Corporation, Tenth Annual Meeting of the Board of Governors, Istanbul, September 15, 1955.*

General Agreement on Tariffs and Trade. *International Trade News Bulletin.* Geneva. Once each six months it contains an *Index of Trade Agreements.*

General Agreement on Tariffs and Trade. *International Trade, 1952.* Geneva, 1953.

González de Cellorigo, Martín. *Memorial de la Política Necessaria y Util Restauración a la República de España.* 1600. (Excerpts are reprinted in Grice-Hutchinson. . . .)

Gordon, Wendell. *Economy of Latin America.* New York: Columbia, 1950.

Gordon, Wendell. *Expropriation of Foreign-Owned Property in Mexico.* Washington: American Council on Public Affairs, 1941.

Goschen, George Joachim Goschen Viscount. *The Theory of the Foreign Exchanges.* 4th ed. London: Pitman, 1932. The first edition was published in 1861.

Great Britain, Central Statistical Office. *Annual Abstract of Statistics, 1937–47.* London: His Majesty's Stationery Office, 1948.

Greaves, H. R. G. *Raw Materials and International Control.* London: Methuen, 1936.

Grice-Hutchinson, Marjorie. *The School of Salamanca, Readings in Spanish Monetary Theory, 1544–1605.* Oxford: Clarendon Press, 1952.

Grove, David L. "Role of the Banking System in the Chilean Inflation," *Staff Papers,* II (September, 1951), 33–59.

Haberler, Gottfried. "Reflections of the Future of the Bretton Woods System," *American Economic Review, Papers and Proceedings,* XLIII (May, 1953), 81–95.

Haberler, Gottfried. *A Survey of International Trade Theory.* Princeton: International Finance Section, Princeton University, 1955.

Haberler, Gottfried. *Theory of International Trade and its Application to Commercial Policy.* London: Hodge, 1936.

Hamilton, Alexander. *Report on Manufactures.* Vol. IV of *The Works of Alexander Hamilton.* Edited by Henry Cabot Lodge. New York: Putnam, 1903.

Hamilton, Earl J. *American Treasure and the Price Revolution in Spain, 1501–1650.* Cambridge: Harvard University Press, 1934.

Harrod, R. F. *International Economics.* Cambridge: University Press, 1933.

Harrod, R. F. *Towards a Dynamic Economics.* London: Macmillan, 1948.

Heckscher, Eli. *Mercantilism.* London: George Allen and Unwin, 1935.

Hicks, J. R. *Value and Capital.* 2d ed.; Oxford: Clarendon Press, 1946.

Hirschman, A. O., "Disinflation, Discrimination, and the Dollar Shortage," *American Economic Review,* XXXVIII (December, 1948), 886–92.

Hispanic American Report. Hispanic American Studies, Stanford University, Ronald Hilton, Director. Stanford, California. A monthly magazine.

Historical Statistics: see United States, Bureau of the Census. *Historical.* . . .

Hobson, C. K. *The Export of Capital.* New York: Macmillan, 1914.

Hobson, J. A. *Imperialism, A Study.* 3rd ed. London: Allen and Unwin, 1938. The first edition was published in 1902.

Hoeffding, Oleg. "Recent Trends in Soviet Foreign Trade," *Annals of the American Academy of Political and Social Science,* CCCIII (January, 1956), 75–88.

Hoffmann, Walther G. *British Industry 1700–1950.* Oxford: Blackwell, 1955.

Hoselitz, Bert F. "The City, The Factory, and Economic Growth," *American Economic Review, Papers and Proceedings,* XLV (May, 1955), 166–84.

Hoselitz, Bert F. (ed.). *The Progress of Under-developed Areas.* Chicago: University of Chicago Press, 1952.

Houston Post. A daily newspaper.

Hume, David. *Political Discourses.* London: Scott, 1906 (?). The work was originally published in 1752.

Humphrey, Don D. *American Imports.* New York: The Twentieth Century Fund, 1955.

Imlah, Albert H. "Real Values in British Foreign Trade, 1798–1853," *Journal of Economic History,* VIII (November, 1948), 133–52.

Imlah, Albert H. "Terms of Trade of the United Kingdom," *Journal of Economic History,* X (November, 1950), 170–94.

International Bank for Reconstruction and Development. *Annual Report.* . . . Washington.

International Bank for Reconstruction and Development. *The Basis of a Development Program for Colombia.* Washington, 1950.

International Bank for Reconstruction and Development. *International Bank for Reconstruction and Development, 1946–1953* (Baltimore: Johns Hopkins Press, 1954).

International Bank for Reconstruction and Development. *Press Releases.* Washington.

International Bank for Reconstruction and Development. *Summary Proceedings, Eighth Annual Meeting of the Board.* . . , *September 9–12, 1953.* Washington, 1953.

International Conciliation. New York. A serial publication of the Carnegie Endowment for International Peace.

International Financial News Survey: See International Monetary Fund. *International Financial News Survey.*

International Financial Statistics: See International Monetary Fund. *International Financial Statistics.*

International Labour Office. *Intergovernmental Commodity Control Agreements.* Montreal, 1943.

International Monetary Fund. *Annual Report on Exchange Restrictions.* Washington.

International Monetary Fund. *International Financial News Survey.* Washington. A weekly bulletin.

International Monetary Fund. *International Financial Statistics.* Washington. Monthly.

International Social Science Bulletin. Paris. A quarterly published by UNESCO.

International Statistical Yearbook: See United Nations, Statistical Office. *Statistical.* . . .

Iversen, Carl. *Aspects of the Theory of International Capital Movements.* Copenhagen: Levin and Munksgaard, 1936.

Izmailov, K. "Torgovlya Imperialisticheskikh Dyerzhav so Slaborazvitimi Stranami—Oroodiye Kolonialnogo Grabyezha," *Voprosi Ekonomiki,* September, 1954, 93–105.

Jevons, W. Stanley. *The Theory of Political Economy.* 4th ed.; London: Macmillan, 1931 (first edition 1871).

Kahn, Alfred E. *Great Britain in the World Economy.* New York: Columbia University Press, 1946.

Kaplan, Norman M., and Wainstein, Eleanor S. "A Comparison of Soviet and American Retail Prices in 1950," *Journal of Political Economy,* LXIV (December, 1956), 470–91.

Keynes, John Maynard. *The Economic Consequences of the Peace.* New York: Harcourt, Brace and Howe, 1920.

Keynes, John Maynard. *The General Theory of Employment, Interest, and Money.* New York: Harcourt, Brace, 1936.

Keynes, John Maynard. "The German Transfer Problem," *Economic Journal,* XXXIX (March, 1929), 1–7.

Keynes, John Maynard. *A Treatise on Money.* London: Macmillan, 1930.

Kindleberger, Charles P. *The Dollar Shortage.* New York: Wiley, 1950.

Kindleberger, Charles P. "Industrial Europe's Terms of Trade on Current Account," *Economic Journal,* LXV (March, 1955), 19–35.

Kindleberger, Charles P. *International Economics.* Homewood, Ill.: Irwin, 1953.

Kindleberger, Charles P. *The Terms of Trade: A European Case Study.* New York: The Technology Press of Massachusetts Institute of Technology and John Wiley, 1956.

Knorr, Klaus E. *Tin under Control.* Stanford: Stanford University Press (Food Research Institute), 1945.

Knorr, Klaus E. *World Rubber and its Regulation.* Stanford: Stanford University Press (Food Research Institute), 1945.

Kravis, Irving B. "The Trade Agreements Escape Clause," *American Economic Review,* XL (June, 1954), 319–38.

Kuznets, Simon. "Population, Income and Capital," *International Social Science Bulletin,* VI (No. 2, 1954), 165–71.

Kuznets, Simon, Moore, Wilbert E., and Spengler, Joseph J. (eds.). *Economic Growth: Brazil, India, Japan.* Durham: Duke University Press, 1955.

Lamont, Thomas W. *Across World Frontiers.* New York: Harcourt, Brace, 1951.

Latin-American Business Highlights. New York. A quarterly publication of the Chase-Manhattan Bank.

Lavergne, Bernard. "Le Redressement de l'Ordre Politique Intérieur," *L'Année Politique et Economique,* April, 1952, 129–38.

League of Nations. *Review of World Trade.* . . . Geneva. Formerly an annual publication.

League of Nations. *Statistical Yearbook.* . . . Geneva. Formerly an annual publication.

Lehfeldt, R. A. "Rate of Interest on British and Foreign Investments," *Journal of the Royal Statistical Society,* LXXVI (January, 1913), 196–207.

Lekachman, Robert (ed.). *National Policy for Economic Welfare at Home and Abroad.* New York: Doubleday, 1955. Conference at Columbia, May, 1954.

Lenin, V. I. *Imperialism, the Highest Stage of Capitalism.* Revised translation. New York: International Publishers, 1933. The work was written in 1916.

Leontief, Wassily W. *Studies in the Structure of the American Economy: Theoretical and Empirical Explorations in Input-Output Analysis.* New York: Oxford University Press, 1953.

Leontief, Wassily W. "The Use of Indifference Curves in the Analysis of Foreign Trade," *Quarterly Journal of Economics,* XLVII (May, 1933), 493–503.

Lerner, Abba P. *Economics of Control.* New York: Macmillan, 1944.

Levi, Leone. *History of British Commerce, 1763–1878.* London: Murray, 1872.

Lewis, W. Arthur. *The Theory of Economic Growth.* Homewood, Illinois: Irwin, 1955.

Liddell Hart, B. H. "Why the H-Bomb Wipes Off the "New Look,'" *World, America's Magazine of World Events,* I (June, 1954), 12–14.

Linton, Ralph. "Cultural and Personality Factors Affecting Economic Growth," *The Progress of Under-developed Areas.* Edited by Bert F. Hoselitz. Chicago: University of Chicago Press, 1952.

List, Friedrich. *National System of Political Economy.* London: Longmans, Green, 1928. The work was originally published in German in 1841.

Looper, Johan H. C. de. "Current Usage of Payments Agreements and Trade Agreements," *International Monetary Fund Staff Papers,* IV (August, 1955), 339–97.

McConnell, Donald W., et al. *Economic Behavior.* Boston: Houghton Mifflin, 1939.

McCulloch, J. R. (ed.). *A Select Collection of Early English Tracts on Commerce. . . .* London: Political Economy Club, 1856. The publication was reissued by the Cambridge University Press in 1954.

McDonald, S. L. Baton Rouge, Louisiana.

McKitterick, Thomas E. M. *Russian Economic Policy in Eastern Europe: Albania, Bulgaria, Czechoslovakia, Hungary, Yugoslavia, Poland, Roumania, and Austria.* London: Fabian Publications, 1948.

McLeod, A. N. "Trade and Investment in Underdeveloped Areas," *American Economic Review,* XLI (June, 1951), 411–19.

Machlup, Fritz. *International Trade and the National Income Multiplier.* Philadelphia: Blakiston, 1943.

Macrae, N. *The London Capital Market—Its Structure, Strains, and Management.* London: Staples, 1955.

Madden, J. T., and Nadler, Marcus. *America's Experience as a Creditor Nation.* New York: Prentice-Hall, 1937.

Maffry, August. "Increasing Private Investment in Foreign Countries," *Comments on Argentine Trade,* July, 1953, 29–31 and 49.

Malynes, Gerard. *A Treatise of the Canker of England's Common Wealth.* 1601.

Marquez, Javier. "Bonos de Poder Adquisitivo Constante," *Trimestre Económico,* XXI (January, 1954), 6–43.

Marshall, Alfred. *Money, Credit and Commerce.* London: Macmillan, 1923.

Marshall, Alfred. *Principles of Economics.* 6th ed. London: Macmillan, 1910.

Marshall, Alfred. *The Pure Theory of Foreign Trade and the Pure Theory of Domestic Values.* Third impression. London: The London School of Economics and Political Science, 1949. Written for private circulation about 1879.

Martin, K., and Thackeray, F. G. "The Terms of Trade of Selected Countries 1870–1938," *Bulletin of the Oxford University Institute of Statisitcs,* X (November, 1948), 373–92.

Marx, Jr., Daniel. *International Shipping Cartels.* Princeton: Princeton University Press, 1952.

Marx, Karl. *Capital, A Critique of Political Economy.* Trans. Ernest Untermann, 4th German ed., 3 vols. Chicago: Kerr, 1906–1909.

Marx, Karl, and Engels, Friedrich. *The Communist Manifesto.* New York: International Publishers, 1948. The work was originally published in 1848.

Meade, James E. *The Balance of Payments.* London: Oxford University Press, 1951.

Meade, James E. *A Geometry of International Trade.* London: George Allen and Unwin, 1952.

Meade, James E. *Problems of Economic Union.* Chicago: University of Chicago, 1953.

Meade, James E. *Trade and Welfare.* London: Oxford University Press, 1955.

Meston, Lord. "Restrictive Business Practices," *Cartel,* VI (October, 1956), 127–9.

Mikesell, Raymond F. *Foreign Exchange in the Postwar World.* New York: The Twentieth Century Fund, 1954.

Mill, John Stuart. *Essays on Some Unsettled Question of Political Economy.* London: Parker, 1844. The work was originally written in 1829 but not published until 1844. It was reprinted by the London School of Economics and Political Science in 1948.

Mill, John Stuart. *Principles of Political Economy.* New impression of the 6th ed. London: Longmans, Green, 1904.

Miller, David L. Austin, Texas.

Miller, Douglas. *You Can't Do Business with Hitler.* Boston: Little, Brown, 1941.

Mining Engineering. New York. Monthly magazine published by the American Institute of Mining and Metallurgical Engineers.

Mintz, Ilse. *Deterioration in the Quality of Foreign Bonds Issued in the United States, 1920–1930.* National Bureau of Economic Research, publication no. 52. New York, 1951.

Misselden, Edward. *The Circle of Commerce, or the Ballance of Trade.* 1623.

Mitchell, Wesley C. *Business Cycles: The Problem and its Setting.* New York: National Bureau of Economic Research, 1927.

Mond, Sir Alfred. *Industry and Politics.* London: Macmillan, 1928.

Monthly Bulletin of Statistics: see United Nations, Statistical Office. *Monthly.* . . .

Moore, Wilbert E. "Labor Attitudes toward Industrialization in Underdeveloped Countries," *American Economic Review, Papers and Proceedings,* XLV (May, 1955), 156–65.

Mosak, Jacob L. *General-Equilibrium Theory in International Trade.* Bloomington, Ind.: Principia Press, 1944.

Mosk, Sanford A. *Industrial Revolution in Mexico.* Berkeley: University of California Press, 1950.

Moulton, Harold G., and Pasvolsky, Leo. *War Debts and World Prosperity.* New York: Century, 1932.

Mun, Thomas. *England's Treasure by Forraign Trade, or the Ballance of our Forraign Trade is the Rule of our Treasure.* 1630 (?).

Myrdal, Gunnar. *An International Economy: Problems and Prospects.* New York: Harper, 1956.

Myrdal, Gunnar. *The Political Element in the Development of Economic Theory.* Trans. Paul Streeten. Cambridge: Harvard University Press, 1954. The original edition in Swedish was published in 1929.

National Industrial Conference Board. *Conference Board Studies in Enterprise and Social Progress.* New York: N.I.C.B., 1939.

Neisser, Hans, and Modigliani, Franco. *National Incomes and International Trade.* Urbana: University of Illinois Press, 1953.

Nelson, Eastin. "Revolution in Economic Policy in Latin America," *Southwestern Social Science Quarterly,* XXXIV (December, 1953), 3–16.

New Republic. New York. A weekly magazine.

New York Times. New York. Daily newspaper.

Nurkse, Ragnar. "Conditions of International Monetary Equilibrium," *Essays in International Finance,* No. 4 (Spring, 1945).

Nurkse, Ragnar. "International Investment Today in the Light of Nineteenth-Century Experience," *Economic Journal,* LXIV (December, 1954), 744–58.

Nurkse, Ragnar. *Problems of Capital Formation in Underdeveloped Countries.* Oxford: Blackwell, 1953.

Ogburn, William F. (ed.) *Technology and International Relations.* Chicago: University of Chicago Press, 1949.

Ohlin, Bertil. *Comercio Exterior y Política Comercial.* Madrid: Aguilar, 1948.

Ohlin, Bertil. *Interregional and International Trade.* Cambridge: Harvard University Press, 1933.

Ohlin, Bertil, "The Reparation Problem: A Discussion," *Economic Journal,* XXXIX (June, 1929), 172–78.

Orcutt, Guy H. "Exchange Rate Adjustment and Relative Size of Depreciating Bloc," *Review of Economics and Statistics,* XXXVII (February, 1955), 1–11.

Orcutt, Guy. "Measurement of Price Elasticities in International Trade," *Review of Economics and Statistics,* XXXII (May, 1950), 117–32.

Organisation for European Economic Co-operation. *Food Consumption Levels in OEEC Countries.* Paris, 1951.

Organisation for European Economic Co-operation. *Liberalisation of Europe's Dollar Trade.* Paris, 1956.

Paish, F. W. "Banking Policy and the Balance of International Payments," *Economica,* III-New Series (November, 1936), 404–22.

Piquet, Howard S. *Aid, Trade and the Tariff.* New York: Crowell, 1953.

Polak, J. J. *An International Economic System.* London: George Allen and Unwin, 1954.

Postan, M. and Rich, E. E. (eds.). *Trade and Industry in the Middle Ages.* (*The Cambridge Economic History of Europe,* Vol. II) Cambridge: University Press, 1952.

Prebisch, Raúl. "Exposición . . . ," *Trimestre Económico,* XX (April, 1953), 351–65.

Progress of Underdeveloped Areas. See: Hoselitz, Bert F.

Ricardo, David. *The Principles of Political Economy and Taxation.* Everyman's Library edition. London: J. M. Dent, 1911. The work was originally published in 1817.

Riesman, David, Glazer, Nathan, and Denny, Reuel. *The Lonely Crowd.* Abridged. New York: Doubleday, 1955.

Rippy, J. Fred. "British Investments in Latin America: A Sample of Profitable Enterprises," *Inter-American Economic Affairs,* VI (Spring, 1953), 3–17.

Roberts, Lewes. *The Treasure of Traffike or a Discourse of Forraigne Trade.* London, 1641. Reproduced in J. R. McCulloch (ed.). *Early English Tracts on Commerce,* 49–113.

Robinson, Joan. "Begger-My-Neighbour Remedies for Unemployment," in *Readings in the Theory of International Trade* (Philadelphia: Blakiston, 1949), 393–407.

Robinson, Joan. "The Foreign Exchanges," *Essays in the Theory of Employment,* 2nd ed. (Oxford: Blackwell, 1947), part III, chap. 1.

Robinson, Joan. "The Pure Theory of International Trade," *Collected Economic Papers.* Oxford: Blackwell, 1951. 182–205.

Robinson, Joan. *The Rate of Interest and Other Essays.* London: Macmillan, 1953.

Rostow, W. W. *Process of Economic Growth.* New York: Norton, 1952.

Rostow, W. W. "The Take-off into Self-sustained Growth," *Economic Journal,* LXVI (March, 1956), 25–48.

Rybalko, G. "Rol Mezhdunarodnovo Valiutnovo Fonda i Mezhdunarodnovo Banka Rekonstruktsii i Razvitiia v Agressivnikh Planakh S.S.A.," *Vneshniaia Torgovlia,* July, 1952, 29–35.

Sailors, Joel W. *Secular Terms of Trade: Theory and Measurement* (Unpublished Ph.D. dissertation, Dept. of Economics, University of Texas, 1956).

Salter, Sir Arthur. *Recovery: The Second Effort.* New York: Century, 1932.

Samuelson, Paul A. *Foundations of Economic Analysis.* Cambridge: Harvard University Press, 1947.

Samuelson, Paul A. "International Factor Price Equalisation Once Again," *Economic Journal,* LIX (June, 1949), 181–97.

Samuelson, Paul A. "International Trade and the Equalisation of Factor Prices," *Economic Journal,* LVIII (June, 1948), 163–84.

Sawyer, Charles. "Secretary Sawyer's Survey of Europe," *Foreign Commerce Weekly,* December 22, 1952.

Schlote, Werner. *British Overseas Trade from 1700 to the 1930's.* Oxford: Blackwell, 1952.

Schultz, Theodore W. "Latin-American Economic Policy Lessons," *American Economic Review, Papers and Proceedings,* XLVI (May, 1956), 425–32.

Schumpeter, Joseph. *Theory of Economic Development.* Cambridge: Harvard University Press, 1934. Translated from the German by Redvers Opie.

Scitovsky, Tibor. "Economies of Scale, Competition, and European Integration," *American Economic Review,* XLVI (March, 1956), 71–91.

Scitovsky, Tibor. "A Reconsideration of the Theory of Tariffs," *Review of Economic Studies,* IX (Summer, 1942), 89–110.

Sedillot, R. *Toutes les Monnaies du Monde—Dictionnaire des Changes.* Paris: Sirey, 1955.

Serra, Antonio. *Breve Trattato delle Cause che Possono Far Abbondare li Regni d'Oro e d'Argento Dove Non Sono Miniere.* 1613.

Sharp, Walter R. *International Technical Assistance, Programs and Organization.* Chicago: Public Administration Service, 1952.

Shaterian, William S. *Export-Import Banking.* New York: Ronald, 1947.

Singer, H. W. "The Distribution of Gains between Investing and Borrowing Countries," *American Economic Review, Papers . . .,* XL (May, 1950), 473–86.

Smith, Adam. *An Inquiry into the Nature and Causes of the Wealth of Nations.* Modern Library edition. New York: Random House, 1937.

Smith, Ralph Elberton. *Customs Valuation in the United States.* Chicago: University of Chicago Press, 1948.

Smith, Warren L. "Effects of Exchange Rate Adjustments on the Standard of Living," *American Economic Review,* XLIV (December, 1954), 808–25.

Snider, Delbert A. *Introduction to International Economics.* Homewood, Ill.: Irwin, 1954.

Solodovnikov, V. "Vivoz Kapitala . . . ," *Voprosi Ekonomiki,* January, 1953, 76–90.

Spulber, Nicolas. "Economic Thinking and its Application and Methodology in Eastern Europe Outside of Soviet Russia," *American Economic Review, Papers . . . ,* XLVI (May, 1956), 367–79.

Staley, Eugene. *The Future of Underdeveloped Countries.* New York: Harper (Council on Foreign Relations), 1954.

Staley, Eugene. *War and the Private Investor.* Garden City: Doubleday, Doran, 1935.

Statistical Abstract: see United States, Bureau of the Census. *Statistical. . . .*

Statistical Yearbook: see United Nations, Statistical Office. *Statistical. . . .*

Steindl, J. *Maturity and Stagnation in American Capitalism.* Oxford University Institute of Statistics, Monograph No. 4. Oxford: Blackwell, 1952.

Stocking, George W., and Watkins, Myron W. *Cartels in Action.* New York: Twentieth Century Fund, 1947.

Stocking, George W., and Watkins, Myron W. *Cartels or Competition.* New York: Twentieth Century Fund, 1948.

Stone, N. I. *One Man's Crusade for an Honest Tariff.* Appleton, Wis.: Lawrence College Press, 1952.

Stowell, Ellery C., and Munro, Henry F. *International Cases.* 2 vols. Boston: Houghton Mifflin, 1916.

Survey of Current Business: see United States, Department of Commerce. *Survey. . . .*

Svennilson, Ingvar. *Growth and Stagnation in the European Economy.* Geneva: United Nations Economic Commission for Europe, 1954.

Sweezy, Paul M. *Theory of Capitalist Development.* New York: Oxford, 1942.

Tannenbaum, Frank. *Mexico, the Struggle for Peace and Bread.* New York: Knopf, 1950.

Taussig, Frank W. *International Trade.* New York: Macmillan, 1928.

Tawney, R. H. *Religion and the Rise of Capitalism.* New York: Penguin, 1947 (first published, 1926).

Teaf, Howard M., Jr., and Franck, Peter G. *Hands across Frontiers—Case Studies in Technical Cooperation.* Ithaca: Cornell University Press. 1955.

Thomas, Brinley. *Migration and Economic Growth.* London: Cambridge University Press, 1954.

Thorp, Willard L. "The Tariff and the Consumer," *Consumer Reports,* XVIII (June, 1953), 267–72.

Towle, Lawrence W. *International Trade and Commercial Policy.* 2d ed.; New York: Harper, 1956.

Trued, Merlyn N., and Mikesell, Raymond F. *Postwar Bilateral Payments Agreements.* Princeton Studies in International Finance No. 4. Princeton: Princeton University Press, 1955.

Twain, Mark. *Pudd'nhead Wilson.* New York: Harper, 1893.

United Nations Bulletin. New York.

United Nations, Department of Economic Affairs. *Instability in Export Markets of Under-developed Countries.* New York, 1952.

United Nations, Department of Economic Affairs. *Measures for the Economic Development of Underdeveloped Countries.* New York, 1951.

United Nations, Department of Economic Affairs. *National and International Measures for Full Employment.* Lake Success, 1949.

United Nations, Department of Economic Affairs. *United States Income Taxation of Private United States Investment in Latin America.* New York, 1953.

United Nations, Department of Economic and Social Affairs. *Analyses and Projections of Economic Development, I. An Introduction to the Technique of programming.* New York, 1955.

United Nations, Department of Economic and Social Affairs. *Foreign Capital in Latin America.* New York, 1955.

United Nations, Department of Economic and Social Affairs. *Processes and Problems of Industrialization in Under-Developed Countries.* New York, 1955.

United Nations, Economic Commission for Latin America. *The Economic Development of Latin America and its Principal Problems.* Lake Success, 1950.

United Nations, Economic Commission for Latin America. *Economic Survey of Latin America. . . .* This is an annual publication.

United Nations, Economic Commission for Latin America. *International Cooperation in a Latin American Development Policy.* New York, 1954.

United Nations, Economic Commission for Latin America. *Relative Prices of Exports and Imports of Under-developed Countries.* Lake Success, 1949.

United Nations, Economic Commission for Latin America. *Study of the Prospects of Inter-Latin-American Trade.* New York, 1954.

United Nations Educational, Scientific and Cultural Organization. *Cultural Patterns and Technical Change.* Paris, 1953.

United Nations Educational, Scientific and Cultural Organization. *Travel Abroad.* Paris, 1953 et seq.

United Nations, Statistical Office. *Monthly Bulletin of Statistics.* New York.

United Nations, Statistical Office. *National Income and its Distribution in Under-developed Countries.* Statistical Papers, Series E, no. 3. New York, 1951.

United Nations, Statistical Office. *Retail Price Comparisons for International Salary Determination.* Statistical Papers, Series M, no. 14. New York, 1952.

United Nations, Statistical Office. *Statistical Yearbook* (various years). New York. Before World War II a similar *Statistical Yearbook* was published by the League of Nations. Some years it was called *International Statistical Yearbook.*

United Nations, Statistical Office. *Yearbook of International Trade Statistics.* New York.

United Nations, Technical Assistance Committee. *Eighth Report of the Technical Assistance Board.* New York, 1956.

United States, Bureau of Foreign and Domestic Commerce. *The Balance of International Payments of the United States, 1946–1948.* Washington: Government Printing Office, 1950.

United States, Bureau of Foreign and Domestic Commerce. *Balance of Payments of the United States, 1949–1951.* Washington: Government Printing Office.

United States, Bureau of Foreign and Domestic Commerce. *Foreign Aid by the United States Government 1940–1951.* Washington: Government Printing Office, 1952.

United States, Bureau of Foreign and Domestic Commerce. *Foreign Trade of the United States, 1936–1949.* Washington: Government Printing Office, 1951.

United States, Bureau of Foreign and Domestic Commerce. *The United States in the World Economy.* Washington: Government Printing Office, 1943.

United States, Bureau of Foreign Commerce. *How to Apply for an Export License and How to Use It.* Business Information Service, World Trade Series, No. 565. Washington, 1954.

United States, Bureau of Foreign Commerce. *Indonesia—Regulations and Procedures Affecting Tourists and Temporary Visitors.* Business Information Service, World Trade Series, No. 600. Washington, 1954.

United States, Bureau of Foreign Commerce. *United States Trade with European and Asiatic Countries in the Soviet Bloc. . . .* Business Information Service, International Trade Statistics Series. Washington, April, 1954.

United States, Bureau of the Census. *Foreign Commerce and Navigation of the United States, 1946.* Washington: Government Printing Office, 1950.

United States, Bureau of the Census. *Historical Statistics of the United States, 1789–1945.* Washington: Government Printing Office, 1949.

United States, Bureau of the Census. *Statistical Abstract of the United States* (various years). Washington: Government Printing Office.

United States, Business and Defense Services Administration. *Area Development Bulletin.* Washington. A monthly magazine.

United States, Commission on Foreign Economic Policy (Randall Commission). *Report.* Washington, 1954. (Mimeographed.)

United States, Commission on Foreign Economic Policy (Randall Commission). *Staff Papers.* Washington: Government Printing Office, 1954.

United States Congress. *Congressional Record*. Washington. Verbatim record of proceedings.

United States Congress, House of Representatives, Committee on Banking and Currency. *Export-Import Bank Loan Guaranty Authority*. Washington: Government Printing Office, 1949.

United States Congress, Joint Committee on the Economic Report. *Foreign Economic Policy*. Hearings, 84th Cong., 1st Sess. Washington: Government Printing Office, 1955.

United States Congress, Senate, Committee on Agriculture and Forestry. *Foreign Trade in Agricultural Products*. Hearings before the Committee on Agriculture and Forestry, U.S. Senate, 83rd Cong., 1st Sess. 5 parts. Washington: Government Printing Office, 1953.

United States Congress, Senate, Committee on Appropriations, Investigations Division. *Foreign-Aid Program in Europe*. 83rd Cong., 1st Sess. Washington: Government Printing Office, 1953.

United States Congress, Senate, Committee on Armed Services. *Essentiality of the American Watch and Clock Industry*. Report of Preparedness Subcommittee No. 6. Washington: Government Printing Office, 1954.

United States Congress, Senate, Committee on Banking and Currency. *Study of Export-Import Bank and World Bank*. Hearings before the . . . , 83rd Cong., 2nd Sess. 2 parts. Washington: Government Printing Office, 1954.

United States Congress, Senate, Committee on Banking and Currency. *Study of Latin American Countries*. Washington: Government Printing Office, 1954.

United States Congress, Senate, Committee on Finance. *Sale of Foreign Bonds or Securities in the United States*. Hearings, 72d Cong., 1st Sess. Washington: Government Printing Office, 1932.

United States Congress, Senate, Committee on Foreign Relations. *Technical Assistance Programs*. Washington: Government Printing Office, 1955.

United States Congress, Senate, Committee on Military Affairs. *Economic and Political Aspects of International Cartels*. Washington: Government Printing Office, 1944. The report was prepared by Corwin D. Edwards.

United States, Department of Commerce. *Factors Limiting U.S. Investment Abroad, Part 2, Business Views on the U.S. Government's Role*. Washington: Government Printing Office, 1954. Part 1 was a *Survey of Factors in Foreign Countries*.

United States, Department of Commerce. *Foreign Commerce Weekly*. Washington.

United States, Department of Commerce. *Handbook on American Underwriting of Foreign Securities*. Washington: Government Printing Office, 1930.

United States, Department of Commerce. *National Income, 1954*. Supplement to the *Survey of Current Business*. Washington, 1954. The National Income Supplement for various other years has also been used.

United States, Department of Commerce. *Survey of Current Business*. Washington. A monthly magazine.

United States, Department of State. *Department of State Bulletin*. Washington. A weekly magazine.

United States, Department of State. *Foreign Legislation concerning Monopoly and Cartel Practices*. Report of the Department of State to the Subcommittee on Monopoly of the Select Committee on Small Business, United States Senate, July 9, 1952, 82d Cong., 2d Sess. Washington: Government Printing Office, 1952.

United States, Department of State. *Friendship, Commerce and Navigation, Treaty and Protocol between the United States of America and Japan (1953)*. Treaties and Other International Acts Series 2863. Washington: Government Printing Office, 1954.

United States, Department of State. *Havana Charter for an International Trade Organization*. Washington: Government Printing Office, 1948.

United States, Department of State. (*Papers relating to*) *the Foreign Relations of the United States*. Washington: Government Printing Office. A serial publication.

United States, Economic Cooperation Administration. *A Report on Recovery Progress and United States Aid*. Washington, 1949.

United States, Federal Trade Commission. *Report of the Federal Trade Commission on International Cartels in the Alkali Industry*. Washington: Government Printing Office, 1950.

United States, Foreign Operations Administration. *European Program, Local Currency Counterpart Funds. . . .* Washington.

United States, International Cooperation Administration. *Counterpart Funds and ICA Foreign Currency Accounts, Data as June 30, 1956*. Washington, 1956.

United States, International Development Advisory Board. *Economic Program for the Americas*. Washington, 1954. The report was prepared by J. Peter Grace.

United States, Public Advisory Board for Mutual Security. *A Trade and Tariff Policy in the National Interest* (Bell Report). Washington: Government Printing Office, 1953.

United States, Tariff Commission. *Toweling, of Flax, Hemp, or Ramie*. Washington, 1956.

United States, Tariff Commission. *Trade Agreements Manual—A Summary of Selected Data Relating to Trade Agreements that the United States Has Negotiated Since 1934*. Washington, 1955.

United States, Temporary National Economic Committee. *Investigation of Concentration of Economic Power, Monograph No. 6, Export Prices and Export Cartels*. Washington: Government Printing Office, 1941. The monograph was prepared by Milton Gilbert, Paul D. Dickens and the staff of the Federal Trade Commission.

United States, Treasury Department. *Census of Foreign-Owned Assets in the United States*. Washington: Government Printing Office, 1945.

United States Code.

Valavanis-Vail, Stefan. "An Econometric Model of Growth—U.S.A.—1869–1953," *American Economic Review, Papers and Proceedings*, XLV (May, 1955), 208–21.

Veblen, Thorstein. *Imperial Germany and the Industrial Revolution*. New York: Macmillan, 1915.

Veblen, Thorstein. *Theory of Business Enterprise*. New York: Scribner's, 1927. First published in 1904.

Veblen, Thorstein. *The Theory of the Leisure Class*. New York: Modern Library, 1934. First published in 1899.

Vernon, Raymond. "Postwar Trends in International Organization," *American Economic Review, Papers and Proceedings*, XXXVIII (May, 1948), 94–108.

Viner, Jacob. *Canada's Balance of International Indebtedness, 1900–1913*. Cambridge: Harvard University Press, 1924.

Viner, Jacob. *Studies in the Theory of International Trade*. New York: Harper, 1937.

Ward, Barbara. *The West at Bay*. New York: Norton, 1948.

Warren, George F., and Pearson, Frank A. *Gold and Prices*. New York: Wiley, 1935.

Warren, George F., and Pearson, Frank A. *Prices*. New York: John Wiley, 1933.

Weir, Ernest T. *Notes on the Foreign Situation Based on a Trip Abroad*. Grant Building, Pittsburgh, Penn., 1953.

Wender, Ira T. "Taxation of Foreign Trade and Investment," in United States Congress, Joint Committee on the Economic Report, *Federal Tax Policy for Economic Growth and Stability*, Papers, 84th Cong., 1st Sess., Washington: Government Printing Office, 1955, 713–24.

Wickizer, V. D. *Coffee, Tea and Cocoa—An Economic and Political Analysis*. Palo Alto: Stanford University Press (Food Research Institute), 1951.

Wickizer, V. D. *Tea under International Regulation*. Stanford: Stanford University Press (Food Research Institute), 1944.

Williamson, Harold F., and Buttrick, John A. *Economic Development: Principles and Patterns*. New York: Prentice-Hall, 1954.

Winslow, E. M. *Pattern of Imperialism*. New York: Columbia University Press, 1948.

Winston, A. P. "Does Trade Follow the Dollar?" *American Economic Review*, XVII (September, 1927), 458–77.

Wolf, Charles, Jr., and Sufrin, Sidney, C. *Capital Formation and Foreign Investment in Underdeveloped Areas*. Syracuse: Syracuse University Press, 1955.

World Almanac. New York. Annual.

Woytinsky, W. S., and Woytinsky, E. S. *World Commerce and Governments—Trends and Outlook*. New York: The Twentieth Century Fund, 1955.

Woytinsky, W. S., and Woytinsky, E. S. *World Population and Production—Trends and Outlook*. New York: Twentieth Century Fund, 1953.

Zimmermann, Erich W. *World Resources and Industries*. Revised Edition; New York: Harper, 1951.

Index

A NOTE ON THE TYPE

This book is set on the Linotype in GRANJON, a type named in compliment to ROBERT GRANJON, but neither a copy of a classic face nor an entirely original creation. The design is based upon the type used by CLAUDE GARAMOND (1510–61) in his beautiful French books, and more closely resembles Garamond's own than do any of the various types that bear his name.

Robert Granjon began his career as type-cutter in 1523. The boldest and most original designer of his time, he was one of the first to practise the trade of type-founder apart from that of printer. Between 1557 and 1562 Granjon printed about twenty books in types designed by himself, following, after the fashion of the day, the cursive handwriting of the time. These types, usually known as "caractères de civilité," he himself called "lettres françaises," as especially appropriate to his own country.

This book was composed, printed, and bound by KINGSPORT PRESS, INC., Kingsport, Tennessee. Paper manufactured by S. D. WARREN COMPANY, Boston. Designed by HARRY FORD